Social Media Tools and Platforms in Learning Environments

Bebo White • Irwin King • Philip Tsang
Editors

Social Media Tools and Platforms in Learning Environments

 Springer

Editors

Bebo White
Stanford Linear Accelerator Center
Scientific Computing
and Computing Services
P.O. Box 20450, MailStop 97
Stanford, CA 94309
USA
bebo@slac.stanford.edu

Philip Tsang
Caritas Institute of Higher Education
Center of Excellence
Chui Ling Road 18
Tseung Kwan O
Hong Kong SAR
drphiliptsang@gmail.com

Irwin King
The Chinese University of Hong Kong
Dept. Computer Science and Engineering
Shatin
NT Hong Kong SAR
king@cse.cuhk.edu.hk

AT&T Labs Research
201 Mission St. Ste 200
San Francisco, CA 94105-1831
USA
irwin@research.att.com

ACM Codes: K.3, H.4, J.4, H.5

ISBN 978-3-642-20391-6   e-ISBN 978-3-642-20392-3
DOI 10.1007/978-3-642-20392-3
Springer Heidelberg Dordrecht London New York

Library of Congress Control Number: 2011938346

Printed on acid-free paper

Springer is part of Springer Science+Business Media (www.springer.com)

Preface

Online social media have transformed the face of human interaction in the twenty-first century. From simple beginnings as a mechanism for sharing photos, discussing common interests, and supplementing traditional social interactions, they have become the agent of change in diverse arenas. Nothing escapes social networking. Everything is affected, from the way we do business (E-Commerce) to our involvement with the government (E-Government). Social tools such as Facebook and Twitter have become dominant drivers of future change in information and network technology along with the very functionality of modern society.

The domain of teaching and learning has always been fertile ground for early adopters of innovation in computing technology. It is, therefore, no surprise that educational practitioners and theorists have begun to eagerly explore how social media can be harnessed to describe and implement new paradigms for communication, learning, and education.

Wikis, blogs, microblogs, online groups and forums, podcasts, Web mashups, virtual worlds, recommender/evaluation systems, social repositories, and social tagging/bookmarking are but a few of the applications enabling innovative behaviors that support the acquisition, access, manipulation, processing, retrieval, presentation, and visualization of information within a teaching/learning space.

Social media for education have become dynamic, ubiquitous, distributed, real time, collaborative, bottom up, many to many, value based, and personalized. Some have referred to this movement as *Education 2.0*, but it should, more likely, be understood as an early glimpse of the future of the entire educational process.

The editors' goal for this book was to identify original research in the application of online social media and related technologies in education, and the emerging applications that might be found in future Internet and Web technologies (not just *Web 2.0*) that could provide educational platforms and policy issues including privacy, risk, and security. These arenas are so critical to the adoption and implementation of these applications. Furthermore, the editors wanted to provide an important reference of current unique, innovative, and effective uses of social media in education for teaching and learning that might stimulate discussion, innovation, and future research.

The contributing chapter authors were challenged with such questions as:

- How can social media truly enrich and enhance learning and teaching experiences in ways not otherwise possible?
- What can be learned from current case studies of state-of-the-art social computing/media systems or platforms being used in the learning/teaching setting?
- What are the necessary policies to balance security, privacy, and risk issues in using social media for education?
- How can learning be integrated in a distributed and ubiquitous social computing environment?
- What methods can be used to assess and evaluate learning and teaching through social media?
- What theories, paradigms, and models are applicable for the support of social computing in education?
- How might social media for education be affected by technological changes such as "smart" mobile devices, ubiquitous networks, rich interfaces, and cloud computing?

The contributing chapter authors met our challenge. Readers of this book will find interesting and provocative chapters on:

- Paradigms and methodologies – Zagenczyk/Bosman, Jeffery/Bani-Salameh, Agarwal, Albors-Garrigos/Ramos Carrasco, Ifenthaler/Pirnay-Dummer, Jahnke, Sigala
- Policy – Liu/Feng, McNaught/Lam/Kwok/Ho
- Virtual educational spaces – Shollen/Brunner, Clarke
- Assessment – Ortega/Aguillo, Purchase/Letch, Gao/Rau, Li/Ma
- Mobile learning spaces – Madjarov/Boucelma, Chang/Lu/Chu
- Social factors – Hernandez-Serrano, Koufaris/Benbunan-Fich, Yamada/Kitamura, Cameron/Finlayson/Wotzko
- Case studies and applications – Denecke/Stewart, Rice/Robinson/Caron, Sampson/Zervas/Kalamatianos, Nosko/Wood, Bailey/Franke

All authors are thanked not only for their outstanding contributions but also for their patience, assistance in peer review, and strict adherence to deadlines. It is their work that defines the value and importance of this volume.

The editors thank Ralf Gerstner of Springer for his belief in the value of this book and his support in its production; James Henri, Sandy Tse, and Mary Ho for their copy editing efforts; and other members of the project program committee who provided valuable reviews and advice.

This book is inspired by the OASISS and the Social Media projects that were funded by the Education Bureau (EDB) under the Quality Enhancement Grant Scheme (QEGS). In addition, special thanks goes to EDB of Hong Kong SAR for its support.

It is the hope of the editors that this book becomes just a first step in addressing the issues surrounding the role of online social media and education. We are pleased to have been able to play a small part in furthering the critical debate into the advancement of this dynamic and critically important technological environment.

Bebo White
Irwin King
Philip Tsang

Contents

Part II   Policy

Part III   Virtual Educational Spaces

Part IV   Assessment

Part V   Mobile Learning Spaces

Contributors

Nitin Agarwal Information Science Department, University of Arkansas, Little Rock 72204, AR, USA, nxagarwal@ualr.edu

Isidro F. Aguillo Cybermetrics Lab, CCHS-CSIC, Madrid, Spain, isidro@cindoc.csic.es

Jose Albors-Garrigos Department of Business Organization, Universidad Politecnica de Valencia, Camino de Vera S/N, 46022 Valencia, Spain, jalbors@doe.upv.es

Nathan Bailey eEducation Centre, Monash University, Melbourne, Australia, Nathan.Bailey@monash.edu

Hani Bani-Salameh University of Idaho, Moscow, ID, USA, hsalameh@vandals.uidaho.edu

Raquel Benbunan-Fich SCIS Department, Zicklin School of Business, Box B11-220, Baruch College, City University of New York, New York, USA, rbfich@baruch.cuny.edu

Lisa Bosman Department of Management, Clemson University, 101 Sirrine Hall, Clemson, SC 29634, USA, lbosman@clemson.edu

Omar Boucelma Laboratoire des Sciences de l'Information et des Systèmes, (LSIS) - UMR CNRS 6168, Aix-Marseille Université, Avenue Escadrille Normandie-Niemen, F-13397 Marseille Cedex 20, France, omar.boucelma@lsis.org

C. Cryss Brunner Department of Organizational Leadership, Policy, and Development, University of Minnesota – Twin Cities, 330 Wulling Hall, 86 Pleasant Street S. E., Minneapolis, MN 55455, USA, brunner@umn.edu

David Cameron University of Newcastle, Callaghan, NSW 2308, Australia, david. cameron@newcastle.edu.au

Bruce Caron New Media Research Institute, Santa Barbara, CA 93105, USA, bruce@nmri.org

Chih-Hung Chang Department of Information Management, Hsiuping Institute of Technology, No. 11, Gongye Rd, Dali City, Taichung County 41280, Taiwan, R.O.C

Juei-Nan Chen Department of Information Networking Technology, Hsiuping Institute of Technology, No. 11, Gongye Rd, Dali City, Taichung County 41280, Taiwan, R.O.C, RNChen@hit.edu.tw

William C. Chu Department of Computer Science and Information Engineering, TungHai University, No. 181 Taichung-Kang Road, Sec. 3, Taichung 40744, Taiwan, R.O.C, cchu@ thu.edu.tw

Christopher Clarke Business school, Nankai University, Tianjin, People's Republic of China, cpclarke123@gmail.com

Kerstin Denecke Leibniz Universität Hannover, Forschungszentrum L3S, Appelstraße 9a, 30167 Hannover, Germany, denecke@L3S.de

Amalie Finlayson Charles Sturt University, Bathurst, NSW, Australia, afinlayson@csu.edu.au

Katharina Franke eEducation Centre, Monash University, Melbourne, Australia, Katharina.Franke@monash.edu

Qin Gao Department of Industrial Engineering, Institute of Human Factors and Ergonomics, Tsinghua University, Beijing 100084, P. R. China, gaoqin@tsinghua. edu.cn

Eric C.L. Ho Centre for Learning Enhancement and Research, The Chinese University of Hong Kong, Shatin, Hong Kong, eric.ho@cuhk.edu.hk

Dirk Ifenthaler University of Freiburg, Rempartstr. 11, 79085 Freiburg, Germany, ifenthaler@ezw.uni-freiburg.de

Isa Jahnke Department of Applied Educational Science, Umeå University, ICT, Media and Learning (IML), SE-90187 Umeå, Sweden, isa.jahnke@tu-dortmund.de

Clinton Jeffery University of Idaho, Moscow, ID, USA, jeffery@uidaho.edu

María José Hernández-Serrano Faculty of Education, University of Salamanca, Paseo de Canalejas 169, 37008 Salamanca, Spain, mjhs@usal.es

Alexandros Kalamatianos Department of Digital Systems, University of Piraeus, Piraeus, Greece

Satoshi Kitamura Tokyo Keizai University, Tokyo, Japan, satkit@satkit-lab.net

Marios Koufaris SCIS Department, Zicklin School of Business, Box B11-220, Baruch College, City University of New York, New York, USA, marios.koufaris@baruch.cuny.edu

Morris Kwok Information Technology Services Centre, The Chinese University of Hong Kong, Shatin, Hong Kong, morris-kwok@cuhk.edu.hk

Paul Lam Centre for Learning Enhancement and Research, The Chinese University of Hong Kong, Shatin, Hong Kong, paul.lam@cuhk.edu.hk

Nick Letch UWA Business School, The University of Western Australia, 35 Stirling Highway, Crawley 6009, Australia, nick.letch@uwa.edu.au

Jerry Z. Li Leaching and Learning Centre, Lifelong Learning, Simon Fraser University, 8888 University Drive, Burnaby BC, V5A 1S6, Canada, jerryli@sfu.ca

Chih-Wei Lu Department of Information Management, Hsiuping Institute of Technology, No. 11, Gongye Rd, Dali City, Taichung County 41280, Taiwan, R.O.C, cwlu@hit.edu.tw

José Luis Ortega R&D Unit, VICYT, CSIC, Madrid, Spain, jortega@orgc.csic.es

Wenting Ma Faculty of Education, Simon Fraser University, 8888 University Drive, Burnaby, BC, Canada, wentingm@sfu.ca

Ivan Madjarov Laboratoire des Sciences de l'Information et des Systèmes, (LSIS) - UMR CNRS 6168, Aix-Marseille Université, Avenue Escadrille Normandie-Niemen, F-13397 Marseille Cedex 20, France, ivan.madjarov@lsis.org

Carmel McNaught Centre for Learning Enhancement And Research, The Chinese University of Hong Kong, Shatin, Hong Kong, carmel.mcnaught@cuhk.edu.hk

Amanda Nosko Department of Psychology, Wilfrid Laurier University, 75 University Ave West, N2L 3C5 Waterloo, ON, Canada, amandanosko@rogers.com

Pei-Luen Patrick Rau Department of Industrial Engineering, Institute of Human Factors and Ergonomics, Tsinghua University, Beijing 100084, P.R. China, rpl@tsinghua.edu.cn

Pablo Pirnay-Dummer University of Freiburg, Rempartstr. 11, 79085 Freiburg, Germany

Sharon Purchase UWA Business School, The University of Western Australia, 35 Stirling Highway, Crawley 6009, Australia, sharon.purchase@uwa.edu.au

Jose Carlos Ramos Carrasco Avanzalis Knowledge Associates, Paseo de Gracia, 12, 1 08007 Barcelona, Spain, jcramos@avanzalis.com

Ronald E. Rice Department of Communication, University of California, Santa Barbara, CA 90106-4020, USA, rrice@comm.ucsb.edu

Julie A. Robinson Bren School of Environmental Science & Management, University of California, Santa Barbara, CA 90106-5131, USA, jrobinson@bren.ucsb.edu

Demetrios G. Sampson Department of Digital Systems, University of Piraeus, Piraeus, Greece; Informatics and Telematics Institute (ITI), Centre for Research and Technology Hellas (CERTH), Athens, Greece

Gordon Sanson eEducation Centre, Monash University, Melbourne, Australia, Gordon.Sanson@monash.edu

S. Lynn Shollen Department of Leadership and American Studies, Christopher Newport University, 1 University Place, Newport News, VA 23606, USA, lynn.shollen@cnu.edu

Marianna Sigala Assistant Professor of Service Management in Tourism, The Business Administration Department, University of the Aegean, Michalon 8. Chios, Greece, GR-82100, m.sigala@aegean.gr

Avaré Stewart Leibniz Universität Hannover, Forschungszentrum L3S, Appelstraße 9a, 30167 Hannover, Germany, stewart@L3S.de

Eileen Wood Department of Psychology, Wilfrid Laurier University, 75 University Ave West, N2L 3C5 Waterloo, ON, Canada, ewood@wlu.ca

Rebecca Wotzko Charles Sturt University, Bathurst, NSW, Australia, rwotzko@csu.edu.au

Masanori Yamada Kanazawa University, Kanazawa, Japan, mark@mark-lab.net

Tom Zagenczyk College of Business and Behavioral Science, Clemson University, 101 Sirrine Hall, Clemson, SC 29634, USA, thomasj@clemson.edu

Panagiotis Zervas Department of Digital Systems, University of Piraeus, Piraeus, Greece; Informatics and Telematics Institute (ITI), Centre for Research and Technology Hellas (CERTH), Athens, Greece

Editors' biographies

Bebo White is a Departmental Associate (Emeritus) at the SLAC National Accelerator Laboratory, the U.S. National laboratory for high-energy physics and basic energy science at Stanford University. Working as a computational physicist, he first became involved with the emerging Web technology while on sabbatical at CERN in 1989.

Upon his return he was part of the team that established the first American Web site at SLAC (the fifth site in the world). Ever since, his academic research interests have evolved in parallel with Web technology. He is often considered to be the "first American Webmaster" and one of the founders of the discipline of Web Engineering.

In addition to his work at SLAC, he also holds faculty appointments at several other institutions, is involved with a number of major conferences series, and is a frequent conference speaker. He is the author (or co-author) of nine books, and over 100 papers and journal articles. His current research interests are Web Science, Social Media in Education, and Cloud Computing. However, given the opportunity, he will talk mercilessly about high-energy physics, jug band music and wine.

Irwin King is Professor at the Department of Computer Science and Engineering, The Chinese University of Hong Kong. Currently, he is on leave to work with AT&T Labs Research in San Francisco. He is also a Visiting Professor at the School of Information, University of California at Berkeley.

As one of the leading experts in Social Computing, Irwin's research interests include machine learning, social computing, web intelligence, data mining, and multimedia information processing. In these research areas, he has over 220 technical publications in top international journals and conferences. In addition, he has contributed over 20 book chapters and edited volumes. He also has over 30 research and applied grants. One notable patented system he has developed is the VeriGuide System, which detects similar sentences to promote academic integrity, honesty, and quality.

Irwin the Book Series Editor for "Social Media and Social Computing" with Taylor and Francis (CRC Press). He is also an Associate Editor of the IEEE Transactions on Neural Networks (TNN) and ACM Transactions on Knowledge

Discovery from Data. In addition, he is a member of the Editorial Board and serves as Guest Editor of several international journals. Currently, he is a Vice-President and Governing Board Member of APNNA. He also serves as the Vice-President for Membership and a member of the Board of Governors with INNS. Professionally, he has served as reviewer and panel member for RGC Hong Kong, Natural Sciences and Engineering Research Council of Canada (NSERC), National Natural Science Foundation of China (NSFC), and Natural Science, and Engineering of Academy of Finland.

Philip Tsang is currently Chair Professor and Vice President (Academic and Research) of the Caritas Institute of Higher Education in Hong Kong. In addition, he also serves as an advisor of the Hong Kong Doctors' Union and as editor of five international journals. He is a prolific and innovative researcher and a prominent practitioner in the important field of ICT in education, and has published over ten books on communication technologies and e-Learning. Prior to his current appointment, Philip was a senior member of the academic staff at the Open University of Hong Kong (OUHK) from 1996–2009, where he won the OUHK President's Award for Excellent Teaching and Research in 2006, 2007 and 2009.

Part I
Paradigms and Methodologies

Chapter 1
Revitalize Your Teaching: Creative Approaches to Applying Social Media in the Classroom

Lisa Bosman and Tom Zagenczyk

Abstract Social media is a widespread phenomenon focused on connecting, sharing, and collaborating. The purpose of this chapter is to focus on the educational opportunities for applying social media in the classroom and this is achieved through an application of Bloom's Taxonomy. A brief description of Bloom's Taxonomy (Bloom, B.S. Taxonomy of Educational Objectives: The Classification of Educational Goals. Susan Fauer Company, Inc., 1956) and a description of its components: remembering, understanding, applying, analyzing, evaluating, and creating is given. It is argued that each of Bloom's components can be highlighted using different social media tools. Finally, a variety of case studies and further ideas demonstrate the effective deployment of social media in the classroom.

1.1 Introduction to Social Media for Education

Social media's capacity to enable people to connect, share, and collaborate has made its use increasingly common in the personal, business, and educational domains. Social media enables people to reconnect with former classmates and coworkers and rekindle past relationships. People share photos, videos, and provide others with frequent updates related to their lives. Further, social media facilitates collaboration for school projects, church gatherings, and community events. In business, social media is useful for virtual marketing, which makes word-of-mouth

L. Bosman
Department of Management, Clemson University, 101 Sirrine Hall, Clemson, SC 29634, USA
e-mail: lbosman@clemson.edu

T. Zagenczyk (✉)
College of Business and Behavioral Science, Clemson University, 101 Sirrine Hall, Clemson, SC 29634, USA
e-mail: thomasj@clemson.edu

B. White et al. (eds.), *Social Media Tools and Platforms in Learning Environments*,
DOI 10.1007/978-3-642-20392-3_1, © Springer-Verlag Berlin Heidelberg 2011

advertising that much easier. Social media provides new approaches for entrepreneurs who wish to reach niche markets, as well as customers who wish to share their evaluations of and recommendations for new products.

In education, social media provides new and exciting opportunities for teaching and learning. Traditionally, education has utilized lectures, written communication, and more recently computers for instruction. Now, the possibilities are endless As Marc Levinson (Levinson 2010) wrote:

> Our education system is in the midst of a paradigm shift, where new methods, environments, and assessment models need to be acquired if schools are to keep pace with our increasingly networked culture. As the conversation about the digital divide shifts from questions of technological access to ones concerning participation, educators must work to ensure that every young person has access to the tools, skills, and experiences needed to join in this new participatory culture. . . . Today's educators have a chance to be courageous and take the risk of jumping off the high dive. Those who do so will give students opportunities to bring their passions into the classroom and encourage them to gain the cultural competencies and social skills they will need in their future roles as 21st-century citizens and workers. Whereas the industrial age prepared many to be workers on assembly lines, today's information age challenges us to be critical thinkers and active citizens, to come together collectively and conceptualize solutions to new problems that didn't exist in the last decade (p. ix).

The purpose of this chapter is to analyze ways in which social media can be used in the classroom through the lens of Bloom's Revised Taxonomy. This is achieved via:

- A brief description of the dimensions of Bloom's Revised Taxonomy, which includes: remember, understand, apply, analyze, evaluate, and create
- Connection of each aspect of Bloom's taxonomy with specific social media tools
- A discussion of strategic tools for obtaining support, for teachers who want to employ social media and, however, have limited resources.

1.2 Bloom's Revised Taxonomy

Bloom's Taxonomy (Bloom et al. 1956) provided a classification of measurable learning objectives for the education system. The taxonomy focused on three main domains, namely, the affective, psychomotor, and cognitive. Within the cognitive domain, the critical thinking objectives included knowledge, comprehension, application, analysis, synthesis, and evaluation.

In the 1990s, Lorin Anderson (Bloom's former student) set out to update the taxonomy for the twenty-first century student and teacher. Changes were made to the terminology and structure to account for the nontraditional knowledge capabilities presented by the Internet. The revised components include: remember, understand, apply, analyze, evaluate, and create, all of which are defined below (Anderson and Krathwohl 2001).

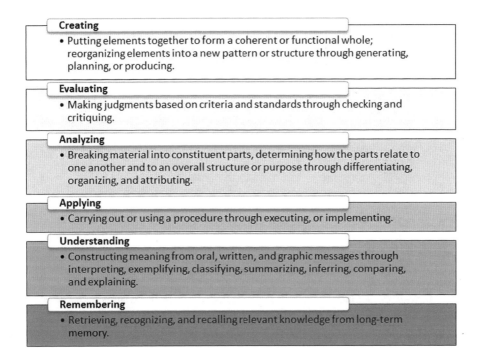

Creating
- Putting elements together to form a coherent or functional whole; reorganizing elements into a new pattern or structure through generating, planning, or producing.

Evaluating
- Making judgments based on criteria and standards through checking and critiquing.

Analyzing
- Breaking material into constituent parts, determining how the parts relate to one another and to an overall structure or purpose through differentiating, organizing, and attributing.

Applying
- Carrying out or using a procedure through executing, or implementing.

Understanding
- Constructing meaning from oral, written, and graphic messages through interpreting, exemplifying, classifying, summarizing, inferring, comparing, and explaining.

Remembering
- Retrieving, recognizing, and recalling relevant knowledge from long-term memory.

1.2.1   Remembering with Social Bookmarking

Remembering is defined as "retrieving, recognizing, and recalling relevant knowledge from long-term memory" (Anderson and Krathwohl 2001). Social bookmarking is a magnificent tool used to *remember* and organize online resources. They provide students and teachers with the ability to save website links to one location, accessible through the Internet. These links allow the students and teachers to easily find the site in the future. Examples of social bookmarking sites include: EdTags, Delicious, Google Reader, and Diigo. As Churches, Crockett and Jukes (Churches et al. 2010) note:

> Using social bookmarking tools, students and teachers are able to harness the huge potential of the Internet's resources by collaborating and sharing sites they have found and validated. The easy accessibility of social bookmarking tools means you can access and search your bookmarks from any computer connected to the Internet. Students are easily able to collaborate with their peers and teachers, which contributes to the learning process and validates their research process (p. 33).

1.2.1.1   Ideas for Social Bookmarking in the Classroom

- Depending on the class topic (science, math, literature...), the student should research the internet and bookmark related links.

- Play Jeopardy using social bookmarks. Give the students a topic and have them work alone to bookmark related links. Next, commence playing, using general statements that should be found on a website. For example, the topic can be the United States and a potential Jeopardy answer could be "This state has the largest population."
- For a student government class, the students use social bookmarks to identify links to debatable topics (websites for gun control and websites against gun control).
- For each new topic, teachers share a new collection of online resources.
- Teachers use social bookmarking to subscribe to RSS feeds to bring the news to one designated location. At the beginning of each class, the teacher can scroll through the new headlines and work with the students to tie a link between the news and the class topic.

1.2.2 Understanding with Social Blogging

Understanding includes "constructing meaning from oral, written, and graphic messages through interpreting, exemplifying, classifying, summarizing, inferring, comparing, and explaining" (Anderson and Krathwohl 2001). Blogs are an efficient method to learn what is known about a specific topic and bring forward new ideas. Typically, blogs are updated and maintained by an individual, rather than a company. Blogs can provide information through writing, pictures, videos, music, and/or audio. Examples of blog publishing tools include EduBlogs, Learner-BlogWordpress, Google Blogger, Tumblr, and PhotoBlog. Specific to education, Richardson (Richardson 2010) suggests:

> Adopters of Weblogs in the classroom have already created a wide variety of ways to use them, and they have shown that blogs can enhance and deepen learning. Even at this still fairly early stage of development, blogs are being used as class portals, online filing cabinets for student work, e-portfolios, collaborative space, knowledge management, and even school Web sites. Through the unique process of blogging, students are learning to read more critically, think about the reading more analytically, and write more clearly. Further, they are building relationships with peers, mentors, and professionals within the Weblog environment (p. 20).

1.2.2.1 Ideas for Social Blogging in the Classroom

- Students use blogs to summarize concepts, articles, and notable resources used within the classroom.
- Teachers use blogs for class management. They help their students understand class requirements better, through posting class assignments, handouts, and by providing a forum for answering questions.
- E-portfolios, summarizing the breadth of a student's work, are created using blogs.

- Blogs are a wonderful tool for students to debate a current topic of interest.
- Teachers use blogs as a way to communicate with parents about computer-use policy, external resources, lesson plans, and class events.
- Teachers have students create a bucket list for the semester – 10 things to accomplish by the end of the semester. Students follow up and summarize the accomplishment with pictures, videos, or writing.
- Teachers challenge students to a food diary, taking a picture of every meal eaten.
- Students create a photoblog – one picture a day for the entire semester.
- Students use blogs as a means of creating a daily response and reflection for a book the class is reading. The students read and respond to each other's blogs.

1.2.3   Applying with Social File Sharing

Applying includes "carrying out or using a procedure through executing, or implementing" (Anderson and Krathwohl 2001). Social file sharing tools are a new way to share information about a specific topic. Examples of social file sharing tools include: Moodle, Google Documents, Wikis, and Keep and Share. Specific to the classroom, Solomon and Schrum (Solomon and Schrum 2010) suggest:

> Imagine this situation: You and your colleagues create a paper, presentation, or report. You pass the file around, each adding the date or your initials, or both. After several iterations, you are not really sure which is the latest version, whose tracking or changes have been accepted and incorporated, or who has made the final decisions on the document. But assuming you end with the correct version, you show up with your thumb drive only to discover that the best version is not the one you have with you! The correct one is really on your home computer or on the thumb drive in your other coat pocket! If this has happened to you, or you know someone for whom this occurred, you might begin to understand the lure of Google Docs (p. 68).

1.2.3.1   Ideas for Social File Sharing in the Classroom

- Google Documents, through spreadsheets, are used as a way to teach probability and statistics. Up to 50 users work on one spreadsheet at a time. In class, users can simultaneously enter data, and the class can then perform statistical analysis.
- Wikis are used to brainstorm new ideas about class projects or debate a hot topic.
- Students work on collaborative projects through file sharing programs.
- Through file sharing programs, the teacher sees exactly who wrote what, to determine project contribution.
- Teachers use file sharing programs to easily share document templates with students.

- File sharing programs create a forum for parents to view and check up on student's work.
- Teachers assign students to edit/comment on each other's documents through the file sharing programs.
- Students use file sharing to fill out a document asking questions about a book review or other topics of interest.
- File sharing programs allow teachers to easily keep track of grades, attendance, and other data for students to review.

1.2.4   Analyzing with Social Collaboration

Analyzing includes "breaking material into constituent parts, determining how the parts relate to one another and to an overall structure or purpose through differentiating, organizing, and attributing" (Anderson and Krathwohl 2001). Social collaboration tools allow groups to meet, discuss, mark-up, and analyze information in one specific playground or workplace. Examples of social collaboration include ePals, Dim Dim, Oovoo, Skype, and Twiddla. Solomon and Schrum (Solomon and Schrum 2010) argue:

> Teachers and other educators have begun using these tools for a variety of activities, and as they become more familiar, they see other ways for students to benefit from them. In general, the goal and purpose has been to make public the types of development, creativity, and other activities that their students typically do individually. These tools have also afforded educators a way in which to promote and encourage collaboration authentically in the development of projects and papers (p. 69).

1.2.4.1   Ideas for Social Collaboration in the Classroom

- Teachers use social collaboration tools to establish virtual classrooms.
- Parent–teacher conferences are achieved using social collaboration tools.
- Social collaboration tools provide a permanent location for distance learning groups to meet about class projects.
- Twiddla is used to increase the functionality associated with collaboration, including screen mark-ups, chat, and a real-time whiteboard.
- Skype allows distance learning student groups the ability to analyze projects and suggest alternatives.
- If students are unable to participate in a fieldtrip, Skype is used to bring the fieldtrip to the students.
- Social collaboration tools are used to virtually bring guest speakers to the classroom.
- Social collaboration tools are used to bring special needs kids into the classroom.
- ePals provide students the ability to create pen pals across the globe and learn about other cultures.

1.2.5 Evaluating with Social Decision Making

Evaluating is defined as "making judgments based on criteria and standards through checking and critiquing" (Anderson and Krathwohl 2001). Social decision-making tools are used to evaluate new ideas, consider multiple options, and gain general consensus through crowd sourcing. Examples of social decision-making tools include: Kluster, Doodle, and User Voice. The Kluster website states the benefit of this tool:

> Kluster is a collaborative decision making platform — a turbo-charged collective wisdom machine that turns questions into answers, ideas into opportunities, and analysis into action. Unlike conventional "crowdsourcing" that pits people and ideas against each other, Kluster brings them together. Our approach is based on real-world group decision-making models, taking into account individual influence and participation. Not only does Kluster identify the best ideas, it actually improves them in the process (Kluster.com).

1.2.5.1 Ideas for Social Decision Making in the Classroom

- Teachers use social decision-making tools to poll the class on upcoming book options.
- Student groups use social decision-making tools to aid in project selection.
- Social decision-making tools are used to brainstorm and select a best idea.
- Students use decision-making tools to judge each other's science projects.
- For a management class, students use Kluster to gain feedback on new product development or business ideas.
- Social decision-making tools can aid in the class project evaluation process through prioritizing objectives and project components.

1.2.6 Creating with Social Creativity Sharing

Creating is described as "putting elements together to form a coherent or functional whole; reorganizing elements into a new pattern or structure through generating, planning, or producing" (Anderson and Krathwohl 2001). Social creativity sharing sites are an exciting venue through which users can share videos, pictures, and personal publications. Examples of social sharing sites include: video sharing (YouTube, Metacafe, and uvouch), picture sharing (Flickr, Photobucket, Snapfish), and publishing (Scribd, Writeboard, Pixton). Relative to the classroom, a workshop attendee described:

> I recently had the privilege of conducting a workshop for about 50 students who were attending a conference with their teachers (something I often advocate, and highly recommend). The setting was a technologically favorable one, in that the kids all had access to a well-stocked computer lab, but the students were an ordinary high school mix, representing high, low, and medium GPAs. We began by working as partners to come up with this guiding question: "What could we make to show our teachers what we are capable

of creating?" Next we spent some time listing all the things that at least some of the students knew how to create – videos, podcasts, games, computer programs, Facebook pages, competitions, and more. Each student then chose his or her preference, and the group divided up into teams. There were, in the end, 10 different tools used, some by more than one team. Even though the students had a total of only three hours to complete the projects (as a model of a weekend homework assignment), the results were extraordinary. One team of a girl and a boy made a podcast in which they did radio interviews with each other, using audio speed-up and slow-down software to reverse their genders! Two teams wrote and shot YouTube-style videos, complete with titles. . . . The point worth taking away is not just the fact that the projects were all great, but also the variety of the projects and the tools the students were able, and preferred, to use (Prensky 2010).

1.2.6.1 Ideas for Social Creativity Sharing in the Classroom

- For a show and tell, using a video camera, the students create a demonstration (science experiment, cooking video, dance lesson) and post to a video sharing site.
- If students go on vacation, ask them to create a video and post to a video sharing site.
- The teacher creates a video demonstration of a science experiment and posts to a video sharing site. Thus, if students have questions, they can just refer to the video.
- If several students are absent from class, the teacher can videotape and post the lectures.
- Students join forces with a local nonprofit and post a photo album of events to a picture sharing site.
- Students use Pixton to create a cartoon depiction of their feelings toward something they like or dislike, relative to the class topic.
- Students use Scribed to collaborate on a writing project, where participants take turns writing without editing. Thus, each person needs to keep the story flowing based on the writings of the previous person.
- Have students research colleges or potential employers through the use of video sharing and picture sharing sites. Then have the students create a video to promote the specific class.
- For a class topic on recycling, have students create a photo album with pictures of common household products that are recyclable.
- Students can use Scribed as a source for brainstorming class project ideas in one central location.

1.2.7 Communicating and Relationship Building with Social Networks

Revisiting Bloom's Taxonomy, the previous six thinking objectives focused almost exclusively on the cognitive domain. However, another important domain for students is the affective – or emotional – domain, which includes communication and relationship building. The ability to effectively network and build relationships is critical to both personal and professional success. An individual's social network includes the individuals with whom that individual maintains relationships, including colleagues, friends, family, and other social contacts. Online social networks, how-ever, can transcend traditional geographic and time-zone limitations. For example, Facebook, Second Life, LinkedIn, Edmodo, and Ning allow individuals to access the network regardless of location and time. Specific to education, Bunzel (Bunzel 2010) writes:

> At the time this is being written, Twitter is extremely hot and is the most significant real-time social media communications tool. "Real time" refers to the immediacy of Twitter's status updates and the responses of followers; because of the brevity of posts, there is almost no lag time between a post and a slew of responses, a viral dissemination of information and opinion. ... But at the moment, Twitter is an important tool for seeing how quickly social media can effect of the outcome of communications strategy, how it comprises a key component of your online identity, and how you interact and are perceived by others (p. 110–111).

1.2.7.1   Ideas for Social Networks in the Classroom

- Through SecondLife, institutions purchase "land" to build and develop structures, and the environment, to create a meeting place for students.
- Students join forces with a local nonprofit and create a fan page in Facebook to promote a cause. Pick teams and make it a competition to see how many people will "Like" the page.
- Host a class discussion using SecondLife.
- For a marketing class, using Ning, the students create a social network centered on a specific product or service and connect with others to gain feedback.
- Have students debate an ethical topic using Facebook and writing on a wall.
- Using LinkedIn, a student may connect with professionals and use their contacts to get a guest speaker in the classroom.
- For a management class, students work in teams to create a business plan using SecondLife to offer a new service in this alternative world.
- For a literature class, have students make an avatar, using SecondLife, based on specific characters in the literature. Then, the students meet in SecondLife to play out the different roles.
- Teachers, students, and parents can stay connected using the different social networks to stay up-to-date on student progress.
- For a law class, teachers use social networks to teach students about privacy. The students read and discuss the different privacy options.
- Facebook etiquette is a great topic for discussion prior to implementing the social media.
- Teachers use social networks to offer a question and answer session prior to taking a test.
- Students use Facebook as a forum for posting book reviews and movie reviews.
- Students use Facebook, through an Event or Fan Page, to organize a community service project.
- Facebook offers a wide variety of educational applications. For example, through a quiz application, the students create quizzes for each other to assist in studying for an upcoming exam.

- Twitter is used to follow famous people (CEOs, president and other political people) to keep current on changes.
- Teachers use Twitter to keep the students updated with information pertaining to absences, upcoming exams...
- Conduct a quantitative study, using probability and statistics, on the type of information tweeted online.
- Teachers use Twitter to focus on writing skills, as tweets are limited to 140 characters.
- Prior to an exam, host a recap quiz where the first student to tweet the correct answer gains a bonus point on the exam.
- Use social information networks to easily find popular articles related to the class topic.

1.2.8   Summary

In conclusion, as exemplified in this chapter, social media is a well-known and widely used mechanism for connecting people and businesses which is now becoming an important part of education as well. Below is a summary of the types of social media tools suggested for using the Bloom's Revised Taxonomy.

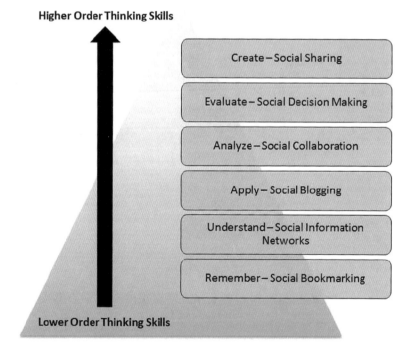

1.3   Strategic Analysis Tool for the Teacher for Implementing Social Media in the Classroom

This section will focus on the advantages, disadvantages, and decisions involved in implementing social media in the classroom. This section will introduce a SWOT Analysis, Feasibility Study, and Project Proposal. Why the fuss? In some institutional settings, obtaining the technology and/or access to technology for all students and staff can be a decision which requires buy-in from the school board, board of directors, or other administration. More often than not, gaining internet access within the school system is a sensitive subject. Use of these strategically focused analysis tools should provide teachers and instructors with the confidence and knowledge to move forward to a twenty-first century classroom.

1.3.1   SWOT Analysis

The SWOT Analysis is used to better understand the strategic benefit of integrating social media into the educational institution's goals and missions. It assesses the institution's (or classroom's) strengths, weaknesses, opportunities, and threats associated with social media. The strengths describe the institution's assets, resources, as well as potential benefits of using the social media. The weaknesses describe the challenges the institution will face in adopting a specific social media. The opportunities describe the institution's possibilities for implementing social media. Finally, the threats describe the potential danger or risk associated with the use of social media. For example, School ABC is considering using Twitter to gain real-time information on political candidates for a class on US Government. A potential SWOT Analysis is shown below.

1.3.2   Feasibility Study

The feasibility study is used to explain the risks and probabilities associated with adopting a new social media tool, with respect to technical, economic, legal, operational, and schedule feasibility, as shown below.

1.3.3   Project Proposal

The project proposal is a summary of the information required to make an accurate and justified decision to move forward and implement the social media in the institution. The components of the proposal include goals and objectives, challenges and opportunities, project feasibility (summarized), project costs, project benefits, and recommendation.

Strengths	Weaknesses
• Twitter is free, thus minimal costs are required for School ABC. • Twitter is RSS-enabled, thus students and teachers can receive information directly to their email inbox or other specified location. • Twitter has a strong brand name and good reputation, thus teachers' and students' familiarity should increase the use and satisfaction. • Twitter is real-time, thus teachers and students can have access to accurate and up-to-date information.	• Twitter is often down due to an overload of tweets (i.e. status updates), which means the potential change in teaching plans. • Twitter requires computer and internet access, which means all teachers and students require access

SWOT Analysis: Adopting Twitter at the School ABC

Opportunities	Threats
• Twitter has the potential to become a search engine for classrooms to search for education-related information. • Twitter continues to grow and is becoming one of the most popular information networking tools. • Twitter has the potential to become a primary tool connect information and users.	• Twitter received a lot of publicity in a short period of time, thus there is a potential for it to be a temporary fad. • Privacy and ethical concerns could result in legal implications for the educational environment. • Twitter has the potential to become a distraction due to overload of information.

Technical Feasibility
• Assessment of whether the social media, including hardware, software, and other system components, can be acquired and maintained in an effort to employ social media in the institution.

Economic Feasibility
• Assessment of whether the implementation of the social media makes financial sense for the institution.

Legal Feasibility
• Assessment of whether laws or regulations prevent the social media from being implemented in the institution.

Operational Feasibility
• Assessment of whether the implementation of the social media can be put into action or operation.

Schedule Feasibility
• Assessment of whether the implementation of using social media in the institution can be completed in a reasonable amount of time.

Goals and Objectives

- Describe the firm's objective. What are the goals and missions of the firm? What service or product is offered by the firm? What is the culture of the firm? How are the firm's goals aligned to the goals of the social networking tool?
- Describe the social media. Include a picture of the tool, website address, purpose, founding information, how the site earns revenue, etc…

Challenges and Opportunities

- Describe the challenges and opportunities faced by the firm in incorporating the social media. Who are the stakeholders? What is the main area for using the social media (e.g. streamline processes, increase communication, etc…)?

Project Feasibility

- Describe the feasibility of the tool with respect to technical, economic, legal, operational, and schedule feasibility.

Project Costs

- Describe the firm's costs of adopting the social media. Think about resources in the aspect of both time and money. How much does the system cost to implement and maintain? How much does training cost? What about process documentation?

Project Benefits

- Use this section to really "sell the idea" including both direct and indirect benefits, as well as both monetary and non-monetary benefits.

Recommendations

- Recommend a start-up option (e.g. direct conversion, pilot start-up, etc…) and timeline for implementation. Will the use of the social media be mandatory or voluntary?

References

Anderson, L.W., Krathwohl, D.R.: A Taxonomy for Learning, Teaching and Assessing: A Revision of Bloom's Taxonomy of Educational Objectives. Complete Edition. Longman, New York (2001)

Bloom, B.S.: Taxonomy of Educational Objectives: The Classification of Educational Goals. Susan Fauer Company, Inc. Boston, MA (1956)

Bunzel, T.: Tools of Engagement: Presenting and Training in a World of Social Media. Wiley, San Francisco (2010)

Churches, A., Crockett, L., Jukes, I.: The Digital Diet: Today's Digital Tools in Small Bytes. Corwin, Kelowna (2010)

Levinson, M.: From Fear to Facebook: One School's Journey. International Society for Technology in Education, Washington, DC (2010)

Prensky, M.: Teaching Digital Natives: Partnering for Real Learning. Corwin, Thousand Oaks (2010)

Richardson, W.: Blogs, Wikis, Podcasts, and Other Powerful Web Tools for Classrooms, 3rd edn. Corwin, Thousand Oaks (2010)

Solomon, G., Schrum, L.: Web 2.0 How-To for Educators: The Indispensable Companion to Web 2.0: New Tools, New Schools. International Society for Technology in Education, Washington, DC (2010)

Chapter 2
Teaching and Learning in a Social Software Development Tool

Hani Bani-Salameh and Clinton Jeffery

Abstract The best practices in the education of software developers require substantial interactions between educator and student, and between students in team projects. Because many students are remote, and colocated students often have different work schedules, their educational needs mirror the needs of distributed software developers. These needs include collaboration tools that replicate the benefits of face-to-face meetings, support real-time tasks such as pair programming, and facilitate asynchronous project-focused communication among team members. Software researchers have invented various development tools that integrate collaborative features. Unfortunately, most of the available collaborative tools have specialized capabilities, such as source-code editing, and developers face numerous collaboration and communication challenges in working with each other.

This chapter presents the core idea and novel design and implementation techniques for a collaborative integrated software development environment with social networking features. The tool, named Social Collaborative IDE (SCI), enables developers to interact with each other within a 3D virtual world. The research results include solutions to problems associated with providing distributed awareness and presence information. SCI addresses the communication and collaboration needs in a variety of different phases in a team software development process, unifies the concepts of social networking and collaborative Integrated Development Environment (IDE), and integrates presence information and collaborative development tools into a single environment.

The SCI system provides software development communities with social activity, presence, and awareness information of team members, other teams, active projects, and current debugging and coding sessions. It also assists developers to find appropriate assistance from inside the development environment. This chapter covers the technical issues in the design and implementation of SCI.

H. Bani-Salameh • C. Jeffery
University of Idaho, Moscow, ID, USA
e-mail: hsalameh@vandals.uidaho.edu; jeffery@uidaho.edu

B. White et al. (eds.), *Social Media Tools and Platforms in Learning Environments*,
DOI 10.1007/978-3-642-20392-3_2, © Springer-Verlag Berlin Heidelberg 2011

2.1 Introduction

Teaching software engineering (SE) and computer science (CS) courses has always been a hard process. Students find it difficult to learn programming languages and write programs for their classes. The difficulties of teaching and learning programming contribute to the low number of students taking computer courses. When it comes to teaching areas that are related to technology and communications such as computer programming, efficient collaboration tools are required for two reasons: first, improving communication techniques is a crucial demand in this era where students depend on computers in most of their tasks and second, those students will be the future software engineers who will need collaboration skills to meet the huge demands for software. Teaching software engineering usually begins with teaching programming prior to teaching advanced topics. Programming is frequently the most difficult part of any computer course (Cubranic and Storey 2005).

Software engineering is a team task where developers have to collaborate and produce a piece of software and semester projects. Such projects aim to help students (a) design, validate, verify, implement, and maintain software systems, (b) understand processes and models, and (c) obtain and improve team and communication skills. Team members may work in different places; thus, they face communication, collaboration, and coordination challenges (Bouillon et al. 2005). To help students and to make it easier for them to collaborate in their software engineering projects, collaboration tools are needed. Integrated Development Environments (IDEs) are one of the programmer's most heavily used tools. A social collaborative development environment (SCDE) is a tool where students can work with each other or a tutor/instructor to design, solve coding problems, share development knowledge, and make them aware of changes to their project artifacts.

Previous research has shown the benefits from using pair programming in collaborative learning for introductory computer science classes (Cubranic and Storey 2005). McKinney and Denton (2006) note that the early use of collaborative learning leads to higher interest, retention, and academic performance in students. Early use of these techniques can also increase the sense of belonging for students and prepare them for team experiences in subsequent courses and future careers.

A major challenge in using pair programming in software engineering classes is that it requires students to work at the same time. Finding time to work together is always hard for students working from different places in a long-term project. The goal of this research is to (a) make it easier for students to experience virtual teamwork and gain some experience with the distributed software development process and the expected challenges and (b) provide a tool that will help students to improve their programming skills.

This project begins by defining the requirements for an efficient collaboration tool for teaching programming. Requirements include features to support: (a) shared editing, compiling and editing tasks; (b) communication, collaboration, and community building; and (c) activity awareness and online presence. SCI was built to address the above requirements, in order to ease the communication and collaboration among the students and allow them to interact, either using text chat or VoIP sessions.

2.2 Social Presence

Social presence is an important factor for a unified vibrant community, where high levels of interaction reflect the group's cohesion. Presence is traditionally defined as the sense of "being in," "existing in," or belonging to a group (Annetta and Holmes 2006). Several definitions are used for presence. Garrison et al. (2000) defined presence as "the ability of participants in a community of inquiry to project themselves socially and emotionally as 'real' people, through the medium of communication being used." Short et al. (1976) stated that social presence is the critical factor in a communication, and the ability to work collaboratively is at the heart of social presence theory.

Previous definitions focused on physical presence. However, other researchers studied social presence and used many definitions. Social presence has been defined as the degree to which a person experiences the feeling of being present, "sense of being with the other," and takes part in the interaction in any community or the degree to which a person is perceived as real in an online conversation (Gunarwardena et al. 1997). Annetta and Holmes (2006) argue that social presence is strongly attached to individuality: If students in an online community feel that they are perceived as an individual, then they feel a sense of presence within that community.

In the context of this work, social presence within social teams and community members is referred to as being aware of the other team members' roles and activities, as well as the resources in the community, relevant to a given project. In order to catch people when they are "in" and focused on a given task, team members need to be aware of the other team member's primary activity windows and/or activity history.

2.3 User and Group Awareness

Awareness is an important factor for a cohesive software development community, where the gathered awareness information supports and reflects the groups' cohesion. *Awareness* has a broad range of meanings.

2.3.1 Definitions

A common definition, from Answers.com (http://www.answers.com/), is "*Awareness refers to the ability to perceive, to feel, or to be conscious of events, objects or patterns, which does not necessarily imply understanding.*" A more specific definition in the context of collaborative work relates awareness to the working environment: "*awareness is an understanding of the activities of others, which provides a context for your own activity*" (Kobylinski 2005). This definition implies a group of people working together. This kind of awareness is often referred to as group awareness in the CSCW research community.

According to that definition, much information can be considered as awareness information. Gutwin and Greenberg (Gutwin and Greenberg 1996) proposed the following list of elements as group awareness relevant information elements. The list shows which of those elements is addressed in SCI.

		Addressed in SCI
Presence	Who is participating in the activity?	X
Location	Where are they working?	X
Activity Level	How active are they in the workplace?	X
Actions	What are they doing?	X
	What are their current activities and tasks?	
Intentions	What will they do next?	X
	Where will they be?	
Changes	What changes are they making, and where?	X
Objects	What objects are they using?	
Extents	What can they see? How far can they reach?	
Abilities	What can they do?	X
Sphere of Influence	Where can they make changes?	X
Expectations	What do they need me to do next?	

Gutwin and others (Gutwin et al. 2004) stated that "*group awareness is the understanding of who is working with you, what they are doing, and how your own actions interact with theirs.*" They also argue that the complexity and interdependency of software systems suggest that group awareness is necessary for collaborative software development.

Awareness in the context of this Chapter refers to a specific kind of awareness called social software awareness and is defined as the "*Combination of passive and active information about developers' activities and artifacts, proportional to their interconnections.*" Awareness is proportional to the user's interconnections in order to avoid information overload. Several levels of friends are needed in order to give closer friends more access to the awareness information than friends-of-friends, which should have more access than the random strangers or other community members.

To summarize, *presence* and *awareness* complement each other. Where presence is the extent to which information about users, their locations, their activities, etc. is available to others, awareness describes the means and extent to which others are informed of this available presence information.

2.3.2 Importance

For many years, software development has presented serious coordination, communication, and collaboration problems, especially, when teams are geographically distributed (Bouillon et al. 2005; Gutwin et al. 2004). This leads to cases where developers affect other team member's code and conflict changes. According to researchers in software engineering and CSCW, this is a result of the lack of awareness about what is happening in other parts of the project and the other team member's activities.

Researchers have found a number of problems that still occur in team projects and software development. They found that it is difficult to: determine when developers are making changes to the same piece of the project, communicate with others due to time-zone barriers and different work schedules, find developers for closer collaboration or assistance, and determine the expert developers who have the knowledge about the project's different artifacts. As Herbsleb and Grinter (Herbsleb and Grinter 1999) state, lack of awareness – *"the inability to share at the same environment and to see what is happening at the other site"* – is one of the major factors in these difficulties. When working with groups who are geographically distributed, awareness of team member's activities provides information that is important to build an effective collaboration. This awareness includes: observing who is working with you and noting their activities or plans. Developers can use the knowledge of team member activities for many other purposes that help the overall cohesion of the project. For example, knowing the specific files and objects on which another developer has been working and the time he/she spent working on them, gives an indication of expertise within the project; tracking who made changes most recently to a particular file gives an indication of whom to ask before making changes; and gathering information about who is currently active can help developers to find a possible closer collaboration and real-time assistance on particular issues (Schneider 2004). A few systems do track and visualize awareness information (e.g., Palantir (Sarma 2003) and TUKAN (Gutwin et al. 2004)).

According to Gutwin and others (Gutwin et al. 2004), in colocated situations, awareness information can be gathered and maintained in three ways: first, when developers tell each other about their activities (explicit communication); second, by watching other work developers gather information about their activities and plans (consequential communication); and last, developers find out about other team member activities, by observing the changes to project artifacts (feed through).

2.3.3 SCI Design

This section presents the novel design techniques for a real-time social collaborative IDE inside CVE, a collaborative virtual environment where users can interact within a 3D virtual world. A subsystem of CVE called Social Collaborative IDE (SCI) supports communication and collaboration within a distributed software development community, and addresses needs in a variety of different phases in a team software development process.

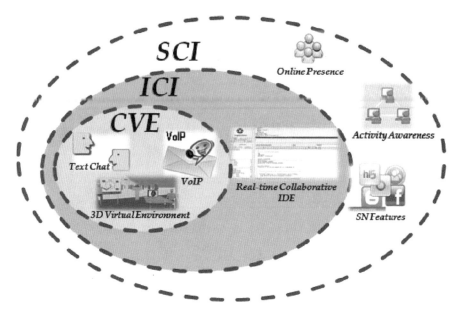

Fig. 2.1 The SCI architecture

Figure 2.1 shows the integration of the presence information, collaboration tools, and software development facilities in a single environment. The inner oval represents the CVE collaborative virtual environment where users can interact within a 3D virtual world. CVE provides developers with a general view of other users and what they are doing. In the middle oval, ICI developers use synchronous collaborative software development tools that extend CVE's generic virtual environmental capabilities to communicate, interact, and collaborate in solving their programming problems. The outer oval provides the developers with group, user, project, and session, presence and awareness information. SCI's asynchronous features help users to select and coordinate their active synchronous collaborations. In general, the asynchronous tools drive the use of the synchronous tools, and the two categories complement each other. CVE, ICI, and SCI are complementary tools that work together to provide a unique single development environment.

2.3.4 User Interface Components

SCI is a desktop application that runs on a variety of operating systems including: Microsoft Windows, Linux, and Mac OS. Figure 2.2 shows the major SCI components. Tabs (F), show social awareness of the users, their status (online, offline, or idle), active collaborative sessions, and members of each session. Information in the tabs allows users to observe the presence of the available teams (groups) and who

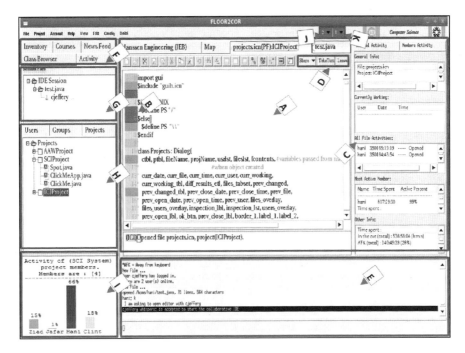

Fig. 2.2 A view of the SCI integrated development environment

belongs to each team. Also, they show the presence of each team member, their activity in the project, and their activity history. The social parts (G, H, and I) represent that subset of the awareness information that users get "for free" while concentrating on their project tasks; it includes a sessions tree, users tree, groups tree, and projects tree. Figure 2.2 I is a bar chart that shows additional information on a project from the user projects list. This detail view cycles semirandomly through the user's projects, allocating more time to projects with high activity. The chart shows the project members' activity and percentage of the time each member spent working in the project. Icons (J) and (K) show passive awareness, user notifications of pending invitations and requests (Fig. 2.2J) and emails (Fig. 2.2K) they receive from friends and other community members. Following is an explanation of these components:

Collaboration Spaces (Fig. 2.2A): The IDE's major collaboration spaces are its text editor and shell areas, where developers and team members collaborate in editing their code and debugging their projects. It uses a color coding to depict the user who committed the most recent updates or changes to each line (see Change Bar Fig. 2.2B), and shows activities on the current collaboration space (Fig. 2.2C). Collaboration icons (Fig. 2.2D) allow users to share their own collaboration space and commence collaboration sessions, take a turn editing the shared space, and leave the collaboration sessions.

Chatting (Fig. 2.2E): This is provided by the CVE virtual environment. It allows developers to chat via text or VoIP with team members and other developers in real-time.

Email: Developers can send private emails to one or more users, and public emails to the whole group. Public emails also appear as an entry inside the news feed, where developers can comment on to the feed entry and share their opinion about the topic of the feed, or respond to the email privately.

Special Interest Groups (Fig. 2.2F): Developers may join special interest groups (SIGs) where they can find other team members or developers who share the same interest. The system began with four original SIGs: Java Group, C++ Group, Unicon Group, and the Software Engineering Group.

Profiles: Users are allowed to view colleague information within the community circle (teams or groups). Profiles show the user's friends, groups of which they are a part, their projects showing the project name, owner, creation date, number of members, number of files, and tree of the project files, and a mini-feed (wall) that will show the user activities, and recent events. The user profile calendar tool keeps everyone informed of items such as project deadlines, holidays, and availability. It also plays a central role informing people at other sites about where someone is, when they might be free, and (when permissions allow it) even with whom they are meeting. Opening a profile, users can view other member's personal information, friends, groups, projects, talks, and any other content they want to display.

News Feed and Discussion Threads (Fig. 2.2F) highlight information that includes new projects, changes to projects, new groups, members who have joined groups, active sessions (debugging or editing sessions), and other updates. The News Feed also shows conversations taking place among the users and their friends (see Fig. 2.3); Each group member can chat with all other members in that group or view and send emails to the discussion feed in the SCI system.

A special kind of news feed (*personal feed*) is available in the user's profile page that shows the updates tailored to that user. This makes it easy for developers, to track changes in projects, and team members. Users are able to control what types of information are shared automatically with friends. Users may prevent friends from seeing updates about several types of private activities. The feed shows people who share interests, so you can easily ask for help. Users have the ability to designate

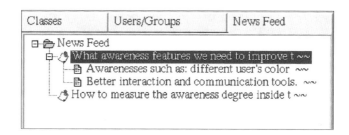

Fig. 2.3 Showing the news feed from inside the development environment

which specific user or list of users can access posted information, if they so choose, so that groups can maintain privacy.

The system provides developers with automatically generated postings about team member activities. These activities include: (a) creating a collaborative editing session; (b) editing a piece of code, compiling a program, and/or starting a collaborative session; and (c) other related topics to the project artifacts.

2.3.5 3D Virtual Environment and Project Presence Features

Developers can create different types of projects with significant permission differences. The owner may set the project to "Group Open," "Group Closed," "Community Open," or "Community Closed" and control access to its files. All the project files are stored in the server. "Group Open" projects allow the owner's friends in the social network to join the project group automatically. "Group Closed" projects require friend status in order to request permission to join the project. "Community Closed" projects require permission but not friend status, to join the project. "Community Open" projects allow any developer to join the project.

The collaboration server is layered on top of an ordinary revision control server that remembers all changes made to the project files. SCI exploits awareness of other team members; its text editor graphically depicts (using distinct background colors) the text lines with (a) pending updates to files that others have committed, lines having uncommitted changes in other developers' copies of the files, and lines that were recently viewed by others. This level of detail minimizes conflicts from concurrent revision of the same code, and helps team members know when consultation or a meeting is in order.

Every project is allocated a space inside the CVE virtual environment when the project is created. Project spaces vary depending on their size; a project begins with a simple room sized for its initial membership.

As the group becomes bigger, the size and number of the project's rooms increase. Project spaces in the 3D environment can be laid out in different ways. If the project is not related to any other virtual spaces, its creator may switch to the 2D map tab, navigate the map and click to reserve an available space, and establish a room at specific coordinates. In many other cases, users can choose to lay out their projects' spaces next to the other rooms that they own or to which they are related, in order to make moving between the rooms easier. For larger projects and closely related projects, their spaces form multiroom complexes that are connected in the virtual world. Also, users may choose to lay out their projects' spaces next to those projects, friends, or community members they share interest with or from whom they wish to ask assistance.

Any user who joins the project causes his/her avatar to be teleported to the project room, and each time the user opens the project within the CVE his/her avatar is teleported there. Users typically will be members of multiple projects. A teleport menu lists the rooms for each of their projects and interest groups.

The presence of the avatars in a virtual room gives the developers the feeling of the team's presence and encourages interaction between them regardless of the variety of locations and cultures. Users can create rooms for specific groups and purposes. Each room's owner controls its membership and access.

2.3.6 Awareness Requirements

Distributed developers need to maintain general awareness of the entire team, as well as more detailed awareness of people of special interest (people with whom a developer is working or from whom he/she wishes to seek assistance). Developers in distributed software development projects maintain their awareness primarily through text-based communication tools, such as mailing lists, email systems, and chat systems, along with voice tools, such as Voice over Internet Protocol (VoIP), and chat systems.

SCI is implemented so developers can maintain awareness of the people working on their project, and in what parts of the code, others are working, what their areas of expertise are, as well as who has joined (or left) the team. Users gain this information from different sources, such as: (1) watching the team news feed; (2) observing the people who access, edit, or change the group project's artifacts; and (3) observing changes to the projects' artifacts and CVS commits. This helps developers keep up-to-date with both changes to the project's artifacts and the activities of other distributed team members. Developers maintain awareness of each other's activities, tasks they are working on, their activity history, and when they are likely to be available.

The system provides the user with a list of the experts in a specific subject. Users who need help reviewing and debugging their code, when trying to share their files, can choose to either share it with an available user or request help from an expert in this piece of code or programming language.

Also, mailing lists and news feeds help developers gather information about others at their convenience, for example, to find out who the experts are in an area. In some cases, developers gather the information by simply initiating a discussion: because the messages go to the entire group, the "right people" will identify themselves by joining the conversation, answering questions, and commenting on the discussion thread. They also can gather information about who are the experts in a specific part of the code, by checking the changes history to this code and the time each team member spent working on it.

2.3.7 Passive and Active Awareness Features

SCI supports two types of awareness: passive and active. Passive awareness describes information that the system provides automatically in order to make the user aware of the surrounding artifacts of interest. Examples of such information are the indications (notifications) to emails and other pending invitations users get for free on their client while focusing on their tasks. Active awareness tools are user directed and provide additional details about other users and projects.

To promote group awareness, SCI supports a tree structure of the available users that provides awareness of one's team members. Developers can view other's status and profile, and check what project they are working on. Each team member is represented by a node in the tree and users can tell who is online and working in the SCI environment at a glance. Clicking on the user icon reveals further details about developer's activities; such as what files they are currently editing or debugging, their active projects, their interest groups, and so on.

Users in the virtual environment, whose avatars reside in the project/group virtual room, can obtain information about other user's tasks. Right-clicking over their avatar's head causes a pop-up menu to appear with a list of the projects of which the member is a user (see Fig. 2.4B). Clicking on any of those projects causes a window to appear with a list of the files he/she accessed in the project decorated with different colors showing the files being modified at the moment (red), files accessed in the last few days (green), and new files he/she added to the project (blue) (see Fig. 2.4C). Files with the same color decoration are listed under a specific section with headers (modified, accessed, or added) to help developers who have problem with colors easily recognize the differences.

Users gather project artifact awareness information by hovering over the project files tree (class browser) and the activity tab, where they can see who is editing a specific file, what files have been edited or are being edited, what kind of sessions have been created, and what are the active sessions (editing, debugging, chatting).

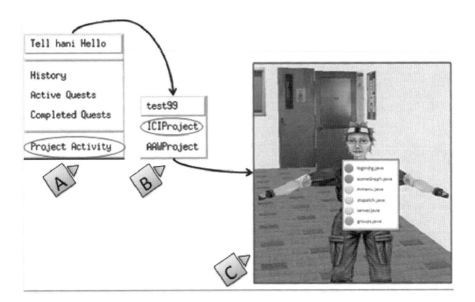

Fig. 2.4 Project artifacts access

From the users/groups tree tab, users can trigger a variety of interactions, including text chat, VoIP session, and inviting others for pair programming, debugging, or code reviews.

Developers who use version control systems (SVN (Subversion), CVS (Concurrent Version System)) can observe others' changes by checking the committed changes history in the software repository, however, their local uncommitted changes to project artifacts are not recorded in the shared repository. Another important example of version control systems is Git (Chacon 2009), and Mercurial are distributed peer-to-peer revision control systems with no central repository. SCI does not yet support decentralized revision control systems.

In addition to the ability to observe changes to the files during the collaborative editing sessions by watching others editing, SCI records each user's uncommitted changes in the shared copy of the code, so changed uncommitted pieces of the code appear highlighted with a different color. Recording local uncommitted changes supports awareness in distributed software development and proactively assists users to avoid changes that conflict with other's changes.

Once developers decide to commit the changes, a window will pop up showing who is currently editing the same file, what time they commenced, who previously changed the file, when they commenced, and when they finished. They can also compare their own version of the file with the previously saved copies after each commit a developer made. This commit-time information helps users check for any conflicts and decide whether they want to commit their changes or not. Figure 2.5 shows the commit window.

Fig. 2.5 Project files commit window

Notations in the left margin of the code inform the user where team members have made changes. These markers help developers maintain awareness of the activities of their community members, including their progress in the coding tasks, and the modifications to specific parts of the code. The supported awareness features introduced here can help team members coordinate their work and avoid conflicts and duplication of effort.

SCI also provides session awareness using a tree structure of the available sessions. By hovering over a session icon (node), a tooltip appears with the session history, showing the owner of the session, who is editing the file at a particular moment, and a list of all the current members and those who made changes to project artifacts and left the session, to help developers gather awareness information about others who may be familiar with a piece of code. Awareness of others' editing and/or debugging of a specific file help to direct the creation of collaborative IDE editing/debugging sessions. Developers, editing a file or needing some assistance while working on a piece of code, benefit from observing others working on the same code. Also, they can invite them to begin a collaborative session.

To summarize, SCI provides activity awareness information that covers the following categories: social awareness (the presence of one's collaborators and community members), action awareness (awareness of what collaborators are doing or what they have recently done), and artifacts awareness (information about all the different files or sub-projects that make up the overall project).

2.4 Implementation

This work uses the CVE virtual environment infrastructure to implement and support SCI. The SCI front end, its editor and shell, is from ICI, while other components and features were implemented from scratch.

2.4.1 Class Model of Social Software Development

SCI's source code is organized into five different groups of classes. Figure 1.6 shows the UML diagram for the classes related to SCI.

The first group is *Social Domain Tools*. This group includes four major classes. (1) *ICI Group* provides group management functionality and describes the behavior and properties of the groups in the SCI system; (2) *NewsFeed* manages the discussion threads and the system generated feeds; (3) *Project,* the main software development projects management class, provides functions and methods to create projects, invite members, join projects, add files to, access (edit) files from, and commit changes to software development projects; (4) *Profile* allows users to create their own personal profiles and view other community member profiles; and (5) *Awareness MC* class that represents the interface between the server and the awareness and social domain tools presented in Fig. 2.6 inside the rounded

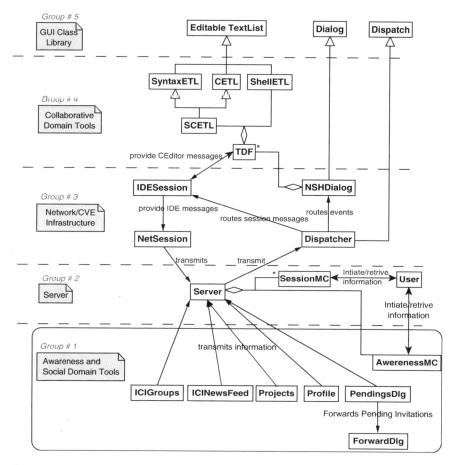

Fig. 2.6 Collaborative IDE class diagram

rectangle. It acts as a protocol coordinator that manages the delivery of the awareness information within the SCI environment.

The second group is *Server Classes*. This group includes three major classes: (1) *Server* as the main collaborative virtual environment server class which has methods for managing the virtual environment. This class is the manager for the collaborative IDE sessions. It creates a session entry there when a user invites another user. Also it adds another user into the users list when additional users are invited into the session. Once users exit the session or log out from the virtual environment, they are removed from the users list. (2) *Session MC* is a class that acts as a protocol manager for the collaboration sessions. (3) *User* is a class that describes the behavior and properties of the user entity in the CVE.

The third group of classes is *Network/CVE Infrastructure Classes*. This group includes the CVE virtual environment classes that provide the context in which SCI executes. The SCI design did not have to establish communications capabilities or create its own window; instead it interfaced with an existing infrastructure. This group includes classes such as (1) *IDESession*, a class responsible of managing the collaborative IDE session (create new sessions; receive events from collaborative IDE); (2) *NSHDialog*, a class which has methods related to the GUI (buttons, trees) that is used by the virtual environment and by the collaborative IDE; (3) *N3Dispatcher*, the client's message reader. The collaborative IDE uses this class to synchronize different events between the clients and the server. This is achieved by sending different types of messages between them (invite user to the session, remove user from a session and fire event in the editor which is currently in a collaborative IDE session); and finally (4) *NetSession*.

The fourth group of classes is *Collaborative Domain Tools*. This group includes the main IDE classes such as (1) *SyntaxETL:* a subclass of the Unicon standard library EditableTextList class provides a multi-language syntax-coloring collaborative editor widget; (2) *CETL:* the main class of the IDE. It provides a scrollable editable text area. This class issues "CETL events" to send the changes through the network to all the collaborating clients; (3) *ShellETL*: this class executes a simple command shell within a collaborative editable textlist widget, in order to fulfill the requirements of the compiling and debugging procedures; and (4) *IDE*: this class is the home for almost all the collaborative IDE functions and methods.

The fifth group *GUI Class Library*. This group includes Unicon standard library classes such as *editableTextList* and Dialog, and other files such as *Dis-patch*.

2.5 Related Work

Several IDEs integrate collaboration and awareness features. This section highlights various existing systems that provide interactive collaboration and awareness for multiple phases of program development.

Eclipse (Object Technology International 2003) is an open source development platform comprised of extensible frameworks, tools and runtimes for building, deploying, and managing software across the lifecycle. Eclipse does not support code-level collaboration, but Eclipse Communication Framework supports the development of distributed Eclipse-based tools and applications and allows the Eclipse code repository and project model to be shared and collaboratively edited.

A number of other Eclipse-based projects integrate additional collaborative features. GILD provides cognitive support for novice programmers and support for instructor activities (Storey et al. 2003). CodeBeamer has plug-ins for integrating collaborative capabilities such as chatting, messaging, project management, and shared data (Ripley et al. 2004). Sangam is a plug-in that features a shared editor and chat for pair programming (Ho et al. 2004).

Stellation (http://www.eclipse.org/stellation) is an open source effort led by IBM Research that introduces a fine-grained source control, supports the notion of activities, aims to simplify collaboration, and provide awareness of changes to team members (Cheng et al. 2003a,b). It enables developers to manage relevant work, notify the team of their current work, be informed of changes pertaining to their own activities, and provides a context for persistent conversations.

Palant´r (Ripley et al. 2004) is another Eclipse plug-in that shows which artifacts have been changed by which developers and by how much. Palant´r provides workspace awareness such that developers can monitor other team activities while working on their current task without the need for switching contexts.

A final related Eclipse-based project is Jazz, a research project at IBM (Cheng et al. 2003a,b). Jazz aims to develop collaboration within the group by providing a facility similar to an IM buddy list to monitor user's status and whether they are coding or not. Developers can chat or use different communication methods such as screen sharing and VoIP telephony. Jazz also provides some awareness features to make developers aware of the activities of other team members (Object Technology International 2003).

Jazz supports many precursors to social networking. As with SCI, Jazz focuses on increasing the user's awareness of people, resources, and activities, and on fostering communication among team members. Both Jazz and SCI support synchronous chat discussions and team-centric discussion boards. User profiles are not supported by Jazz. Jazz supports awareness of the committed code changes with respect to the code repository. In contrast, SCI provides awareness information of the committed and uncommitted code changes, of the currently edited files, and indicates who is responsible for the changes.

In addition to the many Eclipse-based CDE tools, the remainder of this section presents some important related work that (like SCI) is not built on Eclipse. CollabVS (Hegde 2009) allows developers to work together within Visual Studio whether intentional or ad-hoc. For example, a pair of developers can agree to work together at a scheduled time and work together using CollabVS. CollabVS allows for opportunistic collaboration as well. Developers can carry out various activities using the tools provided by CollabVS, including IM, audio and video communication. Also, CollabVS provides two kinds of presence: (1) real-time presence that makes the user aware of what other team members are currently doing (it shows what users are online and whether they are editing, debugging, engaged in an instant messaging session); and (2) contextual presence facilitates finding relevant information and people quickly.

Collab.net (Cook 2007) is a commercial CDE that has both a public and a private face. Collab.net's public face is SourceForge, an open source CDE that focuses on the development of open source software. SourceForge (SourceForge.net) serves as a host to approximately 230,000 projects such as CVE (http://cve.sf.net). Collab.net's private face is SourceCast (http://sourcecast.org/) a CDE that supports a number of important features not in SourceForge, such as greater security that is not a big issue for open source development.

Open source development platforms such as SourceForge provide simple awareness mechanisms along with configuration management (CM) functionality. SourceForge has limitations in terms of what information is shared, when it is shared, and how it is presented to the developers. It is difficult to maintain awareness across SourceForge's multiple communication channels. Perhaps the limitation

Table 2.1 Features of existing CDE systems

		GILD	CodeBeamer	Stellation	Palant'ir	Jazz	JBuilder 2008	CollabVS	SCI
	Synchronous Features	_	Partial	Partial	Partial	X	X	X	X
	Asynchronous Features	_	Partial	Partial	Partial	X	_	X	X
	Artifact Management	X	_			X	X	_	X
	Purpose	EDU	COM	DEV	DEV	COM	GEN	_	GEN
	Multiple Language Support	_	_	_	_	X	_	_	X
	3D Virtual Environment	_	_	_	_	_	_	_	X
Awareness	Social/Presence	_	_		_	X	_	X	X
	Historical	_	_	X	_	X	_	X	X
	Group-Structural	_	_	X	_	X	_	X	X
	Workspace (Artifacts)	_	_	X	_	X	_	X	X
SN Features	Groups	_	_	_	_	X	_	_	X
	Friends	_	_	_	_	X	_	_	X
	Help/Support	_	_	_	_	X	_	_	X

Purpose: EDU (Education), COM(Commercial), DEV(Development), GEN(General)

appears where most open source projects inform developers only of conflicts related to specific project artifacts and ignore the other developer activities (Sarma 2003).

The CDE tools presented previously in this section are categorized in Table 2.1. Table 2.1 shows that CDE tools vary in the number of supported features; most CDE tools are designed for specific purposes and in general do not need to support all software development tasks.

In the design of the SCI framework, a major goal is to provide many CDE features for application developers to utilize. However, instead of writing tools for all purposes of SCI, the research presented in this paper provides a framework that supports key categories listed in the features table, while focusing on the awareness, social presence, and social network features, and mainly the 3D virtual environment integration with the gains from the interaction among user avatars and their online presence.

2.6 Summary

Social support for software development is an important emerging field of research. Conventional single-user tools do not provide the needed environment for smooth collaboration between distributed developers because of the size and complexity of today's development projects. CDE tools that support and provide project artifact updates in real time have the potential to raise the level of communication and coordination between distributed developers.

Most current CDEs have inherent limitations, including a paucity of support for awareness and online presence, missing social networking features, and weak support for source code repository features. The multitude of tools increases the friction that results from switching among different tools.

This chapter presented a social collaborative development environment that addresses these problems and eliminates several current limitations. SCI is composed of a presence and activity awareness information component, an integrated development environment, and collaboration tools that all reside within a single environment. The merger of these tools increases their benefit to the development community.

No existing tool has yet blended full "social networked IDE" features with a 3D virtual environment as found in SCI. The major difference between SCI and almost all the related work cited in this chapter is the integration of social network features inside the software development environment. Most of the cited projects provide some social network-like features, but ignore others such as user profiles and news feed. In contrast, SCI integrates multiple social network information sources and provides the user with broader awareness about the other developers and the project artifacts. It provides what most other open source projects are missing: the overall view of other developer's workspace activities.

SCI supports development in mainstream languages, such as C, C++, and Java. Augmenting related and specific awareness information, online presence, and social network features within a single environment makes SCI a rich environment for both software engineering education and software development teams working in distributed settings.

References

Annetta, L., Holmes, A.S.: Creating presence and community in a synchronous virtual learning environment using Avatars. Int. J. Instr. Technol. Distance Learn 27–43 (2006)

Bouillon, P., Krinke, J., Lukosch, S.: Software engineering projects in Distant Teaching. In: 18th Conference on Software Engineering Education & Training, pp. 147–154 (2005)

Chacon, S.: Pro Git. Apress, 2009. Available from http://progit.org/book/

Cheng, L., de Souza, C., Hupfer, S., Patterson, J., Ross, S.: Building Collaboration into IDEs. ACM Queue 1, pp. 40–50 (2003–2004)

Cheng, L., Hupfer, S., Ross, S., Patterson, J., Clark, B., de Souza, C.: Jazz: a collaborative application development environment. In: 18th Annual ACM SIGPLAN Conference on Object Oriented Programming Systems Languages and Applications, pp. 102–103. Anaheim (2003)

CodeBeamer. http://www.intland.com and http://www.codebeamer.com

Collaborative Development Environment Using Visual Studio. http://research.microsoft.com/enus/projects/collabvs/default.aspx

Cook, C.: Towards computer-supported collaborative software engineering, PhD Thesis, University of Canterbury, Christchurch (2007)

Cubranic, D., Storey, M.A.: Collaboration support for Novice Team Programming. In: ACM GROUP'05, pp. 136–139 (2005)

CVS, Concurrent Version System. http://www.nongnu.org/cvs

Dourish, P., Bellotti, V.: Awareness and coordination in shared workspaces. In: CSCW, ACM (1992)

Eclipse Platform Technical Overview, Object Technology International Incorporated. http://www.eclipse.org/whitepapers/eclipse-overview.pdf (2003)

Garrison, D.R., Anderson, T., Archer, W.: Critical inquiry in a text-based environment: computer conferencing in higher education. Internet Higher Educ 2(2–3), 87–105 (2000)

Gunawardena, C., Zittle, F.: Social presence as a predictor of satisfaction within a computer-mediated conferencing environment. Am J Distance Educ **11**(3):8–26 (1997)

Gutwin, C., Greenberg, S.: Workspace awareness for groupware, Conference on Human Factors in Computing Systems, ACM, New York, pp. 208–209 (1996)

Gutwin, C., Penner, R., Schneider, K.: Group awareness in distributed software development. In: ACM Conference on Computer Supported Cooperative Work, pp. 72–81. Chicago (2004)

Hegde, R.: Collaborative Development Environment using Visual Studio. Available at http://research.microsoft.com/en-us/projects/collabvs/ (2009)

Herbsleb, J.D., Grinter, R.E.: Architectures, coordination, and distance: conway's law and beyond. IEEE Softw. **16**(5), 63–70 (1999)

Ho, C., Raha, S., Gehringer, E., Williams, L.: Sangam: A distributed pair programming plug-in for eclipse. In: Eclipse Technology Exchange (Workshop) at the Object-Oriented Programming, Systems, Languages, and Applications (OOPSLA) (2004)

Kobylinski, R.: Building group awareness in distributed software development projects, PhD Thesis, Technische Universität München (2005)

McKinney, D., Denton, L.: Developing collaborative skills early in the CS curriculum in a laboratory environment. In: 37th SIGCSE Technical Symposium on Computer Science Education, pp. 138–142. Houston (2006)

Ripley, R., Sarma, A., Van der Hoek, A.: Workspace awareness in application development. In: Eclipse Technology eXchange Workshop, pp. 17–21. Vancouver (2004)

Sarma, A., Noroozi, Z., der Hoek, A. Palantír: Raising awareness among configuration management workspaces. In: Twenty-fifth International Conference on Software Engineering, pp. 444–454. Portland, (2003)

Schneider, K., Gutwin, C., Penner, R., Paquette, D.: Mining a software developer's local interaction history. In: International Workshop on Mining Software Repositories (MSR). Saint Louis (2005)

Schümmer, T.: Lost and found in software space. In: 34th Annual Hawaii International Conference on System Sciences (HICSS-34), vol. 9 (2001)

Short, J., Williams, E., Christie, B.: The Social Psychology of Telecommunications. Wiley, London (1976)

SourceForge.net. http://sourceforge.net/

Storey, M.A., Michaud, J., Mindel, M. et al.: Improving the usability of eclipse for Novice Programmers. In: OOPSLA Workshop: Eclipse Technology Exchange, pp. 35–39. Anaheim (2003)

SVN, Subversion. http://subversion.tigris.org

Chapter 3
Collective Learning: An Integrated Use of Social Media in Learning Environment

Nitin Agarwal

Abstract Recent years have seen a much greater emphasis on learning to learn, be it in a classroom environment or an organization. This focus imparts lifelong learning capabilities inducing a formative learning experience. Several studies have reflected that individual learning, which has been a core component around which the education system has been institutionalized, does not fully enable learners to learn the process of learning. It has been observed that people learn faster and in much greater depth in groups, making them familiar with the process of learning. Collective learning is a term that is often used to refer to this concept of learning in groups (dyads, teams, organizations, communities, and societies). However, collective learning encounters several challenges in terms of planning, structuring, managing, and evaluating. With the advent of social media technologies including: blogs, wikis, twitter, social networking sites, social news, social bookmarking, media sharing, virtual worlds, and more, encouraging distributed, collaborative, dynamic, ubiquitous, and personalized experience; new paradigms for communication, learning, and education have emerged. In this chapter, the focus is on social media technology as an enabler for collective learning in a teaching/learning environment. It illustrates a model that leverages the integrated use of social media technologies to support collective learning in a university teaching/learning environment. Moreover, the model is generalizable to other environments. The model demonstrates how various challenges encountered in collective learning (planning, structuring, managing, and evaluating) can be addressed with the help of social media technologies. A case study is presented to showcase the model's applicability, feasibility, utility, and success.

This work is supported in part by grants from the US Office of Naval Research.

N. Agarwal (✉)
Information Science Department, University of Arkansas, Little Rock 72204, AR, USA
e-mail: nxagarwal@ualr.edu

B. White et al. (eds.), *Social Media Tools and Platforms in Learning Environments*,
DOI 10.1007/978-3-642-20392-3_3, © Springer-Verlag Berlin Heidelberg 2011

3.1   Collective Learning

More emphasis should be given to the process of learning regardless of the environment. Pedagogical studies show that individuals learn efficiently by practicing concepts and doing exercises. This paradigm is also known as "learning by doing." Originally proposed as a concept in evolutionary economics theory, learning by doing refers to the ability of individuals to improve the productivity of their actions by practice, self-perfection, and through minor innovations. It has a wide range of applications ranging from explaining the effects of innovation and technical change to explaining increasing returns to embodied human capital. A related and a more relevant concept known as active learning (Bonwell et al. 1991), refers to instruction models that endow the responsibility of learning on the learners. All these paradigms have an essential thing in common – an active engagement of learners with the material. Collectively, individuals can discuss and develop educational material, help each other with questions and exercises, and other similar tasks. Collectively, they can learn by doing. This enhances their capability to learn the process of learning and their ability to retain the material much longer, making it a formative experience.

Collective learning ensures that learners are behaviorally, as well as cognitively, engaged. It is, however, debatable when to introduce collective learning based instruction models depending on the learning environment and the domain. For courses involving foundational concepts, introducing a collective learning based instruction model during initial learning stages is perhaps detrimental to the knowledge acquisition. At initial stages of learning, the learners are required to be cognitively more active, rather than behaviorally active, in such courses. Whereas, in advanced courses the entire learning process can be performed collectively. In this chapter, it is assumed that a collective learning based instruction model is introduced once the initial learning phase is over. This assumption keeps the methodology consistent with the case study that was conducted for a foundational level course. However, the model is unaffected by the choice of learning stage at which it is introduced.

Traditional instruction models divide the participants into two groups, namely teacher and learner. This model has had success, however it has several shortcomings. The learners often do not feel involved in the learning process. Moreover, if the teacher is not following proper instructive strategies, or is not adequately trained, s/he may impart false knowledge to several learners for a substantive period of time. On the contrary, a collective learning approach provides a built-in mechanism to evaluate and verify the instructional material.

The benefits of collective learning stretch beyond the realms of academia. The collective learning paradigm is extremely helpful in organizations, where employees are expected to explore, experience, and teach themselves new technologies without formal training. Specifically, in the Information and Communication Technology (ICT) industry, where new techniques and technologies emerge frequently and quickly attain industry-wide standard recognition, collective learning may prove to be a great tool. Learning to learn, imparted by a collective learning paradigm thus helps train the next generation workforce.

Though there are several benefits of the collective learning based instruction model, to realize them requires overcoming the associated challenges. First, it requires a strong motivation among the learners to work in groups and dedicatedly explore, develop, discuss, and self-perfect the material. As mentioned above, it requires active cognitive, as well as behavioral involvement with the material. Second, establishment of mutual trust is paramount. It is very important to trust all collaborators as peers, overlooking any differences in status or power, suspending assumptions and certainties, and delaying deliberation and decision until everyone is convinced. Lastly, it is extremely challenging to plan, structure, manage, and evaluate learner success and the success of the collective learning model.

To address these challenges, solutions were sought from social media applications such as blogs, wikis, micro-blogging, social bookmarking, social news, and social tagging applications that have spread widely over the past 5 years, attracting more than 100 million visitors each month. Social media applications feature the capability to support social interactions, build social communities, and form social relations. Because these tools offer the potential to foster immediate collaboration and participation, they promise a more conducive platform for supporting collective learning based instruction models. In addition to the challenges of collective learning based instruction models described above, social media applications also present their own set of challenges. Ease of use and a low barrier to publication, however, places serious roadblocks in terms of using social media applications for maintaining quality standards in the material developed collectively. Additionally, social media applications are known to shorten the attention span encouraging instant gratification among the participants.[1] A successful collective learning model needs to factor in such challenges.

In this chapter, the emphasis is on the opportunities and challenges of collective learning and how it differs from traditional learning approaches. In Sect. 3.2, there is a discussion about how social media can assist in addressing challenges by proving to be a promising platform for collective learning based instruction models. Section 3.3 describes a collective learning model that leverages social media in instruction delivery. Assessment and evaluation of the proposed model as well as evaluation of the students, which is both essential and challenging, are described in Sect. 3.4. Section 3.5 describes a case study. The chapter concludes in Sect. 3.6 with the authors' perspective on the evolution of the collective learning model with emphasis on future trends and technologies.

3.2 Social Media Characteristics

This section addresses various questions such as: What are the opportunities and challenges in blending social media with learning environment in terms of its openness and dynamics? How the benefits of social media help in overcoming the

---

[1]http://www.dailymail.co.uk/news/article-1153583/Social-websites-harm-childrens-brains-Chilling-warning-parents-neuroscientist.html

technological challenges with collective learning? What challenges of social media need to be explored for proposing a collective learning model?

Recently, people have developed a strong affinity toward social media sites. This has changed the human–computer interaction paradigm making it more dynamic and responsive. Information on Web sites no longer travels a one-way street (from a chosen few content – producers to consumers) rather it has become a two-way information highway. There is no longer a clear distinction between information producers and consumers. Advent of the Web 2.0 paradigm has encouraged the growth in online participation in mass numbers. Technorati reported a phenomenal 100% growth rate for blogs every 6 months. Twitter, a micro-blogging Web site, has an annual growth rate of 1,342%, with over 105 million users reported recently by Twitter.[2] Over 500 million users have already joined Facebook as reported by the Web site on August 1, 2010.[3]

With so many individuals already using social media technologies, albeit for personal reasons, instructors do not have to spend significant time training the students to use them (Boyd 2007). Social media provides an inexpensive, easy-to-use, interactive, dynamic, collaborative, unregulated, almost ubiquitous and democratic platform for Web denizens to voice opinions, express beliefs, share thoughts, and participate in discussions. The highly dynamic nature of ICT related courses is a very concerning problem both from instructor and learner perspectives. A structured curriculum development process may not be adequate for the constantly evolving discipline (Finlayson et al. 2009). Primary characteristics of social media that help in developing an adaptive and evolving curriculum and make it favorable for collective learning paradigm are:

Accessibility. Social media sites are publicly available for almost free or at no cost. This enables an instructor to develop and share curriculum material in an adaptive fashion and facilitate collaboration among learners.

Permanence. Social media sites can be altered anytime making it an adaptive and evolving platform for curriculum development. Individuals can edit their blogs, profile, and preferences anytime they wish by providing comments.

Reach. Social media sites are hosted on the Internet that provides a global audience.

Recency. The time lag between communications produced by social media sites can be almost zero. The communication on social media sites can be instantaneous and acts as an enabler of collective learning and collaboration among learners.

Usability. Most social media sites do not require any special skills to create content. This assists both instructors and learners to utilize social media for curriculum development and collaboration. Social media sites offer technologies with an almost zero operational cost requiring literally no or minimal training.

---

[2]http://techcrunch.com/2010/04/14/twitter-has-105779710-registered-users-adding-300k-a-day/
[3]http://www.facebook.com/press/info.php?statistics

There have been numerous studies (Agarwal 2010; Agarwal and Liu 2009) highlighting the ongoing research activities on various aspects of social media including community extraction, expert identification, information diffusion, small-world phenomenon, preferential attachment, and scale-free power law distributions manifested in the form of the Long Tail phenomenon. Many of these techniques are useful in reducing/summarizing the extremely large networks providing a vantage point for gaining deeper insights into certain patterns. Specifically, authors (Agarwal et al. 2010) have shown the utility of collective wisdom in developing efficient solutions to some of the research challenges. These research efforts can be leveraged to efficiently and effectively summarize instructional material developed during the collective learning process, identify expert students based on knowledge contributions–solicitations and/or interactions, identify student groups, and so on. These and other research efforts can be explored as a future direction to automatically process the material generated through the collective learning process to enhance the quality.

3.3 Collective Learning Model Leveraging Social Media

In this section, a collective learning model is proposed that leverages the integrated use of social media. However, it is paramount to briefly discuss various social media technologies and identify the various characteristics possessed by them. Different social media technologies could be alike or different in terms of functionality. A brief description of each category and functionality is provided below:

Wikis are publicly edited encyclopedias. Anyone can contribute articles to wikis or edit existing ones. However, most of the wikis are moderated to protect content from vandalism. Wikis provide a great technology for content management, where people with a very basic knowledge of formatting, contribute and produce rich sources of information. Wikis also maintain the history of changes and have the capability to rollback to any previous version. Popular wikis such as Wikipedia[4] also allow people to classify articles under one of the following categories: Featured, Good, Cleanup, and Stub. Wikis are a great example of collective intelligence (Szuba 2001).

Blogs or Web logs, is a collection of articles written by people arranged in reverse chronological order. These articles are known as blog posts. The collection of all the blogs is referred to as Blogosphere. Blogs allow people to share their views, express their opinions, interact, and discuss with each other through linking to other blogs or posting comments. A blog when maintained by an individual is known as an individual blog or when managed by a group of people is known as a community

---

[4]http://www.wikipedia.org/

blog. The authors of blogs are known as bloggers. Some blogs such as BlogCatalog[5] also allow users to create their friendship networks.

Micro-Blogging sites, as the name suggests, are similar to blogs except the fact that the articles can only be of certain length. In the case of Twitter,[6] the articles can be 140 characters in length. These articles are also called messages (or tweets in the case of Twitter) because of the short length. These sites are typically used to share what one is doing. Besides posting messages, people can also create friendship networks. They can follow or become followers of other users.

Media Sharing sites allow people to upload and share their multimedia content on the Web (including but not limited to, images, video, audio) with other people. People can watch the content shared by others, enrich them with tags, and share their thoughts through comments. Some media sharing sites allow users to create friendship networks.

Social Bookmarking sites, also known as collaborative tagging, allow people to tag their favorite Webpages or Web sites and share the results with the other users. This generates a good amount of metadata for the Webpages. People can search through this metadata to find relevant or most favorite Webpages/Web sites. People can also see the most popular tags or the most freshly used tags and freshly favored Web site/Webpage. Some social bookmarking sites such as StumbleUpon[7] allow people to create friendship networks. Social bookmarking is a great example of collective intelligence (Szuba 2001).

Social Friendship Networks allow people to stay in touch with their friends and also create new friends. Individuals create their profile on these sites based on their interests, location, education, work, and so on. Usually the ties are nondirectional, which means that there is a need to reciprocate the friendship relation between two nodes.

Social News sites allow people to share news with others and permit others to vote on these stories. News items that are voted the most emerge as the most popular news stories. People can tag various news stories. They can obtain the most popular stories, fastest upcoming stories for different time periods, and share their thoughts by providing comment.

The description of the social media categories creates a nice segway to a presentation of the collective learning based instruction model as illustrated in Fig. 3.1. Note that the execution sequence of different steps of the model is indicated by number prefixes on the arrows. The learning process is divided in two phases: (1) conceptualization and (2) experience, reflection/observation, and application (Kolb 1984). Conceptualization, or the initial learning phase, involves the instructor preparing the instruction material or the basic educational content (step 1) and delivering it to the students (step 2). Interactive discussion with students (step 3)

---

[5]http://www.blogcatalog.com/

[6]http://www.twitter.com/

[7]http://www.stumbleupon.com/

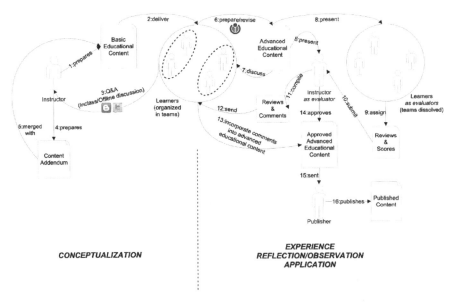

Fig. 3.1 Collective learning based instruction model leveraging social media. The execution sequence of different steps of the model is indicated by *number prefixes on the arrows*

could help the instructor prepare a content addendum (step 4). The interactive discussion could be organized in-class using social media technologies such as Twitter or offline using blogs. While an instructor is teaching, learners can put up questions and/or feedback via twitter posts or tweets. Learners can also post additional resources (in the form of links or previously known facts) in-class on Twitter or offline using blogs. Both twitter and blogs allow instructors and other learners to discuss using the rich interaction paradigm. Instructors can merge the addendum with the basic content (step 5) and make it available to the students. The conceptualization phase is in accordance with the traditional learning model where instructors are solely responsible for educational content preparation and delivery, and most essentially, the learning of the students. The information travels almost one way from instructors to learners. Nonetheless, the conceptualization phase is the vanguard of the collective learning based instruction model because it is paramount that learners build a strong foundation.

The second phase (experience, reflection/observation, and application) as the name suggests, requires more participation from the learners by placing the onus of learning on the learners. Learners are expected to be cognitively and behaviorally active in educational material preparation. Learners invest their basic knowledge and produce an advanced educational content which is moderated by the instructor and their peers, both in a collective manner. This phase is more relevant to the scope of this book and also the objective of this chapter. Learners are organized in teams and are required to prepare an advanced educational content (step 6) using the basic educational content. They discuss and revise the content until it reaches their satisfactory level (step 6 and

7). This can be achieved using a wiki-type interface that provides easy collaborative access to all the team members with the facility of rolling back any changes that seem inappropriate. In addition, wikis are easy to manage and communicate the changes. It avoids bulky and complicated email communications to track changes made by team members. The restricted access controls the security of the content and prevents it from being subjected to vandalism. The advanced educational content is then presented by the teams of learners to instructors and fellow learners (step 8). Both fellow learners and instructors participate in assessment of the material (step 9). The instructor compiles all the reviews and scores from other learners (step 11). These compiled comments and reviews are sent to the respective learner teams (step 12) for them to consider and incorporate into the advanced educational content. The instructor then approves the changes (step 14) and sends the approved advanced educational content to the publisher (step 15). The publisher can publish the content online or elsewhere (step 16). Preparation of a successful advanced educational content warrants experience, observation, and application from the learner perspectives thereby helping them understand the concept much better and retaining it much longer inducing a formative learning experience. The model can be used not only to develop the educational material collectively but also to evaluate or assess its quality collectively. More on assessment and evaluation of the produced educational content as well as the students is discussed in Section 4. The proposed model provides several advantages for leveraging social media technologies:

- Ease of use and intuitive interfaces of social media technologies make it convenient to use these technologies in learning and also for content management. It requires zero or minimal training for learners to begin using social media technologies. Furthermore, as mentioned above, most individuals are already using social media technologies, and this makes blending social media technologies into a learning environment simple and rational.
- Leveraging of social media technologies allows the proposed model to be highly adaptive to an online or e-learning environment. It is not constrained by face time for promoting collective learning.
- Participation being the central tenet of collective learning, the proposed model encourages participatory learning by stimulating discussion in-class and offline.
- Otherwise esoteric concepts or terms can be explained in comfortably conceivable terminology.
- Through collaborative content development, the proposed model encourages communication and team building exercises. The model stimulates within-team and between-team interaction.
- The model takes advantage of the collective learning paradigm inducing a formative learning experience.
- A collective learning based instruction model is well suited for fast-changing curriculum. Educational material development through the proposed collective learning based model can tackle such a dynamic environment.

- Leveraging on the philosophy of collective wisdom, the instruction material is developed from multiple perspectives which may not be entirely possible by a single instructor, which consequently reduces faculty workload.
- The proposed model can readily be taken up by organizations through its ability to handle fast-changing curriculum needs, no face-to-face time constraints, and thus strengthen teamwork.
- Both phases proposed in the model can be decoupled and need not necessarily be interleaved. This could be helpful in situations where the learning is performed in modules.
- The model also proposes a built-in collective wisdom based assessment component explained in more detail in the next section.

3.4   Assessment and Evaluation

Any learning paradigm needs a rigorous assessment methodology to ensure that the desired objectives have been achieved in the most efficient manner. Various assessment methodologies have been proposed for traditional learning approaches. Test scores, grades, exams, and homework have proved to be great assessment strategies over the years. However, in a collective learning paradigm, where participants collectively contribute toward the development of instruction materials, it is extremely critical to assess the success of the model. It is important to evaluate not only the instruction materials but also the participants' intellectual development. The collective learning based instruction model (Fig. 3.1) has a built-in component for assessment of the material (steps 8–14). The assessment relies on the weighted sum of the feedback and scores of the peers, and the instructor with perhaps a larger weight assigned to the instructor's feedback. This assessment strategy builds upon the philosophy of collective wisdom. Learners first organize themselves as teams and develop the advanced educational material (steps 6 and 7). Then they present the material to the instructor and other learners (step 8). At this point, the fellow learners or the peers take on the role of evaluators along with the instructor (steps 9–11). A carefully designed assessment rubric is used to assess the quality and the level of understanding of the learners responsible for the preparation of the material. The feedback and scores thus obtained from the collective assessment strategy generates enormous collective wisdom helping the instructors to assess the educational content and learners to improve their educational content (steps 12–14). The collective wisdom ensures that the variation in scores from any individual outlier assessment is suppressed and the final score converges toward an optimal value (Surowiecki 2004). Bearing upon the central tenet of collective wisdom philosophy, it is paramount to the success of the collective assessment strategy that the evaluators (peer learners in this case) assess and assign scores independently (Landemore and Elster 2008).

The rubric, presented in Table 3.1, is designed to assess the material prepared by the learners along various dimensions of clarity, knowledge, and

Table 3.1 Assessment rubric for the educational content developed by the collective wisdom based instruction model

	1 – (Novice)	2 – (Apprentice)	3 – (Proficient)	4 – (Distinguished)
Content quality of the article				
Organization/structural quality of the article				
Clarity of the article				
Knowledge of the topic reflected by the team				
Extent to which key issues were identified				
Attention to level of details				

understanding. Specifically, the educational material is checked for content quality, proper organization or structural quality, clarity, knowledge of the topic reflected by the team of learners, extent to which key issues are identified, and the attention to detail. Each dimension is calibrated on a scale of 1 to 4, with 4 being the highest. A score of 1 indicates novice, 2 indicates apprentice, 3 indicates proficient, and 4 indicates distinguished level. This set of assessment rubrics is complemented by detailed comments where peers are asked to provide strengths and weaknesses in the material prepared by the learners. Both components constitute toward the assessment as well as further improvement of the educational material.

The collective assessment strategy has the following advantages:

- It introduces learners (especially undergraduate learners) to the peer review process early on in their careers.
- It encourages participation, which is the central tenet for a collective learning based instruction model, not only during material preparation but also during assessment.
- By compelling learners to participate in assessment, it improves student learning.
- Sharing assessment with learners provides different perspectives reducing faculty workload.
- Feedback and comments generate enormous collective wisdom that can be used to improve the educational content.

While the collective assessment strategy presented above helps in the assessment of the educational content, a two-phase process is used for the individual student evaluation, which is independent of the collective assessment strategy. The instructor is solely responsible for the learner's evaluation. Instructors evaluate the learners while they are presenting the material and also request an anonymous member's evaluation report from the team.

3.5   A Case Study: Collective Learning Effort to Develop an Article on Social Media

In this section, a case study is presented to showcase the models applicability, feasibility, utility, and success. The case study refers to a project that was accomplished as a part of a course (IFSC 4360: Social Computing) in a university environment (University of Arkansas at Little Rock) during Fall 2009. The project's aim was to collectively develop a comprehensive article on social media technologies. Students were given a basic lecture on social media technologies as a part of conceptualization phase (steps 1–5 of the proposed model in Fig. 3.1), including various categories (also mentioned in Sect. 3.3), their functionalities, expectations, purpose, and outreach. A course blog was built to answer student queries concerning the lecture or the project as a whole.[8] Students were then asked to form teams and pick at least two categories of social media technologies. During the second phase, they were asked to explore their chosen categories and prepare articles (steps 6 and 7). Students then presented their findings that were peer assessed (steps 8–11). The feedback from the peer assessment was used by the teams to improve their articles (steps 12–14) and shared on the course wiki[9] (steps 15 and 16). The collaboration was not confined within a team but also spanned across multiple teams, since several teams had overlapping social media categories. The outcome of the model was the detailed article on social media technologies that was developed by the students of the class. A few screenshots are shown in Figs. 3.2a, b. Based on the student feedback, their experience with social media technologies was fruitful. The students felt more actively and enthusiastically involved in the exercise. Collaboration within team and across teams was made simpler using wikis. Further, on a larger scale, students were observed to be more behaviorally active in the class. Some students were not as orally expressive as they were in writing on class blogs and twitter, and gradually became less hesitant during in-class discussions.

The proposed model was put to test and the outcome was evaluated according to the collective evaluation plan (steps 8–14 in Fig. 3.1). There were 18 students in the class who were organized into nine teams. For each team, two simultaneous evaluations were performed. One was performed by the instructor and the other was performed by peers using the rubric mentioned in Table 3.1. The peer evaluations were then averaged for each of the six dimensions. Essentially, each team was evaluated by 16 students and the instructor on six dimensions mentioned in the rubric in Table 3.1. Finally, a cumulative evaluation was computed for the teams, both for the peer and instructor evaluation, by averaging evaluation scores for all the six dimensions. The evaluation results for each of the six dimensions are presented

---

[8]The course blog is located at: http://socialcomputing.trojanifsc.net/blog/
[9]The course wiki is located at: http://socialcomputing.trojanifsc.net/wiki/wikka.php?wakka= HomePage

MyWikkaSite : SocialMediaReport
HomePage :: Categories :: PageIndex :: RecentChanges :: Recently
:: Change settings/Logout :: You are admin

What is Social Media?
Social computing is a multi-disciplinary research program that focu
human, cultural, and behavioral aspects. It brings together experts
various disciplines like: anthropology, cognitive science, computer
aaanawlaa, linguistics, mathematics, neuroscience, political science
psychology, sociology, statistics, and theology. Social computing r
intersection of social behavior and computational systems. Social c
is often defined as modeling complex human interactions that are
on a variety of social media. Social media, or commonly known as
Web, consists of an ant-colony of services including blogs, media s
micro blogging, social bookmarking, social news, social friendship
websites, and wikis. Different social media sites could be alike or
terms of functionality. We briefly describe each category and the
functionalities:
Different categories of social media:
- Social Networks
- Media Sharing
- Blogging
- Microblogging
- Virtual World
- Social News
- Social Bookmarking
- Opinions and Ratings

(a) Main page

MyWikkaSite : MediaSharing
HomePage :: Categories :: PageIndex :: RecentChanges :: Recently
:: Change settings/Logout :: You are admin

Edited by: Eric, Tara, Tyler, Yoann

Definition of Media Sharing
Wikipedia states, "media sharing occurs in online social networks i
communities with a comprehensive platform and diversified interfa
aggregate, upload, compress, host and distribute images, text, ap
videos, audio, games and new media. It is the interactive process
via email, instant message, text message, posting or linking to me
website or blog and other methods of sharing media to a targeted
As media is shared, it takes on a variety of different contexts and
The same video posted on YouTube and on Digg will generate diffe
communication outcomes as the same video being sent to a family
and a college buddy. Social commentary usually accompanies shar
Media sharing sustains social networks, web based communities a
digitally supported relationships. It is a communication process tha
the participation of both the sender and receiver."
(http://en.wikipedia.org/wiki/Media_sharing)-Tyler

History
What started as simply sharing your photo album with family and
the couch has transformed into the extremely popular phenomeno
has media sharing on the internet. Media sharing is essentially the
and viewing of different types of media, such as pictures and vide
However, the media sharing phenomenon is comparatively recent,

(b) Sample entry

Fig. 3.2 A collectively developed article on social media technologies using a collective learning based instruction model

in Fig. 3.3a–f, the cumulative evaluation averaged on all the dimensions in Fig. 3.4, and the correlation between student and instructor evaluation in Fig. 3.5. It can be observed that the proposed collective assessment strategy shows a promising result based on the high correlation value ($R^2 = 0.9732$) between instructor and peer evaluation scores.

The results demonstrate that not only the proposed collective learning based instruction model enriched learner experience through social media, but also made an effective evaluation possible by leveraging collective wisdom. This model presents an empirical analysis and a methodology to develop a stronger and foundational underpinning of collective learning, leveraging social media. As a future direction, the authors plan to make this analysis more robust by performing data collection for larger classes with multiple offerings.

3.6 Looking Ahead

As the emphasis is shifting toward learning to learn, putting the focus of learning on the learners, new ways of experimental learning have been explored. Another upcoming technology is the social media where content generation is shifting from a few producers to the consumers. The Web 2.0 paradigm has promoted collaborative content development. The authors attempted to blend

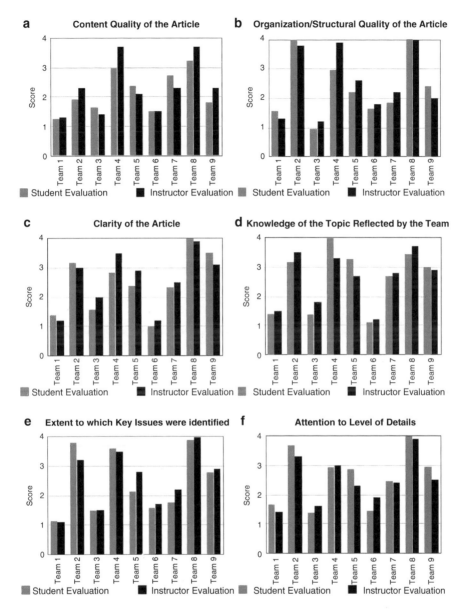

Fig. 3.3 Collective assessment of the material and evaluation of the students based on the proposed collective learning model using the rubrics in Table 3.1. Note that for each of the nine student teams instructor evaluation and average peer evaluation were given on all six dimensions

these two significant paradigm shifts and explore their impacts on learning. Specifically, a collective learning instruction model is proposed that leverages the integrated use of multiple social media. The advantages of the model include

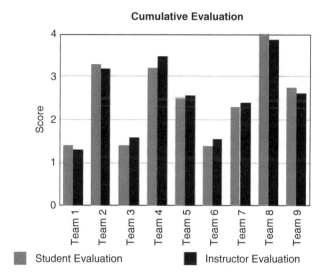

Fig. 3.4 Cumulative evaluation scores for each of the nine student teams averaged on all the six dimensions

Fig. 3.5 Correlation between student and instructor evaluation scores

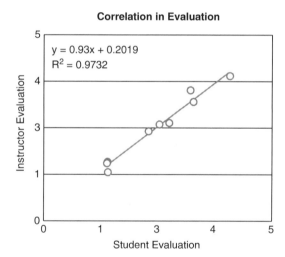

a built-in collective assessment strategy to evaluate the merit of the educational content are highlighted.

Through this model, the authors postulate that learning should not be compartmentalized rather it should be more open. Students learn faster from their peers than the faculty. This is precisely the reason why all the social media technologies do not have a user manual and yet people are able to grasp them quickly. They see, they learn. The main role of faculty should be to give that push to the students and let their creativity feed their imagination. Some students are not as orally expressive as they are in writing. The quietest of the students have often been the most active on

Twitter and the class blog and gradually have become less hesitant during in-class discussions.

As a future direction, the authors will further explore and expand the proposed collective learning model in d-learning, e-learning, and m-learning environments. Furthermore, it is intended to explore various incentive frameworks such as the ones in social applications – Gowalla and Foursquare, to expand the model successfully beyond academia and into more open learning environments.

References

Agarwal, N.: Social Computing in Blogosphere: Challenges, Methodologies, and Opportunities. LAP Lambert Academic Publishing AG & Co. KG (2010)

Agarwal, N., Liu, H.: Modeling and data mining in blogosphere. Synthesis lectures on data mining and knowledge discovery. Morgan & Claypool Publishers (2009)

Agarwal, N., Galan, M., Liu, H., Subramanya, S.: Wiscoll: collective wisdom based blog clustering. J. Inf. Sci. **180**(1), 39–61 (2010)

Bonwell, C., Eison, J.: Active Learning: Creating Excitement in the Classroom, volume AEHE-ERIC Higher Education Report No.1. Jossey-Bass, Washington, DC (1991)

Boyd, D.: Why youth (heart) social network sites: the role of networked publics in teenage social life. In: John, D., Catherine, T. (eds.) MacArthur Foundation Series on Digital Media and Learning, pp. 119–142. MIT Press, Cambridge (2007)

Finlayson, A., Cameron, D., Hardy, M.: Journalism Education as a Perpetual Beta Test: Notes on the Design and Delivery of Tertiary 'Social Media' Subjects (2009)

Kolb, D.A.: Experimental Learning. Experience as a Source of Learning and Development. Prentice Hall, Upper Saddle River (1984)

Landemore, H., Elster, C.M.: Democratic reason: the mechanisms of collective intelligence in politics. In: Collective Wisdom: Principles and Mechanisms Conference, pp. 22–23. Collége de France, Paris (2008)

Surowiecki, J.: The Wisdom of Crowds: Why the Many are Smarter than the Few and How Collective Wisdom Shapes Business, Economies, Societies, and Nations. Doubleday, Random House, Inc, New York (2004)

Szuba, T.M.: Computational Collective Intelligence. Wiley, New York (2001)

Chapter 4
New Learning Paradigms: Open Course Versus Traditional Strategies. The Current Paradox of Learning and Developing Creative Ideas

Jose Albors-Garrigos and Jose Carlos Ramos Carrasco

Abstract This chapter analyses the critical facts related to open course versus classical alternatives for learning and developing creative ideas in a social computing environment. The driving factors, the available tools and the barriers which hinder their utilisation will be discussed. The variables that will have a relevant impact will be analysed within the context of a model that explains this phenomenon. These new learning paradigms will be analysed within the context of learning and their evolution in the last decade.

4.1 Introduction

Learning processes have evolved from the post-industrial to the information technology and knowledge era. Younger individuals, born after the 1980s, also labelled *Digital natives* as opposed to *Digital Immigrants*,[1] learn in a different way (Prensky 2001a, b). As a consequence of the adoption of information technologies, the impact of information input and its instantaneity through search engines such as Google and repositories such as Wikipedia, new learning paradigms such as Open Course have appeared (Sharples 2000). Until now formal education has used IT

---

[1] According to this author, the former 'have learnt with digital language of computers, video games and Internet' while the latter 'were not born into the digital world but have adopted later many or more aspects of new technologies,

J. Albors-Garrigos (✉)
Department of Business Organization, Universidad Politecnica de Valencia, Camino de Vera S/N, 46022 Valencia, Spain
e-mail: jalbors@doe.upv.es

J.C. Ramos Carrasco
Avanzalis Knowledge Associates, Paseo de Gracia, 12, 1, 08007 Barcelona, Spain
e-mail: jcramos@avanzalis.com

B. White et al. (eds.), *Social Media Tools and Platforms in Learning Environments*,
DOI 10.1007/978-3-642-20392-3_4, © Springer-Verlag Berlin Heidelberg 2011

principally to support administration and research and has been slow to adapt it to improve its core business of teaching and learning (Stephenson 2006).

Education[2] is being forced to evolve from providing knowledge to that of training individuals to capture and act on the knowledge they require (Argyrin and Schon, 1996). Society, economy and business are transformed and influenced by the opportunities provided by changes. Individuals have to adapt and develop a well-systematised lifelong learning process to be competitive (Drucker 1966).

The concept of the Open Course is based on the philosophical view of knowledge as a collective social product and the goal of making it a social property (Downes 2007). Additionally, it fits the concept of Lifelong Learning (Gelpi 1985), defined in a practical way by the European Lifelong Learning Initiative (ELLI) as: ... *'a continuously supportive process which stimulates and empowers individuals to acquire all the knowledge, values, skills and understanding they will require throughout their lifetimes and to apply them with confidence, creativity and enjoyment in all roles, circumstances, and environments'* (Peck 1996). There is a transition away from traditional education strategies based on regular and closed structured studies.

Computer-Supported Collaborative Learning (CSCL) has become a relevant discipline based on its own scientific community. CSCL is a learning approach based on social interaction thorough the utilisation of computers and/or through the Internet. This type of learning is characterized by sharing and building knowledge among participants utilising technology as their primary means of communication, or as a common resource. In 2006, the International Society of the Learning Sciences (ISLS) founded the journal 'The International Journal of Computer-Supported Collaborative Learning' (IJCSCL) in order to support their research (Stahl et al. 2006).

This paper will examine how individuals, principally as knowledge workers (Drucker 1966), can benefit from current new learning paradigms in order to stay competitive. The hypothesis is that rapid significant learning through the use of social computing will lead to enhanced creativity, collaboration efficiency and overall learning. On the other hand, learning models have evolved contingently along the development of digital media.

The chapter is structured in the following way. Section 4.2 will review the context of learning theories and models and their contingent relationship with the new digital media and tools. Section 4.3 will analyse the concepts associated with rapid significant learning and how these concepts lead to the new learning paradigms on which open course philosophy has been based. Section 4.4 analyses the relationships of new learning paradigms with the management and stimulation of creativity in a social context. Section 4.5 illustrates the proposed models with actual experiences and finally, Sect. 4.6 draws some conclusions and proposes the future challenges facing collective and digital supported learning.

---

[2]We are referring in this article for higher and professional education contexts.

4.2 Current Learning Contexts

Academic literature and research have discussed individual learning processes extensively. However new technologies have changed the way new generations learn (Prensky 2001b). For the purpose of this section, some common assumptions on the way education is primarily structured and organised, and how these have evolved and led to the upcoming of new learning methods and practices, are reviewed.

According to Gagné (1985), learning is integrated in eight phases; each of them includes events or external conditions that have to be structured by the teacher or learner in order to assure learning efficiency. The following Table 4.1 summarizes them.

In particular, Phases 2 through 5 are based on continuous assimilation between rote and meaningfulness. This author has detailed some typical actions that take place in each of these phases. For example, in Phase 2 of apprehension, asking questions to understand what is being acquired may help to select what really is new knowledge; in Phase 3, the activities relate new concepts with the learner's cognitive structure in a specific action that must be carried out to develop conceptual mental maps.

Gagné (1974, 1985) was one of the first significant educational researchers associating learning processes with media, pointing out how different media have different potentialities for instruction, conceived as the events supporting the learning phases. Therefore, depending on the various kinds of learning outcomes (acquiring information, development of attitude or intellectual skills), the various media will be more or less effective.

Kolb (1984) incorporated experience in his learning paradigm, defining it as the process through which knowledge is created with the elaboration of experience. This experience is transformed into concepts which become guides for new experiences, developing a learning cycle. This cycle is composed of four stages: concrete experience, reflective observation, abstract conceptualization and active experimentation. Schon (1983) adopted this paradigm when he proposed his *reflective practitioner* model showing how professionals learn continuously through challenging experiences.

Table 4.1 Learning phases according to Gagné (Gagné 1974, 1985)

Phase	Learner	Events
Motivation	Expectations	Activating motivation
Apprehension	Selective perception	Attention
Acquisition phase	Encoding storage	Stimulation, Guidance
Retention phase	Memory storage	Enhancing retention
Recall	Retrieval	
Generalisation	Transfer	Promoting transfer of learning
Performance	Response generation	Eliciting performance by providing feedback
Feedback	Reinforcement	

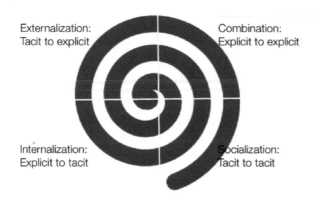

Fig. 4.1 The knowledge creating spiral (Adapted from Nonaka and Takeuchy 1995)

It is interesting to observe how the models mentioned above outline the relevance of the feedback phase. Considering organizational collective learning, Argyris and Schon (1978) suggest their two-way learning approaches: single and double-loop learning. This model proposes that the acquisition of new knowledge involves a feedback loop that leads to a behaviour change in the first mode. A review of self-knowledge and, therefore, the modification of the orientation of our future behaviour and goals will lead to the second mode of learning. However, in general, classical education adopts single-loop learning which impedes innovation and adaptation to new paradigms (Argyris and Schön 1996).

Finally, and from the point of view of knowledge management, most educational systems understand their mission as a task of knowledge transfer from the teacher (seen as experts in a topic) to the student mind (Blank 1978). This means that principally, they use solely *combination processes*, one of the knowledge flows introduced by Nonaka and Takeuchi (1995) in their knowledge generation spiral (see Fig. 4.1). Unfortunately, only few systems apply complementary knowledge flows in their education alternatives, and therefore, this is part of the limitation of traditional education systems.

It could be concluded that learning is an active process of constructing, rather than acquiring knowledge, and instruction is a process of supporting that construction rather than a mere communication of knowledge (Duffy and Cunningham 1996).

4.3   New Learning Paradigms

As a consequence of the drawbacks of traditional learning systems, new educational programmes based on new learning models have been introduced. Authors such as Goleman (1996) incorporated the concept of emotional intelligence for learning success; Peter Senge (1990, 1996), a follower of Argyris, contributed with his seminal contributions on learning organizations. Other authors such as Nelson (1999) have contributed with key ideas for developing content knowledge in complex domains, problem-solving, critical thinking and collaboration skills. Savaneviciene et al. (2008) suggested the relevance of continuous lifelong learning and competencies development. From the point of view of management, Drucker (1996)[3] coined the term 'knowledge worker' pointing out the relevance of education, development and training for his/her success.

The following paragraphs will discuss the new trends which propose new and reviewed learning models.

4.4 Significative Learning, Collaborative Contexts, and Concept Maps

According to Ausubel et al. (1978), significant learning occurs when new information is acquired by a deliberate effort on the part of the learner to tie the new information with concepts, or pre-existent relevant propositions, in his/her cognitive structure. Significant learning has been defined as that which requires some kind of lasting change and relevance in terms of the learner's life (Fink 2003). Several authors, and specially Finkel (1999), argue that most relevant learning is not produced in classical classroom contexts through an expert narrative (a teacher). Rather, profound significant learning occurs in a more natural context based on collaborative factors. Experience corroborates this idea, since it seems that talented people indeed learn more outside of structured courses (and not only in presence contexts). Their expertise updating is higher than that limited to traditional educational institutions (Ausubel et al. 1978).

Novak (1998) designed a tool called Conceptual Maps (Cmaps), based on how children learn at school. It was intended to make explicit what they had learnt after various lessons. Cmaps were remarkable in that they helped people to link new bits of knowledge with their existing cognitive structure in a systematic way. It could be said that, though studying with Cmaps is more demanding than using summaries, schemas or memorizing, the sequence of steps taken to create a Cmap and interiorize knowledge provides reflection and understanding (Buzan and Buzan 2006). Consequently, the achieved reward is substantially higher: a significative learning which is more deeply interiorized and moves routine towards change.

Conceptual Maps use the following steps to develop and achieve significative learning:

1. Generation of a list with main relevant concepts;
2. Sort concepts from general to specific;
3. Develop the map with general concepts on top and specific ones at the bottom;

---

[3]This author defined the term as 'those employees who put knowledge to productive use'.

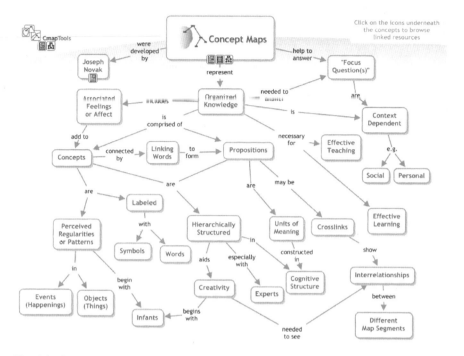

Fig. 4.2 Concept map explaining the idea of concept maps (Source: authors based on Novak (1998) and Buzan and Buzan (2006))

4. Link concepts with lines containing nexus words and
5. Draw crossed links between different hierarchies of the map, which mean significative relationships.

Consequently, concept maps specifically address the reflective observation and abstract conceptualization phases proposed by Kolb. Figure 4.2 represents a conceptual map which explains the main foundations sustaining the idea of what constitutes a concept map. It has been developed with an easy tool called CmapTools from the Florida Institute for Human and Machine Cognition.

4.4.1 Creativity, Brain Laterality and Visual Thinking

Generalisations about certain brain functions (logic, creativity) being lateralised, that is, located in the right or left side of the brain are common in psychology. The existence of functional differences between the two hemispheres of our brain still supports myths (Agor 1989; Hines 1987). These ideas have been controversial and some functionalities are often distributed across both sides (Westen et al. 2006). Table 4.2 summarises some of the theories on the lateralisation of the human brain (Dehaene et al. 1999; Goldberg 2009).

Table 4.2   Left and Right brain hemisphere functions (Dehaene et al. 1999; Goldberg 2009)

Left hemisphere functions	Right hemisphere functions
Numerical computation (exact calculation, numerical comparison, estimation) left hemisphere only: direct fact retrieval	Numerical computation (approximate calculation, numerical comparison, estimates)
Language: grammar/vocabulary, literal	Language: intonation/accentuation, prosody, pragmatic, contextual

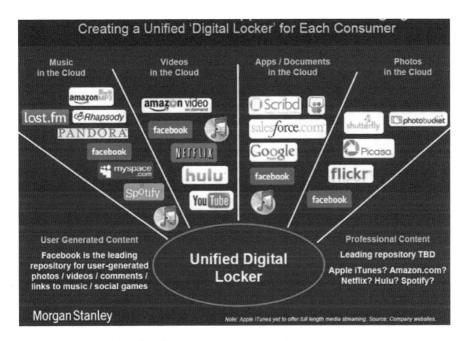

Fig. 4.3   Firms supplying digital services (Source: Morgan 2010)

This research has contributed to enlarging learning boundaries. Other authors such as Mathewson (1999) have introduced the concept of visual or spatial thinking. This scheme is close to the modern concept of hypertext reading and learning (Johnson-Sheehan and Baehr 2001).

In reference to visual thinking and learning, various authors have made efforts to represent concepts graphically in order to more easily convey complex ideas. This drives support of tools such as concept maps (Novak 1998) commented previously, or mental/ idea maps (Buzan and Buzan 2006), among others. These have had an impact on the way information is presented in electronic interfaces such as web pages, reports, presentations and electronic newspapers and also on the way advertising is designed to attract the attention of the consumers. In this line of thinking, Morgan (2010) recently pointed to the importance of document sharing and its mobile trend. Figure 4.3 shows some of the web 2.0 firms supporting various digital services.

4.4.2 Competencies: A New Dimension of Learning

In 1997, the OECD member countries launched the Program for International Student Assessment (PISA), with the aim of monitoring the extent to which students have acquired the knowledge and skills essential for full participation in society. The OECD's Definition and Selection of Competencies (DeSeCo) Project provided a framework for new competency domains for learning (OECD 2005).

The authors (Boyatzis 1982; McClelland 1973) in proposing this term argued that a competency is more than just knowledge and skills. It involves the ability to meet complex demands by drawing on and mobilising psychosocial resources (including skills and attitudes) in a particular context. New active teaching methodologies build on these new contributions to suggest a framework based on three main components:

- Knowledge: Understood as the minimum amount of comprehension of the topic to be able to build on it;
- Skills: Understood as the abilities a person has to have to develop certain activities; and
- Attitudes: Of the individual towards the topic (Fig. 4.4).

The competencies model focuses learning on the experimentation phase (Kolb 1984). Knowing that these pillars sustain competence development, effective and rapid learning will have to incorporate them.

4.4.3 De Treville: Learning Efficiency and Motivation Mechanisms

De Treville (Mumford and Honey 1993) associated learning efficiency with motivation challenges and argued that learning occurs only when the challenge is within certain limits. She argued that maximum learning occurs when the challenge inherent in the problem is consistent with the capabilities of the individual. That is, learning is closely linked to the concept of challenge.

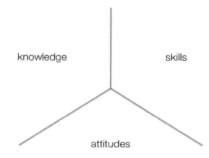

Fig. 4.4 The three pillars of learning competencies (Source: Own elaboration based on Ambrose et al. (2003) and Murray (2003))

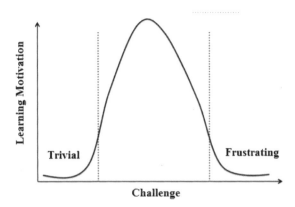

Fig. 4.5 De Treville curve (Adapted from Mumford and Honey 1993)

What takes place when an individual accomplishes by him/herself the task of learning in a significative mode in the Internet? Everything points to the way this margin becomes dynamic. It means that the level of challenge is determined in a variable way by the researcher, in an iterative process, building on the findings and conclusions he/she garners from every approach to the topic (Mumford and Honey 1993) (Fig. 4.5).

4.4.4 Learning as a Creative Process: Bloom's Taxonomy[4]

Bloom and Krathwohl (1956) developed a classification of levels of intellectual behaviour relevant to the learning process. It became a critical tool for structuring and understanding the learning process which was divided into three psychological domains: Cognitive (knowledge, information and mental skills); Affective (attitudes and feelings), and Psychodynamic (manual or physical manipulative skills). Bloom suggested a multi-stage tiered construct of thinking according to six cognitive levels of complexity. These levels have been depicted as a progressive pyramid. The lowest three levels are knowledge, comprehension and application. The highest three levels are analysis, synthesis and evaluation. This is a hierarchical taxonomy: a learner functioning at the application level has also overcome the knowledge and comprehension levels. It could be said that Bloom's pyramid reflects building process competencies according to Ambrose et al. (2003) or Murray (2003).

A new group of cognitive psychologists (Anderson and Krathwohl 2001) updated the taxonomy, reflecting the relevance of new technologies by changing the names of the levels from nouns to active verbs. The two highest, most complex levels – Synthesis and Evaluation – were reversed in the revised model, and were

---

[4]Taxonomy is understood here as the hierarchical classification of human development in knowledge topic.

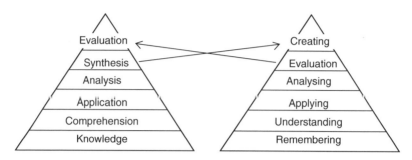

Fig. 4.6 Bloom's original and revised learning taxonomy (Anderson and Krathwohl 2001; Bloom and Krathwohl 1956)

renamed Evaluating and Creating, these two highest levels being essentially equal in level of complexity. It must be highlighted that creating requires learners to put parts together in a new way or to synthesise them into something different, a new form or product.

Based on this reviewed taxonomy, an analysis of the contribution to learning of the digital age shows two important themes: learner participation and creativity and online identity formation which take place in the context of web 2.0. Thus, the process of learning shifts when individuals share ideas built on previous ones that they want to share and to explain to others. This process is facilitated by social computing (Greenhow et al. 2009).

Figure 4.6 shows Bloom's original and revised classification. It has six levels from knowing and evolving to higher skills: understanding, application, analysis and finally, the highest level of knowledge capacity, synthesis and evaluation or, in the new terms, evaluation and creativity. According to this idea and other new learning paradigms reviewed here, the higher the level accomplished, the deeper the learning achieved.

4.4.5 Understanding How Digital Natives Capture Information Bits. "Edutainment"

Today's average recent college graduate has spent over 10,000 h of his/her life playing video games; 20,000 h watching TV (a high percentage high speed MTV); has sent and received 200,000 emails and instant messages; spent over 10,000 h talking on digital cell phones and has watched over 500,000 TV commercials. And, maybe, at the very most, he/she has spent 5,000 h reading books (Prensky 2001a, b). This has led to the term edutainment, 'a form of entertainment designed to educate as well as to amuse' (Okan 2003).

Computer games, email, internet media, cell phones and instant messaging are integral parts of a new language, the digital language. Some educators, aware of this, have made some efforts to re-think the way they teach (Lieberman et al. 1998).

Thus, a new discipline has been developed to use '*digital language*' to motivate students to learn (Merzenich et al. 1996; Tallal and Merzenich 1996).

The Cone of Experience (Dale 1969) and former reviews (Begay et al. 2006) show some evidence of the degree of retention by learners depending on the way learning is achieved. This favours a new way of apparently unstructured learning based on new technologies, channels, tools and communal habits. According to Begay et al. (2006) and Dale (1969) students tend to remember:

- 10% of what they read (comprehension);
- 20% of what they hear (listening);
- 30% of what they see (charts, power points, videos, spreadsheets and reports);
- 50% of what they hear and see (pictures and movies);
- 70% of what they demonstrate and write (oral presentations, explaining, teaching, instructing and participating);
- 90% of what they do (real world practice: becoming aware of what they know, applying what they learn, finding out what they do not know and creating and producing a finished product or service).

Reading and comprehension are vital to the learning process. Academic literature has pointed out that all aspects of the *Cone of Learning* are important when used appropriately by students and instructors in completing a successful project (Begay et al. 2006; Dale 1969). Digital Natives are naturally accustomed to the new interfaces and information sources and they leverage their understanding by taking advantage of these new paradigms (Prensky 2001b).

4.4.6 Instantaneity

Star and Ruhleder (1996) defined Global Information Infrastructure (GII) as: 'both the engine and barrier for change; both customizable and rigid; both inside and outside organizational practices. It is product and process... With the rise of decentralised technologies used across wide geographical distance, both the need for common standards and the need for situated, tailored and flexible technologies grow stronger'.

In a similar rationale, Borgman (2003) points out an interesting reflection on the role of librarians and, in general, libraries in the future. In the present, with a computer and a DSL connection, an individual can access almost all libraries and electronic publications.

Digital Natives are accustomed to capturing important information on a new topic or problem in seconds, in only the time it takes to 'wake up' the laptop or mobile device, enter Google and Wikipedia, and obtain the results (perhaps less than 3 min). That gives them a clue about what they have learnt initially, and ignites a deeper, iterative process to pick up more information (Prensky 2001a, b).

Furthermore, some authors suggest there is no way to return to the former status since universal access to knowledge is inevitable (Lessig 2005). Other aspects about the way to find a balance between creativity protection and availability to ideas have been the subject of discussions and reflections. This instant access and interaction with information has affected the speed and efficiency of the learning process, as well as providing further motivation drivers (Lessig 2005).

4.4.7 Learning as a Continuous Process: Lifelong Learning

At this point, it becomes evident that anyone who aims to be competitive in the knowledge era needs to be ready to learn throughout his/her whole life (Aspin and Chapman 2000; Savaneviciene et al. 2008). Continuous learning has led to the concept of Lifelong learning. Lifelong learning entails education occurring from the integration of formal, non-formal and informal education so as to create the ability for a continuous lifelong development of the individual (Candy 1991).

Figure 4.7 shows two learning curves obtained from an experimental study (Aspin and Chapman 2000). The bottom line represents the regular pattern while the top line represents the learning activity of individuals who continue learning throughout their whole life.

The senior gap, showed here as a red arrow, indicates the outstanding difference in knowledge between lifelong learning versus a regular learning pattern.

With the purpose of relating these new paradigms with each other and with the prevailing theories of learning, these are represented below in Fig. 4.8. It must be mentioned that all of them reinforce the various phases of the Kolb's (1984) learning model (concrete experience; reflective observation, abstract conceptualization and active experimentation) demonstrating their interdependence and their relationship with the basic learning context.

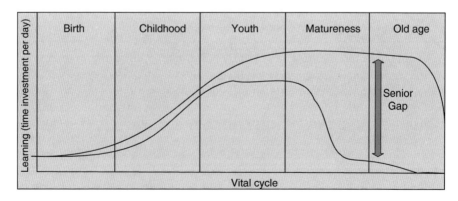

Fig. 4.7 Real learning (*bottom*) and lifelong learning curves (Aspin and Chapman 2000)

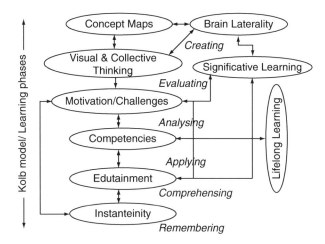

Fig. 4.8 Relationship among new learning paradigms (Source: Authors)

4.5   How New Learning Paradigms Contribute to Managing and Stimulating Creativity

As discussed in previous sections, new paradigms are shifting the way individuals learn and create as a final step of learning. It is intrinsic in 'Digital Natives', and is a handicap to be overcome by 'Digital Immigrants' (Prensky 2001a). Today, individuals can work at home accessing virtually all knowledge resources worldwide, and also access cutting edge trends in any discipline thanks to search engines. This facilitates an individual's development of competencies along the learning cycle. These new skills are well explained in the concept of Actional Intelligence (Albors and Ramos 2010), defined as *the capacity of an individual and, by extension, of a collective organization, to identify useful and necessary knowledge for an activity, learn it and, apply it to better perform.*

Managing creativity, the last step of the learning cycle, is about raising the probability for creative acts to happen by stimulating the factors that work in favour of creativity (Stenmark 2003). The following factors have been considered relevant in information technology contexts:

Since the source of innovation is unpredictable, avoidance of preconceptions is fundamental (Robinson and Stern 1998);

Autonomy is also a relevant factor, given the fact that personal interests are driving factors that regulate the actions of individuals in their daily activities (Stenmark 2003);

Serendipity has also been pointed out as another factor and thus, the probability of accidental findings must be facilitated (Robinson and Stern 1998);

It has also been found that creative persons tend to spend time with people with diverse interests and beliefs. Therefore, variety promotion is another stimulus for creativity as well as a provision for a rich information environment (Stenmark 2003).

4.5.1 Collaboration, Knowledge Sharing, and Creativity Development

Knowledge sharing has been defined as individuals sharing relevant information, ideas, suggestions and expertise (Bartol and Srivastava 2002). It has been emphasized that knowledge sharing constitutes the basis of creative organisations (McAfee 2009; Nonaka and Takeuchi 1995). In fact, it has been emphasised that new ideas may be developed into practice with greater degrees of freedom and speed through the utilisation of the new paradigms posed by new technologies and social networks (Candy 1991; Klemmer et al. 2002; Thomas 2001).

Recent research has shown a more complex context of creativity that highlights the importance of social interactions, mentoring and collaboration in creative work. In this direction, support for the articulation of creative ideas and an enhanced exchange between different disciplines can eliminate some of the barriers in interdisciplinary collaboration (Shirky 2009). Creating an emotional as well as physical environment that encourages creativity is also relevant. Furthermore, trust, encouragement and risk-free exploration, as well as incentives for creative investigation, are a necessary part of any creative culture (Mamykina et al. 2002).

In this direction, Fischer (2005) pointed out that digital media has provided new powers for the individual in the past decade, and in the future, the world's networks will provide enormous unexplored opportunities for groups and communities while cultures of participation provide all learners with the means to become co-creators.

In relation to communication between individuals, informal channels have been found to be richer than formal channels (Bernoff and Groundswell 2008; Shirky 2009). Finally, it seems that when individuals are primarily motivated by their own interests, they are more creative than they are when primarily driven by some goal imposed on them by others (Albors and Ramos 2010; Stenmark 2003).

4.5.2 Telecommunication and Information Technologies (TI) Creativity Support Tools

According to Herrmann (2008), collaborative creativity is a process whereby individuals representing various perspectives communicate, work on shared material and document their mutual results. This process requires alternate phases of individual reflection, asynchronous and highly simultaneous contributions where participants try to produce and synergize ideas so that the results are new and useful in their fields. TI provides a powerful technical support for collaborative creativity, but it becomes a complex task due to the fact that the interacting actors may possess diverse backgrounds and communication patterns or structures. Herrmann (2008) outlines three main factors to be considered: the actor's personal characteristics, the contexts in which ideas may flourish and the processes by which ideas develop.

Conger (1996) has reviewed methodologies oriented towards creative problem solving and pointed out five basic steps: (a) Opportunity and problem definition; (b) Compiling relevant information; (c) Generating ideas; (d) Evaluating and prioritising ideas and (e) Developing an implementation plan.

Shneiderman (2002) proposes a model composed of four basic activities where social interaction has been incorporated in the second and fourth:

- *Collect*: Learn from previous knowledge collected and stored in repositories in the Web;
- *Relate*: Consult with peers and mentors at early, middle and late stages;
- *Create*: Explore, compose and evaluate possible solutions;
- *Donate*: Disseminate the results and contribute to repositories, the Web and other sources.

These activities can be accomplished by software tools through eight tasks:

1. Searching and browsing digital libraries, the Web and other resources;
2. Visualizing data and processes to understand and discover relationships;
3. Consulting with peers and mentors for intellectual and emotional support;
4. Thinking done by free associations to make new combinations of ideas;
5. Exploring solutions – What-if tools and simulation models;
6. Composing artefacts and performances step-by-step;
7. Reviewing and replaying session histories to support reflection; and
8. Disseminating results to gain recognition and add to the searchable resources.

New channels and tools have become unlimited sources for learning and creativity and they have had an impact in almost every known business model (Anderson 2009; Jarvis 2009). Advanced learning organisations (Senge 1996) are integrated by inquiring persons, open to new models and in continuous search for new ideas (Houston 2006). These privileged channels also have a systematic approach to the way knowledge is managed (Albors and Ramos 2008).

There are several tools that significantly facilitate learning and producing creative ideas. Table 4.3 shows the most popular.

4.5.3 Systematising Rapid Significant Learning and Creativity

The current era, known as the knowledge era, requires highly skilled professionals with profound abilities to work productively with knowledge. Edmonds and Candy (Edmonds and Candy 2002) note that creative knowledge work models are based on three requirements:

- Exploration capabilities for accessing data comprising different forms of knowledge;
- Potential for generation of possible solutions and approaches to a problem and sharing them and finally,
- Evaluation of possible solutions by testing them against a set of constraints.

Table 4.3 Tools for rapid significative learning on the internet (Source: Own elaboration based on different web sources)

Name	Tool	Type	Features for learning	Channel
Wired, Fast company, Inc. . .	Electronic magazines of current trends	Web page	Electronic knowledge, technologies and trends diffusion magazines	One way
Executive Sound Review, book reviews, Google books	Summaries of different sources	Web page	Access to book summaries. Relevant ideas synthesised	One way
Wordpress, Blogger	Publication and broadcast of information	Web page	Diffusion of information, interpretations and specialities	One way
Google, Bing. . .	Search engine	Portal	Search engines, prioritisation by use and relevance	One way
ISI Web of Knowledge, Google Academics	Search engine for academic publications	Portal	Search engines, prioritisation by use and relevance. More rigorous content taxonomies	One way
Google Groups, Huddle. . .	Collaborative virtual spaces	Portal	Virtual collaboration environments for workgroup	Collaboration
SlideShare, Webinar. . .	Shared presentations portal	Portal	Sharing visual presentations. It concentrates pure ideas in a very synthesised way	Two ways
Prezi	Design and broadcast of idea maps and presentations	Portal	Presenting ideas in maps, conceptual maps. . .	One way
LinkedIn	Professional networks, social networks	Portal	Access to experts in groups, know about their activities and expertise	Two ways
YouTube	Portal of videos	Portal	Video tutorials, detailed presentations and lecturing	Two ways
Noodle, Blackboard, Moodle. . .	Educational platforms	Portal	Virtual courses, e-learning	Two ways

(continued)

Table 4.3   (continued)

Name	Tool	Type	Features for learning	Channel
Twitter	Brief information broadcast	Portal	Broadcast of events, ideas and links to sources from experts in specific topics	One way
Wikis, DYY, Wikipedia	Collaborative open source environments	Portal	Wikis for sharing knowledge or collaborating in a idea/ project development	Collaboration
Cmap Tools, Mind maps…	Ideas graphical representation	Application	Idea representations, knowledge elicitation and transference	Two ways
Dropbox	File sharing	Application	Sharing editable files in collaborative projects, articles and every kind of contents	Collaboration
RSS feeds, Google alarms	Information update subscription	Application	Be updated on the news in any blog or webpage filtered by topics	One way
Open project, Omniplan…	Project management	Application	Environment for collaborative projects where information is structured and organised	Collaboration

In the case of informal knowledge sharing, this can be motivated by validated contributions to databases, by the general appraisal systems of the sharing context and by the accepted trust of the knowledge node. An interesting example is the participation in communities of practice; here, motivation is driven by organisational citizenship, self-actualisation, learning and advancement of the community (Bartol and Srivastava 2002). Table 4.4 details the main steps involved in learning and generating ideas in a rapid significant way.

Steps IV to VI are not visible in terms of learning tools and collaboration. They are needed in a systematic approach to rapid significative learning. There are always some tasks such as networking, studying, investigating and inquiring that have to be kept up continuously.

Table 4.4 Rapid learning and creativity process (Source: authors)

Step	Tools/ methods	Scope
Evaluate what knowledge is relevant for the organisation or individual work practice	Internal reflection to identify key knowledge areas Cmaps Tool	Tacit. Internal to the organisation
Search in the information oceans to find the precise item. Iterative sub-process till coherent results are extracted Select, synthesise, validate the optimum knowledge Focus on the selected knowledge. Deeper research to get the state of the art on this topic New search based on the results of previous step	Google, Bing LinkedIn SlideShare ISI, on-line / virtual libraries Google academics, books Book summaries, blogs, magazines... Peer support Professional support in forums, communities...	Explicit, applied and tacit. Internal and global
(Optional) Share it, elicitation so it can be enriched across the organisation or with fellows in communities, forums...	SlideShare Prezi Google docs / Groups Dropbox file sharing	Explicit Global (can restrict access to private)
Action it (apply) in a useful and profitable way	Develop new work practices Learning by doing and by teaching Apply new work practices in day to day work and on going projects Slideshare, Prezi Noodle Open project	Practical and tacit
Measure its positive impact	Indicators of improvements Publication of indicators through broadcasting information tools as: blogs, SlideShare, Google groups, Huddle, Twitter Collect feedback and lessons learnt from users, collaborators through open wikis	Explicit and tacit
Review its behaviour in order to improve it in an iterative way	Collaborative After Action Reviews based on wikis, Skype conferences, tweets and blogs Collect feedback and lessons learnt from users, collaborators through open wikis	Practical and tacit

(continued)

Table 4.4 (continued)

Step	Tools/ methods	Scope
Previous / simultaneous	Networking, peer collaborations, professional communities / associations Studying (reading, attending courses...) Attending congresses, conferences Follow active discussion groups in blogs and wikis of experts Participate in webinars and open courses	Tacit

4.6 Examples and Experiences of Open Learning and Problem Solving

4.6.1 Expansion of Social Networks

Various authors have pointed out (Shirky 2009: Bernoff and Groundswell 2008; Albors and Ramos 2008; Barabasi 2009; McAfee 2009) the expansion of social networks and open sourcing in the last 5 years (see Fig. 4.9).

Results and cases from crowdsourcing (Rick 2007; Surowiecki 2004) have been published which confirm the potential of this tool for creative problem solving and innovation. Brabham (2008) has described these. Sharing documents with Dropbox in the web is a powerful sharing tool. YouTube is the leader with more than 104 million visitors (Fig. 4.10 from March 2010). Wikipedia follows with more than 74 million visitors in the same period. Figure 4.11 below shows statistics related to Scribd.com, InnoCentive, SlideShare, and iStockphoto. Scribd is a social publishing site, where tens of millions of people share original writings and documents; SlideShare is a web for sharing, publicly or privately, PowerPoint presentations, Word documents and Adobe PDF Portfolios; iStockphoto, similar to Flickr and having a repository of more than a million files, is a web-based company that sells royalty-free stock photography, animations and video clips compiled from public contributions.

4.6.2 Example: The Case of Air New Zealand Aviation Design Academy

To crowdsource ideas for the finishing touches to their new 777-300 aircraft, Air New Zealand took advantage of the opportunities provided by the direct line

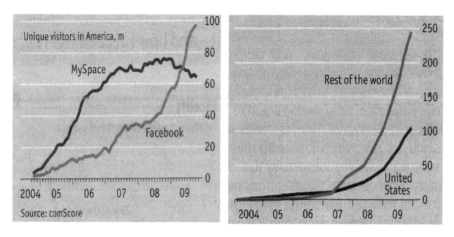

Fig. 4.9 Members and unique visitors for facebook and myspace (Source: www.Comscore.com, 2007)

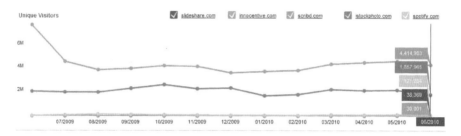

Fig. 4.10 Visitors to most popular digital sharing tools (Source: www.Comscore.com, 2010)

between businesses and consumers opened by social media and interactive websites. Through the Aviation Design Academy, Air New Zealand used the possibilities offered by these sites to reach a greater pool of ideas in order to solicit ideas for several aspects of its in-flight experience: an original cocktail, an in-flight snack, the eye mask design and the proposal of an original idea for a promotional video. The exceptionally well-prepared videos produced by Air New Zealand explain exactly what Air New Zealand is looking for. Although the videos are light, and almost comic in presentation, they make the competition a reality and tell the entrants what to do. The lucky winners will win a seat on the new 777-300 flight in April 2011 from Auckland to London where they will be able to try, first hand, the winning cocktails, snacks and eye mask designs. At the time of writing, more than 1,500 suggestions have been received which demonstrate the success of the initiative.

This could be considered a case of successful collective creativity development.

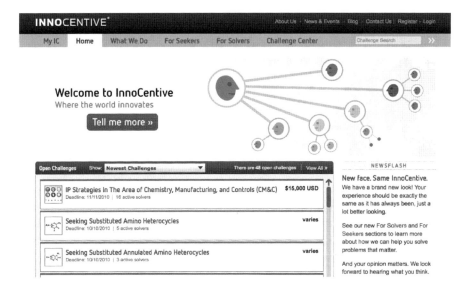

Fig. 4.11   InnoCentive portal

4.6.3   *The Success of Crowdsourcing*

Crowdsourcing offers a good example of managing collective creativity and innovation in the business context (Howe 2006: Albors and Ramos 2008). The web site http://crowdsourcingexamples.pbworks.com lists 144 examples of individual businesses, sites or forums that channel the power of online crowds and the web.

This web http://www.openinnovators.net lists 130 open-innovation crowdsourcing examples classified in R&D platforms – marketing and design sites, collective intelligence and prediction, human resource and freelancers, open innovation software, intermediary services, creative ideas, product development, peer production and public sourcing. As an example, a visit to the website *RedesignMe* shows it has 5,102 Community Members, 54 actual challenges and 2,561 entries.

Another interesting classical approach of crowdsourcing is that of *Lumenogic*, http://www.lumenogic.com/www/index.html an international consultancy that provides technology-enabled consulting services which utilise the power, speed and simplicity of collective intelligence. This company sees themselves as 'transformation agents, combining senior operating experience and strategy consulting with thought leadership in the application of collective intelligence to solve business challenges. [They] deploy a collective intelligence platform and processes to engage stakeholders, harness and align their thinking and set the stage for rapid transformation'.

4.6.4 The Case of InnoCentive

InnoCentive[5] is now a centre of reference in terms of open innovation. Take for example, a large company such as Procter and Gamble (P&G). It solved a great constraint on its capacity to innovate as quickly as the market needed, thanks for using this portal to seek the best of world talent to help them. It is a tool that has helped thousands of companies to embrace open innovation. InnoCentive's mission is as simple as: connect Seekers with Solvers and put them on the shortest, most cost-effective path to finding a solution.

Since its inception in 2001, *InnoCentive* has been building a positive impact on the world, one company at a time. The following figures show evidence of it:

*   Total Solvers: 200,000+ from 200 countries;
*   Total Challenges Posted: 1,044;
*   Project Rooms Opened to Date: 294,865;
*   Total Solution Submissions: 19,346;
*   Total Awards Given: 685;
*   Total Award Dollars Posted: $24.2 million;
*   Range of awards: $5,000 to $1 million based on the complexity of the problem;
*   Total Dollars Awarded: $5.3 million;
*   Average Success Rate: 50%.

4.7 Conclusions and Future Challenges

Several conclusions can be derived from the analysis made in this chapter. On one hand, there are interesting findings on the way learning theory has evolved. On the other hand, collaboration and organisational learning, as well as digital technology, have developed as a new way to develop learning and generate new ideas and have been adopted by mass media, influencing the learning models in a contingent way.

4.7.1 Evolution of Learning Paradigms

Learning paradigms have evolved considerably in the last 20 years. They highlight the relevance of the learning process feedback phase (Gagné 1985), where learning results have influenced the initial learning paradigms, following the double-loop Argyris and Schon (1978) proposal. Learning is conceived as an active process, where initial knowledge and experience are combined, following a spiral cycle,

---

[5]See the web of InnoCentive July 2010.

according to the propositions of various authors (Duffy and Cunningham 1996; Kolb 1984; Nonaka and Takeuchi 1995; Schön 1983). A third conclusion is the relevance of social learning where collaboration becomes a fundamental dimension in the learning process (Albors and Ramos 2008; Argyris and Schon 1978; Fischer 2005; Herrmann 2008; Senge 1990, 1996).

New learning paradigms, supported (or driven) by computing and communication technologies, have developed and adapted to this new environment. The development of tools such as concept maps and the understanding of brain laterality have contributed to facilitating the abstract and conceptualisation learning phases. This fact, combined with a better understanding of learning motivations, the rapid feedback provided by the Internet instantaneity and learning–sharing facilitated by social computing, has made the achievement of significative learning more accomplishable.

Digital Natives have developed a new way of learning, taking advantage of the new reality provided by technology in general and especially by the Internet. On the other hand, to advance, Digital Immigrants have had to evolve to enter into this new reality. Education must evolve to adapt to the needs of Digital Natives and this evolution has become one of the new education challenges. As pointed out by some authors (Albors and Ramos 2008), academic context has been late in adapting to new digital tools and philosophy while, in contrast, social and business contexts were more rapid in their adaptation. 'Edutainment' (Okan 2003) seems to be an evolving paradigm that may facilitate this evolution, and in this direction, the cone of learning (Dale 1969) demonstrates how doing, receiving and participating play an active role and improve the learner's involvement and learning efficiency. Digital interfaces and information tools contribute to this learning leverage (Prensky 2001b).

Any social consideration of learning today must take into account the competencies perspective. The balance of knowledge, skills and attitudes (Boyatzis 1982; McClelland 1973) in any learning system will provide the individual with the adequate tools for his/her full participation and contribution to society (OECD 2005).

Finally, the lifelong learner perspective must be taken into account in a rapidly changing world. Therefore, the concept of Lifelong learning becomes a necessary consideration in any learning paradigm and within the consideration of a knowledge economy (Drucker 1966).

Universal access to almost all human wisdom has become a reality. With an Internet connection and a computer, any individual can access knowledge and share ideas from any side of the planet. Old, slow and meticulous research processes are part of the past. Today 'library rats' are rare ancient vestiges.

4.7.2 Managing and Stimulating Collaborative Creativity

The reviewed model of Bloom's learning taxonomy (Anderson and Krathwohl 2001; Bloom and Krathwohl 1956) provides a clear connection between learning and creation. It is actually the last step in the considered teaching and learning objectives.

Innovation, knowledge management and creativity are connected (Albors and Ramos 2010; Stenmark 2003) and they have a collective dimension. Telecommunication and information technologies are a powerful technical support for collaborative creativity (Herrmann 2008) and clearly business environments have adopted them successfully. Global interaction between peers is easy. Access to experts in certain topics is possible and the supply of innovative and creative ideas and solutions can be outsourced (Albors and Ramos 2008).

New channels enable a speedy broadcast of ideas, which can be enriched, solved or reviewed by thousands of talented brains. New creativity tools and worldwide access have facilitated open innovation and empowered individuals to contribute to the innovation process. Again, business and social contexts have been quick in adapting to these new paradigms, and statistics show that they are becoming an economic success (Brabham 2008; Rick 2007; Surowiecki 2004).

4.7.3   Future Challenges

This chapter has discussed how individuals, mainly as knowledge workers have benefited from current new learning paradigms in order to stay competitive. It has concluded by examining real examples that show that rapid significant learning can be achieved through the use of social computing, and that it leads to enhanced creativity, collaboration, efficiency and overall learning. Learning models have evolved contingently along the development of digital media.

However, there are still some questions open to further research. One could be the analysis of successful evolution models from traditional learning towards digital learning. The other is the key success factors' shift from creativity, new ideas and massive adopted conceptions towards market successes. Although this line of research is more related to the concept of open innovation, still, those aspects related to the process of creativity and crowdsourcing are not yet well-studied. Various research questions still need further attention. What are the drivers that link idea to wealth generation? Are clear references to successful cases building on the new ways of learning and creativity? How can digital immigrants evolve their teaching approach and methodologies in an efficient way in order to serve digital natives?

References

Agor, W.H.: Intuitive Management: Integrating Left and Right Brain Management Skills. Prentice Hall, Englewood Cliffs (1989)

Albors, J., Ramos, J.C.: New learning network paradigms: communities of objectives, crowdsourcing, wikis and open source. Int. J. Inf. Manag. **28**(2), 194–202 (2008)

Albors, J., Ramos, J.C.: Actional intelligence, a critical competence for innovation performance. A research multi-case analysis. Int. J. Technol. Intell. Plan. **6**(3), 211–225 (2010)

Ambrose, D., Cohen, L.M., Tannenbaum, A.J.: Creative Intelligence: Toward Theoretic Integration. Hampton Press, Cresshill (2003)

Anderson, T.: Theory and Practice of Online Learning. Au Press, Montreal (2009)

Anderson, L.W., Krathwohl, D.: A Taxonomy for Learning, Teaching and Assessing: a Revision of Bloom's Taxonomy of Educational Objectives. Longman, New York (2001)

Argyris, C., Schon, S.: Organizational Learning: A Theory in Action Perspective. Addison-Wesley, Reading (1978)

Argyris, C., Schön, D.: Organizational Learning II: Theory, Method and Practice. Addison Wesley, Reading (1996)

Aspin, D.N., Chapman, J.D.: Lifelong Learning: Concepts and Conceptions. Springer, Dordrecht (2000)

Ausubel, D., Novak, J., Hanesian, H.: Educational Psychology: A Cognitive View, 2nd edn. Holt, Rinehart & Winston, New York (1978)

Barabasi, A.: Linked: How Everything Is Connected to Everything Else and What It Means for Business, Science, and Everyday Life. Plume, New York (2009)

Bartol, K.M., Srivastava, A.: Encouraging knowledge sharing: the role of organizational reward systems. J. Leadersh. Organ. Stud. 9(1), 64–75 (2002)

Begay, T., Bender, M., Stemkoski, M., Rainess, D., Walker, T.: Interdisciplinary project-based learning: an experiment to create real world products and services with clients involving the disciplines of business management, multimedia, distance learning, engineering technology, and English. J. Coll. Teach. Learn. 5(5), 1–19 (2006)

Bernoff, J., Groundswell, C.: Winning in a World Transformed by Social Technologies, 1st edn. Harvard Business School Press, Cambridge (2008)

Blank, R.: An organizational model of higher education institutions and faculty teaching goals. Sociol. Inq. 48(1), 23–35 (1978)

Bloom, B., Krathwohl, D.: Taxonomy of Educational Objectives: The Classification of Educational Goals, by a Committee of College and University Examiners. Handbook1: Cognitive Domain. Longmans, New York (1956)

Borgman, C.: From Gutenberg to the Global Information Infrastructure. The MIT Press Cambridge, London (2003)

Boyatzis, R.E.: The Competent Manager. Wiley, New York (1982)

Brabham, D.C.: Crowdsourcing as a model for problem solving an introduction and cases convergence. Int. J. Res. into New Media Technol. 14(1), 75–90 (2008)

Buzan, T., Buzan, B.: The Mind Map Book. Pearson Education, New York (2006)

Candy, P.: Self-Direction for Lifelong Learning. A Comprehensive Guide to Theory and Practice. Jossey-Bass, San Francisco (1991)

Conger, D.: Creativity and Innovation in Information Systems Organizations. Boyd and Fraser, Danvers (1996)

Dale, E.: Audio-Visual Methods in Teaching International. Thomson Publishing, London (1969)

Dehaene, S., Spelke, E., Pinel, P., Stanescu, R., Tsivkin, S.: Sources of mathematical thinking: behavioral and brain-imaging evidence. Science 284, 970–974 (1999)

Downes, S.: Models for sustainable open educational resources. Interdiscip. J. Knowl. Learn. Objects 3, 29–45 (2007)

Drucker, P.: The Effective Executive. Harper Collins, New York (1966)

Duffy, T.M., Cunningham, D.J.: Constructivism: implications for the design and delivery of instruction. In: Jonassen, D.H. (ed.) Handbook of Research for Educational Communications and Technology. Macmillan Library Reference, New York (1996)

Edmonds, E., Candy, L.: Creativity, art practice, and knowledge. Commun. ACM 45(10), 91–95 (2002)

Fink, L.D.: Creating Significant Learning Experiences. Jossey-Bass, San Francisco (2003)

Finkel, D.: Teaching with your Mouth Shut. Bownton/Cook, Postsmouth (1999)

Fischer, G.: Social creativity: turning barriers into opportunities for collaborative design. Int. J. Hum. Comput. Stud. 63(4–5), 210–222 (2005)

Gagné, R.M.: Educational technology and the learning process. Educ. Res. 3, 3–9 (1974)

Gagné, R.M.: The Conditions of Learning and Theory of Instruction. CBS College Publishing, New York (1985)

Gelpi, R.E.: Lifelong education and international relations. In: Wain, K. (ed.) Lifelong Education and Participation. Malta University Press, Msida (1985)

Goldberg, E.: The New Executive Brain: Frontal Lobes in a Complex World. Oxford University Press, New York (2009)

Goleman, D.: On emotional intelligence. Educ. Leadersh. 54(1), 6–10 (1996)

Greenhow, C., Robelia, B., Hughes, J.E.: Learning, teaching, and scholarship in a digital age, web 2.0 and classroom research: what path should we take now? Educ. Res. 38(4), 246–259 (2009)

Herrmann, T.: Design issues for supporting collaborative creativity. In: 8th International Conference on the Design of Cooperative Systems, pp. 179–210 (2008)

Hines, T.: Left brain/right brain mythology and implications for management and training. Acad. Manage. Rev. 12(4), 600–606 (1987)

Houston, J.: Modern Social Work Practice – Teaching and Learning in Practice Settings, Learning in Social Care, 5(1), pp. 57–70, (2006)

Howe, J.: The rise of crowdsourcing. Wired Magazine www.wired.com/wired/archive/14.06/crowds.html (2006)

Jarvis, J.: Adult Education and Lifelong Learning. Routledge, London (2009)

Johnson-Sheehan, R., Baehr, C.: Visual-spatial thinking in hypertexts. Tech. Commun. 48(1), 22–30 (2001)

Klemmer, S. R., Thomsen, M., Phelps-Goodman, E.P., Lee, R., Landay, J.A.: Where Do WebSites Come From? Capturing and Interacting with Design History. In Proceedings of CHI, pp. 1–8 (2002)

Kolb, D.A.: Experiential Learning: Experience as the Source of Learning and Development. Prentice-Hall, Englewood Cliffs (1984)

Lessig, L.: Free Culture. Penguin, London (2005)

Lieberman, Debra A.: Health education video games for children and adolescents: theory, design and research findings. In: Annual Meeting of the International Communications Association, Jerusalem (1998)

Mamykina, L.X., Candy, L., Edmonds, E.: Collaborative creativity. Commun. ACM 45(10), 96–99 (2002)

Mathewson, J.H.: Visual-spatial thinking: an aspect of science overlooked by educators. Sci. Educ. 83(1), 33–54 (1999)

McAfee, A.: Enterprise 2.0: New Collaborative Tools for Your Organization's Toughest Challenges, 1st edn. Harvard Business School Press, Cambridge (2009)

McClelland, D.C.: Testing for competence rather than for intelligence. Am. Psychol. 28, 1–14 (1973)

Merzenich, M.M., Jenkins, W.M., Johnston, P., Schreiner, P., Miller, S.L., Tallal, P.: Temporal processing deficits of language-learning impaired children ameliorated by training. Science 271, 77–81 (1996)

Morgan S.: Internet trends. www.morganstanley.com (2010)

Mumford, A., Honey, P.: Questions and answers on learning styles questionnaire. Ind. Commer. Train. 24(7), 25–32 (1993)

Murray, P.: Organisational learning, competencies, and firm performance: empirical observations. Learn. Organ. 10(5), 305–316 (2003)

Nelson, L.M.: Collaborative problem solving. In: Reigeluth, C.M. (ed.) Instructional Design Theories and Models: A New Paradigm of Instructional Theory, pp. 241–267. Lawrence Erlbaum Associates, Inc., Mahwah (1999)

Nonaka, I., Takeuchi, H.: The Knowledge-Creating Company. Oxford University Press, New York (1995)

Novak, J.: Learning, Creating and Using Knowledge. Routledge, London (1998)

OECD: The Definition and Selection of Key Competencies. OECD, Paris (2005)

Okan, Z.: Edutainment: is learning at risk? Br. J. Educ. Technol. 34(3), 255–264 (2003)

Peck, T.: European lifelong learning initiatives. Phi Delta Kappan **77**, 35–37 (1996)

Prensky, M.: Digital natives digital immigrants. On the Horiz. **9**(5), 5–25 (2001a)

Prensky, M.: Do they think differently? On the Horiz. **9**(6), 25–42 (2001b)

Rick, S.: The wisdom of crowdsourcing. Profit **26**(1), 36–37 (2007)

Robinson, A.G., Stern, S.: Corporate Creativity. Berrett-Koehler Publisher, San Francisco (1998)

Savaneviciene, A., Stukaite, D., Silingiene, V.: Development of strategic individual competences. Inzinerine Ekonomika-Eng. Econ. **3**(1), 81–88 (2008)

Schön, D.: The Reflective Practitioner, How Professionals Think in Action. Basic Books, New York (1983)

Senge, P.: The Fifth Discipline: The Art and Practice of the Learning Organization. Doubleday, New York (1990)

Senge, P.: Leading learning organizations. Train. Dev. **50**(12), 36–4 (1996)

Sharples, M.: The design of personal mobile technologies for lifelong learning. Comput. Educ. **34**(3–4), 177–193 (2000)

Shirky, C.: Here Comes Everybody. The Power of Organizing Without Organizations. Penguin, London (2009)

Shneiderman, B.: Creativity support tools. Commun. ACH **45**(10), 116–120 (2002)

Stahl, G., Koschmann, T., Suthers, D.: Computer-supported collaborative learning: an historical perspective. In: Sawyer, R.K. (ed.) Cambridge Handbook of the Learning Sciences, pp. 409–426. Cambridge University Press, Cambridge (2006)

Star, S.L., Ruhleder, K.: Steps towards an ecology of infrastructure: design and access for large information spaces. Inf. Syst. Res. **7**(1), 111–134 (1996)

Stenmark, D.: Knowledge creation and the web: factors indicating why some intranets succeed where others fail. Knowl. Process Manag. **10**(3), 207–216 (2003)

Stephenson, R.: Open source/open course learning: lessons for educators from free and open source software. Innovate **3**(1), 24–31 (2006)

Surowiecki, J.: The Wisdom of Crowds why the Many are Smarter than the Few and how Collective Wisdom Shapes Business, Economies, Societies, and Nations. Little, London (2004)

Tallal, P., Merzenich, M.M.: Language comprehension in language learning impaired children improved with acoustically modified speech. Science **271**, 88–94 (1996)

Thomas, J.C., Kellogg, W.A., Erickson, T.: The knowledge management puzzle: human and social factors in knowledge management. IBM Systems Journal, 40(4), pp. 863–884 (2001)

Westen, D., Burton, L., Kowalski, R.: Psychology. Wiley, Sydney (2006)

Chapter 5
States and Processes of Learning Communities. Engaging Students in Meaningful Reflection and Learning

Dirk Ifenthaler and Pablo Pirnay-Dummer

Abstract The omnipresence of the Internet and high bandwidth connections has brought about the development of powerful software packages called learning management systems (LMS). An LMS integrates the administration and facilitation of online activities and the distribution of learning materials. In this chapter, it is argued that the use of LMS is limited to only a few technological features and that so far it has failed to promote meaningful learning environments. Therefore, two empirical studies were conducted to investigate these concerns. The first study reports the development of a practicable taxonomy for LMS features. The second study extends the taxonomy for discussion forums. This chapter concludes with future perspectives on the application and extension of the introduced practicable taxonomy for LMS.

5.1 Introduction

The rapid progress of computer technology has introduced a new culture of innovative teaching and learning in schools and higher education, and via lifelong learning. Multimedia technologies implemented in computer-based learning environments provide new opportunities to enhance traditionally taught courses (Alessi and Trollip 2000; Häkkinen 2002; Ifenthaler 2010; Land and Hannafin 1996; Mayer 2001). Web-enhanced features (synchronous and asynchronous communication, document sharing) in particular, grant access to education at any time or place. Additionally, the omnipresence of the internet and high bandwidth connections has brought about the development of powerful software packages called learning management systems (LMS). An LMS integrates the administration and facilitation of online activities and the distribution of learning materials (Falvo and Johnson 2007). LMS provide a stable repository of technological methods for teachers and

D. Ifenthaler (✉) • P. Pirnay-Dummer
University of Freiburg, Rempartstr. 11, 79085 Freiburg, Germany
e-mail: ifenthaler@ezw.uni-freiburg.de

B. White et al. (eds.), *Social Media Tools and Platforms in Learning Environments*,
DOI 10.1007/978-3-642-20392-3_5, © Springer-Verlag Berlin Heidelberg 2011

instructors. Since it is only a matter of time until more social computing aspects are inherited within LMS, it is beneficial to discuss the current framework to prepare and facilitate a transfer of technologies: A real benefit to learning can be expected only if both a conceptual (instructional) framework and the available technological fundament integrate on an operational level of learning. A practical taxonomy of use, as well as a structured understanding (as opposed to simple recipes) of its workings for particular integrated technologies, helps with the current use of LMS by practitioners, providing further integration of technologies, especially social media methods.

Moreover, in this chapter it is argued that the current use of LMS is limited to only a few technological features and that it fails to promote meaningful learning environments so far as its practice is still focused on recipe-style instructional measures. Although an LMS has the technological and instructional potential to support a wide range of learning activities, such as exploring, constructing, and manipulating models, solving authentic problems of the world, or articulating and discussing individual ideas, they are simply used for sharing documents.

5.2 Instructional Support Through Learning Management Systems

LMS integrate interactive learning environments and course and user administration (Black et al. 2007; Waterhouse 2005) and facilitate customized online instructional materials (Koszalka and Ganesan 2004; Schulmeister 2003). Baumgartner et al. (2002) report in their analysis, more than 120 different commercial and open source LMS products (Blackboard, eCollege, Moodle, WebCT...). Another study by Falvo and Johnson (2007) identified the most popular LMS used at colleges and universities in the United States. Based upon a random sample of 100 institutions, the most frequently used LMS were Blackboard (www.blackboard.com) and WebCT (www.webct.com). Beyond these studies, more research is needed to investigate many critical questions about online instruction (Falvo and Johnson 2007).

Similarly, to a content management system (CMS), an LMS consists of a database where various types of information are stored. Figure 5.1 shows the comprehensive characteristics of a LMS. The management and administration of courses, authors, learners, and instructors involves selecting between several possibilities for circulating important information, changing access permissions, and granting privileges of use to certain functions of the LMS. Authoring tools enable instructors and course creators to develop courses, content, and assignments. Numerous evaluation and diagnostic features assist in assessing and analyzing student knowledge, provide examples for feedback, and help instructors with grading of assignments. Additionally, communication via chat, forums, and email connects all users of an LMS (instructors and students; authors and instructors; authors and administrators).

The LMS was developed to support learning in several ways. Accordingly, the technological progression of the LMS offers new opportunities for course

Fig. 5.1 Characteristics of a learning management system

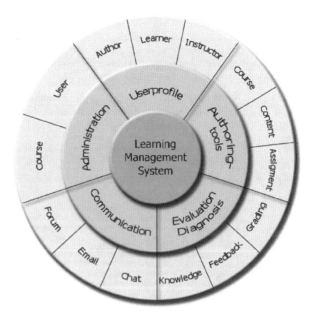

designers, instructors, and students. They provide learning materials, tasks, and exercises; offer synchronous and asynchronous communication tools; evaluate student activities; and support instructors with their course administration. However, the rapid introduction of the LMS into almost every university and organization as a teaching, learning, and management tool (Baumgartner et al. 2002; Bett and Wedekind 2003; see Falvo and Johnson 2007; Trahasch et al. 2002) was not accompanied by a precise investigation of the instructional implications of these technological based systems (see Schulmeister 2003).

For a further investigation of the available features of an LMS and their instructional potential, the authors highlight the LMS Moodle (Modular Object-Oriented Dynamic Learning Environment) which is a widely accepted and used open-source product (Melton 2006). It has features similar to Blackboard and WebCT, and provides various features for the design of online instruction (Cole 2005; Höbarth 2007; Williams et al. 2005). Table 5.1 shows the features of the Moodle Version 1.8.4 (www.moodle.org) that was used in the studies reported in this chapter.

5.3 The LMS in Educational Practice

5.3.1 Empirical Studies on LMS Usage

Particularly in blended learning courses (Kerres and de Witt 2003), the use of a LMS can improve the chance of access to resources. Learners can access them independently without consulting the instructor at any time and from any place.

Table 5.1 Features available in the LMS Moodle (Williams et al. 2005)

Feature	Short description
Assignment	The instructor can provide written feedback or grade assignments submitted online by the student
Chat	The module allows a real-time synchronous discussion
Choice	A question by the instructor with a choice of multiple responses
Files/resources	Uploaded files for download (text documents, spreadsheets, slides, sound, graphic, or video)
Forum	The module allows asynchronous discussions between students and the instructor
Glossary	Allows one to create and maintain a list of definitions
Journal	The module enables students to reflect on a particular topic. The entries can be edited and refined over time
Label	The module enables the instructor to add text or instructions to the content area of the course
Lesson	Content is delivered in an interesting and flexible way, including grading and questions
Quiz	The module allows the instructor to design a set of short tests
Scorm	Uploaded and implemented SCORM packages as part of the course
Survey	Standard surveys for gathering data from students (ATTLS, Critical incidents, COLLES)
Wiki	Enables the authoring of documents collectively in a simple markup language
Workshop	Students are enabled to assess each other's projects in a number of ways

Ifenthaler et al. (2008) gathered and assessed data from 133 courses of an undergraduate program in instructional design ($n = 73$) and a graduate program in educational science ($n = 60$) at a German university, $\chi^2(1, N = 133) = 1.27$, $p > 0.05$. A total of 3,643 students were enrolled in these courses ($M = 27.39$, $SD = 12.93$). An in-depth log-file analysis provided information on student hits, as well as detailed information about individual usage of LMS features and resources. The most frequently implemented LMS feature was the *resource* (PDF documents, PPT slides). Other LMS features (SCORM, workshop) were not implemented at all. Aside from the features *resource* and *forum*, the available features were hardly implemented by the course instructors at all. Accordingly, Ifenthaler et al. (2008) concluded that the LMS was used primarily to share documents. Such low use of the features of the LMS raises the question as to whether such a highly elaborate technical system is necessary at all.

In a second study, Ifenthaler et al. (2008) investigated how students changed their access throughout the 3 years of their course of study. Over 86% of all hits to the LMS Moodle during the six semesters of the bachelor program occurred from outside the university. Interestingly, the frequency of access to the LMS changed during the six semester course of study significantly, $F(5, 122) = 14.89, p < 0.001$, $f = 0.78$. The least access was found for the first semester. Between the second and fifth semester, the frequency of access increased greatly. For the final semester, the most frequent access to the LMS was found. The very frequent access to the LMS outside the institution (university, company), gives high hope that the students are highly motivated to learn within the given learning environment. However, the application of available technological features is far from its limits (see Ifenthaler et al. 2008). Therefore, a qualitative study (with eight expert interviews), which identifies a practicable taxonomy for designing effective online instruction within a LMS, was conducted to further investigate the authors' concerns.

5.3.2   Taxonomy of LMS Features

Following the taxonomy of common CMS features related to resource type and value by Koszalka and Ganesan (2004) and on the basis of empirical findings (Ifenthaler et al. 2008), the authors developed a practical taxonomy of LMS features. The taxonomy contains (1) the name of the LMS feature; (2) a short description of the LMS feature; (3) a classification of the LMS feature with regard to the three design elements *information, instruction,* and *learning* (see Grabowski and Curtis 1991); (4) the LMS feature's association with instructional functions (see Hilgenstock and Jirmann 2005); and (5) exemplary recommendations for instructional use.

5.4   First Empirical Study

Eight interviews with experts (three female and five male) were conducted. The mean age was 41.9 years ($SD = 10.2$). All experts were experienced in using learning management systems for their courses. They had used the LMS Moodle for a mean of 7.6 semesters ($SD = 2.7$) and 19.4 courses ($SD = 21.6$).

The structured online expert interviews consisted of four sections with closed-ended questions: (1) demographic data, (2) teaching experience, (3) user attitudes, and (4) instructional functions of LMS features. In the section *user attitudes*, the respondents were asked how often they used the LMS features in their online courses. The following 11 LMS features were included: *assignment, chat, choice, forum, glossary, lesson, quiz, resources (files), survey, wiki,* and *workshop*. Exclusive technological features (database, SCORM) were not considered in the analysis. The fourth section consisted of 77 pairwise comparisons in which the above mentioned 11 LMS features were paired with seven possible instructional functions (information, communication, cooperation, assessment, self-reflection, feedback, and evaluation) (see Hilgenstock and Jirmann 2005). The interviewees were asked to rate the extent to which each pair, for example, assignment–information, was applicable to the instructional function. Additionally, respondents were asked how confident they were concerning each pairwise comparison.

The collected data were transcribed and categorized for further statistical analysis. In order to build a practicable taxonomy, LMS features that are highly applicable to instructional functions were sought. Additionally, these results have to be supported by a high confidence level on the part of the experts.

The results of all 77 pairwise comparisons between the 11 LMS features and the seven instructional functions are presented in Table 5.2. The expert's confidence (1 = low confidence, 5 = high confidence) with regard to their pairwise ratings was relatively high ($M = 3.66$, $SD = 0.84$). Hence, it was concluded that the experts' knowledge of the LMS features and the instructional function was adequate for our study.

The analysis of usage of LMS features corresponds, in part, to the results of the above described studies. All experts stated that they use the feature *file* ($M = 5.00$, $SD = 0.0$). The feature *forum* is also used in their online courses very often ($M = 4.75$, $SD = 0.46$). The features *assignment* ($M = 3.75$, $SD = 1.16$), *glossary* ($M = 3.00$, $SD = 1.51$), *quiz* ($M = 3.00$, $SD = 1.60$), *choice* ($M = 2.88$, $SD = 1.64$), and *wiki* ($M = 2.88$, $SD = 1.64$) are used moderately. The features *workshop* ($M = 2.13$, $SD = 1.64$), *lesson* ($M = 2.38$, $SD = 1.89$), *chat* ($M = 2.13$, $SD = 1.55$), and *survey* ($M = 1.88$, $SD = 0.99$) are used very seldom.

Table 5.2 Average scores (standard deviations in parenthesis) of pairwise comparison between LMS features and instructional functions rated by experts between 1 (minimal) and 11 (maximum) applicability ($N = 8$)

	Information	Communication	Cooperation	Assessment	Self-reflexion	Feedback	Evaluation
Assignment	7.50 (3.67)	4.38 (3.25)	6.63 (2.77)	10.13 (0.99)	9.88 (0.99)	9.38 (1.06)	8.75 (3.41)
Chat	6.50 (3.12)	10.63 (0.52)	7.75 (4.37)	3.88 (3.76)	6.75 (4.10)	7.88 (2.48)	4.67 (2.42)
Choice	8.50 (3.30)	7.88 (2.17)	6.50 (3.07)	6.67 (3.88)	5.88 (2.30)	8.38 (1.77)	7.75 (2.92)
Files	11.00 (0.00)	4.63 (3.70)	4.63 (4.00)	2.75 (2.44)	4.75 (3.24)	2.50 (2.20)	2.13 (1.81)
Forum	8.63 (2.56)	10.86 (0.38)	10.13 (0.84)	5.00 (3.70)	9.50 (1.38)	10.13 (0.99)	5.38 (3.89)
Glossary	10.63 (0.52)	6.00 (4.07)	8.88 (3.36)	4.63 (2.67)	6.25 (3.28)	4.13 (4.02)	5.25 (3.26)
Lesson	9.38 (1.69)	2.57 (2.07)	4.00 (2.27)	6.43 (2.23)	4.63 (2.07)	6.25 (2.49)	6.25 (3.33)
Quiz	3.13 (3.40)	3.38 (3.89)	3.13 (4.02)	10.50 (0.54)	8.57 (2.23)	10.00 (1.31)	9.88 (1.73)
Survey	5.38 (3.46)	6.00 (2.89)	3.38 (2.83)	3.88 (2.59)	4.88 (2.90)	6.63 (3.89)	6.50 (2.51)
Wiki	9.75 (1.28)	8.50 (3.07)	10.25 (0.89)	5.25 (3.37)	9.63 (1.19)	9.57 (1.51)	5.13 (3.36)
Workshop	7.00 (2.83)	8.00 (2.14)	9.25 (1.49)	7.00 (2.97)	9.17 (1.94)	6.83 (3.76)	7.50 (2.07)

5.5   Designing Effective Online Instruction Within an LMS

The findings of the above reported interview study helped to identify a practicable taxonomy for designing effective online instruction within the LMS. Using the results of the pairwise comparisons and the confidence ratings, the authors identified specific LMS features that are applicable for designated instructional functions.

Table 5.3 shows the taxonomy, which contains (1) the name of the LMS feature; (2) a short description of the LMS feature; (3) a classification of the LMS feature with regard to the three design elements *information*, *instruction*, and *learning* (see Grabowski and Curtis 1991); (4) the LMS feature's association with instructional functions (see Hilgenstock and Jirmann 2005); and (5) exemplary recommendations for instructional use.

5.6   Forums as Asynchronous Extended Applications of Learning Protocols

As a follow up to the first study of this chapter, LMS features like forums need to be integrated into the instructional design. That is, learning protocols are supposed to be instructional interventions to support reflection and elaboration within ongoing learning settings (Nückles et al. 2009). The findings can be transferred into a communication approach where an ongoing reflection on the content is integrated into the asynchronous features of a forum. The design element of the forum is learning, which is fulfilled by methods of interaction/communication. It allows dialogues of any written kind. But the work with the forum also needs to be embedded into the formal structure of the course; into the course requirements. This is not about making people do something that would not make sense otherwise, but rather about anchoring the benefits of use into as many existing design aspects as possible. If the course has formal (external) requirements, then the work will also have to address this issue. Or, from a motivational viewpoint, if the course imposes measures of external regulation (for any given reason), then the work within the course cannot assume otherwise.

5.6.1   Research Questions

There were two research questions:

1. Do the learners in the fully embedded design show a different learning, as regards the structural and semantic progression of their content discussion?
2. Do the fully instructional embedded opportunities to use the LMS features also influence other user behavior within the same tools during comparable courses?

Table 5.3 Practicable taxonomy of LMS features

Feature	Short description	Design element	Instructional function	Recommendation for instructional use
Assignment	The instructor can provide written feedback or grade assignments submitted by the student online	Instruction learning	Assessment Feedback Self-reflection	Assessment of knowledge increase Practice vs. exam assignments Collection of ideas and catchwords
Chat	The module allows a real-time synchronous discussion	Learning	Communication	Intensify the communication among a group of learners Virtual group meetings with direct questions and answers Consultation hours for learners
Choice	A question by the instructor with a choice of multiple responses	Information	Information Communication Feedback	Get opinion on a specific topic Cluster learning groups Short exam
Files/resources	Uploaded files for download (text documents, spreadsheets, slides, sound, graphic, or video)	Information	Information	Provide different types of information to the learners
Forum	The module allows asynchronous discussions between students and the instructor	Learning	Communication Cooperation Feedback	Hub for collaborative learning Exchange of opinions and information Assistance on assignments Feedback on performance and learning progression
Glossary	Allows one to create and maintain a list of definitions	Information	Information	Dictionary for technical terms Connecting course terms with the content with hyperlinks
Lesson	Content is delivered in an interesting and flexible way, including grading and questions	Instruction learning	Information	Collection of information on a specific topic Large texts can be divided into smaller units Differentiated feedback functions / questions and answers

Quiz	The module allows the instructor to design a set of short tests	Instruction learning	Assessment Evaluation Feedback Self-reflection	Self-assessment Exam and rating Repetition of learning content
Survey	Standard surveys to gather data from students (ATTLS, Critical incidents, COLLES)	Information	Communication Feedback	Request expectation and experiences of learners Feedback / Evaluation for instructors, learners, and materials
Wiki	Allows authoring of documents collectively in a simple markup language	Learning	Cooperation Information Self-reflection	Cooperation on joint projects Collate different information on a specific topic Brainstorming
Workshop	Students are enabled to assess each other's projects in a number of ways	Instruction Learning	Communication Cooperation Self-reflection	Complex problem solving Work through a sample solution of exams Feedback within a learning group

5.6.2   Second Empirical Study

The study was conducted within an experimental class for freshmen which contained $N = 34$ instructional design students in their first semester. The control group class consisted of $N = 55$ students in the same year. Among other design features (anchors and highly creative rapid prototyping methods), it was a course requirement within the experimental class to write 30 μ-assignments on a range of subject matters. Ten were designed to open a topic, while 20 of them where answers, comments, and questions on topics that other students opened. The micro-assignments were staggered across the semester and they were a course requirement. Each post was supposed to contain at least 150 words. The authors compared the integrated repeated tasks to a standard free discussion forum – that was embedded as regards to content only – of another class within the same group using a time series analysis on the structural and semantic conceptual change. The experimental class was on "the referring fields of instructional design" and the control class was on "research methods." The control class consisted of students from the experimental class and students who did not participate in the experimental class. In the following documentation, the experimental class is referred to as "*Exp1*," the intersection between the two classes as "*Exp2*," and all the students of the control class who did not take the experimental class are referred to as "*Ctrl*." Exp1 contains $N = 34$ students, Exp2 has $N = 23$ students (who visited both classes and have been tracked in the control group class), and Ctrl contains $N = 32$ students (who only attended the control group class). Copy and paste like actions were not allowed in both classes, and all quotes had to be cited – this requirement was controlled with two common plagiarism-finder software products. The data were collected on ten subsequent measurement time points throughout a 10 week working period, commencing 4 weeks from the beginning of semester and ending 1 week after the semester conclusion. The first measurement time-point was no pre-test, the participants were already writing in their forums on the task at that time. A common pre-test would not make sense, since if there is nothing to compare, then the comparison to the group model is always zero.

For further analysis, the text at the measurement points were first aggregated and then transformed into a graph with the T-MITOCAR (Text Model Inspection Trace of Concepts and Relations) software. Later, the graphs were compared to a *primus–inter–pares solution* that resembled the courses central best performance as compared to all the other students of each course. The comparison was conducted with graph theoretical measures that calculate both structural and semantic similarities (see Pirnay-Dummer and Ifenthaler 2010). Two of the seven available measures were used and are briefly reported in Table 5.4.

The learning curve was traced cumulatively, and the fundamental comparison measures converge to one for at least one participant per group (the primus inter pares) at the last measurement point. It is a suitable representation to see where most of the learning occurs and where the major steps (of convergence) towards the group representation lie. The measures are balanced by overall content quantity at

Table 5.4 Two of the seven similarity measures (Pirnay-Dummer and Ifenthaler 2010)

	Measure	Definition
Structure	Structural matching measure	Compares the complete structures of two graphs without regard to their content. This measure is necessary for all hypotheses which make assumptions about general features of structure (assumptions which state that expert knowledge is structured differently from novice knowledge)
Semantics	Concept matching measure	Compares the sets of concepts within a graph to determine the use of terms. It counts how many concepts are alike. This measure is especially important for different groups operating in the same domain (using the same textbook). It determines differences in language use between the models

each time to account for the amount of information that is represented at each time point within each individual.

5.6.3 Results

To track the differences of the learning development over time, the structural matching measure and the concept matching measure was applied. For Exp1, Exp2 and Ctrl.

Figure 5.2 shows a better learning outcome for the experimental groups over time regarding the group means (MTP stands for time of measurement). Substantially more knowledge is represented under the experimental condition. There is an effect on the Exp2-group, who transfer their experience to other classes they take. The learning curve of Exp1 is also steeper and reaches saturation earlier and on a higher level than Exp 2 or even the control group. Exp2 reaches a comparably high outcome but it takes them longer to get there. The effects are statistically significant over time on a repeated measurement ANOVA, $F(2, 63) = 13.94$, $p < 0.05$, $\eta^2 = 0.442$.

Figure 5.3 shows the group development for the concept matching measure. Semantics usually develops more slowly than does structure. However, very similar effects can be seen. There is clearly also a semantic benefit within the control class if the participants were also in the experimental class. The effects are again statistically significant over time on a repeated measurement ANOVA, $F(2, 63) = 9.52$, $p < 0.05$, $\eta^2 = 0.302$.

Qualitative analysis of the intervention showed that most students tend to dislike the pressure of the micro-assignments, having to write those assignments two to three times a week. This aversion could be observed from the evaluation independent of the grade. In the retrospective, however, this effect had turned. In their final semester, students argued that they had very high benefits from that experience

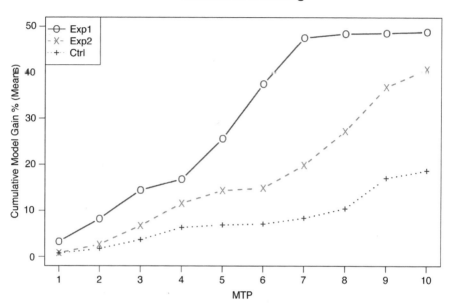

Fig. 5.2 Structural learning development over time

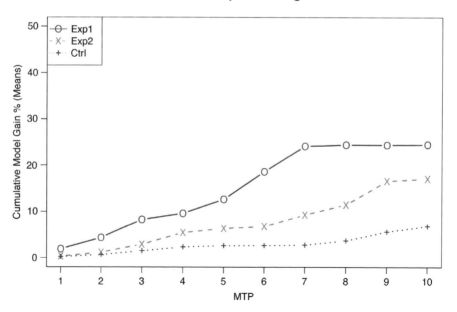

Fig. 5.3 Semantic learning development over time

throughout their studies and that they would not miss the experience. Moreover, they repeatedly stated that they remembered more from that class than from many other comparable classes.

5.7 Conclusions

A theoretically and empirically well-founded practicable taxonomy of instructional use of classic LMS features is provided on the basis of a qualitative study. The second study reported in this chapter extends the taxonomy for forums which were used as a micro-assignment-driven derivate of learning protocols by tracking the individual and group learning over time as compared to classical free use of forums. Whether the work with forum-like tools is embedded into the formal requirements of a course tremendously influences the work and learning outcomes. Concerning the second research question, the data clearly shows the effect of the embedding even on other courses that implement a more disconnected (usual) approach. The results can be interpreted as a clear encouragement to implement single innovations when resources or organizational constraints do not (yet) allow a system-wide change toward new instructional practices. However, the results also show the limits to that effect: The "secondary effect" is lower than the main effect. The innovation is composed of a high *localized benefit* accompanied by a medium additional *innovation halo* into other applications. The latter can be considered as a system effect. The range of such secondary innovation halos is another research question which needs to be addressed in future studies. Based on the results of our study, the above described taxonomy can be extended for the forum technology: The communication process needs to have a meaning throughout all relevant design principles and constraints of the course. The integration of the content is still the most important and also the most obvious prerequisite. It needs to serve both common and in-depth local questions and overall study interests and create accordingly opportunities for all participants. This presupposes a specific focus on a vertical connection between different performers, by encouraging between–peer–groups discussion and allowing/supporting different levels of argument within the same threads. However, the use of the forum also needs to address the qualification aspects of the course, even if that means following the external regulations imposed by assignments and grading, as can be clearly seen on the high effects from the data. Thus, the interaction within a forum will need a constant moderation, as well as the institutional rewards of "not being circumstantial."

In order to extend the practical taxonomy for LMS features, further empirical studies will be conducted for other parts of the taxonomy. This will enable, as shown in the study with discussion forms, understanding of the underlying psychological and educational principles of online learning. On the basis of these results, new instructional design principles for online learning could be introduced for classroom practice.

References

Alessi, S.M., Trollip, S.R.: Multimedia for Learning: Methods and Development. Allyn & Bacon, Inc., Needham Heights (2000)

Baumgartner, P., Häfele, H., Maier-Häfele, K.: E-Learning Praxishandbuch: Auswahl von Lernplattformen. Marktübersicht, Funktionen, Fachbegriffe, Studien Verlag, Innsbruck (2002)

Bett, K., Wedekind, J. (eds.): Lernplattformen in der Praxis. Waxman, Münster (2003)

Black, E.W., Beck, D., Dawson, K., Jinks, S., DiPietro, M.: The other side of the LMS: considering implementation and use in the adoption of an LMS in online and blended learning environments. TechTrends 51(2), 35–53 (2007)

Cole, J.: Using Moodle: Teaching with the Popular Open Source Management System. O'Reilly Community Press, London (2005)

Falvo, D.A., Johnson, B.F.: The use of learning management systems in the United States. TechTrends 51(2), 40–45 (2007)

Grabowski, B.L., Curtis, R.: Information, instruction, and learning: a hypermedia perspective. Perform. Improv. Q. 4(3), 2–12 (1991)

Häkkinen, P.: Challanges for design of computer-based learning environments. Br. J. Edu. Technol. 33(4), 461–469 (2002)

Hilgenstock, R., Jirmann, R.: Gemeinsam Online Lernen mit Moodle: Trainerhandbuch. DIALOGE Verlag, Bonn (2005)

Höbarth, U.: Konstruktivistisches Lernen mit Moodle: Praktische Einsatzmöglichkeiten in Bildungsinstitutionen. Hülsbusch, Boizenburg (2007)

Ifenthaler, D.: Learning and instruction in the digital age. In: Spector, J.M., Ifenthaler, D., Isaías Kinshuk, P., Sampson, D.G. (eds.) Learning and Instruction in the Digital Age: Making a Difference through Cognitive Approaches, Technology-Facilitated Collaboration and Assessment, and Personalized Communications, pp. 3–10. Springer, New York (2010)

Ifenthaler, D.: Implementation of web-enhanced features for successful teaching and learning. The utility of technological progressions of learning management systems. In: Simonson, M.R. (ed.) 31st National Convention of the Association for Educational Communications and Technology, vol. 1, pp. 134–146. AECT, Bloomington (2008)

Kerres, M., de Witt, C.: A didactical framework for the design of blended learning arrangements. Learn. Media Technol. 28(2 & 3), 101–113 (2003)

Koszalka, T.A., Ganesan, R.: Designing online courses: a taxonomy to guide strategic use of features available in course management systems (CMS) in distance education. Distance Educ. 25(2), 243–256 (2004)

Land, S.M., Hannafin, M.J.: A conceptual framework for the development of theories-inaction with open-ended learning environments. Educ. Tech. Res. Dev. 44(3), 37–53 (1996)

Mayer, R.E.: Multimedia Learning. Cambridge University Press, Cambridge (2001)

Melton, J.: The LMS moodle: A usability evaluation. Lang. Issues 11/12(1), 1–24 (2006)

Nückles, M., Hübner, S., Renkl, A.: Enhancing self-regulated learning by writing learning protocols. Learn. Instr. 19(3), 259–271 (2009)

Pirnay-Dummer, P., Ifenthaler, D.: Automated knowledge visualization and assessment. In: Ifenthaler, D., Pirnay-Dummer, P., Seel, N.M. (eds.) Computer-Based Diagnostics and Systematic Analysis of Knowledge, pp. 77–115. Springer, New York (2010)

Schulmeister, R.: Lernplattformen für das virtuelle Lernen – Evaluation und Didaktik. Oldenbourg, München (2003)

Trahasch, S., Kraus, G., Eferth, T.: Lernplattformen – entscheidungen mit weitblick. In: Bachmann, G., Haertel, G.D., Kindt, M. (eds.) Campus 2002. Die Virtuelle Hochschule in der Konsolidierungsphase, pp. 251–261. Waxmann, Münster (2002)

Waterhouse, S.: The Power of Elearning: The Essential Guide for Teaching in the Digital Age. Pearson, Boston (2005)

Williams, B.C.: Moodle: For Teachers, Trainers and Administrators (Version 1.4.3): Moodle.org. (2005)

Chapter 6
How to Foster Creativity in Technology Enhanced Learning?

Isa Jahnke

Abstract Creativity-fostered learning in higher education enhanced by social media is described. The fostering of creativity in teaching and learning is illustrated by three examples: (a) a European project about experimental online learning in production engineering (PeTEX); (b) a longitudinal study about informal learning supported by online forums in a computer science faculty (InPUD); and (c) a mind mapping scenario supported by a Web 2.0 tool. Aspects and conceptions toward a framework about fostering creativity in higher education regarding Media-enhanced education are illustrated.

6.1 Introduction

Teaching and learning in higher education institutions are becoming enhanced by the use of Internet-based technologies (Jahnke and Koch 2009). According to Collins and Halverson (2009), the net generation asks particularly for online social networks with "anytime, anywhere" access. Modern day learning systems are more flexible, adaptable to different existing levels of learning strategies, but are usually controlled by the teacher. They often do not implement concepts that embed the whole learning process into the given curriculum, neither do they empower the students to manage their own learning nor do they foster creative thinking and creative actions. An approach to design technical, social, and educational elements is delivered by the framework of socio-technical systems and networks (Bolisani 2008; Whitworth et al. 2009) and computer-supported collaborative learning. Reshaping blended and co-located learning requires the analysis and design of social processes, technical systems, and educational methods. One essential result

I. Jahnke (✉)
Department of Applied Educational Science, Umeå University, ICT, Media and Learning (IML),
SE-90187 Umeå, Sweden
e-mail: isa.jahnke@tu-dortmund.de

B. White et al. (eds.), *Social Media Tools and Platforms in Learning Environments*,
DOI 10.1007/978-3-642-20392-3_6, © Springer-Verlag Berlin Heidelberg 2011

is that new learning approaches should be situated in a specific context and embedded within social interactions (Lave and Wenger 1990). However, they do not often focus on such educational concepts which promote creativity in learning arrangements.

Universities play a particular role in this context since they are intended to educate people who support the development of creative ideas (generating new ideas) and innovation (enforcement and acceptance of new ideas). In addition to transmitting specialized knowledge to students, institutions of higher education are challenged to develop or even enhance the students' creative potential. Therefore, it is not enough to restrict learning to how expertise, skills, and competencies can be acquired, reproduced, and applied. Students must also be encouraged to learn to think in multiple ways and reach beyond the spectrum of available options to form new relationships between established elements, as well as to discover entirely new concepts or previously unconsidered connections.

This chapter describes creativity in higher education by way of three examples. First, an online learning arrangement called PeTEX in the field of engineering is illustrated, where the three dimensions – technical, social, and educational principles – are designed. In the field of mechanical engineering, remote laboratories are harnessed where creative learning is connected with Internet-supported distance-controlled live experimentation. Second, the socio-technical community called InPUD (a large group with more than 1,500 members at a German university) will be described. The third example concerns a mind mapping tool.

6.2   Theoretical Framework

It is well-known from computer-supported cooperative research (Suchman 1987, 2007) and computer-supported collaborative learning (Wasson et al. 2007), that a successful socio-technical system requires the integration of technical, social, and educational elements (Collins and Halverson 2009; Jahnke and Koch 2009). But what does "successful" mean? This chapter describes a three dimensional framework that addresses that question.

6.2.1   Three Design Dimensions

Designing a socio-technical system must include the design of a technical and of a social system (Herrmann et al. 2007). In addition, when designing computer-supported learning processes, the educational dimension must also be considered. So, there are three essential elements. These are: technical elements (learning management systems; social media, community platforms, Web 2.0 tools), social/ organizational structures (forms of communication and participation, roles of instructors, students), and educational concepts (formal and informal learning, problem-based learning, creativity-supportive concepts).

The following questions illuminate the critical design issues (Jahnke et al. 2010).

- The degree of structural coupling (degree of interdependency) of the three elements and their complex interconnections must be considered: Are the elements strongly connected and formalized, or flexibly usable? How closely or loosely are the elements connected?
- The degree of quality must be considered. This demonstrates how well the elements interact. The greater the unity among these three elements, the more likely that knowledge will be shared and co-construction of knowledge will occur. The better the participants can learn, the more satisfied they become (at least at the end of the learning process).
- "A successful design" depends on a careful description of each user's role. Different target groups, and people in different roles, have different cognitive conceptions of success in mind. Instructors, students, university managers, pedagogical experts, e-learning experts, each define success in different ways. A good design includes different views or at least, supports a common understanding (Herrmann et al. 2007). In addition, a new target group consisting of the "digital natives" (Prensky 2001; Palfrey and Gasser 2008) is arriving at the university. Younger people, who are growing up with social media, are developing different ideas about learning and knowledge. They are networking in many different online communities by using Social Media.

These three dimensions have driven the design process for fostering creativity in learning at higher education institutions. But what exactly is creativity? And what is an appropriate way to foster creativity in higher education?

6.2.2 Creative Thinking and Creative Actions in Higher Education

Creativity has to do with something new, something valuable or *useful* for a particular group (Sternberg 1999, p. 3). "Creativity is the ability to produce work that is both novel (original, unexpected) and appropriate (useful, adaptive concerning task constraints)." This useful novelty is found in an individual and social process of construction or generation: "You cannot be creative without creating something" (Quote by G. Fischer at International Conference CSCL2009, Greece). From this perspective, ideas and idea-generating people are only creative when an external authority assigns this value. But the question is: for whom the creation is something new or valuable? Creativity therefore is relative with regard to the relationship of ideas to individuals and groups who assign value to it. In these approaches, the concepts of creativity (generating ideas) and innovation (acceptance of new ideas by people, society, industry) are not sufficiently separated.

6.2.2.1 Historical Development of "Creativity"

In the early stages of creativity research (Guilford 1956), the dominant approaches for explaining and investigating creativity came from psychology and were focused on individuals. According to the great mind approach (biographical creativity diagnostic or genius theory), creativity is ascribed to new ideas or products when exceptional inventors offer an ingenious solution to a problem at the right time. In contrast, the advocates of psychometric methods regard creativity as a cognitive ability expressed primarily through unorthodox thinking which is available, in principle, to all people. Creativity is also regarded as an individual cognitive ability and as a personality trait according to the experimental methods of psychology, but it is influenced by a number of parameters including: structures of work and space (Amabile et al. 1996), time available (Amabile et al. 2002), and the behavior of leaders (Amabile et al. 2004). As such, a variety of factors affect the generation of ideas in a way that they open up certain possibilities and impose restrictions. According to the systemic understanding, not only the creative person but also the creative process, the creative product, and its evaluation of creativity must be considered. The formative authors for this perspective are Csikszentmihalyi (1996) and Gardner (1993). They view creativity as the result of interaction between an individual (the generator of ideas) and a group who (embedded in a societal context) assess the creative achievement, and a domain containing symbolic rules (Sonnenburg 2007, p. 43).

The rise of the systemic view of creativity has sparked a debate regarding the focus of creativity research. Lenk criticizes the systemic view, maintaining that it describes two distinct concepts, creativity and acceptance of creativity (Lenk 2000, p. 8). Boden (1994) insists that the genesis of creative ideas, rather than their evaluation, is the appropriate focus of research into creativity. Dresler maintains that the "disagreement regarding the focus on psychological or social processes" is an "irreconcilable divide" (Dresler 2008, p. 9). The distinction between individual and (social) environment has become increasingly important in relation to the question of the source of creative ideas.

Elizabeth Watson (2007) provides an initial framework contrasting approaches focused on individuals with those studies which, in addition to individuals, also credit groups, teams, and organizations with an agency in creative achievement (Fischer et al. 2004). Watson identifies three levels of creative agents:

- The individuals in a group are the originators of creative new ideas;
- The product of an individual is socially influenced and therefore a socially constructed creative achievement. Creative production in a team differs from the creative achievement of a single individual. Hermann refers to this as "collaborative creativity" (Herrmann et al. 2009);
- Organizations can also be the agents of creative accomplishment. They make a framework available to groups or teams, within which they can interact with other groups or teams.

Watson's efforts to draw fine distinctions in the tightly woven mesh of studies on creativity, demonstrate the complexity of the current state of the discussion (Greene 2001).

Dresler (2008) attempts to differentiate the term creativity in another way. He lists, among others, every-day creativity, historical creativity, psychological creativity, group creativity, non-human creativity, technological creativity, artistic creativity, and spontaneous creativity. He tries to assign them to the categories process, product, and person. This enumeration could be expanded, but in the end, Dresler demonstrates how little this differentiation helps: "Despite – or even because of – these manifold concepts of creativity, no precise definition of creativity is yet available" (translated by authors, Dresler 2008, p. 15).

6.2.2.2   Multiplicity of Sometimes Contradictory Definitions

Because of the multiplicity of (sometimes mutually exclusive) definitions, many questions remain open in the field of creativity research. In addition to the disagreement about the priority of person-centered or systemic methods, numerous other standpoints remain with regard to a quantitative or qualitative approach to the phenomenon of creativity, the localization of creativity as a general or context-specific phenomenon, as well as less pressing concerns such as the question whether animals or machines can also be creative. Dresler mentions a number of authors who rightly (at times, even sarcastically) criticize the achievements of creativity research against this background, supporting Weitz (1972) in maintaining that creativity should be an open concept. The argument is that creativity is an umbrella concept, not to be exactly defined but offering a common frame of reference for the otherwise very different concepts. This makes it possible to approach the term "creativity" with different perspectives but without conflict. "Instead of looking for a universally valid criterion, a binding definition or a broadly accepted focus, creativity research should accept its inherent diversity" (Dresler 2008, p. 17). At the same time, scientific precision should not be sacrificed.

Brodbeck (2006), like Tosey (2006), advocates the notion that the development of creativity itself should not be the primary focus, rather the question under which conditions creativity can originate should be the focus: "On the other hand, we can say that when we are cramped, pig-headed, agitated, under stress, withdrawn, narrow-minded, then creativity cannot occur; We can limit creativity" (translated by authors, Brodbeck 2006).

Noise, distractions, and disruptions inhibit creativity, and conversely, the absence of these factors *facilitates* the emergence of creativity. Routines and habits, for example, limit creativity, and certain techniques can help break down these barriers. Facilitating creativity always works on two levels: on external influences that inhibit the rise of creativity, and on internal factors in the form of self-imposed thinking barriers such as habits and predetermined opinions. In this context, Brodbeck and De Bono (1992) refer to the fact that according to current models of brain research, the human brain is trained to use patterns and routines. Creative thinking means suspending the use of these patterns.

The "Imaginative Curriculum Network" in Great Britain (Kleiman 2008); Jackson 2003, 2006) aims to change cultures of teaching and learning towards creativity-supported learning. Distancing itself from the scientific discussion in creativity research, the approach is oriented toward the requirements of its target group, the university, and its members. The network does not give a universal definition. But while a few elements of creativity are specifically mentioned ("Creativity is..."), the fact that different concepts of creativity exist for each teacher and each student is emphasized.

For universities, the challenge becomes a matter of designing their cultures of teaching and learning in such a way that as many of these external barriers as possible are removed. At the same time, teaching and learning scenarios should be applied which encourage students to break down their thinking barriers and to think "differently" (away from traditional thinking). Strategies to promote creativity can, in this respect, only succeed as integrated approaches that focus on teaching and learning scenarios, individual factors, as well as institutional and media influences.

6.3   Definition, Study Design (Methods), Results

According to the multiplicity of (sometimes mutually exclusive) definitions (see section above), the authors accept creativity as an open concept. Creativity is subjective; every person has a unique perspective on what a creative effort means. What creative is, or is not, can be different. Majority opinions, about which efforts should be called creative or not creative, can be deceptive. But the open concept does not mean that creativity is "everything." Thus – in order to foster creativity – creativity must be contextualized. The challenge therefore is to define creativity in a specific context (here universities). Against this background, it seems appropriate to educate people involved in higher education with regard to the available, subjective conceptions of creativity. Instead of restricting strategies to promote creativity to specific elements, an effort should be made to do justice to as many different understandings of creativity as possible through a portfolio of different potential approaches.

6.3.1   Methods

To collect the target group's understanding about creativity (here, teachers at universities) and what creativity is for them, the DaVinci sub-project "Didactics" included three phases of data collection and analysis.

The first phase of data collection consisted of ten qualitative, expert interviews with exceptional teachers. These included excellent researchers (Leibniz Prize winners), award-winning teachers (ars legendi or "Professor of the Year" from unicum), as well as professors and research assistants who have been rated highly by students on the website "meinprof.de." In the second phase, ten teachers from the University–Alliance–Metropolis–Ruhr (UAMR, consisting of the universities of Bochum, Dortmund, and Duisburg–Essen, Germany) who are active in the discipline of pedagogy were interviewed. The purpose of the interviews was, among other things, to gain insight into different facets of creativity in teaching in higher education.

The interviews were conducted in the second half of 2009, at the interviewees' places of work and generally with two interviewers. The interviews were audiorecorded and later transcribed. In addition, notes were taken. The interviews were analyzed by means of "open coding" according to the "Grounded Theory" (Strauss and Corbin 1990). Following the Grounded Theory, the empirical data were used to formulate a theoretical model entitled "Conceptual Framework for Fostering Creativity: six Ingredients."

The third phase of data gathering consisted of an online survey of all teachers at UAMR to find out to what extent they would confirm the conceptual framework described in the next section. In the third phase, the framework of six different ingredients has been empirically tested. The first question to the teachers at the universities was: "What is a creative effort (thinking, action) of your students?" And in the second question, the teachers were asked to match their given answers with the framework of the six ingredients. In addition, the answer "nothing matches" and "don't know" were also possible. The main result was that less than 1.5% of all given answers (out a total of $n = 591$ given answers) did not fit to the six levels.

6.3.2   Results: Framework About Creativity in Higher Education

As a result of the interviews, it can be concluded that the concept of creativity in the landscape of higher education is understood in a multitude of ways. The understanding of what creativity is ranges from viewing it:

- As a commonplace phenomenon which can be influenced by a change in one's "attentiveness";
- Through seeing it as the development of one's own ideas (which generally could have already existed but are developed by the individual instead of simply being adopted); and
- As the creative linking of previously unconnected ideas or thoughts, up to considering creativity to be the ability to see objects and relationships from different perspectives, to abandon habitual patterns of thinking, and finally to create and implement entirely new ideas.

This pluralistic character of the conception of creativity in higher education leads back to the question of whether creativity can actually be learned, whether people "create" ideas or whether they "receive" them. The view that creativity can be fostered – or blocked – was also widely represented. But the best way in which creativity could be fostered remained thoroughly subjective; in one case, restrictions were a challenge and motivation, while other experts found restrictions hinder their creative work. Independent of their understanding of creativity, the teachers in the first phase of the interviews thought it important to give students sufficient possibilities to develop ideas, thoughts, and products, to allow them to "create" something themselves, in order to promote the unfolding of their creativity.

In order to do justice to the variety of ways that creativity is conceptualized (pluralistic view) the project team has developed a number of approaches for fostering creativity. Together, they form a conceptual framework which allows academic teachers in higher education institutions to develop individual strategies. In reference to the different facets of creativity identified by the interviewed experts, efforts to foster creativity target the following goals. The six ingredients for fostering creative thinking and creative actions are demonstrated in Table 6.1.

The strengthening of independent, self-reflective learning, or forcing students to work autonomously can be a fundamental improvement in encouraging creativity,

Table 6.1 Fostering creativity in higher education (HE) – a conceptual framework of six ingredients

Richness of creativity in HE	Description (Enabling students to do...)
6. Original, entirely new ideas	The production of many ideas can be encouraged through creativity techniques and an appropriate environment: "enable the possibility of arrival"; allowing and encouraging mistakes.
5. Fostering a new culture of thinking	Change of perspective, break through routines and patterns of habit, take a different attitude, reduce prejudice, integrate provocations, dealing with ambiguities, reflection on one's own creativity and thought-structure, knowledge about the inner-workings of the brain, perpetually scrutinizing.
4. Fostering constructive learning	Where students create something; creation of, for example, interconnections in theses, research-mode learning projects, aid and outreach projects; e.g., planning a congress.
3. Fostering fascination, increasing motivation to learn	Fostering of "research curiosity," learn to ask right questions; enabling situated learning, use experiences of students, developing interesting ways to pose questions or problems; variety; establish a link to practice; use of metaphors, humor; individualization in larger courses.
2. Fostering the ability to work autonomously	Enabling the individual student to set the acquisition of knowledge in motion; enabling students to learn that they are responsible for steering the processes of learning; enabling to make one's own decisions.
1. Fostering independent, self-reflective learning	Critical thinking, learner "constructs" knowledge oneself rather than adopting it; enabling students to hold an internal dialog, breaking out of a receptive posture, supporting lateral and critical thinking.

even under inconvenient conditions (lecture courses with hundreds of students and predetermined content and exams), whereas these goals will essentially fulfill themselves in contexts such as project seminars or workshops. In these cases, higher levels of fostering creativity are appropriate. The decision regarding which level to strive for (and the related questions of how to design the teaching and learning scenarios) depends on the teachers and instructors. In order to make support easier, strategies for fostering creativity can, for example, be integrated into B.A. and M.A. Courses of study.

These six ingredients of the framework require action on multiple levels. Essentially, they address a change in personal attitude and social activity. Students should, in the end, become more "creative" than before (with regard to the six ingredients, students developed competences like reflective and critical thinking, self-autonomous learning, motivation to learn (including research curiosity), ability to do constructive actions, and change of perspectives). This should be achieved through particular teaching and learning scenarios which inspire individuals in the unfolding of their creativity (in the various categories described above) and support them therein. A fundamental distinction must be made between the level of students (level 1) and the level of teaching practice, teachers, and others (level 2). Students need an appropriate teaching and learning scenario where creativity will be fostered. Instructors/teachers need to learn strategies to structure courses toward creativity-supportive learning cultures. This is possible, for example, through faculty development, or workshops in pedagogy. The teaching and learning scenarios (of both levels), personal attitudes, and social actions are embedded in an institutional context (level 3). Through its influence, this context can affect the levels either positively or negatively, and for this reason, adequate measures to promote creativity must also take this level into account and make suitable suggestions to shape it.

6.3.2.1 Changeable Elements at the Level of Teaching

There are many potential starting-points on the level of the teaching practice and learning cultures in higher education which can be implemented. Depending upon the given understanding of creativity and the respective goals, there are many methods of support. Teachers can decide on their goals based on the conceptual framework outlined here. Through working out their own plans, instructors can be inspired to implement appropriate measures. This plan should not be understood as normative; rather it should encourage teachers to become aware of their own understanding of creativity, to reflect on the meaning of creativity for teaching and to consider how creativity can be fostered in their own teaching and learning scenarios regarding the context (like existing curriculum or discipline cultures).

To design a course that fosters creativity requires the integration of short, mid, and long-term measures:

- Elements of a session of a course are changed;
- A complete session of a course is changed;

- Multiple sessions of a course are changed;
- An entire course is changed;
- The curriculum (and its structure) of an entire university is changed.

"Session" in this context means the individual meeting of a course during the semester. Short-term measures include the change of elements in a session of a course (use cognitive techniques or creative thinking methods) and change of a single session of a course (integrate experts or practitioners). Middle-term measures focus on the change of multiple sessions of a course (alter structures) and change of the entire course (the course will be designed like a student's project "Plan an International Congress"). And third, long-term measures consist of a change of the entire curricula or degree program (institutionalize a year of creativity).

Approaches for structuring and therefore the re-structuring of existing courses, as well as the development of new courses so that they foster creativity, can be broken down into four areas:

1. Educational elements:

   1.1 Mode of the course (variable time configurations, physical/virtual spaces, assessments and their mechanisms, pre-defined structure, and student work)
   1.2 Learning process (when, in the learning process, is creativity needed?)

2. Social context (group size, ratio of individual to collaborative learning, group work, learning atmosphere, behavior/role of the teacher)
3. Technical systems; tools (Social Media, Web 2.0, facilitation tools, but also cognitive techniques such as PMI)

These four elements can be used to change a course or a single session to foster creativity-supportive learning processes. They are partly dependent on one another and are not exhaustive. They have not yet been assigned to concrete ingredients (1–6); rather they can be variably applied depending upon the learning scenario.

(Ad 1.1) In the area of the *mode* of the course, a number of different modes can be reflected. For example, the environment can be arranged to better promote creativity: the space can be formatted differently (discussion walls, circular seating arrangements), physical and online meetings can be changed or staggered (one longer meeting per month instead of weekly meetings). In order to shape cultures of learning to help foster creativity, assessment mechanisms must also be critically examined. One of the interviewees emphasized that it is necessary to change the content of assessments. It is not enough to simply test for specialized knowledge. If creative processes have been encouraged in the course, the assessment mechanism must be altered (several assessments instead of one exam; evaluation of progress throughout the course; testing competences and specialized knowledge). Finally, the format of the course can be changed with respect to fostering creativity, adjusting the ratio of formal teacher-provided structures to individual work by the students.

(Ad 1.2) A second area is *shaping the process of teaching and learning*. This can be the case in a wide variety of situations throughout the process:

- The solution to a problem is provided by the teacher and the process of getting there must be creatively developed (creative process);
- The exercise is specified, but the solution and result must be achieved creatively (creative process and creative product);
- Only the topic is defined: the problem, solution and the process of solving the problem must be creatively contested (creative process of defining the problem and the way to solve it as well as a creative product);

(Ad 2) In the area of *social context*, the classroom setting (group size, learning environment, course atmosphere), ratio of (creative) individual and group work as well as the behavior of the teacher must be considered, and depending on the strategy for promoting creativity (compare to the six levels in Table 6.1), perhaps altered.

(Ad 3) *Technical systems* are social media, learning management systems, or combinations. *Tools* for fostering creativity range from cognitive techniques such as the synectic technique, "headstand method," and "thinking-hats" to general discussion techniques, facilitation methods including brainstorming tools, and methods that promote reflection. These tools can be helpful, particularly in achieving the goals in steps four, five, and six (Table 6.1):

- Facilitating a shift in perspective: The challenge "Think the impossible," and assistance in changing one's perspective help to bring about scrutiny of established patterns of thinking and the abandonment of ingrained lines of thought. This allows one to see things from a new, unfamiliar angle in order to encourage creative thinking and arrive at the solutions to problems.
- Encouragement in being able to establish distance between oneself and the situation (and thereby being able to see it from another perspective.)
- Breaking down barriers to creativity: Sometimes expressed through resignation or stagnation, these blockages usually stem from environmental/systemic conditions, economic dependence, and cannot be overcome by logic or rationality, rather by constructive problem-solving strategies (lateral thinking).

Methods for fostering creative thinking are available in many publications (De Bono 1992). Efforts to foster creativity itself can also benefit from the integration of technology (such as the integration of Web 2.0, existing learning management systems at universities, or using modern discussion labs with an interactive wall).

6.4 Technology-Enhanced Creative Learning Cultures – Examples

When designing and implementing creativity concepts in higher education, special courses or classes, the design-based research is one appropriate methodology. It is grounded in empirical data analysis with the aim to improve and change practice including researching the effects of implementation.

The design-based research approach (DBR) fosters collaboration among researchers and teachers (Reeves et al. 2005). Researchers working together with educators and teachers seek to refine theories of teaching and learning by designing, studying, and refining rich, theory-based innovations, in realistic learning environments. DBR is a "systematic but flexible methodology aimed to improve educational practices through iterative analysis, design, development, and implementation, based on collaboration among researchers and practitioners in real-world settings, and leading to contextually-sensitive design principles and theories" (Wang and Hannafin 2005, p. 6). DBR consists of several phases of analysis (reflection) and design (interventions for improving learning) which are alternate and interwoven (cycle of activities). The iterative process enables researchers to understand the socio-technical–pedagogical phenomenon required to improve practice. It is similar to "action research" where researchers and practitioners acting together on a cycle of activities, including action intervention and in this way "*gain feedback from this experience, modify the theory as a result of this feedback, and try it again*" (Avison et al. 1991, pp. 94–95).

The first two studies into fostering creativity in media-enhanced learning were conducted with this methodology. The design-based research procedures regarding these two case studies are illustrated in more detail in Jahnke (2010) (example 2) and Jahnke et al. (2010) (example 1).

6.4.1 PeTEX – Experimental Online Learning

The PeTEX (Platform for eLearning and Telemetric Experimentation) project (2008–2010) aimed to develop online learning within remote laboratories. Interactive live experiments in the fields of forming (tensile tests for characterizing the material behavior), cutting (milling processes), and joining (friction stir welding) were realized. The physical–real laboratories exist in the three European countries Germany (TU Dortmund University, IUL), Italy (University of Palermo, DTMPIG), and Sweden (KTH, Stockholm). As a result of the project's interdisciplinary nature, researchers, educational experts, online learning experts, modeling moderators, and, in particular, the target groups – teachers and students from engineering – have been involved. Table 6.2 shows the educational design, in particular the creativity concept of PeTEX.

PeTEX's objective was to design an experimental online learning prototype that includes experimental design, test set-ups, support, observation, and analysis of acquired measurements and data. The remote experiments are remote controlled and monitored through video cameras. Interfaces to the remote labs provide the possibility to change input parameters and access output results. One challenge was to implement Internet-mediated real experimentations from almost every computer workstation and to customize the pedagogical concept regarding creativity for an e-learning scenario. The central educational concept is the reflective learning approach with instructions for beginners, problem-based learning students at the

Table 6.2 PeTEX scenarios

Elements	Description	PeTEX
Fostering of creativity...	Reflective learning (*focused on No. 1 from 6 ingredients*)	Students get the task to create hypotheses, parameters, and reflect results by observing an online, telemetric experiment in mechanical engineering (cutting)
	Constructive learning (*focused on No. 4 from 6 ingredients*)	Planning and conducting a remote experiment; writing a learning diary about learning progress
Session	Elements of a session of a course are changed	(a) Integrating PeTEX into an existing course
	An entire course is changed	(b) Using PeTEX like a standalone course
Educational elements: Mode of the course	Both physical and online (format which regulates the ratio of formal, pre-defined structure and student work)	(a) Integrating PeTEX into an existing course: from 1 week to next week, give the students homework, a specific questions to guide them through module 1 (later module 2,3 and so forth) (b) PeTEX as standalone course online
	Online assessments	(a) PeTEX as part of existing assessments (40% of the grade) (b) PeTEX as online course: writing a report about results and a learning diary
Learning processes	When in the process is creativity needed	For beginners: learning walkthrough is guided, some tasks support creative thinking For intermediate level: scenario-based, case-based learning (problem solving process), creative thinking and creative actions For advanced level: only the topic is defined: the problem, solution, and the process of solving the problem must be creatively contested (creative process of defining the problem and the way to solve it as well as a creative product)
Social context	Ratio of individual and collaborative learning	Individual learning: first phases of conducting the experiments; community sharing: discussing the results of the remote experiment online with the community members
Technical systems	Social media	Online community platform; portal: learning management system Moodle; for discussions: forums; for reporting: wiki and blogs

intermediate level and research-based learning for advanced level. At all levels, students plan and conduct a remote-configurable experiment in Mechanical Engineering (cutting, welding, or forming). The difference from the pedagogical viewpoint is that (a) the beginners get more support with instructions while the other learning levels get less instructions and (b) within the process, creativity is required at different times: beginners have the task to reflect a given experiment; in the intermediate level, the problem is given but creativity is necessary to solve the problem and in the advanced level, nothing is given, here creativity is required for the entire process (students get the task to find the research lack, an appropriate question, the problem and a solution, and to reflect the process).

A virtual interactive online environment was implemented for using the experimental data. Learners may monitor the progress of the experiments since the equipment is supplemented with synchronized video recording cameras located at different positions and constantly sending the instant images of running experiments. This required the development of an appropriate learning tool, a module oriented layout, instruction, learning tasks, observation, discussions in forums, and experimental tasks. The PeTEX team decided to use Moodle – an online platform that has the potential to integrate modularized teaching objects. The platform is a multi-linguistic, internationally spread Open Source learning management system. It offers the integration of learning materials and learning activities via Internet interfaces. Such an online learning approach also demands an appropriate balance between teaching input, instructions, in particular learning activities, and qualified feedback (from peers as well as instructor): more student activities than in blended learning, or face-to-face settings are required (Jahnke et al. 2010).

6.4.2   InPUD – Informal Learning Supported by Forums

An information and communication system, InPUD, (Informatics Portal University of Dortmund, Germany) was implemented to solve information deficiencies by supporting knowledge sharing among novice (new) and expert (senior) students, study advisors, as well as faculty members (teachers, dean officers, administration officers). The InPUD-community is a community system for computer science students. The InPUD-community differs from other informal, pure online communities which are built in people's spare time and are not a part of an institution. In contrast, InPUD is an extension of a Department (a supplement to the formal structure). According to Preece's four areas (2004) the InPUD-community is (a) characterized by a large size, (b) shares knowledge about computer science, hints about "how to study successfully," and study management at the university, (c) has an extended lifespan, and (d) delivers a space for online communication.

The InPUD-community includes both an information space as well as communication opportunities. InPUD provides an overview of all classes and lectures that are offered during the course of a semester. The way that the information is structured is the same for each lecture or seminar. The information pertains to lectures, including any tutorials that are being held (and when), course materials, notices for examinations, lecturer contact information, and often a free discussion forum, as well as news and search functions. The information portal about the study management domain is combined with online discussion boards. The boards are embedded in an information website that includes facts about course guidance as well as graphical maps of how to study which course at which time.

The communication in InPUD is predominantly online and asynchronous. InPUD has more than 1,500 members (out of 2,000 students at the faculty). It provides private identity (login is possible with nick names, email addresses are not shown) but enables public accessibility. The discussion boards exist for both lectures (to discuss exercises or content) and study organization. The decision about the topic mainly depends on what the students want to discuss. It ranges from discussions about course content, definitions, or solutions for exercises to organizational issues (where/when is the next learning group, what could come up in the examinations?). Table 6.3 demonstrates the InPUD community reflecting the fostering of creativity in higher education.

The community has been analyzed in detail through a longitudinal study (Jahnke 2010). The results show that the InPUD-community is helpful; the degree of the learner satisfaction with the STC; and type and quality of use. The STC is an appropriate and enhanced platform for students to share knowledge. The answer to the question whether the STC is an appropriate means for supporting knowledge sharing is "Yes". The cultivation of such a community has enabled a new learning culture:

Table 6.3 InPUD community with regard to the creativity approach

Elements	Description of elements	InPUD
Fostering of creativity...	Fostering a new thinking culture (*focused on No. 5 from 6 ingredients*)	Knowledge sharing about how to study successfully, discussing aspects, make them available for all students
Session	Elements around the formal curriculum are changed	Online communication space supported by forums
Educational elements: Mode	Online	Online forums
Learning process	When is creativity needed?	Open problems, students post problems, questions, discussions
Social context	Ratio of individual and collaborative learning	Individual problems, group could have answers
	Learning atmosphere	Facilitator, given framework for rules of discussion and posting
Technical system	Social media	Forums (with special topics) and portal (including information by the department)

- The InPUD-community transformed the "jungle of information" in the higher education institution into a "National Park with many ways to go."
- InPUD changed the existing social structures into a flexible communication space for learners.

The community, consisting of both, an information portal (Web 1.0 condition) with flexible communication spaces (Web 2.0 conditions), fosters critical and reflective thinking. Students ask questions, discuss, and reflect about their study planning and conducting. They discuss about exercises and tasks from courses and reflect solutions and own ideas. According to Jahnke's study, more than two-thirds of the community members use InPUD often or very often for "learning to handle different opinions." More than half of the members also use InPUD for exchanging knowledge, information with others, and for helping others. Such a community is an appropriate communication space for learners since it supports me-centricity and personalizes knowledge sharing. The InPUD-community makes it easier for a community member to obtain the relevant information that s/he needs at a given time. This reduces the social complexity and information overload from the official institution.

6.4.3   The Example of Mind Mapping

The third example of fostering creativity in higher education is a more general one. In order to support multi-perspectives (focused on No.1 out of six ingredients of the conceptual framework), a web based online tool for collaborative mind mapping actions can be used (Mindmeister or Freemind). Students are given the task to create a mind map collaboratively. For instance, an appropriate guided question for a physics course is the discussion about a planet: "What is a planet? What properties are essential? Please discuss regarding Mars." The mind map supports different perspectives. Students in small groups with at least one laptop or iPAD get the task to create a definition with arguments and statements of reasons. Then, they have to convince the other students why their own definition is the best one. So, a complex mind map with different perspectives is created. Students learn that they must be flexible and move beyond their own viewpoint during the process of definition finding. They also learn that there is a need to be more open to others.

6.5   Lessons Learned and Next Steps

The conceptual framework of fostering creativity in media-enhanced learning and the three examples installed in higher education show the multi-layered dimensions of creativity in a specific context. Creative action means that people think about new possibilities and solutions when they are in situations where no general and standard solution can be applied. In such situations, self-determination and

Table 6.4 Fostering creativity in higher education (six ingredients)

Fostering creativity in higher education	Description	What instructors/teachers can do to foster creative learning cultures (Jackson 2010)	Supporting students to do "creative thinking and creative actions" (Jackson and Shaw 2006)
Original, entirely new ideas	The production of many ideas can be encouraged through creativity techniques and appropriate environment: "enable the possibility of arrival"'; allowing and encouraging mistakes	"Enabling students to appreciate the significance of being able to deal with situations and to see situations as the fundamental opportunity for being creative. They need to be empowered to create new situations individually and with others by connecting people and transferring, adapting and integrating ideas, resources and opportunities, in an imaginative, willful and productive way, to solve problems and create new value."	"Being original. This embodies the quality of newness, for example inventing and producing new things or doing things no one has done before."
Fostering a new culture of thinking and actions	To take many perspectives; change of perspective, break through routines and patterns of habit, take a different attitude, reduce prejudice, integrate provocations, dealing with ambiguities, reflection on one's own creativity and thought-structure, knowledge about the inner workings of the brain, perpetually scrutinizing	"Helping students develop and explain their understandings of what creativity means in the situations in which they participate or create, and values and recognizes their awareness and application Preparing them for and giving them experiences of adventuring in uncertain and unfamiliar situations, through which they encounter and learn to deal with situations that do not always result in success but which do not penalize 'mistakes' or failure to reach a successful outcome Encouraging participants to behave ethically and with social responsibility, promoting creativity as a means of making a difference to people or adding value to the world. "	"Being imaginative – generating new ideas, thinking out of the boxes we normally inhabit, looking beyond the obvious, seeing the world in different ways so that it can be explored and understood better. Being able to take value from feedback and use it constructively to improve ideas."

(continued)

Table 6.4 (continued)

Fostering creativity in higher education	Description	What instructors/teachers can do to foster creative learning cultures (Jackson 2010)	Supporting students to do "creative thinking and creative actions" (Jackson and Shaw 2006)
Fostering constructive learning, where students create something	Where students create something; creation of, for example, workshops, products designed by students, research-mode learning projects, aid and outreach projects; planning a conference	"Enabling students to experience and appreciate knowledge and knowing in all its forms, and enabling them to experience and appreciate themselves as knower, maker, player, narrator, and enquirer."	"Being able to combine, connect, synthesize complex and incomplete data/ situations/ideas/ contexts in order to see the world freshly/ differently, to understand it better Being able to represent ideas and communicate them to others – the capacity to create and tell stories, pitch and sell ideas, empathize with others, and show people possibilities, opportunities, and solutions in ways that make sense to them or capture their imagination."
Fostering fascination (research curiosity); increasing motivation to learn	Enabling situated learning, use experiences of students, developing interesting ways to pose questions or problems; variety; establish a link to practice; use of metaphors, humor; individualization in larger courses	"Giving students the freedom and empowering them to make choices so that they can find deeply satisfying and personally challenging situations that inspire and require their creativity. A curriculum should nurture their spirit: their will to be and become a better more developed person and create new value in the world around them."	"Being curious with an enquiring disposition – willing to explore, experiment, and take risks, the attitude and motivation to engage in exploration, and the ability to search purposefully in appropriate ways in order to find and discover. It is necessary to work in an uncertain world and often requires people to move from the known to the unknown."
Fostering the ability to work autonomously	Enabling the individual student to set the acquisition of knowledge in motion;	"Engendering a commitment to personal and cooperative learning and the continuing development of capability for the	"Being resourceful – using knowledge, capability, relationships, powers to persuade and influence, and

(continued)

Table 6.4 (continued)

Fostering creativity in higher education	Description	What instructors/teachers can do to foster creative learning cultures (Jackson 2010)	Supporting students to do "creative thinking and creative actions" (Jackson and Shaw 2006)
	Enabling students to learn that they are responsible for steering the processes of learning; enabling to make one's own decisions	demands of any situation and the more strategic development of capability for future learning."	physical resources to overcome whatever challenge or problems are encountered and to exploit opportunities as they arise."
Fostering independent, self-reflective learning (critical thinking)	Learner "constructs" knowledge oneself rather than adopting it; enabling students to hold an internal dialog, breaking out of a receptive posture, supporting lateral and critical thinking	"Enabling students to develop and practice the repertoire of reflective learning including communication and literacy skills they need to be creative in a modern world."	"Being able to think critically and analytically in order to distinguish useful ideas from those that are not so useful and make good decisions Being inventive with someone else's ideas – recreation, reconstruction, re-contextualization, redefinition, adapting things that have been done before, doing things that have been done before but differently; the idea of significance and value – there are different levels, and notions of significance and utility and value are integral to the idea."

responsibility are required – educated people who do break out of the receptive consumption-oriented behavior are needed. With regard to the creativity-model, we have exemplified the diversity and multiplicity of creative thinking and actions in higher education and its fostering with three examples. A proposition for fostering creativity in higher education, which follows Jackson (Jahnke 2010), Jackson and Shaw (2006) as well as the authors' empirical studies, is shown in Table 6.4.

In order to foster creativity, the design of a totally new course is not always required. A small change of just some elements, implementing a mind mapping tool for example, can greatly affect creative efforts. With regard to the level of teaching and learning cultures, changeable elements for fostering creativity in higher education were provided (Sect. 6.3.2). The four elements are: educational elements – mode of course as well as learning process (when, in the process, is creativity needed?), social context and technical systems/tools. Furthermore, elements of a session, a complete session, several sessions, or a complete course can be changed.

Social media can play a significant role in promoting creativity. Online applications have the potential to enable new ideas for fostering creativity in higher education. The barrier for fostering creativity is low when using a simple and easy-to-use Web 2.0 application. So, Social Media can promote creative learning cultures towards education 2.0. But it also needs a creativity approach like the conceptual framework presented in this chapter. The combination of an appropriate educational "ingredient" (Table 6.4) and the right choice of Social Media is needed for successful media-enhanced creativity design.

What kind of creativity do you want to foster in higher education 2.0? This question must be answered first, before designing and implementing socio-technical–educational learning. The conceptual framework developed here means that answers are easier.

One essential next step regarding fostering creativity in higher education is creating a sound feedback questionnaire for both teachers and students. The framework in Table 6 can be operationalized and transformed into a measuring tool for evaluating creativity-designed courses.

References

Amabile, T., Conti, R., Coon, H., Lazenby, J., Herron, M.: Assessing the work environment for creativity. Acad. Manage. J. **19**(5), 1154–1184 (1996)

Amabile, T., Hadley, C., Kramer, S.: Creativity under the gun. Harv. Bus. Rev. **80**, 52–61 (2002)

Amabile, T., Schatzel, E., Moneta, G., Kramer, S.: Leader behaviors and the work environment for creativity: perceived leader support. Leadersh. Q. **15**, 5–32 (2004)

Avison, D., Lau, F., Neilsen, P.A., Myers, M.: Action research. Commun. ACM **42**, 94–97 (1991)

Boden, M.A.: Precis of the creative mind: myths and mechanisms. Behav. Brain Sci. **17**, 519–570 (1994)

Bolisani, E. (ed.): Building the Knowledge Society on the Internet. Information Science Reference. IGI Global, Hershey (2008)

Brodbeck, K.H.: Neue Trends in der Kreativitätsforschung. (New trends in creativity research). Psychol. Österr. **H. 4 & 5**(26), 246–253 (2006)

Collins, A., Halverson, R.: Rethinking Education in the Age of Technology: The Digital Revolution and Schooling in America. Teachers College Press, New York (2009)

Csikszentmihalyi, M.: Creativity: Flow and the Psychology of Discovery and Invention. Harper-Collins, New York (1996)

De Bono, E.: Serious Creativity: Using the Power of Lateral Thinking to Create New Ideas. HarperBusiness, New York (1992)

Dresler, M.: Introduction: Creativity as open concept (Einleitung: Kreativität als offenes Konzept). In: Dresler, M., Baudson, T. (Hsrg.): Kreativität. Beiträge aus den Natur- und Geisteswissenschaften. S. Hirzel, Stuttgart, pp. 7–20 (2008)

Fischer, G., Scharff, E., Ye, Y.: Fostering social creativity by increasing social capital. In: Huysman, M., Wulf, V. (eds.) Social Capital and Information Technology, pp. 355–399. MIT Press, Cambridge (2004)

Gardner, H.: Creating Minds: An Anatomy of Creativity Seen Through the Lives of Freud, Einstein, Picasso, Stravinsky, Eliot, Graham and Gandhi. Basic Books, New York (1993)

Greene, R.: A model of 42 models of creativity. http://www.scribd.com/doc/2149673/A-Model-of-42-Models-of-Creativity-by-Richard-Tabor-Greene-20june06-PDF-for-Global-Distribution-FINAL (2001)

Guilford, J.P.: The structure of intellect. Psychol. Bull. **54**, 267–293 (1956)

Herrmann, T.: Design heuristics for computer supported collaborative creativity. In: 42nd Hawaii International Conference on System Sciences, (HICSS), IEEE Computer Society, pp. 1–10 (2009)

Herrmann, T., Loser, K.U., Jahnke, I.: Socio-technical walkthrough: a means for knowledge integration. Learn. Organ. **14**(5), 450–464 (2007)

Jackson, N.: Imaginative curriculum nurturing creativity project, http://www.surrey.ac.uk/Education/ic/imaginative-curriculum-creativity-project.pdf (2003)

Jackson, N.: Imagining a different world. In: Jackson, N., Oliver, M., Shaw, M., Wisdom, J. (eds.) Developing Creativity in Higher Education. An Imaginative Curriculum, pp. 1–9. Routledge, London (2006)

Jackson, N.: Developing creativity through lifewide education, http://imaginativecurriculumnetwork.pbworks.com/f/Developing+creativity+through+lifewide+education+version+5++15+06.pdf (2010)

Jackson, N., Shaw, M.: Developing subject perspectives on creativity in higher education. In: Jackson, N., et al. (eds.) Developing Creativity in Higher Education: An Imaginative Curriculum, pp. 89–108. Routledge, Abingdon/London (2006)

Jahnke, I., Koch, M.: Web 2.0 goes academia: does web 2.0 make a difference? Int. J. Web Based Communities **5**(4), 484–500 (2009)

Jahnke, I.: A way out of the information jungle: a longitudinal study on a socio-technical community and informal learning in higher education. IN: Int. J. Socio. Technol. Knowl. Dev, **2**(4), pp. 18–38. DOI: 10.4018/jskd.2010100102 (2010)

Jahnke, I., Terkowsky, C., Pleul, Ch., Tekkaya, E.: Online learning with remote-configured experiments. In: Kerres, M., Ojstersek, N., Schroeder, U., Hoppe, U. (eds.) DeLFI. Conference Proceddings. 8. Tagung der Fachgruppe E-Learning der Gesellschaft für Informatik e.V. Bonn: GI e.V.: Köllen Verlag, pp. 265–277 (2010)

Kleiman, P.: Towards transformation: conceptions of creativity in higher education. Innov. Educ. Teach. Int. **3**(45), 209–217 (2008)

Lave, J., Wenger, E.: Situated Learning: Legitimate Peripheral Participation. Cambridge University Press, New York (1990)

Lenk, H.: Creative Ascents (Kreative Aufstiege: zur Philosophie und Psychologie der Kreativität). Suhrkamp, Frankfurt am Main (2000)

Palfrey, J., Gasser, U.: Born Digital. Understanding the First Generation of the Digital Natives. Basic Books, New York (2008)

Prensky, M.: Digital natives, digital immigrants. The Horizon, **9**(5). MCB University Press (2001)

Reeves, T., Herrington, J., Oliver, R.: Design research: a socially responsible approach to instructional technology research in higher education. J. Comput. High. Educ. **16**, 97–116 (2005)

Sonnenburg, St: Cooperative Creativity (Kooperative Kreativität: Theoretische Basisentwürfe und Organisationale Erfolgsfaktoren). Dt. Univ.-Verl, Wiesbaden (2007)

Sternberg, R.J.: Handbook of Creativity. Cambridge University Press, New York (1999)

Strauss, A., Corbin, J.: Basics of Qualitative Research: Grounded Theory Procedures and Techniques. Sage, Newbury Park (1990)

Suchman, L.: Plans and Situated Actions: The Problem of Human-Machine Communication. Cambridge Press, Cambridge (1987)

Suchman, L.: Human-Machine Reconfigurations: Plans and Situated Actions, 2nd edn. Cambridge Press, Cambridge (2007)

Tosey, P.: Interfering with the interference: an emergent perspective on creativity in higher education. In: Jackson, N., Oliver, M., Shaw, M., Wisdom, J. (eds.) Developing Creativity in Higher Education: An Imaginative Curriculum, pp. 29–42. Routledge, New York (2006)

Wang, F., Hannafin, M.J.: Design-based research and technology-enhanced learning environments. Educ. Technol. Res. Dev. **53**(4), 5–23 (2005)

Wasson, B.: Design and use of technology enhanced learning environments. In: The DoCTA experience, **9**(4). Educational Technology & Society (2007)

Watson, E.: Who or what creates? A conceptual framework for social creativity. Hum. Resour. Dev. Rev. **H.** 4(6), 419–441 (2007)

Weitz, M.: Open concepts. Revue Internationale de Philosophie, H. **26**, 86–110 (1972)

Whitworth, B., de Moor, A.: Handbook of Research on Socio-Technical Design and Social Networking Systems. Information Science Reference (IGI Global), New York (2009)

Chapter 7
Exploiting Geocollaborative Portals for Designing Collaborative e-Learning Pedagogies: A Model, Applications and Trends

Marianna Sigala

Abstract The use of digital maps continuously increases, as more than 80% of the data have geospatial references and social technologies are democratising spatial content. As geodata are the lifeblood of tourism, geovisualisation is becoming very important in e-tourism applications. This implies that geodata management needs to be incorporated into tourism curricula and pedagogies in order to assist graduates with career options. However, although research in geovisualisation has examined the impact of geoportals on team-working and cognitive processes, research in education has not examined the role and impact of geocollaborative portals on collaborative e-learning. This chapter addresses this gap by reviewing the related literature and developing a model showing how to exploit geoportals for designing collaborative e-learning. The applicability of the model is shown by analysing the use of a geocollaborative portal for integrating collaborative e-learning in the teaching of a tourism course. Implications and trends for tourism educators and policy makers are discussed.

7.1 Introduction

The use of digital maps is increasing not only in governments, research institutions and businesses but also in education (Jones et al. 2004). This is not surprising when considering the cognitive benefits of digital maps (Davies 1998) and geovisualisation (MacEachren 2005), as well as that 80% of all digital data generated today includes geospatial referencing (MacEachren and Kraak 2001). The wide

M. Sigala (✉)
Assistant Professor of Service Management in Tourism, The Business Administration Department, University of the Aegean, Michalon 8. Chios, Greece, GR-82100
e-mail: m.sigala@aegean.gr

B. White et al. (eds.), *Social Media Tools and Platforms in Learning Environments*,   117
DOI 10.1007/978-3-642-20392-3_7, © Springer-Verlag Berlin Heidelberg 2011

application of digital maps requires educators to incorporate the teaching of spatial skills and geo-data manipulation into their curriculum and pedagogies in order to assist graduates with career options. Specifically, students must develop two major geospatial competencies namely: how to use maps for information discovery, exploration and presentation; and how to design maps to enhance communication and collaboration with peers. However, although research in geovisualisation has advanced, showing how geovisualisation and geoportals can support and enhance group work and collaborative decision making (Brewer et al. 2000; MacEachren and Cai 2006; Sigala 2010), research in education is eliminated in examining the use of digital maps for supporting only individual learning processes (Jones et al. 2004). Hence, educational research has overlooked the opportunities afforded by geospatial and geoportal technologies for developing collaborative e-learning practices. Moreover, as nowadays free web map services and web 2.0 tools – that democratise the creation and dissemination of geographical content and services (Goodchild 2007) – provide numerous tools for spatial decision making and collaboration, research in the area of geovisualisation for collaborative e-learning is a must.

This chapter develops a model for showing university educators how to design an effective collaborative e-learning pedagogy that exploits the tools and functionality of geocollaborative portals. To achieve that, the chapter reviews the related literature and provides examples of learning applications that analyse: first, the features and benefits of geovisualisation for teaching and learning; and then, the impact and role of geoportals and geocollaborative portals in developing collaborative e-learning practices. The chapter presents a holistic model for designing effective collaborative e-learning practices in university education. Finally, trends and suggestions for future research are presented.

7.2 Geovisualisation: Features and Benefits in Education

Geovisualisation is about people, maps, processes, information systems (GIS) and the acquisition of information and knowledge. The aim of geovisualisation is to turn large heterogeneous data into information (interpreted data) and then into knowledge (understanding derived from information). Indeed, as MacEachren and Kraak (2001) argued *geovisualisation integrates approaches from visualization in scientific computing, cartography, image analysis, information visualization, exploratory data analysis and geographic information systems to provide theory, methods and tools for visual exploration, analysis, synthesis and presentation of geospatial data*. Maps are the interface of geospatial data in which, location represents the geography of the studied phenomenon and interactive maps provide flexible geographical interfaces for exploring, analysing, synthesising and presenting spatial information (Table 7.1). Hence, in geovisualisation environments, maps can stimulate visual thinking about geographical patterns, connections or disruptions and trends (Kraak 2003). In this way, users can generate hypotheses, develop problem solutions and construct knowledge (Kwan 2000).

Table 7.1 Views, interactions and tasks of geovisualisation tools (Koua et al. 2006; Lloyd and Dyke 2007)

Exploratory data analysis	(conditional) Histogram and box plot, parallel coordinate plot, table browser, (conditional) Scatter Plot, small multiples, Scatter Plot matrix, time series plot, time plot path, mosaic plot, TreeMap (and other hierarchical plots), sylph/star glyphs, self organising map, bar and pie chart
Mapping (data presentation)	Symbology, thematic/choropleth, density maps, dot maps, cartograms, insets, 3D maps
Interactions with geo-data	Conditioning, brushing, linking, zooming, semantic zooming, animation, sorting, reordering, filtering, multiple views, categorising, extracting, manipulation (rotation, separation), dynamic querying, distortion
Tasks (complexity of tasks increasing from locate to correlate geo-data)	Locate, identify, distinguish, categorise, cluster, distribution, rank, compare, associate, correlate

Because of the benefits of geovisualisation (the ability to dynamically explore spatial-temporal data, the multi-dimensional display of complex datasets, the sequencing and animation of spatial-temporal data to visually uncover trends and identify anomalies), many organisations are using GIS to support their decision making for a range of location-based decisions such as logistics and transportation, location of firms, crisis management and urban planning (Beaumont et al. 2005; Hernandez 2007; Kwan 2000). As a result, a new field has emerged (namely business geomatics) to bring together many disciplines for exploiting geovisualisation for business decision making (Hernandez 2007).

The educational opportunities of geovisualisation are also enormous, as there is a contentious premise that humans learn more effectively and efficiently within a visual as opposed to a textual or numerical setting (Lloyd 1997); for example, Rittschof and Kulhavy (1998) found that regions and information about them were remembered better when learnt from a map rather than from a table. The enhanced educational benefits of digital maps are based on their two major features: (a) digital maps can contain much more (multimedia) information than paper maps; and (b) students have more control over the geo-information displayed on digital maps by choosing what and how is displayed. The features of digital maps and the ways in which they enable visual–cognitive abilities are analysed below (based on Davies 1998):

- Digital maps can contain several layers of geo-information (text labels, reference grids and other explanatory information), which learners can hide or display in order to see various views or relationships between geo-information.
- Digital maps are not constrained by the boundaries of the screen (as paper maps are limited to the size of the paper) and learners can zoom in and out in order to better understand and explore the relations amongst geo-data.

- Learners can choose some or all of the aspects of map appearance for better understanding the geospatial information and its interrelations (symbolisation, colouring, scale, categorisation, description of geo-information).
- Learners can calculate and display spatial correlations and other statistical relationships between features or variables.
- Learners can simulate and model some phenomena (floods, emigration) to investigate the changes and impacts over time.
- Digital maps can be linked to databases so that further (multimedia) information (photographs, spreadsheets, and hypermedia) and explanations about the displayed objects can be provided to the learners.

The underlying information content of a map can alter independent of its visible design, which enables learners to adapt digital maps to their own learning styles and abilities, which in turn allows them to follow their own free style learning flow and speed. For example, learners can link different topics to the same visual display for different learning goals. Indeed, research has shown that the adaptation http://edsserver.ucsd.edu/visualizingearth/ of geovisualisation tools for educational purposes results in 'cognitive amplifiers' that permit people to see what they cannot through direct perception (Bruner 1965). Specifically, geovisualisation tools enable learners to go beyond the provided information by enhancing their five cognitive dimensions: (1) scale (zooming and automatic scales help students to better comprehend the referent space in geographical visualisations); (2) point-of-view visualisation tools (that display the transformation in point-of-view by rotation and top–down view of objects, rotation of north-up orientation of maps) help students adopt alternate points-of-view about the referent space; (3) 3D skills (3D tools enhance students' spatial visualisation skills, such as their ability to understand the relationships between land and atmosphere); (4) representational nature and type, for example, the selection of the presentation of map layers enable students to better understand that the representations of places are just representations and not objective realities; and (5) change-over-time geovisualisation tools (such as user-controlled animations) help students to understand the temporal changes of spatial representations.

Because of these, several efforts have recently emerged to demonstrate to educators how to teach their students on how to use and integrate geo-data in maps to support and enhance student knowledge presentation and exploration processes. Table 7.2 provides a useful collection of geospatial technologies (tools and their providers), as well as of their applications that have been and/or can be used in education. However, as the Table identifies, geovisualisation has been introduced and examined so far mainly in secondary education (K-12) to support individual cognitive knowledge exploration processes. There is very limited research and experience available investigating the use and benefits of geovisualisation and geocollaborative portals on team-based cognitive knowledge creation processes among university learners, and the role of geocollaborative portals as mediators/assistants of collaboration and team-based decision making for enhancing collaborative e-learning processes.

Table 7.2 Tools and applications of geospatial technologies in education

Tools/providers	Applications for educational purposes
Geospatial applications and tools that have been purposefully designed for use in education	
http://www.esri.com/industries/university/index.html The portal for GIS applications in higher education provided by ESRI	http://edcommunity.esri.com/arclessons/arclessons.cfm This website provides links to several case studies for using geospatial technologies in the teaching of many disciplines in higher/university education Educational applications refer to enhancing individual cognitive processes and decision making
http://edina.ac.uk/projects/mapscholar/index.html *e-MapScholar project* aiming to show how to integrate the use of existing geo-data on digital maps for university education	http://edina.ac.uk/projects/mapscholar/casestudies The website provides several case studies demonstrating how university educators from different disciplines have integrated and used geo-data in their teaching practices
Visualise Earth -http://edsserver.ucsd.edu/visualizingearth A website presenting the findings of Visualising Earth, a research project funded by the National Science Foundation, with the goal of better understanding how students learn to work with and make meaning of images and visualisations	http://edsserver.ucsd.edu/visualizingearth/resources/websites.html The website provides several resources of free online geo-data http://edsserver.ucsd.edu/visualizingearth/geo_vis/index.html This website provides examples of geovisualisation projects that can be used for free by school teachers in their teaching practices
http://esipfed.org/about Federation of Earth Science Information Partners *(ESIP Federation)* is a broad-based community comprising researchers and associated groups that produce, interpret and develop applications for Earth and environmental science data	http://esipfed.org/education_products The website provides links to several geovisualisation applications, that teachers can use for enabling their students to engage and interact with geo-data for enhancing their learning abilities and performance http://esipfed.org/resources Again the website provides educational, technological tools as well as geo-data that educators can use for their teaching practices
http://www.fieldscope.us/ *National Geographic FieldScope* is a web-based mapping, analysis and collaboration tool designed to support geographic investigations and engage students as citizen scientists investigating real-world issues – both in the classroom and in outdoor education settings	FieldScope enhances student scientific investigations by providing rich geographic context – through maps, mapping activities and a rich community where student fieldwork and data is integrated with that of peers and professionals, adding analysis opportunities and meaning to student investigations Examples of geo-data that can be used in education are provided at http://www.fieldscope.us/

(continued)

Table 7.2 (continued)

Tools/providers	Applications for educational purposes
http://bird.thewildlab.org/ A collaborative geo-application enabling people to search and share data about birds	http://bird.thewildlab.org/explore With funding from the *MacArthur Foundation* in collaboration with *HASTAC*, the Wildl ab piloted a program in NYC schools that engaged learners in real scientific data collection. Using iPhones, over 500 fifth through 12th-grade students collected thousands of GPS-tagged bird sightings in green spaces near their classrooms. These sightings were then sent to the *Cornell Lab of Ornithology* for use in scientific research
Geospatial applications and tools developed and used in the industry	
http://marinemap.org/ *MarineMap* is a web-based decision support tool for open and participatory spatial planning in the marine environment. MarineMap offers a simple, flexible and powerful means of gathering expertise from resource managers, scientists, stakeholders and public in a process of collaborative decision making	http://marinemap.org/decision-support-tool The website offers a virtual tour to the collaborative decision-making support tool that is based on a digital map and geospatial technologies
http://www.ebmtools.org/ The *EBM* Tools Network is an alliance of EBM tool users, providers and researchers to promote the use and development of an ecosystem approach to manage and enhance environmental sustainability. An ecosystem approach is promoted and supported by the use of geospatial technologies that enable several stakeholders from many backgrounds to interact and contribute related geo-information	http://www.ebmtools.org/about_ebm_tools/ toolkits.html#STAKEHOLDER ENGAGEMENT AND SOCIAL SCIENCE This page currently provides information about other EBM tools resources, such as toolkits, surveys and best practice documents, demonstrating how geospatial tools have been used in decision-making processes in several contexts (eurban development, environmental protection, stakeholders participation in local government)
http://pacmara.org/ The Pacific Marine Analysis and Research Association *(PacMARA)* is an organisation that seeks to develop the use of cross-disciplinary marine science in ecosystem-based decision making. We take an impartial, non-advocacy approach to ocean and marine planning because access to data, good science, and clear results are the heart of sustainable oceans management	http://pacmara.org/marine-planning-resources/ methods-tools This page provides links to a number of on-line tools for creating summaries reports and high level analysis of Marine resources in BC

(continued)

Table 7.2   (continued)

Tools/providers	Applications for educational purposes
http://www.landscapevalues.org/ *The Landscape Values and PPGIS Institute* is a non-profit consortium of international researchers and planners interested in advancing knowledge about landscape values and PPGIS to improve land allocation and management. The consortium provides access to methods and tools that enable multiple stakeholders to search, use and discuss geo-data	http://www.landscapevalues.org/ The website provides and explains several tools for supporting PPGIS PPGIS refers to the aim of the consortium to enhance public participation in GIS

7.3   Geocollaboration: Exploiting Geoportals and Geocollaborative Portals for Collaborative e-Learning

7.3.1   *Geoportals and Geocollaborative Portals: Definitions and Functionality*

Geoportals represent distributed GIS services that use web service standards (Sigala and Marinidis 2009) for integrating and providing user-friendly accessibility to many GIS and other information from a single virtual system. A geoportal is implemented using three distributed GIS components (Tait 2005): a web site presenting the geographic application or portal; web services that publish geographical functionality as a web service and data management software that provides a managed relational environment for geographical content. Geoportals are defined (Maguire and Longley 2005; Tait 2005) as gateways for storing, accessing, sharing, organising and searching web-based geographical content and services such as map rendering; data projection; geographical and attribute-based queries; address geocoding; gazetteer/place name searches; metadata query and management; 3D terrain visualisation; data extraction; routing services and calculations of distance (www.mapquest.com, www.nationalgeographic.com/maps/, www.viamichelin.com).

Traditionally, the development of GIS information and services relied on experts representing a top–down authoritarian, centrist paradigm, in which professional experts produce, dissemination is radial and amateurs consume (Goodchild 2007). Distributed GIS and geoportals allow communities to participate in map development (bottom–up approaches) (Beaumont et al. 2005). Hence, geoportals can be used and co-developed not only by a single user, but also by multiple and distributed users. MacEachren (2001) developed the concept geocollaboration to define collaborative efforts using geospatial information and tools. Geocollaboration was traditionally enabled by technologies integrating groupware and GIS functionality (MacEachren and Cai 2006), while later, research recognised the role and opportunities offered by the web 2.0 for implementing user-friendly geocollaboration and geovisualisation applications to support group work (Sigala 2010;

Rinner et al. 2008). Indeed, web 2.0 advances – such as wiki-mapping, geovisualisation API (Google Maps, Yahoo! Maps and Microsoft Live Maps), geotagging and geoblogging – democratise geoportal development and use by offering Internet users the tools to participate in the development and distribution of web map services. Specifically, web 2.0 users are empowered to (collaboratively) create, disseminate, share, read and combine (mash-up) geographical content, metadata and services. This is referred to as Volunteered Geographic Information (VGI) (Goodchild 2007). The web 2.0 enabled geocollaboration capabilities of geoportals include (Sigala et al. 2009) *social search* referring to the usage of user profiles and user-generated geocontent (geotags, personal maps, favourites, reviews) stored in geoportals for searching geo-content; *social mapping* referring to the dissemination and sharing of maps within social networks; *social publishing* referring to the collaborative creation and publication of maps by a group and *social administration* referring to the collaborative development of new value-added mapping services by combining (mashing-up) and collaboratively administrating multiple geo-information and services. Sigala (2010) defined the geoportals that exploit the web 2.0 enabled geocollaboration capabilities for supporting group work as geocollaborative portals (GCP), which in turn can support the following three roles: storage, searching and representation of spatial information; enabling social practices; supporting collaborative decision making and ways to develop knowledge.

7.3.2   Geoportals and Geocollaborative Portals: Roles and Impact on Collaboration and Collaborative Learning

The literature provides several arguments and evidence about how geoportals and GCP can significantly enhance the success of group work in terms of the processes and outcomes of collaboration (Sigala 2009, 2010). Collaboration involves sharing ideas, knowledge, competencies and information to accomplish a task or goal. Collaborative learning is anchored in the attribute of effective learning that encompasses three distinct elements, namely (Sigala 2004): (1) active learning and construction of knowledge; (2) cooperation and teamwork in learning; and (3) learning via problem solving. Geoportals and GCP can be exploited to support collaborative learning because the Internet has been recognised as an effective tool for developing computer-mediated collaborative learning (Sigala 2005); geovisualisation (and therefore, geoportals and GCP) enhances the cognitive abilities of users/learners that in turn support active and flexible learning in the understanding and construction of knowledge; educators can design collaborative activities/tasks and learning goals that groups can accomplish with the support of GCP and GCP can support and enhance the collaboration, group decision-making processes and constructivism and discussion-based learning activities (geospatial discussion forums) within groups.

GCP increases the information visualisation and visual representations, which increase cognitive resources and abilities, reduce the search complexities, ease the pattern determination and fasten the perceptual inferences, generate hypotheses and construct knowledge. The ability and utility to extend geovisualisation methods and tools to support group work is widely advocated in the literature. External visual representations positively impact group-work task performance, because they provide memory aids, directly perceivable information and structured cognitive behaviour (Sigala 2009). For example, groups can use GCP for sharing, uploading, categorising and saving their social intelligence through the creation of geotags. Geotags and tag clouds systematically categorise group knowledge and allow members to search and identify information based on who knows what, which then increases knowledge exchanges and synergies among members, decreases cognitive processing and redundancy of efforts and directs member efforts to achieve greater group performance (MacEachren and Brewer 2004; Wegner et al. 1991). Research also shows that collaborative geovisualisation facilitates group collaboration, because it enables members to: reduce the cognitive effort to solve a problem; restructure/represent or re-express the problem in a way that makes it more comprehensive; and provide graphical constraining/limits to the problem's interpretation (Brewer et al. 2000; MacEachren and Cai 2006). Hence, GCP is not only a group tool for creating, storing and sharing external representations, but GCP can also address the conceptual barriers and differences in perspectives that may exist amongst group members which in turn facilitates constructivism learning processes (Balram and Dragicevic 2008). GCP should not only be used as an instructional but also as a collective knowledge development tool that is digitally augmented by disseminating, storing, exploring and synthesising collaborator knowledge Resnick (1999). Maps can facilitate group member communication, discussion, divergent thinking and knowledge exchange that can lead to a more complete creation, understanding and synthesis of the collective team knowledge (Resnick 1999; (Shah et al. 2001)). MacEachren and Cai (2005) also showed how geocollaboration enhances the distributed cognition of a group (as maps distribute cognition amongst collaborators, cognitive processes and artefacts and over time) and facilitates geodialogues amongst group members that generate collaborative meaning and knowledge. Rinner (2006) and Rinner et al. (2008) developed argumentation maps; applications to show how geovisualisation can be used for enhancing human-human interaction and facilitating group decision making with spatial connotation. Argumentation maps support the discursive elements in geographic group decision making by providing a geographic visual footprint to geo-referenced debates and the tools for exploring, querying, analysing and participating in the state of discussions.

Overall, GCP supports group work by providing external visual representations to work group tasks, knowledge resources and dialogues, which in turn enable collaborators to create, store and share a collective and easily searchable group memory on maps for referencing it during the decision-making processes MacEachren (1994). GCP also improves group work, because maps can play a crucial role in enhancing the formation, cohesion and collaboration of work groups. MacEachren (2005) identified three roles that maps can play to support group work: an object of the collaboration; a visual depiction to support dialogue and a device to support coordinated activity (information collection, synthesis, decision making and implementation). Several studies in other fields (collaborative software and group support systems, Sigala 2010) provide evidence of these roles and GCP's impact on collaboration. Overall, GCP affords several capabilities for positively influencing the many factors (cognitive, social, cultural and organisational-collaboration setting factors of collaborators) that affect collaborative work.

7.4 An Application of GCP for Collaborative Learning in the Business Field

7.4.1 The GCP Platform

The researcher used Yahoo! Trip Planner (Y!TP) as a GCP for designing and implementing a collaborative e-learning process. Y!TP makes use of web 2.0 and it can be considered as a GCP (Sigala in press), since it enables groups to search, write, assess/comment, discuss and share geo-information that in turn supports their collaborative decision-making processes when designing a trip. Y!TP provides several tools allowing single users and/or multiple users to collaboratively design trips on its platform. Y!TP's geographical services include: geo-data projection on a map (hotels); geographical and attribute-based map search capabilities; map visualisation in hybrid, satellite and normal view and driving directions. Y!TP is integrated with the Yahoo! travel portal databases and so its users can access (www.travel.yahoo.com) and search an enormous amount of travel information (user-generated and commercial content) for selecting, evaluating and adding items into their trips. Y!TP also features the following web 2.0 tools for providing geocollaboration capabilities: geotags for adding geo-information, tags for categorising and searching trips, user-generated content (customer reviews/comments and photos about geo-information – hotels and attractions), user voting system of trips and items, the trip journal and trip plan. Users can create private trips or public trips (Internet users can read, comment on the trip journal and/or copy trip items or whole trips to their own trip). Private trips are useful platforms for multiple users to collaboratively design a trip, while public trips (being user-generated content) represent a vital source of travel information and suggestions/evaluations to all Y!TP users. Two specific Y!TP tools critically support collaboration and communication within user groups. *The trip plan* is a kind of wiki allowing collaborators to add/delete items in the trip collaboratively designed by the group. *The trip journal* represents a kind of a collaborators' geo-forum (argumentation map Rinner 2006), whereby any collaborator can upload comments, photos, weblinks and other geo-related content for discussing with other collaborators the trip design – arguing for the inclusion or not of trip items on the trip map.

7.4.2 The Design of the Collaborative e-Learning Activity

The identification and selection of the location of a restaurant (any business) is affected by numerous factors including size and location of market demand;

existence, location and distances from competitors; proximity to complementary businesses (attractions, hotels, conference centres...); existence and distance from transportation infrastructure (hub stations); demands, preferences and evaluations about different locations; the existence of nearby attractions and so on. Such information is provided on Y!TP, which also enables groups to collaboratively discuss a geo-spatial related problem. The researcher divided students attending a class in services management into several groups, and then asked groups to create private 'trips' whereby they could identify, discuss, evaluate and select ideal locations to establish a Greek cuisine restaurant in Athens, Greece. In this vein, a 'trip design' as named in the Y!TP platform was harnessed to the problem related to the identification of appropriate locations for the establishment of the restaurant. Students were instructed on the functionality of Y!TP in the class. They were also advised to physically visit certain locations in Athens in order to enhance/upload additional and related geo-information on Y!TP (the existence of a competitor, an attraction). Students were allowed 2 months to use Y!TP and discuss the appropriateness and appeal of potential locations for the restaurant.

Students were instructed that their group collaboration performance would be assessed based on a final reflective team report that would analyse the following: (a) the number of identified locations (good and bad locations); and (b) a short argumentation and evaluation report of the appeal of each identified location that would be based on the Y!TP based dialogues and the geo-information identified and uploaded on Y!TP. The assessment design of the collaborative activity aimed to motivate and reward students not only for the outcome of their collaboration (number of potential restaurant locations) but also for the process used to derive the outcome (team discussions and use/debates of geo-information on the map). The collaborative e-learning activity assisted students develop their map reading and designing skills; geocollaboration skills; geovisualisation skills and understanding of the usage of GCP for retail business geomatic problems. Although Y!TP is not a GCP platform purposely designed for e-learning purposes, it is argued that this educational exercise has considerably enhanced student understanding and acquisition of the above mentioned skills in an interactive and entertaining way. However, further research is required to explore the impacts of GCP on collaborative e-learning processes, student skill attainment and learner engagement/satisfaction with the e-learning practice.

7.4.3 Model for Developing Effective (Geo)-Collaborative e-Learning Processes

This chapter has adapted the MacEachren and Brewer (2004) model of geocollaboration for proposing a model for designing effective (geo)-collaborative-learning processes. That model was selected because of: the limited research and lack of models about geocollaboration in education; the application and testing of the selected model in several field and contexts (team based decision making, crisis management, business geomatics, e-government); the model's focus on all three dimensions of geocollaboration (namely, the human/social and technological dimensions) that any pedagogy requires when exploiting technology for learning-educational purposes. Table 7.3 presents the human/social and technological dimensions of this model. It expands and adapts this model within a collaborative e-learning context by identifying and analysing the implications of these two dimensions on the related educational concepts (third column of Table 7.3).

7.5 Conclusions: Implications, Trends and Suggestions for Future Research

This chapter examined the features and benefits of geovisualisation and geocolla-boration for e-learning. To that end, the related literature was reviewed, a model for designing geo-collaborative e-learning processes was proposed and relevant examples and applications were also provided. The discussions have highlighted that in order to exploit the benefits of geovisualisation, educators must structure and design their teaching and learning processes as investigations. They should also employ geovisualisations, digital maps, geoportals and GCP as the source of the investigative questions and the evidence for supporting conjectures and construc-ting knowledge Katterfeld and Paelke (2006). For example, educators need to present maps as rich mysteries to be investigated and to use a tone of inquiry and help learners perceive geovisualisations and GCP as sources of information, generators of hypotheses/questions and assistants of collaboration rather than illustrations of casual viewing.

However, the limited research on geocollaboration in an e-learning context requires that further research is required to investigate a series of questions that have emerged and need to be answered in order to progress and boost the exploi-tation of geovisualisation and GCP in education. Such questions may include: What are the new map reading and designing skills that graduates should gain and develop? Which skills are required by industry and/or research? What are the geocollaboration competencies and abilities that students need to develop to enhance their electronic communication and collaboration skills and career prospects? There is also limited understanding and knowledge about how map reading, design and collaboration skills are learnt and how they can be effectively taught. So, what are the appropriate learning pedagogies for helping (different) students about how to learn to interpret, use and create maps as well as exploit maps for geocollaboration purposes? More studies are also required to explore the effectiveness and efficiency of learning processes based on geovisualisation and geocollaborative tools by measuring the impacts of the former on several dimen-sions such as student satisfaction, learnability (easy use of the system), memora-bility of learnt material, impact on cognitive and communication abilities.

Table 7.3 A model for effective design of geo-collaborative e-learning processes

Dimension	Definition	Educational examples and implications for designing e-learning processes
Definition of the *problem context* in which geocollaboration may be undertaken	There are four types of problem contexts: 1. *Knowledge construction and refinement:* tools facilitating collaborative extraction of information from data and meaning from that information 2. *Design:* supporting the group work directed at creating an entity 3. *Decision-support:* group decision making with spatial connotations that uses geo-information 4. *Training & education:* facilitating group training	1. *Educational activity aimed at knowledge construction and refinement:* Learners using a GCP for debating and exploring the relation and temporal impact of tourism development indices (visitor numbers per week, season) on destinations/locations indices (quality of life, income per capita) 2. *Educational activity aimed at designing:* a regional park, urban development plans, tourism packages, conference offers, a map of the economic activity and productivity of regions 3. *Educational activity aimed at taking decisions about:* facility locations, distribution of staff and supplies in a crisis, logistics network design, the boundaries of a natural reserve, urban planning decisions 4. *Educational activity aimed at training of learners on:* emergency/crisis management, continuous professional development
Collaboration tasks	Identify components/tasks that delineate group work and assist in its completion: • Generate (ideas/options), negotiate, choose, execute • Exploration, analysis, synthesis, presentation	• Explain the stages of group work to learners and use these stages to scaffold and facilitate collaborative group work (Roth et al. 2009) • If necessary, assign learners with roles/stages of group work • Assess learner performance on all tasks of group work, so that learners are motivated to contribute to both the process/ stages and outcomes of the work group (summative and formative assessment) • Identify and use appropriate geovisualisation and GCP tools that can support every stage/ task of the collaboration activity

(continued)

Table 7.3 (continued)

Dimension	Definition	Educational examples and implications for designing e-learning processes
Commonality of perspective	Consider not only the characteristics of individual learners (learning style, personality, perceptual abilities, gender, age) but also the group characteristics regarding the commonality of perspective held by group members about the problem, the choice of appropriate methods and the desired outcomes for the collaborative work	• Decide group size and consistency of groups (collaborators of the same discipline/experience or diverse backgrounds) • Include conflict resolutions tools and approaches (mediation by educator) for competing views • Tools should support innovative thinking and synthesis of what might appear to be divergent ideas • Assess learners on their negotiation/mediation performance
Spatial and temporal context	Geocollaboration can take place: same place and same time (synchronous & co-located); same place different time (asynchronous & co-located); different place same time (synchronous & distributed); and different place different time (asynchronous & distributed)	• Different spatial and temporal contexts within which geo-collaboration takes place require the use of different technological tools to support such (distributed and/or asynchronous) collaboration. For example, collaboration taking place in the same real time for all group members entails the use of geo-chat tools so all members are aware and updated about the activity – location of others • To enhance the social e-presence and collaboration of users (specifically when geocollaboration takes place in distributed locations and times), one has to make use of tools that enable learners to see their and others presence in the GCP as well as their own and other learner actions on objects and discussions. GCP can feature participant watcher tools that not only demonstrate, but also assess learner online (social) presence & contributions

(continued)

Table 7.3 (continued)

Dimension	Definition	Educational examples and implications for designing e-learning processes
		• When learners collaborate from different places/locations, GCP should make sure that everyone has access and sees the same geo-information (the use of tools that control and/or share users' screens)
		• When learners collaborate at different times, the GCP should have tools that can show learners the chronological development and sequence of geo-discussions and arguments/information
Interaction characteristics	Interaction in groups involves three interrelated factors: group size and aggregation (in sub-groups); topology of connections (who connects with whom and how, e.g. hierarchical networks); constraints of flow and form of information among collaborators	Communication networks and tools should respect and follow the three interaction characteristics: In democratic collaboration processes, all learners will be able to submit an argument, in simulation/emergency crisis management training or military/business exercises only learners with specific roles will be able to access and change geo-information and geo-discussions
Tools for mediating group work	Use the appropriate tools for supporting any group tasks that the collaborative activity entails	Technological tools are required to support each type of collaborative group activity: • Knowledge construction: tools for information sharing, group problem conceptualisation, joint knowledge development strategies • Design: tools such as wikis that enable the collaborative design of texts and images • Decision making: tools allowing learners to evaluate, comment or rank options/solutions • Training–learning: tools enabling simulations and experimental learning

Some techniques and dimensions for evaluating geovisualisation in education have been proposed (Marsh et al. 2005) but a more holistic model and methodology for measuring the impact of geovisualisation and geocollaboration on both the learners and the educational processes (more interactive and/or more entertaining education) is required.

Geocollaboration in e-learning has also implications for software developers, who also need to design a purpose-built GCP for collaborative e-learning purposes. Table 7.2 has identified some geospatial tools that currently exist, but these have been developed for professional applications and/or learning activities in school education. Technology developers and consortia (non-profit or open software communities) should develop customised GCP for educational purposes and/or provide their tools in an open basis for further customisation and use by educational communities. The former could also provide technological support and training to educators on using these GCP tools. Access to technology and provision of technological support are two important factors that can inhibit and/or foster the use of GCP in education (specifically in the developing world), as they have been recognised as two major forces creating a digital divide in the exploitation of technology in education (Sigala and Christou 2003).

Use of geospatial applications in education heavily depends not only on available GCP platforms, but also on availability and accessibility of geo-information. Policy makers, governments and research institutions need to increasingly produce and openly/freely distribute geo-data that educators and learners can find, use and integrate into their own geoportals and geocollaborative learning practices. For example, the USA and UK national and local governments have already drafted and adopted a very good policy in producing and disseminating geo-data for public (business and/or research) use, that anyone can download for integrating them and producing any (mash-up) application (http://gos2.geodata.gov/wps/portal/gos, http://datasf.org, http://data.gov.uk/). However, international sharing and dissemination of geo-data requires the development and wide agreement and adoption of geo-data standards and copyright legislation (http://www.geonames.org/ http://geodatacommons.umaine.edu/, http://wiki.creativecommons.org/Geodata).

References

Balram, S., Dragicevic, S.: Collaborative spaces for GIS-based multimedia cartography in blended environments. Comput. Educ. **50**, 371–385 (2008)

Beaumont, P., Longley, P., Maguire, D.: Geographic information portals: UK perspective. Comput. Environ. Urban Syst. **29**, 49–69 (2005)

Brewer, I., MacEachren, A.M., Abdo, H., Gundrum, J., Otto, G.: Collaborative geographic visualization: enabling shared understanding of environmental processes. In: IEEE Information Visualization Symposium, pp. 137–141. Salt Lake City (2000)

Bruner, J.S.: The growth of mind. Am. Psychol. **20**, 1007–1017 (1965)

Davies, C.: Using Digital Geographic Maps in Distance Learning. CAL Research Group Report. Open University (1998)

Goodchild, M.F.: Citizens as voluntary sensors: spatial data infrastructure in the world of web 2.0. Int. J. Spat. Data Infrastructures Res. **2**, 24–32 (2007)

Hernandez, T.: Enhancing retail location decision support: the development and application of geovisualization. J. Retailing Consum. Serv. **14**(4), 249–258 (2007)

Jones, A., Blake, C., Davies, C., Scanlon, E.: Digital maps for learning: a review and prospects. Comput. Educ. **43**(1–2), 91–107 (2004)

Katterfeld, C., Paelke, V.: Interoperable learning environments in geosciences: a virtual learning landscape. In: ISPRS Technical Commission VI Symposium: E-Learning and the Next Steps for Education. Tokyo (2006)

Koua, E.L., MacEachren, A., Kraak, M.J.: Evaluating the usability of visualization methods in an exploratory geovisualization environment. Int. J. Geogr. Info. Sci. **20**(4), 425–448 (2006)

Kraak, M.: Geovisualisation. ISPRS J. Photogramm. Remote Sens. **57**, 390–399 (2003)

Kwan, M.: Interactive geovisualisation of activity-travel patterns using three-dimensional geographical information systems: a methodological exploration with a large data set. Transp. Res. C **8**, 185–203 (2000)

Lloyd, R.: Spatial Cognition, Geographic Environments. Kluwer, Dordrecht (1997)

Lloyd, D. L., Dykes, J.A.: Understanding geovisualization users and their requirements: a user-centred approach. In: Winstanley, A. (ed.) Geographical Information Science Research UK, Conference, pp. 209–214. Maynooth, Ireland (2007)

MacEachren, A.M.: Visualization in modern cartography: setting the Agenda. In: MacEachren, A.M., Taylor, D.R.F. (eds.) Visualization in Modern Cartography, pp. 1–12. Pergamon, Oxford (1994)

MacEachren, A.M.: Moving geovisualization toward support for group work. In: Dykes, J., MacEachren, A.M., Kraak, M. (eds.) Exploring Geovisualization, pp. 445–461. Elsevier Science Ltd., Amsterdam (2005)

MacEachren, A.M., Brewer, I.: Developing a conceptual framework for visually-enabled geocollaboration. Int. J. Geogr. Info. Sci. **18**(1), 1–34 (2004)

MacEachren, A.M., Cai, G.: Supporting group work in crisis management: visually mediated human – GIS – human dialogue. Environmental and Planning B: Planning and Design 33:435–456 (2006)

MacEachren, A.M., Kraak, M.J.: Research challenges in geovisualization. Cartography Geogr. Information Systems 28:(1), 3–12 (2001)

MacEachren, A.M.: Cartography and GIS: facilitating collaboration. Progress in Human Geography. 24:(3), 445–456 (2000)

Maguire, J., Longley, P.: Emergence of geoportals and their role in spatial data infrastructures. Comput. Environ. Urban Syst. **29**, 3–14 (2005)

Marsh, S.L., Dykes, J.A.: Using usability techniques to evaluate geovisualization in learning and teaching. In: Zentai, L., Nunez, J., Fraser, D. (eds.) Internet-based Cartographic Teaching & Learning: Atlases, Map Use, Visual Analytics, pp. 29–34. Joint ICA Commissions Seminar, Madrid (2005)

Resnick, L.B.: Shared Cognition: Thinking as Social Practice. Perspectives on Socially Shared Cognition, pp. 1–20. American Psychological Association, Washington, DC (1999)

Rinner, C.: Argumentation mapping in collaborative spatial decision making. In: Balram, R., Dragicevic, S. (eds.) Collaborative Geographic Information Systems, pp. 85–102. Idea Group Publishing, Hershey (2006)

Rinner, C., Keßler, C., Andrulis, S.: The use of web 2.0 concepts to support deliberation in spatial decision-making. Comput. Environ. Urban Syst. **32**(5), 386–395 (2008)

Rittschof, K.A., Kulhavy, R.W.: Learning and remembering from thematic maps of familiar regions. Educ. Technol. Res. Dev. **46**(1), 19–38 (1998)

Roth, R., MacEachren, A.M., McCabe, C.: A workflow learning model to improve geovisual analytics utility. Int. J. Geogr. Inf. Sci. **21**, 839–857 (2009)

Shah, J., Vargas-Hernandez, N., Summers, J., Kulkarni, S.: Collaborative sketching (C-Sketch): an idea generation technique for engineering design. J. Creat. Behav. **35**(3), 168–198 (2001)

Sigala, M.: Investigating the factors determining e-learning effectiveness in tourism & hospitality education. J. Hospitality Tourism Educ. **16**(2), 11–21 (2004)

Sigala, M.: Developing and Implementing a Model for Assessing Collaborative e-Learning Processes and Products. In: Patricia, Comeaux (ed.) Assessing Online Teaching and Learning, pp. 88–98. Anker Publishing, Bolton (2005)

Sigala, M.: Measuring customer value in online collaborative trip planning processes. Mark. Intell. Plann. **28**(4), 418–443 (2010)

Sigala, M., Christou, E.: Enhancing and complementing the instruction of tourism and hospitality courses through the use of on-line educational tools. J. Hospitality Tourism Educ. **15**(1), 6–16 (2003)

Sigala, M.: Geocollaborative portals and trip planning: users' perceptions of the success of the collaborative decision making processes. In: Proceeding of 4th MCIS 2009, 25–27 September, 2009, Athens (2009)

Sigala, M.: Measuring the impact of geocollaborative portals on collaborative decision making processes for trip planning. Eur. J. Inf. Syst. (in press)

Sigala, M., Marinidis, D.: Exploring the transformation of tourism firms' operations and business models through the use of web map services. In: EMCIS 2009. Izmir, Turkey (2009)

Tait, M.G.: Implementing geoportals: applications of distributed GIS. Comput. Environ. Urban Syst. **29**, 33–47 (2005)

Wegner, D., Erber, R., Raymond, P.: Transactive memory in close relationships. J. Pers. Soc. Psychol. **61**(6), 923–929 (1991)

Part II
Policy

Chapter 8
Building Institutional Capacity for the Use of Social Media

Carmel McNaught, Paul Lam, Morris Kwok, and Eric C.L. Ho

Abstract This chapter is set in the context of a rapidly changing curriculum context in Hong Kong, where a process of educational reform has been working through the school system and is about to reach the universities. The Chinese University of Hong Kong is a traditional, research-intensive university, where there is only a limited uptake of social media in teaching and learning. Eight teachers at The Chinese University of Hong Kong, who have used a range of social-media strategies in their teaching, were interviewed about the successes and challenges of their experiences. As a result of these interviews, a tentative implementation strategy is proposed for action by the eLearning Service.

8.1 Institutional Drivers for Innovation and Change

8.1.1 Overview of Educational Change in Hong Kong

Times of mass change in educational systems can be seen as opportunities for facilitating changes that might be difficult in more stable times. The Hong Kong government has embarked on a comprehensive and ambitious program of educational reform across schools, a range of post-secondary education options, and universities.

C. McNaught (✉) • P. Lam • E.C.L. Ho
Centre for Learning Enhancement And Research, The Chinese University of Hong Kong, Shatin, Hong Kong
e-mail: carmel.mcnaught@cuhk.edu.hk; paul.lam@cuhk.edu.hk; eric.ho@cuhk.edu.hk

M. Kwok
Information Technology Services Centre, The Chinese University of Hong Kong, Shatin, Hong Kong
e-mail: morris-kwok@cuhk.edu.hk

B. White et al. (eds.), *Social Media Tools and Platforms in Learning Environments*, DOI 10.1007/978-3-642-20392-3_8, © Springer-Verlag Berlin Heidelberg 2011

At university level, the University Grants Committee (UGC) of Hong Kong is a non-statutory advisory committee responsible for advising the Government of Hong Kong on the development and funding needs of higher education institutions (HEIs) in Hong Kong. There are eight UGC-funded HEIs, seven of which have university status (http://www.ugc.edu.hk/eng/ugc/site/fund_inst.htm).

Outcome based approaches (OBAs) to teaching and learning have received increasing attention in Hong Kong. There has been a gradual but clearly directed increase in government intervention in ensuring that the Hong Kong HEIs have an OBA that is not merely output-driven but is based on indicators that are recognized as pertaining to student learning. HEIs are increasingly accountable within an OBA framework. The culmination of these more directed government initiatives is the change in Hong Kong's higher education system in 2012 from a 3 year normative undergraduate curriculum to a 4 year normative curriculum. In 2012, undergraduate university student numbers will increase by one third; there will be an intake of students from the "old" secondary 7 year curriculum alongside an intake of students from the "new" 6 year secondary curriculum. This means that during the years 2012–2015 there will be a "double cohort" of students – half doing a 3 year under-graduate degree and half doing a 4 year degree. The "new" curriculum is intended to have an OBA and this undoubtedly will feature in future government audits of teaching and learning. The entire education change initiative for K-12 and beyond is shown diagrammatically in Fig. 8.1. The 4 year curriculum in 2012 is thus a strong driver for curriculum renewal.

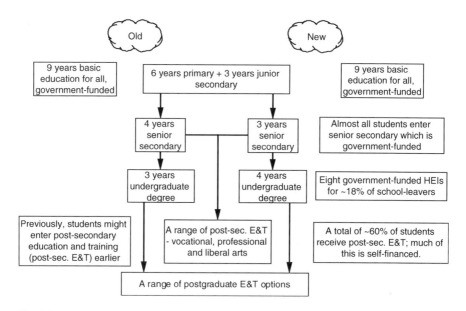

Fig. 8.1 Overview of the new formal education system in Hong Kong

8.1.2 A Model of Drivers for Innovation and Change in Hong Kong Universities

There is evidence in Hong Kong universities that interactions that lead to constructive dialogue (also termed "social exchange" by Lave and Wenger (1991) in their work on situated learning) are more beneficial to learning than students being provided with access to information alone; one example is the empirical study by Kember et al. (2010) who surveyed 595 students in 21 courses with, by Hong Kong standards, high use of eLearning. However, despite the acknowledged significant potential benefits to teaching and learning, more interactive types of eLearning strategies are not widely used by university teachers in Hong Kong. A series of studies at The Chinese University of Hong Kong (CUHK) show that, while the percentage of supplementary online course websites has grown a great deal from ~45% in 2003–2004 to over 80% in 2008–2009, the Web continues to be mostly seen as a convenient storage house for easy distribution of course materials to students, often using existing basic functions in learning management systems (LMSs), such as WebCT and Moodle. Most communications are fed through online forums with simple designs which are not very active; thread lengths are, on average, only one to three messages (McNaught et al. 2006, McNaught and Lam 2009).

One way of understanding this situation is to consider what constitutes a "mutual comfort zone" for all the stakeholders, including teachers, students, and the technical and pedagogical support staff (McNaught et al. 2009). In many universities the mutual comfort zone appears to be quite small. It is therefore easy to see why successful and sustainable cases of complex eLearning are not common and are restricted to highly motivated, pioneering teachers who are comfortable with innovative technologies and may also work within an innovation-friendly environment.

A model of drivers that influence the adoption and sustainability of eLearning strategies, and thus the growth of blended learning, was described in McNaught (2008), and then extended in McNaught and Lam (2009). The development of the model has a synergy with Rogers' (2003) work on the diffusion of innovation. By enabling an understanding of what facilitates and inhibits innovation, the model enables a university to move along the "early adopter"–"mainstream majority" continuum with respect to optimal use of technology for teaching and learning. The model was used to study both positive and negative contextual factors at a research-intensive, comprehensive university (such as CUHK) that positively and negatively influence the adoption of innovation. In this model, the factors of most relevance were commitment of senior management, allocation of time, and a positive cost-benefit decision by teachers that their investment is likely to pay off. These factors can be framed as a set of competing drivers (both internal and external to the University). A summary of the model is given in Fig. 8.2. The arrows indicate that there is always a tension between any process of innovation and change, and the maintenance of the status quo.

The year 2012 is a driver for strengthening IT infrastructure and this has been articulated in a new eLearning Strategy, now endorsed as CUHK policy. There are six key aims:

Factor	Coordinated and supported eLearning		Laissez-faire approach	
	←--------------------------------		-------------------------------→	
	Internal drivers	*External drivers*	*Internal driver*	*External driver*
1. Senior manage- ment	Evidence of institutional research	External government quality audits	Culture of a face-to-face university	Good external rankings
	Implementation of a new student information system with concomitant reviews of internal university processes			
	←--------------------------------		-------------------------------→	
	Internal drivers	*External driver*	*Internal driver*	*External driver*
2. Time	Increased diversity of student profiles Students as 'digital natives'	Changing curriculum mandated at government level	Commitment to a university research life	Frenetic city with a just-in-time philosophy
	←--------------------------------		-------------------------------→	
	Internal drivers	*External driver*	*Internal driver*	*External driver*
3. Teachers' decisions about change	Local support Change in policy for promotion	Strong push for outcomes- based approaches (OBAs) to teaching and learning	Peer groups in departments	Bench- marking within the discipline

Fig. 8.2 Internal and external drivers impinging on decisions about directions for eLearning (Adapted from McNaught and Lam 2009)

1. Clarify the role of eLearning in OBA;
2. Engage in research for planning infrastructure, e.g. University-wide eLearning systems;
3. Support educational design and technology in the 4 year undergraduate curriculum;
4. Continue staff training, support, and collaboration strategies;
5. Continue student induction to eLearning and student IT competence training; and
6. Benchmark eLearning at CUHK against a range of international standards.

There is a detailed action plan, articulated in one section of the eLearning Strategy, which emphasizes the use of social media. This has formalized the use of social media as being more than a "fringe" activity. However, exploration continues about what needs to be achieved at the institutional level in order to fully embed the use of social media as useful teaching and learning tools at CUHK.

8.2   Social Media in Education

Educators are exploring ways to take advantage of students' engagement with social media. Web 2.0 or social software tools such as blogs, wikis, podcasts and media-file-sharing systems such as YouTube are supplementing or even "supplanting" (Gray et al. 2010, p. 33) the basic Web 1.0 strategies such as emails and forums in education. For example, blogs and wikis have been useful tools for facilitating peer collaboration in language teaching and learning (Godwin-Jones 2003), for the interactions among health-care students (Boulos et al. 2006), as well as among students in other disciplines so that they co-construct knowledge through sharing of ideas (Beldarrain 2006). The communications that are facilitated in social software also have the potential to extend communications beyond the boundary of individual universities. For example, Dillon et al. (2007) explored internationalization of learning and teaching through the design of courses where students and teachers, spread across the world, interact and work together as core components of the learning experience. These notions of co-construction of knowledge are not new; for example, they are deeply embedded in the computer-supported collaborative learning community (Stahl et al. 2006).

Educational podcasting is well embedded in universities in many countries, for example, in Australia, Canada, New Zealand, United Kingdom, and the United States (Allen 2006). Madden and Jones (2008) reported findings from the Pew Internet & American Life Project that 19% of internet users downloaded a podcast in August 2008, compared to 12% in August 2006 and 7% in February to April 2006. Podcasting is becoming another possibility for teachers to extend their classes. Hsueh (2007) suggested multiple potential usages of podcasting for teachers. Podcasts with background information can be used to guide students' brainstorming before class and to elicit curiosity. Teachers can assign students to listen to topics through podcasts and then use this material as triggers for in-class discussion and problem solving. Teachers can also record interviews or role-plays in order to share authentic personal experiences with their students. Students can also be involved in making podcasts, for example, to report news, record stories, or prepare "radio shows."

Significant learning benefits are possible if social media is used in ways where students create and share the media and learn through the interactions. Most students are quite familiar with digital devices and are competent in using social-media technologies. Bull et al. (2008) stated that "the majority of all teens are now engaged in active creation of online content" and that "the majority of the video clips posted on YouTube are created by teenagers." It may be incumbent on teachers to design learning tasks that build upon students' media competence in ways that encourage active interrogation of information, leading to shared and personal construction of mental models and knowledge.

8.3   Current Status of Social Media at the Chinese University of Hong Kong

CUHK is a comprehensive, research-intensive university with eight faculties – Arts, Business Administration, Education, Engineering, Law, Medicine, Science, and Social Science – and approximately 22,000 students.

Is the University making full use of these new learning opportunities? There are a number of cases of early adopters using social media at CUHK. In order to investigate the use of social media at CUHK, the abstracts presented at CUHK's annual "innovations in teaching and learning" conference were examined. This conference – commonly called the Expo (http://www.cuhk.edu.hk/elearning/expo) – is a showcase of local initiatives and designed to facilitate conversation and sharing of good practices across the campus. Now in its fourth year, it has proved to be an excellent event for engaging the CUHK community and colleagues from sister HEIs in rich and interactive dialogues. There were 19 presentations in the 2007 Expo, 22 in 2008 and 33 in 2009. There are several other cases of social media in use at CUHK; however, as the Expo presenters had already indicated an interest in sharing their experiences, they were a good sample for this study.

The presentations in the three Expos were analyzed in order to identify innovative strategies that were related to use of social media. There were at least three ways in which social media has been used at CUHK in the context of teaching and learning:

1. A passive mode where *teachers and/or students used resources* built elsewhere to aid teaching and learning.
2. *Teachers creating materials* for sharing. The sharing could be restricted to others within a course or the University or, in some cases, the content was accessible by professional bodies outside the University or by the general public.
3. *Students creating resources* and sharing them. Students learned through the creation and sharing process. The sharing could be restricted to people within a course or within the University. In one case, the content created by students was accessible to a wider audience.

Table 8.1 summarizes the presentations related to the use of social media in the three Expo events. It was noticeable that the notion of social media in teaching and learning has become more pervasive and somewhat more sophisticated over the years. It is interesting to note that several of these teachers are involved in language education for English teachers, an area of high importance in Hong Kong.

In May 2010, the authors contacted the 13 teachers involved in the 15 social-media cases noted above and invited them to a phone or face-to-face interview. The main objectives of the interview were to find out the perceived value of using the various social-media strategies and the challenges that the teachers met. Six teachers were interviewed by phone and two face-to-face. Prior to the interviews, the teachers were emailed a description of the main purpose of the interviews and the main questions to be covered. The telephone conversations lasted from 10 to 20 min

Table 8.1 Presentations over 3 years at Expo that involved social media ($N = 13$, of which eight were interviewed)

	2007 ($n = 2$)	2008 ($n = 6$)	2009 ($n = 7$)
	$N = 13$; two teachers appear in two Expo events in different years.		
	Teachers denoted by A to H were interviewed. *ELE denotes "English language education."		
1. Teachers and students used existing social media as teaching and learning resources			
	• Teacher suggested readings from various social-media sites (*Biology*)	• Teacher used YouTube videos in class (*linguistics*)	
2. Teachers created resources and shared them			
• Restricted	• Teacher recorded podcasts (*ELE**)		• Teachers gave further advice in blogs and on twitter (*Teacher E – information literacy*) • Teachers provided learning objects (*ELE*)
• Open		• Teacher used a wiki to communicate with professionals and students (*Teacher A – ELE*) • Examples of using wikis as collaborative tools (*Teacher D – engineering*)	• Teacher created digital stories for sharing (*Teacher A – ELE*) • Podcast lectures were created and made accessible to public (*Teacher F – law*)
3. Students created resources and shared them			
• Restricted		• Students shared learning portfolios (*Teacher B – biochemistry*) • Students shared video-recorded presentations (*Teacher C – ELE*) • Students shared thoughts in blogs (*physical education*)	• Cases were created by students and shared (*Teacher G – pharmacy*) • Students' thoughts were kept in a wiki/ Twitter/ Facebook (*Teacher H – tutor training*)
• Open			• Students created digital stories that were made public (*Teacher A – ELE*)

each. One face-to-face meeting lasted 15 min and the other one (with a teacher who used three strategies and participated in the Expo in all 3 years) lasted 1 h.

The teachers were marked as "*Teachers A to H*" in Table 8.1. None of the interviewed teachers represented the cases that used existing social media as teaching and learning resources. All interviews were audio-taped. A summary of each interview was made by the interviewer within a few days by recording each separate item (as a descriptive comment, opinion, clarification...) under three headings: (1) details of the use of social media; (2) advantages; and (3) challenges.

8.3.1 Using Existing Social Media

Content created in social-media websites can become teaching and learning resources for both teachers and students. In 2007, a biology teacher began supplementing face-to-face teaching with daily readings and online quizzes. The extra readings enabled students to acquire extended knowledge about aspects of biology. The readings included content from blogs and Wikipedia. In 2008, a linguistics teacher used YouTube videos, e-maps, and e-photos about Papua New Guinea in class when discussing differences in degree of language diversity in a place unknown to the students.

This passive use of social media as a learning resource is straightforward for both teachers and students. Considerable learning benefits can be achieved as the media found on the Web can be rich and diverse. However, teachers and students need ready-to-find sources of appropriate material.

8.3.2 Creation of Social Media by Teachers, Restricted Access

More active uses of social-media technologies involve either the teacher or the students creating content. In 2007, a teacher created podcasting audio-lectures for his English language course. The podcasting technology allowed student subscribers to easily retrieve the listening materials. These materials, however, were not created for public access. In 2009, *Teacher E* reported creating resources for topics in information and IT literacy using blogs and Twitter; this strategy also enhanced interactivity between teacher and students in the course.

Another presentation in 2009 focused on a purpose-designed CUHK system, known as the Learning Objects Repository (LOR), which was developed for sharing teaching resources. Teachers produced metadata, such as the objectives, rationale, and design features, so that the objects could be easily searchable and potentially more readily adopted by other teachers. The project began in English language education but the LOR has now been institutionalized and is open to all disciplines (http://lor.itsc.cuhk.edu.hk/docs/about.html; http://lor.itsc.cuhk.edu.hk/). While not restricted to social-media artifacts, the LOR demonstrates that learning artifacts can encompass a variety of media.

8.3.3   Creation of Social Media by Teachers, Open Access

Teacher and student creations, for access by a wider audience (outside CUHK) have occurred in some cases. In 2008, *Teacher A* used a wiki for professional sharing with students and other teachers in the wider community. He used a wide range of digital materials such as documents, PowerPoints, sound files, and videos to share concepts and topic ideas in English language teaching. *Teacher D* has also used wikis as a collaborative learning environment for collecting, sharing, processing, managing, and disseminating information in the teaching of engineering.

In 2009, the University launched a new podcast service (http://podcast.cuhk.edu.hk/) and *Teacher A* turned a number of teacher-created and student-created digital stories into podcasting materials which were made public on the CUHK podcasting website. *Teacher F* has created an open series of podcasts on law.

8.3.4   Creation of Social Media by Students, Mostly Restricted Access

Students creating content (text and/or multimedia) for sharing is a relatively common strategy at CUHK. Much of the sharing, however, is restricted to members of the one course. In 2008, Teacher B video-taped students while they presented a literature review on a biochemistry topic. These video clips were shared as learning portfolios. Teacher B is a very experienced teacher and she considered that her students were more engaged in learning before and after the presentations, and were also much more able to take ownership of the knowledge they learned.

A physical education teacher has used blogs as learning portfolios. Students can keep track of their own progress, assess their own accomplishments, and determine the extent to which the learning objectives have been achieved. The blogs also provide the teacher with a basis for evaluating his course.

Teacher C has a blog-based eLearning environment and learning community for pre-service and in-service language teachers enrolled in CUHK courses – Platforms for Language Teacher Education (PLaTE) (Tang 2009). The system provides a variety of online reference and learning tools for students, graduates, and teaching professionals. Students in these postgraduate courses have made blog-based teaching portfolios which incorporate video-recorded presentations. There were also exchanges of ideas in online forums.

Student creation and sharing of content was the theme in three presentations in 2009. Teacher G's students developed online cases of authentic pharmacy contexts and problems. Sixteen students worked as case designers and a total of 38 cases were developed. Use of the cases was restricted to use within the course but not limited to one cohort as students in subsequent years used the student-created eCases as self-learning resources (Au Yeung et al. 2008). Both the case developers as well as the case users reported benefits of knowledge consolidation, and enhanced skills in self-learning and critical thinking.

Teacher H is involved in training postgraduate students who will be tutors and laboratory demonstrators. He uses a wiki, Twitter and Facebook to facilitate communications with new teaching assistants in different departments. This strategy enables a learning circle to be formed for participants to share their experiences in teaching and lesson planning after the face-to-face component of the training module.

The Expo sample gave only one example of open access for student work. Teacher A's students (in-service teachers) produced digital stories (short videos made from still images) as reflections of their teaching experiences. The small file size also makes them easy to share with colleagues and students. In this case, the students were in a course about educational technology; the digital-story exercise thus provided training in online publishing skills as an integral component of the course.

8.4   Advantages of Using Social Media in Teaching at CUHK

Motivation is certainly one of the noted advantages. Student creation and sharing of social media improves their motivation to learn. Participation in class is also enhanced when student work is recorded and shared. [Comments are usually translations from Chinese.]

> It leads to high motivation to students in learning. (*Teacher A*)
> It leads to active participation in class. (*Teacher B*)

Social media enable the sharing of experience and ideas with a wider audience, perhaps involving experts or practitioners in the field. It was particularly true when open access was used, or when viewpoints and artifacts from people with various backgrounds were involved.

> It is a convenient way for us to share our views, stories, and resources on the internet. (*Teacher A*)
> It facilitates professionals with similar interest to share their ideas and resources on social platforms. (*Teacher A*)
> Professionals and students could construct knowledge together. (*Teacher C*)
> It could gather a wide range of people interacting together. (*Teacher C*)
> It links up a group of people together. (*Teacher H*)

Social media are engaging, and students spend more time and effort on activities. Engagement is a measure of "time on task" (Chickering and Ehrmann 1996; Chickering and Gamson 1987) and is more easily measurable than motivation which refers to attitudes towards learning. However, the two are closely related. The media can be viewed as many times as the students want.

> Students give a more mature in-class performance if they know that it will be publicized on the internet. (*Teacher B*)
> It provides more chances for students to learn something extra out-of-class. (*Teacher B*)
> It gives more time for students to practice the case studies out-of-class. (*Teacher G*)
> It provides a chance for them to review their presentation after class. (*Teacher B*)
> It provides an opportunity for students to practice what they have learnt in the lectures. (*Teacher G*)

Student–student collaboration is facilitated when students cooperate in creating social-media artifacts. Collaboration is also enhanced when students comment on each other's work through a peer-review process.

> It is very helpful in terms of collaboration in group work. (*Teacher D*)
> It is easy to update, revise, and modify the content. (*Teacher D*)
> It provides instant assistance to students. (*Teacher H*)

Social-media platforms are, by and large, user-friendly. Teachers reported improved convenience in managing content and resources because the platforms facilitated easy uploading, sharing, tagging, and storage of content.

> It is easy to organize different types of resources in hand. (*Teacher A*)

Lastly, the use of social media is fashionable. In Hong Kong, this is quite important. Clearly, this factor overlaps with motivation. Doing this enables teachers to live up to student expectations that new approaches to learning will be adopted.

> It is the current trend of society. (*Teacher E*)
> It is a new promotional channel. (*Teacher E*)

8.5   Challenges in Using Social Media in Teaching at CUHK

Teachers highlighted a number of challenges for the use of social media at CUHK (and similar institutions). For example, creating the social media and then maintaining the media for use and sharing required an investment of time and energy. It can also be technically challenging for some teachers.

> It is time-consuming to maintain it. (*Teacher E*)
> Extra effort in time and resources are needed. (*Teacher F*)
> Sometimes I face technical problems. (*Teacher C*)

There is also additional workload for students if students are to be involved in creating the materials.

> It causes a heavier workload to students. (*Teacher B*)
> Students may find it extra work to participate in the learning platform. (*Teacher H*)

Students find the use of the new media for educational purposes means changes in habits. Although most students may be using the new technologies in their everyday lives, they may still need to be persuaded of the benefits for educational purposes. If students do not sense the real needs and benefits in doing so, the strategies will fail.

> Some students prefer traditional methods to seek help. (*Teacher E*)
> It does not have a popular usage in campus. (*Teacher F*)
> It performs not as well as some specialized education platforms. (*Teacher D*)
> Wikis are not mature enough and not easy to handle. (*Teacher D*)

Teachers need additional support and resources whether they are creating materials themselves or they are monitoring students' creation of materials.

Extra funding and resources are needed to support this learning activity. (*Teacher B*)

When the activities involving creation and sharing of social media are integrated into a course as grade-bearing assignments, students have concerns regarding fairness. In a marks-oriented society where language standards are not high, this is a difficult challenge for which there is no easy solution. One solution used by some teachers is to have such tasks designated as "hurdle" assessments; they are required for course completion but only receive a pass/fail grade.

Students do not want this activity to involve their course marks. (*Teacher G*)
Cheating from students is found if the online activity is counting for marks in the course. (*Teacher G*)

There is a reluctance to share. There are worries regarding leaving a "permanent" record of student performance on the Web. The resistance is even greater if the materials are for open access.

Students are only interested in watching the sharing with their close relationship classmates only. (*Teacher A*)
Students are not active to respond to classmates sharing. (*Teacher A*)
Some students are not willing to share their stories in class. (*Teacher A*)

Lastly, it is not easy for teachers to evaluate the actual learning benefits of the social-media strategies. There are pros and cons of using social media. Students may have varied opinions. Teachers may not get clear-cut evidence that the strategies are leading to better learning outcomes, and that use is worth the effort, unless they spend time collecting evidence in appropriate ways. Partly, this is because the desired learning benefits move beyond understanding and using discipline knowledge to a more explicit focus on generic attributes, the attainment of which is always difficult to gauge. Conducting evaluations is a requirement for attaining a teaching development grant at CUHK and support is provided to all teachers in carrying out evaluation studies.

The effectiveness of using social media in your course may not be as high as your original plan (*Teacher H*).

8.6   Discussion

In this section, we will consider the implications of the interviews for the future work of the eLearning Service. The eLearning Service at CUHK is a collaborative initiative between colleagues in the Information Technology Services Centre (ITSC) and the Centre for Learning Enhancement And Research (CLEAR); it provides institutional support to teachers for fostering the use of technology for teaching and learning. It has six main strategies designed to reinforce the advantages of using eLearning and to support teachers in overcoming the challenges (such as those listed above):

1. Revamp of the eLearning platforms;
2. A range of support services;
3. Seminars and workshops;

4. Support for courseware development;
5. Promotion of eLearning; and
6. Research on new strategies and technologies.

As CUHK moves from a focus on only Web 1.0 services to including Web 2.0 services, a number of evolutionary changes are being discussed in the eLearning Service. The term "evolutionary" is used because it is believed that gently extending a teacher's comfort zone is more effective than mandating rapid "revolutionary" change.

Overall, there is evidence of the beginnings of an interest in using social media to assist teaching and learning. Content in social media is seen as providing useful sources of teaching and learning materials. The conversations with teachers who had concrete experiences using the strategies confirmed that social media has led to multiple, observable learning benefits.

However, the number of courses where social media is used is small – only a few percent of the total courses. Only a few teachers are actively using social media. Also, some of the examples of using social media are in courses about technology, rather than social media where it would be used because of intrinsic potential educational benefits. In addition, access to the materials created was very limited (often to people within a course) so that the real benefits of learning communities are not being fully realized.

Using existing social media as teaching and learning resources by teachers and students may be straightforward enough. What teachers and students need, though, are sources of good materials and ways to minimize the time needed for searching for quality materials.

The creation of social media by teachers and students is challenging and lacks popularity at CUHK. Apart from the few cases reported above, the University has recently begun promoting the use of Echo 360 (http://www.echo360.com/) as a lecture-recording solution for teachers who want: (1) students to review their lectures after class; or (2) to make the recordings publicly accessible as learning modules. The project is slowly building momentum. Reluctance to change and reluctance to share again seem to be factors working against the innovation.

From these interviews and the reflections thereon, a tentative, hopefully pragmatic, implementation strategy for improving the uptake of appropriate uses of social media at CUHK has been developed. The implementation strategy is presented below as a table with action at both local level (with individual teachers and their departments and faculties) and institutional level (university-wide infrastructure and policy) (Table 8.2).

At present, CUHK is at a crossroad. Should a pragmatic approach be adopted, providing limited support to teachers who ask for more service; or a proactive approach where the benefits of using the more advanced technologies are actively promoted?

Two of the strategies noted in Table 8.2, namely, the "eLearning assistant" service and collegial program reviews, are described in some detail below as they may well have wide applicability beyond CUHK.

Table 8.2 Implementation strategy for embedding the use of social media at CUHK

ELearning service strategy	Action at department or faculty level	Action at institutional level
1. Revamp of the eLearning platforms	• Teachers from each of the eight faculties are actively involved in the decision.	• Web 2.0 features will be important criteria in the choice of our next generation eLearning systems.
2. A range of support services	• ELearning assistants (described in more detail below) provide one-on-one service to teachers.	• New criteria for evaluating teaching quality have been drafted and include the benefits of innovation in teaching.
3. Professional development seminars and workshops	• We are using colleagues to present their work in lunch-time seminars.	• Teachers can gain credits for sessions on Web 2.0 towards a professional development certificate in teaching and learning.
4. Support for courseware development	• Individual teachers can apply for courseware development grants to support projects that involve Web 2.0 tools.	• The podcasting service and the learning object repository are examples of institutional support. Other tools are under consideration.
5. Promotion of eLearning	• Decisions to use new eLearning strategies, including social media, are never mandatory. Teachers are supported but not required to use eLearning. This pragmatic approach is, we believe, essential.	• The "new" curriculum for 2012 will be considered by collegial program reviews (described in more detail below). Innovation in eLearning is one of the aspects to receive focused comment.
6. Research on new strategies and technologies	• The new criteria on teaching quality will include reference to the scholarship of teaching and learning (Boyer 1990), which will encourage an evidence-based approach to innovation, including the use of social media.	• This paper will be presented to the University's Academic IT steering committee as an information paper for consideration.

The "eLearning assistant" service began in 2008. A team of 8–10 eLearning assistants (students working part-time as well as fresh graduates working full-time) were recruited and trained to closely work with teachers and to assist them in planning and implementing their eLearning strategies (Lam et al. 2009). Responsibilities include:

• Advising teachers on eLearning strategies that might support expected learning outcomes;
• Providing practical skills and tips in using the strategies;
• Assisting teachers in developing teaching materials and establishing course websites in the learning management platforms (Moodle and WebCT);
• Answering teacher questions during the actual implementation of the strategies;

- Suggesting to teachers the methods to collect feedback and data for evaluation; and
- Informing teachers about basic technical skills so that teachers can achieve simple upgrades to the materials and use the sites independently.

These duties cover more than social media, but viewing social media as one possible change strategy with a wide range of options is useful. The young eLearning assistants are well placed to offer advice and answer questions about how social media might be incorporated into CUHK courses. To date, 12 teachers have been served by the eLearning assistant service in the development of major projects where social media is involved. There also have been numerous short consultations.

During the next 2 years, there will be collegial program reviews for all undergraduate programs (about 60 in number). One example of how social media may be useful is that, in the new curriculum, all students will be expected to engage in a capstone course, designed to be an experience where students can bring together a number of aspects of their studies and consolidate their understanding of what they have achieved in terms of key knowledge, skills, and values. The use of social-media tools can assist students to engage with their peers or with teachers/ professionals/ other students in other places doing similar projects. In the review process, opportunities in this rapidly changing curriculum terrain will be sought to provide suggestions that fit well into overall program design.

8.7 Conclusion

As Web 1.0 is gradually integrated with Web 2.0 technologies, universities need to revisit the practices that have been used to provide institutional support and promotion of eLearning. The use of Web 2.0, or social-media technologies, in teaching and learning is still small at CUHK, but this is a good time to take stock. Eight pioneering teachers who had reported social-media projects in the annual teaching and learning Expo event were interviewed. The teachers affirmed that social-media strategies can support learning outcomes, but teachers also encountered many challenges in implementation.

The findings supported a revision of the eLearning Service. In particular, a pragmatic plan was developed with goals that are believed to be realistic and achievable, and where change is supported, for individual teachers and for policy and resourcing at an institutional level.

References

Allen, B.: Podcasting in education: an intellectual biography http://education.transbat.com/courses/eme6405/IntelBioFinalPaper.pdf (2006)

Au Yeung, M., Lam, P., McNaught, C.: Student-creation of eCases for clinical reasoning in pharmacy. Australas. J. Peer Learn. (2008) http://ro.uow.edu.au/ajpl/vol1/iss1/5/

Beldarrain, Y.: Distance education trends: Integrating new technologies to foster student interaction and collaboration. Distance Educ. **27**(2), 139–153 (2006)

Boulos, M., Moramba, I., Wheeler, S.: Wikis, blogs and podcasts: A new generation of web-based tools for virtual collaborative clinical practice and education. BMC Med. Educ. **6**(41) (2006) http://www.biomedcentral.com/1472-6920/6/41

Boyer, E.L.: Scholarship Reconsidered: Priorities of the Professoriate. Jossey Bass, San Francisco (1990)

Bull, G., Thompson, A., Searson, M., Garofalo, J., Park, J., Young, C., Lee, J.: Connecting informal and formal learning: Experiences in the age of participatory media. Contemp. Issues Technol. Teach. Educ. **8**(2), 100–107 (2008)

Chickering, A.W., Ehrmann, S.C.: Implementing the seven principles: Technology as lever. AAHE Bull. **49**(2), 3–6 (1996)

Chickering, A.W., Gamson, Z.F.: Seven principles for good practice in undergraduate education. AAHE Bull. **39**(7), 8–12 (1987)

Dillon, P., Wang, R., Tearle, P.: Cultural disconnection in virtual education. Pedagogy Cult. Soc. **15**, 153–74 (2007)

Godwin-Jones, R.: Emerging technologies, blogs, and wikis: Environments for online collaboration. Lang. Learn. Technol. **7**(2), 12–16 (2003)

Gray, K., Chang, S., Kennedy, G.: Use of social web technologies by international and domestic undergraduate students: Implications for internationalising learning and teaching in australian universities. Technol. Pedagogy Educ. **19**(1), 31–46 (2010)

Hsueh, S.L.: Teaching and learning with iPods. In Saito-Abbott, Y. (ed.) Convergence in World Language and Culture Learning: Pedagogy, Technology, and Classroom Management. Proceedings of the DigitalStream Conference. California State University, Monterey Bay (2007). http://php.csumb.edu/wlc/ojs/index.php/ds/article/view/55/54

Kember, D., McNaught, C., Chong, F.C.Y., Lam, P., Cheng, K.F.: Understanding the ways in which design features of educational websites impact upon student learning outcomes in blended learning environments. Comput. Educ. **55**, 1183–1192 (2010)

Lam, P., Au Yeung, M., Cheung, E., McNaught, C.: Using the development of eLearning material as challenging and authentic learning experiences for students. In Atkinson, R., McBeath, C. (eds.) Same Places, Different Spaces. In: 26th Annual Australian Society for Computers in Learning in Tertiary Education 2009 Conference (ASCILITE), pp. 548–556 (2009) http://www.ascilite.org.au/conferences/auckland09/procs/lam.pdf

Lave, J., Wenger, E.: Situated Learning. Legitimate Peripheral Participation. University of Cambridge Press, Cambridge (1991)

Madden, M., Jones, S.: Pew internet project data memo – podcast downloading. Pew Internet Am. Life Project (2008) http://www.pewinternet.org/~/media/Files/Reports/2008/PIP_Podcast_2008_Memo.pdf.pdf

McNaught, C.: Towards an institutional eLearning strategy: The long journey. In: Nair, C.S. (ed.) Evidence Based Decision Making: Scholarship and Practice. In: Australasian Higher Education Evaluation Forum (AHEEF), pp. 43–45 (2008) http://pandora.nla.gov.au/tep/103801

McNaught, C., Lam, P.: Institutional strategies for embedding blended learning in a research-intensive university. In: Proceedings of the eLearn 2009 Conference, Bridging the Development Gap through Innovative eLearning Environments (2009)

McNaught, C., Lam, P., Cheng, K.F., Kennedy, D.M., Mohan, J.B.: Challenges in employing complex eLearning strategies in campus-based universities. Int. J. Technol. Enhanced Learn. **1**(4), 266–285 (2009)

McNaught, C., Lam, P., Keing, C., Cheng, K.F.: Improving eLearning support and infrastructure: An evidence-based approach. In: O'Donoghue, J. (ed.) Technology Supported Learning and Teaching: A Staff Perspective, pp. 70–89. Information Science Publishing, Hershey (2006)

Rogers, E.M.: Diffusion of Innovations, 5th edn. Free Press, New York (2003)

Stahl, G., Koschmann, T., Suthers, D.: Computer-Supported collaborative learning: An historical perspective. In: Sawyer, R.K. (ed.) Cambridge Handbook of the Learning Sciences, pp. 409–426. Cambridge University Press, Cambridge (2006)

Tang, E.: Introduction and development of a blog-based teaching portfolio: A case study in a Pre-service teacher education programme. Int. J. Learn. **16**(8), 89–100 (2009)

Part III
Virtual Educational Spaces

Chapter 9
Virtual Environments Leadership: Do Physical Characteristics Matter?

S. Lynn Shollen and C. Cryss Brunner

Abstract Quantitative methods were employed to explore the effect that group member's physical identity had on other member's perceptions of those individuals as leaders during group work in a virtual context. Comparisons were made between perceptions of leadership after a session in which identity was highly anonymous and after a session in which identity was known via avatar photographs. Participants comprised 149 students engaged in a virtual learning environment, designed to develop a variety of leadership capabilities. The results give some indication that age and weight characteristics may affect perceptions of leadership. Overall, the introduction of physically identifying cues after groups had worked together anonymously for a period of time did not affect perceptions of leadership. Implications of these findings relative to availability of identifying cues, impression formation, status-based equalization, and leadership in virtual learning environments are discussed.

9.1 Introduction

Technological advances and the growing need for collaboration across geographic boundaries have contributed to the proliferation of virtual learning environments (Collins and Halverson 2009). Online teaching and learning is increasingly adopted by higher education institutions in response to globalization, scarce funding

S.L. Shollen (✉)
Department of Leadership and American Studies, Christopher Newport University, 1 University Place, Newport News, VA 23606, USA
e-mail: lynn.shollen@cnu.edu

C.C. Brunner
Department of Organizational Leadership, Policy, and Development, University of Minnesota – Twin Cities, 330 Wulling Hall, 86 Pleasant Street S. E., Minneapolis, MN 55455, USA
e-mail: brunner@umn.edu

B. White et al. (eds.), *Social Media Tools and Platforms in Learning Environments*,
DOI 10.1007/978-3-642-20392-3_9, © Springer-Verlag Berlin Heidelberg 2011

resources, and a shift in the population of student and adult learners and their needs (Bennett and Lockyer 2004; Morey 2004; Taylor 1998). Given this shift, along with the increasing diversity of constituents comprising higher education institutions and the current global relationships necessary for institutions to operate (Ashburn 2008; Kezar 2009), an understanding of virtual learning environments, who emerges as leaders in such environments, and understanding the role that identity plays in perceptions of leadership are essential for institutional adaptation and success. Thus, the focus of this chapter is a quantitative study designed to determine the relationship between physical identity and perceptions of leadership within the context of text-based, virtual learning environments. The primary research question was: What effect does introducing the physical characteristics of an individual have on other people's perceptions of that individual as a leader in a virtual learning environment after initial impressions are formed under conditions of anonymity?

9.2   Theoretical Framework and Literature

People interacting in text-based, virtual learning environments use the written word to communicate and do so with various degrees of anonymity. The more restricted the environment, meaning the less social cue information available to users, the higher the degree of ambiguity (Tanis and Postmes 2003). Given a condition of relative ambiguity in virtual contexts, stereotyping is the primary basis of impression formation (Jacobson 1999; Lea et al. 2001). Stereotypes, which are commonly utilized for cognitive efficiency, are relied upon more heavily in the absence of individuating information (Brewer 1996; Kunda and Thagard 1996; Mackie et al. 1996). Most virtual group work requires participants to interact with multiple group members, which increases cognitive load, and to perform tasks with limited time – conditions that enhance stereotyping behavior in impression formation (Brewer 1996).

In the absence of cues typically used in stereotyping and impression formation in face-to-face settings and some virtual contexts, such as physical appearance and voice quality, stereotypes and impressions in text-based, virtual environments are based largely on language and paralanguage (Jacobson 1999; Lea and Spears 1992). Paralinguistic cues, such as typographical marks, typing errors, and emoticons, help to convey communication style. People evaluate language and paralanguage choices and subsequently "make attributions about social and professional status, background and education and even the intent of communication" (Burgoon and Miller 1987, p. 199).

Stereotypes associated with certain social categories inform initial impressions of the *inexplicit* qualities of individuals (Stangor et al. 1992), one quality being leadership ability. Assumptions about who can lead are based on prototypical concepts of leaders – often related to physical identity – that are developed through experience (Lord and Maher 1993; Nye and Forsyth 1991). Stereotypes based on identity may affect perceptions of leadership because people are likely to process information automatically in terms of identity category rather than leadership category (Baumgardner et al. 1993).

The anonymity of physical identity and social status that can be achieved through the reductive capabilities of virtual environments has implications for impression formation and perceptions of leadership in virtual groups (Carte and Chidambaram 2004). Ability to influence is one succinct, customary definition of leadership (Northouse 2004). Status characteristics have been shown to affect an individual's ability to influence others in face-to-face settings, but whether that influence holds in virtual environments is still debated. A status characteristic is "any characteristic of actors around which evaluations of and beliefs about them come to be organized" (Berger et al. 1980, p. 479). The generalization that status differences determine the power and prestige hierarchy in groups has garnered empirical support from Berger and colleagues (1980), whose applied research demonstrated that sex, race, and physical attractiveness function as status characteristics.

Some scholars contend that virtual environments neutralize the effects of social status common in interactions that occur in person, and promote status-based equalization as a result of anonymity and reduced social cues (Bordia 1997; Dubrovsky et al. 1991; Kiesler and Sproull 1992; Siegel et al. 1986). They argue that anonymity and physical isolation are qualities that promote de-individuation of group members (Kiesler et al. 1984). De-individuation equates with the loss of identity, a less complete person-impression, and weakening of social norms and constraints associated with identity (Spears and Lea 1992; Tanis and Postmes 2003).

Other scholars argue that the anonymity offered by virtual environments *heightens* the salience of social identity, such that de-individuation enhances status effects rather than promotes equality (Matheson 1992; Postmes and Spears 2002; Postmes et al. 1998; Spears and Lea 1992, 1994; Spears et al. 1990; Weisband et al. 1995). For example, the Social Identity model of De-individuation Effects (SIDE) proposes that when social cues are scarce but relevant social identities are known (gender, for example), stereotypical social identity group characteristics will be attributed to individuals and accentuated "because the relative lack of individuation in CMC [computer-mediated communication] can provide a context in which individual differences between group members are ignored because individual distinctions within the group are obscured and less likely to be made" (Tanis and Postmes 2003, p. 679). Consequently, social identity and status can play a role in the numerous facets of virtual group work (Postmes and Spears 2002; Spears and Lea 1992; Weisband et al. 1995). Further, Spears and Lea argue that there is little empirical evidence to support a view that participants are less aware of status differences in a virtual context. They caution the "dangers of romanticizing the effects of CMC by viewing it as a sort of virtual reality where the individual can escape from the strictures of ordinary identity and interaction" (1994, p. 449).

Although research specifically on perceptions of leadership in virtual groups is underway (Miller and Brunner 2008; Misiolek and Heckman 2005; Shollen and Brunner 2009; Wickham and Walther 2007; Yoo and Alavi 2004), limited research on *identity* and perceptions of leadership has been conducted with groups in text-based, virtual learning environments (Sarker et al. 2002). Further, no studies have highly controlled for full participant anonymity. This chapter focuses specifically on virtual learning environments that allow participant's true identity to remain highly anonymous, initially by keeping any identifying information from being revealed, and then by representing participants with avatar (false) photographs.

Now that social media tools allow for teaching and learning in a virtual space that permits identity to be fully hidden, questions arise about impressions of group members. What happens to impressions when information about physical identity is presented after people have worked together for a period of time without identifying information? Specifically, do perceptions of group members *as leaders* change once physical identity is revealed, even after people have had time to form impressions in the absence of identifying cues?

9.3 Methods and Design[1]

This quantitative study addressed the research question: What effect does introducing the physical characteristics of an individual have on other people's perceptions of that individual as a leader in a virtual learning environment, after initial impressions are formed under conditions of anonymity? The study was designed to reveal the extent of the shift in participant perceptions of leadership between a context in which physically identifying cues were absent and one in which they were present.

9.3.1 Participants and Context

About 75% of the 149 participants – graduate students enrolled in one of two virtual leadership courses at a Midwestern research university – self-reported as women and 83% as Caucasian/white. Ages ranged from 21–60 years. (See Table 9.1 for group size and composition.) The courses focused on the relationship between power, identity, and leadership using Experiential Simulations[©].[2] During the online sessions, "interactions occurred in carefully designed leadership/policy forming situations, intended to illustrate how perceptions and understandings of others' identity shape the way leaders enhance or restrict others' participation in

---

[1]Because the data used for this study are a subset of data from a larger study, material in the Methods and Design section is very similar, and at times verbatim, to other works presented, submitted, or published from the larger study.

[2]An online leadership preparation process developed in 2001 by C. Cryss Brunner at the University of Minnesota. For a detailed description of the Experiential Simulations[©] process, see Brunner et al. (2006).

Table 9.1 Number, reported gender, and reported race/ethnicity of participants by group and course type

Group	N	Gender (W:M)	Race/ethnicity (white:of color)
Course 1 – Section 1	15	9:6	13:2
Course 1 – Section 2	12	6:6	10:2
Course 1 – Section 3	11	7:4	9:2
Course 1 – Section 4	9	3:6	7:2
Course 1 – Section 5	8	4:4	7:1
Course 1 – Section 6	7	3:4	5:2
Course 1 – Section 7	10	4:6	9:1
Course 1 – Section 8	9	6:3	7:2
Subtotal	81	42:39	67:14
Course 2 – Section 1	13	13:0	9:4
Course 2 – Section 2	12	12:0	11:1
Course 2 – Section 3	10	10:0	9:1
Course 2 – Section 4	8	8:0	8:0
Course 2 – Section 5	7	7:0	6:1
Course 2 – Section 6	5	4:1	3:2
Course 2 – Section 7	13	13:0	11:2
Subtotal	68	67:1	57:11
Total	149	109:40	124:25

decision-making" (Brunner et al. 2003, p. 75). Upon enrollment, participants were instructed to hide their identities from other participants until a time identified by the instructor.[3]

9.3.2   Study Design

This study focused on the first two sessions of the Experiential Simulations process[©], in which participants logged into a virtual chat space with assigned IDs and passwords – from different, self-chosen, and undisclosed locations – and used only synchronous, text-based communication to work on a group task for 4–5 h per session. For the first session, identities remained fully hidden. Participants did not meet each other before the session and were instructed to avoid identifying themselves in any way during the session. They were identified in the chat space by assigned IDs only; for example, Student10. Between the first and second sessions, participants were given access to electronic photographs that appeared to be of the

---

[3]Participants signed informed consent forms and were made aware that identity would shift as part of the learning experience.

group members. However, unbeknown to the participants, the photographs in use were randomly assigned avatars (faces of other ordinary people in place of the participant's actual faces). Avatars replaced all group member's photographs, except in the case of each individual group member who saw her/his own *true* photograph. In other words, when a participant viewed photographs of the entire class, s/he saw her/his own *true* photo while all other photos were *false* avatars. To be clear, if Kate (pseudonym) was a member of a group, when she viewed the photos of her group she would see her own photo, and the rest of the photos would be avatar photographs that she would assume to be true depictions of the other group members. Participants were instructed not to discuss the photographs or identify themselves in any way during the second session, but were to keep a copy of the photographs adjacent to their computers.

9.3.3 Data Collection

Data were generated and collected from transcripts of chats, threaded discussions between each participant and the course instructor, and an initial on-line interview – all were archived within an online course management system. Specifically, the data came from three sets of reflective questions on issues of power and identity in relation to the group decision-making process.

9.3.4 Data Analysis

As leadership has been defined as the social–perceptual process of being perceived by others as a leader (Lord and Maher 1993), participant perceptions of leadership were analyzed. Given the nature of the questions from which the data for this study were drawn, leadership was operationalized with nominations based on the constructs of directivity and influence (Bass 1990; Northouse 2004). At no time were the terms *directive* and *influential* pre-defined for the participants; thus, they based their responses on their own interpretations.

To determine the effects of physical identity, the perceptions of leadership gathered through reflective questions after session one (when only text-based communication cues were available) were compared to perceptions of leadership gathered after session two (when both text-based communication and physical identity cues were available). After each session, participants were asked to nominate the group member(s) they felt was the most (1) directive, and (2) influential. During data analysis, the dependent variables represented the *change* in proportion of nominations a participant received – from after session one to after session two – for being directive and for being influential. For each participant, after session one and after session two, the proportion of nominations for being directive was calculated as the number of nominations the participant received divided by the total number of nominations that were made in that participant's group. The same calculation was performed to determine the proportion of nominations for being influential after each session. The dependent variables were analyzed as continuous; however, they also were constructed and analyzed as dichotomous to reflect only the direction of change in nominations (increase or decrease).

The independent variables were the physical identity characteristics of the avatar photographs, including gender, race, age, clothing, facial expression, and weight. In some analyses, independent variables also included (1) true gender (as self-reported), and (2) proportion of nominations avatars received for *looking* directive and *looking* influential. (After viewing the photographs but prior to the second session, participants were asked to identify which group member(s) *looks* the most directive and which group member(s) *looks* the most influential, based solely on the photographs.) Analyses-of-variance, and correlation and regression analyses were performed to determine the extent to which physical identity characteristics affected perceptions of leader emergence.

9.4   Results[4]

One-way analysis-of-variance tests were conducted to reveal the relationship between each independent variable, when considered alone, and the two dependent variables (change in proportion of nominations for being directive and for being influential from after session one to after session two). When considered alone, none of the perceived physical characteristics or true gender were statistically significantly related to changes in proportions of nominations for being directive or for being influential.

Pearson correlation analyses with a two-tailed test of significance were performed to elucidate the bivariate relationships between the variables (Table 9.2). Being medium in age was significantly, positively related to having a *change* in proportion of nominations for being directive. Aside from being medium in age, no other physical characteristics were significantly related to a *change* in perceptions of being directive or of being influential from session one to session two. Participants who were perceived as looking directive or as looking influential (via avatars) were more likely to have been perceived as being directive *after session two*. None of the perceived physical characteristic variables were significantly related to perceptions of being directive or being influential *after session two*.

Multiple linear regressions were performed to determine the extent to which the physical characteristics of the avatar photographs predicted changes in proportions of nominations for (1) being directive, and (2) being influential. In both cases, all of the independent variables were entered simultaneously. Neither model proved statistically significant overall, nor were any independent variables in either model

---

[4]Portions of the material in the Results section appeared verbatim previously in Shollen (2009).

Table 9.2 Correlation matrix of all variables

Variables	1	2	3	4	5	6	7	8	9
1 Being directive session 1	—								
2 Being influential session 1	.65***	—							
3 Looking directive	.11	.16	—						
4 Looking influential	.15	.24**	.51***	—					
5 Being directive session 2	.51***	.46***	.22**	.23**	—				
6 Being influential session 2	.47***	.46***	.08	.15	.52***	—			
7 Change in being directive	-.49***	-.19*	.12	.09	.50***	.05	—		
8 Change in being influential	-.29***	-.68***	-.11	-.13	-.05	.34***	.25**	—	
9 Change directive increase	-.05	.13	.19	.14	.65	.27**	.71***	.09	—
10 Change directive decrease	.52***	.27**	-.08	-.05	-.16*	.16	-.69***	-.15	-.52***
11 Change influential increase	-.12	-.37***	.00	-.05	.08	.35***	.20*	.63***	.18*
12 Change influential decrease	.33***	.64***	.09	.12	.10	-.01	-.23**	-.69***	-.04
13 Self-reported gender man	.03	.07	-.09	-.11	.02	.11	-.01	.02	.00
14 Perceived gender man	-.13	-.05	.13	.18*	-.02	.02	.11	.07	.11
15 Perceived race of color	.01	-.06	-.17*	-.03	.00	-.05	-.01	.05	-.03
16 Perceived age medium	-.11	.00	-.02	-.01	.06	.01	.17*	.01	.15
17 Perceived age young	.12	.03	-.14	-.21*	-.03	.01	-.15	-.02	-.15
18 Perceived age old	.01	-.03	.22**	.31***	-.04	-.03	-.05	.01	-.02
19 Perceived clothing business	-.04	.03	.58***	.47***	.04	.07	.08	.03	.04
20 Perceived expression neutral	.00	-.03	.02	.03	.02	-.06	.02	-.02	.02
21 Perceived expression smiling	.06	.03	-.40***	-.19*	-.06	.06	-.12	.03	-.10
22 Perceived expression serious	-.07	.01	.44***	.18*	.05	.00	.12	-.01	.08
23 Perceived weight heavy	.05	.05	-.04	-.11	.07	-.08	.02	-.12	.01
24 Course type the school superintendent	-.02	-.02	-.02	-.02	-.02	-.02	.00	.00	-.03

Variables	10	11	12	13	14	15	16	17	18
10 Change directive decrease	–								
11 Change influential increase	-.13	–							
12 Change influential decrease	.29***	-.69***	–						
13 Self-reported gender man	-.02	-.14	.06	–					
14 Perceived gender man	-.10	.18	-.13	.04	–				
15 Perceived race of color	-.04	-.09	.05	-.01	-.24**	–			
16 Perceived age medium	-.10	-.07	.08	.06	-.06	-.03	–		
17 Perceived age young	.18	.07	.03	-.01	-.27**	.22**	-.77***	–	
18 Perceived age old	-.01	.08	-.17	-.08	.48***	-.26**	-.44***	-.23**	–
19 Perceived clothing business	-.02	.01	.03	-.03	.20*	-.04	.15	-.28**	.16*
20 Perceived expression neutral	.00	-.11	.03	.11	-.21*	.26**	.40***	-.22**	-.31***
21 Perceived expression smiling	.12	.13	-.06	-.05	.00	-.20*	-.19*	.12	.12
22 Perceived expression serious	-.14	-.02	.03	-.08	.26**	-.09	-.28**	.13	.24**
23 Perceived weight heavy	.05	-.11	.01	-.02	.01	-.33***	.06	-.28**	.30***
24 Course type the school superintendent	-.10	-.10	.01	.53***	.14	-.08	.03	-.09	.08

Significance level: $*p < .05$; $**p < .01$; $***p < .001$

significant predictors of the dependent variable. Both models failed to gain significance when the independent variables of proportion of nominations for looking directive and for looking influential were added. With the addition of these variables, however, the independent variable of perceived old age emerged as a significant predictor of change in the proportion of nominations for being directive at the $p < 0.05$ level.

As discussed in the Methods and Design section, four dependent variables that represented a shift up or down in perceptions of being directive and of being influential also were constructed. Chi-squared tests revealed that the only statistically significant relationship between the dichotomous, dependent variables and any of the independent variables was between a decrease in nominations for being influential and perceived old age (Table 9.3). Logistic regressions revealed that none of the models proved statistically significant overall. Independent variables were significant predictors in only two of the models tested; both were models

Table 9.3 Relationship between perceived old age and decrease in nominations for being influential from after session one to after session two

Perceived Old age	N	Decrease in nominations for being influential		
		Yes	No	
		n (%)	n (%)	Total (%)
Yes	17	3 (18)	14 (82)	100
No	132	57 (43)	75 (57)	100
Total	149	60 (40)	89 (60)	100

$X^2 = 4.08, p < .05$

Table 9.4 Logistic regression coefficients for direction of change in proportion of nominations for being directive and in proportion of nominations for being influential

	Directive		Influential	
	Increase	Decrease	Increase	Decrease
Man	.575	−.421	.478	−.248
Person of color	.056	−.400	−.453	.280
Young age	−.810	.846	.082	.067
Old age	−1.302	.513	.884	−2.228*
Business clothing	−.527	.747	.149	−.066
Smiling expression	.027	.193	.268	.483
Serious expression	.601	−.730	−.546	.694
Heavy weight	.310	.231	−1.346*	1.048
The school superintendent course type	−.284	−.458	−.339	.008
Reported gender man	.233	.203	−.642	.444
Looking directive	1.118	−1.125	.940	.759
Looking influential	2.956	−.312	−3.307	4.777*
X^2	11.480	10.360	15.195	15.278

Significance level: *$p < .05$

that included variables for proportion of nominations for looking directive and for looking influential (Table 9.4). Perceived heavy weight was a negative predictor of an increase in proportion of nominations for being influential. Perceived older age was a negative predictor of a decrease in proportion of nominations for being influential.

The analyses indicate that the revealing of age and weight identities may affect changes in perceptions of leadership, and provide a compelling reason for further study of these variables. Judging from the omnibus tests of the regression models, however, perceptions of leadership – compared from after a highly anonymous session to after a session with identity revealed – did not change related to exposure to the physical characteristics of gender, race, age, facial expression, clothing, and weight. Further, perceptions of a person as looking directive or as looking influential did not contribute to changes in perceptions of that person as a leader. It appears from these results that the introduction of physically identifying cues, after groups had worked together anonymously for a period of time in a virtual learning environment, did not affect perceptions of leadership.

9.5   Discussion and Implications

While not fully convincing, the results give some indication that an individual's age and weight may affect other people's perceptions of that individual as a leader after initial impressions have been formed in the absence of identifying cues. The sample size was small when groups were disaggregated by age and weight characteristics, thus the results are provocative but neither generalizable nor conclusive. Although stereotypes and biases do exist based on age and weight (Kite et al. 2005; Puhl and Heuer 2009), and trait theories of leadership have long considered age and weight as traits that may affect leadership (Northouse 2004), there is no conclusive evidence on the effect of age and weight on perceptions of leadership – particularly in virtual environments. Future research that investigates the relationship between perceptions of leadership and the characteristics of age and weight in virtual environments is indicated.

It is remarkable that while age and weight may have affected perceptions of leadership in the virtual learning environment studied, gender did not – at least explicitly. Gender is often the first characteristic noticed and is highly utilized in person perception (Brewer 1996; Stangor et al. 1992). The relationship between gender and perceptions of leadership in face-to-face settings is well-documented (Eagly and Karau 1991; Karau and Eagly 1999; Ritter and Yoder 2004; Walker et al. 1996). Sarker and colleagues (2002) showed that gender played a significant role in perceptions of leadership during the initial stages of group work in a text-based, virtual environment, but not during the later stages. Given the salience of gender identity and the ubiquity of related stereotypes, along with the findings of the current study that gender – once revealed – did not change perceptions of individuals as leaders, further research is needed on gender and perceptions of leadership in virtual learning environments. A complexity to consider is that it may not be possible to extricate fully the effects of one physical characteristic from another (hooks 1989).

The more compelling case made by this study is that impressions that participants formed of others during the first session – based solely on text-based communication – may have been strong enough to prevail over the effect of subsequent exposure to physically identifying cues. Indeed, an analysis of the reasons participants gave for their nominations of leaders after session one were similar to the reasons given after session two. The reasons given pointed to a member's participation in the process rather than to identity (Shollen and Brunner 2009). The findings support Carte and Chidambaram's (2004) theory that when the reductive capabilities of virtual environments – such as visual anonymity – are used early on during group work, the salience of physical and social identity characteristics are reduced; thereby leading participants to focus on the task and judge group members on merit and contributions over identifying characteristics (Lim et al. 2008; Yoo and Alavi 2004). Similarly, Sarker and colleagues (2002) posit that individuals collaborating in a virtual environment in which physical identity is not readily visible may attend less to the known characteristics of others as they become focused on task productivity.

Prior to the revealing of the photographs, participants had only language and paralanguage on which to form impressions of other group members (Burgoon and Miller 1987; Jacobson 1999). The way a person interacted with the group arguably gave individuating information about that individual, even though the information was not about identity. As stereotypes have less of an effect on impressions when observed after individuating information rather than before, the revealing of the photographs may not have changed perceptions that were based on the individuating information gathered (Kunda and Thagard 1996).

The findings of this study align with the impression formation literature (conducted in face-to-face settings) that contends that preliminary impressions persevere (Anderson 1965), and that once initial hypotheses are formed, additional evidence tends to be ignored or misconstrued to support those hypotheses (Rabin and Schrag 1999). The findings also contribute to the literature on impression formation in virtual environments. In an experimental study to examine the influence of social cues on the reduction of ambiguity of impressions, Tanis and Postmes (2003) found that social cues in the form of photographs led participants to feel they had clearer impressions of potential virtual work partners. In their study, the participants had no prior interaction with the people depicted by the photographs. The current study adds the dimension of participants having highly anonymous interactions working on a task prior to exposure to photographs. The results indicate that subsequent exposure to social cues via photographs may not change impressions – at least in terms of leadership. It could be argued, however, that participant perceptions of leadership – although overall unchanged by introduction of the photographs – may have become clearer once social cues could be gleaned from photographs.

The results also support the position that virtual environments can promote de-individuation and status-based equalization (Dubrovsky et al. 1991; Kiesler et al. 1984), in this case with regard to perceptions of leadership. The apparent equalization, however, was preceded by a period of time during which participants interacted with a high degree of anonymity. Without access to social status cues typically used to make assumptions about an individual's leadership potential (Berger et al. 1980), group members could not process information about an individual's identity to form perceptions of leadership. The results do not necessarily contradict the perspectives of scholars who contend that de-individuation enhances status effects (Postmes and Spears 2002; Spears and Lea 1992, 1994). The reasoning is that during the first session social cues were scarce *and* social identity was unknown, thereby leaving very little information on which to base individual attributions of stereotypical group characteristics. By the time social identity (via avatars) was known, participants already had time to form impressions and learn some individuating information regarding how participants interacted.

9.6 Conclusion

This study highly suggests that allowing participants to interact for 4–5 h under highly anonymous conditions in a virtual learning environment played a role in impression formation, such that subsequent revealing of social identity information did not significantly shift perceptions of leadership in the particular context of this study. Questions related to the relationship between length of highly anonymous interaction time, degree of anonymity, impression formation, and status-based equalization in virtual contexts are relevant for teaching and learning in virtual environments. The relationship between interaction time and impression development has been found in groups using asynchronous, text-based, virtual communication over a period of 5 weeks, such that impressions developed more fully as participants exchanged more messages over time. The participants, however, were not instructed to refrain from asking questions or socializing as a means of exchanging potentially individuating information (Walther 1993). Questions for further research in virtual contexts – in particular, virtual learning environments– include: (1) How long must participants interact with scarce social and physical identity cues before lasting impressions are formed? (2) To what extent must social and physical identity cues be initially anonymous in order for the revealing of physical identity not to affect impressions in general, and perceptions of leadership in specific? and (3) Is it possible to create a virtual learning environment that truly achieves status-based equalization (gender, race, age, ...) with regard to leadership and other facets of group work? The current study provides a foundation for future studies that address these questions, by offering preliminary evidence that social media tools can be used to develop learning environments in which diverse learners could be judged less on their physical identities, with regard to leadership.

References

Anderson, N.H.: Primacy effects in personality impression formation using a generalized order effect paradigm. J. Personal. Soc. Psychol. **2**(1), 1–9 (1965)

Ashburn, E.: New data predict major shifts in student population, requiring colleges to change strategies [Electronic version]. The Chronicle of Higher Education. http://chronicle.com/article/New-Data-Predict-Major-Shifts/606/ (2008)

Bass, B.M.: Bass & Stogdill's Handbook of Leadership: Theory, Research, and Managerial Applications, 3rd edn. The Free Press, New York (1990)

Baumgardner, T.L., Lord, R.G., Maher, K.J.: Perceptions of Women in Management. In: Lord, R. G., Maher, K.J. (eds.) Leadership and Information Processing: Linking Perceptions and Performance, pp. 95–113. Routledge, New York (1993)

Bennett, S., Lockyer, L.: Becoming an online teacher: adapting to a changing environment in teaching and learning in higher education. Educ. Media Int. **41**(3), 231–244 (2004)

Berger, J., Rosenholtz, S.J., Zelditch Jr., M.: Status organizing processes. Annual Rev. Sociol. **6**, 479–508 (1980)

Bordia, P.: Face-to-face versus computer-mediated communication: a synthesis of the experimental literature. J. Bus. Commun. **34**(1), 99–120 (1997)

Brewer, M.B.: When stereotypes lead to stereotyping: the use of stereotypes in person perception. In: Macrae, C.N., Stangor, C., Hewstone, M. (eds.) Stereotypes and Stereotyping, pp. 254–275. The Guilford Press, New York (1996)

Brunner, C.C., Hammel, K., Miller, M.D.: Transforming leadership preparation for social justice: dissatisfaction, inspiration, and rebirth – an exemplar. In: Lunenburg, F.C., Carr, C.S. (eds.) Shaping the Future: Policy, Partnerships, and Emerging Perspectives, pp. 70–84. Scarecrow Education, Lanham/Toronto/Oxford (2003)

Brunner, C.C., Opsal, C., Oliva, M.: Disrupting identity: fertile soil for raising social consciousness in educational leaders. In: Marshall, C., Oliva, M. (eds.) Leading for Social Justice: Making Revolutions in Education, pp. 214–232. Sage Publications, Thousand Oaks (2006)

Burgoon, M., Miller, G.R.: An expectancy interpretation of language and persuasion. In: Giles, H., St Clair, R.N. (eds.) Recent Advances in Language, Communication, and Social Psychology, pp. 199–229. Lawrence Erlbaum Associates, Publishers, Hillsdale (1987)

Carte, T., Chidambaram, L.: A capabilities-based theory of technology deployment in diverse teams: leapfrogging the pitfalls of diversity and leveraging its potential with collaborative technology. J. Assoc. Inf. Syst. **5**(11–12), 448–471 (2004)

Collins, A., Halverson, R.: Rethinking Education in the Age of Technology: The Digital Revolution and Schooling in America. Teachers College Press, New York (2009)

Dubrovsky, V.J., Kiesler, S., Sethna, B.N.: The equalization phenomenon: status effects in computer-mediated and face-to-face decision-making groups. Hum. Comput. Interact. **6**(2), 119–146 (1991)

Eagly, A.H., Karau, S.J.: Gender and the emergence of leaders: a meta-analysis. J. Personal. Soc. Psychol. **60**(5), 685–710 (1991)

hooks, b.: Talking Back: Thinking Feminist, Thinking Black. South End Press, Boston (1989)

Jacobson, D.: Impression formation in cyberspace: online expectations and offline experiences in text-based virtual communities. J. Comput.-Mediated Commun, **5**(1) (1999)

Karau, S.J., Eagly, A.H.: Invited reaction: gender, social roles, and the emergence of leaders. Hum. Resour. Dev. Q. **10**(4), 321–327 (1999)

Kezar, A. (ed.): Rethinking Leadership in a Complex, Multicultural, and Global Environment: New Concepts and Models for Higher Education. Stylus Publishing, Sterling (2009)

Kiesler, S., Sproull, L.: Group decision making and communication technology. Org. Behav. Hum. Decis. Process. **52**(1), 96–123 (1992)

Kiesler, S., Siegel, J., McGuire, T.W.: Social psychological aspects of computer-mediated communication. Am. Psychol. **39**(10), 1123–1134 (1984)

Kite, M.E., Stockdale, G.D., Whitley Jr., B.E., Johnson, B.T.: Attitudes toward younger and older adults: an updated meta-analytic review. J. Soc. Issues **61**(2), 241–266 (2005)

Kunda, Z., Thagard, P.: Forming impressions from stereotypes, traits, and behaviors: a parallel-constraint-satisfaction theory. Psychol. Rev. **103**(2), 284–308 (1996)

Lea, M., Spears, R.: Paralanguage and social perception in computer-mediated communication. J. Org. Comput. **2**(3/4), 321–341 (1992)

Lea, M., Spears, R., de Groot, D.: Knowing me, knowing you: anonymity effects on social identity processes within groups. Personal. Soc. Psychol. Bull. **27**(5), 526–537 (2001)

Lim, J., Chidambaram, L., Carte, T.: Impression management and leadership emergence in virtual settings: the role of gender and media. In: JAIS Theory Development Workshop. Sprouts: Working Papers on Information Systems, vol. 8, p. 22. Paris (2008)

Lord, R.G., Maher, K.J.: Leadership and Information Processing: Linking Perceptions and Performance. Routledge, New York (1993)

Mackie, D.M., Hamilton, D.L., Susskind, J., Rosselli, F.: Social psychological foundations of stereotype formation. In: Macrae, C.N., Stangor, C., Hewstone, M. (eds.) Stereotypes and Stereotyping, pp. 44–71. The Guilford Press, New York (1996)

Matheson, K.: Women and computer technology: communicating for herself. In: Lea, M. (ed.) Contexts of Computer-Mediated Communication, pp. 66–88. Harvester Wheatsheaf, Hemel Hempstead (1992)

Miller, M.D., Brunner, C.C.: Social impact in technologically-mediated communication: an examination of online influence. Comput. Hum. Behav. **24**(6), 2972–2991 (2008)

Misiolek, N.I., Heckman, R.: Patterns of emergent leadership in virtual teams. In: 38th Hawaii International Conference on System Sciences, Waikoloa (2005)

Morey, A.I.: Globalization and the emergence of for-profit higher education. High. Educ. **48**(1), 131–150 (2004)

Northouse, P.G.: Leadership: Theory and Practice, 3rd edn. Sage Publications, Inc., Thousand Oaks (2004)

Nye, J.L., Forsyth, D.R.: The effects of prototype-based biases on leadership appraisals: a test of leadership categorization theory. Small Group Res. **22**(3), 360–379 (1991)

Postmes, T., Spears, R.: Behavior online: does anonymous computer communication reduce gender inequality? Personal. Soc. Psychol. Bull. **28**(8), 1073–1083 (2002)

Postmes, T., Spears, R., Lea, M.: Breaching or building social boundaries? SIDE-effects of computer-mediated communication. Commun. Res. **25**(6), 689–715 (1998)

Puhl, R.M., Heuer, C.A.: The stigma of obesity: a review and update. Obesity **17**(5), 941–964 (2009)

Rabin, M., Schrag, J.L.: First impressions matter: a model of confirmatory bias. Q. J. Econ. **114**(1), 37–82 (1999)

Ritter, B.A., Yoder, J.D.: Gender differences in leader emergence persist even for dominant women: an updated confirmation of role congruity theory. Psychol. Women Q. **28**(3), 187–193 (2004)

Sarker, S., Grewal, R., Sarker, S.: Emergence of leaders in virtual teams: what matters? In: 35th Hawaii International Conference on System Sciences, Waikoloa (2002)

Shollen, S.L.: Perceptions of gender and leader emergence in computer-mediated decision-making. Unpublished Doctoral Dissertation, University of Minnesota, Minneapolis (2009)

Shollen, S.L., Brunner, C.C.: Leader emergence in virtual groups: effects of text-based communication under highly anonymous conditions. In: Annual Meeting of the American Educational Research Association, San Diego (2009)

Siegel, J., Dubrovsky, V., Kiesler, S., McGuire, T.W.: Group processes in computer-mediated communication. Org. Behav. Hum. Decis. Process. **37**(2), 157–187 (1986)

Spears, R., Lea, M.: Social influence and the influence of 'social' in computer-mediated communication. In: Lea, M. (ed.) Contexts of Computer-Mediated Communication, pp. 30–65. Harvester Wheatsheaf, Hemel Hempstead (1992)

Spears, R., Lea, M.: Panacea or panopticon? the hidden power in computer-mediated communication. Commun. Res. **21**(4), 427–459 (1994)

Spears, R., Lea, M., Lee, S.: De-individuation and group polarization in computer-mediated communication. Br. .J. Soc. Psychol. **29**, 121–134 (1990)

Stangor, C., Lynch, L., Duan, C., Glass, B.: Categorization of individuals on the basis of multiple social features. J. Personal. Soc. Psychol. **62**(2), 207–218 (1992)

Tanis, M., Postmes, T.: Social cues and impression formation in CMC. J. Commun. **53**(4), 676–693 (2003)

Taylor, P.G.: Institutional change in uncertain times: lone ranging is not enough. Stud. High. Educ. **23**(3), 269–279 (1998)

Walker, H.A., Ilardi, B.C., McMahon, A.M., Fennell, M.L.: Gender, interaction, and leadership. Soc. Psychol. Q. **59**(3), 255–272 (1996)

Walther, J.B.: Impression development in computer-mediated interaction. West. J. Commun. **57**(4), 381–398 (1993)

Weisband, S.P., Schneider, S.K., Connolly, T.: Computer-mediated communication and social information: status salience and status differences. Acad. Manage. J. **38**(4), 1124–1151 (1995)

Wickham, K., Walther, J.B.: Perceived behaviors of emergent and assigned leaders in virtual groups. Int. J. e-Collab. **3**(1), 1–17 (2007)

Yoo, Y., Alavi, M.: Emergent leadership in virtual teams: what do emergent leaders do? Inf. Org. **14**(1), 27–58 (2004)

Chapter 10
Virtual Worlds: Spaces for Education or Places for Play?

Christopher Clarke

Abstract Virtual worlds are gaining in popularity day by day, for a variety of uses. This chapter explores the current and potential applications of 3-D virtual learning environments and the barriers to their potential expansion into a mainstream educational tool. A brief history of virtual worlds is given, followed by an examination into current research on their educational applications, a discussion of the research project undertaken here, and a look at the potential developments of virtual worlds in education. The research study involved the observation of four participants who were new to virtual worlds and analyzing their first 10 h of immersion in both Second-Life (SL) and World of Warcraft (WOW). The findings revealed that each participant preferred the game play based WOW, that none sought out educational opportunities within SL, and that what they did experience there was mostly negative.

10.1 The Synthetic and the Virtual: New Worlds to Explore

Virtual or synthetic worlds, Massively Multiplayer Online Role Playing Games, Multi User Dungeons, and virtual reality, all of these terms refer broadly to the same thing: online persistent environments in which multiple individuals are free to act and interact in a variety of ways. From the early 1980s, experiments such as Multi User Dungeons (MUDs) to EverQuest, WOW and SL, There, and Active Worlds, these environments have evolved and developed, creating a new culture and the potential to alter the way people communicate and socialize, as well as teach and learn. Environments that can simulate anything imaginable and put a user in that situation; that can present information in all forms of media; and that can be used to create virtual constructs of any design are all on the horizon or already here – are we

C. Clarke (✉)
Business school, Nankai University, Tianjin, People's Republic of China
e-mail: cpclarke123@gmail.com

B. White et al. (eds.), *Social Media Tools and Platforms in Learning Environments*,
DOI 10.1007/978-3-642-20392-3_10, © Springer-Verlag Berlin Heidelberg 2011

witnessing a revolution in education? This study examined the potential for virtual worlds to become ubiquitous, ways of accessing information and interacting with others by examining the ways new users interacted with both the game play WOW and non-game play SL, and compared the two. It aimed to identify the barriers that prevent virtual worlds opening to a wider audience. The positives that could help were also considered, while determining whether game play based worlds or open-ended creative worlds are more appealing to the average non-user.

10.2   A Brief History of Virtual Time

The big bang of virtual worlds came with the creation of the first Multi User Dungeon or MUD in 1980 by Richard Bartle and Roy Trubshaw at Essex University (Taylor 2006). Inspired by the table-top Dungeons and Dragons role-playing games that were popular at the time they developed a primitive text-based virtual world which users could log onto through the university's network and interact with other users by entering commands. This was popular with computer programmers throughout the 1980s and led to them looking for new ways to exploit the networking technology. In 1986, Lucasarts created a graphical online virtual world called "Habitat" which allowed its users to have property and complete quests in a 2-D rendered environment. From then on, the technology evolved through gradual advances in design until TinyMUD in 1989. This changed the dynamic of virtual worlds by placing the emphasis on object creation and socialization with other users, rather than combat and role-play which had dominated previous attempts. This would pave the way for the later emergence of worlds like SL, There, and Active Worlds.

In 1997, Ultima Online was released and became the most popular virtual world ever, with 100,000 subscribers reached quickly (Taylor 2006) and enough longevity that it is still running today. This was a fantasy based two dimensional world which gained good reviews and attention within the gaming community. The appeal of Massively Multiplayer Online Role Playing Games (MMORPGS) was broadened further with the release of Sony Online Entertainment's EverQuest in 1999. This added the third dimension to the graphical appearance of virtual worlds and led to it eclipsing Ultima Online in terms of subscriptions. In 2003, Linden Labs launched SL, which has gone on to become the most popular and recognizable non-game play based virtual world and one of the worlds chosen for use in this study. This was followed in 2004 by the release of WOW by Blizzard Entertainment, which would go on to become, by some distance, the most popular MMORPG of all time and see a movement of virtual worlds from niche hobby to mainstream form of entertainment. New developments are occurring rapidly and new worlds are released all the time, with worlds based on Star Trek and Star Wars, two of the real worlds' largest media franchises, either recently released or due to be released soon.

10.3   Education and Learning in a Virtual Reality

Virtual worlds have long been seen as interesting environments for sociological research, as they develop their own economies, societies, and cultures (Castronova 2005; Taylor 2006), but the popularity of SL brought an explosion of interest from educators keen to harness the potential of a world that gave creative freedom to its users and didn't try to get them to hunt Orcs or shoot their friends' spaceships. There are now over 700 educational institutions operating in-world, and the number is growing by the day (Simteach Wiki 2010), and with virtual worlds now being perceived in a more serious light, their myriad educational applications are becoming apparent.

A virtual world allows for the replication and simulation of environments and situations which, in reality, may hold dangers or costs that make them prohibitive. Simulations of various natural and man-made disasters have already been conducted in virtual worlds in order to give some sense of the pandemonium and various hazards that may have impact on the work of rescue workers or victims of these scenarios (Foster 2007). Play2Train and Virtual Public Health offer disaster management training in-world and have run scenarios on flu pandemics and other emergency preparedness procedures using scripts built within SL (Play2Train 2010; University of Illinois 2009). Historical sites have been recreated abd users can effectively travel to recreations of anywhere in the world at any time in history. Architecture departments at universities have long been using SL to build 3-D representations of designs (Fang and Lee 2009). In less extreme scenarios, virtual worlds have already been used to provide virtual tours of existing places to allow people to familiarize themselves with places before they go there, such as potential Hajj pilgrims, thus preventing any dangers that may arise from large numbers of people congregating in a new environment (Widyarto and Latiff 2007). This simulation also stretches to role-play. Powerful avatar creation tools allow users to become anyone they like within world. They can take on new hairstyles, new clothing, a new race or gender, or even a new species and experience what it is like to interact in a different manner. Language learners can also log in and use VOIP to interact with native speakers and explore cultural information resources from across the world.

The 3-D virtual space provided by worlds such as SL allows for collaboration in ways 2-D environments simply cannot. Lectures can be given and virtually attended by interested parties from across the world, meetings can be held in representations of board rooms using multimedia presentations, and training classes demonstrating all manner of things can take place in a simulation of anywhere imaginable. "Attendance" involves merely logging in and searching for the right virtual space. Distance learning is transformed by the technology, by allowing students, who would normally have to meet up for seminars in the real world, to avoid the necessary complications associated with this. Virtual worlds also allow for disparate communities to come together and share their ideas in environments in which they are comfortable (Abeles 2007; Tebbutt 2007), and are in theory never closed, environmental friendly, and can pool global knowledge in one space (Morris 2008).

SL also allows learners to collaborate in their learning in a productive manner, by being able to manipulate the world and adding their own input and information (Cheal 2007; Steinkuehler and Squire 2009). The potential for collaboration within the business world is also being explored by Aalto University's VinCo and ProViWo projects, which aim to monitor the performance of geographically dispersed teams within virtual environments (Aalto University 2004-2008). Once the tools of virtual worlds are mastered, they offer learners the ability to make their own worlds. Anything can be constructed there, from avatars of historical figures to buildings of the distant future, and this flexibility can lead to highly experimental learning methods that are prohibited in the real world by cost and the laws of physics.

Librarians have become a prominent educational prescence in SL as they look to utilize the world to deliver information services, provide reference and enquiry desks, and support other educational endeavors (Blankenship and Hollingsworth 2009; Hill and Lee 2009; Hurst-Wahl 2007; Ostrander 2008; Tebbutt 2007). The Info Islands utilize the skills of over 400 librarians to respond to virtual reference enquiries and assist in-world users in meeting their information needs (Abram 2007). Librarians are also creating virtual exhibits for anything from artworks to architecture at a fraction of their real world costs (Hill and Lee 2009). Interactive games have been developed that help educate about nutrition and genetics, and there exists even a heart murmur simulation, allowing medical students to listen to various heart murmurs and put into practice their knowledge in a safe environment (Kamel Boulos et al. 2007). They have also been used to help doctors understand the hallucinations of schizophrenia patients by replicating them within the virtual environments (Yellowlees and Cook 2006) and to help individuals understand the effects on neurological disability through simulating them on their avatar (Kamel Boulos et al. 2007) (Fig. 10.1).

Education has now become such an important application of SL that Linden Labs has recently launched its own educational portal for educators to find the information they need to help set up their own virtual institution (SL Education Directory: http://education.secondlife.com), offering support for Twitter and blogging, and educators themselves have collaborated on a wiki project to share

Fig. 10.1 The location of the heart murmur simulation designed to educate and train medical students in SL

ideas and locate in-world educational opportunities (Sim Teach Wiki: http://www. simteach.com).

Of concern is the potential for the exposure of students to sexual content, and other disruptive behavior or influences which occur in SL as they do in the real world (Sidorko 2009). Harassment can take place as users hide behind the apparent anonymity of their avatars, and "griefers" have been known to interrupt presentations and interviews in a variety of colorful ways. Teen SecondLife moves around these problems to an extent, and improved policies and security can help make the world as safe as possible, but in a free-form world designed to be creative, the potential for mischief still exists.

10.4   Methodology

The main goal of the research was to examine how new users interacted with virtual worlds to determine what barriers to immersion they came across, and therefore what barriers to an expansion of the audiences beyond the traditional core users exist. It was also a stated aim to examine the differences in users' perceptions of, and feelings toward, game play based worlds and open-ended worlds. In order to do this, four participants were chosen using a convenience sample of availability due to the investment of time required, and the difficulty of identifying participants with no previous experience of virtual worlds. The only criterion other than availability and willingness necessary in participants was no previous experience of virtual world environments; other than these they ran the full spectrum of information literacy, differences of age and gender, and different levels of apathy toward virtual environments.

Participants were asked to immerse themselves in two virtual worlds, SL and WOW, for five 2-h sessions, for a total of 10 h in each world. With regards to the 10 h spent in WOW, all participants created their characters on the same USA based server, Aggramar, for the purpose of unifying the experiences of the server culture for each participant. This server is categorized as player versus environment, rather than player versus player, meaning that players from either side cannot engage each other in combat unless certain criteria are met or they are in certain zones, and it is also non-role-playing, meaning that during interactions the participants would not be expected to act in character. In SL, all users are present on the same server with the same general set of rules with regard to interaction with other users.

SL and WOW were chosen as opposed to other worlds because of their higher user numbers and therefore relative success in attracting and keeping "players." WOW is the leading MMORPG on the market, and SL is the leading non-game play world, and both by some distance. The two worlds differ in several key aspects with regards to structure, design, and experience. WOW is specifically designed around video game parameters, with a quest structure in place in order to keep users playing and paying, whereas SL is focused on the creation of 3-D objects and socializing within a virtual economy and community. Participants were asked to engage with the worlds in any way they saw fit with the only guidance being in the form of short statements outlining the nature of each world. They were free to pursue any goals to which they felt drawn and to choose to interact with other users or engage in solo play. Within SL, they were not given the specific locations of any points of interest, but were told they could use in-world navigation tools or the Internet to locate them.

Data were collected through a variety of methods. Before immersing themselves, participants completed an open ended questionnaire about their preconceptions of virtual worlds. The first 2 h and last 2 h of immersion in each world were observed using non-participant overt observation and extensive notes were taken based on a set of predetermined criteria. Participants were also asked to complete an online diary detailing their actions in-world and their feelings about their experiences (available for viewing at: *http://virtualworldsdiss.blogspot.com*). After the 20 h (ten in WOW, ten in SL), post-immersion questionnaires were completed and 20 min interviews were conducted to compliment them and expand on any points of interest from the observational periods or diaries.

During the observation sessions, the researchers noted any instances of the following broad criteria, as well as any other notable events or responses: Deviation from guided paths; Identification; and implementation of in-world terminologies.

Interaction with other users within the environment and reaction to interactions; Response to stimuli elicited within the world; Improvements made to or care taken with avatar appearance; Identification of goals and objectives and subjects' use for their time in the world; Use of outside/community resources to complete task or desire to do so. The interviews and questionnaires asked participants about their opinions of the worlds and their users, their enjoyment of the worlds and the differences between the two styles, any interactions they had, and any surprises they encountered.

10.5 Results

The clearest result of the comparison between SL and WOW was the preference that all participants had for WOW's game play environments over the less structured non-game play world of SL. This was unanimously expressed, and in the observation sessions it was clearly seen in the responses of the participants to the situations and stimuli encountered within the worlds. While in SL, all users sought out some form of game or activity that allowed them to feel the sense of achievement offered by WOW, and viewed the world on the same terms without exploring the other uses it could have. Two users attempted to earn money in order to buy in game items while others wandered with the aim of activating a game. None attempted to travel to areas offering education or learning facilities or programs beyond the initial tutorial which trains users how to use their avatar and how to navigate the world.

The major barriers that appeared in SL were the lack of obvious goals and game play elements, a confusing and over-complicated user interface, the less appealing "home-made" appearance of the world, the time and cost required to sufficiently enjoy the environment, and the image of users of the worlds and of usage in itself that appears to currently reside in mainstream society. Participants clearly preferred the stylized and carefully constructed world that Warcraft presented rather than anything that goes by the look of SL, which can in places and on less powerful machines look homemade (as it is). Leveling up the player character appealed to the more competitive-minded participants and all of them spent their time in SL attempting to find games to engage with or activities which had end goals. Previous to their time within the worlds and even after their immersion, the participants highlighted a perception of virtual worlds as *"geeky"* and of users as *"people who spend a lot of time alone… people without a life"* and said that this was one reason for them not having engaged with worlds previously and even for having avoided interaction during their immersion time. Indeed, it would seem that a major barrier to the participant's entry to the worlds previous to the study was this perception they had of them. They unanimously believed that users of virtual worlds chose to spend time there because their real lives were unsatisfactory in some way, and so viewed them in a negative light.

The Massively Multiplayer aspect of the worlds only had any real appeal for one participant, with the others finding the experience of approaching strangers sometimes intimidating and often, a little strange. The interviews, however, revealed this may have been a result of a lack of understanding with regards to the norms and values of the environment and the preconceptions the participants had of online interaction and the users of MMORPGS and virtual worlds. This may have also been an aspect of the participant's preference for WOW over SL, as SL is designed primarily as a creative and social space for its inhabitants. Two of the participants also stated that they would only consider going back into SL if some of their friends used the world as a communication tool over distances. This suggests that social networks could influence the non-user to enter virtual worlds, and that as they become more ubiquitous, more people could be drawn to them.

Several implications for short-term educational opportunities within virtual worlds and, SL in particular, can be drawn from this study. When attempting to offer courses or education within SL to those with little or no experience of non-game play virtual worlds, it is important to provide enough tutorial time that learners can familiarize themselves with how to use the technology. The control systems in both SL and WOW can be off-putting to new users unfamiliar with such interfaces and without the motivation to learn all of their complexities. In the future, users will have become more attuned to using complex computer programs when compared to the current older generation (including one participant from this study) and will therefore not be as daunted by the level of understanding required.

Interface problems and the complexity of interacting in virtual spaces could be reduced by the new generation of instruments currently entering the video game market. Sony has recently released "PlayStation Move," a similar controller to the Wii's now-famous remote that combines with cameras to produce even more interactional opportunities, and Microsoft's "Kinect" system uses sensors and cameras to capture body movements and translate them to onscreen avatar movements: "You are the Controller" as the tag line goes (Microsoft 2010; Sony 2010). These are the interfaces of today, not tomorrow, and their integration with virtual worlds such as SL will inevitably lead to myriad new educational applications, all within the reach of educational institutions as regards cost. Indeed, the Wii-mote can already be used in SL with a few open source hacks.

Two of the participants encountered virtual exhibits in areas where information could be extracted and found the experience sterile and *not as good as a real gallery or museum*. It appears that the graphics and construction are not evolved enough to enthrall the casual visitor. In order to engage learners fully and meet their expectation that simulated computer environments are equivalent to video games, any educational simulations or experiences should incorporate aspects of game design. When using virtual worlds in the curriculum, educators should seek to combine aspects of the game play based worlds with the creative freedom offered by worlds such as SL. Tasks should be given and the learning experience should be as engaging and immersive as possible. By combining a quest structure and reward generation with relevant educational settings and content, student interest is more likely to be maintained. Each student in a class or on a course could be assigned an avatar with which to participate in all their virtual classes, and would keep the rewards and develop their character as they progress through the course. Rewarding successfully answered pop-quizzes with virtual loot and leveling their avatar with each successful exam or class attended would motivate those users who otherwise might be put off by the world's complexity.

One aspect of both worlds that appealed to all participants was the creation of their avatar. All of them spent at least 30 min in SL crafting their appearance, and expressed their enjoyment of it in their post-immersion interviews and questionnaires. Despite the relative complexity of the program facilitating the avatar design, the time required for them to be satisfied with the result was not an issue. This indicates that the creative aspects of SL may have a wider appeal if simplified for the user and presented to them in an easier manner, and for creative students the possibilities may outweigh the difficulties already (Fig. 10.2).

Fig. 10.2 Tomorrows university? The SL campus of Edinburgh University

Overcoming the image problem of virtual worlds is also hopefully only a matter of time. As their use in education grows, and new generations grow up used to interacting in these sorts of environments, they will move into mainstream acceptance. With rudimentary 2-D worlds such as Maple Story and even to some extent Farmville and Mafia Wars attracting unprecedented numbers of users, it appears as if this is already happening. The number of devices capable of access is growing all the time (SL is already accessible from certain mobile phones and Xbox and PlayStation) and the process of gaining access is becoming simplified. This, coupled with the growth in user numbers, should allow the negative image of users to be shed, much as it appears the once "geeky" image of video games players has diminished.

10.6   The Present and the Future: The Possibilities Are Endless

The barriers pinpointed by this study represent a challenge to the integration of virtual worlds into contemporary education. The complexity of the interface, the preconceptions of non-users of the worlds and their inhabitants, the time required to properly engage with the worlds, the costs, and the nature of social interaction within them all inhibit potential users and negatively affect their use in the classroom. On a positive note, the game play elements of WOW such as leveling a character and achieving in-world goals were attractive and could potentially be incorporated into future generations of educational worlds. The appeal of the avatar creation, parts of both WOW and SL, also suggests that creativity is something that non-users would be interested in, if it were simpler.

For now, virtual worlds such as SL present a new frontier of educational opportunities, and while not without its flaws, the chances to collaborate, simulate, and experiment are many. The benefits of the technology for language students, medical students, architects, and distance learners are already being explored and are obvious, but new potential ideas may have yet to be considered. By adding game play elements into course designs and simulations, educators can help maintain the interest of learners and maybe even foster a desire for them to spend more time in world, as this study demonstrates the frustrations of the experience for the casual user. Interfaces in future generations of worlds will no doubt be simplified, and come with better tools of access, and as new technologies further add to it, virtual worlds clearly have a chance of becoming key areas of many curricula.

Future research should focus on the positive aspects of worlds such as SL and examine how the creative aspects can be simplified and harnessed by relatively casual users. The impact of the barriers identified in this research for the casual user should be measured on the more intense users of SL and WOW. Identifying how they cope with these constructs that put-off the more casual users and what motivates them to initially overcome them may help in developing new worlds which can appeal to a wider audience and help to engage students in virtual classrooms. As the technology develops, the opportunities for educating in these spaces will no doubt increase. The realism achievable will only increase and with that the level of immersion and appeal to the user. Students could log in from across the world to partake in history classes that recreate the battle of Waterloo, drama classes that involve playing a part in Romeo and Juliet at the Globe Theatre, or French classes in a perfect recreation of Paris. They could create and grow their own course avatars to reflect their standing in the class and take them out into other virtual worlds to show their friends. By engaging the learner in a fun, interesting, and simple manner the barriers identified in this study can be overcome and the potential for educating can be realized in fantastical ways that are unachievable in the real classroom at a relatively low cost. While the present clearly has its limitations, the future is virtually limitless in its possibilities.

References

Aalto University: Virtual and mobile work research unit – vmwork. www.vmwork.net

Abeles, T.: Synthetic worlds and the university: approaching the unknown. On the Horiz. 15(1), 3–6 (2007)

Abram, S.: At second life, info pros will find much to see, do, learn, play with try out. Inf. Outlook 11(4), 34–36 (2007)

Blankenship, Emily, Hollingsworth, Y.: Balancing both lives: issues facing librarians working in second life and real life worlds. New Libr. World 110(9/10), 430–440 (2009)

Castronova, E.: Synthetic Worlds: The Business and Culture of Online Worlds. The University of Chicago Press, Chicago (2005)

Cheal, C.: Second life: hype or hyperlearning? On the Horiz. 15(4), 204–210 (2007)

Fang, Y.S., Lee, L.S.: A review and synthesis of recent research in second life. Interact. Technol. Smart Educ. 6(4), 261–267 (2009)

Foster, A.L.: Teaching geography in second life. Chron. High. Educ. 54(10), 36 (2007)

Hill, V., Lee, H.J.: Libraries and immersive learning environments unite in second life. Libr. Hi Tech 27(3), 338–356 (2009)

Hurst-Wahl, J.: Librarians and second life. Inf. Outlook 11(6), 45–50 (2007)

Kamel Boulos, M.N., Hetherington, L., Wheeler, S.: Second life: an overview of the potential of 3-D virtual worlds in medical and health education. Health Infor. Libr. J. 24(4), 233–245 (2007)

Microsoft: Microsoft Xbox Kinect. http://www.xbox.com/en-us/kinect

Morris, S.: Virtual team working: making it happen. Ind. Commer. Train. 40(3), 129–133 (2008)

Ostrander, M.: Talking, looking, flying searching: information seeking behaviour in second life. Libr. Hi Tech 26(4), 512–524 (2008)

Play2Train: Play2train. http://www.play2train.org

Sidorko, P.E.: Virtually there almost: educational and informational possibilities in virtual worlds. Libr. Manage. 30(6/7), 404–418 (2009)

Simteach: Second life education wiki. http://www.simteach.com

Sony: Sony playstation move. http://us.playstation.com/ps3/playstation-move/index.htm

Steinkuehler, C., Squire, K.: Virtual worlds and Learning. On the Horiz. 17(1), 8–11 (2009)

Taylor, T.L.: Play between Worlds: Exploring Online Game Culture. MIT Press, Cambridge (2006)

Tebbutt, D.: Brave new worlds. Infor. World Rev. 233, 12 (2007)

University of Illinois: Virtual public health. www.virtualpublichealth.com

Widyarto, S., Latiff, Muhammad Shafie Abd: The use of virtual tours for cognitive preparation of visitors: a case study for VHE. Facilities **25**(7/8), 271–285 (2007)

Yellowlees, P.M., Cook, J.N.: Education about hallucinations using an internet virtual reality system: a qualitative survey. Acad. Psychiatry **30**(6), 534–539 (2006)

Part IV
Assessment

Chapter 11
Social Network Tools for the Assessment of the University Web Performance

José Luis Ortega and Isidro F. Aguillo

Abstract This chapter introduces Webometrics as an emerging discipline focused on the understanding and assessment of the flow of Web based academic information. It describes the principal web-based techniques and tools used to evaluate the performance of higher education websites and to explain how these information networks are created and modelled. The chapter begins with an introduction to Webometrics: its origin and evolution, its theoretical framework and its relationship with other web disciplines. The principal indicators and measures used to quantify the development of several web units (web domains, sites and pages) are described. Emphasis is placed on the properties of social-network measures in order to describe the visibility of a web site and to characterise the structure of a web space. Major developments, such as the Ranking of World universities on the Web and visualisations of web regions, are considered. Finally, there is a discussion about the implications of this discipline on the improvement of web performance and visibility of the university institutions on the Web and its impact on the development of the higher education web-based policies according to open access and e-learning initiatives.

Webometrics: a discipline devoted to the quantification of the performance of the Web

Webometrics is a young discipline born around the mid-1990s with the seminal work of Almind and Ingwersen (1997) and the creation of the first specialised e-journal on webometric studies, *Cybermetrics*. It emerged at a moment when the

J.L. Ortega (✉)
R&D Unit, VICYT, CSIC, Madrid, Spain
e-mail: jortega@orgc.csic.es

I.F. Aguillo
Cybermetrics Lab, CCHS-CSIC, Madrid, Spain
e-mail: isidro@cindoc.csic.es

B. White et al. (eds.), *Social Media Tools and Platforms in Learning Environments*,
DOI 10.1007/978-3-642-20392-3_11, © Springer-Verlag Berlin Heidelberg 2011

Web had gained credibility within the academic world and emerged as a new and powerful way to communicate scientific results. As scientometrics is focussed on the assessment of print-based communication processes (papers, patents, citations), Webometrics targets web-based communication units such as web domains, pages and hyperlinks as a way to understand new scientific activities including those unrelated to the print world. Thus, Webometrics is defined as 'the study of the quantitative aspects of the construction and use of information resources, structures and technologies on the Web drawing on bibliometric and informetric approaches' (Björneborn and Ingwersen 2004). Early work focussed on the research evaluation, seeking relationships between web production and visibility with scientific activity and impact. Thus, a strong correlation was found between the web pages/link ratio and the scores of the research assessment exercises in the United Kingdom and Australia (Smith and Thelwall 2002; Thelwall 2001). Significant relationship was also found between links and journal citations (Vaughan and Thelwall 2003) and between web-based university rankings and rankings built on bibliometric data (Aguillo et al. 2006). These papers gave the discipline credibility, enabling an understanding of the non-formal scientific communication process on the Web and relationships with other scientific outputs (papers, books, patents). The growth of the Web and the incorporation of these traditional formats to the Web prompted the appearance of studies about formal scientific communication on the Web such as the impact of e-journals (Harter and Ford 2000), scientific repositories (Antelman 2004) and web-based citation indexes (Google Scholar, Scirus) (Bar-Ilan 2008).

One of the most concerning issues related to the Web studies was the reliability of the data sources used to develop quantitative analysis and the meaning of the results obtained. Basically, search engines and crawler data were used to carry out web researches. The appearance of AltaVista in 1995 and its search operators suggested that the search engines may be used as a web citation index (Rodriguez Gairín 1997). Later, several studies showed that the search engines were unstable along short time periods (Rousseau 1998); their operators were weak and their databases frequently outdated (Sullivan 2003). Other contributions detected linguistic biases in non-Latin languages (Bar-Ilan 2005) and a low overlap between search engines (Lawrence and Giles 1998). This situation favoured the use of web crawlers, customised for the harvesting process and direct extraction of exhaustive information about a website. This approach consumed much time and technical resources. In addition, it was difficult to extract and follow links from non-textual formats (Chakrabarti 2002). Following the search engines war of 2003, the largest engines improved in stability and their search operators reported more consistent results (Bar-Ilan and Peritz 2009). Thus, search engine data are used to develop broad scope studies. In this way, it is possible to obtain huge amounts of quantitative data at the level of countries and domains, while the crawler data are suitable to carry out micro studies on web sites and link content.

However, Webometrics has to face the volatile nature of the Web in which the contents appear, change and vanish in a short time period (Ortega et al. 2006) and where a rate of web page disappearance of 0.25–0.50% per week is evidence of a fast changing world (Fetterly et al. 2003). This instability attracted the attention of many studies that sought to understand such phenomena, investigating the ephemeral existence of incoming links in e-journals (Harter and Kim 1996), web citations in scientific repositories (Lawrence et al. 2001) and web content decay (Payne and Thelwall 2008). These studies can be defined as Web demography because they observe the web as a population of contents that are born, grow and die. There are studies that calculate the age of the Web (Ortega et al. 2009) the ratio of change of web pages (Cho et al. 2000) or the death of web pages (Koehler et al. 2004).

The analysis of the information usage of web sites has attracted early attention from business and commercial web sites interested in gathering and processing information about the behaviour of their customers (Gomory et al. 1999) as an extension of the data mining techniques applied to their client databases. This field has not been exploited in depth by scholars as a result of the difficulty of obtaining the log data and comparing similar patterns of different web log sources. Several works focussed on analysing the search skill and attitudes of the principal search engine users such as AltaVista (Silverstein et al. 1998), Excite and Alltheweb (Jansen et al. 2005) and Yahoo! (Teevan et al. 2006), while others targeted methodological problems such as the definition of web sessions and the advantages of using them instead of the number of hits. Data mining was used for the identification of web sessions; to estimate their duration and their length in clicks (Pitkow et al. 1997); to classify content according to the pages requested by their visitors (Wang and Zaiane 2002) and to show navigational differences between different points of access (Ortega and Aguillo 2010).

Recently, a new way of understanding web services and relationships has emerged, the so-called Web 2.0 Boyd and Ellison (2007). In this new paradigm, the Web is becoming a way of collaborative creation of content in which the freely active web surfers contribute personal experiences and own the content. This favours the emergence of web sites where the personal interaction in the content design and the participative relationships between those users is the focus. This new environment gives the opportunity to study how online environments affect social relationships (Lenhart and Madden 2007); what structural differences exist with other large-scale networks (Kumar et al. 2006); and what content characterise these networks (Thelwall 2008).

11.1 Structural Indicators: Social Network Measures as Web Indicators

The Web is essentially a huge network of interconnected webpages through hyperlinks which allow navigation of sites and domains across world. The degree of interconnection of a web site makes possible to be reached by potential users, as the more incoming links (visibility) a web site receives, the larger is the likelihood that it achieves visitors (popularity). Furthermore, if the link popularity of the websites connected to the nominated site is higher, the probability of being located and visited increases. Hence, not only is it important to be connected but also to know who are creating the links. Understanding this structural characteristic of the Web is essential to understand the position and successful of a web site. So, the use of the Social Network Analysis (SNA) has been crucial for in-depth assessment of web sites.

11.1.1   The Web as a Graph

When Tim Berners-Lee gave the name 'World Wide Web' to the hypertextual information system developed in the CERN (*Conseil Européen pour la Recherche Nucléaire*), he sensed that the system would be a complex web-shape network in which each html document would be a node connected to the whole repository through hyperlinks. But what would be the shape of that network? And what importance would be the shape of that system? The large size of the Web, in number of pages and links, and the ease of harvesting this information through web crawlers attracted the attention of many scientists who sought to empirically observe if the Web followed a random network shape. They were surprised to discover that there was not a constant parameter or scale in the degree distribution such as in random networks but rather a potential distribution (power law), in which there are a small number of highly connected nodes while the remaining ones have barely a few links (Barabási and Albert 1999). These scale-free networks also show a high clustering coefficient and a short average path length as the small world networks. This means that the Web is a decentralised environment where there are a high density of links and where highly connected nodes (hubs) supporting that density emerge. Barabási and Albert (1999) suggested that the formation and evolution of the scale-free networks results from the 'preferential attachment' phenomenon, which states that the best connected nodes are more likely to obtain new links than the less connected ones. This phenomenon provokes skewed distributions and the emergence of large hubs that bring together the network. Other factors that affect the emergence of scale-free networks such as competition and fitness (Bianconi and Barabasi 2001), optimisation (Valverde et al. 2002) and uniform attachment (Pennock et al. 2002) were found. However, these factors do not take into account web contents and other socio-cultural phenomena that would explain the dawning of search engines or web 2.0 sites. Thelwall (2002) found that there is a geographical pattern in the link relationship between British university web sites and Ortega et al. (2008) observed that the language is a strong variable for explaining interlinking among university web domains (Fig. 11.1).

Nevertheless, the Web is a directed network in which the orientation of the links does not need to be reciprocal. Thus, a web site may be linked by many web pages but it does not link to any other. Taking this into account, several models were proposed in order to study the web topology. The 'bow-tie' model (Broder et al. 2000) localises the web pages in four regions according to their link relationship

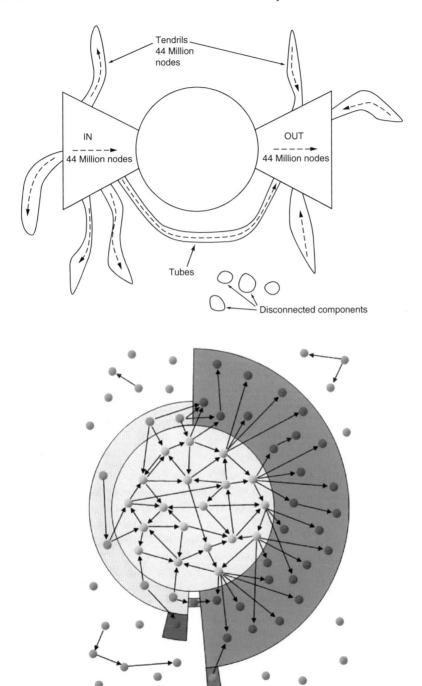

Fig. 11.1 Topological proposals about the form of the Web: 'Bow-tie' model (Broder et al. 2000) and 'corona' model (Bjornerborn 2004)

with others: the SCC or Strong Connected Component is the zone where all the nodes are connected among themselves; The IN component shows nodes that link to SCC but they are not reached from SCC; in the OUT component, the nodes are linked from SCC but they do not tie to SCC; and the TENDRILS are nodes that link to other nodes outside the sample. This model allowed characterisation of a web space (geographical, thematic) through study of the size of its components. Hence, a very large SCC component shows a highly compact environment while a big OUT component is a sign of dependency with other web space. The 'corona' model (Björneborn 2004) is a variation in which the IN and OUT zones are directly related.

11.1.2 Social Network Indicators

The interconnected nature of the Web forces web researchers to adopt structural indicators to measure the web activity of a web site, domain or space. These structural indicators allow the defining of properties of the analysis units and comparison of their performance into the Web. SNA techniques have pushed the development of web indicators that measure the structural relationship of a web site with its surroundings or to study the main characteristics of a web space.

The following are the most important social network indicators used in Webometrics Ortega and Aguillo (2008a):

Individual Indicators

These indicators are focussed in the situation of a node in the network; they describe the importance and meaning of a vertex in the context of the entire network.

• *Centrality degree*: Measures the number of lines incident with a node, that is, the total number of links that a web site, domain or space receives. This can be normalised (InDegree) by the total number of nodes in the network. Since the Web is a directed network, it is possible to count the incoming links (InDegree) or the outgoing links (OutDegree). The incoming links are signs of visibility because they generate traffic and visits to a web site, raising its popularity. Furthermore, the in-links are considered as a prestige indicator because they can be interpreted as an authoritative citation. On the other hand, the outgoing links show the mediator property of a website which directs the navigation to new web sites, domains or spaces. Following Kleinberg's (1999) nomenclature, the very in-linked sites are defined as Authorities, while the greatest out-linkers web sites are called Hubs. When a network is built from aggregated data (network of web domains, countries, regions), each tie between two nodes represents the total amount of links from all the web sites of a domain, country or region to another. In this weighted network, the centrality degree is calculated as the sum of the weight of each tie connected to a node. It was used by Kretschmer and Aguillo (2005) to highlight the scientist presence on the Web and gender differences. Ortega et al. (Ortega et al. 2008) used it to rank the most out and in-linked European universities.

- *Betweenness centrality*: Measures the intermediation degree of a node to keep the network connected, that is, the capacity of one node to connect only those nodes that are not directly connected to each other. In a weighted network, the Dijkstra's algorithm informs the shortest path and enables the calculation of the betweenness centrality according to that path. From a webometric point of view, this measure enables detection of hubs or gateways that connect different web sub-networks. It was used by Björneborn (2004) to observe small world phenomena in the British academic web and by Ortega et al. (2008) to detect European web universities that mediate between their local sub-network and the European one.
- *Closeness centrality*: It is an indicator that measures the average distance in number of clicks of a node with every node in the network. It is a good indicator to study infection processes and information flows, because this centrality is based on the proximity of a single web site with the rest. A high closeness shows a high reachability of a website during a navigational process. Dijkstra's algorithm is also used in weighted networks to calculate the closeness centrality. This index was used by Chen et al. (2006) to detect prominent members in a mailing list.
- *Eigenvector centrality*: Indicates the relevance of a node according to the importance of other nodes that link it. This is a recursive indicator that transmits the value of a node to acquaintances. It is a prestige index that not only values the quantity of partners but also their importance. An adaptation of this indicator was the popular PageRank (Brin and Page 1998) developed for positioning the most valuable pages in the top of the query results of Google.

Network Indicators

These indicators measure the main characteristics of the network and describe the relationships of the whole to the constituent members. They enable comparison of network structures.

- *P-Cliques*: A *p*-clique is a sub-network where every node is directly connected with the other ones. It shows groups with a high density and it is a way to detect underlying sub-networks. The value of *p* corresponds with the number of nodes that constitute a clique. It was used by Cothey et al. (2006) to uncover web site structures clustering web pages. Ortega et al. (2008) used it to identify national and regional groups in the European web space.
- *K-Cores*: Is a sub-network in which each node has *k* degree in that sub-network. Unlike the *p*-cliques the *k*-cores allow detection of groups with a strong link density. In scale-free networks, such as the Web, the core with the highest degree is the central nucleus of the network. Detecting the set of nodes where the network rests is highly critical. Ortega and Aguillo (2009) used this measure to detect which universities constitute the centre of the world academic network.

- *Distance*: Is the number of steps in the shortest path that connects two nodes. The average among all the shortest paths in the network is the average distance. A short mean average distance is a good indicator of network density. Broder et al. (2000) applied this measure to show the density of the Web, finding an average distance of 16 clicks.
- *Diameter*. Is the number of steps in the longest path, just like how the distance allows one to measure the cohesion of a network because it shows the largest distance that a node has to cover to reach the most distant node. Diameter was also used by Broder et al. (2000) to measure the thickness of the Web. Björneborn (2004) applied it to detect 'small-worlds' properties on the Web.
- *Global clustering coefficient*: Is a measure that shows the density or cohesion of the Web. It shows the proportion of nodes that tend to group together. Mathematically, it is the proportion of closed triads by open triads; a triad being a group of three linked nodes. This measure is important to detect 'small world' phenomena on the Web.

11.2   Visualising the Web

Several approaches have been used to present a visual picture of the Web that allows understanding of how their elements are related and the principal structural characteristics of the Web. Below is a summary of some of the most important tools.

11.2.1   Co-link Analysis

The first attempt was to represent web sites relationships through co-links. This technique studies the number of co-occurrences of linked web pages, sites or domains on a certain link corpus. Co-link Analysis assumes that if two web units appeared together then they are somehow related. To apply this technique, a co-occurrence matrix has to be built from search engines or crawler data. When collecting data from a search engine, the use of asymmetrical matrices is recommended. This follows from the fact that links analysed belong to the study population, while a symmetric matrix counts the links from all the web sites indexed in the search engine database which introduces noise and biases. A proximity measure (Salton's cosine, Spearman's rank correlation coefficient) is applied to transform the data into a distance matrix. Finally, a statistical model is used to project these distances in two dimensions, usually Principal Component Analysis (PCA), a method to reduce several correlated variables to a few components, or Multidimensional Scaling (MDS), which builds a point map according to the distances between the objects in an iterative process.

This technique is really more of a location method than a visualisation one, because their proximities are presented as (x, y) coordinates and may be plotted with other visual elements such as links, size and shape (Fig. 11.2). Co-link is

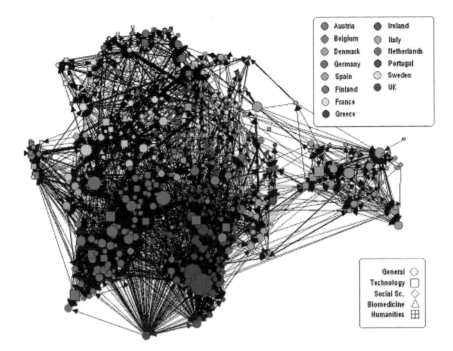

Fig. 11.2 (continued)

mainly used to detect content relationships between web units. Hence, Larson et al. (1996) observed thematic clusters in web pages about geographic information systems, while Vaughan (2006) detected clusters in the Canadian university web sets by their cultural and linguistic relationships.

11.2.2 Network Graphs

Network modelling allows the visual representation of the link structure of a space web according to the web unit used. It makes it possible to uncover structural properties of the nodes using social network indicators. Just as the Co-link Analysis, the network graphs may be generated through search engine and crawler data, building a weighted matrix of directed links. However, the network can be directly plotted because it does not need any statistical processing but rather a network visualisation programme such as Pajek or NetDraw. There are several energising algorithms (Kamada–Kawai and Fruchterman–Reingold), that optimise the graph visualisation when it is complex and densely packed. These algorithms assume that the nodes are attracted or repelled according to their energy, which makes closer or further the location of these nodes regarding to the number of links that they have.

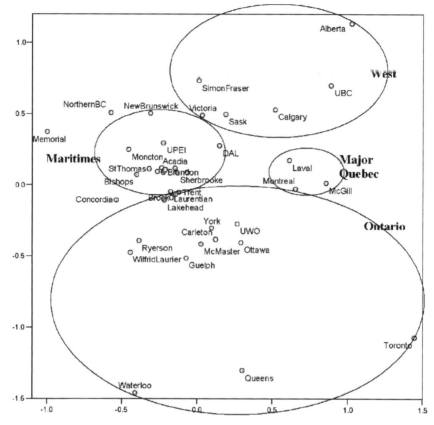

Fig. 11.2 Co-link technique results: (*up*) Map of the Canadian (Vaughan 2006) and the (*before*) European (Ortega et al. 2008) academic web space

The Kamada–Kawai algorithm is more suitable to small networks and only one component, while Fruchterman–Reingold is appropriate for large networks and many components.

Both Network graphs and Co-link analysis allows the addition of properties to the nodes in order to observe relationships between the network configuration and other qualitative or quantitative variables. For example, the size of the nodes may represent the number of web pages; colour and shape can apply to any classification scheme such as country, type or discipline. These added variables permit the observance of relationships between the centrality of a university and the number of web pages, or the colours make it possible to identify national sub-networks in the World-class universities (Fig. 11.3).

The network visualisation has been mainly used at the level of web university domain, although there are others works at the web page level (Björneborn 2004; Cothey et al. 2006). Heimeriks and Van den Besselaar (2006) used it to detect four

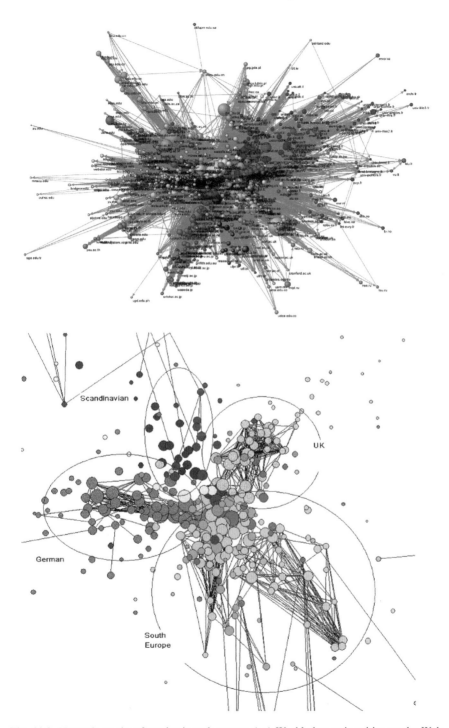

Fig. 11.3 Network graphs of academic web spaces: (*up*) World-class universities on the Web (Ortega and Aguillo 2009), (*down*) EU-15 universities hyperlink network (Heimeriks et al. 2006)

clusters in the EU-15 university web: German, British, Scandinavian and South European, while Ortega et al. (2008) observed that these clusters or national sub-networks are linked to the complete networks through prominent gateway universities.

11.2.3 Geographical Maps

A third way to visualise web data is through a geographical metaphor. Geographical maps allow the presentation of information at the macro level and assign web magnitudes to a certain region of the World Ortega and Aguillo (2008b). It makes possible observation of geographical patterns in the web content and links distribution. To design a geographical map, there are two essential elements: a base map and data. The base map is an empty map where each region boundary is associated to an index in a database, while the data are grouped by regions and linked to that index. These maps are usually built using Geographical Information System (GIS) software, which allows the addition of layers, classification methods and different map projections. Although multiple layers can be aggregated, it is recommended for simplicity to use only two: a hutch map which represents the number of web pages by region and a flow map which shows the links between those regions. There are several classification methods which distribute the data in classes (Standard deviation, Jenks' natural breaks, Percentiles), but the most usual and effective is the Jenks' natural breaks. This method determines the best arrangement of values into classes by iteratively comparing sums of the squared difference between observed values within each class and class means. This method improves the visualisation and the interpretation of the results, because it creates more significant differences between classes (Fig. 11.4).

11.3 Relevance of the University Performance on the Web

Link analysis is a powerful tool for evaluating performance of institutions, especially those with a diverse group of stakeholders. Academic organisations are usually evaluated using peer review, by consulting scholars or indirectly through bibliometric citation analysis. In each case, only colleagues are taken into account, the impact of other-than-research university missions is ignored. Even more important, these scientometric techniques explicitly exclude the economic, sociological, cultural or political impact of the academia and as already pointed out in many papers with strong biases against developing countries contribution.

External in-links distribution to university websites provides a rich and diverse source of information about the visibility and impact of the university web presence. If this reflects the whole set of activities of the university, its global output, its performance according to its excellence and prestige, then webometric indicators are the easiest and most powerful academic and research policy tool (Aguillo 2009).

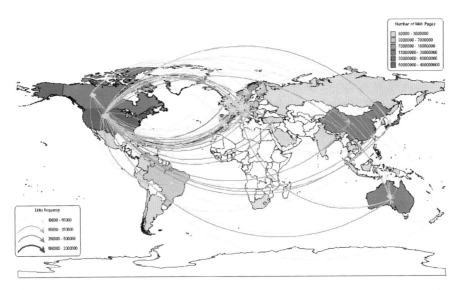

Fig. 11.4 Geographical representation of web data: The 1000 most important universities on the Web grouped by countries and link flows (Ortega and Aguillo 2009)

In order to take advantage of this situation, a Ranking of institutions was built using a composite webometric indicator. The aim is to increase digital presence of universities by considering web indicators in academic evaluation.

The Ranking Web has several technical advantages: Most of the universities have only one main web domain, so affiliation normalisation is no longer a problem. The data are collected from the huge databases of the main search engines; with different geographic coverage but limited overlap among them. Both activity and impact can be computed from the number of Webpages and documents and the number of external in-links received in the university webdomain.

Since 2004 the Ranking Web of World Universities, also known as the Webometrics Ranking (www.webometrics.info), has been published twice per year (January and July) and analyses the web presence of over 20,000 higher education institutions worldwide (Aguillo et al. 2008). Since 2006, the number of Open Access papers published is collected from the Google Scholar bibliographic citation database. During the last decades, the ISI/Thomson databases were the only source for this information, being challenged only very recently by the SCOPUS/Elsevier database. The popularity of free alternatives, such as Google Scholar, is promoting many institutions to publish their papers in web directories indexed by Scholar crawler increasing significantly the coverage and reducing the (still very relevant) biases and shortcomings of this Google database.

An ongoing global network analysis of the webometrics ranking results is showing both expected and unexpected results:

• There is an academic digital divide between North American universities that appear far better positioned than their European counterparts.

- US and Canadian universities are grouped forming a unit in the WebSpace, with French-speaking institutions not far from the core.
- European universities are split in several national or linguistic (Austria and Germany) groups not closely related to each other.
- In many countries, a single university acts as a central gateway to the international academic network.

This global approach, considering the whole set of in and out-links, has many advantages as it allows uncovering of relationships with other non academic stakeholders, but also a few shortcomings as probably some of the links coming from third parties are spurious. So, the future research on link networks will require classifying 'a priori' the links according to their motivations (Wilkinson et al. 2003). Academic web networks could be cleaned allowing the identification of invisible colleges at a global level previously not achieved.

But the effort for identifying the different groups of motivations can be very high, so perhaps other alternatives could be also explored. According to link topology, it is possible to identify shallow links from deep links (Vasileiadou and van den Besselaar 2006). The former refer to links between main homepages such as the central page of an academic institution. In this case, the institutional interlinking could be driven by perception of prestige, the sense of community or common interests. An application for these links is to identify the pattern of out-links of a page and to build a set of webpages with a similar pattern. Using a quantitative approach one can use a helping tool in search recovery (like the related operator in Google) or to visualise the neighbourhood of an institution, as it is developed by TouchGraph (www.touchgraph.com) in Fig. 11.5.

Deep linking refers to links among the contents published in the web directories. They are important in academia as the websites gets richer and more diverse allowing the building of complex networks and answering new questions. A short list of some of these questions is proposed for future research:

- Is it possible to estimate the relative contribution of each of the university missions to the global web performance of the university? What are the reasons explaining possible discrepancies between obtained and failed results?
- What is the importance of the disciplines in the self-organisations of web networks, specially targeting the problems related to the humanities and social sciences?
- According to central measures, what is most relevant for the web domain, the formal or the informal scholarly communication processes and outputs?
- What is the impact of Web 2.0? How is it affecting publishing, use and linkages to media content?
- What is the relative contribution to the WebSpace of the non-academic activities? For example, is the Ivy League a group of elite universities or just a sports league?
- Are technical and information guidelines being applied correctly and what is the impact of bad web practices?

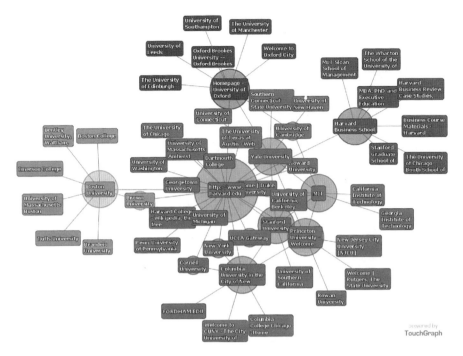

Fig. 11.5 Neighbourhood of the Harvard University according to its out-link pattern, showing affinities with other Ivy League universities and international relationships with UK universities

References

Aguillo, I.: Measuring the institution's footprint in the web. Libr. Hi Tech **27**(4), 540–556 (2009)

Aguillo, I.F., Granadino, B., Ortega, J.L., Prieto, J.A.: Scientific research activity and communication measured with cybermetrics indicators. Am. Soc. Info. Sci. Technol. **57**(10), 1296–1302 (2006)

Aguillo, I.F., Ortega, J.L., Fernández, M.: Webometric ranking of world universities: introduction, methodology, and future developments. High. Educ. Eur. **33**(2/3), 234–244 (2008)

Almind, T.C., Ingwersen, P.: Informetric analyses on the world wide web: methodological approaches to 'webometrics'. Documentation **53**(4), 404–426 (1997)

Antelman, K.: Do open-access articles have a greater research impact? Coll. Res. Libr. **65**(5), 372–382 (2004)

Barabási, A.L., Albert, R.: Emergence of scaling in random networks. Science **286**, 509–512 (1999)

Bar-Ilan, J.: Which h-index? – a comparison of WoS, scopus and google scholar. Scientometrics **74**(2), 257–271 (2008)

Bar-Ilan, J.: Expectations versus reality – search engine features needed for web research at mid 2005. Cybermetrics **9**(1) (2005). http://cybermetrics.cindoc.csic.es/cybermetrics/articles/v9i1p2.html

Bar-Ilan, J., Peritz, B.C.: The lifespan of 'Informetrics' on the web: an eight year study (1998-2006). Scientometrics **79**(1), 7–25 (2009)

Bianconi, G., Barabasi, A.L.: Competition and multiscaling in evolving networks. Europhys. Lett. **54**, 43M42 (2001)

Björneborn, L., Ingwersen, P.: Toward a basic framework for webometrics. Am. Soc. Info. Sci. Technol. **55**(14), 1216–1227 (2004)

Björneborn, L.: Small-world link structures across an academic web space: a library and information science approach. Dissertation, Royal School of Library and Information Science (2004)

Boyd, D.M., Ellison, N.B.: Social Network Sites: Definition, history, and scholarship. J. Comput.-Mediated Commun. **13**(1), article 11 (2007)

Brin, S., Page, L.: The anatomy of a large-scale hypertextual web search engine. Comput. Netw. ISDN Syst. **30**(1–7), 107–117 (1998)

Broder, A., Kumar, R., Maghoul, F., et al.: Graph structure in the web. Comput. Netw. **33**(1–6), 309–320 (2000)

Chakrabarti, S.: Mining the Web: Discovering Knowledge from Hypertext Data. Morgan-Kaufmann Publishers, San Francisco (2002)

Chen, H., Shen, H., Xiong, J. et al.: Social network structure behind the mailing lists: ICT-IIIS. In: TREC 2006 Expert Finding Track. Gaithersburg, Maryland (2006)

Cho, J., Garcia-Molina, H.: The evolution of the web and implications for an incremental crawler. In: 26th International Conference on Very Large Data Bases, San Francisco (2000)

Cothey, V., Aguillo, I.F., Arroyo, N.: Operationalising "websites": lexically, semantically or topologically? Cybermetrics **10**(1), Paper 4 (2006)

Fetterly, D., Manasse, M., Najork, M. et al.: A large-scale study of the evolution of web pages. In: 12th International World Wide Web Conference, ACM Press, Budapest (2003)

Gomory, S., Hoch, R., Lee, J., et al.: Analysis and visualization of metrics for online merchandizing. In: Hochheiser, H., Shneiderman, B. (eds.) Understanding Patterns of User Visits to Web Sites: Interactive Starfield Visualization of WWW Log Data. Springer, San Diego (1999)

Harter, S.P., Ford, C.E.: Web-based analyses of E-journal impact: approaches, problems, and issues. Am. Soc. Info. Sci. **51**(13), 1159–1176 (2000)

Harter, S., Kim, H.: Electronic journals and scholarly communication: a citation and reference study. Inf. Res. **2**(1), paper 9a (1996)

Heimeriks, G., Van Den Besselaar, P.: Analyzing hyperlinks networks: the meaning of hyperlink based indicators of knowledge production. Cybermetrics **10**(1,1) (2006)

Jansen, B.J., Spink, A., Pederson, J.: A temporal comparison of AltaVista web searching. Am. Soc. Info. Sci. Technol. **56**(6), 559–570 (2005)

Kleinberg, J.: Authoritative sources in a hyperlinked environment. ACM **46**(5), 604–632 (1999)

Koehler, W.: A longitudinal study of web pages continued: a consideration of document persistence. Inf. Res. **9**(2), paper 174 (2004)

Kretschmer, H., Aguillo, I.F.: New indicators for gender studies in web networks. Info. Process. Manage. **41**(6), 1481–1494 (2005)

Kumar, R., Novak, J., Tomkins, A.: Structure and evolution of online social networks. In: 12th ACM SIGKDD International Conference on Knowledge Discovery and Data Mining. ACM Press, Philadelphia (2006)

Larson, R.: Bibliometrics of the world wide web: an exploratory analysis of the intellectual structure of cyberspace. In: ASIS96, pp. 71–78 (1996)

Lawrence, S., Giles, C.L.: Searching the world wide web. Science **280**(5360), 98–100 (1998)

Lawrence, S., Pennock, D.M., Flake, G.W., et al.: Persistence of web references in scientific research. Computer **34**(2), 26–31 (2001)

Lenhart, A., Madden, M.: Teens, Privacy, & Online Social Networks. Pew Internet and American Life Project Report. Washington, DC (2007)

Ortega, J.L., Aguillo, I.F.: Visualization of the Nordic academic web: link analysis using social network tools. Info. Process. Manage. **44**(4), 1624–1633 (2008a)

Ortega, J.L., Aguillo, I.F.: Linking patterns in the European union's countries: geographical maps of the European academic web space. J. Info. Sci. **34**(5), 705–714 (2008b)

Ortega, J.L., Aguillo, I.F.: Mapping world-class universities on the web. Info. Process. Manage. **45**(2), 272–279 (2009)

Ortega, J.L., Aguillo, I.F.: Differences between web sessions according to the origin of their visits. J. Informetrics **4**(3), 331–337 (2010)

Ortega, J.L., Aguillo, I.F., Prieto, J.A.: Longitudinal study of contents and elements in the scientific Web environment. J. Info. Sci. **32**(4), 344–351 (2006)

Ortega, J.L., Aguillo, I.F., Cothey, V., Scharnhorst, A.: Maps of the academic web in the European higher education area - an exploration of visual web indicators. Scientometrics **74**(2), 295–308 (2008)

Ortega, J.L., Cothey, V., Aguillo, I.F.: How old is the web? Characterizing the age and the currency of the European scientific web. Scientometrics **81**(1), 295–309 (2009)

Payne, N., Thelwall, M.: Do academic link types change over time? J. Doc. **64**(5), 707–720 (2008)

Pennock, D.M., Flake, G.W., Lawrence, S., et al.: Winners don't take all: characterizing the competition for links on the web. Natl. Acad. Sci. **99**(8), 5207–5211 (2002)

Pitkow, J.: In search of reliable usage data on the WWW. In: Sixth International World Wide Web Conference, pp. 451–463. Santa Clara (1997)

Rodriguez Gairín, J.M.: Valorando el impacto de la información en Internet AltaVista, el "Citation Index" de la Red. Revista Española de Documentación Científica **20**(2), 175–181 (1997)

Rousseau, R.: Daily time series of common single word searches in AltaVista and NorthernLight. Cybermetrics **2**(3), Paper 2 (1998)

Silverstein, C., Henzinger, M., Marais, H., Moricz, M.: Analysis of a very large AltaVista query log. SRC Technical Note, 14 (1998)

Smith, A., Thelwall, M.: Web impact factors for Australasian universities. Scientometrics **54**(1–2), 363–380 (2002)

Sullivan, D.: Google dance syndrome strikes again. SearchEngineWatch.com, http://searchenginewatch.com/showPage.html?page=3114531 (2003)

Teevan, J., Adar, E., Jones, R., Potts, M.: History repeats itself: repeat queries in Yahoo's logs. In: 29th Annual International ACM SIGIR. Seattle (2006)

Thelwall, M.: Extracting macroscopic information from web links. Am. Soc. Info. Sci. Technol. **52**(13), 1157–1168 (2001)

Thelwall, M.: Evidence for the existence of geographic trends in university web site interlinking. Documentation **58**(5), 563–574 (2002)

Thelwall, M.: Social networks, gender and friending: an analysis of MySpace member profiles. Am. Soc. Info. Sci. Technol. **59**(8), 1321–1330 (2008)

Thelwall, M., Klitkou, A., Verbeek, A., et al.: Policy-relevant webometrics for individual scientific fields. Am. Soc. Info. Sci. Technol. **61**(7), 1464–1475 (2010)

Valverde, S., Ferrer-Cancho, R., Sole, R.V.: Scale free networks from optimal design. Europhys. Lett. **60**, 512–517 (2002)

Vasileiadou, E., van den Besselaar, P.: Linking shallow, linking deep. How scientific intermediaries use the web for their network of collaborators. Cybermetrics **10**(1), paper 4 (2006)

Vaughan, L.: Visualizing linguistic and cultural differences using web co-link data. Am. Soc. Info. Sci. Technol. **57**(9), 1178–1193 (2006)

Vaughan, L., Thelwall, M.: Scholarly use of the web: what are the key inducers of links to journal web sites? Am. Soc. Info. Sci. Technol. **54**(1), 29–38 (2003)

Wang, W., Zaiane, O.R.: Clustering web sessions by sequence alignment. In: 13th International Workshop on Database and Expert Systems Applications, Aix-en-Provence (2002)

Wilkinson, D., Harries, G., Thelwall, M., et al.: Motivations for academic web site interlinking: evidence for the web as a novel source of information on informal scholarly communication. Info. Sci. **29**(1), 49–56 (2003)

Chapter 12
Social Capital in Electronic Networks of Practice: An Analysis of University Blogging Communities

Sharon Purchase and Nick Letch

Abstract Weblogs are a popular social communication technology enabling individuals to collaborate and share knowledge. This paper investigates how universities use blogging to facilitate student information exchange that is not directly moderated within a classroom environment. Social capital has been identified as a powerful indicator facilitating the transfer of knowledge (Nahapiet and Ghoshal 1998) and is used as the theoretical underpinnings for investigating why students participate in un-moderated university blogging communities. It is postulated that students with higher levels of social capital are more likely to participate within university blogging communities. Results suggest that *the following aspects of social capital*: trust; personal reputation and the enjoyment derived from helping others; significantly influence student participation in un-moderated blogging communities.

12.1 Introduction

Information and communication technologies are important tools that support student learning and the use of learning management systems is now common practice (McGill and Klobas 2009). Managed learning environments are the norm in Australian universities as a means of delivering curricula and sharing knowledge – the most commonly used being WebCT. In addition to managed learning environments, universities are increasingly investigating the potential for emerging technologies under the banner of Web 2.0 to enhance student learning and experience (Cronin 2009).

There is a significant body of research demonstrating that learning management systems do impact student learning and that instructors strongly influence a student's attitude towards use (e.g. (McGill and Klobas 2009)). However, most previous

S. Purchase (✉) • N. Letch
UWA Business School, The University of Western Australia, 35 Stirling Highway, Crawley 6009, Australia
e-mail: sharon.purchase@uwa.edu.au; nick.letch@uwa.edu.au

B. White et al. (eds.), *Social Media Tools and Platforms in Learning Environments*,
DOI 10.1007/978-3-642-20392-3_12, © Springer-Verlag Berlin Heidelberg 2011

research investigates online practices linked to assessment or instructor moderation (Chen et al. 2008; McGill and Klobas 2009) and only a relatively few articles discuss behaviour not linked to instructor influences (see Phang et al. 2009). We take the view that the educational benefits of knowledge exchange and sharing within universities are not limited to discrete areas of study in which community participation is bounded by enrolment. Rather, students and faculty alike can additionally benefit from sharing and exchanging knowledge about a range of experiences encountered in university life. The research presented in this paper is concerned with online technologies in university settings but rather than focussing on specific units of study or assessment, we investigate the blogging behaviours which facilitate knowledge sharing at either the course level or at the university-wide level. Thus, for this research, participation in online interactions is voluntary, not influenced by the normative practice of instructors and is not linked to any form of assessment. This focus is where our paper differs to previous research and offers unique insights into voluntary student participation in blogging communities. We argue that current students already participate and use these tools extensively within the social arena and that universities need to leverage off these practices to enhance student learning outside of the classroom experience.

The inherently social nature of knowledge exchange in voluntary university blogging communities is investigated through the lens of *social capital* which is used to develop a survey of blogging communities in five Australian universities. Therefore, our research question is: *How does social capital affect student online knowledge sharing within voluntary university blogging communities?* In the following section, we examine the emerging research into knowledge exchange in blogging communities, with specific reference to higher education, and explore how the sociability aspects of the networks of knowledge interactions can be studied. In this chapter, we review the literature on social capital in relation to blogging and discussion forums; develop a conceptual model of social influences on knowledge sharing and subsequently derive eight hypotheses. These hypotheses are tested using a survey of blogging community participants from five Australian universities. The results of the survey are discussed in the context of the previous literature and recommendations for research and practice are proposed.

12.2 Background

Among the variety of applications available which facilitate online learning and collaboration, weblogs or 'blogs' are a form of social software being used to support individual learning in university environments (Du and Wagner 2005; Huffaker 2005; Kim 2008). Weblogs allow individuals to develop personal content and connect with an online community enabling individuals to collaborate and share knowledge. Weblogs offer advantages over other types of social media (i.e. Wikis) in that they allow different view points on the same subject to be posted as each user can post their own argument and link to other blogs with a similar theme (Huang and Yang 2009). Weblogs are beginning to proliferate in universities as a means for students to share experiences and knowledge in the course of their studies (Chen et al. 2008; Huang and Yang 2009; Kim 2008; Phang et al. 2009). Given the emergence of blogs in this context and the likelihood that the factors influencing intentions to participate are likely to vary according to the blogging community characteristics (Hsu and Lin 2008), more research is required to improve our understanding of student intentions to participate in university blogging communities. Furthermore, if we gain a better understanding of voluntary use rather than instructor influenced use of weblogs, we can enhance student experiences across the university outside of the classroom.

Social media or Web 2.0 technologies have a growing popularity for facilitating knowledge sharing, particularly within university contexts (Huang and Yang 2009; Kim 2008). Results of research conducted for online knowledge sharing behaviour of students is inconsistent, with students using the systems differently. For example, some students benefit from only reading other student's postings, while others actively participate in the posting process for sharing knowledge (Kim 2008). Research conducted within another type of voluntary blogging community shows that both readers and posters value the information contained within the community (Taylor and Murthy 2009). Therefore, improving participation ensures that the discussion evolves rather than stagnates, benefiting all participants. This suggests that research on how to improve student participation for both reading and posting within weblog communities is required. Particularly, if universities are to develop blogging communities that have a self sustaining mass of active participants – a current issue faced by universities implementing Web 2.0 technologies.

Social capital theory or social influences are often used to explain behavioural intentions (see Chiu et al. 2006; Chow and Chan 2008; Hsu and Lin 2008; Kankanhalli et al. 2005; Wasko and Faraj 2005; Taylor and Murthy 2009). The range of different types of blogging communities researched and their differing community characteristics means that research should be conducted into various types of blogging communities, as well as the factors influencing participant intentions which vary across different blogging situations. In addition, the concepts used to measure social influences vary widely among previous research articles. The focus of this study is on investigating how the three dimensions of social capital: structural, relational and cognitive, influence participants' behavioural intentions within a voluntary university blogging community.

12.3 Weblogs as Conversational Knowledge Networks

The conversational nature of blogs takes advantage of Web 2.0 technologies for knowledge sharing in that they are inherently social media. A weblog conversation is a series of interrelated (interlinked) weblog posts and comments on a specific topic, usually not planned, but emerging spontaneously (Efimova and Moor 2005). These social characteristics allow individuals to connect to all other weblog participants generating an emerging sense of community and belonging. Thus, the informal social system contains social characteristics such as trust, friendship which facilitate the knowledge sharing process (Chiu et al. 2006; Davenport and Prusak 1998; Taylor and Murthy 2009). Yet, these results are inconsistent with other research indicating that trust is not significant (Chow and Chan 2008; Hsu and Lin 2008).

Weblogs are used in a variety of contexts where different environments may affect how people participate in blogging communities (Hsu and Lin 2008). Most of the research conducted within education environments are in different contexts to this research. For example: case-based learning within a single unit and used for assessment (Chen et al. 2008); academic staff (Taylor and Murthy 2009); undergraduate course moderated via academic staff (Phang et al. 2009); and discussion forum within a single unit moderated by the lecturer (McGill and Klobas 2009). This research concentrates on non-moderated blogs that operate at the course level such that lecturer influence is minimised and does not contribute to unit assessment. The research therefore contributes to understanding the influence of different environments on blogging behaviour.

12.4   Social Capital

Social Capital is a set of social resources embedded in relationships (Nahapiet and Ghoshal 1998). It is a concept that has been applied to a number of fields from sociology to management and has more recently been used in investigations of information and communication technologies and knowledge management (Huysman and Wulf 2004). We use social capital in the context of this study because we seek to understand sociability aspects of blogs in student learning environments. Nahapiet and Ghoshal (1998, p. 243) define social capital as '*the sum of the actual and potential resources embedded within, available through and derived from the network of relationships possessed by an individual or social unit*'. The social capital concept can be used to describe how the social context (represented as social ties, trust, relationships and values systems) facilitates interactions between individuals (Nahapiet and Ghoshal 1998). It is appropriate in the context of this study of blogging communities because it allows examination of the relationships between individuals interacting through blogging conversations.

Social capital is commonly described along three dimensions: structural; cognitive and relational dimensions (Nahapiet and Ghoshal 1998). The structural dimension refers to the form and number of connections between actors. The cognitive dimension relates to how actors in networks understand each other and create meaning; whereas the relational dimension describes mutual trust and reciprocity between network actors. Some researchers also argue that the relational dimension includes the aspect of motivation (Adler and Kwon 2002).

Within the notion of social capital, social community is a crucial factor which facilitates the transfer of knowledge (Tsai and Ghoshal 1998). In relation to the context of knowledge management, social capital extends the prospect of sharing knowledge from individuals to communities. Communities of practice and social networks are seen as embodying a sense of membership and commitment, acting as a source of trust and a place in organisations where people feel responsible for one another.

Given that the literature reveals links between communities of practice, social capital and knowledge management (Wasko and Faraj 2005) and that communities of practice contribute to the development of social capital, which in turn is an essential condition for knowledge sharing (Lesser and Prusak 2000), for the use of online technologies in higher education, the following research question is developed:

How does social capital affect student online knowledge sharing within voluntary university blogging communities?

12.5 Conceptual MODEL

The framework used in this research investigates the role of social capital in knowledge sharing within university blogging communities and describes the three dimensions of social capital (structural, cognitive and relational) as independent variables with online knowledge sharing as a dependent variable.

12.5.1 Hypotheses

Viewing blog communities as networks of conversation, the location of actors in the network becomes important for knowledge sharing. The structural dimension of social capital is used to describe the form that connections between actors take with indicative measures including density, connectivity and the hierarchy of network ties (Wasserman and Faust 1994). Centrality however is the most commonly measured aspect of the structural dimension of social capital. An individual who is central in a network of social interactions has a greater capacity to collaborate and share resources with other members (Tsai and Ghoshal 1998; Wasko and Faraj 2005). Furthermore, individuals who are centrally embedded in a collective, willingly cooperate with other members in electronic networks (Wasko and Faraj 2005). Previously, Wasko and Faraj (2005) found that centrality significantly influenced both quality / helpfulness and quantity of the contribution, while Chiu et al. (2006) found the structural dimension to influence quantity but not quality. It should be noted that Chiu et al. (2006) measured the structural dimension of social capital via closeness, interaction intensity and time, rather than the number of ties relative to all other ties as per the common measurement of centrality (Wasserman and Faust (1994). Bearing in mind these differences in measures, we hypothesise:

H_1: Centrality is positively associated with online knowledge sharing.

The cognitive dimension of social capital includes shared meaning and understanding between network members (Nahapiet and Ghoshal 1998). Two constructs present in the cognitive dimension are *expertise* and *shared vision (shared norms and shared goals)*. Individuals share their expertise because of the belief that their knowledge adds value to other members in the group (Constant et al. 1996). However, they are probably unlikely to share any knowledge with the group if they do not perceive themselves as an expert in their chosen area. Previous research in electronic networks indicates that individuals who are confident in their skills are willing to share knowledge with others (Constant et al. 1996; Wasko and Faraj 2000). Lu and Hsiao (2007) also show that perceived expertise – moderated by knowledge self-efficacy – influences blogging behaviour intentions. While Wasko and Faraj (2005) find that expertise does not influence blogging behaviour. The following hypothesis is therefore proposed:

H₂: Individual expertise is positively associated with online knowledge sharing.

Shared vision facilitates appropriate ways of acting in a social system (Nahapiet and Ghoshal 1998) and norms represent a level of agreement in the social system. Norms influence human behaviour based on the expectations of the group or community. Community norms are thus formed by the manners of influential individuals to the group as well as the group to its members (Chavis et al. 1986). Previous research has shown mixed results with both significant influences of shared norms on behaviour (Lu and Hsiao 2007; Chen et al. 2008; Chiu et al. 2006; Wasko and Faraj 2005) and insignificant influences on behaviour (Hsu and Lin 2008; McGill and Klobas 2009). It is also noted that Chiu et al. (2006) found a negative influence between shared norms and blogging volume. Therefore these inconsistent results lead to the hypothesis:

H₃ₐ: Shared norms are positively associated with online knowledge sharing.

When individuals have the same understanding of interactions with one another, they can effectively communicate and exchange their ideas or resources (Tsai and Ghoshal 1998). In other words, individuals who share a common goal become partners in sharing or exchanging their resources and members who willingly help others have a collective goal orientation (Leana and Van Buren 1999). Many studies have found that individuals who exchange their ideas or resources have common interests and achieve goals (Chow and Chan 2008; Kankanhalli et al. 2005; Lochner et al. 1999; Wasko and Faraj 2000; Tsai and Ghoshal 1998). The following hypothesis is therefore derived:

H₃ᵦ: Shared goals are positively associated with online knowledge sharing.

The relational dimension of social capital describes mutual trust and reciprocity between network actors. Trust is the extent to which individuals believe in others and are willing to act based on others' words, actions and decisions (McAllister 1995). The relational dimension includes motivation which identifies individuals' self-interest (Adler and Kwon 2002). Having a willingness to contribute to the relationship between members provides individuals with their intrinsic motivation to share knowledge with each other in the group (Huysman and Wulf 2004). Trust is a key component of the relational dimension in social capital (Adler and

Kwon 2002). Trust does not rest with a specific individual but instead on the behaviour of a social unit as a whole (Kankanhalli et al. 2005). Prior research indicates that trust is an important factor supporting cooperation and effective knowledge exchange (Tsai and Ghoshal 1998). Trust is measured as trust in others' competence, reliability and good intentions relating to knowledge sharing (Kankanhalli et al. 2005; Kim and Lee 2006; Ridings et al. 2002). Previous research has shown that trust positively influences the quality of information share (Chiu et al. 2006) while others have found no influence at all (Chow and Chan 2008; Hsu and Lin 2008). Wasko and Faraj (2005) found a significant negative relationship between commitment and quality of postings. Therefore, for this study we represent trust in the following hypothesis:

H_4: *Trust is positively associated with online knowledge sharing.*

Reciprocity has been noted as a measure of the relational dimension in social capital (Huysman and Wulf 2004; Wasko and Faraj 2005). Reciprocity enables individuals to participate in social exchange since it influences individuals' expectation of help from others in the future. Individuals contribute to online knowledge sharing if they believe that their requests for knowledge will be met in future (Kankanhalli et al. 2005; Wasko and Faraj 2005). Yet, previous research has found no significant influence between reciprocity and online knowledge sharing behaviour (Hsu and Lin 2008; Wasko and Faraj 2005; Taylor and Murthy 2009) with Chiu et al. (2006) only finding a positive influence with quantity and not quality. Therefore, the following hypothesis is suggested:

H_5: *Reciprocity is positively associated with online knowledge sharing.*

Individuals are motivated to share their knowledge because they expect to build their reputation. In an organisation, knowledge contributors gain respect from others when they contribute their knowledge (Constant et al. 1994). Employees are willing to share their best practice when they are recognised by their colleagues as experts. In the same manner, individuals who share their high-level of technical knowledge are more likely to gain better prestige in the workplace. Research within blogging communities has shown mixed results with Taylor and Murthy (2009) showing no significant influence while significant influences are found by Hsu and Lin (2008) and Wasko and Faraj (2005). The hypothesis is shown as follows:

H_{6a}: *Personal reputation is positively associated with online knowledge sharing.*

Enjoyment from helping is a measure of the relational dimension in individual online knowledge sharing. Individuals enjoy helping others because of their intrinsic motivations. Knowledge contributors help others because they are motivated by relative altruism (Davenport and Prusak 1998). Knowledge contributors gain satisfaction from their intrinsic enjoyment in helping others (Constant et al. 1994). Previous research in electronic networks indicates that individuals simply enjoy helping others; and individuals are thus willing to share knowledge with others (Wasko and Faraj 2000). Altruism and enjoy helping have been shown to significantly influence blogging behaviour (Taylor and Murthy 2009; Hsu and Lin 2008) while others have found an insignificant relationship (Wasko and Faraj 2005). The hypothesis is shown as follows:

H_{6b}: *Enjoy helping is positively associated with online knowledge sharing.*

With the notion of knowledge management, knowledge sharing is the process of acquiring knowledge and, in turn, sharing the learned knowledge. The dependent variable of this study is online knowledge sharing. Online knowledge sharing is the activity when individuals share knowledge and pass along information they consider useful and timely to others in their university weblog communities.

12.5.2 Methodology

In order to investigate the hypothesised relationships, a survey was conducted of participants in blogging communities in five Australian universities. To improve the validity and reliability of the research, items in the survey instrument were adapted from previous sources and were available from the authors upon request. Multiple items were used to measure each construct. The questionnaire items were pre-tested on a group of ten students with the aim of determining whether questions were seen as ambiguous or difficult to interpret. Feedback from the pre-test resulted in no changes to item wording although the layout of the questionnaire was adapted as a result of the feedback from the pre-test.

The questionnaire was organised into three main sections. The first section included questions on social capital and knowledge sharing. Survey respondents were asked to select an answer for each question from the seven-point Likert scale (from strongly disagree = 1 to strongly agree = 7) based on their blogging behaviour and experience with their university's weblog community. Next, the respondents were asked to answer the questions regarding their own blogging activities. The last section of this questionnaire was designed to determine the bloggers' demographics by asking questions about their gender, age, nationality, occupation and discipline area of study.

Centrality is frequently used to measure the structural dimension of social capital (Wasko and Faraj 2005; Wasserman and Faust 1994). We adapted the questionnaire items used to measure centrality from previous work (Kim and Lee 2006; Moody 2001) and given that the researcher did not have full access to the interactions of all blog communities, respondent perceptions of centrality were used.

The cognitive dimension consists of two main constructs: expertise and shared vision. Expertise is an individual's abilities and skills in the context of relevant knowledge adapted from Kankanhalli et al. (2005). Shared vision includes shared norms and shared goals adapted from literature (Kankanhalli et al. 2005; Lochner et al. 1999; Tsai and Ghoshal 1998).

Trust is measured in terms of a willingness to rely on other members of the electronic network (Kankanhalli et al. 2005; Ridings et al. 2002). Motivation is measured in terms of reputation and enjoyment from helping (Wasko and

Faraj 2000; Wang and Fesenmaier 2003). Reciprocity measures are adapted from Kankanhalli et al. (2005).

Online knowledge sharing is the dependent variable of this research. Consistent with previous research, online knowledge sharing is measured by the extent of knowledge transferred from one person to another (Jarvenpaa and Staples 2000; Kim and Lee 2006). Items measured knowledge sharing behaviours such as whether they share knowledge, whether they use the blog site, publish on the blog site and access documents from the site.

12.5.3 Data Collection and Sample

The participants in the survey were selected from people who work or study in Australian educational institutions and were restricted to those who were familiar with weblogs as a medium for communicating with other members of the same institution. In this study, the electronic network of practice refers to the blog community as the system provided by universities around Australia. To ensure adequate sample size, a number of educational institutions were selected and included: The University of Sydney; Griffith University; Victoria University, Edith Cowan University, Curtin University of Technology and The University of Western Australia. Although blogging technology is currently used for a variety of purposes, all blogs are aimed at sharing knowledge across a broad scope of topics and not associated with individual learning units. For example, the blogging community at the University of Western Australia is available to all higher degree research students to discuss their issues regardless of the faculty in which the student is located.

The IT administrators of the university blog communities within Australia were contacted to ask for permission to post a blog which asked respondents to complete an online survey. The online survey was then published in various weblog communities in order to ensure that respondents were bloggers of an Australian university weblog community.

Both male and female participants ranging in age from 18 to over 70 years of age responded to the survey. The total number of respondents was 179, of which 76% completed the questionnaire. Surveys with more than 30% of values missing were eliminated from the analysis and a final 136 questionnaires were used in the analysis. The percentage of male and female respondents was 46.6% and 53.4% respectively. The majority of the respondents (50.4%) were between the ages of 26 and 35 years old. Doctoral students were the largest number of respondents with 40.5% of responses followed by postgraduate coursework (29.8%), academic staff (9.9%); university staff (9.9%) and undergraduate students (9.2%). Perhaps given the relatively new implementation of weblogs, a third (33.8%) of respondents had only participated in the community for 1 month (Table 12.1).

Table 12.1 Participation of respondents in university blog community

Frequency	% of valid responses
Less than 1 month	33.8
1–3 months	16.9
3–6 months	22.3
6–12 months	16.9
1–3 years	9.2
More than 3 years	0.8

Table 12.2 Model fit summary

Construct	Composite reliability	RMSEA	RMSR	GFI	AGFI	NFI	CFI	CMIN/DF
Centrality	0.953	0.106	0.038	0.970	0.887	0.973	0.983	2.503
Expertise	0.987	0.118	0.018	0.978	0.892	0.989	0.992	2.887
Norms	0.975	0.000	0.001	1.00	0.998	1.00	1.00	0.057
Goals	0.951	0.117	0.051	0.986	0.917	0.992	0.995	2.857
Trust	0.917	0.110	0.007	0.978	0.888	0.989	0.993	2.634
Reciprocity	0.964	0.045	0.032	0.994	0.963	0.997	0.999	1.275
Reputation	0.901	0.045	0.021	0.986	0.955	0.991	0.998	1.279
Enjoy helping	0.962	0.099	0.012	0.968	0.887	0.989	0.994	2.318
Online knowledge sharing	0.949	0.000	0.010	0.995	0.960	0.997	1.00	0.898

12.5.4 Results

The measurement items were analysed for correlation, reliability and validity analysis. Items that did not represent the constructs were eliminated. Prelis in LISREL was used to determine the polyserial correlations between interval and ordinal variables. This matrix was then supporting AMOS to conduct the confirmatory factor analysis. Confirmatory factor analysis (CFA) was applied to investigate whether the measured variables represented the constructs well. Factor loadings ranged from 0.636 to 0.993 which are greater than 0.5 indicating convergent validity (Hair et al. 2006). The results from confirmatory factor analysis indicate that all construct models have a good fit and showed evidence of construct validity (Table 12.2). The estimate standardised regression weights calculated from AMOS analysis showed that all items were higher than 0.5 and, therefore possessed convergent validity. The factors proposed in this study have also been tested for its composite reliability (0.901–0.987). The results showed that all constructs were reliable. Variance extracted estimates ranged from 0.612 to 0.811 and exceeded the squared correlations across all pairs of constructs, showing that discriminant validity is achieved.

In summary, overall model fit indices have met their threshold requirements. Although this study assesses fit on multiple measures, most measures indicate that constructs achieve overall excellent model fit.

Table 12.3 Multiple regression coefficients

	Standardised coefficients	t	Sig.	Collinearity statistics	
	Beta			Tolerance	VIF
(Constant)		−3.056	0.003		
Centrality	0.049	0.897	0.372	0.613	1.632
Expertise	0.079	1.299	0.196	0.500	2.001
Norms	0.053	0.878	0.381	0.516	1.937
Goals	0.068	1.028	0.306	0.432	2.315
Trust	0.143	2.696	0.008	0.663	1.508
Reciprocity	0.061	0.979	0.329	0.478	2.091
Reputation	0.193	2.839	0.005	0.404	2.477
Enjoy helping	0.431	5.258	0.000	0.278	3.601

A dependent variable: online knowledge sharing

12.6   Hypotheses Testing

Multiple regression was used to test the hypotheses given that the limited sample size made it unsuitable for structural equation modelling (Hair et al. 2006). The factor score of each construct is calculated from the confirmatory factor analysis and is used in the model to test the relationship between online knowledge sharing and its antecedents. Overall, the R indicates that 76.3% of the variance in online knowledge sharing is explained by the eight independent variables. The collinearity statistics are within acceptable range of tolerance (>0.1) and VIF (<10) indicating multicollinearity is not a problem.

Table 12.3 reports the results obtained by regression knowledge sharing on the independent variables. Four hypotheses (H_4, H_{6a} and H_{6b}) were supported while the remaining four hypotheses (H_1, H_2, H_{3a}, H_{3b} and H_5) were rejected. In summary, the empirical study showed that the hypotheses of individual expertise, trust, personal reputation and enjoy helping were accepted.

12.7   Discussion

This study investigates dimensions of social capital that affect individual knowledge sharing in electronic networks of practice. It fills a gap in the literature by exploring the impact of social capital dimensions on an individual's capability to share knowledge in university blog communities. The study found that 'Enjoy helping' had the strongest influence on online knowledge sharing which is similar to Taylor and Murphy (2008) who also found that altruism significantly influences blogging behaviour. The interesting aspect is that both studies were conducted on blogging communities within an academic context that were not related directly to student assessment. Therefore, within the context of knowledge sharing, we suggest that altruism or 'enjoy helping' plays a significant role in knowledge sharing behaviours. 'Enjoy helping' is an internal motivation resulting from individual characteristics rather than behaviours that can be influenced by academic institutions. To improve active participation through students who 'enjoy helping', universities can recruit participants who currently display these characteristics such as: student mentors; student volunteers for open days and students participating in guild activities. By generating a critical mass of students who enjoy helping and who enjoy participating, the blogging community is more likely to become a sustainable online space where students can meet and discuss their issues.

Trust is not often included within educational contexts although Taylor and Murphy (2008) included commitment which is strongly correlated to trust in their study, though it was found to be insignificant. Outside of educational contexts, Chiu et al. (2006) is the only other study that has found trust to be significant. Their study was conducted within an IT knowledge community and an open learning type of culture. From this, we can infer that when significant learning opportunities emerge from the blogging community then people need to 'trust' what the other participants post. To improve the students trust with other participants, universities can recruit students who currently have a high profile within the university community and get these students to post discussions. Students with high profiles are likely to engender trust thus attracting others to either post or read the blogging discussions.

In our study, reputation was also found to significantly influence online knowledge sharing, but Taylor and Murphy (2008) found reputation an insignificant influence. This difference could be due to Taylor and Murphy (2008) conducting their research within an academic staff blogging community (accounting education), whereas our study was conducted within a student blogging community. Students might place more emphasis on their reputation through the knowledge contributed while academic staff reputation is built on publications and research. Students who have a desire to improve their reputation may also be those who have an existing high level reputation within the university community. Therefore, similar to the previous discussion, recruiting students who currently have a credible reputation – participating in the blogging community will further enhance their reputation – thus supplying a motivation to continue posting.

A major objective of this study was to investigate social capital as a lens for understanding knowledge exchange in blog sites. While three dimensions of social capital were investigated (structural, cognitive and relational), only constructs within the relational dimension of social capital were found to have a positive influence on online knowledge sharing. One possible explanation might be the relative infancy of the blog sites that were studied. One third of respondents had participated in the blog communities for less than 1 month. An individual's cognitive capital develops over time as s/he interacts with others in the community. Familiar narratives that develop through interaction in a common set of practices or problems encountered in a community of practice require time to develop. Similarly, structural capital and measures of centrality are dependent on the structural links created through social interactions. If participants were relative newcomers to the blog site, the opportunity to develop cognitive and structural capital may not have been afforded sufficient time. Hence, interaction in the online community is more likely to be driven by personal factors such as personal reputation and enjoyment in helping others. Furthermore, the voluntaristic nature of the blog sites from which the respondents were drawn may also be a factor which would emphasise relational capital over structural and cognitive dimensions.

Findings of this study offer practical implications for Australian universities. While the use of blogs in universities for knowledge sharing is still in its infancy, the findings from this study do provide the basis for Australian universities to consider how they might encourage greater use of voluntary blog sites. For example, encouraging students who are motivated by helping others and the enhancement of personal reputation to become active in the blog community may (at least in initial stages) promote wider adoption. The model could also be specifically applied by individual Australian universities to study the characteristics of their individual university settings. This would allow them to gain an insight into the significant social dimensions that could enhance their staff and students' behaviour in knowledge sharing within weblog communities.

While the findings of the research provide direction for further study, there are limitations to this study which would need to be addressed in subsequent studies. Firstly, the study is based on online settings in Australian universities; given differences in university contexts around the world, results generated from this study may not be applicable to other university online settings in different countries. Secondly, the sample size is small and limited to university blog communities. The small sample size may in part be a reflection of the relative youth of the sampled communities and therefore generalisation of the findings should be taken with caution. Furthermore, the small sample size might suggest that these results may not be applicable to business organisations in some industries. A third limitation of the study relates to the survey items. Given that it was not possible to gain access to logs of the online communities, the study relied on self-reporting of knowledge sharing behaviour and dimensions of social capital. Therefore, an element of bias may have been introduced in the responses of the self-reporting questionnaire. Finally, previous research shows that the knowledge context is linked with the culture in organisations (De Long and Fahey 2000; Ford and Chan 2003). Hence, the findings may be different if the study applies in different organisational, cultural and national settings.

12.8   Conclusion

This study set out to investigate the role of social capital in influencing knowledge sharing in voluntary online communities in university settings. Results highlighted that students who trust the other blogging participants; want to improve their personal reputation and enjoy helping others are more likely to participate in blogs relating to courses where there is no link to assessment or unit instruction.

As online communities develop further and Web 2.0 technologies take on a more prominent role in the lives of students and university communities in general, understanding the impact of social capital and online knowledge sharing by using new technologies will continue to be a significant topic within the information systems education literature. Future studies should examine how social capital affects organisational knowledge sharing in different workplaces and online settings. One limitation of our study is that our sample is based on Australian universities and future research should consider universities from other countries. Each social capital dimension should be independently tested for its effect on online knowledge sharing. Future research should also examine how the differences in organisational cultures affect individual online knowledge sharing.

References

Adler, P.S., Kwon, S.W.: Social capital: prospects for a new concept. Acad. Manage. Rev. **27**(1), 17–40 (2002)

Chavis, D.M., Hogge, J.H., McMillion, D.W., Wandersman, A.: Sense of Community Through Brunswik's Lens: A First Look', Journal of Community Psychology, **14**(1), pp 24–40 (1986)

Chen, C., Wu, J., Yang, S.: Accelerating the use of weblogs as an alternative method to deliver case-based learning. Int. J. E Learn. **7**(2), 331–349 (2008)

Chiu, C.M., Hsu, M.H., Wang, E.T.G.: Understanding knowledge sharing in virtual communities: an integration of social capital and social cognitive theories. Decis. Support Syst. **42**, 1872–1888 (2006)

Chow, W.S., Chan, L.S.: Social network, social trust and shared goals in organizational knowledge sharing. Inf. Manage. **45**, 458–465 (2008)

Constant, D., Kiesler, S., Sproull, L.: What's mine is ours, or is it? A study of attitudes about information sharing. Inf. Syst. Res. **5**(4), 400–421 (1994)

Constant, D., Sproull, L., Kiesler, S.: The kindness of strangers: the usefulness of electronic weak ties for technical advice. Organ. Sci. **7**(2), 119–135 (1996)

Cronin, J.J.: Upgrading to web 2.0: an experiential project to build a marketing wiki. J. Mark. Educ. **31**(1), 66–75 (2009)

Davenport, T.H., Prusak, L.: Working Knowledge: How Organizations Manage What They Know. Harvard Business School Press, Boston (1998)

De Long, D.W., Fahey, L.: Diagnosing cultural barriers to knowledge management. Acad. Manag. Exec. **14**(4), 113–127 (2000)

Du, H.S., Wagner, C.: Learning with weblogs: an empirical investigation, in system sciences. In: HICSS '05, 38th Annual Hawaii International Conference, pp. 7b–7b (2005)

Efimova, L., Moor, A.D.: Beyond personal webpublishing: an exploratory study of conventional blogging practices. In: 38th Hawaii International Conference on System Sciences, IEEE, pp. 107a–107a (2005)

Ford, D.P., Chan, Y.E.: Knowledge sharing in a multi-cultural setting: a case study. Knowl. Manag. Res. Pract. **1**(1), 11–27 (2003)

Hair, J.J.F., Black, W.C., Babin, B.J., Anderson, R.E., Tatham, R.L.: Multivariate Data Analysis, 6th edn. Pearson Prentice Hall, Upper Saddle River (2006)

Hsu, C.L., Lin, J.C.: Acceptance of blog usage: the roles of technology acceptance social influences and knowledge sharing motivation. Inf. Manage. **45**, 65–74 (2008)

Huang, S.L., Yang, C.W.: Designing a semantic Bliki system to support different types of knowledge and adaptive learning. Comput. Educ. **53**, 701–712 (2009)

Huffaker, D.: The educated blogger: using weblogs to promote literacy in the classroom. Assoc. Adv. Comput. Educ. J. **13**(2), 91–98 (2005)

Huysman, M., Wulf, V.: Social Capital and Information Technology. The MIT Press, Cambridge (2004)

Jarvenpaa, S.L., Staples, D.S.: The use of collaborative electronic media for information sharing: an exploratory study of determinants. J. Strateg. Inf. Syst. **9**(2–3), 129–154 (2000)

Kankanhalli, A., Tan, B.C.Y., Kwok-Kee, W.: Contributing knowledge to electronic knowledge repositories: an empirical investigation. MIS Q. **29**(1), 113–143 (2005)

Kim, S.: The phenomenon of blogs and theoretical model of blog use in educational contexts. Comput. Educ. **51**, 1342–1352 (2008)

Kim, S., Lee, H.: The impact of organizational context and information technology on employee knowledge-sharing capabilities. Public Adm. Rev. **66**(3), 370–385 (2006)

Leana, C.R., Van Buren, H.J.I.I.I.: Organizational social capital and employment practices. Acad. Manage. Rev. **24**(3), 538–555 (1999)

Lee, J.K., Kang, J., Park, J.H., Park, K.: Excellence of knowledge management comes only when combined with corporate culture: LG CNS. In: Lee, J.K., Siew, B.G.K., Sethi, V. (eds.) Premier e-Business Cases from Asia: Problem-Solution-Challenge-Impact Approach, pp. 189–219. Prentice Hall, Pearson Education South Asia Pte Ltd, Singapore (2007)

Lesser, E., Prusak, L.: Communities of Practice, Social Capital and Organizational knowledge in Knowledge and Communities, (eds.) Leasser E.L., Fontaine M., Slusher A.J., Butterworth-Heinemann A., Boston, pp 123–132 (2000)

Lochner, K., Kawachi, I., Kennedy, B.P.: Social capital: a guide to its measurement. Health Place **5**(4), 259–270 (1999)

Lu, H.-P, Hsiao, K.-L.: Understanding intention to continuously share information on weblogs. Internet Research **17**(4), 345–361 (2007)

McAllister, D.J.: Affect- and cognition-based trust as foundations for interpersonal cooperation in organizations. Acad. Manage. J. **38**(1), 24–59 (1995)

McGill, T.J., Klobas, J.E.: A task-technology fit view of learning management system impact. Comput. Educ. **52**, 496–508 (2009)

McLure Wasko, M., Faraj, S.: It is what one does: why people participate and help others in electronic communities of practice. J. Strateg. Inf. Syst. **9**(2–3), 155–173 (2000)

McLure Wasko, M., Faraj, S.: Why should I share? Examining social capital and knowledge contribution in electronic networks of practice. MIS Q. **29**(1), 35–57 (2005)

Moody, E.J.: Internet use and its relationship to loneliness. Cyberpsychol. Behav. **4**(3), 393–401 (2001)

Nahapiet, J., Ghoshal, S.: Social capital, intellectual capital, and the organizational advantage academy of management. Acad. Manage. Rev. **23**(2), 242–266 (1998)

Nonaka, I., Takeuchi, H.: The Knowledge-Creating Company: How Japanese Companies Create the Dynamics of Innovation. Oxford University Press, New York (1995)

Parks, M.R., Floyd, K.: Making friends in cyberspace. J. Commun. **46**(1), 80–97 (1996)

Phang, C.W., Kankanhalli, A., Sabherwal, R.: Usability and sociability in online communities: a comparative study of knowledge seeking and contribution. J. Assoc. Inf. Syst. **10**(10), 721–747 (2009)

Ridings, C.M., Gefen, D., Arinze, B.: Some antecedents and effects of trust in virtual communities. J. Strateg. Inf. Syst. **11**(3–4), 271–295 (2002)

Szulanski, G.: The process of knowledge transfer: a diachronic analysis of stickiness. Organ. Behav. Hum. Decis. Process. **82**(1), 9–27 (2000)

Taylor, E., Murthy, U.S.: Knowledge sharing among accounting academics in an electronic network of practice. Acc. Horiz. **23**(2), 151–179 (2009)

Tsai, W., Ghoshal, S.: Social capital and value creation: the role of intrafirm networks. Acad. Manage. J. **41**(4), 464–476 (1998)

Walsham, G.: Knowledge management: the benefits and limitations of computer systems. Eur. Manage. J. **19**(6), 599–608 (2001)

Wang, Y., Fesenmaier, D.R.: Assessing motivation of contribution in online communities: an empirical investigation of an online travel community. Electron. Mark. **13**(1), 33–45 (2003)

Wasserman, S., Faust, K.: Social Network Analysis: Methods and Applications. Cambridge University Press, Cambridge (1994)

Wellman, B., Haase, A.Q., Witte, J., Hampton, K.: Does the internet increase, decrease, or supplement social capital? Social networks, participation, and community commitment Am. Behav Sci **45**(3), 136 155 (2001)

Chapter 13
Understanding Online Sociability: Investigations on Sociability Determinants and Cultural Differences in Sociability Perception

Qin Gao and Pei-Luen Patrick Rau

Abstract New online social tools provide more opportunities for social interaction between learners and instructors and among learners. The extent that a computer-supported communication environment supports online social interaction is referred to as the sociability of the environment. In this chapter, an integrated and user-centered approach to understand sociability of social media is presented. Based upon a wide review of literature, a framework of sociability is developed with five major components: purpose and benefit, people, social climate, mediated communication, and technological system. Then significant factors that affect the sociability of social media are identified based upon three empirical studies. The relationship between these factors and the user attitudes and behavior intentions are examined. The influence of culture on sociability is examined and an empirical comparison between German and Chinese internet users with regards to perceived importance of sociability items is presented. Finally, implications for design and use of social media for learning are discussed.

13.1 Introduction: Social Media, CSCL, and Sociability

Social interaction between learners and instructors or among learners is considered a central component of learner-centered pedagogies, and the positive relationship between interaction and learning has been confirmed in both online and offline learning (Gunawardena 1995; Johnson and Johnson 1994; Johnson et al. 1985; Menzel and Carrell 1999; Rovai and Barnum 2003; Wenger 2007). Empirical studies provide evidence that the quantity and the quality of social interactions influence perceived learning and learner/instructor satisfaction in computer-supported

Q. Gao (✉) • P.-L.P. Rau
Department of Industrial Engineering, Institute of Human Factors and Ergonomics, Tsinghua University, Beijing 100084, P.R. China
e-mail: gaoqin@tsinghua.edu.cn; rpl@tsinghua.edu.cn

B. White et al. (eds.), *Social Media Tools and Platforms in Learning Environments*,
DOI 10.1007/978-3-642-20392-3_13, © Springer-Verlag Berlin Heidelberg 2011

collaborative learning (CSCL) significantly (Fredericksen et al. 1999; Picciano 2002; Rovai and Barnum 2003; Zhou et al. 2007). Previous research on collaborative learning investigated the influence of social interaction from two perspectives. From the cognition perspective, the social constructivist model and the theory of community of practices claims that social interaction is a fundamental process of cognition development and knowledge construction (Vygotskǐ 1978; Wenger 2007). Analyses of dialogues among students and with faculty provide evidence of the mediating role of such interactions in the development of thinking and learning (Ven der Linden and Renshaw 2004). From the socio-emotional perspective, social interaction plays an important role in social relationship development, social identity building, trust and belongingness development, and development of a sense of community. Earlier studies underlined the importance of a warm and supportive social–emotional environment that provides learners a condition in which they are willing to discuss, to critique, and to be critiqued (Bogdan et al. 2002; Kollock 1998; Rourke and Anderson 2002). In particular, Wegerif's study (1998) found that individual success or failure is associated with whether students felt like outsiders or insiders of the community. The result suggested that lack of a sense of community is likely to make learners anxious, defensive, and unwilling to take the risks involved in collaborative learning.

The recent rapid development of online communication tools, especially the new social media, provides more possibilities for online social interaction. The term "social media" or "social software" refers to internet software which enables groups of people to communicate and to collaborate, from something very familiar such as email, instant messengers (IM), and group forums, to new applications such as blogs, social networking services (SNS), and web-based collaborative editing tools (Boyd et al. 2007; Davis 2003). These new tools provide support for geographically distributed learners to share ideas and resources, collaborate and create content, and develop relationships and communities of practices with others. It is expected that enhanced social affordance will facilitate learner-centered pedagogies and give rise to alternative education paradigms, such as knowledge building paradigm (Anderson 2008; Frydenberg 2006; McLoughlin et al. 2007).

The availability of more possibilities for online social interaction, however, does not guarantee that social interaction does occur (Kreijns et al. 2003). Many researchers argue that what really matters is not the technology, but how the technology is used. To foster social interaction within online communities, both technological and sociological properties of online communication systems should be planned and designed carefully (Godwin 1994; Kollock 1998; Millen and Patterson 2002; Preece and Maloney-Krichmar 2003; Whitaker and Parker 2000). The issue of facilitating online social interaction is discussed in studies from different areas (CSCL, online communities, e-commerce, computer-supported collaborative working), and related but different concepts are used to address the social property of communication technologies, such as social presence, social affordance, social space, sociality, and sociability (Beenen et al. 2004; Bouman et al. 2008; Chatti et al. 2007; De Souza and Preece 2004; Gunawardena 1995; Kreijns et al. 2002; Wellman et al. 2001). This leads to the need for an integrated approach to understand what makes a computer-supported communication (CMC) environment sociable. In addition, sociability design guidelines based upon empirical studies are desirable.

This chapter presents an integrated and user-centered approach to understand sociability of social media and its implications for educational use of social media. Section 13.2 discusses the concept of sociability and its measurements. Following a wide review of literature, a framework of sociability of social media consisting of five components is proposed and illustrated in Sect. 13.3. Following this, Sect. 13.4 presents a series of empirical studies, in which factors that affect the sociability of social media were identified and the influence of sociability on user attitudes was examined. In Sect. 13.5, the impact of cultures on user perceptions of sociability is explored and exemplified by an empirical comparison between German and Chinese internet users with regard to their perceived perceptions of sociability.

13.2 Online Sociability: Definitions and Measurements

Socialization is an essential human need. Simmel (1949) claimed that although individuals enter into human association because of special interests, there is always a component of pure socialization within this motivation. In sociology and psychology, sociability is referred to as either the amount of socialization activities or the psychological tendency to socially interact with other people (Nie 2001; Rubin et al. 1989). In a technical context, where socialization is mediated by information and communication technologies, the term can be used to describe the property of the technical systems to enhance user socialization both for task-oriented and non-task-oriented purposes.

The discussion about the competency of online communication tools for human–human socialization is nothing new. As early as 1976, when the use of computer networks was still limited to the army and universities, researchers were discussing the ability of telecommunication to provide enough presence of other people and to support the formation of interpersonal relationships (Short et al. 1976). Since then, the socialization ability of the technology has been discussed for various purposes (community building, marketing, collaborative learning, social-support exchanging, social recommendation, and collaborative filtering) using different concepts, such as media richness, social presence, social space, and sociality. Some concepts focus on functional properties of the technology required to convey cues for effective social interaction (media richness Daft and Lengel 1984), some emphasize the importance of user perception and subjective assessment of the sociability of a mediated environment (social presence Short et al. 1976), and others view system sociability as a high-level construct consisting of social and political components (sociability in Preece 2001).

All of these concepts are related in one way or another to one single key element: online social interaction, although they differ in perspective. All these perspectives are indispensable to support online social interaction. To provide an integrated understanding of the impact of mediated technology on socialization, online sociability is defined as: *the extent to which the communication environment mediated by social media is perceived to facilitate social interaction and to enhance social connectivity.* This definition is adapted from Keijins et al. (2002) but with a wider scope to contain more general social interaction other than those taking place in groups and communities with clear group boundaries.

As a pioneer of online sociability studies, Preece (2000) proposed three components of sociability related to social policies: purpose (a community's shared focus that provides a reason for individual members to belong to the community), people (the people who interact with each other in the community and who have individual, social, and organization needs), and policies (the language and protocols that guide people's interactions). Based on these components, he proposed a battery of measures of sociability, including obvious measures such as the number of participants in a community, the number of messages per unit of time, member satisfaction, and some less obvious measures such as the amount of reciprocity, the number of on-topic messages, and trustworthiness among others. Most of Preece's measures are objective, focusing on collective activities and properties of online communities, and are useful for predicting the success of online communities. But they do not directly measure user perceptions of sociability. Kreijns et al. (2007), on the contrary, developed a sociability measure based on subjective assessments. This one-dimensional measure using self-reported scales is able to determine the perceived degree of sociability of an online environment which may not be reflected accurately through objective measures.

13.3   A Framework of Online Sociability

Online sociability inherently involves both human–human interaction and human–technology interaction, and both social issues (trust, reciprocation, intimacy) and technological issues (the infrastructure of information technology, speed, the ease of use). Past research from multiple disciplines (sociology, communications, computer science, e-commerce, information systems, and online communities) discussed online social interaction from either one of the two perspectives or both. Based upon a review of this literature, a sociability framework is proposed consisting of five major components, each addressing an essential perspective for the design of a sociable online environment. As shown in Fig. 13.1, the five components are: the purpose and benefits individuals expect from interaction, mediated technology they interact through, people they interact with, social climate and moderations, and the technology system that supports the networked interaction.

13.3.1   Purpose and Benefit

Social media users interact with others to achieve a purpose. The purpose could be either instrumental (acquiring useful information) or social (social networking)

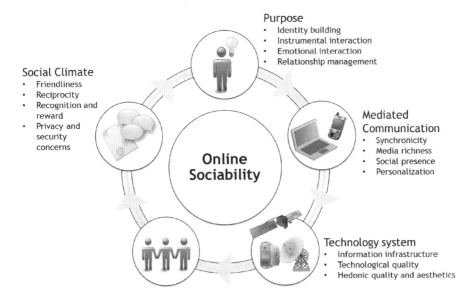

Fig. 13.1 Key components of online sociability

(Bouman et al. 2008). The level of user-need fulfillment or perceived benefits was found to influence user satisfaction and participation in online activities (Kim et al. 2004; Whitaker et al. 2000). Some research suggests that online community developers should provide a strong statement of purpose so users know what to expect (Kim 2000; Preece 2000; Preece and Maloney-Krichmar 2003). Purposes of online social interaction could be categorized according to the type of social support users want to exchange through the interaction. There are essentially five types of social support: esteem, informational, emotional, social network, and tangible support (Cobb 1979; Cutrona and Russell 1990). In online social networks, tangible support is often not direct. Rather, people may request or confirm information about such support (meeting offline) through online social interaction. Combining tangible support with informational support, and classified purposes for using social media identifies four categories:

- Identity building for esteem support: Identity building is a fundamental condition for any cooperative relationships to emerge and persist (Axelrod and Hamilton 1981). The impoverished communication and potentially asynchronous nature of CMC environments, on the one hand, limit the number of interpersonal cues for self-presentation; on the other hand, give users more opportunities to present themselves selectively (Gibbs et al. 2006; Toma et al. 2008). In distributed learning groups, the need for self-presentation was found to affect learner collaboration (Kimmerle and Cress 2007). Providing proper mechanisms for self-presentation (individual contribution behavior) is an opportunity for designers and instructors to stimulate interaction among learners.

- Instrumental interaction for Informational support and tangible support: Information acquisition and exchange is a major motivation of online participation (Ardichvili et al. 2003; Koh et al. 2007; Whitaker et al. 2000). The new social media make the task even easier. They allow every common user to compose and share their own knowledge or ideas in a range of modalities (through websites: flickr.com, youtube.com, and services: podcast), to aggregate knowledge from many sources for personal use (use of RSS), and to mix, amend, and recombine micro-content from the community (mashup).
- Emotional interaction for emotional support: Despite the lack of nonverbal cues, online communication tools provide some disparate opportunities for emotional interaction, such as the accessibility of computer technology, the gathering of like-minded people with similar interests or problems, the anonymity that enables deep and intimate disclosures, and the low barriers to disclosure of negative aspects of one's self (Bargh and McKenna 2004; Tidwell and Walther 2002). Research has shown that online tools, if utilized properly, can effectively support the exchange of emotional-support and empathy among people who do not know each other, as well as among people who are closely related (Maloney-Krichmar and Preece 2005; Rice and Love 1987; Vetere et al. 2005). Exchange of social–emotional support is also considered a major ingredient of learner-centered instruction in CSCL as it is critical to encourage students to share their experience and beliefs (Gunawardena 1995).
- Relationship management for social network support: Numerous studies show that social media can be used to develop and intensify tightly-knit relationships, to stay connected with loosely connected contacts, and to expand one's social network through linkages of like-minded people (Davis 2003; Ellison et al. 2007; Koku et al. 2001). For learners, relationship development within the group can improve group cohesiveness and promote collaborative learning, and the extended capability of linking weakly-tied people through new social media enables the discovery of new friends and resources (McLoughlin et al. 2007).

13.3.2 *People*

An individual's use of a type of communication technology cannot be separated from his/her communication partner's use (Markus 1987). From the group level, user perceptions of the total amount of users will influence the perceived usefulness of the communication media, and will further influence user participation behaviors (Koh et al. 2007; Li et al. 2005; Lou et al. 2000). As argued by Short et al. (1976), "the evidence that the other is attending" is important for promoting socially meaningful interaction. In addition, it was found that the similarity of participant interests has a significant effect on user satisfaction and loyalty to an online community (Kim et al. 2004), although having no significant effect on participation behaviors (Beenen et al. 2004). At the interpersonal level, the user attitudes towards the online community and participation intentions are influenced by the strength of relationship with other members of the community, the level of intimacy among them, and whether they are acquainted in real life or not (Cho et al. 2007; Lento et al. 2006; Li et al. 2005; Rau et al. 2008).

13.3.3 Social Climate

There are a number of social–contextual factors that may encourage or limit online social interaction:

- Friendliness – a warm and friendly atmosphere is important to foster open communication among users. Whereas researchers proposed certain guidelines for fostering friendly social climates, the proper implementation relies on a deep understanding of group dynamics and how social influence will take place. For example, a moderation policy is considered to be necessary to deter uncivil behavior, such as flaming (Andrews 2002; Preece 2001), but improper implementation of such policies may inhibit open discussion in cyberspace.
- Reciprocity – reciprocity refers to a pattern of behavior where people respond to friendly or hostile actions with similar actions even if no material gains are expected (Fehr and Gächter 2000). The expectation of reciprocation from partners is a main factor in the voluntary contribution to virtual groups and a strong norm of reciprocity is a vital factor for the survival of self-sustaining online communities (Andrews 2002; Chan et al. 2004; Dellarocas et al. 2003; Maloney-Krichmar and Preece 2005).
- Recognition and reward program – recognition from others, either in an intangible form such as identity reinforcement and reputation building or in a tangible form, was found to positively influence user participation behavior (Butler et al. 2002; Chan et al. 2004). A direct implication is that recognition and reward programs should be developed to stimulate active participation (Andrews 2002; Koh et al. 2007).
- Concern for privacy and security – The privacy concern in online communities is just as prevalent as it is for real-world interaction (Cranor et al. 2000). However, web users, especially young people, are found often providing personal data generously and unconcernedly, which may expose them to various physical and cyber risks (Gross and Acquisti 2005). A plausible reason for this is that they find the benefits from public disclosure of certain information in certain situations outweigh its costs. An effective privacy protection policy for social media should consider the dynamic social contexts and the changing information needs and uses (Dourish and Anderson 2006).

13.3.4 Mediated-Communication

The research shows differences between CMC and face-to-face communications. CMC allows social interactions with less constrains of geographic distance or temporal differences. It enables both synchronous and asynchronous communication modes, and the two modes create different social climates for interaction. Whereas synchronous communication allows spontaneous and immediate feedback, the asynchronous mode can reduce the pressure for an immediate response and allow more thoughtful and organized conversations (Hiltz and Turoff 1981; Walther 1996). Furthermore, the lack of nonverbal cues and the low information bandwidth limit the level of social presence in CMC. Social presence refers to the degree to which a person is perceived as a real person in CMC (Short et al. 1976). There is a relationship between the amount of online interaction and learner satisfaction in CSCL environments (Gunawardena 1995; Gunawardena and Zittle 1997; Tu 2001). Social presence can be enhanced by including nonverbal cues in CMC, such as avatars, graphics, videos, and gestures (Bente and Krämer 2002; Bente et al. 2008; Fish et al. 1992; Smith et al. 2002; Yoo and Alavi 2001). Another closely related concept is media richness, which refers to the ability of information to change understanding within a time interval or provide substantial new consensual understanding (Daft and Lengel 1984). An interesting conclusion held by richness theory is that matching media richness with a task will improve communication performance. Performance improves when rich media are used for equivocal tasks and lean media are used for non-equivocal tasks. Empirical studies, however, yield both supportive and conflicting results for this conclusion (Dennis and Kinney 1998; Panteli 2002; Schliemann et al. 2002). In addition, different users tend to perceive the same verbal cues differently depending on the environment. Thus customizability of CMC is important to compensate for this difference and to enhance user enjoyment (Li et al. 2005; Tractinsky et al. 2004).

13.3.5   Technological System

Online social interaction is inevitably influenced by the technological system, which provides a context for people to meet and communicate. Problems related to the technical infrastructure such as cost, accessibility, speed, and information search facilities, were identified by community moderators to be barriers of online community development (Whitaker and Parker 2000). Technological qualities of the system, such as reliability, usability, and flexibility, are also found to influencing user willingness to interact with others and their satisfaction with the interaction (Kim 2000; Lin and Lee 2006; Preece 2001). For new technologies to be adopted, simplicity and ease of learning are particularly important to support interaction among non-expert web users with diverse technical backgrounds (Avram 2006; Bross et al. 2007; Chatti et al. 2007).

Interaction tools which are often used for leisure purposes should also be fun and engaging. Van der Heijen (2004) and Li et al. (2005) found that the fun aspect of IM motivates people to use it more than its usefulness deserves. IM users were found motivated more intrinsically by the pleasures they experienced from the interaction itself rather than extrinsically for the instrumental purpose. This suggests that social media designers should consider joy of use and the hedonistic values of the technology. Furthermore, the aesthetic design of social media is also important for satisfactory social interaction. People are affected by the physical attractiveness of other people and artifacts and this further affects their social interaction with others and the consequent relationship development (Bloch 1995; Coates 2003; Dion et al. 1972; Hamermesh and Biddle 1994).

13.4   Factors Influencing Online Sociability

The framework presented above provides a systematic approach for designers and instructors to understand the dynamics of social interaction from all relevant perspectives and a basis to empirically identify and validate factors that influence online sociability. This section presents a series of qualitative and quantitative Chinese studies by which to explore, identify, and validate factors that influence online sociability (Gao et al. 2010).

13.4.1   Pilot Study

A pilot study was conducted to obtain qualitative understanding of how online social tools are utilized to support people's social life and what factors influence perceived sociability. Thirty-five social media users, including 20 students, were interviewed. The majority were selected from the researchers' social networks and several were recruited by posting advertisements on Xiaonei.com (a Chinese SNS for college students) and on personal blogs. Among the participants were 17 females and 18 males, and their ages ranged from 17 to 49 ($M = 24.7$). Within the sample, there were a variety of Internet usage patterns and experiences, from 2 years of experience and using the Internet for 1 h a week, to 10 years of experience and using the Internet for more than 40 h a week. During the interviews, participants were asked to describe how they used communication channels (FTF, telephone, SMS, email, IM, blog, BBS, SNS, and online games) in their daily social life; their usage and attitude towards different social media applications; and the factors that influence their decisions to try a new social media application, to continue using social media applications and to abandon social media applications. Permanent audio records of the interview process were obtained for all interview sessions with the permission of the participant. All the interviews were transcribed and coded for further analysis.

As shown in Table 13.1, social media serves many different purposes in various social contexts. Email is primarily used for formal communication, such as work-related or study-related issues. It is often used to communicate with weakly connected people or workmates but is rarely used with familiar friends, especially with young people. However, three participants mentioned that email can also be

Table 13.1 Communication contexts, audience, and purposes of different media

Tool	contexts	Identity building	Instrumental interaction	Emotional interaction	Relationship management
Email	Used more in work life, dealing with formal issues (not instantly needing a reply)	Low support	Strong support for work/study due to its convenience to use, high accessibility of the service, capability to transfer big files, and provision of a permanent log of conversation	Some support for deep communication in intimate relationships; rarely used in daily emotional support exchange due to the lack of contextual information and possible misunderstandings	Some support for maintaining relations with distant people
IM	Used more in personal life	Low support	Strong support for distributed work, convenient and cost saving; good for sending big files which cannot be sent by email	Strong interaction richness due to its synchronized communication and informal communication style, but it also leads to aimless conversation	Strong support for maintaining connections due to the popularity of usage and the buddy list function
Blog	Used more in personal life	Strong support for building virtual and real identities	Strong support due to the ease of publishing and commenting, encourages deep communication, as the writer needs to elaborate feelings or ideas	Some support for deep communication, but the lack of immediacy and interactivity limits the effect of emotional supports	Some support for maintaining connections due to the buddy list function, but the unequal status of blogger and reader may limit the development of the relationship between users
BBS	Used both for work life and personal life	Some support for building virtual identities	Strong support due to the high informational value and searchability of BBS posts	Some emotional support, depending on if the user is willing to disclose personal issues to unknown people	Low support, anonymity, and low social responsibility make public BBS places lacking of trust and it is difficult to build real and lasting relationships

SNS	Personal life	Strong support for building real identities	Some support for weak connections among acquaintances	Strong emotional support, due to the trustful and relaxing atmosphere	Strong support for relationship maintenance due to the high authenticity of user population and the high level of trust
Online game	Personal life	Strong support for building totally different virtual identity	–	Some support for intimate interactions since game players share common interests, but it is difficult to transfer friendship built in online gaming to real life	–

used for deep communication regarding critical issues in an intimate relationship. IM is considered to be a versatile tool that is useful in both work and personal life, and is believed to be superior in emotional communication, such as exchanging support and gaining friends. Among the 28 blog users, 13 participants reported that the primary reason for maintaining a blog was self-presentation, and three participants mentioned that visiting a friend's blog with whom they had not kept frequent contact helped them to stay close in the relationship. Most of the participants joined a BBS primarily to seek information or for entertainment purposes rather than to socialize (in fact, only two participants reported socialization in BBSs). The results are consistent with previous studies that found that selection of communication media is influenced by the purpose and the partner's choice of communication (Haythornthwaite and Wellman 1998; Haythornthwaite 2002; Kim et al. 2007).

13.4.2   Study 1: Identifying Factors Affecting Perceived Sociability

The initial pool of sociability items contains items from previous studies together with items from the pilot study. These items were then pruned to ensure the centrality of the concepts, to minimize overlap and incompatibility between items, and to minimize the ambiguity of wording. Finally 34 items were retained. Based on the 34 items, an online survey consisting of two sections was constructed. The first section included questions about background, Internet experience, and experience and attitude regarding social software. In the second section, participants were asked to use a seven-point scale, anchored by the responses "very important" and "not important at all," to evaluate the importance of the 34 items as they related to their use of social software.

Undergraduate students at Tsinghua University and Beihang University were invited through emails to participate in the study. Out of the 195 collected responses, 163 responses were valid. Of the participants, 36% were females and 64% were males. The average age of participants was 20.2 years (SD = 1.29). The average length of Internet experience was 5.4 years (SD = 2.35), and the average, use of Internet was 18.5 h/week (SD = 13.26). An average of 4.9 h (SD = 4.6) was spent on online social activities per week. The large variance in weekly online socializing time indicates a wide variety of social media usage patterns and experiences within the sample.

Exploratory factor analysis (EFA) with varimax rotation was applied to identify the latent factor structure which gave an interpretable seven-factor structure as presented in Table 13.2. Nine items that did not load strongly on any factor with a loading over 0.45 or items that had cross-loadings were deleted. Altogether, 63.4% of the variance was explained. Factor 1, which was labeled *system competency*, explains most of variance, or 11.5% of the total. The items in this factor address the necessary system components that are required to deliver interactive, smooth, and

Table 13.2 Factor analysis result of study one

Factor	Item	Loading	Explained variance (%)	Mean
System performance	Speed	0.83	11.5	5.82
	Reliability	0.69		
	Disturbance prevention	0.68		
	Privacy	0.65		
	Information bandwidth	0.61		
Social climate	Open communication	0.73	10.8	5.67
	Immediacy	0.73		
	Friendliness	0.69		
	Security	0.64		
	Affective communication	0.55		
Benefits and reciprocity	Meaning to reality	0.68	9.3	4.29
	Reciprocity	0.66		
	Tangible rewards	0.65		
	Control of content quality	0.62		
People	Number of existing contacts	0.86	8.7	4.69
	Amount of users	0.74		
	Relations to existing contacts in the system	0.71		
Interaction richness	Customizability	0.67	8.1	5.01
	Information richness	0.65		
	Socio-emotional rewards	0.56		
Self presentation	Self-image building	0.70	8.0	4.25
	Reputation building	0.66		
Support for formal interaction	Authenticity	0.73	7.0	4.93
	Operation flexibility	0.57		
	Support for group activity	0.46		

reliable online interaction. It is interesting to note that *privacy* and *disturbance prevention* also loaded strongly on this factor. This indicates that the prevention of privacy intrusion and disturbance is assumed to be a basic competency of social media. Factor 2 was labeled *social climate*. Belonging to this factor are items describing a social atmosphere as being suitable and comfortable for social interaction. Factor 3 was labeled *benefits and reciprocity*. It describes the benefits that users expect from online social interaction. Users expect their input to be rewarded fairly, and their efforts can have an impact on their real life relationships in addition to their "virtual" relationships. Content quality control also matters, as the lack of such control will harm the benefits that users might gain from the system. Factor 4 was labeled *people*. Perception of sociability is also influenced by the number of members they can easily reach through the software, the number of people they know who are using the software, and the closeness of the relationship they have with these people. Factor 5 was labeled *interaction richness*. This factor is about how rich information representation can be and how easily users can customize the way that they interact with others. Additionally, the user perceptions of interaction richness are influenced by whether the socializing effort in the system can be recognized and whether socio-emotional rewards can be obtained. Factor 6, labeled *self-presentation*, addresses how well social media helps the users to convey an impression of themselves to other users, and consequently, how well the users can develop their reputation through verbal or non-verbal communication via the system. Factor 7 was labeled *support for formal interactions* since the items that are included in this factor are related to formal communication. To support formal communication, the *authenticity* of the user's identification and the content of the quality should be protected. Users should find it easy to organize group activities, such as initiating a discussion or arranging a meeting among a group. In addition, *operational flexibility* is also required to support formal communication, in which relationships are structured and communication rules exist, either explicitly or implicitly.

13.4.3 Study 2: Validating Sociability Factors and Relationship Between Sociability and Users' Attitude

The second study was designed to verify the relationship between design factors identified in the first study and the perceived sociability, and to examine the impact of sociability on user attitudes and behavioral intentions. Ten social-media applications, popular in China, were selected from five types of social media: email, IM, forum, blog, and SNS, with two applications in each genre. Participants were asked to select one application and to evaluate it with regards to its performance in terms of the seven dimensions that were extracted in the first study, using a seven-point Likert scale. Perceived sociability, user attitude towards the software, and intention to use the software, were also measured. The questionnaire was administered online. Participants were recruited by posting advertisements on: campus BBS at Tsinghua University and Beihang University, personal blogs, two Chinese SNSs (Xiaonei.com and kaixin001.com), and two public BBSs. Within 2 weeks, 298 responses were collected, which included 246 valid responses. The majority of the respondents were students (65%), but there were also 92 non-student respondents. There were 83 females and 163 males, with an age range from 16 to 40 ($M = 23.0$, SD $= 3.53$). The sample had a good Internet experience and many were heavy users. The average length of Internet experience was 6.7 years (SD $= 2.03$), spending an average of 14.4 h (SD $= 13.31$) in online social activities per week. The sample included both users that spent less than 2 h with social media (14%) and users that spent more than 30 h with social media (5%). The respondents reflected a wide range of possible user attitudes and opinions.

Multiple regression analyses were applied to examine the impact of each factor on the sociability of software. The coefficients of *social climate*, *benefits and reciprocity*, and *self presentation* and *support of weak connections* are significant at the $p < 0.01$ level, and the coefficient of *people* is significant at the $p < 0.05$ level. However, the coefficients of *system competency* and *interaction richness* are not significant in the model. Since different social-media applications support different types of social interaction, an examination of the relationship between sociability and design factors for each type of applications except for online forum (there were too few responses for running regression) was undertaken. The results show that the goodness-of-fit of all these models is sufficiently acceptable. The R^2 ranges from 0.56 to 0.73, which indicates the models have a high level of explanatory power. However, for different types of applications, the impact of different factors varies.

- For email applications, *social climate* and *support of weak connections* contribute significantly to *sociability*.
- For IM applications, all of the factors contribute significantly to *sociability*, except for *system competency*.
- For blog applications, only *interaction richness* contributes to *sociability*.
- For SNS, *people* contribute significantly to sociability and *social climate* has a marginal impact on *sociability*.

Interaction richness contributes significantly to the sociability of IM, and is the only contributing factor for blog sociability. In all of these models, the *system competency* is not a significant predictor of sociability. Therefore *system competency* was removed from the influencing factors. The remaining six factors can explain 61% of *sociability*.

Figure 13.2 presents the validated model of sociability. It shows that *sociability* has a significant and strong impact on both the attitude towards the application ($b = 0.37$, $t = 7.03$, $p < 0.001$) and the intention to use it ($b = 0.49$, $t = 8.05$,

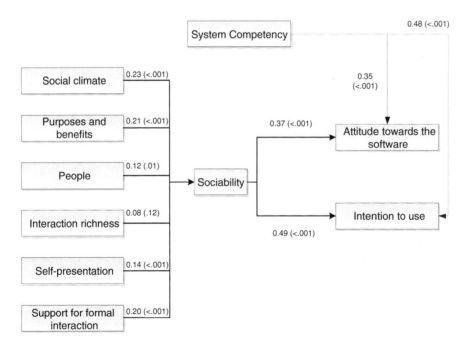

Fig. 13.2 Relationships between design factors, sociability, and user attitude

$p < 0.001$). *Sociability* itself can predict 34% of the attitude towards the application and 40% of the intention to use it. With *system competency* included in the model, 43% of user attitudes towards social media and 51% of the intention to use can be explained. The coefficients of *sociability* and *system competency* in the two regression formulas were very close, which indicates that *sociability* is as important as the *system competency* features (speed, reliability, and information bandwidth). This result advocates the importance of supporting sociability in system design by integrating sociological, psychological, and technological considerations with the overall goal to facilitate online social interaction.

13.5 Cross-Cultural Differences in Sociability Perception and Consequent Design Implications

13.5.1 Cross-Cultural Difference and Implications for Online Sociability

People from different cultures think and behave differently, and they interact with each other in different ways (Adler et al. 1992; Hinton et al. 2000; Norenzayan and Nisbett 2000). It is very probable that they perceive the sociability of technical systems in different ways. Social media designed for one culture may not work well for another. In addition, the development of new social media enables people from different cultural backgrounds to share knowledge and collaborate with each other. Therefore understanding of cultural differences in sociability perception is desired not only for cross-cultural software design but also for cross-cultural knowledge construction and collaborative learning.

This section explores the impact of cultures on user perceptions of sociability. Cross-cultural literature discusses differences in cognitive styles between eastern and western cultures. People from eastern cultures such as China are characterized as thinking in a holistic, relational, and concrete way, and the western cognitive style is depicted as analytic, functional, and abstract (Nisbett et al. 2001; Stewart and Bennett 1991). On the basis of a wide survey of IBM employees in 53 countries, Hofstede proposed five dimensions which quantify cross-cultural differences (Hofstede and Hofstede 1997; Hofstede and Bond 1988), as discussed below:

- *Power distance* refers to the extent to which the less powerful members of groups or categories expect and accept that power is distributed unequally. In small distance index countries, the degree of dependence in hierarchical relationships is low, and the emotional distance between subordinates and their superiors is low, which is just the opposite of countries with high power distance index.
- *Individualism/collectivism* refers to the extent to which the ties between individuals are loose/tight. In individual societies, people care mainly about themselves and their immediate connections like family members; on the contrary, in collective societies, people are integrated into powerful groups and the

sacrifice of freedom in exchange for support and protection from the group is often considered necessary.

- *Masculinity/femininity* refers to the extent to which social gender roles are distinct/ overlap. This indicator mainly quantifies the tendency of either favoring an assertive and competitive social role or a caring, social–environment–oriented social role of men.
- *Uncertainty avoidance* refers to the extent to which the members of groups or categories feel threatened by uncertain or unknown situations. Uncertainty avoiding cultures try to minimize the certainties by explicit and strict rules and formally structured relationships and activities are favored. The opposite type, uncertainty accepting cultures, tends to have as few rules as possible and rules are often implicit and flexible. Changes are more acceptable.
- *Long/short-term orientation* refers to the extent to which virtues are oriented. Long-term oriented cultures place emphasis on persistence, ordering relationships by status, thrift, and sense of fame, whereas short-term oriented cultures attend to personal steadiness and stability, respect of tradition, and reciprocation of greetings, favors, and gifts.

Hall (1997) suggested people from different cultures use different communication. Communication styles of different cultures can be grouped along a continuum from low-context to high-context. The former refers to communications in which the mass of the information is mainly communicated through explicit statements in text and speech, while the latter refers to the opposite, which need other communicative cues (for example, context information, authority of the speaker, body language) to pass the message. Indirect style is preferred in high-context cultures (Yum 1997), and low-context cultures prefer problem-oriented, direct, explicit, personal, and informal communications (Stewart and Bennett 1991). These differences will lead to different requirements for online communication tools and different socialization strategies of different culture groups.

13.5.2   Cross-Cultural Differences in Sociability Perception: Chinese and German

To demonstrate how cultures may influence the perception of online sociability, this section presents an empirical study (Raue 2008) which compares students from China and students from Germany with regards to their perceived importance of sociability features of social media. The questionnaire of sociability factors used in the Gao et al. study (2010) as presented in 4.2 was translated into German and distributed to German students enrolled at RWTH-Aachen University. Altogether 165 responses from German students were collected, consisting of 32% females and 68% males. The average age was 23.5 years (SD = 3.28). Compared with the Chinese group, German participants had longer internet experience, partly the result of the different development status of information technology in the two countries. But there is no significant difference in the weekly hours spent on the Internet.

A first look at the responses shows that for Chinese users, *security*, *privacy*, and *speed* had the highest mean values; *reputation building*, *material rewards*, and *meaning to reality* had the lowest mean values, just above the neutral point. For German users, *privacy*, *prevention from disturbance*, and *security* were considered as most important to online sociability; *material rewards*, *reputation building*, and *self image building* had the lowest ratings. It is noteworthy that Chinese participant scores of most items were higher than those of German participants and the dispersion of German responses was larger than that of Chinese responses. This indicates that participants from the two cultures may have different tendencies in responding to questionnaires. To remove this response bias, each participant's score of each item was converted to a culturally standardized score (Ralston et al. 2001; van de Vliert and Janssen 2002). From the comparisons of the standardized scores, the following differences between Chinese and German users were identified:

Maintaining existing social relationships in online systems is more important for German users than for Chinese users. The results show that German students were more concerned with the *meaning of online socialization to real social life* ($M = 0.08$, $SD = 0.96$) than were Chinese students users ($M = -0.56$, $SD = 1.08$; $F = 32.51$, $p < 0.001$). The *authenticity* of the online communication was more important for German students ($M = 0.32$, $SD = 0.85$) than for the Chinese ($M = -0.34$, $SD = 1.04$; $F = 38.26$, $p < 0.001$). German students also credited significantly higher importance to *the number of existing social contacts in the system* ($M = 0.24$, $SD = 0.85$) and *the relationship they had with these existing contacts* ($M = 0.29$, $SD = 0.83$) than did Chinese students (*the number of existing social contacts*: $M = -0.20$, $SD = 0.96$, $F = 19.19$, $p < 0.001$; *the relationship they have with these existing contacts*: $M = -0.24$, $SD = 0.95$, $p = 28.82$, $p < 0.001$). These results suggest that German social media user have a stronger tendency to use online social media for existing contacts with the aim to supplement their real social life than do Chinese students.

German students care more about privacy and disturbance issues than Chinese students. Though *prevention from disturbance* and *privacy* were important to both Chinese and German students, German students assigned significantly higher importance to both items (*prevention from disturbance*: $M = 0.91$, $SD = 0.57$; *privacy*: $M = 0.99$, $SD = 0.58$) than did the Chinese students (*prevention from disturbance*: $M = 0.40$, $SD = 0.89$, $F = 38.36$, $p < 0.001$; *privacy*: $M = 0.69$, $SD = 0.74$, $F = 12.32$, $p < 0.001$). The results suggest that German students are more conservative with social media use resulting from privacy and spam concerns. The findings are consistent with those of Hofstede (Hofstede and Hoftstede 1997) showing that Germans have a higher level of uncertainty avoidance (Uncertainty avoidance index: 65) than do Chinese (Uncertainty avoidance index: 65).

Supporting informational interactions is more important for Chinese students than for German students. Chinese students rated *information interaction* higher ($M = 0.48$, $SD = 0.80$) than German students ($M = -0.01$, $SD = 0.91$, $F = 26.60$, $p < 0.001$). Whether the system supports transfer of large volume of information was also more important to Chinese students ($M = 0.27$, $SD = 0.93$) than to German students ($M = -0.06$, $SD = 0.88$, $F = 10.76$, $p = 0.001$).

Compared with German students, Chinese students *cared more about the activeness of the system* ($F = 14.74$, $p < 0.001$) *and the originality of the content* in the system ($F = 11.46$, $p < 0.001$).

Chinese students are more concerned about immediacy and affective communication than are German students. The *immediacy of mediated communication* was more important to Chinese students ($M = 0.23$, SD $= 0.86$) than to German students ($M = -0.55$, SD $= 0.91$, $F = 63.6$, $p < 0.001$). Furthermore, *affective communication* was rated more important by Chinese students ($M = 0.12$, SD $= 0.81$) than by German students ($M = -0.47$, SD $= 0.94$, $F = 36.72$, $p < 0.001$). An explanation might be that the Chinese culture insists more on relatedness to each other, with an emphasis on attending to others, fitting in, and demanding a particularly harmonious interdependence. On the contrary, German social behavior is characterized with formality and reservation.

For Chinese students, simultaneous communication is more important than non-simultaneous communication; for German students, no significant difference was found between these two items. German student ratings on both simultaneous and non-simultaneous communications are significantly higher than found among Chinese students. It is interesting to note that *simultaneous communication* ($M = 0.18$, SD $= 0.80$) is significantly more important than *non-simultaneous communication* ($M = -0.11$, SD $= 0.95$, $t = 3.53$, $p < 0.001$) for Chinese students; for German students, however, the difference between *simultaneous communication* ($M = 0.46$, SD $= 0.69$) and *non-simultaneous communication* ($M = 0.33$, SD $= 0.75$, $t = 1.88$, $p = 0.06$) is not significant.

The results imply that Chinese and German students have different understanding of what constitutes a sociable tool. For German users, online social interaction is more about a supplement to their social life in reality. They are also more serious towards online social interaction. The extent to which online social relationships resemble real life relationships, the authenticity of such relationships, and the impact upon real life relationships are important for them. Chinese users, however, have more flexible views about online social interaction. It seems that they make clearer distinction between online and real life social networking. They do not care so much about whether online social networks resemble those in real life, and have little expectation for any relationship of online social interaction with real life. They do care, however, about whether the system supports effective and efficient informational interaction more than do German users. Whether the system helps them to obtain useful information is, for Chinese, an important measure of the usefulness of the system.

Regarding communication styles, Chinese users care more about the immediacy and affective communication capabilities of the media, and consider simultaneous communication as more important than non-simultaneous communication. This is consistent with culture literature, which suggests that Chinese rely on a high-context culture, requiring more interpersonal and contextual cues to transfer a message from one to another. It is also interesting to note the fact that many popular social networking tools developed by Chinese companies, such as QQ messenger, feature rich emoticons, affective gestures, and decorative accessories and ornaments for the avatars and homepages. In fact, selling decorative avatar accessories is a big source of benefit for the company. German users, on the contrary, do not think immediacy and affective communication are important, as indicated by the negative values given to these two items. However, they are very sensitive with privacy protection and the distance prevention capabilities of the system.

13.6 Conclusions

New online communication tools, especially the so-called social media that emphasize active participation, connectivity, collaboration, and sharing ideas among users, is expected to enhance social interaction in CSCL environments and support learner-centered pedagogical approaches. However, in order for these goals to be realized, designers and instructors need a deep understanding of the sociability of social media. The aim of this chapter is to provide an integrated approach to understand sociability of social media combining both social and technological perspectives.

The chapter begins with a discussion of the role of social interaction in CSCL and an introduction of the potentials of social media for supporting social interaction. A social-interaction-centered definition of sociability is proposed by authors based on a review of literature. Objective and subjective measures of sociability are then introduced. Based on the definition, the chapter continues with a conceptual framework for sociability of social media. Then a series of qualitative and quantitative studies was presented with the aim to identify and validate factors that influence the perception of online sociability. The results show that online sociability is influenced by six important factors: *social climate*, *purpose and benefits*, *people*, *interaction richness*, *self-presentation*, and *support for formal interaction*. The studies also show that the sociability and system competency issues, although closely related in practice, are still distinguishable aspects of social media. Then a discussion of the impact of culture on sociability design is presented, emphasizing the importance of considering cultural differences when designing and analyzing online communication systems. A cross-cultural comparison between Chinese and German shows significant differences in perception of sociability between Chinese and German engineering students. The results provide numerous implications for CSCL designers and instructors, and some of them are discussed below.

Social climate is an important component of online sociability for both Chinese and German users. In CSCL, a secured and friendly environment is critical to foster open discussions and critics among learners. Joining public and formal discussions seems to require a big amount of courage. Especially when focusing on the participant's own work, it is important to create an atmosphere of confidentiality and trust among the participants (Saarenkunnas et al. 2008). Kitsantas and Chow's study (2007) indicated that feeling embarrassed, fear of being perceived as "dumb" by others, and perceived threat to self-esteem may prevent the students from seeking help in CSCL. In addition to a stable and secured technological system and policies against unfriendly or flaming behavior, instructors also play an impor-tant role in moderation. It is noteworthy that to sustain and guide online discussion requires different moderation styles compared with sustaining face-to-face discussions in classrooms (Gil et al. 2007). The instructor should be aware of the complexity of such moderation and proper training should be provided.

People with whom users can interact with through a technical system is an important issue for users to adopt the technology. If there are too few people contributing to an online community discussion, the community will cease to exist. For learners, having other learners as listeners is important for reflection development (Knights 1985); In CSCL, there is empirical evidence showing that presence of the instructor and other students correlates with students' attitude towards the course and satisfaction with their own learning (Russo and Benson 2005). In particular, satisfaction with learning is found correlated more strongly with perception of other students than perceptions of the instructor. Furthermore, presence of other people also means presence of expertise available for help and support, and is important to peer-based learning. It is interesting to note that there is in expectation regarding *people* between Chinese and German. Whether a user knows other users in real life and how well they know them is more important for German users than for Chinese users. Results also suggest that CSCL environments provide support for adequate *self-presentation*. Whether a user can build up an identifiable self-image and develop his/her reputation in the virtual space is funda-mental to his/her commitment to online interaction. Russo and Benson (2005) found that students' perception of their own presence in a CSCL environment significantly correlated with the performance in the class.

Benefits and purposes refers to the capability of the tool to address and support users' true needs. In addition to content-based interaction, reciprocity and recogni-tion from others are also benefits expected from users. Preece (2001) suggests online community developers to provide a clear statement of the purpose of their community so that users know what to expect. This may well apply to CSCL. Especially when students are expected to join in the teaching, share information with others, and actively construct with others, proper statement of the benefits and purpose of this working method should be clearly communicated to students. As Saarenkunnas et al. (2008) found in their study, some users who joined an online course for their first time found it confusing that that the online module had no ready-made content to be studied, but that instead they themselves formed a community of experts which then chose interesting themes to cover.

Results about cross-cultural difference in sociability perception highlight the importance of cultural considerations when a social application is to accommodate users from different cultures. It is important to decide whether these cultural-specific details should incorporate into the design or not. If yes, what should be culture-specific and what should be kept cultural-neutral? If cross-cultural knowledge sharing or learning is to be fostered, how could the communication software and community policy help to reduce bias and misunderstandings caused cross-cultural differences? These questions are not only questions practitioners need to answer, but also interesting topics for future research.

References

Adler, N.J., Brahm, R., Graham, J.L.: Strategy implementation: a comparison of face-to-face negotiations in the People's Republic of China and the United States. Strateg. Manage. J. **13**(6), 449–466 (1992). doi:10.1002/smj.4250130605

Anderson, T.: Toward a theory of online learning. In: Anderson, T., Elloumi, F. (eds.) Theory and Practice of Online Learning, pp. 33–60. AU Press, Edmonton (2008)

Andrews, D.C.: Audience-specific online community design. Commun. ACM **45**(4), 64–68 (2002). doi:10.1145/505248.505275

Ardichvili, A., Page, V., Wentling, T.: Motivation and barriers to participation in virtual knowledge-sharing communities of practice. J. Knowl. Manage. **7**(1), 64–77 (2003). doi:10.1108/13673270310463626

Avram, G.: At the crossroads of knowledge management and social software. Electron. J. Knowl. Manage. **4**(1), 1–10 (2006)

Axelrod, R., Hamilton, W.D.: The evolution of cooperation. Science **211**(4489), 1390–1396 (1981)

Bargh, J.A., McKenna, K.Y.A.: The internet and social life. Annu. Rev. Psychol. **55**(1), 573–590 (2004). doi:10.1146/annurev.psych.55.090902.141922

Beenen, G., Ling, K., Wang, X., Chang, K., Frankowski, D., Resnick, P., Kraut, R.E.: Using social psychology to motivate contributions to online communities. In: 2004 ACM Conference on Computer Supported Cooperative Work, pp. 221. ACM, Chicago (2004)

Bente, G., Krämer, N.C.: Virtual gestures: analyzing social presence effects of computer-mediated and computer-generated nonverbal behaviour. In: Fifth Annual International Workshop Presence 2002. Porto (2002)

Bente, G., Rüggenberg, S., Krämer, N.C., Eschenburg, F.: Avatar-mediated networking: increasing social presence and interpersonal trust in net-based collaborations. Hum. Commun. Res. **34**(2), 287–318 (2008). doi:10.1111/j.1468-2958.2008.00322.x

Bloch, P.H.: Seeking the ideal form: product design and consumer response. J. Mark. **59**(3), 16–29 (1995)

Bogdan, C., Pargman, T.C.: Reconsidering support for the members of specialized online communities. In: 34th Congress of the Nordic Ergonomics Society, NES, pp. 121–126 (2002)

Bouman, W., Hoogenboom, T., Jansen, R., Schoondorp, M., Bruin, B.D., Huizing, A.: The realm of sociality: notes on the design of social software. In: ICIS Conference, International Conference on Information Systems. Montreal (2008) http://sprouts.aisnet.org/8-1/

Boyd, D.: The significance of social software. BlogTalks reloaded: social software research & cases, pp. 15–30, Norderstedt (2007)

Bross, J., Sack, H., Meinel, C.: Encouraging participation in virtual communities: the "IT-summit-blog" case. In: IADIS e-Society 2007. Lisbon (2007)

Butler, B., Sproull, L., Kiesler, S., Kraut, R.: Community effort in online groups: who does the work and why? In: Weisban, S.P. (ed.) Leadership at a Distance. Erlbaum, Mahwah (2002)

Chan, C.M., Bhandar, M., Oh, L.B., Chan, H.C.: Recognition and participation in a virtual community. In: 37th Annual Hawaii International Conference on System Sciences. Big Island (2004)

Chatti, M.A., Jarke, M., Frosch-Wilke, D.: The future of e-learning: a shift to knowledge networking and social software. Int. J. Knowl. Learn. **3**(4), 404–420 (2007)

Cho, H., Gay, G., Davidson, B., Ingraffea, A.: Social networks, communication styles, and learning performance in a CSCL community. Comput. Educ. **49**(2), 309–329 (2007)

Coates, D.: Watches Tell More than Time: Product Design, Information, and the Quest for Elegance. McGraw-Hill, New York (2003)

Cobb, S.: Social support and health through the life course. In: Riley, M.W. (ed.) Aging from Birth to Death: Interdisciplinary Perspectives, pp. 93–106. Westview Press, Boulder (1979)

Cranor, L.F., Reagle, J., Ackerman, M.S.: Beyond concern: understanding net users' attitudes about online privacy. In: Vogelsang, I., Companine, B.J. (eds.) The Internet Upheaval: Raising

Questions, Seeking Answers in Communications Policy, pp. 47–70. MIT Press, Cambridge (2000)

Cutrona, C.E., Russell, D.: Type of social support and specific stress: toward a theory of optimal matching. In: Sarason, I.G., Sarason, B.R., Pierce, G.R. (eds.) Social Support: An Interactional View, pp. 319–366. Wiley, New York (1990)

Daft, R.L., Lengel, R.H.: Information richness: a new approach to managerial behavior and organizational design. Res. Org. Behav. **6**, 191–233 (1984)

Davis, W.: You Don't Know Me, But. . . Social Capital and Social Software. iSociety, The Work Foundation, London (2003)

De Souza, C.S., Preece, J.: A framework for analyzing and understanding online communities. Interact. Comput. **16**(3), 579–610 (2004)

Dellarocas, C., Fan, M., Wood, C.: Self-interest, reciprocity, and participation in online reputation systems. In: 2003 Workshop in Information Systems and Economics (WISE). Seattle (2003)

Dennis, A., Kinney, S.: Testing media richness theory in the new media: the effects of cues, feedback, and task equivocality. Inf. Syst. Res. **9**, 256–274 (1998)

Dion, K., Berscheid, E., Walster, E.: What is beautiful is good. J. Pers. Soc. Psychol. **24**(3), 285–290 (1972)

Dourish, P., Anderson, K.: Collective information practice: exploring privacy and security as social and cultural phenomena. Hum. Comput. Interact. **21**(3), 319–342 (2006)

Ellison, N.B., Steinfield, C., Lampe, C.: The benefits of facebook "Friends:" social capital and college students' use of online social network sites. J. Comput. Mediat. Commun. **12**(4), 1143–1168 (2007). doi:10.1111/j.1083-6101.2007.00367.x

Fehr, E., Gächter, S.: Fairness and retaliation: the economics of reciprocity. J. Econ. Perspect. **14**(3), 159–181 (2000)

Fish, R.S., Kraut, R.E., Root, R.W., Rice, R.E.: Evaluating video as a technology for informal communication. In: SIGCHI Conference on Human Factors in Computing Systems, pp. 37–48. ACM, Monterey (1992). doi: 10.1145/142750.142755

Fredericksen, E., Pickett, A., Shea, P., Pelz, W., Swan, K.: Student satisfaction and perceived learning with on-line courses-principles and examples from the SUNY learning network. In: Learning Effectiveness and Faculty Satisfaction: Proceedings of the 1999 Sloan Summer Workshop on Asynchronous Learning Networks, pp. 7. SCOLE (2000)

Frydenberg, M.: Principles and pedagogy: the two P's of podcasting in the information technology classroom. In: The Proceedings of ISECON 2006, vol. 23 (2006)

Gao, Q., Dai, Y., Fan, Z., Kang, R.: Understanding factors affecting perceived sociability of social software. Comput. Hum. Behav. **26**(6), 1846–1861 (2010)

Gibbs, J.L., Ellison, N.B., Heino, R.D.: Self-presentation in online personals: the role of anticipated future interaction, self-disclosure, and perceived success in internet dating. Commun. Res. **33**(2), 152–177 (2006)

Gil, J., Schwarz, B.B., Asterhan, C.S.C.: Intuitive moderation styles and beliefs of teachers in CSCL-based argumentation. In: 8th International Conference on Computer Supported Collaborative Learning, pp. 222–231. International Society of the Learning Sciences, New Brunswick (2007)

Godwin, M.: Nine principles for making virtual communities work. Wired **2**, 72–73 (1994)

Gross, R., Acquisti, A.: Information revelation and privacy in online social networks. In: 2005 ACM Workshop on Privacy in the Electronic Society, pp. 71–80. Alexandria (2005)

Gunawardena, C.N.: Social presence theory and implications for interaction and collaborative learning in computer conferences. Int. J. Educ. Telecommun. **1**(2/3), 147–166 (1995)

Gunawardena, C.N., Zittle, F.J.: Social presence as a predictor of satisfaction within a computer-mediated conferencing environment. Am. J. Dist. Educ. **11**(3), 8–26 (1997)

Hall, E.T., Hall, M.R.: Understanding cultural differences: Germans, French and Americans. Intercultural Press (1997)

Hamermesh, D.S., Biddle, J.E.: Beauty and the labor market. Am. Econ. Rev. **84**(5), 1174–1194 (1994)

Haythornthwaite, C., Wellman, B.: Work, friendship, and media use for information exchange in a networked organization. Journal of the American Society for Information Science. 49, 1101–1114 (1998)

Haythornthwaite, C.: Strong, Weak, and Latent Ties and the Impact of New Media. The Information Society. 18, 385–401 (2002)

Hiltz, S.R., Turoff, M.: The evolution of user behavior in a computerized conferencing system. Commun. ACM 24(11), 739–751 (1981). doi:10.1145/358790.358794

Hinton, L., Guo, Z., Hillygus, J., Levkoff, S.: Working with culture: a qualitative analysis of barriers to the recruitment of Chinese–American family caregivers for Dementia research. J Cross-Cult. Gerontol. 15(2), 119–137 (2000). doi:10.1023/A:1006798316654

Hofstede, G.H., Hoftstede, G.J.: Cultures and organizations: Software of the mind. McGraw-Hill, New York (1997)

Johnson, D.W., Johnson, R.T.: Learning Together and Alone: Cooperative, Competitive, and Individualistic Learning. Allyn and Baconv, Boston (1994)

Johnson, R.T., Johnson, D.W., Stanne, M.B.: Effects of cooperative, competitive, and individualistic goal structures on computer-assisted instruction. J. Educ. Psychol. 77(6), 668–677 (1985)

Kim, A.J.: Community Building on the Web: Secret Strategies for Successful Online Communities. Peachpit Press, Berkeley (2000)

Kim, H., Kim, G.J., Park, H.W., Rice, R.E.: Configurations of relationships in different media: FtF, email, instant messenger, mobile phone, and SMS. Journal of Computer-Mediated Communication. 12, (2007).

Kim, W.G., Lee, C., Hiemstra, S.J.: Effects of an online virtual community on customer loyalty and travel product purchases. Tourism Manage. 25(3), 343–355 (2004). doi:10.1016/S0261-5177(03)00142-0

Kimmerle, J., Cress, U.: Group awareness and self-presentation in computer-supported information exchange. Int. J. Comput. Support. Collab. Learn. 3(1), 85–97 (2007). doi:10.1007/s11412-007-9027-z

Kitsantas, A., Chow, A.: College students' perceived threat and preference for seeking help in traditional, distributed, and distance learning environments. Comput. Educ. 48(3), 383–395 (2007)

Knights, S.: Reflection and learning: the importance of a listener. In: Boud, D., Keogh, R., Walker, D. (eds.) Reflection: Turning Experience into Learning, pp. 85–90. Kogan Page, London (1985)

Koh, J., Kim, Y.G., Butler, B., Bock, G.W.: Encouraging participation in virtual communities. Commun. ACM 50(2), 69–73 (2007). doi:10.1145/1216016.1216023

Koku, E., Nazer, N., Wellman, B.: Netting scholars: online and offline. Am. Behav. Sci. 44(10), 1752–1774 (2001)

Kollock, P.: Design principles for online communities. PC Update 15(5), 58–60 (1998)

Kreijns, K., Kirschner, P.A., Jochems, W.: The sociability of computer-supported collaborative learning environments. Educ. Technol. Soc. 5, 8–22 (2002)

Kreijns, K., Kirschner, P.A., Jochems, W.: Identifying the pitfalls for social interaction in computer-supported collaborative learning environments: a review of the research. Comput. Hum. Behav. 19, 335–353 (2003)

Kreijns, K., Kirschner, P.A., Jochems, W., Buuren, H.: Measuring perceived sociability of computer-supported collaborative learning environments. Computers & Education. 49, 176–192 (2007)

Lento, T., Welser, H.T., Gu, L., Smith, M.: The ties that blog: examining the relationship between social ties and continued participation in the wallop weblogging system. In: 3 rd Annual Workshop on the Weblogging Ecosystem. Edinburgh (2006)

Li, D., Chau, P.Y., Lou, H.: Understanding individual adoption of instant messaging: an empirical investigation. J. Assoc. Inf. Syst. 6(4), 102–129 (2005)

Lin, H., Lee, G.: Determinants of success for online communities: an empirical study. Behav. Inf. Technol. 25, 479–488 (2006)

Lou, H., Luo, W., Strong, D.: Perceived critical mass effect on groupware acceptance. Europ. J. Inf. Syst. 9(2), 91–103 (2000)

Maloney-Krichmar, D., Preece, J.: A multilevel analysis of sociability, usability, and community dynamics in an online health community. ACM Trans. Comput. Hum. Interact. **12**(2), 201–232 (2005). doi:10.1145/1067860.1067864

Markus, M.L.: Toward a 'critical mass' theory of interactive media. Commun. Res. **14**(5), 491–511 (1987)

McLoughlin, C., Lee, M.: Social software and participatory learning: pedagogical choices with technology affordances in the web 2.0 Era. In: ICT: Providing Choices for Learners and Learning. Ascilite, Singapore (2007)

Menzel, K.E., Carrell, L.J.: The impact of gender and immediacy on willingness to talk and perceived learning. Commun. Educ. **48**(1), 31 (1999). doi:10.1080/03634529909379150

Millen, D.R., Patterson, J.F.: Stimulating social engagement in a community network. In: 2002 ACM Conference on Computer Supported Cooperative Work. ACM, New Orleans, pp. 306–313 (2002) doi: 10.1145/587078.587121

Nie, N.H.: Sociability, interpersonal relations, and the internet: reconciling conflicting findings. Am. Behav. Sci. **45**, 420–435 (2001)

Nisbett, R.E., Peng, K., Choi, I., Norenzayan, A.: Culture and systems of thought: holistic versus analytic cognition. Psychological Review. 108, 291-310 (2001).

Norenzayan, A., Nisbett, R.E.: Culture and causal cognition. Curr. Dir. Psychol. Sci. **9**(4), 132–135 (2000). doi:10.1111/1467-8721.00077

Panteli, N.: Richness power cues and email text. Inf. Manage. **40**, 75–86 (2002)

Picciano, A.G.: Beyond student perceptions: issues of interaction, presence, and performance in an online course. J. Asynchronous Learn. Netw. **6**(1), 21–40 (2002)

Preece, J.: Sociability and usability in online communities: determining and measuring success. Behav. Inf. Technol. **20**, 347–356 (2001)

Preece, J.: Online communities: designing usability and supporting sociability. Wiley, New York (2000) http://books.google.com/books?hl=zh-CN&lr=&id=ReBu5l74DpoC&oi=fnd &pg= PA3&dq=definition+of+%22sociability%22&ots=nO4w5yoFyh&sig=aIfYCQyvRLAbDm A2flWBikvzvUI

Preece, J., Maloney-Krichmar, D.: Online communities: focusing on sociability and usability. In: Jacko, J.A., Sears, A. (eds.) The Human-Computer Interaction Handbook: Fundamentals, Evolving Technologies and Emerging Applications, pp. 596–620. Lawrence Erlbaum Associates, Mahwah (2003)

Ralston, D.A., Vollmer, G.R., Srinvasan, N., Nicholson, J.D., Tang, M., Wan, P.: Strategies of upward influence: a study of six cultures from Europe, Asia, and America. J. Cross-Cult. Psychol. **32**(6), 728–735 (2001). doi:10.1177/0022022101032006006

Rau, P.P., Gao, Q., Ding, Y.: Relationship between the level of intimacy and lurking in online social network services. Comput. Hum. Behav. **24**, 2757–2770 (2008)

Raue, N.: Factors Influencing Online Sociability: A Cross-Cultural Study (Unpublished Master Thesis). Tsinghua University, Beijing, China (2008)

Rice, R.E., Love, G.: Electronic emotion: socioemotional content in a computer-mediated communication network. Commun. Res. **14**(1), 85–108 (1987)

Rourke, L., Anderson, T.: Exploring social communication in asynchronous, Text-Based Computer Conferencing. J. Inter. Learn. Res. **13**, 259–275 (2002)

Rovai, A.P., Barnum, K.T.: On-line course effectiveness: an analysis of student interactions and perceptions of learning. J. Dist. Educ. **18**(1), 57–73 (2003)

Rubin, K.H., Hymel, S., Mills, R.S.L.: Sociability and social withdrawal in childhood: stability and outcomes. J. Pers. **57**(2), 237–255 (1989). doi:10.1111/j.1467-6494.1989.tb00482.x

Russo, T., Benson, S.: Learning with invisible others: perceptions of online presence and their relationship to cognitive and affective learning. Educ. Technol. Soc. **8**(1), 54–62 (2005)

Saarenkunnas, M., Taalas, P., Tenhula, T.: It is the atmosphere that matters-enhancing local pedagogical change through shared online work. In: Training University Personnel for the Information Society–the Finnish TieVie Project, pp. 59–70. Service Unit, Finnish Virtual University (2008)

Schliemann, T., Asting, T., Folstad, A., Heim, J.: Medium preference and medium effects in person-person communication. In: CHI' 02 Extended Abstracts on Human Factors in Computing Systems. Minneapolis (2002)

Short, J., Williams, E., Christie, B.: The Social Psychology of Telecommunications. Wiley, New York (1976)

Simmel, G., Hughes, E.C.: The sociology of sociability. Am. J. Sociol. 55(3), 254–261 (1949)

Smith, M., Farnham, S., Drucker, S.: The social life of small graphical chat spaces. In: The Social Life of Avatars: Presence and Interaction in Shared Virtual Environments, pp. 205–220. Springer, New York (2002)

Stewart, E.C., Bennett, M.J.: American cultural patterns: a cross-cultural perspective. Intercultural Press, Chicago, US (1991).

Tidwell, L.C., Walther, J.B.: Computer-mediated communication effects on disclosure, impressions, and interpersonal evaluations: getting to know one another a bit at a time. Hum. Commun. Res. 28(3), 317–348 (2002)

Toma, C.L., Hancock, J.T., Ellison, N.B.: Separating fact from fiction: an examination of deceptive self-presentation in online dating profiles. Pers Soc Psychol Bull 34(8), 1023–1036 (2008). doi:10.1177/0146167208318067

Tractinsky, N.: Toward the study of aesthetics in information technology. In: Twenty-Fifth International Conference on Information Systems, pp. 771–780 (2004)

Tu, C.H.: How Chinese perceive social presence: an examination of interaction in online learning environment. Educ. Media Int. 38(1), 45–60 (2001)

van de Vliert, E., Janssen, O.: Better than performance motives as roots of satisfaction across more and less developed countries. J. Cross-Cult. Psychol. 33(4), 380–397 (2002). doi:10.1177/00222102033004002

Van der Heijden, H.V.D.: User acceptance of hedonic information systems. MIS Quart. 28(4), 695–704 (2004)

Ven der Linden, J., Renshaw, P.: Dialogic Learning: Shifting Perspectives to Learning, Instruction, and Teaching. Kluwer Academic Publishers, Dordrecht (2004)

Vetere, F., Gibbs, M.R., Kjeldskov, J., Howard, S., Mueller, F.F., Pedell, S., Mecoles, K., et al.: Mediating intimacy: designing technologies to support strong-tie relationships. In: Proceedings of the 2005 SIGCHI Conference on Human Factors in Computing Systems, pp. 471–480. Portland (2005)

Vygotskǐ, L.S.: Mind in Society. Harvard University Press, Cambridge (1978)

Walther, J.B.: Computer-mediated communication: impersonal, interpersonal, and hyperpersonal interaction. Commun. Res. 23(1), 3–43 (1996). doi:10.1177/009365096023001001

Wegerif, R.: The social dimension of asynchronous learning networks. J. Asynchronous Learn. Networks 2, 34–49 (1998)

Wellman, B., Haase, A.Q., Witte, J., Hampton, K.: Does the internet increase, decrease, or supplement social capital? social networks, participation, and community commitment. Am. Behav. Sci. 45(3), 436–455 (2001). doi:10.1177/00027640121957286

Wenger, E.: Communities of Practice: Learning, Meanings, and Identity. Cambridge University Press, Cambridge (2007)

Whitaker, V.M., Parker, C.M.: The factors enabling and inhibiting the development of agricultural internet virtual communities: an Australian case study. In: 8th European Conference on Information Systems, Trends in Information and Communication Systems for the 21st Century (ECIS 2000), pp. 148–155. Vienna (2000)

Yoo, Y., Alavi, M.: Media and group cohesion: relative influences on social presence, task participation, and group consensus. MIS Quar. 25(3), 371–390 (2001)

Yum, J.O., Samover, L.A., Porter, B.: The impact of Confucianism on interpersonal relationships and communication patterns in east Asia. Intercultural Communication. pp. 78-88 The impact of Confucianism on interpersonal relationships and communication patterns in East Asia., CA (1997)

Zhou, N., Zemel, A., Stahl, G.: Information as a social achievement: collaborative information behavior in CSCL. In: 8th International Conference on Computer Supported Collaborative Learning, pp. 814–816. International Society of the Learning Sciences, New Brunswick, (2007)

Chapter 14
Using Social Media to Empower Learning Resources Evaluation and Recommendation Across Boundaries

Jerry Z. Li and Wenting Ma

Abstract The increasing availability of digital learning resources on the Web is changing the nature of information retrieval (IR) in education. Educators and learners are often faced with two challenges in selecting appropriate online learning resources: the sheer number of learning resources and the variety of educational quality among them. This chapter provides an examination of the current approaches employed to improve the quality of learning resources, which include the current state of the field and typical evaluation approaches adopted in major learning resource repositories. The impact of Web 2.0 and social bookmarking on learning resource evaluation is also considered. A recommender system that uses an ontology-mapping approach is examined and consideration given as to how it can facilitate learning resource evaluation across diverse communities of practice and cultures.

14.1 The Need for Learning Object Evaluation Across Communities

With the advancement of personal computing and Internet technologies, information technology has made a monumental shift in knowledge representation from paper to digital. Along with this advancement, there is a rapid increase in the creation and collection of online learning resources which are consequently playing an increasingly crucial role in teaching and learning. Specifically, education

J.Z. Li (✉)
Leaching and Learning Centre, Lifelong Learning, Simon Fraser University, 8888 University Drive, Burnaby BC, V5A 1S6, Canada
e-mail: jerryli@sfu.ca

W. Ma
Faculty of Education, Simon Fraser University, 8888 University Drive, Burnaby, BC, Canada
e-mail: wentingm@sfu.ca

B. White et al. (eds.), *Social Media Tools and Platforms in Learning Environments*, 245
DOI 10.1007/978-3-642-20392-3_14, © Springer-Verlag Berlin Heidelberg 2011

institutions have invested significant resources in the creation of Web-based content for delivery through Learning Management Systems (LMS). With e-learning standards and the emergence of learning resource repositories, a new paradigm of learning is emerging.

Online learning resources are distinguished from traditional educational resources by their immediate availability through Web-based repositories that are searchable with standardized metadata. Compared to conventional educational products, they are more flexible in serving student learning styles and preferences, supporting a rich multimedia learning environment and offering a new paradigm of learning. Unfortunately, the quality of online learning resources varies greatly, presumably because the production processes often lack quality-control procedures or guidelines. Designers may fail to apply design principles that have been established in the fields of instructional design, instructional psychology, and learning sciences (Nesbit and Belfer 2004). Therefore, there is a pressing need for systematic methods that promote the development, evaluation, and dissemination of high-quality resources.

14.2 Current Evaluation Approaches and Models

To facilitate the process of searching and utilizing online learning resources, rating systems are often used to evaluate the resource quality and guide the selection process. Four evaluation models that feature rating systems are discussed in the following section. In those systems, users are required to specify their estimates of quality on a multilevel rating scale that is mapped to numeric values (Knowledge Base 2006). The final score for the respondents on a given scale is the sum of their ratings for all items on that scale. Most repositories have evaluation models that combine technical tools, evaluation rubrics, and community practices.

14.2.1 CLOE

The Co-operative Learning Object Exchange (CLOE) was jointly developed by 17 Ontario universities to facilitate the design and application of multimedia-rich learning resources, and operates on a structured review process (Clarke 2003). CLOE provides three broad evaluative dimensions: quality of content, effectiveness as a teaching/learning tool, and ease of use.

14.2.2 MERLOT

MERLOT (www.merlot.org) is a learning object repository containing educational resources classified into more than 500 subject categories. MERLOT provides tools for both individual and peer reviews on learning resources based on a five-point Likert scale.

14.2.3   DLNET

The U.S. National Sciences Digital Library is a federated repository that includes DLNET, the Digital Library Network for Engineering and Technology (www.dlnet. vt.edu). DLNET uses a subject taxonomy that was adapted from the INSPEC taxonomy of scientific and technical literature (www.iee.org/Publish/Inspec). DLNET currently allows members to publish multiple reviews but does not provide statistical aggregation of rating data.

14.2.4   eLera

The eLera Web site allows users to evaluate resources with the Learning Object Review Instrument (LORI) (Nesbit et al. 2003). LORI consists of eight dimensions of quality: content quality, learning gaol alignment, feedback and adaptation, motivation, presentation design, interaction usability, accessibility, and standard compliance. For each dimension, reviewers are able to provide comments and ratings based on a five-level rating scale. The complete individual review is then published in eLera.

The evaluation approaches (CLOE, MERLOT, DLNET, and eLera) in those repositories share several communalities. Each is formed from: (a) a searchable database of learning resource metadata that more or less conforms to the IEEE learning object metadata standard, (b) a subject taxonomy constituting a single component of the metadata, (c) evaluation criteria in the form of guidelines or a structured instrument, (d) a process for conducting and publishing reviews including restrictions on who can review, and (e) a structured form in which all reviews are published. Such systems are socio-technical phenomena that can be analyzed and empirically researched.

However, the evaluation processes in those repositories provide few opportunities for interaction among expert reviewers (content experts and instructional designers) and even fewer opportunities for interaction between experts and individual reviewers (learners and teachers). The eLera model, mentioned above (Vargo et al. 2003), does provide review forms that present the reviews of experts and individuals and allows them to interact with each other. Such interactions are potentially crucial because, in research settings, reviewers have been consistently observed to modify their evaluation on a learning resource after being presented with reviews different from their own (Vargo et al. 2003). This lends weight to the view that experts and individual reviewers can affect each others' opinions and form a convergent evaluation, which demonstrates a greater validity than either could achieve independently. The support of interactions in the eLera model in fact is a form of social media. The social media discussed in this chapter extends and amplifies the social interactions in the eLera model.

14.3   Social Tagging and Bookmarking

With the advent of Web 2.0 and social media technologies, a user is not only a reader, but also a contributor when surfing on the Web. Social bookmarking is becoming a popular social media for users to search, store, and manage bookmarks to quickly locate useful online resources. Bookmarks can be saved privately or shared among specific groups of people in a community or a subject domain and are usually presented in the form of metadata, which enable a user to select the resource without the need to browse or search through its content. The most popular metadata in the social bookmarking is social tagging, which is also called folksonomy. The idea of folksonomy is that tags are generated by individual users and reflect personal points of views for a resource. By assigning free-form labels as tags to a resource, users attribute meanings to the resource and make it readily searchable and sharable among communities of similar interests and perspectives in a collective manner (Bi et al. 2009). Some popular social bookmarking sites, such as Delicious (delicious.com/) and citeulike (www.citeulike.org), have been used for education purposes, primarily to create online collections of learning resources.

Many social bookmarking services provide information about the number of users who have bookmarked them and also draw inferences from the relationships among tags to create clusters of tags or bookmarks, which are known as tag clouds. Tag clouds provide a new way to classify learning resources in that they contain meaningful and contextual descriptions of the resources which reflect multiple users' collective understanding and thoughts on them (Yanbe et al. 2007). It holds the promise that more intelligent search engines will utilize the tags created by humans to search for and recommend personalized learning resources to individual learners as opposed to the traditional crawling programs used in search engines to extract and categorize Web pages (Godwin-Jones 2006).

Despite the perceived advantages that social bookmarking services offer – users from different communities usually adopt different classification systems – it occurs that users often categorize resources using different tags that have similar meanings. This makes it challenging to search and share all relevant resources among users across various communities and cultures when many associated tags are not included in the search queries (Bi et al. 2009). Therefore, there arises a great need to map different classification systems at a semantic level so all tags of similar meanings are included in search engines. One of the viable solutions to tackle the problem is to use ontology mapping.

14.4 Ontology Mapping

As discussed previously, on one hand, social bookmarking enables users to retrieve and share learning resources more easily within a community; on the other hand, each community has its own tagging system to classify learning resources. Requiring all communities and learning resource repositories to adopt a single classification system is not a viable solution. It is commonly understood that teachers, instructional designers, and students adopt terms that have been shared in a local community of practice for subject matters, learning objectives, and achievement levels. When teachers search for appropriate resources for students, they need to evaluate and determine whether the resources meet particular learning goals and can be readily used by students. These aims are difficult to achieve when the learning resources are presented in unfamiliar terms (Li et al. 2005).

Systems are needed that allow use of community-specific terms to categorize learning resources while supporting search of unfamiliar terms for sharing ideas across various communities. The techniques of mapping domain ontologies could be a feasible solution to this problem as ontologies are a formal way to represent a shared conceptualization of a domain under study (Gruber 1993). Domain ontologies are very effective for describing relations, especially when the relations are multidimensional. The term "domain ontology" is used to represent both subject taxonomies and subject classification systems. It refers to "an explicit list and organization of all the terms, relations and objects that constitute the representational scheme for that domain" (Gennari et al. 1994, p. 402). Ontology mapping is a means to support semantic interoperability among different domain ontologies. It involves modifying one domain ontology to match the expectations or requirements of another to fulfill the task at hand. By the use of various relations, ontology mapping relates similar concepts or relations from different sources to each other (Klein 2001).

Li et al. (2005), developed a modified Dewey Decimal Classification (DDC), called eLera-Dewey Decimal Classification (DDC), which was used as a general taxonomy into which a large number of local ontologies could be mapped. In the design, the Simple Knowledge Organization System (SKOS) is used to define different types of ontologies (classifications, taxonomies, thesaurus, curriculum) and to apply mappings among different domain ontologies (Miles and Brickley 2005). SKOS is a W3C RDF-based standard which supports the use of knowledge organization systems such as taxonomies, terminologies, glossaries, and other types of controlled vocabulary within the framework of the Semantic Web (W3C 2005).

In Fig. 14.1, the excerpts of two ontologies defined in SKOS are presented. Figure 14.1a shows a snippet of the ontology based on British Columbia's school curriculum (BC IRP), suggested approaches to instruction, a list of recommended learning resources, and possible assessment methods (BC Ministry of Education 2005). Figure 14.1b contains a sample part of the eLera-DDC as a subject

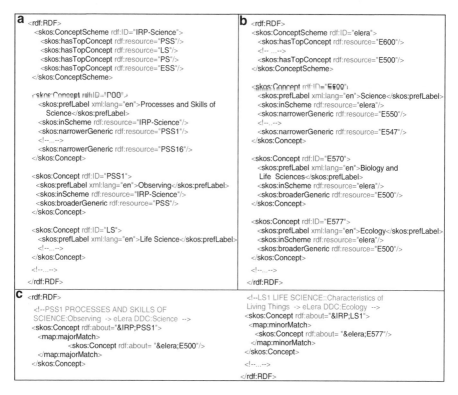

Fig. 14.1 The RDF/XML snippets of the SKOS-based ontologies: (**a**) a part of the learning outcomes defined in British Columbia Integrated Resource Packages (BC IRP); (**b**) an excerpt of the eLera-Dewey Decimal Classification (DDC); (**c**) an excerpt of mappings between BC IRP and eLera encoded using the SKOS mapping vocabulary

classification system. Figure 14.1c exemplifies the use of SKOS mapping vocabulary to define the mappings between the BC IRP and eLera-DDC ontologies.

The deployment of the search algorithm in ontology mapping on the eLera system (Li et al. 2005) is shown in Fig. 14.2. The implementation uses OWLJessKB, which is a description logic reasoner for Web Ontology Language (OWL) based on the JESS rule-based reasoning engine. In the implementation, OWLJessKB works with ontologies, which are defined by SKOS, by taking a concept from the local ontology (BC IRP) as an argument to search for concepts in the target ontology (eLera-DDC). It uses the SKOS mapping relations defined between these ontologies and generates a sequence of concepts compliant with the eLera-DDC, which the eLera learning object repository can interpret. When a request is received from a user who uses the selected local ontology (in our case BC IRP), the system translates the query argument to eLera-DDC ontology in run time. Then, the eLera system generates an SQL query to search its learning object repository.

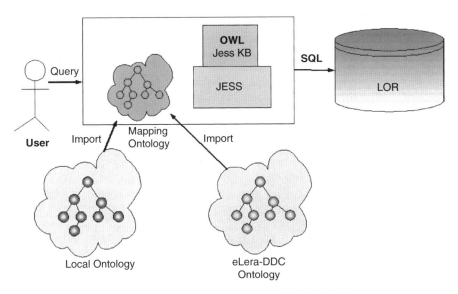

Fig. 14.2 Using SKOS-based ontologies and ontology mappings in the eLera system

Refer to Li et al. (2005) for the implementation details of the ontology mapping in eLera. The algorithm of ontology mapping can also be applied to mappings between tag clouds in a social bookmarking system. In this way, resources tagged by different communities, or different languages, can be shared across communities or countries. Ideally, this mapping relationship can be dynamic and adjusted automatically according to the collective efforts of users. Then, an intelligent agent can interpret the relations and recommend learning resources across communities and cultures.

14.5 Recommender Systems

Recommender systems emerged in the mid-1990s. Such systems usually rely on a ratings system to estimate ratings for an item that have not been seen and rated by a user. The likelihood of recommending a specific item to a user is based on a group of other users who share similar interests. When the ratings for the unrated items are estimated according to the user, the item(s) with the highest estimated ratings are then recommended to the user (Adomavicius and Tuzhilin 2005). For example, this is the way that books are recommended based on other reader ratings and reviews on Amazon.com. The underlying idea behind such systems is to "use the opinions of a community of users to help individuals in that community more effectively identify content of interest from a potentially overwhelming set of choices" (Herlocker et al. 2004, p. 5).

To deal with the increasing heterogeneity of learning resources, recommender systems are emerging as a promising paradigm which provides personalized suggestions for learning resources. Specifically, relevant learning resources are automatically recommended to a user instead of the user explicitly searching for these resources. There are a few recommendation models for learning resources recommendation. For instance, Recker and Wiley (2001) propose a system that included multi-record, non-authoritative metadata in an instructional context. It provided evaluative metadata such as quality and educational relevance. The system incorporated a Presentation, Inspection, and Recommendation Tool (PIRT), which uses the nearest neighbor approach to compare information regarding objects previously used together by its neighbor and the group of objects a user has selected so that the system can recommend additional objects. The PIRT system supports the automatic recommendation of relevant learning objects and locates users that share similar interests for communication and collaboration.

Another example is the collaborative filtering systems, which have been widely used for recommendations in many areas, such as music albums (Upendra et al. 1995), jokes (Gupta et al. 1999), and radio programs (Hauver 2001). Collaborative filtering recommendations are based on the ratings of items, instead of the content of the items. The algorithms of collaborative filtering are developed to identify users who have relevant interests and preferences by calculating similarities and dissimilarities between user profiles (Herlocker et al. 2004). Interest similarity is defined as having rated many items in common, and having assigned similar ratings to each of these items. The idea behind this method is that it is beneficial to a search for information to consult the behavior of other users who share the same, or relevant, interests and whose opinion can thus be trusted as being similar.

A more advanced recommender system may use collaborative filtering systems, especially those that use explicit and implicit sources as a basis, and integrate collaborative filtering systems with ontology-based recommendations, which builds on the ideas discussed in the previous sections. Through applying the socially created tags which are based on the technique of ontology mapping to capture all tags bearing similar meanings, learning resources are classified according to the individual's understanding and assigned meanings to them from broader groups of users across various communities, and it thus makes the recommendations more readily applicable and meaningful to new users.

However, recommendation algorithms may be computationally expensive and the complexity grows nonlinearly with the number of users and items. Therefore, the design of a recommender system needs to balance the sophistication of the data structures with the requirement of providing recommendations within acceptable quality and time frame (Cosley 2002). In addition to the scalability issue, collaborative filtering also faces sparsity issues; Sparsity occurs when there are only a few rated items among the total number of items in a database since the recommendation algorithms are based on similarity measures computed over the co-rated set of items. An item cannot be recommended unless it has been rated by a substantial number of users (Melville et al. 2002; Schein et al. 2002).

14.6   Future Direction

"The effect of recommender systems will be one of the most important changes in the next decade," says University of Minnesota computer science professor John Riedl, who built one of the first recommendation engines in the mid-1990s. "The social web is going to be driven by these systems." (O''Brien et al. 2006).

The ever-expanding volume and increasing complexity of online learning resources have created a great demand for effective resource retrieval. It will soon be seen that recommender systems will recommend learning resources of interest to users based on their preferences, either explicitly or implicitly. Such systems will help tackle information overload problems through recommending users the most relevant resources with high quality instead of users explicitly searching for these resources. With the availability of Web 2.0 tools as social bookmarking and tagging, recommendation technology represents a new paradigm of information searching, management, and sharing through a socially enabled collective effort across communities.

Acknowledgment   With a deep respect, we extend our sincere thanks to Dr. John Nesbit, whose encouragement, contribution, and support enabled us to complete this chapter.

References

Adomavicius, G., Tuzhilin, A.: Toward the next generation of recommender systems: a survey of the state-of-the-art and possible extensions. IEEE Trans. Knowl. Data Eng. **17**(6), 734–749 (2005)

BC Ministry of Education. Integrated Resource Packages (IRPs).www.bced.gov.bc.ca.proxy.lib.sfu.ca/irp/irp.htm (2005)

Bi, B., Shang, L.F., Kao, B.: Collaborative resource discovery in social tagging systems. In: CIKM 2009, 18th ACM Conference on Information and Knowledge Management, pp. 1919–1922. ACM, New York (2009)

Clarke, M.: CLOE Peer Review. Co-operative learning object exchange. http://cloe.on.ca/documents.html (2003)

Cosley, D., Lawrence, S., Pennock, D. M.: REFEREE: an open framework for practical testing of recommender systems using ResearchIndex. Proceedings of the 28th Very Large Data Bases Conference, (2002)

Gennari, J.H., Tu, S.W., Rothenfluh, T.E., Musen, M.A.: Mapping domains to methods in support of reuse. Int. J. Hum. Comput. Stud. **41**, 399–424 (1994)

Godwin-Jones, R.: Tag clouds in the blogosphere: electronic literacy and social networking. Lang. Learn. Technol. **10**(2), 8–15 (2006)

Gruber, T.R.: A translation approach to portable ontology specifications. Knowl. Acquisition **5**(2), 199–220 (1993)

Gupta, D., Digiovanni, M., Narita, H., Goldberg, K.: Jester 2.0: evaluation of a new linear time collaborative filtering algorithm. In: SIGIR-99, pp. 291–292 (1999)

Hauver, D.B.: Flycasting: using collaborative filtering to generate a play list for online radio. In: International Conference on Web Delivery of Music (2001)

Herlocker, J., Konstan, J.A., Terveen, L., Reidl, J.: Evaluating collaborative filtering recommender system. ACM Trans. Info. Syst. **22**(1), 5–53 (2004)

Klein, M.: Combining and relating ontologies: An analysis of problems and solutions. In: Proc. of IJCAI'01-Workshop on Ontologies and Information Sharing, A. Gomez-Perez, A. et al., (eds.), Seattle, USA, Aug. 4–5 (2001)

Li, J., Nesbit, J.C., Belfer, K.: Collaborative evaluation of learning objects. In: McGreal, R. (ed.) Online Education Using Learning Objects. Routledge/Falmer, London (2004)

Li, J., Gašević, D., Nesbit, J., Richards, G.: Ontology mappings to enable interoperation of knowledge domain taxonomies. In: 2nd Annual LORNET Conference on Intelligent, Interactive, Learning Object Repositories Network (CD Edition), Vancouver (2005)

Likert Scale. Knowledge Base. http://www.socialresearchmethods.net/kb/scallik.php (2006)

Melville, P., Mooney, R.J., Nagarajan, R.: Content-boosted collaborative filtering for improved recommendations. In: 18th National Conference Artificial Intelligence, pp. 187–192. American Association for Artificial Intelligence, Menlo Park (2002)

Miles, A., Brickley, D.: SKOS Core Vocabulary Specification, W3C Working Draft (2005). http://www.w3.org/TR/swbp-skos-core-guide

Nesbit, J.C., Belfer, K., Leacock, T.: Learning Object Review Instrument (LORI). In: E-Learning Research and Assessment Network. www.elera.net (2003)

Nesbit, J.C., Belfer, K.: Collaborative evaluation of learning objects. In: McGreal, R. (ed.) Online Education Using Learning Objects. Routledge/Falmer, London (2004)

O'Brien, Jeffrey M.: The Race to Create a 'Smart' Google CNN Money. http://money.cnn.com/magazines/fortune/fortune_archive/2006/11/27/8394347/index.htm?section=money_latest (2006)

Recker, M.M., Wiley, D.A.: A non-authoritative educational metadata ontology for filtering and recommending learning objects. Interact. Learn. Environ. 9(3), 255–271 (2001)

Schein, A.I., Popescul, A., Ungar, L.H., Pennock, D.M.: Methods and metrics for cold-start recommendations. In: 25th Intl. ACM SIGIT Conference Inf. Retr., pp. 253–260. ACM Press, New York (2002)

Upendra, S., Maes, P.: Social information filtering: algorithms for automating "word of mouth". In: ACM CHI _95, pp. 210–217 (1995)

Vargo, J., Nesbit, J.C., Belfer, K., Archambault, A.: Learning object evaluation: computer mediated collaboration and inter-rater reliability. Int. J. Comput. Appl. 25, 198–205 (2003)

W3C. http://www.w3.org/Submission/WSMO/ (2005)

Yanbe, Y., Jatowt, A., Nakamura, S., Tanaka, K.: Can social bookmarking enhance search in the web? In: JCDL '07: 7th ACM/IEEE-CS Joint Conference on Digital Libraries, pp. 107–116. ACM, Vancouver. http://dx.doi.org/10.1145/1255175.1255198 (2007)

Part V
Mobile Learning Spaces

Chapter 15
Multimodality and Context Adaptation for Mobile Learning

Ivan Madjarov and Omar Boucelma

Abstract The new e-Learning 2.0 approach combines the use of social software, complementary tools, and mobile Web services to support the creation of ad hoc learning communities. The ubiquitous availability of mobile communication devices which are connected to the Internet makes it possible to use small amounts of spare time for mobile learning. The limited screen size and resolution makes current mobile devices quite hard to visualize multifaceted Web pages, so this kind of content could be adjusted to meet the device needs. This means the contextualization of learning contents for m-Learning usage. A Web services-based framework is presented for adapting, displaying, and manipulating learning objects on small handheld devices. A speech solution allows learners to turn any written text into natural speech files, using standard voices.

15.1 Introduction

The traditional e-Learning approach consists in using *Virtual Learning Environment* (VLE), a software that is often cumbersome and expensive and which tends to be structured around courses, timetables, and testing. In contrast, new e-Learning 2.0 combines the use of complementary tools, social software, and mobile Web services to support the creation of ad hoc learning communities.

New capabilities for social networking and communicating as exemplified by tools for *syndication, tagging, blogging, wikis. . . .* are having a significant impact on both working and social lives. This rapid pace of change in Web usage under the banner of Web 2.0 and the widespread availability of new tools are significant for

I. Madjarov (✉) • O. Boucelma
Laboratoire des Sciences de l'Information et des Systèmes, (LSIS) – UMR CNRS 6168,
Aix-Marseille Université, Avenue Escadrille Normandie-Niemen, F-13397 Marseille Cedex 20,
France
e-mail: ivan.madjarov@lsis.org; omar.boucelma@lsis.org

B. White et al. (eds.), *Social Media Tools and Platforms in Learning Environments*,   257
DOI 10.1007/978-3-642-20392-3_15, © Springer-Verlag Berlin Heidelberg 2011

Learning Management System (LMS) extension. The educational potential of social software and Web services is huge. The development of Web technologies has influenced the emergence of e-Learning 2.0 more specifically with implementing *blogging, podcasting*, and *mobile devices access* as new pedagogical services. Although not designed specifically for use in education, these tools and media are helping to make e-Learning 2.0 far more personal, social, flexible, and anywhere accessible.

Teachers are beginning to explore the potential of *blogs*, media-sharing services, and other social software which can be used to empower students and create new learning opportunities. *Podcasting* has become a popular technology in education, in particular because it provides a way of pushing educational content to learners.

Mobile Internet is becoming a regular companion for young people through the rapid development of computer technologies, the availability of services, and the falling decreasing prices for data transmission. Travel and latency times can be used not only for Internet surfing, but also for learning. One major challenge for mobile learning systems is that mobile device displays are small while the user interfaces for typical desktop applications are large and complex.

Flexible reuse and adaptation of learning content in this more dynamic environment requires modular structuring of *Learning Objects* (LOs) (Hwang et al. 2008). The use of *XML* as a medium-neutral data format for data storage and processing allows the learning contents to be classified hierarchically, to be structured at the desired level of granularity and to be adjusted to different contexts, situations, and devices.

The process of dynamic text adjustment refers to the *contextualization* and the *multimodality* in learning content (Kukulska-Hulme 2002). *Context* is associated for the most part to the current situation in connection with mobile information and communications systems. The *situation* is specified by the time, the place, the physical and social environment, the technical device, and the technical infrastructure [39].

With the successful development of Bluetooth, Wi-Fi (*IEEE 802.11*), *Wireless Application Protocol* (WAP), *General Packet Radio System* (GPRS), and *Universal Mobile Telecommunications System* (UMTS), the technological structures for wireless telephony and wireless computing are now firmly in place. This includes the personal and technical mobility, where mobile devices, including cell phones, Smart phones, handheld PCs, and PDAs, are carried everywhere (Sharma and Kitchens 2004). Taking advantage of their hardware characteristics, mobile devices are ideal tools to support the learning process (Trifanova et al. 2004), especially given their pervasive nature and personal use (Sharples et al. 2008).

Basically m-Learning is considered as any form of learning that is delivered through a mobile device (Sharples et al. 2008). M-Learning is seen, by several authors Sharma and Kitchens (2004), Petrova and Li (2009), Sharples et al. (2008), and Quint and Vatton (2004) as the natural evolution of e-Learning. For example, delays during commuting and traveling become potential learning moments. Some researchers (LineZine 2000) and Trifanova et al. (2004) think that mobile devices should be seen more like an extension, rather than as a replacement of the existing learning tools (Kinshuk et al. 2009). Moreover, not all kinds of learning content or learning activities are appropriate for mobile devices (Glover and Davies 2005). Some researchers are adapting LMS (Alier et al. 2008) by modifying the source code to the needs of mobility. The application of new, mostly mobile, technologies to e-Learning raises new problems that require innovative solutions from both pedagogical and technological points of view.

LOs, which are the basic component of e-Learning and m-Learning systems, usually target modifications in contexts and formats. The device-dependent applications of handheld devices have proven to be ineffective for creating m-Learning courseware. LOM (Hwang et al. 2008) is the most popular standard specification for LOs but lacks the ability to facilitate platforms descriptions.

This chapter raises various aspects of design and implementation of *Web Services Oriented Framework* (WSOF) which combines our *Open Semantic Editor Suite* (OSES) (IMS 2999) with a set of developed Web services. The objective is to make a device-independent m-Learning gateway between different mobile devices and the vast area of LOs available on a plethora of LMSs. The key technologies behind OSES are extending the LOM base *scheme structure* (IMS 2999), device-independent LOs *generator*, and *Web services*. The major advantage of the authors' proposal is to give mobile units of different types direct access to LOs customarily designed for desktop Web browsers. The authors propose a *Web Service-based semantic content adaptation tool* that uses templates to automatically and efficiently adapt content for *mobile Web browsers*. An additional *speech solution* allows learners to turn any written text into natural speech files, when using standard voices. This approach allows the generation of text- and audio-based learning material dynamically for m-Learning and ubiquitous access. The deployment of audio data to the mobile Web user *via progressive download* is also discussed.

15.2 M-Learning Technologies

E-Learning is defined by Madjarov and Boucelma (2006) as the convergence of the Internet and learning or Internet-enabled learning of network technologies to create, foster, deliver, and facilitate learning, anytime and anywhere. M-Learning is seen by several authors as the natural evolution of e-Learning, but Web pages, in general, are designed to be visualized on larger screens and, when one attempts to fit it on a small-screen device, most of its content is not visible.

The authors believe that m-Learning can be presented as a mobile extension of e-Learning through mobile computational devices with Internet connectivity. At the same time, mobile devices significantly differ from each other in their characteristics:

– *Mobile units:* cell phones, Smart phones, PDAs, handheld PCs
– *Application platforms:* Java2ME, Symbian, iPhone, Windows Mobile, Android
– *Web browsers:* Opera Mobile and Mini, Safari, S60, Microsoft IE for Mobile
– *Mark-up languages:* XHTML MP (*XHTML Mobile Profile*), WML, XML
– *Script languages:* JavaScript, VBScript

- *Development tools:* Nokia's Ovi SDK, Samsung Bada SDK, Sweb Apps for iPhone
- *File* formats and *screen* resolution

This heterogeneity of mobile units and different parameters does not contribute to the creation of a unified model for *Mobile Learning Content* (MLC) and requires a tailored approach for content restructuring and correct visualization of already developed pedagogical units (LOs). While m-Learning is a growing research area, aspects of *adaptivity* and *personalization* become more and more important. Incorporating adaptivity and personalization issues in m-Learning (Graf et al. 2008) allows these systems to provide learners with an environment that is not only accessible anytime and anywhere, but also accommodating to the individual preferences and needs of learners (FreeTTS 2005). Mobile learning systems have started to emerge as potential educational environments but still suffer from various technological and access related problems.

15.2.1 Mobile Learning Content and Mobile Applications

There are some standardization efforts in the world of e-Learning systems, so SCORM proposed by ADL (ADL-SCORM 2004) integrates a set of related technical standards, specifications, and guidelines that makes learning content accessible, interoperable, durable, and reusable. SCORM content can be delivered to learners via any SCORM compliant LMS or *Learning Content Management System* (LCMS). Both LMS/LCMS applications and SCORM content lack life cycle maintenance, offer poor support for mobile devices and were developed with the desktop browser in mind. There are few LMS vendors that provide a mobile version or fully support W3C standards.

LOs delivered on mobile devices become *Mobile Learning Objects* (MLOs) and have the potential to move learning use beyond computer labs. At the same time, MLOs must not be designed and developed as LOs for desktop computers, becoming just an adaptation to the restrictions of the interface of mobile devices. They should be designed, developed, and used, taking into consideration the advantages of mobile devices and the learning approaches that support *Mobile Learning Environments* (MLE). Pedagogical and other types of metadata are important in the implementation of LMSs for use by mobile devices. MLOs represent a means of rendering mobile learning content interoperable on a wide range of devices in different formats using XML for usability on small and large screens. Based on XML data and technologies, all kind of MLOs could be produced.

Several features of mobile technologies make them attractive in learning environments, among them: portability, communication capabilities, relatively low cost of mobile devices. To provide access to different student profiles, course authors can imagine various configurations and common options that can be used to *interact* (text input, multiple choices), to *visualize* the pedagogical content (images, video), or to combine *multimodal elements* (MEs) (Kukulska-Hulme 2002).

Research report (Petrova and Li 2009) shows that the most important constraining factors for widespread mobile learning adoption, along with *battery life*, are the *screen size* and *user interface* of most portable devices. In order to assist users in managing mobile devices, user interface designers are starting to combine the traditional keyboard or pen input with "hands free" speech input, adding other modes of interaction such as speech-based interfaces that are capable of interpreting voice commands (W3C 2004). This permits multimodal interaction (Kukulska-Hulme 2002), where the user has more than one means of accessing data from the mobile device. By definition, students seek different modes (text, voice, multimedia, etc.) to understand a delivered content.

MEs include TTS (*text-to-speech*) features which recreate the content through audio output (Quint et al. 2004). For instance, a text paragraph can be automatically recreated as an audio file. Other types of content can also be converted into audio: images can be tagged with a description which will be transformed into audio or can contain an audio-only description directly recorded by the course author. The same principle applies to all other pedagogical elements that can be used to create *Multimodal Mobile Learning Objects* (MMLOs). Speech generation is the process which allows the transformation of a string of phonetic and prosodic symbols into a synthetic speech signal. Synthesized speech can be created by concatenating pieces of recorded speech that are stored in a database. Synthetic speech systems differ in the size of the stored speech units.

Web services are an integration technology with best demonstration of its value when integrating heterogeneous systems because it supports many kinds of programming languages, run times, and networks (Waycott et al. 2002). Web services use XML data to transfer messages and SOAP protocol to transfer objects (Quint et al. 2004) (Fig.15.1). Web services capabilities are standard on desktop and server

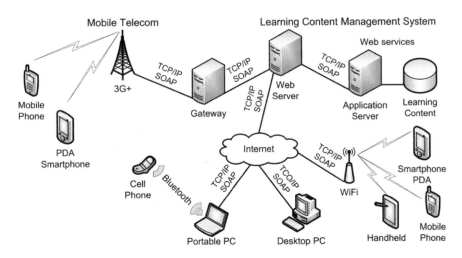

Fig. 15.1 Handheld, PDA, and smart phone connections through Internet (Adapted from Sá et al. 2009)

systems, but are increasingly available on mobile devices, enabling direct communication between devices, network operators, and content providers.

Mobile Web Services (MWS) are the application of Web services technology to the mobile environment (Sá et al. 2009). MWS is mainly designed so embedded devices can consume the *service* provided by the *server*. However, the direct application of Web service technology is unlikely to meet the full requirements of the mobile application and its user. A MWS application will typically differ from a traditional Web service (Chang et al. 2008). The developed service must take into account the constraints imposed by the limitations of the device and the personalization of the application to the user. Such a service is usually developed in Java2ME.[1] The application is downloaded to a mobile device and then it can exchange data via Web services.

A *Mobile Web Browser* is a semi-consistent network-based thin client designed for use on a mobile device to display Web content most effectively for small screens. Mobile browser software is smaller and accommodated to the low memory capacity and low bandwidth of wireless mobile devices. The mobile browser usually connects via a cellular network, or via Wireless LAN, using standard HTTP over TCP/IP and displays Web pages written in XHTML, XHTML MP, with WCSS support, XML-based documents with XSL Transformation styles, or WML (WAP 2.0). Technically, recent versions of some mobile browsers can handle more advanced Web technologies such as SVG, MathML, JavaScript, and Ajax.

For audio and video formats, to avoid the download of a huge file on the client side prior to playback, a streaming technique is recommended. *Progressive download* (pseudostreaming) is a UDP-based protocol extension that delivers audio and/or video "on demand" to a computer and can be installed on regular HTTP servers.

Podcasting refers to the automatic distribution of *media files* using standard Web technologies. The *Web feed* is an XML document that contains information that references the media files belonging to the podcast and it is updated every time new content is published. This is an automatic content distribution mechanism that differs from traditional vertical integrated media distribution such as Radio and Television. With the transformation of cell phones and Smart phones into portable information devices, this kind of services is also used in mobile networks and offers large possibilities for learning content distribution.

15.2.2 *M-Learning Architectures and Device-Independent Content*

There are two known approaches that address m-Learning issues: (1) the first considers that, due to the dominant role of Internet access via wireless devices,

---

[1]http://java.sun.com/javame/index.jsp

e-Learning simply becomes m-Learning, without any particular changes in content (Sá et al. 2009) and (2) the second encourages the development of LOs separately for each mode of use: *LOs* specific for e-Learning systems and desktop computing and *MLOs* specific for m-Learning systems and portable units. The authors believe that *adaptation* and *development* of the second approach could be more productive for all stakeholders (authors, learners, and administrators). MLOs could be produced dynamically for a specific mobile unit by processing (*transcoding*) (Glover and Davies 2005) existing LOs. Actually, LMS applications and LOs lack life cycle maintenance, offer poor support for mobile devices, and were developed with the desktop browser in mind. The major challenge for mobile learning systems is that mobile device displays are small while the user interfaces for typical desktop applications are large and complex. The challenge of reducing the complex interface to a small display in a manner that does not impair user performance and student learning can be managed (Bischoff et al. 2007).

The evolution of the Web-based education platforms goes toward a mix Web–mobile scenario (Fig. 15.1). Users will continue to access the LMS platforms using the Web for major tasks, but more and more often the access to the learning platform will shift to mobile devices. This will lead to a whole new kind of learning applications that will take advantage of the unique conditions of mobility and location of the mobile devices. However, these applications need to be integrated into the current generation of LMSs (Fig. 15.1). One of the possible solutions is presented in (Chen et al. 2005; IMS 2004) as a method for exploiting Web services architecture for m-Learning and e-Learning.

The challenge of *device independence* is to produce *Web-accessible* information that can be browsed in a readable and effective way on different devices and software platforms (Farley and Capp 2005). In order to reach this goal, methods are needed for (1) effective mobile device recognition and (2) mobile Web browsers functionalities identification. This means that application of an effective *Mobile Device Recognition Method* (MDRM) should be possible. Currently, servers and proxies can determine the identity of a particular device using the request header field in the *HTTP* protocol. In addition, there are three alternative methods:

– W3C composite capability/preferences profile (CC/PP) (Kondratova et al. 2009)
– WAP User Agent Profile (UAPROF) (Openmobilealliance) standard
– Wireless Universal Resource File (WURFL) (Wilson 2004)

The WURFL is an XML file (database) which contains information about device capabilities, features and various APIs (Java, PHP, Python, XSLT) for a variety of mobile devices. Currently, a complex and standard method for mobile Web browser functionalities identification is unavailable.

15.2.3 Methods for Mobile Learning Content Adaptation

Most LMSs are Web-based systems with HTML-based pedagogical content. Web pages are designed to be visualized on larger screens and, when one attempts to fit it on a small-screen device, most of its content is not visible. In general, *mobile Web browsers* provide a linearized version of the HTML page, leading to a large amount of scrolling and difficulty in finding the desired content. To better visualize page content, different approaches can be taken. The adaptation approach technically may be automatic, semiautomatic, or manual. The transformation process may be located either server side (XML/XSLT), either proxy side (Web clipping), or client side (XHTML/CSS). The process itself can be managed by server-side Web services (IMS 2004), by client-side mobile Web services (Sá et al. 2009), or by another interposed solution.

In Graf and Kinshuk (2008), characteristics of m-Learning systems are discussed, focusing more on aspects of context-awareness and adaptation. According to them, an m-Learning system could actively provide personalized support in the right way, at the right place, and at the right time, based on the personal and environmental contexts in the real world, as well as the learner's profile. Another characteristic is that the m-Learning system enables seamless learning, allowing students to move around in the real world. Furthermore, an m-Learning system is able to adapt the learning material according to the functions of the mobile device the student is using (FreeTTS 2005).

Regarding learning content presentation, different methods exist for providing students with adapted and personalized learning material. These methods determine how learning material is presented differently for units with different characteristics. In Brown et al. (2008), author classified these methods regarding to their aim into two groups, namely, for *adaptive presentation* and *adaptive navigation* support, whereby navigation in this context means how students navigate through the learning material.

In Kiss (2007), authors present a personalization process via two adaptive approaches: (1) the learning service could adapt to learner characteristics and profiles and (2) the learning service could adapt to the context surrounding the learners. In the development of these two approaches, the content adaptation process itself is not discussed.

Some studies describe different automatic, or manual mechanisms (Brusilovsky 2001; Zbozhna et al. 2008) and architecture (Buyukkokten et al. 2002) for adapting learning content to overcome the drawbacks of browsing content with mobile devices. Adapting the content through transcoding (Glover and Davies 2005) servers or proxies is one of the most used techniques: for simply translating from one presentation language to another (W3C 2004), or by modifying the HTML page tree structure (Glover and Davies 2005).

Certain methods for content summarization are introduced in Bischoff et al. (2007) to handle Web pages and HTML forms before displaying on a mobile device. A page is separated into text units that can each be hidden or partially displayed. Another study (WURFL 2010) developed an adaptation technique that analyzes a HTML page's structure and splits it into smaller, logically related units, which can be displayed on a mobile device screen.

The majority of proposed solutions are HTML-based in semantically poor format. The adaptation is applied to whole pedagogical content (Web page) so deprived of extraction possibilities of selected parts of content by a query language according to dynamically adopted criteria of personalization. Techniques of contextualization are generally limited to screen size adjustment and do not consider functional specificities of mobile browsers. An *XML-based solution* would be simpler, more tailored, dynamic, and flexible.

For a suitable choice of an appropriate adaptation technique, it is important to *identify* the nature of the *mobile device* and the specificity of the installed *mobile Web browser*. For mobile device system identification, there are some server-side or proxy-side standard methods. To check how well a *Web browser* (desktop or mobile) adheres to some W3C standards, especially those related to Web 2.0 technologies, an Acid3[2] test suite is available. Tests are focused on the feasibility of CSS, JavaScript and DOM 2 scripts and techniques. A few subtests also concern SVG, XML, and data URIs. As a result, a gradually increasing percentage counter is displayed without precision on subtests. This is not sufficient to evaluate the mobile Web browser reproduction accuracy for a multimedia learning content.

In Kukulska-Hulme (2002), the author explores possible improvements by utilization of *natural user interfaces* to enhance interaction with mobile devices. *Multimodal* speech-based content presentation is discussed. A *speech output* solution is presented in [39] when used in mobile applications for solving the problem of small displays. Some LMSs (Dokeos[3] or Moodle[4]) offer plug-ins for speech generation of a manually imported text. The result is stored in an audio file. So, the TTS framework is not integrated into the LMS system architecture. The authors consider *speech-based presentation* of learning content as an important option that could be integrated into the automatic content adaptation process as a server-side Web service.

15.3 Learning Content Adaptation and Service Integration

Today, a persistent connection is generally offered by handheld devices using a telecommunication protocol, so browsing the Web and reading e-mails while on the move has become usual. This has been possible due to cheaper and faster wireless network interfaces and the availability of mobile devices with augmented power, memory, and battery capacity. The problem of offline connecting does not arise given the packages proposed by the mobile providers and the multiple possibilities of free connections on public places. On the other hand, the limited screen size and resolution makes current mobile devices quite hard to visualize multifaceted HTML pages, so this kind of content could be adjusted to meet the device needs and user preferences.

---

[2]http://acid3.acidtests.org/

[3]http://www.dokeos.com

[4]http://moodlemodules.netcourse.org/2007/08/16/text-to-speech-block/

The main contribution of our work is to propose a *Web service-based framework* for adapting learning content on small-screen devices by content *restructuring, summarizing,* and *customization* according to the user needs and device profiles. In addition, for more usability and learning mobility, a TTS (*text-to-speech*) *conversion service* is proposed which may be initiated by the user.

Learning environments are supported by a number of key services such as *content creation* which require an *authoring tool*. Authoring tools are used to create and distribute content in diverse domains. LMSs (Moodle, Dokeos, Atutor, or Claroline) are complex software platforms designed for planning and managing learning activities online. They usually contain traditional authoring tools that use hypertext and multimedia features for content creation in HTML format not tailored for direct displaying on small screens.

The authors' technique for *mobile learning content creation* and *applications integration* is based on *flexible authoring* which involves *automatic adaptation* of content for different devices (desktop devices, mobile devices) on demand. The m-Learning system becomes an extension of an e-Learning system. There are two types of solution for such an extension:

- Web-based solutions, where mobile Web browsers are completed with plug-ins
- Java2ME or Flash downloadable mobile application with reduced compatibility following the model of phone

The authors propose a *Web-based approach* with *Web service support*. The *OSES editor suite* (FreeTTS 2005) is able to generate pages on the fly in different output formats (text or audio) depending on the mobile browser's profile. Different parts of a course can be broken into *separate units* and *summarized* before displaying on the small handheld device because *navigation* is an essential condition for assessing the effectiveness of a *visualization* method (Brusilovsky 2001). In connection with multimodal characteristics of m-Learning content, an additional *TTS service* is proposed. Speech is perceived as a modality which offers different output processes and tools.

15.3.1 Learning Content Creation and Applications Integration

The *Xesop* open source software (IMS) becomes a central piece of the system. Xesop provides a flexible XML-based suite of tools for author *customization, editing, storage,* and *publication* of LOs compliant with existing e-Learning standards (SCORM (ADL-SCORM), IMS (IEEE et al. 1484), and LOM (Hwang et al. 2008)). The content aggregation specification (ADL-SCORM) comprises two models: a metadata model specifying the metadata elements of learning resources and a content packaging model representing content structure. Both are hierarchical, which is convenient for representing data consisting of many elements and sub-elements. XML is perfectly suited for representing hierarchical models, as exemplified by the LOM and content packaging XML binding specifications published by IMS, both of which are adopted in SCORM.

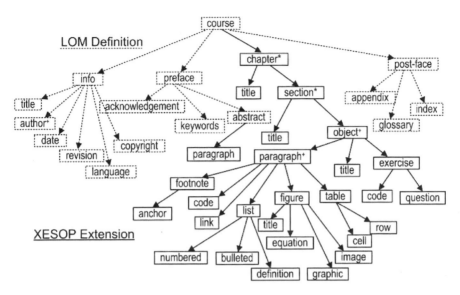

Fig. 15.2   The Xesop course structure

In Fig. 15.2, the structure of the created course content with the Xesop project's semantic tools is presented. The original LOM structure is extended with new elements that seem important for more homogeneous and identifiable pedagogical content.

For encoding textual information and content assembly, an XML *semantic editor* is used and a tree structure of a generic learning document is generated, while a *validation grammar* of XML Schema type is used. Depending on course specificity, (mathematics or informatics course), the author can represent texts, diagrams, mathematical formulas, or data in tables. A *MathML* editor was created for mathematical expressions, a *SVG* editor for vector graphics creation, a *QTI* editor for student's progression evaluation, a schema for *table* generation, and a *chart* editor for data presentation. In this case, XML is used for encoding non-textual information (Pham et al. 2004) such as vector graphics, mathematical expressions, multimedia documents, complex forms.

An XML document has a hierarchical structure naturally and to achieve maximum flexibility, XML is used for internal representation of learning materials. In our authoring suite, binary data of multimedia content is embedded directly into XML course data. During the editing process, if the author inserts an image or any binary data into the edited content, the semantic editor will encode it using the *Base64* encoding method. As a result, the course collection can be managed easily since all materials relating to the course are stored in a single XML collection. A large number of media-rich content can be stored using the abundant set of available XML Schemas. By providing proper XSLT transformation files, the XML content can be presented in many forms, such as XHTML for Web-based desktop users, XHTML MP or WML for Web-based mobile users.

Once created, a course can be saved as an XML document and shared by making local copies, or by using HTTP protocols. That does not imply the creation of a course warehouse, ready to be shared by several LMS or LCMS. According to the evolution of the course, authors may need to modify its content. Therefore, the correct operation of a collaborative authoring system imposes the storage of learning collections, possibly in an appropriate database, for a better reuse and diffusion of these documents. The choice of an appropriate database is essential: the authors have chosen a *native XML database* which allows the storage of XML documents in their native format. This choice, in opposition to that of a relational database, is explained by the nature of learning documents which are, in general, of narrative types – *document centric* and not data centric. Although relational database products today provide built-in XML document and query support, native XML databases are arguably the best choice for metadata storage. As far as the query language is concerned, IMS recommends XQuery. If necessary, formatted XHTML and PDF versions of extracted learning content can be published in a LCMS via Web services (IMS). Existing and old pedagogical documents can be adapted in the compliant XML format via importing Web services as external input in the XML semantic editor. M-Learning pedagogical content can be given in the form of a visual presentation as text, pictures, tables in XML, XHTML MP format, or as PDF data. Optionally, m-Learning content can be given as sound data in the form of an acoustic presentation in an MP3 or WAV format.

There are several possibilities and a large number of tools such as *FreeTTS speech synthesizer* written in Java (Dutoit et al. 1393) for the integration of acoustic presentation in m-Learning materials. Synthetic speech output offers a free and flexible alternative to prerecorded speaking by a professional speaker (Caetano et al. 2007). As a first step, a learning content has to be preprocessed. A rule set for preprocessing of text paragraphs is necessary to cover special cases like spoken numbers, abbreviations, and text formatting (Andronico et al. 2003). Spoken language consists of a set of phonemes and the generation of these phonemes out of text paragraphs varies largely between different languages (Andronico et al. 2003). After identifying all phonemes, every single phoneme must be synthesized as digital audio output. A free digitally available pronunciation encyclopedia for every target language is required. For this purpose, a free (Mbrola) *speech synthesizer* is used as a universal solution for voice files from different languages. As a next step, the generated audio output may be addressed to the *client audio player*.

To avoid the download of a huge file on the client-side before the playback begins, a *streaming* technique is recommended. Streaming is defined as UDP-based transmission of IP packets. *Progressive download* is a UDP-based protocol extension that delivers audio and/or video "on demand" to the user's computer in a simple way and can be installed on regular HTTP servers. Progressive download is usually initiated by a client player and uses a server-side script for communication. The audio player sends a HTTP request to the server with a start-time parameter in the request URL's query string and the server script responds with the audio stream so that its start position corresponds to the requested parameter. The advantage of using pseudostreaming is the simplicity of client–server communication like any other HTTP download from a Web site. The full streaming is more powerful but more complex technology to setting up. It requires an appropriate server-side software configuration.

15.3.2 Learning Content Adaptation for Mobile Web Browsers

The adaptation process on a mobile client is associated with complex algorithms and techniques for *splitting* (Zbozhna et al. 2008), *restructuring* (Glover and Davies 2005), *extraction* (Buyukkokten et al. 2002), and/or *summarizing* (Brusilovsky 2001) of proposed learning content. This results from the fact that a LMS provides resources in HTML format with no semantic notations. This type of notation is specific to an XML data source. By using an XML-based content, the authors could select, via XPath or XQuery, and dispatch extracted parts of learning content in an appropriate format by using simple *transformation* (XSLT). Alternatively, one could distribute the same object as an *audio* sequence. Finally, the adapted content can be "*displayed*" on the mobile unit *via* a *mobile Web browser*.

A series of *tests* were conducted to proof the LOs portability on *mobile browsers*. In this experiment, several mobile browsers were sent through a series of test pages. These represent some of the common design types that are in use, and like most real Web pages, not all of them were designed to work with small screens. To compare our test results with another popular test, the authors applied Acid3 for each tested browser. The main objective of the tests was to highlight the capabilities of popular mobile browsers to interpret and to visualize heterogeneous LOs. Each page contains a *test element*:

1. *Styled text*: *XHTML Mobile Profile* (XHTML MP) text paragraph with *Wireless Cascading Style Sheets* (WCSS).
2. *Tables*: XHTML MP page with Table and styled cells.
3. *Scripting*: XHTML MP form with JavaScript function.
4. *DOM and Ajax*: XHTML MP page with Ajax technique invocation.
5. *Device recognition*: Mobile user identification via HTTP headers: HTTP_USER_AGENT, HTTP_X_WAP_PROFILE and HTTP_ACCEPT.
6. *Object*: MathML page with formula equation example.
7. *Vector graphics*: XHTML MP page with SVG graphic.
8. *Video*: XHTML MP page with image and embedded sound file.
9. *Image:* Pages with an animated GIF graphic, PNG and JPEG images.
10. *Sound*: Pages with an WAV sound file on background and embedded object with MP3 sound file on auto play mode.
11. *XML*: XML document with an XSLT definition for presentation generation.
12. *Events*: XHTML MP page testing click events support.
13. *Acid3*: It is written in ECMAScript and consists of 100 subtests in six groups of selected elements from W3C standards. The result is expressed as a percentage.

Table 15.1 Mobile browser's common characteristics and tests results

Browser/Test item	Opera Mobile	S60 WebKit	Safari	Opera Mini	IE Mobile	BOLT WebKit	Blazer
XHTML MP	✓	✓	✓	✓	✓	✓	✓
WCSS	✓	✓	✓	×	✓	✓	✓
Tables	✓	✓	✓	✓	✓	✓	✓
JavaScript	✓	✓	✓	✓	✓	✓	✓
Image	✓	✓	✓	✓	✓	✓	✓
Sound	✓	✓	✓	✓	✓	✓	✓
Video	✓	✓	✓	×	✓	✓	✓
XML	✓	×	✓	✓	×	✓	×
XSLT	✓	×	✓	✓	×	✓	×
MathML	✓	×	✓	×	×	✓	×
SVG 1.1	✓	×	✓	×	×	✓	×
AJAX	✓	✓	✓	✓	×	✓	×
Java2ME	✓	✓	✓	✓	✓	✓	×
Events	✓	✓	✓	×	✓	✓	×
Acid3	99/100	47/100	100/100	64/100	20/100	100/100	73/100

The authors tested several *mobile Web browsers* on different models of *PDAs*, *Smart phones*, and *cell phones* with the objective to identify their compatibility with desktop Web browsers. The results of the tests are in Table 15.1.

Analysis of the *test results* shows that some mobile browsers are compatible to desktop browsers functionality. Thus, a multimedia pedagogical content, which is especially appreciated by students (Petrova and Li 2009), is suitable on mobile browsers. The main problem to address here is to tailor the *presentation* on small-screen mobile devices, rather than focusing on the complexity of pedagogical hypermedia content. This process includes the development of a suitable page-adaptation technique that analyzes XML course structure and generated pages into smaller, logically related units that can fit into a mobile device's browser. The page sequence should be generated in a suitable format (XML or XHTML) accordingly to the browser's profile.

On the other hand, the nature of mobile devices, with their small screens and poor input capabilities leads to the assumption that they cannot replace the standard desktop computers or laptops. However, the same properties can make them efficient in learning domain, if certain constraints are kept (Alier et al. 2008):

- *Short modules*: Authors should prepare flexible learning materials that can be accessed across contexts.
- *Simple functionality*: Authors should create pages with simple interactions to avoid the complexity of the rich multimedia content.
- *Summarize*: Authors may divide pages into smaller chunks and place them on multiple hyperlinked pages surrounded by an *index* to facilitate the access to a requested content.

– *Browser profile*: Authors should adapt the diffused page in a format according to the browser's profile.
– *Text-to-speech*: Authors should propose this feature for ease of access to users on the move and/or with small display capabilities associated with mobile devices.

To achieve the goal, the authors have extended the functionality of the *Web service-based OSES suite* (IMS) with three additional services. The first one (XICT) is able to create a hypertext *index* on the basis of the course tree structure. The second service represents an *XML content adaptation tool* (XCAT) that uses *profiles* (XML metadata files) for automatic content adaptation displayed on the mobile browser. Profiles are adjusted in the function of detection: (1) mobile device profile issue from WURFL database (Wilson 2004) and (2) of mobile browser profile (Table 15.1). The third service is developed on the base of the (Mbrola) speech synthesizer free library to produce speech output from a text paragraph. The *XML speech adaptation tool* (XSAT) converts the associated text to index item content to an audio output.

The course content adaptation process is an overall index of hyperlinks. Each link points to a node in the hierarchical structure of a created course. On a "click," the corresponding content is first adapted, then downloaded and displayed on the mobile screen. The navigation process is provided in two dimensions: top-level index entries and hyperlinks to the next/previous page. If a text item is highlighted, then the *XCAT service* is executed, otherwise the *XSAT service* is executed when the sound icon is highlighted for the same item.

In Fig. 15.3, the course content adaptation process is presented. The result is displayed on the mobile Web browser. Section 1 shows the *course tree structure* developed in accordance with the definition presented on Fig. 15.2. All elements of the tree are *labeled* at their creation time. Thus, they become easily identifiable and locatable along the depth of the tree, which defines their *hierarchical position* in the generated index. Section 15.2 presents the *semantic editor* defining any pedagogical component edited by the author. Section 15.3 is an additional and optional *view* of the course content in native XML format. Screen 4 shows the results of *summarization* in the form of indexes corresponding to each node of the hierarchical structure of the course. This page is initially sent to the mobile Web browser. Screen 5 shows a possible learner interaction by choosing items from *index* and receiving corresponding *adapted content*, while screen 6 shows an *audio* file played by the client-side player. If the audio icon is selected from screen 4 instead of text link, the associated text content is processed in audio output. If a binary content is chosen, a standard audio message is send.

15.3.3 Web Services Implementation

A Web service application interaction is quite simple as defined by W3C (Caetano et al. 2007). A requester entity might connect and use a Web service as follows: (1) the requester and provider entities become known to each other, (2) the requester

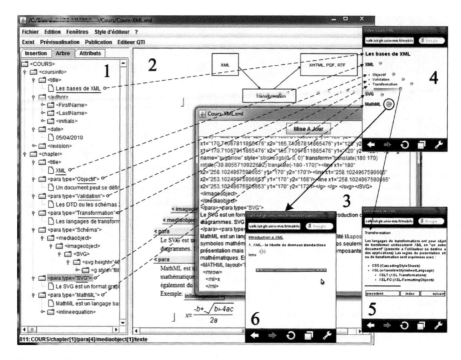

Fig. 15.3 Learning content adaptation process

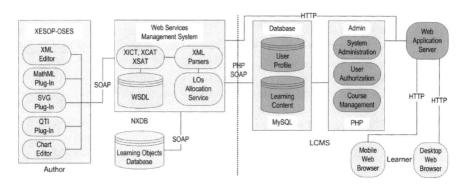

Fig. 15.4 Web service-based system architecture (Adapted from FreeTTS)

and provider entities agree on the service description and semantics that will manage the interaction between them, and (3) the requester and provider entities exchange messages.

Developed Web services may be implemented on LCMS as showed on Fig. 15.4, and then may include: *authoring, content managing and publishing, remote exercising, service discovering*, etc.

The left side of Fig. 15.4 highlights the OSES application, while the right side illustrates a Web-based LCMS. The interconnection of these two parts is carried out by a *Web Services Management System* (WSMS). Thus, many Web service-based external applications can be integrated with a LCMS. The publication of an XML collection created by OSES in the learning space of a LMS/LCMS is achieved by the creation of a SCORM conformant *imsmanifest.xml* file and optional *zipped SCO package*. A Web service is responsible for integrating XML data into internal data structures of the LMS/LCMS.

As shown in Fig. 15.4, the *learning-centric* data and the *management-centric* data are clearly separated. LOs are developed by the author in OSES section of the Xesop system and thereafter are stored in a NXDB. The information relevant to learner personal data, learner profiles, course maps, LOs sequencing, data presentation, and general user data is stored in the relational database (RDB) of LMS/LCMS. The publication process of learning content is carried out by the WSMS (*Web Services Management System*). This represents the authors' *method* for external applications *integration* through Web services. This allows extending existing e-Learning systems without modifications of their own source code. In practice, this may *extend* infinitely the system's features. In the authors' case, content adaptation Web service-based modules make the *bridge* from e-Learning to m-Learning system in a simple and effective way.

As a proof of concept, the authors used eCUME (Moodle-based) e-Learning system adopted by their university. The authors integrated the PHP-based LCMS interface via Web services. An implementation of the LCMS interface via Web services offers a high degree of flexibility and ease of use, in particular as SOAP libraries for PHP already exist, which leads to an easily extensible PHP and MySQL-based LCMS. For services registration, *Apache Axis*[5] as *SOAP engine* was employed. This tool facilitates the deployment of Web services, and it offers functionality to automatically generate a WSDL description of a service. For storing and managing LOs *eXist*,[6] a Java-based open source *native XML database* was used. It can be run in the *Apache Tomcat*[7] *Servlet engine* as Web application. For searching and updating data, eXist supports XQuery, XPath, and XUpdate. eXist can also be invoked via XML-RPC, a REST-style Web services API, SOAP.

15.4 Conclusion and Future Work

With the advent of Web 2.0 and related technologies, social computing has become a new paradigm for communication and learning. Social platforms such as wikis, blogs, podcasts, and sites for social networking are generating novel ways for

---

[5]http://ws.apache.org/axis/

[6]http://exist.sourceforge.net/

[7]http://tomcat.apache.org/

access and visualization of information in the teaching and learning space. Social media uses Web-based technologies to turn communication into interactive dialogue. The social media for education has become ubiquitous, distributed, collaborative, and personalized. Much like Web-based social networking, mobile social networking occurs in virtual communities through a mobile phone. The challenge of mobile networking is the context-aware content adaptation. There is steady growth in the number of mobile multimedia services. Usage of multimedia services and especially the presentation of multimedia content is more challenging in a mobile environment than on stationary devices as a result of the diversity of mobile devices and their parameters, the sparse resources of the air interface, or the changing context.

This chapter described *personalization* in mobile learning via an adaptive approach, by adapting to the context of the learner's surroundings. This chapter described a *Web service-based approach* to an integrated Web-based learning and mobile learning environment. The authors *tested* several mobile Web browsers to proof the LOs portability. An adaptive course customization strategy for an m-Learning environment was analyzed. The authors introduced a *framework* that utilizes the hierarchical displaying multimedia units with index extraction and content summarization. Web services technology was adapted to provide a flexible *integration model* in which all the learning components and applications are well defined and loosely connected. The advantages of using a *mobile Web browser* as universal communication environment were noted. The authors combined textual content adaptation with alternative audio transcoding to better fulfill student needs. An adaptive technique which is better suited for a large content of LOs, because it is XML-based, relies on Web service-based processing and is along the line of recent trends in e-Learning 2.0, was proposed. The target objective of this technological contribution is to improve the achievement of learning outcomes.

Finally, this proposal is oriented toward system engineering based on independent components to ensure not only the reuse of LOs but also the interoperability and the reuse of the applications in any kind of environment: e-Learning or m-Learning.

Future research efforts will be focused on: (1) the development of a generic Web service-based architecture integration with the AJAX technique for a LCMS Web-based desktop and mobile clients; (2) the feasibility of personalizing and adapting the m-Learning applications and contents to learner preferences, in regard to the increasing capabilities of mobile devices; and (3) the development of an adapted learning–podcasting service that will be used in mobile pedagogical (social) networks.

References

ADL-SCORM, Advanced Distributed Learning, The Sharable Content Object Reference Model (SCORM). http://www.adlnet.gov/Technologies/scorm/default.aspx (2004)
Alier, F.M. Guerrero, J.C.: Moodlbile: extending moodle to the mobile on/offline scenario. In: IADIS International Conference Mobile Learning, Algarve (2008)

Andronico A. et al.: Designing models and services for learning management systems in mobile settings. In: Crestani, F. et al. (eds.) Mobile and Ubiquitous Info. Access Ws 2003, LNCS, vol. 2954, pp. 90–106. Springer, Verlag/Berlin/Heidelberg (2004)

Bischoff, A.: Context-aware mobile learning with pediaphon – a text-to-speech interface to the free wikipedia encyclopedia for cell phones and MP3-players. In: Inmaculada Arnedillo Sánchez (ed.) IADIS International Conference Mobile Learning, pp. 228–232. Lisbon (2007)

Brown, Q., Lee, F.J., Salvucci, D.D., Aleven, V.: Interface challenges for mobile tutoring systems. In: Woolf, B. et al. (eds.) ITS 2008, LNCS, vol. 5091, pp. 693–695. Springer, Verlag/Berlin/ Heidelberg (2008)

Brusilovsky, P.: Adaptive hypermedia. User Model. User-Adapt. Interact. **11**, 87–110 (2001)

Buyukkokten, O., Kaljuvee, O., Garcia-Molina, H., Paepcke, A., Winograd, T.: Efficient web browsing on handheld devices using page and form summarization. ACM Trans. Info. Syst. **20**(1), 82–115 (2002)

Caetano, M.F., Fialho, A.L.F., Bordim, J.L., Castanho, C.D., Jacobi, R.P., Nakano, K.: Proteus: an architecture for adapting web page on small-screen devices. In: Li, K. et al. (eds.) NPC 2007, LNCS, vol. 4672, pp. 161–170, Dalian, China (2007)

Chang, H.P., Wang, C.C., Shih, T.K., Chao, L.R., Yeh, S.W., Lee, C.Y.: A semiautomatic content adaptation authoring tool for mobile learning. In: Li, F. et al. (eds.) ICWL 2008. LNCS, vol. 5145, pp. 529–540. Springer, Verlag (2008)

Chen, Y., Xie, X., Ma, W.Y., Zhang, H.J.: Adapting web pages for small-screen devices. IEEE Internet Comput. **9**(1), 50–56 (2005)

Dutoit, T., Pagel, V., Pierret, N., Bataille, F., van der Vreken, O.: The MBROLA project: towards a set of high-quality speech synthesizers free of use for non-commercial purposes. In: ICSLP'96, vol. 3, pp. 1393–1396. Philadelphia (1996)

Farley, P., Capp, M.: Mobile web services. BT Technol. J. **23**(2), 202–213 (2005)

FreeTTS, Speech Integration Group, Sun Microsystems Laboratories. http://freetts.source-forge. net/docs/index.php (2005)

Glover, T., Davies, J.: Integrating device independence and user profiles on the web export find similar. BT Technol. J. **23**(3), 239–248 (2005)

Graf, S., Kinshuk: Adaptivity and personalization in ubiquitous learning systems. In: Holzinger, A. (ed.) Symposium on Usability and Human Computer Interaction for Education and Work. USAB 2008, LNCS, vol. 5298, pp. 331–338 (2008)

Hwang, G.J., Tsai, C.C., Yang, S.J.H.: Criteria, strategies and research issues of context-aware ubiquitous learning. Educ. Technol. Soc. **11**(2), 81–91 (2008)

IEEE LOM, Draft Standard for Learning Object Metadata, IEEE 1484.12.1-2002 (2002)

IMS Content Packaging v1.2 Public Draft v2.0, Content Packaging Specification. http://www. imsglobal.org/content/packaging/ (2004)

Kinshuk Chang, M.G., Graf, S., Yang, G.B.: Adaptivity and personalization in mobile learning. In: Annual Meeting of the American Educational Research Association, San Diego (2009)

Kiss, C.: W3C, Composite Capability/Preference Profiles (CC/PP): Structure and Vocabularies 2.0, W3C Working Draft 30 April 2007, http://www.w3.org/TR/2007/WD-CCPP-struct-vocab2-20070430

Kondratova, I.: Multimodal interaction for mobile learning. In: Stephanidis, C. (ed.) ICWL 2009, Universal Access in HCI, Part II, HCII 2009, LNCS, vol. 5615, pp. 327–334 (2009)

Kukulska-Hulme, A.: Cognitive, ergonomic and affective aspects of PDA use for learning. In: European Workshop on Mobile and Contextual Learning, pp. 32–33. Birmingham (2002)

LineZine, Learning in the New Economy. http://www.linezine.com/elearning.htm (2000)

Madjarov, I., Boucelma, O.: Data and application integration in learning content management systems: a web services approach. In: Nejdl, W., Tochtermann, K. (eds.) LNCS, vol. 4227, pp. 272–286. Springer, Verlag/Berlin/Heidelberg (2006)

Mbrola, N.N.: MBROLA Project, TCTS Lab, http://tcts.fpms.ac.be/synthesis/mbrola.html (2010)

Openmobilealliance, UAProf spec. http://www.openmobilealliance.org/tech/affiliates/wap/wap-248-uaprof-20011020-a.pdf (2001)

Petrova, K., Li, C.: Focus and setting in mobile learning research: a review of the literature. Commun. IBIMA **10**(28), 219–226 (2009)

Pham, B., Wong, O.: Handheld devices for applications using dynamic multimedia data, computer graphics and interactive techniques in Australasia and South East Asia. In: 2nd International Conference on Computer Graphics and Interactive Techniques in Australasia and South East Asia. ACM Press, New York (2004)

Quint, V., Vatton, I.. Techniques for authoring complex XML documents. In: ACM Symposium on Document Engineering, pp. 115–123. Milwaukee (2004)

Sá, M., Carriço, L.: Supporting end-user development of personalized mobile learning tools. In: Jacko, J.A. (ed.) Human-Computer Interaction, Part IV, HCII 2009, LNCS, vol. 5613, pp. 217–225. Springer, Verlag/Berlin/Heidelberg (2009)

Sharma, S.K., Kitchens, F.L.: Web services architecture for M-learning. Electr. J. e-Learning **2**(1), 203–216 (2004)

Sharples, M., Milrad, M., Arnedillo-Sánchez, I., Vavoula, G.: Mobile learning: small devices, big issues. In: Balacheff, N., et al. (eds.) Technology Enhanced Learning: Principles and Products. Springer, Berlin (2008)

Trifanova, A., Knapp, J., Ronchetti, M., Gamper, J.: Mobile ELDIT: challenges in the transitions from an e-learning to an m-learning system. University of Trento, Trento (2004). http://eprints.biblio.unitn.it/archive/00000532/01/paper4911.pdf

Waycott, J., Scanlon, E., Jones, A.: Evaluating the use of PDAs as learning and workplace tools: an activity theory perspective. In: European Workshop on Mobile and Contextual Learning, pp. 34–35. Birmingham (2002)

W3C, Web Services Architecture, W3C Working Group Note. http://www.w3.org/TR/ws-arch/ (2004)

Wilson, L., Look Ma Bell, No Hands! – VoiceXML, X + V, and the Mobile Device, Journal, SysCon Media, http://xml.sys-con.com/node/45792 (2004)

WURFL, Wireless Universal Resource File. http://wurfl. sourceforge.net/ (2010)

Zbozhna, O., Vatterrott, H.R., Martens, A., Tavangarian, D.: Mobile learning using text-to-speech technologies. Gen. Aspects Assess. ICT Use Educ. **1**, 554–557 (2008)

Chapter 16
Context-Sensitive Content Representation for Mobile Learning

Chih-Hung Chang, Chih-Wei Lu, William C. Chu, and Juei-Nan Chen

Abstract Mobile learning enables learning content to be displayed anytime, anywhere, and with any kind of presentation device. Learning Content Management Systems (LCMSs) usually provide convenient authoring tools to help instructors construct learning content, which may include static documents such as PowerPoint, Word, PDFs, etc. Dynamic multimedia documents such as video and audio files can also be managed and created. Static and dynamic files can be integrated to enable users to access rich content. Most LCMSs are designed around desktop computer environments, rather than on mobile-device-driven environments. Context-Sensitivity is an application of software system's ability to sense and analyze context from various sources. Context-Sensitivity enables actions to be taken based on the current context. The action could involve adapting to the new environment, notifying the user, communicating with other another device to exchange information, a change of content, or performing other tasks. Context-Sensitive environments should provide the facilities for application software to define such context-triggered actions so as to transparently invoke them whenever the corresponding contexts are valid. This chapter illustrates how a Context-Sensitive Middleware (CSM) for an LCMS is able to transform the same learning content to different mobile devices, so mobile learning can be supported.

C.-H. Chang • C.-W. Lu
Department of Information Management, Hsiuping Institute of Technology, No. 11, Gongye Rd, Dali City, Taichung County 41280, Taiwan, R.O.C
e-mail: cwlu@hit.edu.tw

W.C. Chu (✉)
Department of Computer Science and Information Engineering, TungHai University, No. 181, Taichung-Kang Road, Sec. 3, Taichung 40744, Taiwan, R.O.C
e-mail: cchu@thu.edu.tw

J.-N. Chen
Department of Information Networking Technology, Hsiuping Institute of Technology, No. 11, Gongye Rd, Dali City, Taichung County 41280, Taiwan, R.O.C
e-mail: RNChen@hit.edu.tw

B. White et al. (eds.), *Social Media Tools and Platforms in Learning Environments*,
DOI 10.1007/978-3-642-20392-3_16, © Springer-Verlag Berlin Heidelberg 2011

16.1   Introduction

The purpose of a good learning environment is to enable the absorption of knowledge in an efficient manner. In traditional learning environments, study habits may be affected by the restriction of time and space to the detriment of learning quality. Mobile learning enables learning content to be accessed anytime, anywhere, and with any kind of devices, thereby addressing the issues associated with traditional learning environments.

Many Learning Content Management Systems (LCMSs) 1 offer convenient authoring tools to help instructors construct learning content. Content may be static files (slides, word documents, PDF files), and it may be dynamic multimedia files (video and audio files). Static and dynamic files can be integrated to provide rich content accessible through mobile devices.

However, most LCMSs are based on desktop computer environments, rather than on mobile device environments. Context-Sensitivity is an application of the software system's ability to sense and analyze context from various sources. This chapter describes a study that developed Context-Sensitive Middleware (CSM) for an LCMS to transform the same learning content to different mobile devices, to enable mobile learning.

16.2   Related Studies

During the past 15 years, techniques such as learner customized courses (Tatar et al. 2003), curriculum sequencing, and intelligent analysis of student solutions have all supported the Web Tutoring System (WTS) (Brusilovsky et al. 1996). WTS tends to develop more intelligent and interactive learning. Therefore, it is argued that many innovative WTSs are able to facilitate learning outcomes through information technology.

16.2.1   LCMS and LMS

Figure 16.1 shows a tutoring system in a Web learning ecosystem. The Learning Content Management System (LCMS) is responsible for standardizing author processing and learning objects management services. In other words, the core function of the WTS must be to package learning content into the Learning Object (LO). WTS will then reorganize the LOs into a learning sequence determined by the learner's query.

There are many working groups engaged in learning content specification for reusability and exchange, and these well-known specifications are like Content Packaging and Simply Sequencing (IMS 2003), LOM (IEEE LTSC 2002), CMI (AICC 2003). The specifications of Sharable Course Object Reference Model (SCORM) (Advanced Distributed Learning (ADL), SCORM 2004) were

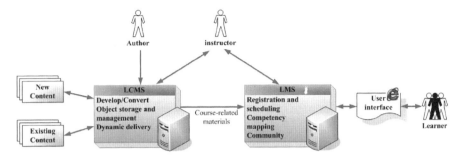

Fig. 16.1 LMS–LCMS integration within a Web learning ecosystem (IDC 2001)

collectively developed by the White House Office of Science and Technology Policy (OSTP) and the Department of Defense's Advanced Distributed Learning (ADL) initiatives. SCORM is the most widely accepted e-Learning specification, and is applied to WTS because it combines other content specifications to enhance digital content allowing reusability and exchange among LMS and LCMS. The structure of SCORM divides learning content into three levels:

1. Sharable Assets (SA). This is the smallest unit of LO as a piece of text or information, image, or multimedia.
2. Sharable Content Objects (SCO). One SA or several SAs are packaged as the building block of a topic, a lesson, or a course.
3. Content reorganization. Depending on different learning activities, some SCOs are organized as learning sequences by instructional design, which allows LMS to guide the behavior of learners to archive learning objectives (Fig. 16.2).

There are many proposals for a learning sequence involving many SCOs that would enable existing learning mechanisms to offer cost-effective ways of enabling learning anywhere and anytime. However, none of these proposals have sufficient intelligent ability to support a process of learning scenario. These mechanisms still use a "one-size-fits-all" process called "learning from technology but learning with technology" (Brusilovsky et al. 1996; Hooper et al. 1995). Three interesting issues have developed: Automatic Construction of Concept Maps (Tatar et al. 2003), Intelligent Course Tailoring, and Case-Based Reasoning (Capuano et al. 2003). Each emphasizes analytic reasoning/learning and relevant information filtering.

16.2.2   Learning Object Metadata (LOM)

Learning Object Metadata (Wikipedia, http://en.wikipedia.org/wiki/Learning_object_metadata) is a data model, usually encoded in XML, which is used to describe a learning object and similar digital resources that are used to support learning. The purpose of learning object metadata is to support the reusability of learning objects, to aid discoverability, and to facilitate their interoperability, usually in the context of online LMS.

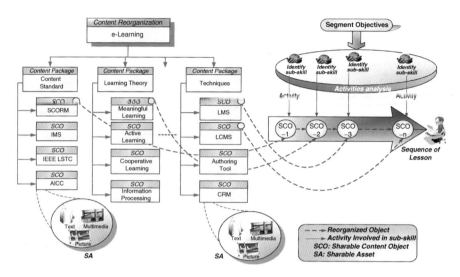

Fig. 16.2 An e-Learning curriculum containing hierarchical content objects where the content is reorganized into the learning sequence by defined learning activities

The aim of the LOMs (Zurita and Nussbaum 2004) is:

- To enable learners or instructors to search, evaluate, acquire, and utilize LOs
- To enable the sharing and exchange of LOs across technology-supported learning systems
- To enable the development of LOs in units that can be combined and decomposed in meaningful ways
- To enable computer agents to automatically and dynamically compose personalized lessons for individual learners
- To compliment the direct work on standards that is focused on enabling multiple LOs to collaborate within an open, distributed learning environment
- To enable, where desired, the documentation and recognition of the completion of existing or new learning and performance objectives associated with LOs
- To enable a strong and growing economy for LO that supports and sustains all forms of distribution: nonprofit, not-for-profit, and for profit
- To enable education, training and learning organizations, governments, public and private, to express educational content and performance standards in a standardized format that is independent of the content itself
- To provide researchers with standards that support the collection and sharing of comparable data concerning the applicability and effectiveness of LOs
- To define a standard that is simple yet extensible to multiple domains and jurisdictions so as to be most easily and broadly adopted and applied
- To support necessary security and authentication for the distribution and use of LOs

LOM defines a set of elements that describe the learning resource; they are General, Life cycle, Meta-metadata, Technical, Educational, Rights, Relation,

Annotation, and Classification. There are five data types in LOM, which are CharacterString, LangString, DataTime, Duration, and Vocabulary.

16.2.3   Mobile Learning

The rapid emergence of wireless communication technology and mobile devices has meant, in recent years, that the use of handheld technology in education settings has increasingly been the object of study. From laptops to wireless phones and handheld devices (or W/H devices for short) (Lai and Wu 2006), the nature of higher education has been altered through the massive infusion of computing devices and the rapid improvement of Internet capabilities (Green 2000). Via wireless technology, W/H devices can be synchronized with or connected to computers or wireless networks (WiFi, GPRS, 3G). Research has shown that W/H devices provide new opportunities for communication and innovative user interaction both inside and outside learning environments (Roschelle and Pea 2002). W/H devices have also provided a unique opportunity for enhancing cooperative learning (Imielinsky and Badrinath 1994). Because W/H devices can support cooperative learning environments (Mai 2005), they greatly enhance mobility, coordination, communication, and organization of materials, negotiation, and interactivity in ways not possible in conventional cooperative learning environments (Tseng et al. 2007). Roschelle and Pea (2002) have suggested five reasons for using W/H devices in cooperative learning environments: (1) augmenting physical space, (2) leveraging topological space, (3) aggregating coherently across student's individual contributions, (4) facilitating evaluation of student performance, and (5) providing an easy and instant way to archive student work for future reference. The mobility and connectivity of W/H devices allows group members to work on a task and to discuss topics with each other even while they are away from the group. Overall, W/H devices provide a natural mobile collaboration environment (Danesh et al. 2001; http://www.ieeeltsc.org:8080/Plone/working-group/learning-object-metadata-working-group-12/learning-object-metadata-lom-working-group-12).

16.3   Context-Sensitive Mobile Learning Environment

The mobile computing environment consists of LCMS, rendering devices, and Context-Sensitive Middleware (CSM), as shown in Fig. 16.3. The major functionality of CSM is to provide learners with proper content format when they access content from a range of mobile devices.

In the current study, an MVC pattern was applied to the system design phase and to the system implementation phase. In order to promote the reusability of mobile content, this research replicates SCORM 2004 2, where learning content was subdivided into Asset, SCO, SCA, and Content Packaging; meanwhile, the linking relationship of these elements is defined by XML description.

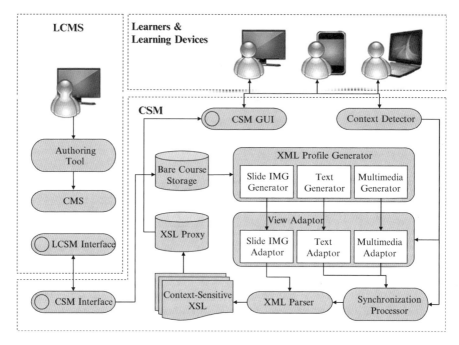

Fig. 16.3 System architecture for CSM learning

16.3.1 XML Profile Generator

The limitation of the resources of mobile devices, such as the smaller screen size, means that the learning content (e.g., slides in Microsoft PowerPoint format) which were originally designed for a PC environment, cannot be properly rendered in mobile devices and need to be analyzed and transformed to the appropriate format. In order to make learners acquire proper contents by their mobile devices, all learning resources are transformed to XML profiles via XML Profile Generator in Fig. 16.3.

XML Profile Generator classifies the learning content into three formats: Slide IMG, Text, and Multimedia. Slide IMG is the image and picture, Text is the text, and Multimedia is the attached multimedia files from slides. These three types of content are extracted from original slides and transformed into their corresponding profiles in XML format. Based on these profiles, View Adaptor can adapt them into an appropriate format appropriate for a range of devices.

16.3.1.1 Transformation of Learning Content

The transformation steps needed to convert learning content into XML profile are the following:

1. *Parse and analyze the slide.* When the learning content is acquired from LCMS, this system parses and analyzes the slide element according to the Slide Element Table (SET).
2. *Extract the text and image from slide.* After parsing and analyzing the slide, one of the slide templates is selected. Then, the text and image are extracted from the slide. Since the Microsoft PowerPoint file format supports Text mode (shown in Fig. 16.4), this problem can be solved. In addition, if it contains some images in the slide, it can be extracted directly since Microsoft PowerPoint regards images as independent objects. The image extracting process discards other objects in the slide, as shown in Fig. 16.5. The elements of the slide can be extracted effectively and reused in CSM.
3. *Generate the XML profiles based on analyzed result.* Finally, since the text can be extracted successfully, the Text Generator can transform Text into XML profiles. The complete process is shown in Fig. 16.6.

16.3.1.2   Transformation of Slide IMG and Multimedia

The purpose of generating Slide IMG is to make learners hold the full view of the content when learning in mobile devices. Slide IMG Profiles are transformed via a Slide IMG Generator, as shown in Fig. 16.7.

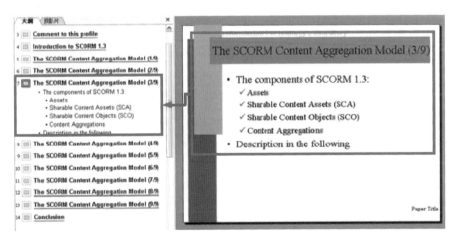

Fig. 16.4 Extract text from PowerPoint

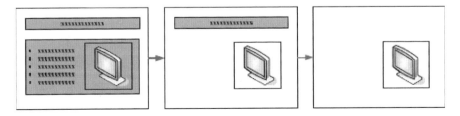

Fig. 16.5 Image extraction process

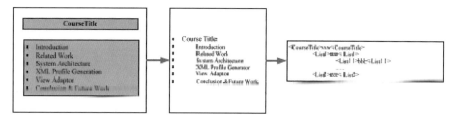

Fig. 16.6 Slide transformation process

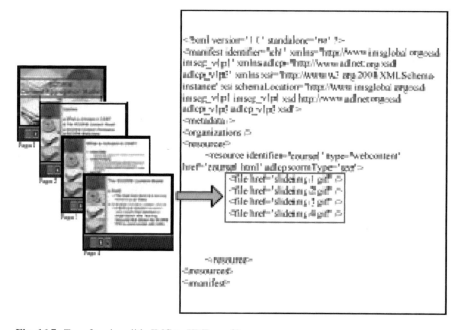

Fig. 16.7 Transforming slide IMG to XML profiles

16.3.2 View Adaptor

This section describes how to transform the XML profiles into adaptive files by use of the Context Detector and View Adaptor, and then integrating these files into customized learning content.

16.3.2.1 Context-Sensitive Content Rearrangement

As a result of the Text format containing rich information, the learner should be acquired with the full view of learning contents. When learners select one Slide

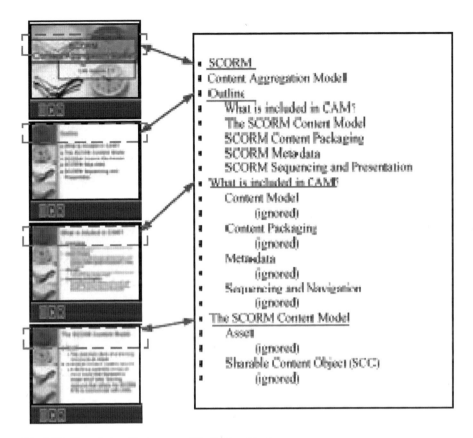

Fig. 16.8 The relationship between slide IMG and text

IMG, the Text of the image is matched to Text Mode. The technique to attain this is to use a Double Anchor Hyperlink between Text and Slide IMG, as shown in Fig. 16.8.

16.3.2.2   Context-Sensitive Content Transformation

Some XSL, which describe device context, are stored in the Context Detector. When learners study online, the Context Detector selects the proper XSL and then integrates this with XML profiles generated by the XML Profile Generator. Finally, the customized mobile learning content is transformed according to the browsers that mobile devices support. This process results in Context-Sensitive XSL. Context-Sensitive XSL is placed into the XSL Proxy, so that it is convenient for learners to learn by the same mobile device.

16.4 Conclusion and Future Work

Most LCMS can integrate static and dynamic files, but they only pay attention to systems based on desktop computer environments, rather than on mobile devices. In this study, the XML profiles of the three learning resources are generated by an XML Profile Generator. Adaptive XML profiles are transformed via a View Adaptor and Context Detector that detects device context of the mobile devices. Finally, a customized mobile learning content is packaged to enhance the reusability of learning resources. In the future, the project will extend "Context-Sensitive Content Representation" to include "Interactive Learning" and "Offline Learning."

References

Advanced Distributed Learning (ADL): SCORM 2004 2nd Edn. Overview. www.ADLNet.gov (2004)

AICC (Aviation Industry CBT Committee). Available at: http://www.aicc.org/(2003)

Brusilovsky, P., Schwarz, E., Weber, G.: ELM-ART: An intelligent tutoring system on world wide web. In: Frasson, C., Gauthier, G., Lesgold, G. (eds.) Third International Conference on Intelligent Tutoring Systems. LNCS, vol. 1086, pp. 261–269 (1996)

Capuano, N., Gaeta, M., Pappacena, L.: An e-learning platform for SME manager upgrade and its evolution toward a distributed training environment. In: 2nd International LeGE-WG Workshop (2003)

Danesh, A., Inkpen, K.M., Lau, F., Shu, K., Booth, K.S., Geney, T.M.: Designing a collaborative activity for the palm handheld computer. In: Conference on Human Factors in Computing Systems, pp. 388–395 (2001)

Green, K.C.: Technology and instruction: compelling, competing, and complementary visions for the instructional role of technology in higher education. http://www.campuscomputing.net (2000)

Hooper, S., Rieber, L.P.: Teaching with technology. In: Ornstein, C.A. (ed.), Teaching: Theory into Practice, pp. 154–170 (1995)

IEEE LTSC (IEEE Learning Technology Standards Committee). Available at: http://ltsc.ieee.org/ (2002)

Imielinsky, T, Badrinath, B: Mobile wireless computing: challenges in data management. Commun. ACM 37, 18–28 (1994)

IMS (Instructional Management Systems) Content Packaging Best Practice Guide, Version 1.1.3 Final Specification. Available at: http://www.imsglobal.org/ (2003)

Lai, C Y, Wu, C C: Using handhelds in a jigsaw cooperative learning environment. J. Comput. Assist. Learn. 22, 284–297 (2006)

Mai, N: Engaging students in group-based cooperative learning - a Malaysian perspective. Educ. Technol. Soc. 8(4), 220–232 (2005)

Roschelle, J., Pea, R.: A walk on the WILD side: how wireless handhelds may change computer-supported collaborative learning. Int. J. Cogn. Technol. 1(1), 145–168 (2002)

Tatar, D, Roschelle, J, Vahey, P, Penuel, W R: Handhelds go to school: lessons learned. IEEE Comput. 36, 30–37 (2003)

Tseng, S.S., Sue, P.C., Su, J.M., Weng, J.F., Tsai, W.N.: A new approach for constructing the concept map. Comput. Educ. 49(3), 691–707 (2007)

SCORM (Shareable Content Object Reference Model) Version 1.3, Advanced Distributed Learning. Available at: http://www.adlnet.org/ (2004)

Zurita, G, Nussbaum, M: Computer supported collaborative learning using wirelessly interconnected handhelds computers. Comput. Educ. 42, 289–314 (2004)

Part VI
Social Factors

Chapter 17
Progressing the Social Dimension Toward the Collaborative Construction of Knowledge in 2.0 Learning Environments: A Pedagogical Approach

María José Hernández-Serrano

Abstract The chapter proposes an optimization of the opportunities for learning via social media through the progression of the social dimension toward collaboration. The key question is how to map this progression when using 2.0 environments for achieving meaningful processes of collaborative construction of knowledge. A pedagogical framework with three mediating elements is developed: social interaction (technology promoted) and participation or collaboration (educationally aimed). The main changes in the participatory scenario and the new forms of participation that are relevant for learning are explored. Subsequently, there is a description of the social dimension with the main variables involved. Finally, once the variables have become visible, some light is shed on pedagogical guidelines concerning how the facilitator has to manage the variables explored in order to promote effective processes of collaboration in the construction of knowledge via contemporary social media.

17.1 Introduction

Web evolution toward collaborative approaches is considered one of the main advancements of the last decade. The influence of a strong social approach (Widén-Wulff 2007); has emerged with the extension, both quantitative and qualitative, of the participatory scenario of the Internet. A new collective imaginary (Mattelart 2000; Castoriadis 2008) has been created with new social structures, which promote innovative forms of socialization that go far beyond traditional spaces for exchanging knowledge.

The second Web generation, or Web 2.0 (O'Reilly et al. 2005), offers numerous tools and services to promote social interaction. More than a simple technological

M.J. Hernández-Serrano (✉)
Faculty of Education, University of Salamanca, Paseo de Canalejas 169, 37008 Salamanca, Spain
e-mail: mjhs@usal.es

B. White et al. (eds.), *Social Media Tools and Platforms in Learning Environments*, 289
DOI 10.1007/978-3-642-20392-3_17, © Springer-Verlag Berlin Heidelberg 2011

change, what most characterizes the new wave of social media is an evolution in the *use* of technologies through an *increase of participation* (Hernández-Serrano and González 2008). Hence, the Web has changed from a showcase – created by a minority – toward a space for the collaborative construction of information and knowledge.

New communication channels and new sociability modes are expanding the dimensions for understanding the participatory process in virtual environments, and by extension, the virtual learning environments. Consequently, educators should act on the potentialities of these new social media for learning, fundamentally because, as explored in this chapter, the construction of knowledge is affected by social engagement, which inevitably occurs during the course of participation among individuals.

As a result, the interpretation of the new educational reality, where technological and social processes converge with the learning processes, requires the incorporation of collaborative processes, promoting the Collaborative Construction of Knowledge (hereafter, CCK).

Learning theories (Scardamalia and Bereiter 1991; Stahl 2006; Stahl et al. 2006) enable CCK to be understood as a dynamic action, generated by the influences of different mediating elements of two types: symbolic (in this case, mediation of technologies by artifacts and tools, according to socio-constructivist theories) and social (mediation of individual's interaction).

More precisely, together with these two mediating elements, participation is indispensable for the CCK, which is visibly linked with the other elements. CCK is generated under the influence of social media, by mediating artifacts and tools that create a context for interaction. Here, the distinction between *interaction* and *participation* put forward by Jenkins (2009) is clearly important: while interaction is a technological mediating element, participation is cultural. In other words, artifacts and social interactions can exist, but CCK necessitates that individuals are explicit about their willingness to collaborate and construct knowledge.

Therefore, the theoretical framework involves three mediating elements for CCK (see Fig. 17.1). First, CCK can be generated by symbolic mediation in a

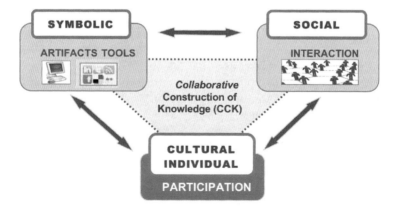

Fig. 17.1 Mediating elements in the collaborative construction of knowledge (CCK)

technological context of tools and artifacts. Interestingly, tools allow interaction and communication (language modalities: oral, textual, hypermedial. . .); artifacts (technologies, specifically social media) promote different levels of participation, representing an interrelationship among the three mediating elements (as depicted by the blue arrows).

Second, CCK necessitates the existence of a social reference; knowledge is constructed collaboratively and requires *interaction* with others (social mediation).

Third, CCK implies a joint action inextricably requiring *participation* with others, in order to share or generate knowledge (individual or cultural mediation).

In terms of meaningful learning, the three elements are indispensable and interdependent. When knowledge construction is aimed collaboratively, only by the mere use of technologies, even if they are social media or provide group interaction, it is not sufficient to guarantee the desired results. CCK is highly determined by the third factor, individual and cultural intertwined, related to participation and sense of inclusion in a community for collaboration and learning.

Accordingly, the aim of this chapter is central to understanding the necessary progression from the technological mediation toward the social mediation, fundamentally based on participation for the collaborative construction of knowledge in 2.0 environments.

Thus, in the following sections, the two second mediating elements (individual/ cultural and social) are analyzed in more detail within the context of social media. On one hand, it is necessary to deconstruct *the participative component*, as the driving force of each and every one of the social actions and, consequently, of the learning actions. Taking into consideration that at the present time participation acquired several forms, the discussion is focused on the main social media participation forms. On the other hand, the critical value of interactions relies upon *the social nature of cognitive processes*, according to several learning theories, as will be explained. The understanding of a new learning scenario seeks a reflection about how CCK is different in social media, compared to face-to-face settings. Additionally, this scenario is not only affected by some of the most important traditional learning factors, but also by new phenomena associated to the context of social media.

After explaining this introductory framework, the chapter provides an insight into new factors that require mapping educational practices and managing social variables differently in order to achieve desired learning results via social media. So, the main pedagogical concern is how to design a virtual environment able to generate significant participation and collaboration. For this purpose, identification of the main variables involved in social dimension will be explored.

Finally, once the variables of the social dimension have become visible, the chapter intends to shed some light on pedagogical guidelines about how to map those variables to ensure an effective progression in the process of collaboration. The aim of these guidelines is to illustrate ways of empowering individuals in the meaningful construction of knowledge using social media.

17.2 Understanding Participatory Scenario Within Social Media

Social media have generated an expansion of the participatory scenario, so much so that nowadays living and participating on the Internet is invaluable. Most traditional participative processes have an online equivalent: associating, meeting people, voting, motivating others to participate, keeping a profile, and attracting followers. However, online participation is complex; there are many constraints, as in the face-to-face participation.

Participation is primarily a systemic process in which different factors contribute to success or failure. It relies on each individual's socialization, development, and situational factors. At the same time, the concept of participation is hardly unequivocal. Depending on the starting point, it is possible to define it as a procedure or a target, or even as a value, or a technique.

In the field of education, the meaning of participation is twofold. First, participation is understood as *implication*, to be with others; sometimes merely a perception (sense of integration in a group) rather than an action itself. This dimension is extremely necessary, however it is not sufficient. Second, from a more productive perspective, participation denotes *realization*, actively doing something with others (creating, sharing, reflecting... learning); in this sense, participation involves generating a product by a joint action, either cooperatively or collaboratively.

Social media can promote both dimensions of participation, although there are many barriers regarding personal conditions or social facilities and opportunities. Likewise, it is assumed that the strategies and skills necessary for online social development differ to some extent from those that are face-to-face. First, online participation turns people into citizens of the world, influencing their sense of belonging and their roots. They are participants of a network in the process of expansion that, in principle, has no restrictions based on geographical criteria. Second, the minority rules and interests for participating are eroded through globalization, by the development of a common Internet culture. Third, in a changing and ephemeral world, online participation today will be radically different that in 5 years time. It is important to consider the fact that the constantly evolving participatory possibilities are influencing younger generations, for whom social media is a genuine fashion, along with an appealing source for sociability.

Technologies, and especially social media, affect the traditional idea of participation, leading us to rethink the importance of participation in educational settings. However the real point is: To what extent is participation determining learning by means of the collaborative construction of knowledge?

Jonassen (2000) argues that technologies make the construction of knowledge possible by means of articulation, contextualization, or cooperation, which imply participation. At present, social media go beyond this, by moving participation forward to collaboration, specifically by making possible the collaborative construction of knowledge. To understand this idea in greater depth, it is necessary to consider the diverse forms of participation in social media, as depicted in Fig. 17.2.

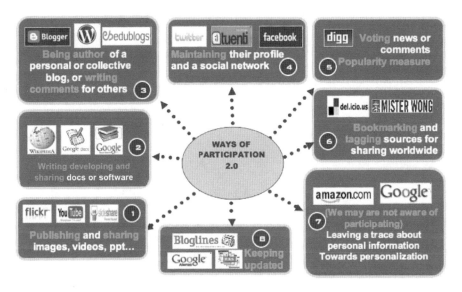

Fig. 17.2 Current forms of participation in social media

1. The prime form of participation is by using social media as a repository, making public different multimedia resources (videos, images, PowerPoint presentations, movies, etc.). In this modality, participation means to *transmit* information, as a basic condition for learning.
2. The next stage is the collaborative edition of information, sharing ideas world-wide, such as contributing in open wikispaces. Also, in Web development, a combination/synthesis of software (mash-up and fast aggregation). Here, partic-ipation means contribution, but also relations with others. There is a component of consensus and respect. It deals, fundamentally, with the construction of knowledge collaboratively.
3. As author, the blog phenomenon means a commitment and a responsibility with an audience. As contributors, making commentaries evolve through stages of comprehension, reflection, and finally contribution. As reviewers, by linking or forwarding user-generated content, users lead to a discussion and feedback with the original author. So, participation implies negotiation of meanings, as an essential element in the collaborative construction of knowledge.
4. Also, social networking systems such as Facebook facilitate microblogging for sharing information among users, in the form of permanent profile updating or retwittering. Besides new forms of communications, social networks motivate others to participate in the construction of personal profiles and online identities. Participation involves, consequently, a process of selection and sharing common interests.
5. Online sites inviting evaluation, or specifically platforms for voting such as Digg, require users to contribute a rating or an opinion. Thus, voting involves

a process of decision making, based on information synthesis and contrast, and making a judgment.

6. Sharing bookmarks, replaying posts or logs, categorizing through one or several tags, generate a browsable personal or public tagging map, as in Delicious. Categorizing entails also a process of decision making and a judgment. These involve higher level cognitive processes contributing to the construction of a meta-knowledge, which is shared and compared with others, learning from other people's judgments.

7. Leaving a trace about personal information contributes toward personalization, sometimes without the individual being aware. Any kind of data (interest, preferences, timetables, links with colleagues...) is given to the media and returns to us in the form of tailored information. So, media creates a personal likeness, motivating successive participation. At the same time, media share this information, offering collective suggestions that may meet someone's individual requirements. It is a form of pseudocollaboration with others, which allows one to take advantage of others preferences and experiences (even their errors, such as when Google suggests what was typed for searching).

8. Finally, through news readers and e-mail alerts, the information superhighway has allowed users to participate by choosing the relevant information they want updated and then personalizing the information selected.

From the above considerations, possibilities to share and collaborate with others are changing the use of technologies and most importantly, the ways of maintaining relationships and taking advantage of other people's knowledge and experiences. Different ways of participation are therefore paramount. New ways of interacting through social media pilot the evolution of collaboration and learning. However, technologies can enhance meaningful learning only if envisaged as a participatory ecosystem, in terms of Brown and Adler (2008), with emergent interconnections between individuals and context, where the sense of community is an indispensable condition to collaborate for learning.

17.3   The Social Nature of the Construction of Knowledge

Pedagogical disciplines have begun to reflect on how new ways of interacting with social media are capable of evolving processes of collaboration and construction of knowledge. This debate raises interesting questions, such as: Can social media generate a new evolution in ways of meaningful learning? Will social media recreate appropriate contexts for social learning by the use of virtual learning communities? Most importantly, what is the best way to combine the social and technological possibilities for promoting and channeling participation toward meaningful social learning?

Answering these questions concerning the potential learning evolution, it is of the utmost importance to mention the *socio-constructivist theories* (Vygotsky 1962/1978; Leontiev 1983; Engeström 1993; Wertsch 1993; Cole 1996) from which knowledge is conceived as an object that is built from cognitive mechanisms and operations introduced in social interaction and negotiation.

An individual's cognitive activity develops through interaction. Thus, if cognition is not to be limited to inner mental processes, but rather to a system of interactions, then pedagogical interests should be twofold. They should focus not only on the processes taking place inside the mind of an individual, but also, more importantly, on the influences provided by the surrounding *context*, such as social *activities* and the sense of presence of *others* or their roles.

Emphasis on the influence of context and social activities are both perspectives represented by relevant theories: *situated cognition theory* (Brown et al. 1998; Suchman 1988) and *distributed cognition theory* (Lave and Wenger 1991; Salomon, 1993; Wenger, 1998). Situated cognition is focused on the context; and distributed cognition on the distributed resources that make possible the construction of knowledge. From these two theories, learning is understood as a situated and distributed practice that takes place in a context, when meaningful activities are socially shared.

Cognitive process is developed and shaped by interactions among individuals with different levels of knowledge. More specifically, contemporary learning theories revolve around the importance of interactions. *Connectivist learning theory* (Siemens 2004) insists on the importance of interactions, noting that knowledge is formed and projected through connections generated in networks, where opportunities for connecting knowledge are more important than the current state of knowledge.

In the context of social media, individuals interact in both synchronic and asynchronic ways. These interactions strengthen the central role of sharing knowledge and accelerate its collective production (Fainholc 2008). Accordingly, access to shared collective knowledge is promoted (Rheingold 2002). The most representative ideas are displayed in the notions of collective intelligence (Levy 1999), and crowd wisdom (Surowiecki 2004).

The most important consideration for learning collaboratively is that the interactions within the social media reinforce the *community* character, if common practices and values exist (responsibility, commitment, support...) and if all stakeholders have similar hierarchical positions, which facilitate enough closeness for sharing knowledge and the collaborative (re)construction of meanings.

According to Tu and Blocher (2010) different types of learning communities can be generated by the media: communities of interest, communities of purpose, communities of passion, and communities of practice. These four communities provide different sets/stages upon which individuals act. Specifically, the context for CCK is related to a community of purpose, as one of the common purposes in a community can be the focus on learning, as an integral and indispensable aspect of social practice (Rovai 2002). In these virtual communities, members are learners who build knowledge together throughout the use of social media.

The construction of communities has noticeably strengthened with social media through the main participatory of "being" online and working together. However, social connectedness mediated by technologies, or social technologies, does not necessarily imply participation. Enhancing community character necessitates the explicit participation of the individuals, related to individual and cultural mediating elements.

Community is a space where interactions arise and develop from an implicit/ explicit sense of sharing (Kuo and Young 2008). This is especially important for education because unlike naturally or quickly formed relationships, complex interactions for learning necessitate a certain level of interdependence together with the existence of different social elements.

Therefore, in educational contexts, providing a successful interrelationship between the individual and the virtual space requires a significant dimension, which is mainly based on social variables related to the *sense of community*.

Description of the social variables involved in the sense of community is not an unproblematic task. Despite the lengthy history of research on the topic of community, it is becoming increasingly difficult to define the term. Traditional definitions of community are not always valid for online environments because these definitions referred to physical social presence and geographic territories. However, in the Network Society, the configuration of social links is based on similarity of interests, much more than similarity to the immediate environment (Castells 2000). Community is changing from geographic specific to relation specific, defined not in terms of physical proximity, but in terms of social networks (Smith and Kollock 2002). Spatiality is expressed by connectivity, and thus, virtual space is experienced as a network of interactions (Hine 2000). As a result, from the three traditional elements of community defined by Hillery (1955) – spatial consciousness (geographically), common ties, and social interaction – contemporary understandings of community emphasize the interactions, while the perception of a shared space is envisaged through the media.

Spatial consciousness exists now in the form of connectivity, as a result of the fact that when the Net absorbs a process, that process is recreated in "likeness," as a reticular image with multiple connections. Hence, the Internet enables social interactions presenting a spatial character, which can be manifested throughout perceptual, emotional, and socio-cognitive aspects evidenced by individuals when they are interacting in a virtual environment (Hernández-Serrano et al. 2009).

It is not the author's intention to deliberate whether online communities fulfill the characteristics and requirements of off-line communities – this has been well debated by Wellman and Gulia (1999). The aim is to dwell upon the dynamic relationship between the sense of community and the enhancement of learning experiences in 2.0 environments.

A progression in the social dimension, from interaction to participation and collaboration for learning, is proposed (Fig. 17.3). The proposal encompasses the three mediating elements through a macro-*environmental context*, consisting of social media interactions, with regard to the symbolic mediation previously stated. Then, regarding both the social and individual/cultural mediating elements, consideration is given to two contexts: a *community context*, which provides participation, affected by two main factors and new considerations regarding to social media and

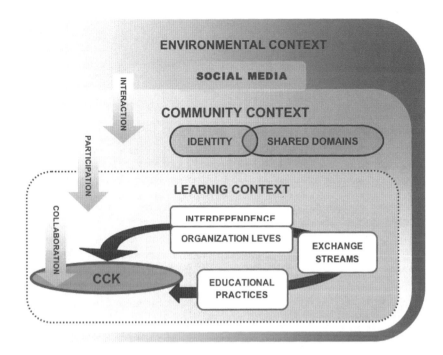

Fig. 17.3 Community context and social variables for CCK in 2.0 learning environments

a third context specifically regarding to a *learning context* for collaborative construction of knowledge.

Interestingly, the column on the right in the framework represents the required progression in the social dimension; interaction turns into participation within a community context; and, when community variables are accomplished, socially situated learning turns participation into collaboration, by means of several factors essential for successful CCK.

17.4 Community Variables via Social Media

Generally, community is defined as a group of individuals who have at least one common feature that identifies them in their interactions. Wellman and Gulia (1999) and Purcell (2006) define a community as a "network of interpersonal ties that provide sociability, support, information, a sense of belonging and social identity." Further to mutual support, there are also common concerns, which imply commitment and decision making (Smith and Pellegrini 2000) with agreement on certain shared goals (Bickford et al. 2006).

According to the above authors and other commonly cited definitions of community (Tönnies 1957; McMillan and Chavis 1986; Smith and Kollock 2002) there are two main variables involved – the shared domain and the identity – which are clearly relevant for promoting not only participation, but also collaboration.

17.4.1 Shared Domain

Either in face-to-face or virtually, emergence of a community is based on a shared domain of *interests*, *needs*, and/or *expectations*, by means of explicit or implicit agreements between individuals. However, in a virtual setting, this shared domain acquires distinctive characteristics that may affect the learning goals:

- *Ways of sharing.* In an online community, everything that is shared necessarily has to be public and explicit. Interests, needs, or expectations have to be visible and noticeable for others, in order to share commonalities. Media provide an opportunity for sharing by the description in their profiles. That which is invisible is not shareable (personal data, shows of affection, or cognitive levels of reasoning). Conversely, the more shared domains the greater the linkages with others online. Finding similarities and a sense of community cohesion is important for collaborative learning.
- *Expectations about what is shared online.* The quantity or quality of issues being shared may evoke perceptions of dissimilar levels of participation, which may lead to a failure to meet expectations of homogeneity. This is central because the amount of visible data confirms an identity to others, which can also differ from original intentions, affecting further interactions. For membership and cohesion, participants have to be perceived as being of similar, but not necessarily equal status. For successful collaborative learning, the similarity of previous knowledge and attitudes need to be ensured before being shared in the public domain.
- *Those with whom the domain is shared.* In an online community, a shared domain gains a global dimension. Individuals from very different backgrounds are bridging to build a community. Thus, similarity converges with diversity. The shared domain is reshaped by the enrichment of different cultures, with ways of understanding, varied interest and needs, which enhances learning exchanges. The needs of individuals and their interest for sharing are similar whether on or offline, but virtuality enlarges social space (Turkle 1995) and enhances, extends, and supplements the offline (Howard and Jones 2004) creating greater diversity.
- *A shared domain needs to be modified over the time.* The volatility of online communities relies on the sustainability of the shared domain. A change of community and the exploration of new interests are at the click of a mouse. Consequently, if what is shared is not nurtured with practices that imply identification with others, the shared domain will stagnate and therefore the community will become extinct with zero learning results.

As can be observed, collaborative learning via social media turns into an organic process of sharing and development. Evolving over time, the common, shared aspects are promoters of a more or less strong sense of cohesion, as a sense of individual adaptation and well-being, along with the perception of this in others. As a result, cohesion turns into a process more than a condition or end state, which requires a shared legitimacy, recognition, participation, inclusion, and a sense of belonging (Jenson 1998).

Regarding learning goals, outcomes are reliant on effective educational practices to promote and maintain significant shared domains and higher levels of cohesion between individuals.

17.4.2 Identity

Identity is a sense of belonging, a recognition of being part of a community with shared needs, interests, or expectations. Rovai (2002) claims that identity has two dimensions: spirit (feelings of connectedness and inclusion) and trust (reliance on others and motivation to assist them). The former is an *inner* dimension, which is at the same time recreated online based on community belonging; and the latter is *external*, depending on what is perceived of one's identity online. Thus, online identity is sometimes merely a part of the visible shared domain, but for trust and support to flourish, identity needs to be shared by all the members, shaping a consensual sense of belonging.

Global networks can increase relationships, in both quantity and diversity, or at least, provide access to relationships more easily. However, this mode of sociability may undervalue the sense of belonging, as individuals can register in many different groups. Virtual communities require active individual involvement. The main condition of belonging to a group is participation, although, merely involvement does not automatically provide a membership identity. Identity is based on common understandings *among* and *with* others.

With reference to the perception of others in virtuality, the idea of social presence requires reevaluation. In virtual environments, social presence has been defined by Garrison and Akyol (2009) as: "the ability of individuals to project themselves on others' social and emotional development, with community members who are 'believed as true.'" In this respect, technologies can enhance social presence incorporating different forms of interaction among stakeholders, synchronic and asynchronic. Specifically, Burbulles and Callister (2001) differentiate between explicit self-identity (choosing a nickname) and imaginary (an avatar). Additionally, technologies endorse dynamism through the ease with which different identities can continuously move forward and adapt, depending on the tool or platform chosen.

Arguably, virtual interaction promotes and increases the flow of information and collaboration among individuals, resulting from a sense of social proximity existing beyond the physical boundaries, now based on similarities. More precisely, this sense of social identification encourages individuals to cooperate, offer assistance, and share with others (Brickson and Brewer 2001); in this way, collaboration and learning can be promoted in virtual spaces.

Moreover, virtual identification is created within a space, where identity is projected. So, what turns a space into a personal space is everything about oneself that is perceived in such space, even perception of others, with whom close bonds should exist. For this reason, personalizing services in social media generate the individual's feeling of being (re)presented in a space, by continuous selection and leaking of personal information (Burbules and Callister 2001), with a diversity of activities facilitating social closeness as a prerequisite for collaboration.

17.5 Collaborative Factors for Learning in 2.0 Environments

Building a context for learning within social media requires consideration of the emerging field of Computer-Supported Collaborative Learning (CSCL), in which different learning sciences are involved (Stahl et al. 2006) to identify how collaborative phenomena can be described and achieved by the use of technologies. However, to create artifacts, activities, and environments that enhance the practices of learning collaboratively involves considerable intricacy. Knowledge construction in the CSCL literature (Stahl 2000) shows that collaborative learning with technology is related to numerous factors. Here, three of the more relevant factors, widely cited in the specialized literature on collective activities supported by learning environments, are considered. These are: (1) the required basis for collaboration by means of *organization activities* (Dillenbourg 1999; Dillenbourg and Jermann 2007; Dillenbourg and Hong 2008; Dillenbourg et al. 2009) and *positive interdependence* (Johnson et al. 1998; Janz and Prasarnphanich 2003; Nistor 2003), (2) the way different *exchange streams* are used (Baker and Lund 1997; Hron et al. 2000; McInnerney and Roberts 2004), and (3) the quality/quantity of *educational practices* provided (Koschmann 2002).

In addition, it is necessary to consider the initial attitude toward technologies that may prevent individuals from socializing or learning collaboratively, as meaningful collaboration requires a positive perception of *efficacy* in the available media. That is, the individual has to perceive that the mediating technology, particularly social media, is effective for the development and success of the collaboration and learning. As Bandura (2002) notes, new electronic technologies provide opportunities for individuals to bring their influence to bear on collective actions. In addition, as Kavanaugh et al. (2005) elaborates, Bandura's assertions also warn that ready access to technologies will not necessarily enlist active participation unless individuals believe that they can achieve the desired results by this means. Thus, how the Internet changes the features of social participation and collaboration depends on the perceived efficacy of the media for learning and engaging in collaborative activity.

17.5.1 Collaboration Basis

Collaboration using technologies requires a productive setting to promote knowledge construction. Fundamental to this is the individual's sense of positive interdependence, along with organizational levels in a culture for learning (Hernández-Serrano and Jones 2010).

Generating a strong social cohesion in a community, with the idea of achieving mutual goals, does not itself move learning forward. Cohesion is only a condition for activating responsibility in the construction of knowledge. A further step is necessary, a sense of *positive interdependence*: "linking students together so one cannot succeed unless all group members succeed" (Johnson et al. 1998: 4).

Individuals should understand that each group member's efforts are required and indispensable for the success of the group, where everyone is responsible for each other's performance. Within a learning context, these joint efforts are focused on a common goal of constructing and sharing knowledge collaboratively; its goals can only be achieved when individuals work in collaboration. This is accomplished when the context has a level of organization, which involves and permits negotiation and joint decision making.

Collaboration, thus, is also affected by supplementary factors, either external (educationally designed by a facilitator) or community built, referring to different levels of organization, including a definition of a shared culture. Organization is a central aspect in collaboration, as successful decision making is easier when individuals are organized (Dillenbourg et al. 2009). Sometimes, an external facilitator defines organizational levels, although these must be shared by the whole learning community (Dillenbourg and Jermann 2007; Dillenbourg and Hong 2008). Organization deals with a shared culture of collaboration, which should be based on norms and values. Norms establish attitudes of respect among individuals and are based on a set of main shared values such as: solidarity, participation, and coherence (Purcell 2006). Organization, thus, seeks to stimulate the capacity for the communication, transmission, and construction of knowledge. Degrees of formality in collaboration will depend on contextual factors; they can vary progressively and can take into account many aspects: the age of individuals, the establishment of subgroups according to computer skills, the work timetables, and the focused interests.

17.5.2 Exchange Streams

CCK is developed through different transfer mechanisms, which offer diverse levels of communication and collaboration (Warschauer 1997). Exchanges, as confirmed by Jarvis (2009) can be of four different forms: among individuals, between individuals and phenomena, between individuals and future phenomena, and between the individual and the self. CCK necessitates dynamic streams mainly for the first three exchanges, although it is important to consider the idea of the virtual self.

As the virtual self can be different from the off-line represented self, in roles, scripts, or appropriate interactions (McInnerney and Roberts 2004), thus, the virtual environment should encourage different forms for self-representation in order to facilitate synchronization. Transposition in an avatar is the most evolved form, but is it important to promote resources for personalization and activities for space appropriation.

Exchanges between individuals should also be diverse, preferably synchronous. However, a considerable part of technology-mediated communication is based on writing. Online participants are mostly represented by text on a screen, which constrains the expansion of the interaction, in comparison to face-to-face encounters, losing visual cues or nonverbal references, critical for message understanding. Preece (2000) has reflected on Goleman's ideas by showing the importance of empathy in communication, which is mostly conveyed nonverbally. Empathy is also central for effective collaboration, so, after ensuring there are no barriers to communication, social cues must be visible through media exchanges. In view of this, some current virtual communities have evolved to 3D environments, or platforms for videoconferencing that allow individuals to participate in a more complete sense.

17.5.3 Educational Practices

Providing an enabling learning environment is much more than making some documents accessible online or introducing a virtual forum in class. Meaningful and authentic activities "bond students and teachers collectively to catalyze social interaction into skills and knowledge acquisition" (Tu and Blocher 2010 135).

In the learning community context, individuals should interact through a variety of learning practices, offering different levels of adaptation, interaction/participation, and collaboration. Members engage in joint activities and discussions, to help each other and share information. They build relationships that enable them to learn from each other (Wenger et al. 2009).

Practices mean resources and activities whose main focus is to collaborate in the construction of knowledge among individuals. It is important to consider that social dimension in CCK requires not only task-based practices, but also emotionally driven tasks, as pointed out by Rovai (2002). The latter improves the socio-affective dimension and facilitates social well-being (Liu et al. 2007).

Table 17.1 gives some examples of collaborative practices for these two dimensions according to different levels of participation (as analyzed in Fig. 17.2).

17.6 How to Optimize Individual Participation in Social Media?

The current revolution around social media poses a challenge for educators in the promotion of meaningful learning. It involves a step forward in the use of technologies, through new forms of participation that lead to a reevaluation of the traditional spaces for the collaborative construction of knowledge.

Table 17.1 Educational practices in a learning community context using social media

Level of participation	Knowledge construction tasks	Emotionally driven tasks
1/2	Sharing in a virtual collaborative whiteboard	Creating and publishing a video with initial expectations about learning
Transmission, contribution, relation	Building a lesson by a wiki Sharing materials (e.g., own shelves on Google Books)	
3	Changing the leadership of a blog (author, contributor)	Performing a chat on personal needs and discussing the feelings involved
Negotiation of meanings	Creating a code of feedback in blog exchanges	
4	A social networking forum discussion	Tweeting about previous feelings on a topic
Selection and sharing	Turning a personal page into a learning portfolio	Sharing events of interest
5/6/7	Guiding individuals (re)search by supporting with social bookmarks	Rating profiles or individual's activities based on prosocial criteria
Making or exploring judgment		
8	Subscribing to relevant sites by RSS	Sending information alerts regarding personal interest to others
Information updating	Creating a social news reader	

Technologies have the ability to transform educational practices by creating new environments, which are increasingly diverse, influential, and critical. However, merely exposing individuals to technologies is not a sufficient guarantee for learning empowerment. The effective construction of knowledge necessitates a certain level of organization with opportunities for collaboration and learning through a variety of practices.

According to the progression proposed, from interaction to collaboration, a reflection on how to optimize the participation of students via social media is needed. So, in educational context, what can truly create the difference between a disappointment or a highly productive learning experience is the supporting actions of the *online facilitator* to consider and map the social variables to effective learning outcomes. This support is achieved through strong encouragement, along with the necessary time and effort to make individuals feel adapted to the online community. So, it is critical to be aware that the social dimension will ensure collaborative learning. For this reason, in this section some pedagogical guidelines for promoting effective processes of collaboration for learning are considered.

The first consideration relates to the technological environment, by selecting the specific 2.0 tool. Each different virtual space involves social meanings, cultural, physical, personal, emotional... and all these meanings are the result, as McKie has reported (2000), not only of what technology *provokes* for individuals because of its structure, possibilities, limitations, or social features, but also what the technology *evokes*, that is, the memory of what traditional environments represent, compared to the virtual ones. So, the principal goal is to choose the appropriate social media, in order that students can experience and enjoy the virtual exchanges in a clear *social sense*, by feelings of proximity, comparison, identification... for sharing experiences in sociability (Bickford and Wright, 2006).

In this regard, it is noted (Hernández-Serrano et al. 2009) that in virtuality, adaptation is based on familiarity, as students feel a greater level of adaptation in spaces that resemble off-line social activities, and not ones where they have to invent new patterns of behavior. Thus, conceiving and organizing a virtual space from a known space metaphor allows students to develop a sense of recognition and adaptation (Peraya and Dumont 2003). Spatial metaphors (boarding news, shared whiteboard, or "cafeteria") facilitate the transference of knowledge, routines, and behavior. Taking advantage of the learner's evocations from traditional spaces and activities, makes them feel more adapted, thus promoting successful exchanges.

It is expected that the skills learned in a noneducational context are transferred to learning in educational contexts, albeit, as Trinder et al. (2008) note, there are inhibiting factors for transference, mainly based on expectations. Students are used to the paradigm of the instructor as teacher from whom they expect a great deal of input. However, it is important to clarify the changing roles within a context of collaboration, with greater expectation on learner self-direction and mutual commitments.

The second step is the creation of a community context. Facilitating a sense of online community correlates with perceived learning gains, learner engagement, and satisfaction as observed by Liu et al. (2007). It is essential for the facilitator to reflect about the sense of community. Bacon (2009) defines four issues in planning an online community: mission, opportunities, areas for collaboration, and required skills. In an online community, opportunities and areas for collaboration are necessarily related to the technological possibilities, as well as requiring a minimum background of computer literacy, besides other more specific content skills.

From the above considerations, it is necessary to ensure that there are no obstacles for online communication, and individuals are able to handle the different channels, languages, and media. Effective decoding and communicative fluency is essential for virtual understandings, otherwise the level of media efficacy will be lower, limiting the chances of a successful outcome.

In this stage, the facilitator must construct a shared domain. This enables the individual's identification with the community. Some authors suggest commencing with an initial welcome to the group (Brown 2001; Salmon 2004) in which an online identity is established. This first moment serves to provoke the initial necessities, interests, and expectations, shaping the sense of community by obtaining feedback about shared characteristics. Also by understanding each individual's perception of the sense of community, it is possible to offer participation levels that match personal learning styles. In the first stages, it is essential to offer sufficient information about the participative process, the different possibilities available, and the level of involvement that can lead individuals to a variety of collaborative results. Making this information explicit allows individuals to assess the participative situations and make conscious decisions, which contribute to the enrichment of the interactions.

Thus, after the first exchanges and the endorsement of community identification, the next activities aim to create an atmosphere of collaboration related to the organizational levels. It is necessary to define the norms and values of the community, in which the sense of collaboration plays a central role. This can be achieved through a code of behavior or intentions. One general model could be the six critical points for the establishment of virtual learning communities described by Palloff and Pratt (2007: 145–148), which seek to ensure:

1. Sense of security and the confidence to provide and receive sincere feedback among the members of the community (clear norms for avoiding fake identities, making consensus about correct/incorrect methods of feedback).
2. Sensitivity and mutual responsiveness among members, with the facilitator also engaged in the exchanges (controlling the norms).
3. Relevance and connection with everyday life experiences by sharing examples.
4. Support equality among members and respect the participative personal styles (observant, participant).
5. Promote a climate of sincerity and freedom to express thoughts and arguments.
6. Empower and strengthen the autonomy of learning, by adopting new roles and responsibilities in the learning process, along with the encouragement of self-motivation to seek and construct their own knowledge independently of the facilitator.

The level of organization in a virtual learning community is also related to the establishment of different virtual spaces: for collaboration, for sharing, for individual learning, for expressing emotion, which means a variety in exchange streams and practices for pursuing the learning goals.

For the consolidation of collaborative learning, the facilitator should continuously evaluate in three main areas. The first is the evaluation of the shared domain, by assessing whether individuals are engaged in the same common goal of learning, as well as focusing on domains not previously considered, which offer further chances for learning.

The second is the evaluation of the exchanges, by assessing whether participation meets expectations and whether, according to personal styles, the desirable collaboration is accomplished. It can be useful for the facilitator to explore data offered by embedded statistical tools, which record the history of activities, permitting the identification of less motivated individuals, or those with technical problems. However, monitoring the social process by observation and involvement in the collaborative activities can improve practice by offering immediate support, or by planning strategic actions. So, in order to guide students from being passive spectators to active participants, it is useful to provide them with gradual opportunities, which trigger their level of participation, as well as its maintenance. Participation can be enhanced when individuals use virtual spaces they have handled before, turning their use from personal purposes to academic ones, with specific learning goals and methodologies.

In addition, the facilitator can serve as model for the individuals, so participation relies on his/her skills. It is extremely important to support the exchanges by recognizing individual contributions and providing immediate feedback, which encourages further participation.

The third area for evaluation is the construction of knowledge, by assessing what individuals explicitly learnt, along with non-explicit results such as: learning to reason by reading the reflections of others written in the comments of a blog post, learning to confront a new sharing situation by observing initial attitudes or behaviors in a social network, and learning to manage with social bookmarking.

17.7 Implications and Future Research

This chapter has contributed to an insight into the variables involved in the social process that underpin the importance of progression from simple interaction toward collaboration in learning 2.0 environments.

Social media offer enough opportunities for learning, with different degrees of participation. The most important consideration is that social media can generate significant interactions between the individuals and, most of the time, the way individuals are experiencing their interactions within the context of technologies may transcend how or what is learned. Pedagogical guidelines focus on current ways of participation and their possibilities for collaboration in learning. Whether these recommendations can or should lead to a coherent implementation for collaborative learning requires practical evidence by future research. This would lead to a more comprehensive understanding of the social dimension.

In the constantly evolving field of social media, it is impossible to prescribe or speculate on future practices and possibilities for learning. Social media is a constantly developing field. Thus, it will be necessary to continually identify and update new variables, which affect collaboration, as well as analyzing the forthcoming tools to exploit new interactions that foster learning.

In the future, creating new tools and methods for monitoring and evaluating the practices of sharing and their impact on learning will be required, fundamentally because, as stated by Stahl et al. (2006) the metaphor of social learning is continuously changing, and by extension, so is the metaphor of collaborative learning in virtual environments.

Having appropriate methods for analyzing the social practices will be useful, as methodologies for self-regulatory knowledge sharing (Monteserin et al. 2010; Tseng and Kuo 2010). In this regard, it is necessary to develop more optimized learning assessment mechanisms, which are not based solely on verbal statements, by providing monitoring activities as noted by Persico et al. (2010). New specific tools are needed, which combine procedures to observe and measure the knowledge that can be constructed collaboratively.

The way the use of virtual reality or a 3D world can support collaborative learning is hardly foreseeable at the present moment, but some interesting studies have emerged in this field (Edirisingha et al. 2009; Jarmon et al. 2009; Andreas et al. 2010), which may offer fruitful grounds for further research.

References

Andreas, K., Tsiatsos, T., Terzidou, T., et al.: Fostering collaborative learning in second life: metaphors and affordances. Comput. Educ. **55**(2), 603–615 (2010)

Bacon, J.: The Art of Community: Building the New Age of Participation. O'Reilly Media, Sebastopol (2009)

Baker, M., Lund, K.: Promoting reflective interactions in a CSCL environment. J. Comput. Assist. Learn. **13**(3), 175–193 (1997)

Bandura, A.: Growing primacy of human agency in adaptation and change in the electronic era. Europ. Psychol. **7**(1), 2–16 (2002)

Bickford, D.J., Wright, D.J.: Community: the hidden context for learning. In Oblinger D. (ed.) Learning Spaces , http://www.educause.edu/ir/library/pdf/PUB7102d.pdf (2006)

Brickson, S.L., Brewer, M.B.: Identity orientation and intergroup relations in organizations. In: Hogg, M.A., Terry, D.J. (eds.) Social Identity Processes in Organizational Contexts, pp. 49–66. Psychology Press, Philadelphia (2001)

Brown, J.S.: The Social Life of Information. Harvard Business School, Boston (2001)

Brown, R.: The process of community-building in distance learning classes. J. Asynchron. Learn. Netw. **5**(4), 18–35 (2001)

Brown, J.S., Collins, A., Duguid, P.: Situated cognition and the culture of learning. Educ. Res. **18**(1), 32–41 (1998)

Brown, J.S., Adler, R.P.: Minds on fire: open education, the long tail, and learning 2.0. EDUCAUSE Review, **43**(1), 16–32, http://net.educause.edu/ir/library/pdf/ERM0811.pdf (2008)

Burbulles, N., Callister, T.: Educación: Riesgos y promesas de las nuevas tecnologías. Granica, Barcelona (2001)

Castells, M.: The Rise of Network Society. Blackwell, New York (2001)

Castoriadis, C.: L'imaginaire comme tel. Hermann, Paris (2008)

Cole, M.: Culture in mind. Cambridge, Harvard University Press (1996)

Dillenbourg, P. (ed.): Collaborative Learning. Cognitive and Computational Approaches. Elsevier, Amsterdam (1999)

Dillenbourg, P., Hong, F.: The mechanics of CSCL macro scripts. Int. J. Comput.-Support. Collab. Learn. **3**(1), 5–24 (2008)

Dillenbourg, P., Jermann, P.: Designing integrative scripts. In: Fischer, F., Kollar, I., Mandl, H., Haake, J.M. (eds.) Scripting Computer-Supported Collaborative Learning – Cognitive, Computational, and Educational Perspectives. Computer-Supported Collaborative Learning Series, pp. 275–301. Springer, New York (2007)

Dillenbourg, P., Järvelä, S., Fischer, F.: The evolution of research on computer-supported collaborative learning: from design to orchestration. In: Balacheff, N., Ludvigsen, S., de Jong, T., Lazonder, T.A., Barnes, S. (eds.) Technology-Enhanced Learning. Principles and Products, pp. 3–19. Springer, Berlin (2009)

Edirisingha, P., Nie, M., Pluciennik, M., et al.: Socialisation for learning at a distance in a 3-D multi-user virtual environment. Br. J. Educ. Technol. **40**(3), 458–479 (2009)

Engeström, Y.: Developmental studies of work as a test bench of activity theory: the case of primary care medical practice. In: Chaiklin, S., Lave, J. (eds.) Understanding Practice. Cambridge University Press, Cambridge (1993)

Fainholc, B.: ¿Cuáles son los pro y los contras de la web 2.0 o web participativa en educación? http://www.cediproe.org.ar/new/newsletter1._nota1.php (2008)

Garrison, D.R., Akyol, Z.: Role of instructional technology in the transformation of higher education. J. Comput. High. Educ. **21**(1), 19–30 (2009)

Hernández-Serrano, M.J., Jones, B.: Innovation, informational literacy and lifelong learning culture. eLearning Papers, 21, http://www.elearningeuropa.info/out/?doc_id=23511&rsr_id=23706 (2010)

Hernández-Serrano, M.J., González, M.: Un nuevo escenario de información: el espacio 2.0. Revista Portuguesa de Pedagogía 42(2, II), 139–153 (2008)

Hernández-Serrano, M.J., González-Sánchez, M., Muñoz-Rodríguez, J.M.: Designing learning environments improving social interactions: essential variables for a virtual training space. Procedia – Soc. Behav. Sci. (ISSHP/ISI Proceedings-SSCI) 1(1), 2411–2415 (2009)

Hillery, G.A.: Definitions of community: areas of agreement, Rural Sociol. 20(?), 111–123 (1955)

Hine, C.: Virtual Etnography. Sage, London (2000)

Howard, P.N., Jones, S. (eds.): Society Online: The Internet in Context. Sage, Thousand Oaks (2004)

Hron, A., Hesse, F.W., Cress, U., Giovis, C.: Implicit and explicit dialogue structuring in virtual learning groups. Br. J. Educ. Psychol. 70(1), 51–64 (2000)

Janz, B.D., Prasarnphanich, P.: Understanding the antecedents of effective knowledge management: the importance of a knowledge-centered culture. Decis. Sci. 34(2), 351–384 (2003)

Jarmon, L., Traphagan, T., Mayrath, M., et al.: Virtual world teaching, experiential learning, and assessment: an interdisciplinary communication course in second life. Comput. Educ. 53(1), 169–182 (2009)

Jarvis, P.: Learning to be a Person in Society. Routledge, London (2009)

Jenkins, H. (ed.): Confronting the Challenges of Participatory Culture: Media Education for the 21st Century. MIT Press, Cambridge (2009)

Jenson, J.: Mapping social cohesion: the state of Canadian research. Canadian policy research network: study No. F-03. 48. Ottawa (1998)

Johnson, D., Johnson, R., Holubec, E.: Cooperation in the Classroom. Allyn and Bacon, Boston (1998)

Jonassen, D.: Therethical Foundations of Learning Environments. Lawrence Erlbaum, Mahwah (2000)

Kavanaugh, A., Carroll, J.M., Rosson, M.B., Reese, D.D., Zin, T.T.: Participating in civil society: the case of networked communities. Int. Comput. 17(1), 9–33 (2005)

Koschmann, T.: Dewey's contribution to the foundations of CSCL research. In: Stahl, G. (ed.) Computer Support for Collaborative Learning (CSCL): Foundations for a CSCL Community, pp. 17–22. Lawrence Erlbaum Associates, Boulder (2002)

Kuo, F.Y., Young, M.L.: A study of the intention–action gap in knowledge sharing practices. J. Am. Soc. Inf. Sci. Technol. 59(8), 1224–1237 (2008)

Lave, J., Wenger, E. Situated learning. New York, Cambridge University Press (1991)

Leontiev, A.N.: El desarrollo del psiquismo. Akal, Madrid (1983)

Levy, P.: Collective Intelligence: Mankind's Emerging World in Cyberspace. Plenium Press, New York (1999)

Liu, X., Magjuka, R.J., Bonk, C.J., Seung-Jee, L.: Does sense of community matter? an examination of participants' perceptions of building learning communities in online courses. Quart. Rev. Dist. Educ. 8(1), 9–24 (2007)

Mattelart, A.: Networking the World: 1794–2000. University of Minnesota Press, Minneapolis (2000)

McInnerney, J.M., Roberts, T.S.: Online learning: social interaction and the creation of a sense of community. Educ. Technol. Soc. 7(3), 73–81 (2004)

McKie, J.: Conjuring notions of place. J. Philos. Educ. 34(1), 111–122 (2000)

McMillan, D.W., Chavis, D.M.: Sense of community: a definition and theory. Am. J. Community Psychol. 14(1), 6–23 (1986)

Monteserin, A., Schiaffino, S., Amandi, A.: Assisting students with argumentation plans when solving problems in CSCL. Compute. Educ. 54(2), 416–426 (2010)

Nistor, N.: Toward the Virtual University: International Online Perspectives. Perspectives in Instructional Technology and Distance Learning. IAP, Greenwihc (2003)

O'Reilly, T.: What is web 2.0: design patterns and business models for the next generation, http://www.oreillynet.com/pub/a/oreilly/tim/news/2005/09/30/what-is-web-20.html (2005)

Pallof, R.M., Pratt, K.: Building Online Learning Communities: Effective Strategies for the Virtual Classroom. Jossey-Bass, San Francisco (2007)

Peraya, D., Dumont, P.: Interagir dans une classe virtuelle: analyse des interactions verbales médiatisées dans un environnement synchrone. La revue française de pédagogie **145**, 51–61 (2003)

Persico, D., Pozzi, F., Sarti, L.: Monitoring collaborative activities in computer supported collaborative learning. Dist. Educ. **31**(1), 5–22 (2010)

Preece, J.: Online Communities: Designing Usability, Supporting Sociability. Wiley, New York (2000)

Purcell, P.A.: Networked Neighbourhoods: The Connected Community in Context. Springer, London (2006)

Rheingold, H.: Smart Mobs: The Next Social Revolution. Perseus, Cambridge (2002)

Rovai, A.P.: Building sense of community at a distance. Int. Rev. Res. Open and Dist. Learn. **3**(1), 1–16 (2002)

Salmon, G.: E-moderating: The Key to Teaching and Learning Online. Routledge, London (2004)

Salomon, G.: Distributed Cognitions. Cambridge University Press, New York (1993)

Scardamalia, M., Bereiter, C.: Higher levels of agency in knowledge building: a challenge for the design of new knowledge media. J. Learn. Sci. **1**, 37–68 (1991)

Siemens, G.: Connectivism: a learning theory for the digital age, http://www.elearnspace.org/Articles/connectivism.htm, eLearnSpace (2004)

Smith, M.A., Kollock, P.: Communities in the Cyberspace. EdiUOC, Barcelona (2002)

Smith, P.K., Pellegrini, A.D. (eds.): Major Writings in the Psychology of Education. Taylor & Francis, London (2000)

Stahl, G.: Collaborative information environments to support knowledge construction by communities. AI Soc. **14**, 1–27 (2000)

Stahl, G.: Group Cognition: Computer Support for Building Collaborative Knowledge. MIT Press, Cambridge (2006)

Stahl, G., Koschmann, T., Suthers, D.: Computer-supported collaborative learning: a historical perspective. In: Sawyer, R.K. (ed.) Cambridge Handbook of the Learning Sciences, pp. 409–426. Cambridge University Press, Cambridge (2006)

Suchman, L.: Plans and Situated Actions: The Problem of Human/Machine Communication. Cambridge University Press, Cambridge (1988)

Surowiecki, J.: The Wisdom of Crowds. Random House, New York (2004)

Tönnies, F.: Community and Society. (C.P. Loomis, Trans.) Routledge and Kegan Paul, London (1957)

Trinder, K., Guiller, J., Margaryan, A., Littlejohn, A., Nicol, D.: Learning from Digital Natives: Bridging Formal and Informal Learning. Research Project Report. The Higher Education Academy, Glasgow (2008)

Tseng, F., Kuo, F.: The way we share and learn: an exploratory study of the self-regulatory mechanisms in the professional online learning community. Comput. Hum. Behav. **26**, 1043–1053 (2010)

Tu, C., Blocher, M.: Web 2.0 learning environment in distance learning. In: Papas, R. (ed.) Technology Leadership for School Improvement, pp. 129–125. Sage, London (2010)

Turkle, S.: Life on the Screen: Identity in the Age of the Internet. Touchstone, New York (1995)

Vygotsky, L.: Mind in Society. Harvard University Press, Cambridge (1962/1978)

Warschauer, M.: Computer-mediated collaborative learning: theory and practice. Modern Lang. J. **81**, 470–481 (1997)

Wellman, B., Gulia, M.: Virtual communities as communities: net surfers don't ride alone. In: Smith, M.A., Kollock, P. (eds.) Communities in Cyberspace, pp. 167–194. Routledge, New York (1999)

Wenger, E.: Communities of Practice: Learning, Meaning, and Identity. Cambridge University Press, Cambridge (1998)

Wenger, E., White, N., Smith, J.D.: Digital Habitats: Stewarding Technology for Communities. Cpsquare, Portland (2009)

Wertsch, J.: Voces de la mente. Un enfoque sociocultural para el estudio de la acción mediada. Visor, Madrid (1993)

Widén-Wulff, G.: Challenges of Knowledge Sharing in Practice: a Social Approach. Chandos Publishing, Oxford (2007)

Chapter 18
Contributions to Social Bookmarking Systems: Integration of Three Empirical Studies

Raquel Benbunan-Fich and Marios Koufaris

Abstract Web-based bookmarking systems offer users the option to post and tag Web resources privately or to make their tagged resources publicly available to other users of the site. While these systems can exist solely as private tools to organize personal bookmarks, when users share their bookmarks with others, an online social structure emerges. Given the voluntary nature of public contributions in social bookmarking systems, three empirical studies were designed to understand why users contribute to the public repository of tagged bookmarks when it is not mandatory to do so. This is an integrated report of the results of these three empirical studies. Overall, it was found that while some people use bookmarking systems for their own private benefit, most users intentionally contribute resources for other users when they believe that those resources will be potentially useful for others. Taken together, the results suggest that the collective action model underlying social bookmarking systems is characterized by voluntary contributions of high-quality resources (self-regulated voluntarism).

18.1 Introduction

Web 2.0 is an environment characterized by innovative applications that allow users to upload their own content and share it with others. This content can be in the form of videos (YouTube), photographs (Flickr), knowledge on a specific subject (Wikipedia), product reviews (Amazon), bookmarks (del.icio.us), and any other type of digital information (Aguiton and Cardon 2007). In order to facilitate the sharing of user-generated content, some sites allow users to organize information

R. Benbunan-Fich (✉) • M. Koufaris
SCIS Department, Zicklin School of Business, Box B11-220, Baruch College, City University of
New York, New York, USA
e-mail: rbfich@baruch.cuny.edu; marios.koufaris@baruch.cuny.edu

B. White et al. (eds.), *Social Media Tools and Platforms in Learning Environments*,   311
DOI 10.1007/978-3-642-20392-3_18, © Springer-Verlag Berlin Heidelberg 2011

with user-generated meta-information (or tags). In Flickr, for example, users can tag photos posted by themselves and others by assigning their own explanatory keywords. In social bookmarking systems, such as del.icio.us, Furl, Spurl, Simpy, and Ma.gnolia, users store their Web bookmarks on a central server and label them with descriptive words (tags) of their choice (Marlow et al. 2006).

Bookmarking sites provide an alternative to traditional browser-based storage of favorite bookmarks or links. When users store Web addresses in their local computer, they cannot access their links from another location. In contrast, with Web-based bookmarking, users have the advantage of portability when trying to access or find their previously discovered Web resources. Additionally, the use of tags facilitates future retrieval or "findability." Many bookmarking sites offer users the option of keeping their tagged bookmarks private or sharing some (or all) of them with other users, thereby creating a social bookmarking system.

As a result of the public/private option, Web-based bookmarking systems can fulfill two purposes: organizational and social (Marlow et al. 2006). On one hand, tagging bookmarks is a mechanism to file and organize resources for future retrieval. On the other hand, users may share their resources with others through the tags they choose. Those who make their tagged resources available to others help create and maintain an online public repository of cataloged bookmarks. When users search this repository using tags, they can find their own bookmarks along with those stored by others under the same tags. This serendipity effect, where users discover or find unexpected collocated resources sharing the same tag (Bryant 2006) is a significant collective benefit of social bookmarking systems (Golder and Huberman 2006).

Since contributing to the public pool of tagged resources is entirely optional, both for the users and for the continued existence of the bookmarking system, these systems offer a unique setting to study the dynamics of public contributions in online communities. To investigate this issue, the authors designed a series of complementary studies whose rationale, findings, and integration are discussed in this chapter. Study 1 (Benbunan-Fich and Koufaris 2010) uses a resource-based view to explain contribution activity as a function of the benefits that members obtain from the social bookmarking system. Study 2 (Arakji et al. 2009) examines whether contributions to the public repository are unintentional by-products of contributing for oneself or intentional acts aimed at benefiting others. Study 3 (Benbunan-Fich and Koufaris 2008) explores the balance between the quantity and quality of the contributions for self and for others in social bookmarking systems. The first study is based on objective measures of user activity, while the second and the third use subjective measures collected via a survey of actual users at popular social bookmarking sites.

The remainder of this chapter provides a description of the theoretical background guiding the research program along with a brief review of the relevant literature. It also provides a description of each study and its findings and concludes with the discussion of their integration, implications, and future research directions.

18.2   Theoretical Background

A key challenge for the success of bookmarking sites as social structures is ensuring a growing pool of publicly tagged bookmarks that brings benefits to users. The site must attract and maintain a large enough user population – or critical mass – that is actively contributing to the public pool of resources. According to the theory of critical mass, a community or social network is sustainable only when it reaches a sizeable number of members or resources (Markus 1987; Butler 2001). This theory also suggests that a community will also be favored by heterogeneity of interests (Markus 1987). In bookmarking sites, the joint action of individual users with varied backgrounds, resources, and interests will bring to the attention of the community more online sources than a homogeneous group of participants tagging the same sources. Like other Web 2.0 sites, bookmarking systems allow a potentially wide range of individuals to participate and contribute. Open participation increases the heterogeneity of users and the variety of resources made available to the community. Since bookmarking systems are free to join and use, it would seem that achieving critical mass of users and resources to ensure their success is easy.

Social bookmarking systems are unique because they can exist solely as private tools for storing and organizing personal resources, without any communal contributions or social benefits. For example, members can use bookmarking sites as their own private storage of favorite links. If all users choose to keep their contributions private, however, the public pool of resources will be impoverished and the collective benefits of the site will not materialize. A poorly populated repository of public tagged resources may reduce the motivation to use the bookmarking site, thus eliminating the positive social effects, and creating a negative spiral that would result in the demise of the site as a social structure. Conversely, a large and rich public repository of tagged resources will entice more people to use it and add their own contributions, ensuring the growth of the social bookmarking site.

Butler (Butler 2001) developed a resource-based model of sustainability for online social structures based on communication such as discussion boards and forums. In this model, a community or social network is sustainable only when it reaches a critical mass of members and resources. Sustainability is thus achieved through the contribution of resources that provide benefits to the members. Resource availability is a function of membership size which is, in turn, affected by the net growth of members (attraction minus loss). The original model was developed for online social structures based on interpersonal interaction where the benefit creation process depends on the level of communication activity among users and where all contributions are automatically public. Since contributions to social bookmarking sites are not based on communication activity, it was adapted for this study. The benefit creation process was reframed in terms of contributions to the public repository. Second, availability of public resources as an explicit element affected by contribution activity was added. The benefit creation process was transformed into a decision node influencing changes in membership. These two latter modifications are indicated in the dotted box (Fig. 18.1).

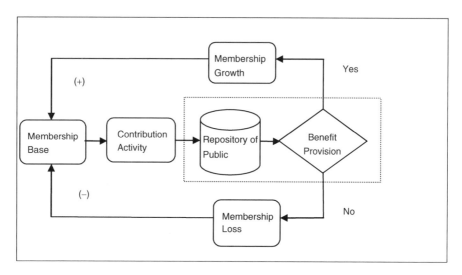

Fig. 18.1 A resource-based model of sustainable social structures (Adapted from Butler (2001))

In social bookmarking systems, sustainability refers to a social structure that is able to be maintained indefinitely by the continuous collective action of its members. Although the system may grow as a private storage of personal bookmarks for a number of people acting individually, as a social structure it will be sustainable if it remains as a mechanism for sharing bookmarks across users. A resource-based view of social bookmarking systems thus suggests that the provision of collective benefits results from contributions to the public repository of tagged bookmarks. A constantly growing body of public tagged bookmarks requires active members who continuously add resources to the common repository. If this is not the case, the private advantage of findability and portability would not result in the public benefits of collocation and serendipity (finding similar resources tagged by others), which is the essence of a social bookmarking system. The adapted model suggests four different mechanisms for the sustainability of the social structure: membership base, contribution activity, membership growth (attraction of new members), and membership loss (retention of existing members). These mechanisms were examined in Benbunan-Fich and Koufaris (Benbunan-Fich and Koufaris 2010), a study of contribution activity at Simpy.com, a social bookmarking Web site.

18.2.1 Motivations for Contributing to the Public Repository

An intriguing question is what motivates users to share information in these impersonal contexts, where users have no direct interaction or communication with each other. Users of social bookmarking systems may derive a personal benefit from storing their own bookmarks but when they decide to share their contributions, they help other users with whom they have no direct ties. In some respects, the act of contributing tagged resources for others is similar to the voluntary contributions of movie reviews at MovieLens (Ling et al. 2005) and product reviews at Amazon. com (Peddibohtla and Subramani 2007). Those contributions are independently initiated by an individual contributor who interacts with the Web site but not with other specific users.

One important difference, however, between individual contributions to review sites and to social bookmarking systems, is in the nature of the contributions and the level of effort required for their production. While writing a product or movie review is a more demanding task that requires writing a document to express subjective and personal opinions, storing and tagging a bookmark is much simpler. Humans naturally and automatically categorize objects and information based on an assessment of similarity, and tagging bookmarks is a manifestation of that ability.

As social structures, bookmarking systems rely on privately produced contributions for public consumption. Since users are able to benefit from their own contributions (by storing, organizing, and easily accessing their own bookmarks in the future from any computer), there are two possible explanations for making resources available to others in the public repository. The first explanation is that users primarily contribute resources for themselves but allow their contributions to be placed in the public repository. The second explanation is that users intentionally tag resources for others, according to the premises of social exchange theory. Thus, contributions to the public repository can be the by-product of storing resources for personal use or the result of deliberate contributions provided for other users. Figure 18.2 illustrates these two alternative paths for public contributions. Arakji et al. (Arakji et al. 2009) investigated whether public contributions are unintentional side effects of contributing for oneself, or intentional contributions intended for others.

A public repository of tagged bookmarks is sustained with voluntary contributions from individuals. In such voluntary repositories, different types of

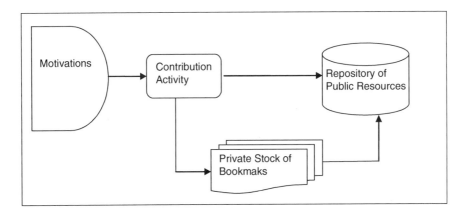

Fig. 18.2 Intentional and unintentional public contributions

contributors coexist (Peddibohtla and Subramani 2007). At the extremes, individual contributors have been considered either selfish or altruistic. Selfish contributors are conceived as utilitarian agents concerned with the maximization of their own personal interests. In contrast, altruistic individuals are motivated by collective action, volunteering, community belonging, public interest, and knowledge sharing (Aguiton and Cardon 2007).

Empirical research findings on the motivations for volunteering indicate that individuals are driven by a mix of self-oriented motives and other-oriented motivations (Clary et al. 1998), and that the interaction among altruists and selfish individuals is essential for achieving human cooperation (Fehr and Fischbacher 2003). The interplay between self-oriented and other-oriented motivations is likely to affect the quantity and quality of public contributions to social bookmarking systems.

18.3 Study 1: Sustainability of Social Bookmarking[1]

To understand the dynamics of contribution activity at social bookmarking systems, activity data was collected from a sample of users of a popular bookmarking site and used to test the adaptation of Butler's (Butler 2001) model. The adapted model suggests four mechanisms (active membership base, prevalence of public contribution activity, attraction of new users, and retention of regular contributors) to explain the sustainability of bookmarking sites as social structures. Ultimately, they result in a continuously growing pool of public resources that enhance the collective benefits of the bookmarking system.

To examine these potential mechanisms for sustainability, activity data were collected from a sample of users of Simpy (www.simpy.com), a popular social bookmarking site. Simpy maintains a profile page for each user showing join date and contribution activity statistics, and a links page showing a list of bookmarks posted by the user along with up to seven most recent dates (add dates) in which the user has made contributions to the repository. An initial roster of users was assembled by collecting user names from three sources: (1) names associated with each tag in the tag cloud (the cloud is a visual representation of the most popular tags used on the site, where the font size of each tag indicates how many times it has been used in relation to the others), (2) the names featured on Simpy's homepage as new users and more active users, and (3) the names shown in user groups. After removing duplicates and invalid users, the final sample consisted of 933 users.

The percentage of individual contributions made to the public repository ranged from 0% to 100%, with an average of 92%, indicating that some individuals used

---

[1]This study is reported in Benbunan-Fich and Koufaris (2010).

the site only as a private keepsake of their own bookmarks, while others contributed their entire bookmark collection to the public pool. The plotting of all users in the sample according to their number of public contributions and ranking them from highest (top contributors) to lowest according to their level of contribution, resulted in a curve with a long tail. The curve indicates that few top-ranked users made very large contributions of public bookmarks and that the amount of visible contributions drastically declined for the remaining users. Thus, there was a minority of users making disproportionately large contributions of publicly tagged bookmarks and a long tail of small contributors.

A total of 670 users were *pure public contributors* because 100% of their bookmarks were available in the public repository. At the other extreme, there were 23 *private users* who contributed 0% to the public repository because they were using the site only as a private keepsake of personal bookmarks. The 240 remaining members were mixed users with a combination of public and private contributions. The average public contribution made by these mixed members was 79%. A total of 134 users in the sample were newcomers (members of the site for a month or less). These new users made, on average, 92% of their contributions visible (or public). Overall, the proportion of recurrent contributors was significantly higher than the proportion of one-time contributors. Therefore, there was evidence of membership maintenance through constant contributions.

These findings suggest a range of reasons why publicly tagged resources continue to grow in a self-perpetuating cycle that ensures the sustainability of social bookmarking systems. An active membership base that is making mostly public contributions produces an abundance of resources in the public repository. This public repository, in turn, enhances the social benefits of the bookmarking system, which serves to attract new members and retain existing ones, ensuring a positive net growth of members.

This study is limited to objective activity information, stored at the user page profile of Simpy and therefore lacks information about the demographic characteristics or psychological motivations that could explain different levels of user contribution. To overcome this limitation, other research studies were conducted to shed light on the motivational drivers of social bookmarking users.

18.4   Study 2: Intentional or Unintentional Public Contributions?[2]

Unlike other systems based on collective action, bookmarking sites offer the option to post and tag bookmarks privately without contributing them to the public repository. Given the possibility of pure private behavior by users of these systems,

---

[2]This study is reported in Arakji et al. (2009).

studying what motivates users to make contributions to the public repository of tagged bookmarks is crucial. While some may be contributing for themselves (for portability or findability) but allowing others to see and benefit, it is possible that other users are deliberately making public contributions for the benefit of others (Weinberger 2007).

In his article on online communities, Kollock (1999) discusses the existence of intentional vis-à-vis unintentional contributions by members of those communities. Based on his discussion, the first path leading to a sustainable social bookmarking system indicates that individual contributions to the public pool of bookmarked resources are not intentional, but rather circumstantial and the by-products of bookmarking for personal use. As Kollock (1999. p. 229) explains "while it may be the case that many people spend time and effort producing goods they intend to contribute to the group, another path to the production of public goods is as a simple side-effect of private behavior." In most bookmarking systems, since the default is to bookmark resources publicly, bookmarking for personal use unintentionally feeds into the pool of public bookmarks. This spillover is automatic, unless the user chooses to restrict accessibility to his/her personal bookmarks. Since keeping bookmarks public generally does not decrease the private benefit that users derives from the resources they contribute, users do not have the incentive to make the bookmarks private except when they point to information that is valuable only if it is not widely disseminated. However, the second path leading to a sustainable social bookmarking system indicates that contributions to social bookmarking systems are intentionally made for other users. In this study, we investigated which path (or both) was stronger.

A survey was conducted to test whether contributions to the public repository are intentionally aimed at others, or circumstantial by-products of contributing for oneself. The survey was available online through a commercial Web hosting service. Participants were recruited from two popular social bookmarking sites. No incentives were offered to the respondents for completing the survey. From 381 users who accepted the invitation to participate, a sample of 94 complete and usable responses was received (25% response rate).

The results only supported the intentional explanation of public contributions. No support was found for the spillover of private bookmarking. Thus, in social bookmarking systems, the contribution of public resources was the product of deliberate and voluntary sharing of resources specifically intended for other users. It was also found that this sharing of resources with other users was driven by two factors. The first factor was the belief that a user had resources that were perceived as valuable to other users. The second factor was the contextual influence of the site: the more a user perceived that other users contributed to the public repository, the more likely that user was to contribute resources specifically for other users.

Although circumstantial contributions were insignificant in this study, it cannot be concluded that users of social bookmarking sites are not contributing resources for themselves, as this is the primary purpose of bookmarking sites (to allow people to store and classify their own bookmarks). It is possible that a large number of users are contributing for themselves and keeping their contributions private or contributing them to the public pool but not in large numbers. While individuals may be using the bookmarking system for their own purposes (as a keepsake of personal bookmarks), the results suggest that their level of contribution for others does not appear to be simply a side effect of the storage of private bookmarks. A significant predictor of public contribution is actually the intentional and voluntary sharing of resources specifically intended for other users.

18.5   Study 3: Quantity vs. Quality of Contributions for Self and Others[3]

The results of the study described in Arakji et al. (2009) indicate that users separate the contributions intended for themselves from those made for others, suggesting that there are two distinct sets of motives driving contributors: self-oriented motives and other-oriented motives. It was hypothesized that self-oriented motives were related to the quantity and quality of contributions for personal use, while other-oriented motives were related to the quantity and quality of contributions to the public repository. A negative relation between quantity and quality of contributions was hypothesized in both cases.

When individuals voluntarily contribute to online repositories, they are investing their time, energy, attention, and knowledge (Butler 2001). Therefore, when contributors focus on the quality of their postings, the quantity of postings tends to be lower, due to time constraints associated with producing contributions. Similarly, in a social bookmarking system, users who are evaluating the relevance of the resources they tag are expected to produce fewer contributions than those who are not carefully evaluating the quality of such resources.

These relationships were tested through an online survey of actual users of two popular social bookmarking sites with similar functionality. This is the same survey described in Study 2 but different constructs were used in this case. The results indicated that self-oriented motives were related to both quantity and quality of contributions for self. Users who employed social bookmarking systems as a personal and portable repository of their own bookmark collections (with self-oriented motives) contributed more tagged resources for themselves as well as resources that were more relevant to them. On the other hand, it was found that other-oriented motives were only associated with quality of contributions for others and not with quantity. Thus, users who contributed resources for use by other users (with other-oriented motives) contributed only resources that they believed would be useful to the other users but did not contribute more resources for others overall.

Contrary to expectation, the hypothesized negative path between quality and quantity of contributions for self and for others was not supported. In fact, the path

---

[3]This study is reported in Benbunan-Fich and Koufaris (2008).

coefficients were positive and significant, indicating the absence of a trade-off between quantity and quality of contributions. Given the simplicity of producing contributions for social bookmarking sites, users can increase their amount of contributions without sacrificing quality.

In terms of spillover effect from contributions aimed at oneself vis-à-vis contributions aimed at others, it was found that the higher the quality of tagged resources contributed for self, the higher the quality of contributions for others. However, this spillover effect did not manifest itself in terms of quantity, as large contributions for oneself were not significantly related to more volume of contribution for others. Thus, users who contributed a large number of tagged resources for personal use did not necessarily contribute at the same level for others.

These results imply that users are much more discriminating when contributing tagged resources specifically for other users. When using the social bookmarking site as a personal bookmarking tool, users may add as many bookmarks as they can think of without limiting their contributions to ones that are more relevant to their needs. In this way, they may create a less focused but more extensive collection of tagged bookmarks. However, when considering their contributions to the public repository of information, they prefer to add only what might be highly relevant to other users. This may result from efforts to preserve the quality of public repositories or to conserve private resources (such as time and effort). More research is necessary to test these alternative explanations.

The findings indicate that self-oriented motives are not related to the quality or quantity of contributions for others, and that other-oriented motives are not related to the quality and quality of contributions for self. Each category of motives is solely related to their respective type of contributions (self-oriented motives with contributions for self and other-oriented motives with contributions for others). This reinforces the notion that contributions for self and for others are independent activities.

18.6 Discussion: Integration of Empirical Studies

By investigating motivations and contribution behavior, this research program has to date addressed the supply side of social bookmarking systems with the use of objective measures of user activity (Study 1) and of subjective measures (Studies 2 and 3). Because social bookmarking systems give users the option of designating their contributions as public or private, users can separate the contribution intended for themselves from those intended for others. In this unique context, the research agenda explored: (1) whether users contribute for others even when it is not mandatory for them to do so in Study 1, (2) whether contributions for others are intentional or unintentional in Study 2, and (3) the interaction between the quantity and quality of contributions for self and for others in Study 3.

Having sufficient resources available in the public repository of tagged bookmarks is a necessary condition for the sustainability of a social bookmarking site. The first study analyzed objective activity data to test four potential mechanisms for the sustainability of social bookmarking sites. It was found that users are indeed contributing tagged bookmarks to the public repository, that the predominant user profile is that of the public contributor, and that the net growth of members is positive. All of these signs are positive indicators of the long-term survival prospects of bookmarking sites as social structures.

Given the nature of social bookmarking systems and their private and public option, it is not obvious whether public contributions are intentional or unintentional by-products of contributing for oneself. Study 1 employed a resource-based view of social bookmarking where members obtain benefits from the resources available in the public repository. It is also possible that the act of making a contribution is what brings benefits to the members and motivates them to contribute. This was the rationale for Study 2, where it was found that users intentionally contribute for others because of the perceived value of those resources or because of contextual influences (social norms) they perceive from the site. The findings of this study suggest that contributions are deliberately made for the benefit of others. In terms of Marlow et al.'s (2006) high-level objectives, users tend to emphasize the social aspects of Web-based bookmarking systems.

The findings of Study 1 and 2 together indicate that both organizational and social uses of bookmarking systems coexist. While some individuals use bookmarking systems for the purpose of organizing their own Web resources, others use it as a mechanism to bring Web resources to the attention of others. Thus, in Study 3, we explored the balance between the quantity and quality of the contributions for self and for others. The findings suggest that when using the social bookmarking site as a personal tool, users add as many bookmarks as they can think of without limiting their contributions to ones that are more relevant to their needs (focus on quantity). However, when contributing to the public repository of information, they prefer to add only what might be highly relevant to other users (focus on quality). This tendency to contribute for others only resources that are deemed potentially useful will tend to preserve the quality of public repositories.

This result suggests that the collective action model underlying social bookmarking systems is sustained by voluntary contributions of high-quality resources (self-regulated voluntarism). Furthermore, because in social bookmarking systems the quality of contributions does not constrain their quantity, both the personal and the prosocial motives for contribution result in a sizeable volume of high-quality contributions.

18.7   Conclusion

The findings of these three empirical studies have important implications for bookmarking systems as online social structures. The sustainability of these sites depends on user willingness to publicize at least a part of their personal production of bookmarks. The collective effects of cooperation can only be accomplished if there is a critical mass of individual contributors. This form of cooperation based on individual contributions is possible in a specific context that attracts a large number of participants that make very small contributions.

The key question is what motivates these individuals to make their contributions public? The results suggest that users deliberately contribute for others because they are driven by a combination of selfish and altruistic motives. As in other Web 2.0 sites, the success of social bookmarking systems results from hybrid motivations, where personal goals can be pursued in a context that affords the opportunity for sharing individual contributions in a public repository.

However, the ultimate success of these types of systems will be determined by the extent to which the resources they provide are actually used by others. Therefore, future research should examine the demand side of these systems. In particular, the extent to which public resources are useful and actually used by others and how usage in turn affects contribution levels of individual users. Understanding when people use bookmarks produced by others and what they learn from them may also have important implications for the use of social software in academia and social bookmarking in teaching and learning environments.

References

Aguiton, C., Cardon, D.: The strength of weak cooperation: an attempt to understand the meaning of web 2.0. Commun. Strateg. **65**, 51–65 (2007)

Arakji, R., Benbunan-Fich, R., Koufaris, M.: Exploring contributions of public resources in social bookmarking systems. Decis. Supp. Syst. **47**(3), 245–253 (2009)

Benbunan-Fich, R., Koufaris, M.: Motivations and contribution behavior in social bookmarking systems. Electron. Market **18**(2), 150–160 (2008)

Benbunan-Fich, R., Koufaris, M.: An empirical examination of the sustainability of social bookmarking websites. J. Inf. Syst. E-Business Manage. **8**(2), 131–148 (2010)

Bryant, T.: Social software in academia. Educ. Q. **29**(2), 61–64 (2006)

Butler, B.S.: Membership size, communication activity and sustainability: a resource-based model of online social structures. Inf. Syst. Res. **12**(4), 346–362 (2001)

Clary, E.G., Snyder, M., Ridge, R.D., Copeland, J., Stukas, A.A., Haugen, J., Miene, P.: Understanding and assessing the motivations of volunteers: a functional approach. J. Person. Soc. Psychol. **74**, 1516–1530 (1998)

Fehr, E., Fischbacher, U.: The nature of human altruism. Nature **425**, 785–791 (2003)

Golder, S.A., Huberman, B.A.: Usage patterns of collaborative tagging systems. J. Inf. Sci. **32**(2), 198–208 (2006)

Kollock, P.: The economies of online cooperation: gifts and public goods in cyberspace. In: Smith, M.A., Kollock, P. (eds.) Communities in Cyberspace. Routledge, London (1999)

Ling, K., Beenen, G., Ludford, P., Wang, X., Chang, K., Li, X., Cosley, D., Frankowski, D., Terveen, L., Rashid, A. M., Resnick, P., Kraut, R.: Using social psychology to motivate contributions to online communities. J. Comput. Mediat. Commun., **10**(4), article 10. http://jcmc.indiana.edu/vol10/issue4/ling.html (2005)

Markus, L.: Towards a critical mass theory of interactive media: universal access, interdependence and diffusion. Commun. Res. **14**, 491–511 (1987)

Marlow, C., Naaman, M., Boyd, D., Davis, M.: HT06, Tagging paper, taxonomy, flickr, academic article, toread. In: Hypertext'06, pp. 31–40 (2006)

Peddibohtla, N.B., Subramani, M.R.: Contributing to public document repositories: a critical mass theory perspective. Org. Stud. **28**(3), 327–346 (2007)

Weinberger, D.: Everything Is Miscellaneous: The Power of the New Digital Disorder. Henry Holt and Company, New York (2007)

Chapter 19
The Role of Social Presence in Interactive Learning with Social Software

Masanori Yamada and Satoshi Kitamura

Abstract This chapter presents the effect of social presence in learning with social media. It is divided into four parts: introduction, theoretical background, effect of social presence in learning, and conclusion. The introductory section provides the historical background to computer-mediated communication (CMC) research in educational technology with special attention to the concept of social presence. The second section reviews previous research on social presence from the viewpoints of social psychology and educational technology. The third section presents the effects of social presence within social media as described in previous research, particularly Yamada (Comput Educ 52(4):820–833, 2009). Social presence appears to have an effect on motivation and other aspects of the affective side of learning. Avenues for future research are considered.

19.1 Introduction: Computer-Mediated Communication in Educational Settings

As information and communication technology advances, universities and other educational organizations throughout the world have shown increased interest in using computer-supported collaborative learning (CSCL), to facilitate active interaction among learners. Computer-mediated communication (CMC) tools such as asynchronous CMC (e.g., e-mail, Bulletin Board System [BBS]) and synchronous CMC (e.g., text chat, videoconferencing) are often used in CSCL. Recently, social networking services (SNS) such as Facebook and Twitter, also known as "social

M. Yamada (✉)
Kanazawa University, Kanazawa, Japan
e-mail: mark@mark-lab.net

S. Kitamura
Tokyo Keizai University, Tokyo, Japan
e-mail: satkit@satkit-lab.net

B. White et al. (eds.), *Social Media Tools and Platforms in Learning Environments*,
DOI 10.1007/978-3-642-20392-3_19, © Springer-Verlag Berlin Heidelberg 2011

media," have been the focus of attention not only in social psychology (e.g., Walther et al. 2008) but also in educational settings.

Learning activities in social media are based on interpersonal interactions and (computer)-mediated communication. Most interactions in social media are multiparty interactions, and understanding of these interactions is supported by theories of dyadic interactions, which are interactions between two persons. Although many studies in CMC focus on dyadic interactions, their findings can be important for researchers interested in learning via social media.

The foundation of CMC research was formed by a group of researchers based at University College London. Their findings culminated in *The Social Psychology of Telecommunications* (Short et al. 1976). The most important construct in their findings is social presence. Their argument has been critiqued on a number of counts in the context of CMC studies. However, since the 1990s, social presence has attracted educational researchers, especially in distance education and learning (e.g., Gunawardena 1995).

19.2 Theoretical Background: Social Presence

There are two primary issues in CSCL: first, how to improve interactions between learners, and second, how to evaluate the effectiveness of CSCL. Because the pedagogy of CSCL is based on socio-constructivism, the central point for both issues is the importance of the learning process during interactions. The relationship between learners enhances learning motivation, which promotes participation (Garrison and Anderson 2003). Using discourse analysis, Savignon and Roithmeier (Savignon and Roithmeier 2004) found that the use of quotation and personal names in CMC communication promotes continuing and collaborative discussion. However, the precise factors that cause increased interaction, awareness of the relationship with learners, and improved learning performance are not clear.

In light of the spread of CSCL, one useful conceptual tool for evaluating CSCL use in learning is social presence. Social presence is the degree to which one person perceives the presence of others when their communications are mediated by tools such as a telephone or letter. Short et al. (1976) define social presence as the "degree of salience of the other person in the interaction and the consequent salience of the interpersonal relationship." That is, the perceived proximity to real-time communication in face-to-face settings. Short et al. (1976) suggest that the two factors that promote social presence are "immediacy"(Wiener and Mehrabian 1968), which is the psychological proximity of the interlocutors, and "intimacy" (Argyle and Dean 1965), which is the perceived familiarity caused by social behavior such as eye gazing, nodding, and smiling. Short et al. conducted their research in the 1970s under the auspices of social psychology. During the 1990s, researchers found that the concept of social presence was relevant to their investigations on distance learning. Social presence is a significant concept when considering methods of connecting interaction to learning. In particular, social presence is an important factor in enhancing distance learning (McIsaac and Gunawardena 1996) and is considered to be emotionally effective, as a means to enhancing learner satisfaction with the process of learning (Gunawardena and Zittle 1997).

Garrison and Anderson (2003) suggest that social presence is a fundamental factor for promoting collaborative learning in a "community of inquiry." It is a "dynamic learning process model designed to define, describe, and measure elements supporting the development of an online learning community" (Swan and Ice 2010) with the use of asynchronous CMC, because it can motivate users and lead to serious discussions. For example, the use of greetings and participant's names (rather than pronouns), and asking questions, all enhance the sense of intimacy and coherency within a "community of inquiry." This leads to active discussions in online communication.

Social presence is a central theoretical concept for the design and evaluation of social software for learning. There appears to be three distinct perspectives from which to evaluate relative levels of social presence: the type of media, the type of interaction among learners, and the quality of learner utterances. (These are displayed in Table 19.1.)

The first viewpoint is derived from the findings of Short et al. (1976). They introduced the original concept of social presence to explain how the particular features of a given media affect the direction or outcome of a conversation. From this viewpoint, the perceived comfort level associated with a type of communication media, which could be social or isolating, warm or cool, affects participant perception of social presence.

The second view of social presence depends on the quality of interaction among learners. Gunawardena and Zittle (1997) argued that with the widespread use of CSCL, the role of instructors is no longer that of a "teacher," but rather a "facilitator." They redefined social presence as the degree to which a person is perceived as real in an online mediated conversation. Gunawardena and Zittle emphasize that it is the quality of the interaction that influences the perception of social presence. In their view, self-disclosures such as introductions and support from other learners are constitutive of social presence.

The third viewpoint reflects the research findings of Garrison et al. (2000). They redefined social presence as "the ability of participants in a community of inquiry to project themselves socially and emotionally, as 'real' people, through the medium

Table 19.1 Three viewpoints of social presence

	Researchers	Factor that enhances social presence	Aspect of social presence
The first stance	Short et al. (1976), etc.	The feature of media	Perceived
The second stance	Gunawardena and Zittle (1997), Tu and McIssac (2002), etc.	Interaction between learners and mutual recognition	Perceived
The third stance	Garrison et al. (2002), etc.	Learner's ability and utterances	Expressive

of communication being used." This viewpoint emphasizes that social presence is dependent on participant ability to "express" themselves as engaged by "referring to other learner's opinion" and "expressing emotion with the use of emoticon." Expressing social presence promotes collaborative learning by enhancing group coherence. Garrison et al. (2000) studied conversations in text-based asynchronous CMC. Like Gunawardena and Zittle (1997), they focused on learner's interactions, but their findings emphasize the importance of participation for interactive CSCL conversations.

19.3   Effect of Social Presence in Learning

The previous section described three distinct viewpoints on the significance of social presence for communication. This section provides a review of the literature on the effect of social presence in collaborative learning with social media. In particular, the authors explain their research, which indicated a causal relationship between social media type, psychological perception, and learning performance.

Kies et al. (1997) suggest that high-quality video enhances social presence, and leads to higher satisfaction with learning activity, as compared to lower quality video. In traditional text-based CMC, which lacks social cues, learners tend to increase their social presence in continuous communication by expressing their emotions in various ways, such as using emoticons. Derks et al. (2008) suggest that nonverbal devices have social meaning, such as feelings, which they transmit from person to person. Annetta and Holmes (2006) investigate the effect of avatar design on the perception of social presence. They suggest that individual design of avatar and displaying other's avatar promotes the perception of social presence. Social presence plays an important role in this transmittance. However, in situations in which the interlocutor is not visible, learners may have trouble understanding the interlocutor's feelings. This results from the absence of social cues associated with the messages sent by the interlocutor (Derks et al. 2008). In some types of SCMC, such as audio conferencing and text chat, learners cannot use social cues such as eye contact and nodding, and as a result, they "are not aware when one person starts to type a message and may continue with a topic, or else may change the direction of the discussion while a potential contributor to the discussion types his or her message" (Levy and Stockwell 2006).

Richardson and Swan (2003) used data from 369 online course learners to survey the correlation between social presence, learning consciousness, and satisfaction with the lectures, and found a high correlation between these points. Hughes et al. (2007) investigated the effect of social presence on the sense of group unity in learner-centered learning with BBS. The results of their research revealed that increased expression of social presence (e.g., the use of emoticons, the use of other member's names, and self-disclosure such as relating personal experiences) promoted learner's sense of community.

As mentioned above, there appears to be three distinct viewpoints on what creates social presence. One common thread found in all three viewpoints is the finding that social presence enhances participant's motivation to learn and their satisfaction with the process. However, these findings do not tell us if enhancing social presence affects learning output. They do not explain how social presence leads to the promotion of learning motivation and performance. Recent advances in technology have created a new type of SCMC using video conferencing, enabling interlocutors to feel other's presence to a much greater degree than in text-based communication. Yamada (2009) investigated the relationship between communication media, psychological perception, and learning performance in a communicative language learning setting, from the vantage points of both perceptive and expressive social presence. He used four types of communication media (videoconferencing software, audio conferencing software, text chat with images, and plain text chat) for learning tasks in learner-centered instruction. All these software have a communication assistance function; target expression display, which learners can use when they face communication problems such as the difficulty to transfer the desired meaning. He evaluated and discussed the relationship between media, learner's affective side and output. The study participants were 40 university students who were randomly divided into four groups: the video conferencing group, the audio conferencing group, the text chat with images group, and the plain text chat group. The participants were then randomly formed, by lottery, into pairs. Each pair engaged in a learner-centered discussion for 15 min. Each of the pairs were given the same topic—choosing a new schoolteacher from among four candidates—while taking into consideration certain given conditions (a decision-making task). Information about the school and candidates and their backgrounds were provided in the learning material displayed in each system (see the explanation of the system interface above). Each pair tried to make a decision through communication: in voice-based communication, learners exchanged their opinions and argued verbally; in text chat, they discussed this theme via text-based communication. In order to investigate the relationship between affective evaluation, communication media, and learning performance, Yamada used path analysis.

Figure 19.1 shows the relationship between factors, communication medium, and overall performance, according to the path analysis. Before the path analysis was conducted, three psychological factors were determined. Results from factor analysis conducted in 2007, extracted four factors (Yamada and Akahori 2007). However, only three factors were used for the 2009 investigation because the eigenvalue of the fourth factor is low, and contains only one item. Table 19.2 shows question items and factors for the 2007 research.

In this path analysis, significant relationships between some psychological perceptions and interactive performance were confirmed. The presence of the partner's image stimulated more active communication, enhancing the perceived ease of communication in English. Language learners tended to speak English actively even in learner-centered communication, finding it easier to speak because of the partner's image (factor 1). The presence of the partner's image had an indirect effect on factor 2, "consciousness of natural communication," which helped learners to understand their partner's situation. For example, in the case of miscommunication, learners were able to recognize when their partner failed to comprehend their utterance, and modified the utterance to avoid the miscommunication.

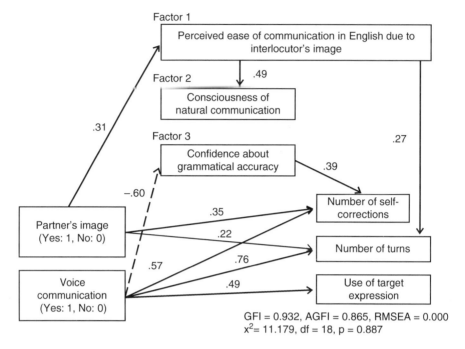

Fig. 19.1 The relationship between media, psychological factors, and performance metrics (*dotted line* means negative effect)

Table 19.2 Factor name and items (Yamada and Akahori 2007)

Factors	Items
Perceived ease of communication in English due to interlocutors' image	Rate your perceived ease of understanding your partner's utterances
	Rate your perceived consciousness of your partner's presence
	Rate the perceived relief in communication while using SCMC
	Rate your perceived ease of communication in English
	Rate your perceived feeling of the similarity between face-to-face and SCMC
Consciousness of natural communication	Rate the frequency of your utterances while using SCMC
	Rate your perceived ease of initiating communication
	Rate your perceived ease of saying what you want to say
	Rate your perceived consciousness responding as soon as possible
	Rate your perceived consciousness of the grammatical accuracy of your partner's utterances
Confidence about grammatical accuracy	Rate your perceived consciousness of accuracy in English communication
	Rate your perceived consciousness of communicating the desired meaning in English, even if you made a grammatical mistake
	Rate your perceived consciousness of the response speed of your partner

Voice communication has a clear influence on all aspects of learning. It has the added advantage that it enables learners to speak naturally, as in face-to-face communication. In voice-based CMC, learners can use fillers, which indicate communication problems or signal ongoing sentence construction, much like they would in face-to-face communication. Moreover, judging from the dialogue data, learners could interrupt their partner's utterances because verbal social cues eased their comprehension of their partner's meaning, thus promoting active English communication. Voice communication also promotes self-correction. The use of nonverbal devices, such as facial expressions, enabled learners to understand their partner's comprehension. When a learner's partner shook their head, it was easy for the learner to understand that their partner was unable to comprehend what was being said.

As the results of this research reveal, interactive media such as video conferencing helps promote social presence, which in turn encourages active communicative language learning. Moreover, social cues seem to affect reflective learning. In fact, learners tried to modify grammatical errors in their utterances in response to the facial expressions of their partners. Nonverbal devices play an important role in compensating for the lack of oral proficiency. However, it is difficult for learners to transfer their desired meaning through verbal expressions alone. The same logic can be applied to understand the effect of target expressions on voice communications. This point suggests social presence leads to learning consciousness, enhancing learning performance as a result. According to previous studies (Gunawardena 1995; Garrison and Anderson 2003), social presence affects the will to learn. This research demonstrates that social presence effectively promotes interaction in communicative language learning and raises participant consciousness of learning. It also leads to enhanced learning performance, which was demonstrated by the participant's increased frequency of utterances and grammatical modifications.

On the other hand, the negative relationship found between voice communication and grammatical accuracy is significant. That is, the lack of social cues in text chat encourages learners to be conscious of whether or not they are accurately transferring their meaning during communication. Learners can, however, use nonverbal devices in video conferencing sessions to insure the transfer of their desired meaning (Garrison and Anderson 2003). The only relationship found for target expression usage was the relationship with voice communication. Psychological perception had no significant effect on expression usage. The use of voice-only communication makes learners feel burdened when communicating in English. In this situation, learners have the opportunity to use target expressions related to communication strategies and theme-specific expressions.

The following qualitative data reveals that the use of social cues, which play an important role in the enhancement of social presence, leads to learning output, through the solution of a communication problem with the use of a target expression and modification of an utterance.

Subject 6 (S6): Okay . . . right. But it takes some cost to teach him how to teach. (looking at the ground)
Subject 5 (S5): Uh? Uh?(cocking head)
S6: (2 seconds) Ahhh but, it costs us in teaching him how to teach, right?
S5: Uhmmm . . .

This example indicates social cues helping the learner to understand the interlocutor's situation in video conferencing. Subject 6 made a grammatical error. Subject 6 did not seem to have confidence in his grammatical accuracy, and spoke in a soft voice. Subject 5 asked subject 6 to repeat his utterance by saying "uh? uh?" because subject 5 could not hear subject 6. Subject 6 translated subject 5's response and gesture as a sign of difficulty in comprehension. Therefore, subject 6 modified his previous utterance. The filler was used, together with social cues, as an indirect trigger for feedback.

The effects of the presence of the partner's image on communication were revealed not only in perceived presence, but also in perceived consciousness of second language communication skills and in productive performance. The next example shows the effect of this presence in video conferencing.

> Subject 7 (S7): Yes. Horiike (Candidate's name in this task) is the best one for this work.
>   Subject 8 (S8): Hai ("yes" in Japanese) (with laughing)
>   S7: His life and ability is very good. And the...
>   S8: (interrupting) Yeah (nodding)
>   S7: And he can go to work not take long time.
>   S8: Ummm (with nodding) (41 seconds), is our choice Miss Horiike (cocking inclining head)? (S8 mistook the gender of the character "Mr. Horiike" in the task)
>   S7: Yes.
>   S8: Yeah. (with laughing)
>   S7: (laughing)

This dialogue indicates that nonverbal behavior seemed to help subjects speak English without the usual frustration associated with grammatical and lexical errors. In this communication, there are several grammatical errors (use of the singular "is" in subject 7's utterance). However, behaviors such as nodding and laughing allowed them to relax and speak positively. Moreover, such behaviors facilitate the transfer of intention to their interlocutors. In subject 8's utterance, we can see the concrete functions of nonverbal behavior. In order to confirm their decision, subject 8 asked with uncertainty "is our choice Miss Horiike?" while expressing a sign of negative intention. Subject 7 responded to this question, they relaxed and began laughing, having confirmed their agreement. As can be seen from this example, the partner's image seemed to play an important role in facilitating communication. However, in text chat with image, such behaviors were not confirmed. Immediacy, which is one of the features of social presence, seems to facilitate communication in both video conferencing and text chat. But nonverbal behavior not only carries the strength of immediacy but also negative feedback, which may lead to effective learning (Lou et al. 2003).

> Subject 13 (S13): (17 seconds) Why?
>   S13: (37 seconds) She have the knowledge, but she have no experience.
>   Subject 14 (S14): (91 seconds) She have been study the skill, but her has not the experiences
>   S14: (12 seconds) I'm sorry. "She has"
>   S13: (14 seconds) All right. "She has"
>   S13: (73 seconds) But I think the communication skill is the most important thing for this job.

S14: (33 seconds) Then I think the best election is the member 2.
S14: (7 seconds) Why?

This example displays the feature of modification in communicative language learning using plain text chat. Both subjects 13 and 14 made grammatical errors about the third person singular, writing "She have" in their utterances (subject 14 also made a nominative error, "her has. . ."). However, the reflective feature of text chat seemed to raise consciousness of grammatical accuracy, as a result of the display of their utterances. In fact, subject 14 apologized for the grammatical error and modified her response. In this experiment, comparative research on four types of SCMC was conducted, in order to find the relationship between medium, perceived evaluation, and learning performance. This research found two types of consciousness: consciousness of the proximity to face-to-face communication, which is concerned with factors 1 and 2, and consciousness of language learning, as reflected in factor 3. The results of this experiment reveal that the combination of the interlocutor's image and voice affects the perceived consciousness of natural communication in SCMC use. On the other hand, the communication tool used (voice vs. text) influences the consciousness of learning, in this case, grammatical accuracy. It seems that learners in text chat were relaxed and satisfied with comprehensive communication. As the results of this research reveal, interactive media such as video conferencing, which promotes social presence, promotes active communicative language learning from the viewpoint of the affective side. Moreover, social cues appear to affect reflective learning. In fact, learners tried to modify grammatical errors in their utterances in response to the facial expressions made by their partners. Nonverbal devices played an important role in compensating for the lack of oral proficiency. However, it is difficult for learners to transfer their desired meaning through verbal expressions alone. The use of social cues enabled by social presence such as facial expression makes it easier for learners to transfer their intention to other learners (McIsaac and Gunawardena 1996; Gunawardena and Zittle 1997). Comprehension of other learner's utterances and intentions appears to relate to learning output.

19.4   Conclusion

This chapter discussed the relationships between social media type, psychological perception, and learning output, and reviewed previous research on social presence from the disciplines of social psychology and educational technology. However, when evaluating social software, one should also consider potential differences in outcomes between experiments and practical situations. Various factors influence learning during the practical use of social software. Whereas in an experimental situation, many factors, such as the number of participants can be controlled. In real life, multiple participants may take part in online discussions, even if only two participants initiate the discussion. In this situation, each and every participant may not be able to keep up with, and assess the direction of, discussion, which is different from experimental situations. On "Twitter," a social software used world-wide, the number of followers is different from the number of users. Therefore, one issue of interest is that the quality and quantity of information found online with Twitter depends on the users. Some can read tweets, while others cannot tweet, a phenomenon that is due to the difference between followers and following users. Every discussant in Twitter does not follow each other. Thus, when a discussant tweets, one can receive the tweet, other cannot. It is very important to understand the usage and features of social software in practical situations, in order to design a learning system that utilizes social software. Nevertheless, experimental findings contribute to the design of social software for learning.

Research findings, such as the effectiveness of emoticons in promoting social presence have recently been applied to learning system designs. The handwriting capability of tablet computers affects the perception of social presence, motivating learners in writing education (Li et al. 2007). Tactile communications, such as a tangible interface also seems to serve as an effective adjunct in helping learners express personal experience. Capabilities such as these, which allow learners to express and perceive social presence, are likely to continue being developed in the future. As social media is increasingly deployed in education, social presence will be one of the theoretical frameworks for the design and evaluation of social media for learning. Further research will be required to discover relationships between social presence, capabilities of social media, and learning performance.

References

Annetta, L.A., Holmes, S.: Creating presence and community in a synchronous virtual learning environment using avatars. Int. J. Instruct. Technol. Dist. Learn. 3(8), 27–43 (2006)

Argyle, M., Dean, J.: Eye-contact distance and affiliation. Sociometry 28, 289–304 (1965)

Derks, D., Fischer, A.H., Bos, A.E.R.: The role of emotion in computer-mediated communication: a review. Comput. Hum. Behav. 24, 766–785 (2008)

Garrison, D.R., Anderson, T.: E-learning in the 21st Century: A Framework for Research and Practice. Routledge-Falmar, London (2003)

Garrison, D.R., Anderson, T., Archer, W.: Critical inquiry in a text-based environment: computer conferencing in higher education. Internet High. Educ. 2(2/3), 87–105 (2000)

Gunawardena, C.N.: Social presence theory and implications for interaction and collaborative learning in computer conferences. Int. J. Educ. Telecommun. 1(2/3), 147–166 (1995)

Gunawardena, C.N., Zittle, F.J.: Social presence as a predictor of satisfaction within a computer-mediated conferencing environment. Am. J. Dist. Educ. 11(3), 8–26 (1997)

Kies, J.K., Willges, R.C., Rosson, M.B.: Evaluating desktop videoconferencing for distance learning. Comput. Educ. 28(2), 79–91 (1997)

Levy, M., Stockwell, G.: CALL Dimensions: Options & Issues in Computer Assisted Language Learning. Lawrence Erlbaum Associates, Mahwah (2006)

Li, K., Akahori, K.: Development and evaluation on a writing correction system with audio and playback stroke. In: World Conference on Educational Multimedia, Hypermedia and Telecommunications 2007, Vancouver, pp. 3944–3950 (2007)

Lomicka, L., Lord, G.: Social presence in virtual communities of foreign language (FL) teachers. System **35**, 208–228 (2007)

McIsaac, M.S., Gunawardena, C.N.: Research in distance education. In: Jonassen, D. (ed.) Handbook of Research for Educational Communications and Technology, pp. 403–437. Scholastic Press, New York (1996)

Richardson, J.C., Swan, K.: Examining social presence in online courses in relation to students' perceived learning and satisfaction. J. Asynchronous Learn. Network **7**(1), 68–88 (2003)

Savignon, S.J., Roithmeier, W.: Computer-mediated communication: texts and strategies. CALICO J. **21**(2), 265–290 (2004)

Short, J., Williams, E., Christie, B.: The Social Psychology of Telecommunications. Wiley, London (1976)

Swan, K., Ice, P.: The community of inquiry framework ten years later: introduction to the special issue. Internet High. Educ. **13**, 1–4 (2010)

Tu, C.H., McIssac, M.: The relationship of social presence and interaction in online classes. Am. J. Dist. Educ. **16**(3), 131–150 (2002)

Walther, J.B., Van Der Hide, B., Kim, S.-Y., Westerman, D., Tong, S.T.: The role of friends' appearance and behavior on evaluations of individuals on facebook: are we known by the company we keep? Hum. Commun. Res. **34**, 28–49 (2008)

Wiener, M., Mehrabian, A.: Language Within Language: Immediacy, a Channel Verbal Communication. Appleton, New York (1968)

Yamada, M.: The role of social presence in learner-centered communicative language learning using synchronous computer-mediated communication: experimental study. Comput. Educ. **52**(4), 820–833 (2009)

Yamada, M., Akahori, K.: An analysis of the relationship between presence, consciousness and performance in learner-centered communicative learning using SCMC - experimental study. J. Asia TEFL **4**(4), 59–91 (2007)

Chapter 20
Visualising Social Computing Output: Mapping Student Blogs and Tweets

David Cameron, Amalie Finlayson, and Rebecca Wotzko

Abstract This chapter provides a case study in the development of a data mining approach to assess blogging and microblogging ('tweets') in a higher education setting. Data mining is the use of computational algorithms to analyse large datasets, and this chapter describes the use of the Leximancer software tool to perform a conceptual analysis of the blogs and tweets published by students in an undergraduate course about social media. A Leximancer analysis is represented visually as a 'concept map' showing the relationships between the concepts and ideas drawn out of the data automatically, rather than using predefined terms and keywords. In this chapter, Leximancer is used to produce a concept map of the student blogs and tweets to enhance the evaluation of conceptual understanding of the syllabus, as well as more general observations about the use of these social media tools in higher education. This suggests a possible approach to analysing the potentially large volume of text-based information that can be produced by students in these social computing settings.

20.1 Teaching Social Media with Social Media

Social computing technology is now constantly evolving in a process described as 'perpetual beta', in which it is 'developed in the open, with new features slipstreamed in on a monthly, weekly, or even daily basis' (O'Reilly 2005). Teachers working with these tools can find themselves also constantly evaluating, maintaining and updating subject matter in a similar perpetual beta model

D. Cameron (✉)
University of Newcastle, Callaghan, NSW 2308, Australia
e-mail: david.cameron@newcastle.edu.au

A. Finlayson • R. Wotzko
Charles Sturt University, Bathurst, NSW, Australia
e-mail: afinlayson@csu.edu.au; rwotzko@csu.edu.au

B. White et al. (eds.), *Social Media Tools and Platforms in Learning Environments*,
DOI 10.1007/978-3-642-20392-3_20, © Springer-Verlag Berlin Heidelberg 2011

(Finlayson et al. 2009). In addition, the assumption that so-called digital native learners have a natural and homogeneous affinity for using these technologies in their education has increasingly been questioned (Kennedy et al. 2008). For example, the authors have noted significant variations in skills and comfort levels with different applications, and a tendency for students to equate their frequent but often unsophisticated use of some sites, such as Facebook, with mastery of social media generally. This self-assessment can lead to attitudes of resistance from some learners when they are asked to apply these tools in educational settings. A third factor for consideration is that the ease with which content can be produced with these tools can potentially leave educators and researchers with a large volume of student output to review or assess. Increasingly sophisticated data mining and visualisation tools and techniques are emerging to explore these data sets (e.g. Java et al. 2007).

At Charles Sturt University, the course titled COM340 Social Media is delivered to undergraduate Communication and Media students, with the aim of engaging them with the potential professional applications of social computing tools such as social networks (Facebook), blogs, wikis, microblogs (Twitter), and mobile media. The 2010 cohort of students taking COM340 Social Media was introduced to concepts and practise around social media, with an emphasis on the journalism and public relations industries. The students were required to use blogging and microblogging tools to report on their own use of and attitudes towards Web 2.0 and social media applications, and to reflect on the potential impact of these technologies on their future careers in the media and communication industries. Many also chose to comment on the integration of social media into the course's delivery, providing a critique of the syllabus and the teaching and learning strategies.

20.2 The CSU Interact Collaboration and Learning Environment

The COM340 Social Media course is delivered simultaneously to both on-campus (face-to-face) and distance education (online) cohorts. Charles Sturt University's teaching and learning strategies are focused on a collaborative learning environment (CLE), called CSU Interact, which is based on the open source Sakai project (http://sakaiproject.org/portal). CSU Interact is a mandatory teaching resource for all courses taught at Charles Sturt, including those still considered to be delivered primarily in a face-to-face mode. The CLE provides a default set of online tools such as a discussion forum, course outline, announcements, a course evaluation survey and electronic assignment submission. Teaching staff may then select additional online teaching and learning tools from a suite of options, including a weblog, a wiki, lesson modules, RSS feeds, links to external Web sites, chat, e-portfolios and file sharing. The tool used for COM340 Social Media in 2010 and discussed in this chapter is the blog publication tool integrated into the Sakai CLE. In addition, the course made use of the external microblogging application Twitter (www.twitter.com).

20.2.1   The Blogging Tool and Task

The CSU Interact online environment contains a blog tool that students use as a reflective learning journal. In COM340 Social Media, students used this tool for an assessment task requiring them to:

- Post regular entries to their own personal weblog, hosted within the CSU Interact site for COM340, focusing on content related to social media
- Focus on producing quality, compelling and rich Web content as well as a regular quantity of content
- Utilise the blog as a space to engage with weekly reflection on readings and the course content
- Provide critical feedback and comment on other students' blog posts

Students used the CSU Interact blog tool in class to document the completion of tutorial activities, and outside of class to reflect on the course content. It was hoped that the simplicity of the blog tool would make it easy for students to create posts, upload their own media and link to external media content.

20.2.2   Microblogging Task via Twitter

In addition to the blog assessment task, the instructors decided to explore the emerging principles and practise of microblogging as they related to the journalism and public relations industries. Twitter was chosen because of its widespread uptake and use in the communication industry.

The introduction of Twitter to the course was initially met with resistance from the 2010 cohort of students. A survey of their social media use at the beginning of the course indicated that almost 70% of students had never used Twitter, with many respondents also indicating that they were not planning to ever use it. However, students were required to sign up for an account to enable participation in a collaborative lecture focused on the topic of blogging and microblogging. This environment allowed students to experiment with Twitter communication conventions, and to contribute to an ongoing conversation about the Social Media course by using the 'hashtag' (a keyword that categorises tweets) '#com340'.

The Twitter tasks were not set as summative assessment tasks, in part reflecting privacy, intellectual property and academic governance issues that might be raised by forcing students to make use of an externally hosted online publication medium. While the authors acknowledge that there are advantages to be gained by engaging students with social computing applications 'in the wild', it was not considered crucial for the learning objectives of this course. For similar reasons, it was decided to make use of the internally hosted blog tool within the CSU Interact CLE, although throughout the course students were exposed to externally hosted blogs as examples of current practise.

20.3 Methodology

The objective in this small study was to explore the application of a data mining approach to evaluating student engagement with the syllabus, as reflected in their course-related blog and microblogging output.

The methodology for this chapter falls into the qualitative paradigm and utilises a 'reflective practitioner' or autoethnographic perspective, on the basis that autoethnographies are recognised as providing a solid footing for qualitative research in the social sciences (Hustler 2005).

Further, in this study, the use of a grounded theory approach is used to enable a theoretical stance to be developed from the data (Strauss and Corbin 1990). Given that theory generation is the principle aim (Corbin 2005), the research in this study was not conducted with a predefined theory in mind, as the rapid change and ongoing developments in the area of social media education mean that there is as yet little theoretical or conceptual apparatus to draw on when conducting studies of this kind. Importantly, therefore, careful delimitation was also a part of the methodological process. The data in this instance is limited, as a result, to that generated within a specific context: student blogging and microblogging output for the COM340 course in 2010. The sample was further refined to include only those students studying in the on-campus mode, as they were engaged more directly with the blogging and microblogging exercises through lecture and tutorial content.

Multiple forms of data in the form of raw text from both student blogs and student tweets were collected and analysed for this case study, primarily using the open-coding software analysis tool known as Leximancer. Visual representations of this data, or 'themic maps', along with lists of primary themes relating to this data, were then created.

20.4 Leximancer

Leximancer is a software tool used to find meaning in text-based documents. It automatically identifies key themes and ideas by data mining texts, and visually representing information in 'themic maps', showing the relationships between these themes and ideas. In these maps, the thematic groups are surrounded by colour-coded circles, where the size of the circle indicates the frequency of the occurrence of the theme throughout the data, and the position of the circle indicates the relationship of that theme to the other themes.

This form of textual analysis was identified as suitable for this study as it adds a quantitative, scientific analysis component to the method. The benefits of using the Leximancer tool are evident: as a form of analysis it is highly inclusive as all articles within the text are treated as important. Every article contributes to the analysis and to overall understanding. The picture that emerges from this analysis is, in essence, a user-driven representation of meaning.

Leximancer is a commercial product, though a number of pricing options are provided for academic use. The authors are not aware of any open source alternatives that provide the same functionality.

20.5 Concept Mapping

The concepts that Leximancer produces in the primary themic maps are generated through thousands of iterations, as the software observes clusters of words that move with key terms in the data. As Leximancer identifies some words appearing frequently with certain terms and less frequently with others, the software 'learns' that the words that travel together with a term, frames the profile of that term and defines that term to be a key theme in the data.

Another feature of Leximancer is that 'it also allows the user to request overviews of text sources and key segments of texts in relation to specific concepts and relationships between concepts' (Fisk et al. 2009). This feature was seen as a highly useful facet of the Leximancer data mining approach, as it helped single out text sources and key segments of texts in relation to specific concepts under discussion without needing to search through large samples of student blog and microblog text.

The authors therefore worked with the highly inclusive analysis tool Leximancer, coupled with their own conceptual sensitivity and practical experiential knowledge, to identify themes and formulate valid and representative themic maps based on the blogging and microblogging output of students enrolled in the COM340 course for 2010.

20.6 Collecting and Processing the Data

Two data sets were collected for the purposes of this study: the blog content produced by students as part of their work in the COM340 session for 2010, and the microblog or 'tweet' content produced by students on the Twitter microblogging application for the same COM340 session. For this study, the authors collected both sets of data manually by copying and pasting the content into text files, in preparation for analysis using the Leximancer tool.

In order to comply with ethical considerations, no individual names or aliases were included in the analytical output of the study, so as to guarantee student anonymity. The omission of names in this way was a deliberate act, in recognition of the tension that currently exists in new forms of digital publishing (such as blogs and microblogs) around the public/private nature of information made available by individuals in these mediums (Viégas 2005). Indeed, one of the key learning objectives of COM340 is to raise students' awareness of the personal risks of publishing in these 'networked publics' (Boyd 2007).

20.6.1 Results

All of the blog text was grouped into one data set, and all of the microblog or tweet text into another, so as to create two separate data sets for analysis by Leximancer. These were then run through the analysis process to create a separate concept map for each.

20.7   Concept Map of Student Blogs

The analysis of the student blogs was initially conducted by bundling all of the student blog content together. For the purposes of the study, the sample was limited to the 60 students who completed the course in the on-campus mode. The content of all 60 blogs was treated as one set of data, and running all the text from these created an initial exploratory map.

Few of the preprocessing options allowed by Leximancer were adjusted in the initial phase of analysis. The prose test threshold, which usually defaults to a value of one to allow the software to skip parts of the text that it sees as redundant or extraneous, was reduced to zero to ensure that Leximancer checked every single part of the blog texts under analysis. The default setting suits the analysis of texts that are comprised of full sentences in a prose format, as it would be advisable to ignore any sentences that are not full prose sentences. However, as this particular set of text data contained student blog entries of more casual or informal language, the prose test threshold was removed.

In the Automatic Concept Identification options, it was decided to allow Leximancer to automatically identify the concepts existing within the data set of the text of the 60 student blogs. All other settings were also left on the default setting at this point.

An initial themic map was then generated, with a view to having something to which to refer and alter so as to produce a final, relevant map or data visualisation. After consulting this initial resulting map, and the list of themes that the software generated automatically from the blog text data, some unnecessary and redundant concepts were removed. It was necessary to delete some concepts and merge others in the primary themic maps as the data under analysis were, as described above, produced by analysis of the text of a collection of student blog entries. As such, the data contained several informal elements: words that were adjectival, for example, or that were used as part of the casual vernacular of students, or which were simply irrelevant. These words included 'able', 'access', 'Bathurst', 'become', 'best', 'check', 'day', 'example', 'fact', 'group', 'interesting', 'look', 'name', 'post', 'probably', 'someone', 'sure', 'take', 'things', 'thought', 'use', 'used', 'users', 'using', 'via' and 'year'.

Further review revealed that some other Leximancer-identified words or concepts belonged together or were very similar to each other, and could be merged so as to create a simpler and clearer themic map. It was necessary to manually merge these concepts within the data – these included 'social' and 'media', 'friend' and 'friends', 'people' and 'person' and 'site', 'sites' and 'Web sites'.

After these changes had been made in terms of the instructions instructing Leximancer how to analyse the data set, the second and final map was more stable. These general maps and broad analysis techniques represented the initial stage of analysis for this part of the student blog data set.

From this point, it was possible to generate a useful and viable map to help to identify the major themes within the data, as part of the grounded theory methodology identified earlier in this section. This is shown as Fig. 20.1.

The concept map provides a starting point for the researcher to begin generating theories from the data. In Fig. 20.1, it can be seen that given its size that 'social

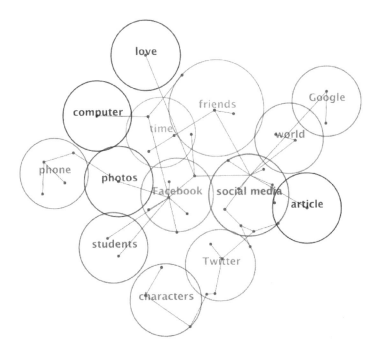

Fig. 20.1 Leximancer map – primary themes in student blogs (n = 60)

Table 20.1 Themes and connectivity for student blogs (n = 60)

Theme	Connectivity (%)
Social media	100
Facebook	69
Twitter	23
Time	19
Friends	19
Phone	14
Google	14
Characters	10
World	9
Students	5
Photo	4
Article	2
Computer	2
Love	2

media' is a major theme. However, in a colour map it is presented as red, which indicates that it is possibly less significant to the researcher than, for example, the smaller themes of Facebook and Twitter which are in hues more towards the blue end of the spectrum. This is actually quite intuitive, as the theme of social media could be expected to be common across the data set as a result of the name and content of the course, and the frequency, therefore, that these terms are used in the student blogs. At an initial glance, the theme of 'friends' could be considered more worthy of further investigation, as it is indicated as significant in the data set through both size and colour coding (it is presented as a green/blue hue).

For the researcher, the concept map can therefore provide the launching point for other tools within Leximancer. The next step in this study was to consider the concept map in parallel with Leximancer's list of the main themes identified as applicable to this unique student blog data set. These themes were organised in order of connectivity, or relevance, and the percentage next to them indicates the level of connectivity or relevance. That is, the top theme, social media, was chosen as the most relevant theme of all the available themes from the data, and was scaled as being 100% connected. Leximancer scaled all the other themes accordingly.

The top three themes were not surprising to the authors given their own knowledge of the topics and the subject matter of the course, and this provides a simple check of the validity of the Leximancer output. However, as noted earlier in the discussion on colour coding in the concept map, ranking alone does not necessarily offer a guide as to the nature of these themes. The third step in this analysis was to use Leximancer's linking feature that enables the researcher to click into examples of the themes and concepts from the data set, to investigate at a highly granular level the contexts in which the terms are used. By moving in this way between concept map, theme rankings and examples of use, a clearer picture of the emerging themes can be quickly developed from a large data set.

20.8   Concept Map of Student Tweets

The analysis process for the student microblogs or tweets was initially conducted within Leximancer by once again bundling all of the student microblog content together. For the purposes of the study, the number of students who engaged with the Twitter application numbered much lower at 35 students, presumably because this was not an assessable part of student output for the COM340 course in 2010. Therefore, for this part of the analysis, the quantity of student blogs included was $n = 35$. The manually copied content of all 35 Twitter streams was treated as one set of data, and running all the text from these 35 Twitter streams created an initial exploratory map.

Once again, only the minimum Leximancer settings were adjusted in the initial phase of analysis. The prose test threshold was again reduced to zero to ensure that Leximancer checked every single part of the microblog text under analysis. Leximancer was again allowed to automatically identify the concepts existing within the data set, and all other settings were left at the default level.

A working themic map was then generated, and then some unnecessary and redundant words or concepts were removed. These words included 'amazing', 'best', 'bring', 'coming', 'feel', 'makes', 'RT', 'use', 'used', 'via', 'wait', 'watching' and 'year'. For this data set, just two words or concepts were merged: 'social' and 'media'.

A more relevant map was then generated for use by the authors to help identify the major themes and the relationship of these themes, and can be seen below in Fig. 20.2.

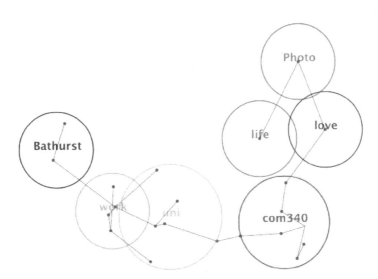

Fig. 20.2 Leximancer concept map – primary themes identified in the student microblogs $(n = 35)$

Theme	Connectivity (%)
COM340	100
Uni	60
Work	35
Life	7
Photo	7
Love	6
Bathurst	6

Table 20.2 Leximancer themes and connectivity for student microblogs (n = 35)

Leximancer also produced a list of the major themes that were applicable to this unique student microblog or tweet data set. The top theme, social media, was chosen as the most relevant theme of all the available themes from the data, and was scaled as being 100% connected. Leximancer scaled all the other themes accordingly.

The dominance of COM340 theme was not unexpected by the authors. However, the other top themes of 'uni' and 'work' had not been anticipated, which illustrates how Leximancer can point investigators to unexpected themes emerging from a data set. At this stage, having generated a broad themic map and list, and a more specific concept list for both the blog and microblog data sets, the conceptual data was further interrogated.

20.9 Discussion

As noted earlier, the Leximancer concept map provides a visualisation of the relevance and connectivity of themes and concepts emerging from the text data; however, more detailed investigation is then required to explore the context in which these themes appear within the data set. Leximancer does not provide 'answers', but instead provides a set of tools to help the researcher traverse the data set in search of meaning. An initial observation of the concept maps and theme rankings produced in this study shows that the student reflections centred on 'social media', 'Facebook', 'Twitter' and 'COM340'. At a casual level, these would not be unexpected given the subject matter, but drilling down to some sample examples of usage draws the researcher to a range of interesting observations.

Conversely, deeper examination of less obvious themes such as 'friends', 'article', 'characters' and 'love' revealed that they often referred to the outputs of one-off class exercises and were therefore less relevant to the investigation. For example, in a tutorial, the students were asked to devise a proposal for a transmedia drama that used social media to tell a dramatic narrative. Subsequent blog reflections therefore made frequent mention to the terms 'characters' and 'friends' in describing the plot synopses. Another tutorial prompted students to reflect on a reading, which boosted the perceived significance of the concept of 'article'.

The theme of 'love' emerged from the common use of the term in a verbal form to indicate a liking or preference for something, as in these examples:

> I'm pretty sure that after a big night people love going online and checking out what happened the night before (Student 1, blog post).
>
> I'd love to hear from all my fellow COM340ers and your experiences with twitter (Student 2, blog post).
>
> Would love to have a shower with hot water for once and some heating. Damn #Uni! (Student 3, tweet).

20.9.1   Students' Conceptual Understanding of the Syllabus

From the beginning of the course it was clear that many students perceived COM340 Social Media as 'the Facebook course'. This was partly reinforced by the timetabling of a 2 h tutorial each week in a computer laboratory, which placed social media tools at the students' fingertips and proved both a convenience and distraction for teaching. Also apparent was the students' general resistance to Twitter, which was revealed in a survey of their social media habits undertaken at the start of the course and then reflected in their class discussions, blog posts and tweets. A typical comment was:

> If everybody is connected to facebook do I really need to get my head around twitter? Apparently so, if only for the lecture for this subject in two weeks (Student 4, blog post).

However, the ability of Leximancer to link themes with contextual examples in the data set allowed the authors to identify moments of direct engagement with the syllabus. Student blogs would reflect directly on issues raised in the weekly lectures and tutorial sessions, such as the use of Twitter by journalists trying to track a breaking news story:

> I was at work in a radio newsroom when Michael Jackson died and found Twitter especially useful during this busy morning … I used a variety of tweets to find credible sources (Student 5, blog post).

Other examples of direct reflection on the syllabus included students' posts on privacy issues in social networking sites, and the topic of online memorials:

> Although education is important I think the creators of sites like Facebook need to take greater responsibility (Student 6, blog post).
>
> I think that i would definitely prefer it if my social media footprint was deleted. While my social media sites are fairly secure and don't allow strangers to see my information, there are still things hidden away on my Facebook page that i don't think i would like other people to see, or have access to (student 7, blog post).

Another observation that can be made from comparing the two data sets is that the bulk of tweets from the COM340 students could be categorised as personal rather than course-focused. This can in part be explained by the fact that the tweeting exercise was not assessable, and that the students had been quite clearly told to use the blog as the main platform for their reflections. For the majority of students, as noted in a survey conducted at the beginning of the course, this was also the first time they had used Twitter and so many of their tweets had an air of being guarded, or superficially exploring how the application works. This was interesting to the authors, given that the student resistance to Twitter was often articulated in terms of it being a channel for irrelevant and banal personal observations. Ironically, they failed to perceive the same elements in their own tweets, such as:

> So... I went out last night, and got home @ 11am today - Instead of doing work (Student 8, tweet).
> Check out the fog that has swept over Bathurst this morning... Winter is on its way! (Student 9, tweet).

20.9.2   Student Reflections on Their Own Social Media Use

A key teaching strategy used in COM340 Social Media was to encourage students to evaluate and reflect on their own use of social media tools, and to compare that with the defined demographics of some of the more popular applications. The course also focused on the use of social media tools by media and communication industries. The aim of this strategy was to help students, as consumers, acknowledge their own – often heavily biased – perceptions of social media, and engage with broader concepts as producers and content creators. From the Leximancer examination of the blog and tweet data sets, and triangulated with other sources such as tutorial discussions and other tasks in the course, it was clear that this strategy had mixed results with this cohort. Some students had difficulty overcoming their personal preferences for certain applications, as evidenced in the superficial 'Facebook vs. Twitter' debates that dominated their blog posts. Their reflections were also heavily based on their own current usage at a consumer level, rather than their application or potential usage by media or communication content producers. Typical of this introspective commentary are these reflections:

> There are certain aspects of Facebook that I am simply not interested in using, for example facebookchat, and 'become a fan of'. I am also quite hesitant to join certain groups, for example Political or Religious advocacy groups (Student 10, blog post).
> I use Twitter to tweet randomly when I'm in a class with a computer or if I'm stuck late at the uni and bored. I'm only following 2 other people and they tweet rarely as well (Student 11, blog post).

20.9.3   Student Observations on the Use of Social Media Tools in Higher Education

Reflections on the subject content of COM340 inevitably included commentary on the delivery of the course itself. These did include some positive observations, particularly from those students who made a connection between social media and their career aspirations in the media and communication industries. As noted above, there was at times bitter resistance to the idea that the course would require examination and use of microblogging, and more particularly, Twitter. Educators need to be wary of assuming that all social media tools are equally popular, or that students will automatically be willing experimenters with online tools. These students had difficulty detaching themselves from their personal social media habits. While a handful of students were already prolific Twitter users, the majority indicated little or no experience, and some were opposed to trying it at all:

> YOU WANT ME TO JOIN TWITTER!? THE SAME TWITTER THAT I'VE BEEN MOCKING AND FIGHTING AGAINST SINCE IT FIRST STARTED? (Student x, tweet).

Along similar lines, the heavy use of online resources in a face-to-face setting produced some comments from students. It was clear that some felt that the requirement to attend face-to-face classes that demonstrated the affordances of social media tools did not make sense, as with this tweeted note:

> I'm at uni, in the maclabs, for a lecture being delivered by Twitter. Why couldn't I do this from bed? (Student 12, tweet).

The Leximancer analysis also provided links to more general observations about the delivery of the course, for example, the timetabling of classes was a regular source of comments:

> mmmm 8 am lecture for @com340. Loving life (Student 13, tweet).

20.10 Conclusion

The sample size in this study is small, and therefore no generalised claims can be made about the specific experiences of these students or their engagement with the subject matter. Rather, the authors argue that the adoption of a data mining approach may provide educators with a set of tools and techniques to assist them when working with the large volume of output that can be generated in some social media publishing forms.

From this trial, the authors found that the use of a data mining approach to student social media output provided some useful insights into student engagement with the syllabus, and the course delivery strategies. The authors could apply broader knowledge of what was going on in class with the themes and concepts emerging from the data analysis, and use this to inform reflections on the course content and delivery. Leximancer's visualisation of the themes and concepts as a graphic map was a useful starting point for our analysis of the large volume of text generated by the use of blogs and tweets in COM340 Social Media. Although there were preconceived notions as to what the dominant themes would be in the student responses, the use of Leximancer to draw out meaning from the text provided a useful means by which to test those views, and to identify unexpected themes.

The ability of Leximancer to then allow the researcher to drill down to examples of the themes and concepts in context within the data set also provided a useful means by which to explore the meaning of the themes and concepts in terms of the course as a whole. It enabled the authors to navigate through large volumes of blog and tweet text to become sensitised to the types of comments being made by the cohort about aspects of the syllabus and the delivery of the course itself.

One area that presents itself as an area for future research is the potential use of data mining tools more directly in the assessment process. This study concentrated on a post-assessment analysis of the textual output from the students. However, the ability of software tools such as Leximancer to collate and analyse the work of individual students is worthy of further investigation. Similarly, processes for automatically collecting the output of students using blogs and microblogs – either hosted within a CLE or externally hosted – are also worth considering to enhance the use of data mining tools in educational settings.

References

Boyd, D.: Why youth (Heart) social network sites: The role of networked Publics in teenage social life. In: Buckingham, D. (ed.) Macarthur Foundation Series on Digital Learning: Youth, Identity, and Digital Media Volume. MIT Press, Cambridge (2007)

Corbin, J.: Grounded theory. In: Somekh, B., Lewin, C. (eds.) Research Methods in the Social Sciences, pp. 49–55. Sage Publications, London/Thousand Oaks/New Delhi (2005)

Finlayson, A., Cameron, D., Hardy, M.: Journalism education as a perpetual beta test: notes on the design and delivery of tertiary 'Social Media' subjects. In: Journalism Education Association of Australia. Perth (2009)

Fisk, K., Cherney, A., Hornsey. M., Smith, A.: Rebuilding institutional legitimacy in Post-conflict societies: an Asia Pacific case study – phase 1a. Air Force Office of Scientific Research (AFOSR), Asian Office of Aerospace Research and Development (AOARD), University of Queensland (2009)

Hustler, D.: Ethnography. In: Somekh, B., Lewin, C. (eds.) Research Methods in the Social Sciences. Sage Publications, London (2005)

Java, A., Song, X., Finin, T., Tseng, B.: Why we twitter: understanding microblogging usage and communities. In: Joint 9th WEBKDD and 1st SNA – KDD Workshop (2007)

Kennedy, G.E., Judd, T.S., Churchward, A., Gray, K., Krause, K.L.: First year students' experiences with technology: Are they really digital natives? Australas. J. Educ. Technol. **24** (1), 108–122 (2008)

O'Reilly, T.: What is web 2.0?. http://oreilly.com/pub/a/web2/archive/what-is-web-20.html? page=4(2005)

Strauss, A.L., Corbin, J.: Basics of Qualitative Research. Sage Publications, Newbury Park (1990)

Viégas, F.B.: Bloggers' expectations of privacy and accountability: an initial survey. In: Computer-Mediated Communication, **10**(3) p. 120 (2005)

Part VII
Case Studies and Applications

Chapter 21
Learning from Medical Social Media Data: Current State and Future Challenges

Kerstin Denecke and Avaré Stewart

Abstract The amount of social media data dealing with medical and health issues increased significantly in the last couple of years. Patients, physicians, and other health professionals are willing to share their knowledge and experiences in the Web. Medical social media data now provides a new source of information within a learning context, for various learners. The variety of such content provides opportunities for a broad range of applications to exploit this data and support these learners in gaining knowledge. A potential benefit is that communication barriers are much lower for social media tools than communication through traditional channels. The objective of this chapter is to highlight the potentials for learning from medical social media data. Various characteristics of learning from this data will be presented and their impact to groups of learners is highlighted. Further, potential real-world applications are described. Taking this as a basis, the challenges for technology development in this context will be discussed.

21.1 Introduction

The Internet and other electronic communication tools are changing the way patients, health care providers, and health officials exchange information. The growing number of social sites enables people to share text, images, and video with others around the world, instantaneously. "Health 2.0" or "Medicine 2.0" are seen as developing trends that could lead – among others – to the empowerment of patients, as patients have easier access to health-related information and thereby have better understanding of choices that can be made (Kovic et al. 2008; Lagu

K. Denecke (✉) • A. Stewart
Leibniz Universität Hannover, Forschungszentrum L3S, Appelstraße 9a, 30167 Hannover, Germany
e-mail: denecke@L3S.de; stewart@L3S.de

B. White et al. (eds.), *Social Media Tools and Platforms in Learning Environments*,
DOI 10.1007/978-3-642-20392-3_21, © Springer-Verlag Berlin Heidelberg 2011

et al. 2008). It creates a new arena for the stakeholders in an online medical community with new opportunities and challenges (Mehta and Hofmann 2007; Narismatsu 2008; Randeree 2009).

Breaking away from older practices, physicians now blog about their experiences in treating patients or diagnosing diseases. They communicate with each other sharing experiences and knowledge (e.g., through Web sites such as http://www.doctors.net.uk, http://www.doc2doc.bmj.com). Patients provide personal accounts about their medical conditions and the treatments they receive. They share their health data anonymously with the public (e.g., at http://www.curetogether.com). Relatives of patients participate in question and answer portals to receive support for issues of concern. Researchers and practitioners receive up-to-date information on the best practices and latest research results from the (medical) Web.

In such a setting, there is an every growing opportunity for different types of actors to collaborate and learn. Learning is the act, process, or experience of gaining knowledge or skill. Besides facts on a specific topic, this knowledge might include personal information about individual opinions, preferences about groups and their behavior, or general trends and patterns. There are a number of compelling reasons for learning from Medical Social Media Data (MSMD). The foremost reason is the timeliness of the information. Compared to classical printed books and journals, the publication barrier (and cost) is much lower. The ease with which content can be created allows the roles of the content consumers and content creators to be seamlessly interchanged. So, many types of participants can rapidly generate a broad spectrum of data. An additional reason for learning from social media data is that the potential reading audience is wide reaching, allowing a global audience to be reached in a matter of seconds.

In this chapter, a vision of what characterizes learning within an MSMD environment is presented. An overview of the available medical social media data is given. We focus on the learners within this environment and what they can learn from MSMD. The different types of learners and the role that MSMD plays in closing the information gap among these learner groups is discussed. A variety of applications and scenarios is also presented to show how medical social media data can be exploited for fostering collaboration within an online medical community. Finally, given the nature of the social media data, it is often difficult to automatically process such content, due to the peculiarities inherent in human language text, or limitations of processing audio–visual content. These challenges will be summarized and the demands they make on enabling technologies that deal with medical social media data will be highlighted.

In summary, the questions to be addressed are:

- What medical social media content is available?
- Who can learn from MSMD?
- What does learning from medical social media comprise?
- What technological challenges need to be addressed?

21.2 Medical Social Media Data Space

21.2.1 Definition of Medical Social Media Data

Social media is the use of technology combined with social interaction in which individuals can engage in one-to-many conversations, using electronic communication tools. Social media data includes various kinds of publicly available content that is produced by end users, rather than by the operator of a Web site, and has been uploaded without a commercial, marketing or promotional purpose in mind. Medical social media data (MSMD) is a subset of the social media data space, in which the interests of the participants are specifically devoted to medicine and health issues. The content is characterized by a mix between expert knowledge, lay knowledge, and empirical findings (Randeree 2009).

MSMD does not exist in isolation. It can be viewed as a set of resources that are embedded within a system of collaborating learners (see Fig. 21.1). In this context, MSMD serves as a conduit through which the exchange of information between the different types of learners takes place. It also serves a foundation upon which numerous applications are built to foster the exchange of information within an online medical community.

This chapter explores MSMD within this embedded context. In this section, the different types of MSMD are outlined and an overview of the available medical social media data is given. In Sect. 21.3, MSMD is viewed within the context of

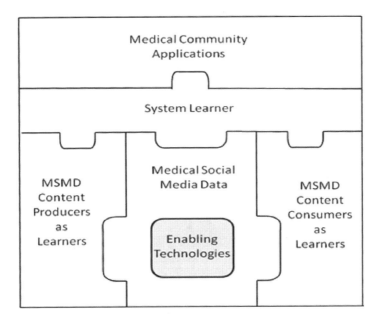

Fig. 21.1 Medical social media data space

learning and finally in Sect. 21.4, applications which exploit MSMD for these various learners are discussed. Challenges and their implications to technology development are summarized in Sect. 21.5.

21.2.2 Types of MSMD

The types of MSMD can be broadly placed into two categories. Users can either generate their own content, or alternatively annotate the content created by others. To make the distinction clear, we refer to the former as (user-generated) *content*, and the latter as *metadata*. Each MSMD can be further defined based on the degree to which different individuals collaborate to create the content or metadata (see Table 21.1). In a *collaborative mode*, the actual content, or the metadata associated with the content, is created or edited by multiple users. Users collaborate to annotate or create metadata for the original content. In a *non-collaborative mode*, the content is created and edited by one author(s). In the following, an overview on existing MSMD for these categories is given. Table 21.2 provides examples for each category.

21.2.2.1 Collaborative Content

Medical wikis offer the opportunity to get information about diseases, human anatomy, and medical procedures. They are either directed to health professionals, students of medicine, or the general public. Medical wiki authors are mainly health professionals, who are specialized in a given area of medicine. For example, Flu Wiki (http://www.fluwikie.com) aims at helping local communities to prepare for and perhaps cope with a possible influenza pandemic. Another example is Radiopaedia (http://radiopaedia.org), a wiki dealing with issues related to radiology.

21.2.2.2 Non-collaborative Content

Medical Weblogs, i.e., Weblogs specifically focusing on medicine or health care can be differentiated by the role of the content producer within the medical community; for example, doctor, nurse, or patient. The main topics in medical Weblogs are medications, physiology, and disorders (Allison 2009).

Table 21.1 Types of medical social media data

	Collaborative	Non-collaborative
Content	Medical wiki	Weblog, microblog, video-blog, podcasts, person health records
Metadata	Social bookmarking, Social networks	Review and rating portals, question and answer portal

Table 21.2 Examples of medical social media data

Types	Examples
Wiki	• *AskDrWiki* (http://askdrwiki.com) is a nonprofit educational Web site made by physicians for physicians, medical students, and health care providers focusing on cardiology and electrophysiology
Medical Weblogs	• *Physician-written:* http://www.webmd.com • *Patient-written:* http://www.diabetesmine.com • *Nurse-written:* http://mediblogopathy.blogspot.com/
Microblogs	• *CDC emergency:* http://twitter.com/CDCEMERGENCY • *WHO news:* http://twitter.com/WHONEWS • *Diabetes community:* http://twitter.com/tudiabetes
V-logs	• *Health channel from Center of Disease Control (CDC):* http://www.youtube.com/CDCstreaminghealth
Medical podcasts	• *Medical education:* http://www.podmetrics.com • *Patient information:* http://www2c.cdc.gov/podcasts/ • *Ophthalmology podcast:* http://www.asseenfromhere.com/
Personal health records	• *Microsoft health vault:* http://www.healthvault.com/ • *Google health:* www.google.com/health/
Social networks	• In *PatientsLikeMe* (http://www.patientslikeme.com/), patients can anonymously share treatment, symptom, progression and outcome data with the entire community, facilitating knowledge management and transfer for all to benefit (Brownstein et al. 2009) • *Dailystrength* (http://www.dailystrength.org/) is a platform to share treatment reviews, discuss with each other, or get expert's help • *Medpedia* (http://www.medpedia.com) combines a wiki-like knowledge base on medical concepts and a database of clinical trials with aggregated news collected from various sources and enables people to connect and exchange knowledge • *Sermo* (http://www.sermo.com) is an online physician community in the USA
Social bookmarking	• *PeerClip* (http://www.PeerClip.com) allows physicians and nurses to organize data and make them visible to others sharing the same interest. Opinions can be exchanged on single items • *Meddlinks* (http://meddlinks.com/) is a community resource to gather health and medical articles
Query and answer portals	• *Netdoctor* (http://www.netdoctor.co.uk) is a collaboration between physicians, health care professionals, and patients. The Web site delivers information related to health as well as various services like query facilities
Reviews and ratings	• At *Drugratingz.com*, users can anonymously rate drugs in several categories, including effectiveness, side effects, convenience, and value; they can post and read comments • *Patient opinion* (http://www.PatientOpinion.org.uk) allows for providing opinions on the UK National Health System (NHS)

Patients use blogs to discuss disease issues, share personal stories, or connect with friends or persons suffering from the same disease. The content is typically specific to personalized disease matters, i.e., to blogger's own experience with the disease. The focus is mainly on chronic diseases (e.g., asthma, allergies) or on life changing or threatening diseases (e.g., cancer).

Health care professionals (i.e., physicians and nurses) provide informative health updates, personal stories, information about health care technology, and other areas of clinical or practice interest (Hardey 2008). They may blog in order to target patients, the general public, or each other. The doctors who blog often want to share practical knowledge and skills or influence medical and health policy (Denecke and Nejdl 2009).

Microblogs are another source for distributing information. Through the microblog *Twitter*, people discuss issues related to medicine. Health organizations such as the Center of Disease Control in the USA. provide information on the latest disease outbreaks. Twitter communities exist that are devoted to a specific health topic (e.g., http://www.twitter.com/tudiabetes). Further, people distribute links to Webpages on latest research results related to medicine or treatments. In this way, Twitter offers a new way for communication and sharing of information among health care professionals (Lupiáñez-Villanueva et al. 2009).

Medical Video-Blogs (VLog) provide information on medical issues in an audio–visual manner. A huge source of videos is available within the YouTube portal. The variety of videos ranges from recorded surgeries, educational video for patients or medical students, to reports on medical issues in news channels. Authors of VLogs are health professionals, official health institutions and organizations, or universities.

Medical Podcasts are examples of audio data with medical content. Podcasts provided by physicians inform patients about concrete health questions. Patient information on treatments (e.g., endoscopy, coronary angiography) or explanations of symptoms or diseases (e.g., obstructive sleep apnea) are provided through Web sites of official organizations such as the Mayo Clinic (http://www.mayoclinic. com). Podcasts directed to physicians help to inform them about general issues or latest news such as medical informatics or electronic prescription. In addition, podcasts and video lectures are available for medical education purposes (e.g., http://www.podmetrics.com).

Personal health records are exploited by patients to keep their own health data. They allow individuals to organize health information, gather medical records from doctors, hospitals, and pharmacies; and share this information securely with a family member, doctors, or caregivers. Access to the stored data is mainly restricted to persons directly related to the patient.

21.2.2.3 Collaborative Metadata

Content communities and social networking sites related to health and medicine enable people with similar interests to connect. More specifically, patients who suffer from diseases can share health data in order to empathize with each other or learn about techniques or medication other sufferers are trying in order to improve their health status. Health professionals exploit social networking sites to connect with other professionals who also share common (medical) interests. Yet other social networking sites such as *HelloHealth* connect patients to physicians.

Social bookmarking systems restricted to the medical domain allow users to easily read and gather medical literature, while fostering interaction with persons via an online tool. Clinicians and clinical students can instantly rate and discuss medical literature online, and share their thoughts on any scientific paper. This has the potential of improving communication amongst physicians and can lead to a better understanding and interpretation of the ever growing amount of medical literature.

21.2.2.4   Non-collaborative Metadata

Forums and Query–Answer Portals (Q&A) with a medical focus offer the opportunity to post queries or engage in discussions. Expert forums enable users to get a qualified answer to a question regarding a disease or treatment. In Q&A portals, people's objective of posting is mainly to receive information related to drugs and disorders, with some attention also given to treatment-related issues (Allison 2009). Depending on the portal, answers can be provided either by health professionals or by the general public.

Reviews and rating portals enable users to present experiences with medical devices, hospitals, or drugs. A broad range of user experiences with medications are available in drug reviews. Reviews on medical devices report on the functionality of the device. Portals are available that even allow individuals to rate and share their experiences with the health care system (e.g., *PatientOpinion.org.uk*) or with medical doctors (e.g., *Ratemd.com*).

21.2.3   Enabling Technologies

In order to realize an MSMD environment, an extensive infrastructure of enabling technologies is required. This infrastructure offers a satisfying user experience by providing responsiveness and the timely availability of data. There is a broad range of Web 2.0 social media technologies available. Some of them are specific for MSMD (Denecke 2008), while others are used throughout various domains.

These technologies impact the users' experience at several levels. *User authentication* is needed to allow appropriately restricting and managing user's registration, passwords, and accounts. Once access to an MSMD site is obtained, *effective user interfaces and interactivity* are required. Technologies such as Ajax allow highly interactive and user-friendly interactions with Web applications. Facilities for interaction include voting, rating, or tagging facilities.

The MSMD environment must also support *performance and scalability,* so that slowdowns are not experienced by multiple users. S*upport for media-rich content* provides a seamless usage for the multiple types of non-textual media (e.g., audio and visual).

Specialized search engines facilitate the access to Web content dealing with medical issues. The results of the search are limited to health Web sites. The search results can also be restricted to only trustworthy sources. A Custom Search Engine by Google uses authoritative and trusted consumer health information and patient education resources recommended by the U.S. National Library of Medicine or by the Consumer and Patient Health Information Section of the Medical Library Association (CAPHIS). Medworm (http://www.medworm.com) allows search for medical blogs, forums, podcasts, or news. *Folksonomies,* i.e., collaboratively, user-generated free form metadata tags that categorize Web content, can be used to discover similar items.

Further, technologies are required to *process and analyze the content* of MSMD. For processing clinical documents, some technologies have been developed already (Kim 2009; Scherer et al. 2010). But, as we will see in Sect. 21.5, there are a couple of challenges to deal with when processing MSMD. These problems have not yet been solved with existing tools which are specialized in processing clinical documents.

Standard *technologies for clustering and classification* are required for filtering and grouping content according to various criteria. Some progress toward this direction has been made already. A classification approach to separate information from experiences in medical Weblogs is presented in (Rice 2001). Various methods for classifying lay requests to an Internet medical expert forum have also been tested (Kamel Boulos and Wheelert 2007).

In summary, enabling technologies are at the core of an MSMD environment and are essential for supporting learning and building MSMD applications.

21.3   Learning Within an MSMD Context

Viewed as resources embedded within a system of collaborating learners, MSMD can support the creation of communities, in which information exchange between the different types of learners takes place. According to the Oxford Dictionary, learning is simply defined as the process of "*acquiring knowledge*" (Oxford). In an *MSMD* environment, the knowledge acquired by the learners is related to the behaviors or preferences of individuals or groups. It is accomplished by synthesizing different types of information across the social media data space and may include machine or system learners. In an MSMD environment, the following learners are distinguished (Table 21.3).

When dealing with MSMD, these different groups of learners pursue various objectives. They are summarized in Table 21.4. For each group of learner, more details on what they can learn from MSMD are provided in the following discussion.

Table 21.3 Learner groups in the medical domain

	Learner groups	Description
Content producer and consumer	1. Researchers	Persons doing research in the medical domain (e.g., clinical research, epidemiological research, medical students)
	2. Health professionals	Persons working in the medical practice, for example, physicians, nurses
	3. Patients and relatives	Persons suffering from a medical condition or their relatives, persons interested in medical issues
	4. Health officials and policy makers	Institutions operating in the medical area, caring about public health
	5. Corporations	Enterprises operating in the medical domain, for example, companies of medical devices, health insurances, pharmaceutical companies
System	6. Software agents	Computer systems interacting with persons, providing information and knowledge, for example, recommender systems

Table 21.4 Learning objectives per learner

Group \ Goals	Acquire information	Share and disseminate information	Social intervention	Evaluate information
Researchers	x	x		x
Health professionals	x	x	x	x
Patients and relatives	x	x	x	
Health officials	x			x
Corporations	x	x		
Software agents	x			x

21.3.1 Content Producer and Consumers as Learner

Given the nature of medical social media tools, learners are required who produce content and also consume content. These roles are not only interchangeable, both user groups are considered to be learners within an MSMD environment.

Medical researchers can learn from MSMD in several ways. First, they can access the research results presented by other researchers in their blogs, etc. Second, research results are presented often as summaries in blogs of other author groups (e.g., in patient-written blogs) together with discussions, opinions, and experiences. Further, MSMD provides an opportunity to compare real-world experiences on a medication or treatment with those reported by clinical trials. From such analysis, medical researchers can learn about the real-world outcomes of medical treatments.

Health professionals such as physicians or nurses use MSMD for learning for professional purposes. Valuable information on new treatments is available as well as experiences about medical procedures. Clinical cases are presented and discussed online (e.g., http://radiopaedia.org/). In this way, physicians can learn from each other daily and in innovative ways. They can learn about clinical outcomes and best practices, but more importantly from patient experiences. In this way, health professionals gain an increased awareness of patients or family satisfaction. They can browse through relevant texts, look at automatically analyzed and visualized data (e.g., tag clouds) which facilitates the individual learning process. Social media is also useful with regards to acquiring information about local health care services that are recommended by a physician, in order to help to manage a patient's condition.

Patients, their relatives, or friends or even the general public have a personal interest in learning from MSMD. When people come home from the doctor, they often seek additional information regarding the long-term impact of a condition on their life. Using MSMD, patients can expand their disease-related knowledge, seek opinions, validate information received (Eysenbach 2008), or search for recent news on diagnostic and prognostic information (Friedman 2000; Hanif et al. 2009). Information on diseases and their treatments is not only provided by physicians or hospitals blogs. Also, experiences of persons in a similar situation might be relevant. The patient becomes, in this way, informed through other patients who are aware of the disease and its influencing factors. Thus, patients are empowered to make better decisions – such as selecting one of several suggested treatments. Further, learning from the experiences of others as well as writing about their own experiences, can help patients to deal with the psychological consequences of illnesses. Health information-seeking behavior of patients has already been studied extensively (Terry 2009). If patients become better informed as a result of accessing information from health sites and health communities, they may be better prepared and ask more critical questions when they meet their doctors. This clearly affects the doctor–patient relationship, moving power and initiative from the former to the latter (Van De Belt et al. 2010).

Another group of learners are *health organizations or political institutions* related to public health and medicine. MSMD can support them in obtaining information about the health status of a population (of a specific region or even globally). Medicine 2.0, social medical blogs, and other forms of user-generated content can be seen as an additional source for gathering epidemic intelligence. These sources are of significance, since those who experience as well as treat disease first hand, describe their experiences in blogs and other forms of social media (Rice 2006).

Corporations and companies including pharmaceutical companies, producers of medical devices, but also health insurances and hospitals can learn from medical social media content about the experiences of their customers, become aware of unsatisfied patients families, employees, and the public. In particular, pharmaceutical companies and producers of medical devices are normally not in direct contact with the patients. Through MSMD, a bridge is built and the experiences of customers are accessible. Learning from customer experiences includes becoming aware of complications, contraindications, or difficulties in handling a medical device. Companies can use this new knowledge in product development and improvement, adapting the marketing strategies, reacting to latest trends. They learn about customers and what they do online and can use this information for targeting products to existing customers. For example, PatientsLikeMe provides services to the pharmaceutical industry that permit them to "listen" to patients on their medications in a real-world setting while also allowing submission of adverse event data to the U.S. Food and Drug Administration.

Hospital ratings allow others (e.g., corporations, companies, but also patients and health professionals) to gain insight into the public (patient-) view and experiences. Grievances in institution can be identified and can then be used to react in an appropriate manner.

In summary, content producer and consumers can, from MSMD, get knowledge on:

• People's behavior, interests, views, and opinions
• Working and living experiences
• Diseases and treatments

21.3.2 System Learner

Besides persons or institutions, another type of learner in an MSMD environment is the system. A system can learn about personal preferences of individuals and groups or can learn data patterns and time-dependent trends. The knowledge acquired by human learners can be augmented with that obtained from the system learner (or vice versa) for mutual benefit and the exchange of information. Through MSMD, the system learner can facilitate matchmaking and foster the creation of a virtual community of like-minded participants. Different stakeholders can be united in ways that otherwise might not have achieved, without a great deal of time and effort. The advantage of the system learner is that it can automatically synthesize

Table 21.5 Types of knowledge acquired by the system learner

Information type	Description
Implicit user (group) profile	Information about the user (group) gathered indirectly from associations, affiliations, or behavior
Explicit user (group) profiles	Information about the user gathered directly based on explicit information such as from surveys, comments, ratings, or content produced by the user
Temporal pattern	Time series information describing variations over time such as the popularity of a topic, the commodity, or resource. This may also include sequential patterns with respect to time
Clustering of patterns	Underlying patterns, which define natural groupings of individuals, resources, keywords

vast amounts of data, on a large scale. There are several types of information a system can learn (see Table 21.5).

Using the different types of knowledge, the system learner is capable of adapting to the user or *personalizing* the information presented to help improve their information-seeking experience. This can be done by providing a *recommendation* for different resources. For example, a social networking system should only recommend connecting to people that share similar interests.

MSMD could be used by a system to learn more about the single user and to adapt to his interests automatically over time. In order to realize this, systems learn from people's search behavior, which is recorded and analyzed for recommendation and personalization purposes. Result presentations are adapted to the user interests based on what the systems have learned. In addition to directly monitoring the user behavior in terms of user clicks, queries, etc., social media data provides an additional source for learning more about the user and his preferences.

In the context of the system as learner, the concept of apomediaries in the information gathering process introduced by Eysenbach (Lagu et al. 2008) is relevant. Apomediaries are tools or peers standing by to guide the consumer to trustworthy information. Examples for apomediaries are technologies enabling machine processable dissemination of consumer ratings, collaborative filtering, or recommender systems. In this context, evaluation of the trustworthiness of information is crucial. In the medical domain, one mean is the HON code (see Sect. 21.5.1) that owners of Web sites can place on their page when their Web page fulfills certain requirements. Other criteria that could be used for deciding about the trustworthiness are the author of the provided content (e.g., health organizations might be more trustworthy sources than patients).

In summary, the system as a learner is a valuable asset in the dynamic information space of MSMD. Without such considerations, users can quickly become overloaded and unable to find relevant information in a timely manner.

21.4 Medical Community Applications

This section will provide an overview of visions of various applications that make use of medical social media data for learning. The applications are structured according to learner groups presented in Sect. 21.3.

21.4.1 Patients and Physicians as Users

There are numerous applications geared toward patient treatment (Brownstein et al. 2009; Denecke 2008; Eysenbach 2002; Himmel et al. 2009). Some possible applications are described in the following.

21.4.1.1 Decision Support for Diagnosis and Treatment

Given the abundance of information, it is crucial for doctors to be able to make appropriate decisions for treatment and drug prescription. A major portion of the relevant information is recorded as narrative text, for example, in clinical observations, radiology reports, operative notes, or in discharge summaries, and is normally stored in hospital information systems (HIS). In contrast, the latest research results and experiences gained by physicians from their treatments are accessible in the medical Web. A decision support system could integrate information relevant for the treatment of a current "case" from the HIS and from online sources, identify relevant literature and information on best practices from MSMD. The collected information could be presented to a physician in a structured way, separating research results from experiences.

21.4.1.2 Retrieval of Medical Information

The content provided in the medical Web is highly diverse and the information seekers (content consumers) are unaware of most information that is relevant to their interests. A diversity-aware search engine could provide a more sophisticated overview on the various aspects of a query. It could cluster relevant Web content according to information related to diseases or treatments, or even separate informative from opinionated content (i.e., experiences). To realize this new type of domain-specific search, text analysis and other mechanisms are needed to extract relevant content from content sources and to identify groups of concepts. Similarly, users could be alerted automatically with relevant information. For example, a social networking system could be exploited for alerting patients to new, off-label uses of existing approved drugs, and for identifying potentially new safety issues (Brownstein et al. 2009).

21.4.1.3 Patient–Doctor Communication

Another MSMD application could support the communication between patient and physicians in an indirect way (Denecke 2008). If patients are storing their health data in an online personal health record, this data could also be linked to the patient blog or to an online patient diary. In this way, the doctor would know more about the patient's experiences with an affliction and the treatments undergo. The physician could get a more complete overview on the physical and mental state of the patient. To avoid extra work for the physician through reading long patient stories, the system should summarize and prepare the blog data in an easily understandable way and could extract only those aspects that are of interest for the treatment. Such a system could also allow the physician to offer additional resources to the patient such as podcasts or links to Web pages with related content.

21.4.2 Health Officials as Users

21.4.2.1 Outbreak Detection

The early detection of disease outbreaks is important to prevent spread of diseases. In addition to data from hospitals and laboratories, unofficial sources such as news articles or social media data (e.g., blogs, forums) have become an important source for health care officials to monitor. An outbreak detection system could identify and collect relevant information from MSMD. This includes monitoring the frequencies of symptoms that are mentioned. This information could then be analyzed using text analysis technologies. In this way, information on health events could be extracted, validated, and linked to relevant official data (e.g., laboratory data). Finally, alerts could be generated and sent to users in health organizations.

21.4.3 Corporations as Users

21.4.3.1 Collecting Competitive Data

People write about their experiences with medical devices and drugs in customer reviews, blogs, and forums. In order to obtain an overview of customer satisfaction (i.e., problems, experiences, or opinions), a system could monitor relevant Web sources. It could identify the opinions and link them to a product or service. As a result, an overview of customer satisfaction would be presented in a structured way. Trends in opinions could be identified and statistics on described problems with a product or service could be created.

21.4.4 Medical Researchers as Users

21.4.4.1 Nontraditional Research

By collecting and analyzing MSMD, a system could gain information to establish clinical trials or to recruit patients for clinical trials (Eysenbach 2002). In such scenario, patient data as provided in patient social networks, or other sources of MSMD, need to be integrated, analyzed, and the results need to be interpreted.

21.5 Challenges and Implications to Technology Development

In the previous sections, learning from MSMD has been highlighted from various perspectives: Who is the learner? What can be learned and which applications might be possible? Using MSMD in the envisioned applications outlined in Sect. 21.4

is still challenging, since this data places several demands on the technologies with respect to appropriate analysis and interpretation. In this section, an overview on these challenges is given together with implications for technology development. The challenges can be classified into three groups: social challenges, media-specific challenges, and systemic challenges.

21.5.1 Social Challenges

MSMD content highly depends on the willingness of people to share their health data, experiences, and opinions. There is a trade-off between personal transparency and privacy. The current size of patient social networks shows that some people are willing to share. Those who contribute believe that they have more to gain when others know more about their current health state. Clearly, others want to keep their privacy and hesitate to share their data with others. It is still unclear what criteria determine their willingness to share information and what impact this limitation presents.

Further, people might be rather willing to share general information on a concrete disease or possible treatments, but resist on personal experiences In applications such as those sketched in Sect. 21.4, we must be aware that the information and knowledge acquired from MSMD might be incomplete, highly subjective, and might not even reflect all relevant points of view.

Another challenge to deal with is spam and so-called splogs (spam blogs). Sources of MSMD are used to distribute advertisements, and are subject to spam attacks. This includes irrelevant content, i.e., content unrelated to medicine or content from sources that intend to gain in influence or attention (e.g., pharmaceutical companies that advertise about their products with masses of postings). Further, an important issue is the trustworthiness and quality of the data of health information in the Internet. Some people might post incorrect data in their blog. Although some researchers have applied codes of conduct to monitor the quality of health Web sites (Narismatsu 2008), there are still no methods available for automatically assessing the trustworthiness of information provided. Therefore, applications dealing with MSMD need to account for: reporting errors, bias, misinformation, and the proper interpretation of unstructured information (Brownstein et al. 2009).

However, warnings have also been raised, concerning primarily the quality of the information available on the Internet. These concerns have led to concerted efforts to assess the quality of e-health information and to create quality standards for Internet health sites (e.g., HON code, http://www.healthonnet.org, (Stewart et al. 2009)).

21.5.2 Media-Specific Challenges

Given the nature of social media data, it is often difficult to automatically process such content due to the peculiarities inherent in human language text, or limitations of processing audio–visual content. These challenges will be summarized and the demands they make on enabling technologies that deal with medical social media data will be highlighted in this section.

21.5.2.1 Natural Language Text

Applications that exploit MSMD clearly need technologies that allow for dealing with and analyze the unstructured content of MSMD. Thus, natural language is challenging. The language used in MSMD is highly diverse. Authors may express information in different languages; use medical sublanguage. In addition, consumer health terminology, slang, and common language is also used. Applications, therefore, require methods and terminological resources that support the identification of medical and medical-related terms and expressions (e.g., description of symptoms). In the medical domain, ontologies, controlled vocabularies, and thesauri have been created over a long period of time. However, even the scholarly terminologies, which are controlled by various medical thesauri, cannot easily represent the narrative of bloggers (patients) or authors of MSMD content (Hillan 2003). Another vocabulary is required as well as possibilities to map to existing medical terminologies (e.g., UMLS or SNOMED CT) to connect research work and clinical results with nonprofessional experiences.

There are many content providers with different styles and they often write topic drifting prose. From the linguistic point of view, medical Weblogs and other MSMD usually consist of syntactically correct sentences, but can contain verbless clauses (e.g., the phrase *"Paperwork, paperwork, and paperwork"*) or sentences without subject (like in the phrase *Take out the garbage*). In addition, medical abbreviations (e.g., *CLL (chronic lymphocytic leukemia)*), enumerations and citations of conversations; as well as common speech, medical terms, and opinion-related words are frequently used in medical blog posts. This increases the complexity for text analysis tools to process MSMD.

Opinions-related words (e.g., *terribly painful*) can be found throughout MSMD, in particular in blog and forum postings, as well as in reviews. Social media data is typically informal and contains an interspersing of subjective and factual information. Depending on the application, the informative and affective information needs to be separated from each other. Also required is filtering for the huge number of noisy, irrelevant, hypothetical, or opinionated sentences – which all may be presented within the text as facts. Due to all these peculiarities, a potential analysis tool has to deal with medical and affective content appropriately, and it has to be robust regarding language and syntax errors.

Redundancy is another characteristic in MSMD. Given the large amount of information available, information on the same event might be reported from various sources. Therefore, for some applications, it is crucial to aggregate information on the same event and to cluster events.

21.5.2.2   Audio Data and the Spoken Web

Even though audio data and the spoken medical Web might be a valuable source of information, this data needs, at first, to be transformed into a computer-processable format. Creating transcriptions automatically from audio data that has been produced by nonspecialists (layman) is challenging. There might be background noise, or unclear voices that complicate the automatic speech recognition. Further, existing speech recognition tools need to be trained on both: common language and clinical terminology, and consumer health vocabulary. Once the audio data has been transcribed, the challenges of processing unstructured, noisy text need to be addressed.

21.5.2.3   Video Data

Video data dealing with medical issues is also challenging. First, when searching for relevant videos, applications might need additional textual information associated with the video for the search algorithms, but this textual content is hidden in the video. Although it is possible to produce transcripts for the audio portion of a video, depending on the original quality, the transcripts may contain numerous errors. Videos produced by layman as found in YouTube, for example, are much noisier. Second, the language used can be slang, dialect, accent, or common language, all of which make speech recognition challenging. Further, transcription technology is often specialized to a specific domain. As for audio data dealing with medicine, the underlying vocabulary of the transcription technology needs to be extended with consumer health vocabulary and common language on medical and health issues. While producing transcripts, the visual information gets lost which could make (automatic) content analysis more difficult.

21.5.3   Systemic Challenges

From a systemic point of view, four groups of challenges can be identified: Filtering, open social networking, cross-system personalization, and social media search.

21.5.3.1   Filtering

There is an ever-increasing volume of MSMD and user-generated content. So, the methods for processing MSMD have to be scalable and more importantly, capable of filtering irrelevant information. Only a small subset of the content available is relevant for the single applications. For example, for outbreak detection, patient experiences on living with asthma are irrelevant. Beyond relevance filtering, there is a need to filter, for example, historical information from actual information (e.g., swine flu in 1918 vs. swine flu in 2005) or distinguish reports of actual events (e.g., an influenza outbreak) from reports on hypothetical discussions. Clustering and classification methods need to be applied to this data for filtering purposes.

21.5.3.2 Open Social Networking

The social networking phenomena have attracted many millions of users, and have resulted in a proliferation of sites. These sites intentionally seek to distinguish themselves by a set of community practices (social activities) and what they offer members. However, given the sheer number, it is often the case that there is redundancy or overlap with respect to the type of media, resources, or topics to which the sites are devoted. Although overlap exists, it is untapped to the benefit of those who actually constitute the social networking ecosystem. The result is a social networking divide. The momentum is swinging in favor of truly open social networking (OSN) – where data can be ported across various sites – not only limited to classical social networks (e.g., between Google Health and PatientsLikeMe). These sites seek to establish de-facto standards, to handle issues related to the portability and interoperability of data, personal identities, as well as social graphs. Recent advances toward a more open social networking paradigm are also prevalent in the Semantic Web community and in cross-folksonomy platforms where the user's multiple identities are consolidated.

21.5.3.3 Cross-System Personalization

User profiles and knowledge on user behavior in search or system use is normally linked to one concrete tool (social networking site, search engine, etc.). In reality, people interact with various social media tools. Health data uploaded to a social network site or even to a personal health record could be used to personalize search. For such applications, cross-system personalization is crucial. In recommender systems, cross-system personalization is a body of work, which enables personal information across different systems to be shared (Stewart et al. 2010). MSMD applications could also benefit from such cross-system personalization techniques to improve the user's experience and provide enhanced access to medical information.

21.5.3.4 Social Media Search

Finding relevant content in MSMD is crucial for all the applications introduced in Sect. 21.4. For example, how can patients find the hospital with the largest experience in treating a specific disease? In order to identify relevant content, tags have been proven a successful mean to label unstructured data (Kim and Chung 2007). Capitalizing on the success of user-defined tags – *medical tagging* systems could be employed. It is an open question how existing clinical vocabularies can be used for tagging purposes and how *medical tags* help users finding the information of interest. Retrieval systems need to be extended to allow for using MSMD to make recommendation on treatment possibilities, hospitals, or physicians. The required information is out there, in the medical Web. But, there is still much work to be done, in order to automatically identify such information in MSMD.

In summary, to address the challenges given by the nature of MSMD, the following technologies are necessary:

- Various filtering mechanisms (relevance, importance, content...)
- Robust text analysis technologies that can deal with the language peculiarities and specific language
- Methods for analyzing and processing video and audio content
- More sophisticated personalization technologies
- Facilities to connect knowledge and information from various social media tools

21.6 Conclusions

Learning from medical social media data is a complex field and can involve diverse types of content and learners, such as patients and physicians, corporations and health officials. MSMD has a real-world impact on improving the quality of life and as a tool for:

- Helping medical corporations to improve their products and services
- Empowering patients and providing opportunity for them to improve their physical and psychological condition
- Catalyzing and ultimately changing the pace and quality of evidence-based medicine

Many challenges still need to be addressed in order to realize applications that exploit medical social media data. Future developments need to consider these aspects, providing technologies that can cope with the linguistic and systemic peculiarities of this data. There is also a need to test the applicability of existing technologies to deal with MSMD and – where necessary – to adapt the methods to deal with the peculiarities of MSMD. Even though there are still lots of open challenges in dealing and processing medical social media data in real-world applications, the benefit for stakeholders in the medical area is compelling.

References

Allison, M.: Can web 2.0 reboot clinical trials? Nat. Biotechnol. **27**(10), 895–902 (2009)

Brownstein, C.A., Brownstein, J.S., Williams III, D.S., Wicks, P., Heywood, J.A.: The power of social networking in medicine. Nat. Biotechnol. **27**(10), 888–890 (2009)

Denecke, K.: Accessing medical experiences and information. European Conference on Artificial Intelligence, Workshop on Mining Social Data (2008)

Denecke, K.: Semantic structuring of and information extraction from medical documents using the UMLS. Method Inf. Med. **47**(5), 425–434 (2008)

Denecke, K., Nejdl, W.: How valuable is medical social media data? Content analysis of the medical web. J. Inf. Sci. **179**, 1870–1880 (2009)

Eysenbach, G.: Infodemiology: the epidemiology of (mis)information. Am. J. Med. **113**, 763–765 (2002)

Eysenbach, G.: Medicine 2.0: social networking, collaboration, participation, apomediation, and openness. J. Med. Internet Res. **10**(3), e22 (2008)

Friedman, C.: A broad-coverage natural language processing system. AMIA Annu Symp (2000)

Hanif, F., Read, J.C., Goodacre, J.A., Chaudhry, A., Gibbs, P.: The role of quality tools in assessing reliability of the internet for health information. Inform. Health Soc. Care **34**(4), 231–243 (2009)

Hardey, M.: Public health and web 2.0. J. R. Soc. Promot. Health **128**(4), 181–189 (2008)

Hillan, J.: Physician use of patient-centred weblogs and online journals. Clin. Med. Res. **1**(4), 333–335 (2003)

Himmel, W., Reincke, U., Michelmann, H.W.: Text mining and natural language processing approaches for automatic categorization of lay requests to web-based expert forums. J. Med. Internet Res. **11**(3), e25 (2009)

Kamel Boulos, M.N., Wheelert, S.: The emerging web 2.0 social software: an enabling suite of sociable technologies in health and health care education. Health Inf. Libr. J. **24**, 2–23 (2007)

Kim, S.: Content analysis of cancer blog posts. J. Med. Libr. Assoc. **97**(4), 260–266 (2009)

Kim, S., Chung, D.S.: Characteristics of cancer blog users. J. Med. Libr. Assoc. **95**(4), 445–450 (2007)

Kovic, I., Lulic, I., Brumini, G.: Examining the medical blogosphere: an online survey of medical bloggers. J. Med. Internet Res. **10**(3), e28 (2008)

Lagu, T., Kaufman, E.J., Asch, D.A., Armstrong, K.: Content of weblogs written by health professionals. J. Gen. Intern. Med. **23**(10), 1642–1646 (2008)

Lupiáñez-Villanueva, F., Mayer, M.A., Torrent, J.: Opportunities and challenges of web 2.0 within the health care systems: an empirical exploration. Inf. Health Soc. Care. **34**(3), 117–126 (2009)

Mehta, B., Hofmann, T.: Cross system personalization and collaborative filtering by learning manifold alignments. In: KI 2006: Advances in Artificial Intelligence, pp. 244–259. Springer, Berlin (2007)

Narismatsu, H.: Detailed analysis of visitors to cancer-related web sites. J. Clin. Oncol. **26**(25), 4219–4223 (2008)

Randeree, E.: Exploring technology impacts of healthcare 2.0 initiatives. Telemed. J. E. Health **15**(3), 255–260 (2009)

Rice, R.E.: The internet and health communication: a framework of experiences. In: Rice, R.E., Katz, J.E. (eds.) The Internet and Health Communication: Expectations and Experiences, pp. 5–46. Sage, Thousand Oaks (2001)

Rice, R.E.: Influences, usage, and outcomes of internet health information searching: multivariate results from the pew surveys. Int. J. Med. Inform. **75**(1), 8–28 (2006)

Scherer, M., Zitterbart, S., Mildenstein, K., Himmelm, W.: What questions do headache patients pose in the internet? Content analysis of an internet expert forum. Gesundheitswesen **72**(5), 28–32 (2010)

Stewart, A., Denecke, K.: Can ProMED-mail bootstrap blogs? automatic labelling of victim-reporting sentences. In: First International Workshop on Web Science and Information Exchange in the Medical Web, MedEx 2010, Raleigh (2010)

Stewart, A., Diaz-Aviles, E., Nejdl, W., Marinho, L. B., Nanopoulos, A., Schmidt-Thieme, L.: Cross-tagging for personalized open social networking. In: HT '09: 20th ACM Conference on Hypertext and Hypermedia, pp. 271–278. Torino (2009)

Terry, M.: Twittering healthcare: social media and medicine. Telemed. J. E. Health **15**(6), 507–510 (2009)

Van De Belt, T.H., Engelen, L.J., Berben, S.A.A., Schoonhoven, L.: Definition of health 2.0 and medicine 2.0: a systematic review. J. Med. Internet Res. **12**(2), e18 (2010)

Chapter 22
Sampling the Sea: Using Social Media for an Online Ocean Sustainability Curriculum

Ronald E. Rice, Julie A. Robinson, and Bruce Caron

Abstract The Sampling the Sea Project is a pilot online resource for teachers and students in grades 9–12, designed to improve learning beyond traditionally targeted cognitive dimensions such as *knowledge*, to include affective dimensions of learning such as *attitudes*, *skills*, *intention*, and *efficacy*, outcomes of sea food sustainability science, by means of specially designed curricula and active social media participation, with a multisource evaluation component. The chapter provides overviews of the need for ocean sustainability curricula, the Sampling the Sea Project, pedagogic foundations, the ocean science sustainability curriculum, the infrastructure/platform, the justification for and nature of social media activities within the curriculum, the evaluation approach, and summary results.

22.1 The Need for Engaging and Participative Ocean Sustainability Curricula

The purpose of this chapter is to summarize how an online ocean sustainability curriculum can be developed within a pedagogical framework and in accord with ocean science education standards, integrated into an online secure K-12 platform

R.E. Rice (✉)
Department of Communication, University of California, Santa Barbara, CA 90106-4020, USA
e-mail: rrice@comm.ucsb.edu

J.A. Robinson
Bren School of Environmental Science & Management, University of California, Santa Barbara, CA 90106-5131, USA
e-mail: jrobinson@bren.ucsb.edu

B. Caron
New Media Research Institute, Santa Barbara, CA 93105, USA
e-mail: bruce@nmri.org

B. White et al. (eds.), *Social Media Tools and Platforms in Learning Environments*,
DOI 10.1007/978-3-642-20392-3_22, © Springer-Verlag Berlin Heidelberg 2011

employing social media, and evaluated for both outcomes and process, using multiple data sources, as a model approach for similar projects.

The worldwide collapse of fisheries and subsequent impact on ocean health has reached crisis proportions (Halpern et al. 2008). One fifth of the protein humans consume comes from the sea. The global seafood catch has dramatically declined for two decades while human populations grow, commercial fishing extends farther into the oceans, and pollutants and misuse damage ocean ecologies. Many marine species are now threatened or endangered. It has been estimated that 90% of the world's large predatory fishes (tuna, swordfish, shark, and cod) have been removed from the ocean (Myers and Worm 2003). The pending global crisis dwarfs other food issues, yet oceans garner little attention. Most people are too removed from the sea in their daily lives to understand that crises exist; hence, the demand for sustainable solutions is limited. Thus, it is vital to engage the next generation of consumers in a global dialogue about the way seafood is harvested and consumed so as to create a cultural consensus to address this problem (Cava et al. 2005).

Ocean literacy curriculum units, lessons, and activities centered in issue-based learning can be used to increase opportunities to engage students in active and authentic ocean science inquiry (Wilmes and Howarth 2009). These opportunities can now be enhanced through the use of online social media in support of participatory learning in, across, and outside of classrooms. Students can share data, stories, and media while they learn from other students and their own content creation. This process also engages the same social media skills they are learning and developing outside of the classroom. Empirical research is needed to gather data and test theoretical predictions to support the design and integration of best practices for use of social media tools in education pedagogies.

This chapter briefly summarizes the Sampling the Sea project—its objectives, theoretical foundations, curriculum and activities, platform and social media, participants, and outcome and process evaluation plan, and summary results.

22.2 The Sampling the Sea Project

22.2.1 Overview

Sampling the Sea (StS) is a pilot project of Digital Ocean, an ocean science education and social networking infrastructure project designed to create international, multigenerational communities working for ocean conservation, developing in interdisciplinary collaboration among the Carsey-Wolf Center, the Bren School for Environmental Science and Management, the Marine Science Institute, the New Media Research Institute, the Department of Communication, and the Department of Film and Media Studies, all at the University of California, Santa Barbara (see http://www.carseywolf.ucsb.edu/emi/sampling-sea). This chapter reports on the first year, a 1-year pilot project including 10 months of development and 2 months of test usage. Ongoing development, usage, and evaluation will depend on funding.

StS determined that other efforts to inform the public about sustainable fisheries were available online (more than 120 Facebook groups on this topic in July 2010) and through informal education venues (Seafood Watch, Marine Stewardship Council, Seafood Choices Alliance), and through a small number of restaurants aligned with the philosophy of the sustainable food movement. But few efforts were focused in the schools. Furthermore, as the consumption of seafood is not limited to coastal communities, this topic could be used in schools nationwide.

StS uses collaborative digital technologies to create a dynamic social learning environment that introduces middle and high school students in classes in the USA and beyond using a secure online environment (ePals) to collect and share scientific data, media, and stories about human impacts on the ocean in ways that are fun, intellectually challenging, and rooted in peer interaction. The general goals of the long-term StS project are that student participants from around the world learn about seafood sustainability through curriculum unit lessons and activities, collect and share data about seafood choices in their communities, learn how these choices affect the health of the world's ocean, and discuss and create (within their classes and across classes) materials about the curriculum topics through social media.

22.2.2 Pedagogic Perspectives

From the early development stages, the StS project was guided by a model that elaborated participation through social media as a process for improved ocean literacy. Developing the curriculum and evaluation of learning required integrating multiple theories of learning (*constructivism, cooperative learning, connectivism, transformative learning, community of inquiry*, and the *unified theory of online learning*); as well as an environmental education framework (NAAEE 2004) and the Ocean Literacy Principles (http://www.coexploration. org/oceanliteracy/documents/OceanLitChart.pdf). The goal of the developers was to provide a curriculum that met U.S. National Science Education Standards (NSES) for teaching, and targeted cognitive dimensions of learning such *knowledge*, as well as *affective* dimensions such as *attitudes, skills, intention*, and *efficacy*; important but often overlooked aspects of environmental science learning (McBeth et al. 2008; NAAEE 2004; NSTA Position Statement: Environmental Education 2010; Ramsey and Hungerford 2002). This section briefly defines and describes how these theoretical frameworks and perspectives were integrated into the project.

Teaching skills and issue-based science has been endorsed as a best practice by the National Council of Teachers of Mathematics, the American Association for the

Advancement of Science, and the National Council for the Social Studies (Ivers and Barren 2002). Skill-based science learning is grounded in *constructivism* which relates the process of active learning through the construction of knowledge, weighing new information against previous understandings, thinking about and working through discrepancies (individually and with others), and coming to new understandings (ASCD 1992). With a focus on sustainable seafood as context for an issue-based approach for teaching ocean science, StS was able to incorporate constructivist theory into the curricula design.

One of the central goals of StS was to provide a platform for students to learn through the *cooperative* sharing of knowledge (seafood science and stories). A *cooperative learning group* is defined by five characteristics: positive interdependence, individual accountability, face-to-face promotive interaction, social skills, and group processing (Ivers and Barren 2002; Johnson and Johnson 1999). In StS, group participation through curriculum activities was emphasized to foster enhanced individual and group-level learning opportunities.

Connectivism posits that learning (defined as actionable knowledge) is not entirely under the control of the student and can occur under shifting conditions where new information is continually being acquired (Siemens 2005). Learners need to draw distinctions between important and unimportant information, and recognize when new information alters the landscape. Erickson et al. (2010) argue that *transformative learning* (changes in perspectives) about sustainability requires understanding of the interrelationships of environment, economic, and social factors, at individual and societal levels. Students participating in the StS pilot project were exposed to a blended curriculum of "in-seat," extracurricular, and online experiences. Further, the complexity and connectivity of seafood sustainability issues (consumerism, methods of harvest, and trophic level feedback, e.g.) are linked intrinsically through connectivist and transformative perspectives.

A final need for StS was to integrate traditional theories of learning with emerging and evolving theories that describe learning interactions that occur online. A *community of inquiry* is one theoretical framework developed for describing how online learning technology is used to create online learning communities and networks (Benbunan-Fich et al. 2005; Garrison et al. 2000). Anderson's (2008) *Unified Theory of Online Learning* claims that quality online learning, like all learning, should be knowledge-, community-, assessment-, and learner-centered, and include feedback, assessment, and reflection. Anderson's model of e-Learning illustrates a relationship between human actors as teachers and learners, their interactions with each other, and with content and proposes that the major modes of online learning that should always be considered are collaborative, community-of-inquiry, and community-of-learning models.

These theories and frameworks provided the structure and support for the StS curriculum development, and a foundation for the evaluation.

22.2.3 Ocean Literacy: Sustainability Through Environmental Education

Educators and policy makers have proposed that tackling the problem of rapidly declining ocean health requires a massive effort at developing an "ocean literate society"—in other words, broader awareness, knowledge, and concern for the ocean's influence on human health and our influence on the ocean among the world's citizenry ("America's living oceans: Charting a course for sea change," 2003; U.S. Commission on Ocean Policy 2004; Cava et al. 2005; Day 2003).

One path to achieving this goal is through the development and integration of an ocean-oriented approach to teaching science in K-12 education. Ocean literacy integrates research and perspectives from constructivist, connectivist, and environmental education frameworks, and targets both cognitive and affective dimensions of learning (e.g., attitudes and skills). Both social media and ocean literacy can be linked *theoretically* to cognitive and affective learning; both are in need, however, of *evaluation research* to determine whether, and under what conditions, they can or should be integrated into the formal science curriculum.

Developing a curriculum for high school students—near-future decision makers—about the relationship between sustainable seafood issues and ocean health contributes toward building a foundation for the improved stewardship of these resources. Until recently however, ocean science curricula have been largely ignored in K-12 classrooms. In the USA, this problem began to be addressed in 2004, when a consortium of government and nongovernmental agencies (NGOs) including the National Geographic Society and National Oceanographic and Atmospheric Administration, and some 100 members of the ocean sciences and education communities, crafted the ocean literacy framework. Comprised of seven essential principles and a subset of fundamental concepts, these guidelines support an ocean-centered approach to teaching science standards (Cava et al. 2005).

An early goal of StS's lead curriculum developer was to integrate the ocean literacy principles (based on an environmental education framework) into the StS curriculum. One of the key distinctions between environmental education (EE) and formal science education is that EE attempts to target other domains of learning in addition to knowledge (Pooley and O'Connor 2000; Stapp et al. 1969). These objectives are often referred to as affect outcomes (attitudes, feelings, sensitivity), skill outcomes (issue analysis and skill building), intention outcomes (willingness to act), and behavior (participation) (Final Report 1979; Hungerford and Volk 1990; McBeth et al. 2008; Ramsey and Hungerford 2002; Simmons et al. 2004).

Therefore, from an evaluation standpoint, integrating traditional and online theories of learning, the ocean literacy principles, EE, and sustainable seafood science, supported the twin goals of providing a curriculum that targeted cognitive *and* affective learning, and a coherent model for assessing student's short-term ocean literacy learning outcomes. An organizational matrix linking StS units and activities with their associated EE domains, Ocean Literacy Principles, and NSES standards was created as a reference for the development of the before–after teacher and student survey instruments.

22.2.4 StS Curriculum

Through a series of informal workshops and discussions with educators held at the outset of the project, it became apparent that in order to make the Sampling the Sea program accessible to, and adopted by, science educators in the formal classroom, the curriculum would need to support several key but disparate needs. Three of these were chosen as most important. First, the curriculum must be oriented toward the National Science Education Standards (in the U.S., educators teaching at primary and secondary schools are required to teach to a set of national and state science standards and administer standardized statewide tests). Second, the curriculum would need to be designed with enough flexibility to allow use by students under a variety of technology configurations (and barriers such as limited computer access). And third, the project must be designed and presented in such a way that student and teacher "downtime" in learning and navigating the online interface is minimized, with the aim of maximizing participatory learning duration and outcomes.

An expert panel of ocean science educators developed five curriculum units, each with 3–5 activities, involving classroom content, media, and projects, out-of-classroom experiences, and online social media involvement. For the teachers, the activities include an overview, key concepts, learning objectives, time required, social media opportunity, materials required, student instructions, and additional print and online resources (see http://www.stsproject.org/).

1. *What's in the water?* Students play a game modeling the life cycle and migration patterns of the Pacific salmon. Students compare and contrast ocean life in the epipelagic zone of the ocean. Students share information gathered as part of an in-class newsletter project with students partnered through ePals. They critique each other's work and cocreate a collaborative blog on ocean life. Students participate in an online simulation following the migration of a young salmon to the ocean. They use online discussion forums and the ePals media gallery to compare and share results with students in other classrooms.
2. *Ocean ecology.* Students are introduced to the concepts of ocean ecology through a series of interactive games and activities. Students share what they know about ecosystems with others by posting and describing photos of local ecosystems and/or components of their local ecosystems on a shared gallery space within ePals.
3. *Who's fishing?* Students compare and contrast the techniques and challenges of fishing via several labs and activities. Students collect and graph data. Students analyze maps of worldwide fish imports and exports and discuss the impacts of the global fish trade. After learning about the pros and cons of various types of fishing, students use an online forum to discuss ways to make sustainability a marketable feature of seafood products.

4. *Fisheries management.* Students engage in a mock fishing derby that simultaneously explores the history of the New England Cod fishery and illustrates the tragedy of the commons. Students use Google Earth to examine fisheries data from the Sea Around Us Project and the US National Marine Fisheries. Students read and share articles and case studies explaining fisheries management strategies. Students use the Internet to visit marine protected areas around the world.

5. *Sustainable seas.* Students formulate a research plan to study local seafood consumption and collect fish and seafood market observations to test their hypotheses. Within the ePals environment, students share data, observations, and results along with images, video, and/or text with their class and the Sampling the Sea community. Students design and create educational posters and bumper stickers to share, and comment on, and revise.

22.2.5 The StS Platform

One of the perceived risks for social media sharing inside the classroom is the potential for inappropriate content sharing, such as cyberbullying or "sexting." One response to this risk is to allow for moderated interactions within a closed network. Social networking platforms such as Ning and widely used course management systems such as Blackboard and Moodle now provide a range of moderation tools for content, from moderation queues for pre-posted content, to flags for inappropriate content. A classroom-specific social network platform, ePals (http://epals.com), has made teacher moderation the hallmark of its service. StS chose to partner with ePals as its initial social network platform. The ePals™ platform is built on an enterprise-level instance of the Telligent Community (http://telligent.com/) software platform. However, the StS curriculum and other tools are not hosted directly within ePals, so other platforms are possible in the future. ePals™ offered StS an early version of its LearningSpace™ service, which is a project-based learning environment designed for school districts. The chief advantages of the LearningSpace™ service, beyond its teacher moderation capabilities, are a combination of social media tools: wikis, forums, and image and video uploading/linking and commenting. In its early stage development and the pilot StS implementation, the LearningSpace™ suffered from some usability and other user interface issues, which will be improved in future versions.

The central activity of collecting fish names from local suppliers is supported by an online Data Collection Tool built in Adobe Flash™. The DCT was designed to help the student move from the common name of the seafood to its scientific name. This step was important for the tool to programmatically interface with other databases (FishBase and Seafood Watch). The DCT also creates a custom data visualization layer in Google Earth. The tool is connected programmatically to the uBio database of scientific names, the FishBase species database, and to the Monterey Bay Aquarium's Seafood Watch database. The uBio database maps species (and subspecies) names onto common names in dozens of languages. This was very useful for international schools.

22.2.6   Social Media

A basic proposition of Sampling the Sea is that the use of social media and social networking within the curriculum should allow students to bring their outside-of-school media sharing expertise and interests into the classroom (Rheingold 2008) and enhance opportunities for peer-to-peer, or cooperative learning. StS embeds U.S. National Science Education Standards and essential ocean literacy principles within a philosophy and networked platform of asynchronous learning, social media, convergence, and participation.

Asynchronous learning networks (Anderson 2008; Hiltz and Goldman 2005) and collaborative media, such as online social media (Jenkins 2006; Kaplan and Haenlein 2010; Shirky 2009), can complement *conveyance* pedagogies (lectures) with *convergence* approaches (mutual construction of knowledge) (Hiltz and Goldman 2005; Siemens 2005). (2006, p. 4) propose that social media can offer students possibilities to integrate important new skills: distributed cognition, collective intelligence, transmedia navigation, and even play, as several examples.

The curriculum units listed in the Ocean Sustainability section provide suggestions, tools, and resources for integrating social media as ways of discussing, sharing, and creating experiences related to ocean sustainability. For example (one activity from each unit):

- 1B Students within their class engage in online conversations using the class discussion list about the pros and cons of salmon fishing.
- 2B Students photograph a meal eaten in a typical day, upload it to the ePals LearningSpace, and research the origin(s) of one component of another student's meal. Using the online discussion forums, they discuss the process of finding out from where a food item comes.
- 3C Students obtain a dozen digital photos tell a "fishing story" from somewhere in the world, and then create a short music video showing how people catch fish in different parts of the world.
- 4B Students search online for seafood choices available in local restaurants. They place the results of their search into a group-edited Web page (wiki).
- 5A Students share fish consumption data (common and scientific names, origin of catch, cost per unit, sustainability rating), photos/videos of fish, fishing, and fish markets, stories of fish as a family food choice, and of fishing as a hobby or occupation. Student's comment on other students offerings. The fish data upload form available in StS is connected to online resources about sustainability (Monterey Bay Aquarium's Seafood Watch.org) and fish species information (Fishbase.org). The uploaded data can be used to create sharable research objects in the form of Google Earth layers and spreadsheets.

22.2.7 Evaluation Plan

As with other new technologies, the use of social media in the classroom requires careful studies to weigh its pedagogical benefits and associated risks. The StS project is designed to contribute to this effort through an integrated evaluation process. Outcome and process evaluation data were integrated from ePals and StS teacher and student usage data aggregated at the classroom and curriculum levels, and across relevant time periods; teacher and student surveys at the beginning and end of the StS pilot; teacher e-mails and responses to open-ended survey questions; insights from the curriculum developers; and experiences from all the project members. The teachers were self-selected, volunteering to participate in the project as a way to obtain additional ocean science curriculum knowledge and to continue using the online ePals system. Participation in the surveys by both teachers and students was anonymous (though linked across surveys and usage), voluntary, and in accordance with University and high school human subjects procedures.

The sets of survey questions for teachers, and for students, were developed after extensive review of other ocean literacy project evaluation efforts. This pilot study obtained selected ePals and StS usage measures, ranging from user logins, media uploads, forum activity, posts and comments per blog, conversations, and wiki activity, as ePals provided StS full access to the underlying code and database for its LearningSpace™ instance. Thus, it was possible to programmatically integrate user login and activities usage data with pre- and post-survey responses (through SurveyMonkey) from both teachers and students. This integrated approach allowed analysis at the teacher, student, class, curriculum, and overall levels of analysis.

The general outcomes of interest at the student level of analysis were (a) the short-term influences (from classes, other students, and teachers) on student seafood sustainability learning outcomes, as (b) moderated by participatory learning (student and teacher use of social media as part of their course sustainability activities). For example, different classes have different levels of accessibility to computers and networking, students have different levels of social media expertise, and teachers have different levels of ocean science and online classroom training.

As derived from the pedagogical perspectives, the measured effects included: *Knowledge* (change in student knowledge of seafood sustainability concepts), *Affect* (change in student attitudes, sensitivity, and feelings about seafood sustainability concepts), *Skills* (change in student cognitive skills related to analysis about seafood sustainability concepts), *Intention* (change in student verbal commitment and willingness to act on sustainable seafood issues), and *Efficacy* or locus of control (perceived ability to perform the intentions and change attitudes and behaviors about seafood sustainability), as well as more general assessments of the StS system and project.

The project included the teacher level of analysis, including outcomes such as *Affect* toward seafood sustainability, and of the overall validity of providing social media as course tools in the formal classroom (considering barriers to use such as time, technology, and/or access, and perceived value and acceptance by educators and administrators as an effective learning tool) and general assessments of the StS system and project.

Finally, formative and process evaluations were built in, to use initial results to revise the system and content, and to understand the challenges and opportunities of the social, pedagogical, technical, management, resource, and analysis aspects for future projects.

22.2.8   Lessons Learned

1. The work produced by the curriculum development team resulted in a very high-quality curriculum centered on sustainable seafood science. Each curriculum unit and activity was linked to NSES and Ocean Literacy Principles. Additionally, the curriculum was skills-based, which provided students with an opportunity to engage in real field research related to consumer impacts (supermarket and fish market data collection and analysis, and the collection and sharing of images and other media and stories).
2. Over 200 classrooms were preregistered through outreach efforts using NASA GLOBE and ePals resources. Unfortunately, there was a high rate of attrition by the end of the program, resulting from aspects of each of the five foundational themes noted in section 8 below.
3. Through the development of a Rich Internet Application (Teacher's Assistant) for the LearningSpace™ platform, registered teachers (and their classes) and students accessed the StS curriculum on the project's Google site.
4. The development of the Data Collection Tool (DCT), a cornerstone feature of the StS curriculum (Unit 5a), created the capability for uploading and displaying collected fish and seafood survey data into a custom Google Earth KML file. The scientific names provided by the Data Collection Tool that map to Seafood Watch are often species or subspecies (coho salmon) that might require the student to know more information than was collected (harvest location). Also, the late delivery of the DCT precluded the majority of registered students from being able to use the DCT.
5. In the future, Sampling the Sea will likely need to glean information from the standard analysis tools that services expose to their customers. The experiment in total access to the ePals database gives StS a better understanding of the limits of what is possible, and will inform future evaluation efforts.
6. The goal of supporting cross-classroom collaboration through social media was not achieved. Students were not inclined to talk with each other in the LearningSpace™ (as reported by teachers and actual usage), and since most of the social media features in what turned out to be a beta version of LearningSpace™ did not function well, it was difficult for students to share materials. Further, because of time pressures, and insufficient documentation of the procedures, teachers were not able to design shared classes.

7. The process evaluation provided important information related to how teachers, classes, and students did or didn't use Sampling the Sea, and how certain features could be improved for future runs. Data collected for those teachers and students who did use the system and responded to both before and after surveys indicated small but statistically significant increases in some learning outcomes related to the five EE domains, including sustainable seafood knowledge. A regression analysis revealed that student's self-reported improved understanding of seafood sustainability and ocean health were partially explained by the *sharing* and *viewing* of stories and media, and science content. While these results are encouraging, it is emphasized here that they are based on a very small portion of teachers ($n = 6$) and students ($n = 54 - 55$).
8. As an example of one data source and the related process evaluation insights, the teacher comments were initially coded into 228 separate topics (one e-mail might include two or three topics), then into 132 distinct codes (after standardizing across variants), and iteratively into a set of 13 general categories. These *general* categories reflect five foundational themes of *authorization* (5 topics), *curriculum* (28), *project* (38), *social media* (7), and *technology problems* (53).
9. Overall, the project's process flows, the data collection procedures, and the evaluation components were all successful models for rigorous future evaluations of the DigitalOcean: Sampling the Sea project, and similar projects.

22.3 Conclusion

Sampling the Sea was designed to support the critical need for improved ocean literacy, especially concerning sustainability. It seems unique in several respects. First, it may be one of the earliest projects to explicitly integrate National Science Education Standards and ocean literacy principles into a curriculum design for high school students. Second, it addresses existing recommendations put forward by the Centers for Ocean Science Education Excellence, the U.S. Environmental Protection Agency, the National Environmental Education Council, the National Science Teachers Association, North American Association for Environmental Education, and the National Oceanic and Atmospheric Organization, to empirically investigate the effectiveness of instructional materials in meeting the goals of environmental education and environmental literacy. Third, it builds on existing ocean-related curricula to achieve the highest possible success at meeting academic objectives and provides some measures to compare future measures. Fourth, the operationalization of the evaluation model as a proof-of-concept design illustrates how the linkages and variables related to environmental literacy could be tested in a full (pilot) project implementation. And fifth, the outcomes obtained point to interesting insights into how new digital teaching tools and technologies like social media may affect learning outcomes in the five domains critical to environmental literacy (knowledge, affect, skills, intention, and efficacy), and point to how to refine the curriculum and evaluation model for a full implementation in a Phase II of StS.

Online learning environments that support participatory learning through social media tools hold promise for ocean literacy and other subjects in which knowledge sharing and the exchange of ideas among students can increase academic performance, skill building, and expanded learning opportunities, Yet, funding and research to support the inclusion of digital tools in the classroom means many schools in the USA have only limited computer access. Further, the shifting focus from the use of the Internet and computers as purely research tools, to collaborative online learning environments, has not, as yet, been integrated into teaching practices. Cost, time, and effort for technology adoption are certainly barriers to acquisition, as is the need to guarantee security for students working in online environments.

It is hoped that these early results in an emergent, transdisciplinary field of research will generate interest in developing and funding a full project implementation and Phase II evaluation of the Sampling the Sea program.

Acknowledgments This project was funded by a MacArthur Foundation Digital Media and Learning Innovation Grant, 2009–2010, and the Paul G. Allen Family Foundation. All project members contributed extensively, including Dr. Constance Penley, Department of Film and Media Studies and Principal Investigator; Arthur Clifford, technical analyst/programmer; Betsy Youngman, lead curriculum developer; Lissa Edelman, Peggy Lubchenco, Dr. George Matsumoto (also science advisor), Rebecca Reid, and Meghan Saxer, curriculum developers; Dr. Sue Johnson, science education pedagogy advisor, Department of Education; Dr. Cathy Boggs, Carsey-Wolf Center Associate Director; Linda Dozier, CTO ePals; Ryan Fuller, Center Graduate Student Associate; Rebekah Pure, Assistant; Nicole Klanfer, UCSB Assistant Dean for Development in Arts and Humanities; and of course, the teachers and students who participated.

References

Anderson, T. (ed.): Theory and Practice of Online Learning. AU Press, Athabasca University, Edmonton (2008)

ASCD: Wanted: deep understanding. Constructivism posits new conception of learning. ASCD Update **34**(3), 1–5 (1992)

Benbunan-Fich, R., Hiltz, S.R., Harasim, L.: The online interaction learning model: an integrated theoretical framework for learning networks. In: Hiltz, S.R., Goldman, R. (eds.) Learning Together Online: Research on Asynchronous Learning Networks, pp. 19–37. Lawrence Erlbaum Associates, Mahwah (2005)

Cava, F., Schoedinger, S., Strang, C., Tuddenham, P.: Science Content and standards for ocean literacy: A Report on Ocean Literacy. National Geographic Society, National Oceanic and Atmospheric Administration, Lawrence Hall of Science, University of California College of Exploration. http://www.coexploration.org/oceanliteracy/documents/OceanLitConcepts_10.11.05.pdf (2005)

Day, B.A.: Defying oceans end: A massive need for environmental communication and education. Applied Environmental Education and Communication 2(4), 189–190 (2003)

Erickson, L.E., Griswold, W., Hohn, K., Saulters, O.S.: Enriching and evaluating sustainability education. J. Sustain. Educ. **1**. http://www.journalofsustainabilityeducation.org/wordpress/content/enriching-and-evaluating-sustainability-education_2010_05/ (2010)

An ocean blueprint for the Twent-First century. Final report: Intergovernmental Conference on Environmental Education. Organized by UNESCO in Cooperation with UNEP, Tblisi, USSR. (No. UNESCO ED/MD/49) (1979)

Garrison, D.R., Anderson, T., Archer, W.: Critical inquiry in a text-based environment: computer conferencing in higher education. Internet High. Educ. 2(3), 87–105 (2000)

Halpern, B.S., Walbridge, S., Selkoe, K.A., Kappel, C.V., Micheli, F., D'Agrosa, C., et al.: A global map of human impact on marine ecosystems. Science 319(948), 948–952 (2008)

Hiltz, S.R., Goldman, R. (eds.): Learning Together Online: Research on Asynchronous Learning Networks. Lawrence Erlbaum Associates, Mahwah (2005)

Hungerford, H.R., Volk, T.L.: Changing learner behavior through environmental education. J. Environ. Educ. 21(3), 8–21 (1990)

Ivers, K.S., Barren, A.E.: Multimedia Projects in Education: Designing, Producing and Assessing. Libraries Unlimited, Teacher Ideas Press, Westport (2002)

Jenkins, H.: Convergence Culture: Where Old and New Media Collide. New York University Press, New York (2006)

Jenkins, H., Clinton, K., Purushotma, R., Robison, A.J., Weigel, M.: Confronting the Challenges of Participatory Culture: Media Education for the 21st Century. Comparative Media Studies Program. Massachusetts Institute of Technology, Cambridge (2006)

Johnson, D.W., Johnson, R.T.: Learning Together Online: Cooperative, Competitive, and Individualistic Learning, 5th edn. Allyn & Bacon, Needham Heights (1999)

Kaplan, A.M., Haenlein, M.: Users of the world, Unite! The challenges and opportunities of social media. Bus. Horiz. 53, 59–68 (2010)

McBeth, B., Hungerford, H., Marcinkowski, T., Volk, T., Myers, R.: National Environmental Literacy Assessment Project: Final Research Report. http://www.peecworks.org/PEEC/PEEC_Research/S03DFD1F6-03DFD369 (2008)

Myers, R.A., Worm, B.: Rapid worldwide depletion of predatory fish communities. Nature 423, 280–283 (2003)

North American Association for Environmental Education (NAAEE). Excellence in Environmental Education Guidelines for Learning (Pre K-12). http://www.naaee.org/publications/guidelines-for-excellence (2004)

Pooley, J.A., O'Connor, M.: Environmental education and attitudes: emotions and beliefs are what is needed. Environ. Behav. 32(5), 711–723 (2000)

NSTA Position Statement: Environmental Education. http://www.nsta.org/about/positions/environmental.aspx (2010)

Ramsey, J., Hungerford, H.R.: Perspectives on environmental education in the united states. In: Dietz, T., Stern, P.C. (eds.) New Tools for Environmental Protection: Education, Information, and Voluntary Measures, pp. 147–160. National Academy Press, Washington, DC (2002)

Rheingold, H.: Using social media to teach social media. N. Engl. J. High. Educ. 23(1), 25–26 (2008)

Seafood Watch. http://www.montereybayaquarium.org/cr/seafoodwatch.aspx

Shirky, C.: Here Comes Everybody: The Power of Organizing without Organizations. Penguin Press, New York (2009)

Siemens, G.: Connectivism: a learning theory for the digital age. Int. J. Instr. Technol. Distance Learn. http://www.itdl.org/Journal/Jan_05/article01.htm (2005)

Stapp, W.B., Bennett, D., Bryan, W., Jr., Fulton, J., MacGregor, J., Nowak, P., et al.: The concept of environmental education. J. Environ. Educ. 1(1), 30–31 (1969)

U.S. Commission on Ocean Policy: An ocean blueprint for the 21st century. Final report. Washington, DC: U.S. Commission on Ocean Policy. http://www.oceancommission.gov/documents/full_color_rpt/welcome.html (2004)

Wilmes, S., Howarth, J.: Using issues-based science in the classroom. Sci. Teach. 76, 24–29 (2009)

Chapter 23
ASK-LOST 2.0: A Web-Based Tool for Social Tagging Digital Educational Resources in Learning Environments

Demetrios G. Sampson, Panagiotis Zervas, and Alexandros Kalamatianos

Abstract Digital educational resources have gained attention as the means for supporting educational activities in the context of Technology Enhanced Learning. A number of international initiatives have recently emerged and recognized the importance of sharing and reusing digital educational resources among educational communities worldwide. As a result, organizing, managing, offering, and accessing these resources over the Web have been key issues for both the research and the educational community. Within this framework, a popular way for describing digital educational resources is by using a formal and centrally agreed classification system, such as the IEEE Learning Objects Metadata (LOM). The emerging Web 2.0 applications have increased the amount of user-generated educational resources on the Web. As a result, the issue of socially tagging these resources, beyond predefined metadata schemas, has attracted both research and practical attention. In this book chapter, we discuss issues related to Social Tagging as a means for describing digital educational resources and we present the ASK Learning Objects Social Tagging 2.0 (ASK-LOST 2.0), a Web-based tool that can be used for social tagging digital educational resources in learning environments.

23.1 Introduction

Web 2.0 applications and user behaviors are becoming the mainstream paradigm on the World Wide Web. Tim O' Reilly describes Web 2.0 as a platform: "...delivering software as a continually-updated service that gets better the more people use it,

D.G. Sampson (✉) • P. Zervas
Department of Digital Systems, University of Piraeus, Piraeus, Greece

Informatics and Telematics Institute (ITI), Centre for Research and Technology Hellas (CERTH), Athens, Greece

A. Kalamatianos
Department of Digital Systems, University of Piraeus, Piraeus, Greece

B. White et al. (eds.), *Social Media Tools and Platforms in Learning Environments*,
DOI 10.1007/978-3-642-20392-3_23, © Springer-Verlag Berlin Heidelberg 2011

consuming and remixing data from multiple sources, including individual users, while providing their own data and services in a form that allows remixing by others, creating network effects through an architecture of participation, and going beyond the page metaphor of web 1.0 to deliver rich user experiences" (O' and T.: What is Web 2.0 2005). Thus, Web 2.0 bares the potential to implement Tim-Berners Lee original vision for a "read-write Web" where everyone could add, edit, and comment Web pages and resources (Berners-Lee 1999).

This has led to an enormous increase of the digital resources available on the Web today. As a result, both the discovery of new resources and the retrieval of known ones on the World Wide Web, become an increasingly complex problem (Heymann et al. 2008; Yande et al. 2007).

Within this context, the issue of characterizing digital resources tents to move from the expert-based description based on formal classification systems (e.g., with metadata such as the IEEE Learning Objects Metadata for educational resources) to a less formal user-based tagging (i.e., adding keywords to digital resources) (Bi et al. 2009).

Adding keywords, also known as tags, to any type of digital resource by users (rather than resources' authors) is referred to as *Social Tagging* (Bonino 2009; Vossen and Hageman 2007). The term of social tagging has emerged for those applications that encourage groups of individuals to openly share their private descriptions (or tags) of digital resources with other users, either by using a collection of tags created by the individual for his/her personal use (referred to as *folksonomy*) or by using a collective vocabulary (referred to as *collabulary*) (Anderson 2007).

23.2   Social Tagging of Digital Educational Resources

In the field of Technology Enhanced Learning, Learning Objects (LO) are a common format for sharing educational resources and can be defined as *"Potential reusable digital or non-digital resources or a collection of linked resources that are characterized by metadata, and have been designed and developed for a specific audience, their scope is to achieve one or more specified learning goals and they are used in order to support one or more educational activities which feature specified criteria that measure the achievement of the learning goals that have been defined"* (Sampson and Papanikou 2009).

A number of international initiatives, such as the leading initiative of Open Educational Resources (OER) movement, have recognized the importance of digital educational resources to be shared and possibly reused among educational communities (Caswell et al. 2008).

Traditionally, digital educational resources are organized using formal descriptions from centrally designed and agreed classification systems using metadata. The IEEE Learning Object Metadata (IEEE LOM) Standard is such an example (IEEE LTSC). As a result, digital educational resources and their associated metadata are organized, classified, and stored in Web-based repositories which are referred to as Learning Object Repositories (LORs) (McGreal 2004).

Despite the use of well-defined metadata for digital educational resources, the end users have difficulties to find suitable digital educational resources from LORs (Vuorikari 2007). With the emergence of Web2.0 and the increased volume of user-generated educational resources on the Web, other means (commonly used in popular Web 2.0 applications) for describing digital educational resources are investigated. More specifically, social bookmarking and social tagging of digital educational resources are proposed (Bateman et al. 2007).

The creators of metadata need no longer be metadata experts or authors of resources. Instead, the generation of metadata is now done by individual users, who might primarily see private benefits, like an easy way to search and retrieve already used and known resources using meaningful terms (Dahl and Vossen 2008).

Anticipated benefits expected from the use of social tagging of digital educational resources are (Vuorikari 2007; Bateman et al. 2007; Ullrich et al. 2008; Hayman 2007; Seldow 2006):

- *Advantage 1:* Individual users (teachers and/or learners) are able to provide and use terms that are meaningful to them and create a personal collection of tags. This can facilitate the searching and recalling of previously used and already known resources.
- *Advantage 2:* Personal tags pay attention to the individual users' intents, reflecting their personal way of organizing and locating learning objects. This offers a unique and personalized way of classification which is delivered by users' tags and not by an externally defined classification system.
- *Advantage 3:* By sharing these tags in an open manner with other users and groups of users with common perception on vocabularies can act as a "human filter" for each other and/or between community members.
- *Advantage 4:* By identifying the most popular tags within a given educational community of users, a community-based vocabulary can be built eliminating redundant and irrelevant to the community description elements.
- *Advantage 5:* Tags generated by highly populated educational communities bare the potential to discern contextual information from tags' aggregation, facilitating an educational wisdom of the hoi polloi.
- *Advantage 6:* Social tagging can enable the formation of social networks around educational tags. These networks can reflect the interests and expertise of users contributing to the tag development.
- *Advantage 7:* Analyzing user-generated tags can enrich peer interaction and peer awareness around educational content.

On the other hand, common disadvantages with social bookmarking and social tagging of digital educational resources are (Vuorikari 2007; Bateman et al. 2007; Ullrich et al. 2008; Hayman 2007; Seldow 2006):

- *Disadvantage 1:* The use of tags with personal meaning from different users can create difficulties in the process of reusing digital educational resources. These tags could be misleading for a user when searches for digital educational resources in Web-based repositories.

- *Disadvantage 2:* Unclear tags due to spelling errors and synonym tags can create difficulties in the process of searching and retrieving digital educational resources that have been characterized with these tags.
- *Disadvantage 3:* The lack of "rules" for the structure of tags (e.g., singular vs. plural, capitalization, etc.) can cause additional problems in searching and retrieving appropriate digital educational resources.
- *Disadvantage 4:* Overall, tags are not connected to each other by a reference structure, which in formal systems is used to link related terms and narrower or broader terms.

23.3 Existing Tools for Social Tagging of Digital Educational Resources

Within this context, during the last years, a number of tools for facilitating social tagging of digital educational resources have been developed. Typically, these tools allow users to create their own tags and share digital educational resources, as well as to browse the resources categorized by others. The main tools in this category are presented in the following sections.

23.3.1 Connotea

Connotea[1] is an open-source, Web-based reference management and social bookmarking tool for scientists created by Nature Publishing Group (Lund et al. 2005). Its main functionalities are: (1) online storage of bookmarks, (2) simple, nonhierarchical structuring of bookmarks, (3) access to the bookmarks list of different users, and finally, (4) automatic discovery of citation details for any article or book that is added to the system.

23.3.2 CiteULike

CiteULike[2] (Emamy and Cameron 2007) is a Web-based tool for facilitating scientists, researchers, and academics to store, organize, share, and discover links to academic scientific and research papers. Similar to Connotea, CiteULike automatically extracts citation details and stores a link to the paper, along with a set of user-defined tags. By tagging scientific papers, users are building an explicit

---

[1]Connotea: http://www.connotea.org
[2]CiteULike: http://www.citeulike.org

domain-specific folksonomy that describes this paper in a potentially meaningful manner to the other members of the scientific community.

23.3.3 MELT

MELT[3] is a product of a Content Enrichment project supported by the European Commission's eContentplus Programme that builds on the existing technical architectures developed in the earlier CALIBRATE project. MELT aims to address the problem that metadata created by an expert indexer related to the learning resources may not always reflect how a resource is really used in classrooms by experienced practicing teachers. MELT facilitates teachers who have used a digital educational resource to create their own tags by providing a social tagging system for this purpose.

23.3.4 Comparison of Social Tagging Tools

Table 23.1 summarizes the main functionalities of the aforementioned tools. It can be noted that Connotea and CiteULike are online reference management and social bookmarking services, while MELT is using CALIBRATE's learning object repository[4] allowing users to add their own tags to the resources of this repository. The scope of the first seven functionalities, presented in Table 23.1, is to support the advantages of social tagging as described in the previous section. On the other hand, searching digital educational resources via tag cloud and social networking support are techniques that aim to eliminate Disadvantages 3 and 4 of social tagging as presented

Table 23.1 Main functionalities of existing social tagging tools

Functionalities	Connotea	CiteULike	MELT
Submit digital educational resources	√ [Only URL]	√ [Only URL]	–
Tagging digital educational resources	√	√	√
Comment digital educational resources	√	√	√
Rate digital educational resources	–	–	√
Search digital educational resources (via tag cloud or free text)	√	√	√
Create social network	√	√	√
RSS feed	√	√	√
Autosuggested tagging	–	–	√

---

[3]MELT: http://info.melt-project.eu

[4]CALIBRATE's Learning Resources Repository: http://calibrate.eun.org/merlin/index.cfm

earlier. Additionally, Autosuggested Tagging is a technique that provides suggested values to a text field aiming to eliminate Disadvantages 1 and 2 of social tagging.

However, as it can be noted from Table 23.1, none of the aforementioned tools allow:

- Social tagging of digital educational resources of any format, i.e., image, video, text, URLs, etc.
- Searching of digital educational resources via autosuggested tags
- Guided tagging, which is a technique that presents to the user (during the tagging process) his/her tags previously used for characterizing other digital educational resources (refereed to as Personal Tags), as well as the tags that are most frequently used by other users regarding this specific digital educational resource (refereed to as Popular Tags)

The last two identified functionalities aim to eliminate Disadvantages 1 and 2 of social tagging and they are used in well-known tools for facilitating social tagging of general digital resources (e.g., bookmarks, images, videos, etc.). These tools include: (a) delicious,[5] which is used for management, sharing, and social tagging of bookmarks on the Web; (b) flickr,[6] which is used for management, sharing, and social tagging of photographs and images; and (c) youtube,[7] which is used for management, sharing, and social tagging of videos.

In order to address all identified problems of existing social tagging tools, which are presented in Table 23.1, we have designed and developed ASK-LOST 2.0, a Web-based tool that fully supports the process of social tagging of any type of digital educational resources. Next, we present ASK-LOST 2.0.

23.4 ASK-Learning Objects Social Tagging 2.0 (ASK-LOST 2.0)

ASK-LOST 2.0[8] is a newly developed Web-based tool fully supporting the process of social tagging of any type of digital educational resources by offering facilities for authoring and management of tags and resources. The main objectives of ASK-LOST 2.0 are the following:

- *Objective 1:* The development of a learning object repository with any type of digital educational resources submitted and annotated by end users.
- *Objective 2:* The creation of personal collections of digital educational resources for every user and the provision of access to personal vocabularies created by user's tags.

---

[5]http://www.delicious.com/

[6]http://www.flickr.com/

[7]http://www.youtube.com/

[8]http://www.ask4research.info/ask-lost/

- *Objective 3:* The provision of facilities for search and retrieval of digital educational resources based on users' tags.
- *Objective 4:* The provision of facilities for building social networks between users, aiming to enrich user's interaction and awareness around the available digital educational resources.

The main functionalities of ASK-LOST 2.0 can be summarized as follows:

- *Submit and tag digital educational resources:* The user can submit and characterize with his/her selected tags any kind (URL or digital file) of educational resource. This functionality is not supported by other existing tools and enables the user to enrich the repository of the tool with his/her digital educational resources.
- *Guided Tagging:* During the tagging process of a digital educational resource, the user is presented with his/her tags previously used for characterizing other digital educational resources (refereed to as *Personal Tags*), as well as with tags that are most frequently used by other users regarding this specific digital educational resource (referred to as *Popular Tags*). This functionality is not supported by other existing tools and enables the user to easily reuse his/her personal tags, as well as the tags offered by other users aiming to tackle Disadvantage 1 and Disadvantage 2 of Social Tagging.
- *Autosuggested Tagging:* During the tagging process, the user is presented with suggested tags that have been used by other users and are relevant with the tag that the user is typing. This functionality aims to tackle Disadvantage 1 and Disadvantage 2 of Social Tagging.
- *Creation of user's personal digital education resources collection:* The user has the capability to save to his/her personal list, digital educational resources uploaded by other users, and browse the tags that these users have used.

Table 23.2 Mapping of main functionalities with ASK-LOST 2.0 objectives

ASK-LOST 2.0	
Submit and tag	*Objective 1:* The development of learning object repository with any type of digital educational resources submitted and annotated by end users
Guided tagging Creation of user's personal collection Autosuggested tagging	*Objective 2:* The creation of personal collections of digital educational resources for every user and access to personal vocabularies created by user's tags
Browse via tag cloud Search Comment Rate	*Objective 3:* Facilities for search and retrieval of these digital educational resources based on users' tags
Social networking support	*Objective 4:* Facilities for building social network between users, aiming to enrich user's interaction and awareness around the available digital educational resources

- *Browse digital educational resources via tag cloud:* The user can search and browse digital educational resources using an appropriately formatted tag cloud produced by the tags that all users of the tool have offered. This functionality aims to tackle Disadvantage 3 of Social Tagging.
- *Search, rate, and comment digital educational resources:* The user can search via tag cloud, free text, and autosuggested tags, available digital educational resources tagged by other users and provide his/her ratings and comments. This functionality aims to tackle Disadvantage 3 of Social Tagging.
- *Social networking support:* The user can create watchlists, which include other users' profiles, so as to be able to monitor (through RSS feeds) the tags that these users are using, as well as the digital educational resources that they are submitting to the repository of ASK-LOST 2.0. This functionality aims to tackle Disadvantage 4 of Social Tagging.

Table 23.2 presents the main functionalities of ASK-LOST 2.0 in relation to the objectives that have been set.

23.5 ASK-LOST 2.0 Scenarios of Use

In this section, we present three (3) scenarios of ASK-LOST 2.0 use, so as to demonstrate: (a) the contribution of ASK-LOST 2.0 toward supporting social tagging advantages and (b) the contribution of ASK-LOST 2.0 toward tackling social tagging disadvantages as identified in previous sections. The scenarios of use are described next in detail.

23.5.1 Submit and Guided Tag of a Digital Educational Resource

The scope of this scenario of use is to present the process of submitting and guided tagging of digital educational resources toward supporting *Advantage 1* and *Advantage 2*, as well as tackling *Disadvantage 1* and *Disadvantage 2* of Social Tagging. More specifically, the process includes three (3) steps:

1st step: During the 1st step, the user has the capability to characterize the digital educational resource, which is going to be uploaded to the ASK-LOST 2.0 repository, with the following information: (1) the title of the educational resource, (2) the type of the educational resource (i.e., exercise, simulation experiment), (3) the technical format of the educational resource, (4) the intended user role for the educational resource, (5) the context where the use of the educational resource is intended to take place, and (6) the subject domain of the educational resource.

2nd step: Next, the user has the capability to upload the file of the digital educational resource or to submit the URL which depicts the location of the digital educational resource from where it can be accessed.

3rd step: During the final step, the user can insert free tags to the digital educational resource. As it is depicted in Fig. 23.1, during the tagging process, the user is presented with his/her tags that have been previously used for characterizing other digital educational resources (referred to as *Your Tags*), as well as with tags that have been mostly used by other users (referred to as *Popular Tags*). Furthermore, Autosuggested Tagging is provided to the user. More precisely, the user is presented with suggested tags that have been used by other users and are relevant with the word that the user is typing to the "tags" field.

This scenario of use enables the user to create personal collections of tags and it organizes in a personal manner his/her digital educational resources, which he/she has contributed to the tool's repository. Moreover, the user is able to tag the specific educational resource in a more consistent way by preventing him/her from making spelling or other mistakes during the tagging process. However, it is important to be noted that the guided tagging process does not prevent the user to insert different tags from those suggested from the tool, and as a result, this tagging technique does not constrain the quantity of the tags that are contributed from the users to the digital educational resources stored in the tool's repository.

Fig. 23.1 The process of guided and autosuggested tagging

23.5.2   Search Digital Educational Resources via Tag Cloud

The scope of this scenario of use is to present the process of searching digital educational resources via the tag cloud feature of ASK-LOST 2.0 toward supporting *Advantage 3* and *Advantage 4*, as well as tackling *Disadvantage 3* of Social Tagging.

In this scenario of use, the user can select a specific tag and browse digital educational resources that have been tagged by other users of the tool with the selected tag (Fig. 23.2). Furthermore, additional tags (referred to as *Related Tags*) are presented to the user. These tags have been previously used by other users for tagging digital educational resources along with the previously selected tag from the tag cloud.

This scenario of use enables the users to share their tags and obtain a common understanding for different educational resources. Additionally, the feature of related tags creates an internal structure within the available tags of the tool and the users are able to browse and find digital educational resources, which have been tagged with the related tags of the initially selected one, making search and retrieval of digital educational resources more efficient for the users.

23.5.3   Create Social Network Connections

The scope of this scenario of use is to present the process of creating social network connections toward supporting *Advantage 5*, *Advantage 6*, and *Advantage 7*, as well as tackling *Disadvantage 4* of Social Tagging.

Fig. 23.2 The process of searching and browsing digital educational resources from tag cloud feature of the ASK-LOST 2.0 tool

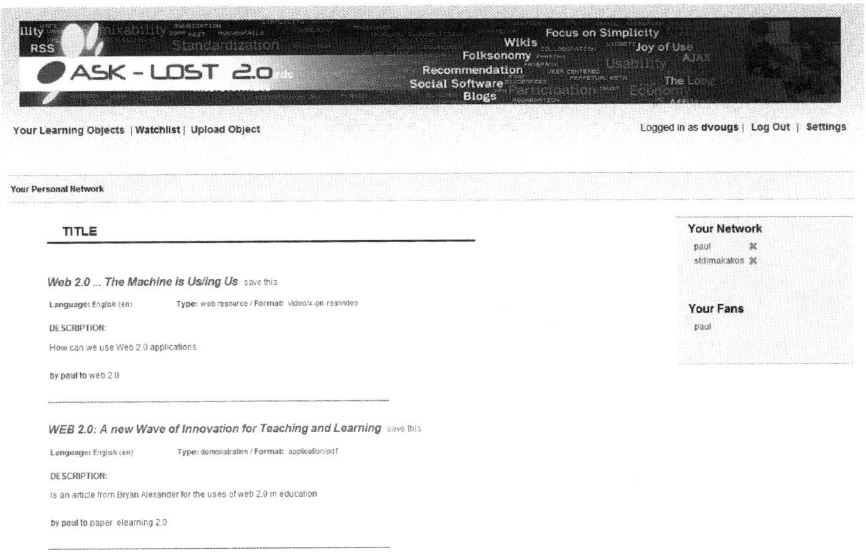

Fig. 23.3 Presentation of a user's personal network

In this scenario of use, the user can browse digital educational resources that other users have uploaded to the tool's repository and, moreover, to connect with them by adding them to his/her watchlist (Fig. 23.3). This will enable them to monitor (through RSS feed) the tags that these users are offering to the tool, as well as the digital educational resources that they are uploading.

This scenario of use enables the users to formulate and/or joint existing social networks around their contributed tags and enrich their interaction and collaboration. Additionally, users that are connected through social networks can obtain a common understating about the usage of specific tags for particular educational resources. This could be reflected in their future tagging behavior on other digital educational resources that they might want to contribute to the tool's repository.

23.6   Conclusion

In this book chapter, we discussed issues related to social tagging as a means for describing digital educational resources in learning environments and we examined existing tools in relation to known advantages and potential problems of social tagging in technology-enhanced learning. We, then, presented ASK-LOST 2.0, a newly developed Web-based tool fully supporting the process of social tagging of any type of digital educational resources by offering facilities for authoring and management of tags and digital educational resources. ASK-LOST 2.0 incorporates all available functionalities of existing tools and it supports additional functionalities such as guided tagging and searching via autosuggested tags. Finally, we examined the potential of ASK-LOST 2.0 Web-based tool to support the identified advantages of social tagging, as well as to tackle the identified known disadvantages of social tagging.

Acknowledgments The work presented in this book chapter is supported by the OpenScienceResources Project (http://www.openscienceresources.eu/) that is funded by European Commission's eContentPlus programme. Contract No: ECP- 2008 – EDU- 428045

References

Anderson, P.: What is web2.0? Ideas, Technologies and Implications for Education. JISC Technology and Standards Watch. (2007) http://www.jisc.ac.uk/media/documents/techwatch/tsw0701b.pdf

Bateman, S., Brooks, C., McCalla, G., Brusilovsky, P.: Applying collaborative tagging to E-Learning. In: 16th International World Wide Web Conference (WWW 2007). Banff (2007)

Berners-Lee, T.: Weaving the Web. Oricon Business Books, London (1999)

Bi, B., Shang, L., Kao, B.: Collaborative resource discovery in social tagging systems. In: 18th ACM Conference on Information and Knowledge Management. Hong Kong (2009)

Bonino, S.: Social Tagging as a Classification and Search Strategy. VDM, Germany (2009)

Caswell, T., Henson, S., Jensen, M., Wiley, D.: Open educational resources: Enabling universal education. In Int. Rev. Res. Open Distance Learn. **9**(1), 1–11 (2008)

Dahl, D., Vossen, G.: Evolution of learning folksonomies: Social tagging in e-Learning repositories. Technol. Enhanced Learn. **1**(2), 35–46 (2008)

Emamy, K., Cameron, R.: Citeulike: A researcher's social bookmarking service (2007) http://www.ariadne.ac.uk/issue51/emamy-cameron

Hayman, S.: Folksonomies and tagging: new development in social bookmarking. Education.au. (2007) http://www.educationau.edu.au/jahia/webdav/site/myjahiasite/shared/papers/arkhayman.pdf

Heymann, P., Koutrika, G., Molina, H.: Can social bookmarking improve web search? In: 1st International Conference on Web Search and Data Mining (WSDM 2008), pp. 195–205. Palo Alto (2008)

IEEE LTSC : Draft Standard for Learning Object Metadata, IEEE Learning Technology Standards Committee (LTSC), http://ltsc.ieee.org/wg12/files/LOM_1484_12_1_v1_Final_Draft.pdf

Lund, B., Hammond, T., Flack, M., Hannay, T.: Social bookmarking tools (II) – A case study connotea. D – Lib Mag. **11**(4) (2005) http://www.dlib.org/dlib/april05/lund/04lund.html

McGreal, R.: Online Education Using Learning Objects. Falmer Press, Washington, DC (2004)

O' Reilly, T.: What is Web 2.0. (2005) http://www.oreillynet.com/pub/a/oreilly/tim/news/2005/09/30/what-is-web-20.html

Sampson, D., Papanikou, C.: A framework for learning objects reusability within learning activities. In: 9th IEEE International Conference on Advanced Learning Technologies (ICALT 2009), pp. 32–36. Riga, Latvia (2009)

Seldow, ç.: Social tagging in K-12 education: Folksonomies for student folk (2006) http://mrseldow.gradeweb.com/custom/Social_tagging_in_K12_Education_Seldow_4_3_06.pdf

Ullrich, C., Kerstin, B., Heng, L., Xiaohong, T., Liping, S., Ruimin, S.: Why web 2.0 is good for learning and for research: Principles and prototypes. In: 17th International World Wide Web Conference. Beijing (2008)

Vossen, G., Hageman, S.: Unleashing Web 2.0 From Concept to Creativity. Morgan Kaufmann (2007)

Vuorikari, R.: Folksonomies, Social Bookmarking and Tagging: State of the art. European Schoolnet (2007) http://info.melt-project.eu

Yande, Y., Jatowt, A., Nakamura, S., Tanaka, K.: Can social bookmarking enhance search in the web? In: Joint Conference on Digital Libraries (JCDL 2007), pp. 107–116. Vancouver (2007)

Chapter 24
Learning in the Digital Age with SNSs: Creating a Profile

Amanda Nosko and Eileen Wood

Abstract In the proposed chapter, we will start off by introducing social media and some of the features of social networking sites. We will go on to highlight why these technologies are so pervasive, and how/why people are using them. We will expand our discussion to include studies that have examined Facebook as a social networking and learning tool. Specifically, we will go on to present studies that relate to the integration of technology and social media as a means for encouraging learning across the life span, and will use social learning as a theoretical base. We will also present how social media such as Facebook can enrich learning, and offer some suggestions and insights into the policies that may help to balance security, privacy, and risk issues associated with using social media in education. Next, we will present information about risks associated with using social media, and will continue by highlighting how users can protect their information online. We will then present some potential privacy and policy considerations within the educational context that examine social learning contexts, and the implications that these contexts have for the learner and educator. Lastly, we will conclude by offering some suggestions about how to best integrate this technology within the classroom.

24.1 Learning in the Digital Age with SNSs: Creating a Profile

24.1.1 What Are Social Networking Sites?

Social networking sites (SNSs) are Web-based social communication tools designed to allow users to contact and communicate with other users. The three

A. Nosko (✉) • E. Wood
Department of Psychology, Wilfrid Laurier University, 75 University Ave West, N2L 3C5
Waterloo, ON, Canada
e-mail: amandanosko@rogers.com; ewood@wlu.ca

B. White et al. (eds.), *Social Media Tools and Platforms in Learning Environments*,
DOI 10.1007/978-3-642-20392-3_24, © Springer-Verlag Berlin Heidelberg 2011

key features that define SNSs according to Boyd and Ellison (2007) are that the sites
"allow individuals to (1) construct a public or semi-public profile within a bounded
system, (2) articulate a list of other users with whom they share a connection, and
(3) view and traverse their list of connections and those made by others within the
system" (p. 2). Personal Web pages and online profile networks have emerged at an
increasing rate on SNSs and continue to gain popularity (Yum 2007). Two prevalent SNSs are MySpace and Facebook.

MySpace, developed in 2003, emerged from a previous SNS called "Friendster"
(History of MySpace 2008). As of June 2010, MySpace had 140 million members
(www.myspace.com). MySpace allows users to create personal profiles and to add a
variety of content (pictures, display emoticons, comments) (www.myspace.com).
Facebook founded in 2004, was originally designed as an SNS for students at
Harvard University. Its popularity has grown immensely and expanded beyond
the initial Harvard setting with the potential to include anyone anywhere in the
world who is older than 13 years of age. Facebook currently has over 400 million
active users (www.Facebook.com) and as such is the leading social network site in
the world. The infrastructure of Facebook is comprised of a variety of networks.
Each network represents a company, school (university/college), or geographical
region (city, state, or province). Individuals create a profile within one network.
Creation of an account is necessary for membership and requires that the user
provides basic information including a valid e-mail address, gender, and birth date.
Once a member, users can create a personal profile for themselves which may
include information such as their age, gender, personal preferences, and location.
They can also upload photos, describe interests, education, relationships, and more.
Facebook offers users the opportunity to search for friends by typing their names
into the search bar (these can be actual friends, acquaintances, or even strangers)
and add them to their "friends list." Users can interact with one another either
through a personal message, similar to an e-mail inbox, or by posting more public
messages on the profile wall, a feature similar to a bulletin board. Another attractive
feature of Facebook is the capacity to create and join groups that may be based on
similar interests, mutual causes, or are simply for fun.

24.1.2   How and Why Do People Use SNSs?

I like FACEBOOK™ because I can post things about myself, and also see what other
people have posted (female, 23)

Researchers have begun to examine how and why people are drawn to SNSs and
social media platforms. Research examining Facebook, for example, has identified
that multiple reasons explain why users establish and maintain personal profiles
including: interconnection and the desire to bridge off-line and online relationships
(Boyd and Ellison 2007), maintenance of existing off-line friendships (Ellison et al.
2007; Lenhart and Madden 2007; Madge et al. 2009; Wiley and Sisson 2006),

identity formation (Selwyn 2009; Stutzman 2006; Valkenburg et al. 2005), self-expression and self-disclosure (Nosko et al. 2010; Wiley and Sisson 2006), and "lurking" or browsing information of other users (Pempek et al. 2009). Additionally, SNSs allow users to express themselves openly and freely, and in fact, encourage just that (www.Facebook.com).

24.1.3 Taking Facebook to School: Challenges, Successes, and Considerations

At all levels of education, access to computers and the Internet as teaching tools continues to increase as parents, educators, school boards, and universities/colleges push for the adoption of new technologies. In part, the impetus for this growth stems from the understanding that digital technologies capture the interest of learners from preschool to adults and that many learners are much more motivated and persistent with learning tasks presented through digital technologies than traditional teaching formats (Willoughby and Wood 2008). Despite the anticipated and potential learning gains, computer integration in the classroom continues to fall below expectations (Paraskeva et al. 2008). This problem has been evident for some time and continues to be an issue internationally (Aduwa-Ogiegbaen 2009; Birch 2009; Cuban et al. 2001; Drent and Meelissen 2008; Lim and Khine 2006; Sang et al. 2010; Shapley et al. 2010).

Recent models suggest that computer integration in formal learning environments, that is school or classroom-based contexts, is predicted by a complex interaction of individual and situational variables. For example, Koehler and Mishra proposed a model of successful integration (2009) that outlines how educators must simultaneously integrate content, pedagogical, and technological knowledge (TPACK). Educators must also navigate logistical issues related to computer access, classroom management, and personal concerns of confidence, comfort, and experience with technology (Granger et al. 2002; Mueller et al. 2008; Watson 2006). Given the relative recency and popularity of SNSs and the challenges to computer integration in the classroom in general, it is not surprising that, as of yet, there is little empirical work or evidence-based practice demonstrating the impact of using SNSs as an instructional tool in formal learning contexts. Available research, however, tends to support the notion that integration of social network sites in the classroom will be a complex process.

To date, much of what we know about SNSs in educational contexts has been based upon informal (nonschool or classroom) learning opportunities and experiences. It is important to note that SNSs originated in informal contexts and predominantly exist in informal contexts. Informal learning situations tend to be self-directed, less structured, and often more spontaneous than formal learning contexts (Bartlett-Bragg 2006; Bull et al. 2008). Informal learning contexts are often overlooked as credible and important learning environments; however, informal contexts can provide sophisticated opportunities that promote cognitive and social development (Willoughby and Wood 2008).

24.1.3.1 How Can SNSs Promote Learning?

The natural application of traditional social/instructional and developmental theories to SNSs has been noted by several investigators (Ajjan and Hartshorne 2008; Bandura 2001; Bartlett-Bragg 2006; Olson and Bruner 1996; Maloney 2007; Mazman and Usluel 2010). For example, Bandura's theory of mass communication (2001) and constructivist theory (Olson and Bruner 1996) have both been applied to this novel digital technology. Bandura's theory of mass communication (2001) centers around the idea that media acts as a link between the individual and their social networks and communities. Social models (whether in the form of a fictional or real person) provided by online media display new ideas, values, and social practices, which can be transmitted almost instantly across the globe. According to Bandura (2001), this new global consciousness transmitted by electronic media helps to shape the social realities of the individual and engages users in social learning. Constructivist theory endorses learning as a social activity where peers learn from one another during interactive exchanges (Olson and Bruner 1996). SNSs which are based in social interaction and information sharing may present a whole new world of learning possibilities.

One of the key strengths of social network sites is the instant connectivity among multiple users. Students have used Facebook to learn outside of the classroom by joining discussion or interest groups and sharing information, ideas, and opinions among themselves in these settings. In addition, users can share visual (photos, art, and videos) and verbal information and this provides an ideal forum for learning from others. Together, these activities can encourage collaborative learning, learning from peers, providing and responding to peer feedback, and being an active engaged learner (Ajjan and Hartshorne 2008; Bartlett-Bragg 2006; Mason 2006; Mejias 2005; Selwyn 2007), which are skills consistent with pedagogical goals in formal learning contexts. In addition, engaging in these key skills in a highly motivating social networking environment suggests that SNSs would be ideal for promoting development of these skills (Bugeja 2006; Maloney 2007; Mason 2006; Mazer et al. 2009; Ziegler 2007). An additional advantage in employing social network sites is the level of participation that can be elicited from a greater number of learners. The integration of reluctant, shy, and less communicative students is a concern for educators. Social media may present a way to circumvent some of the issues that shy students face. Web-based classroom discussions are considered more welcoming and allow shy or less outgoing students to engage in discussions in which they would otherwise not participate (Sullivan 2001).

In general, males tend to dominate face-to-face classroom discussion (Crombie et al. 2003; Sadker and Sadker 1994).This poses a challenge for educators who are trying to engage students in active discussion, interaction, or collaborative exercises. The online learning environment may provide a solution to this gender-based participation issue, by providing a more female-friendly environment (Savicki et al. 1996; Sullivan 2001). Research outcomes suggest that females have a preference for online communication more than males do (Boneva et al. 2001; Bostock and Lizhi 2005; Jackson et al. 2001), and when teaching is shifted to an online forum, females tend to express themselves more strongly, which in turn contributes to greater learning (Anderson and Haddad 2005).

24.1.4 What Predicts Who Is Likely to Adopt Social Network Sites as an Educational Tool?

The complexity inherent in integrating SNSs into the formal educational context has been borne out in recent research. Specifically, three studies suggest an array of variables that predict when and by whom SNSs will be adopted and used in educational settings. The first two studies employed survey data collected from university instructors and students ((Ajjan and Hartshorne 2008; Hartshorne and Ajjan 2009), respectively). This data was examined through path analyses to identify which variables predicted the intention to use and then actually use an array of Web 2.0 technologies (blogs, wikis, SNSs, etc.) for formal education purposes. In both studies, intention to use Web 2.0 technologies was related to attitudes and perceived behavioral control. Specifically, if instructors/students felt that the technologies were useful, easy to use, and compatible with their existing values, they were more likely to think about using the technologies. Similarly, if the conditions were right and there was sufficient support such that faculty/students would feel comfortable using the technology, they would also be more likely to intend to use the technology. In addition, students, unlike instructors, were subject to the social influence of their peers and instructors as to whether they intended to use the technologies. As expected, intention to use the technology positively impacted actual behavior, with those *intending* to use the technologies more likely to adopt and *use* the technologies.

These outcomes are consistent with previous findings given in the literature addressing the complex considerations associated with the integration of computer technology. Specifically, potential adoption of social media and use of social media are influenced by individual variables (comfort, ease), pedagogical considerations (perceived usefulness, learning), and technological knowledge/support. In addition, students were influenced by their peers and perceptions about their peers. The failure for instructors to be affected by social influences was suggested to be a function of the relatively independent nature of faculty teaching assignments (Ajjan and Hartshorne 2008). Together, these findings suggest that adoption of Web 2.0 technologies is contingent upon the fostering of positive attitudes toward the technologies as well as providing the necessary support to execute integration. Interestingly, these studies drew upon respondents who were not necessarily required to use Web 2.0 technologies in their formal educational contexts; therefore, caution is required in applying these outcomes in broader contexts.

Descriptive data in each of these studies provided some specific insights regarding use of SNSs in these samples. In terms of faculty members' beliefs about the instructional benefits of SNSs, only 16% thought social networking would improve learning; 24% thought that use of SNSs would increase interaction among students; and 32% thought students satisfaction with their course would improve. These numbers suggest that about a quarter of the faculty saw potential in using SNSs as part of their instructional approach. Why were the evaluations so low? In part, it could be that instructors perceived this technology to be a difficult one to integrate. Indeed, only 23% thought social network sites could be easily integrated. More likely, however, these responses reflect lack of familiarity with SNSs. In fact, 60% of the faculty reported that they had never used SNSs. Given these perceptions and the general lack of knowledge about SNSs, it is not surprising that 74% of the faculty do not currently use SNSs in their classes and do not plan to use them. When students were polled, just under half (46%) of the sample did not currently use SNSs and did not plan to use these for educational purposes. Clearly, more students were open to using SNSs than faculty, perhaps reflecting greater familiarity with this technology. Even so, these outcomes suggest that in order to encourage greater integration, universities need to foster positive attitudes toward the technologies. This may require training and support in the use of the technology. In addition, faculty and students may require concrete demonstrations where SNSs are used effectively in practical ways as part of the classroom structure.

One concern with these two studies is that social networking was considered as one of many Web 2.0 technologies and it is possible that attitudes toward other technologies may have influenced responses regarding social networking. A third study, investigating Facebook, clarifies potential confusion or interference from these grouped technologies (Mazman and Usluel 2010). When students were surveyed to see what variables impacted on their educational use of Facebook, some of the same variables in the previous two studies involving faculty and students also appeared when only adoption of Facebook was considered (Mazman and Usluel 2010). Specifically, when students perceived Facebook to be useful, easy, and comfortable to use, and they experienced a sense of community or identity with others, there was a positive impact on the students' social, work, and daily use of Facebook. These three purposes for Facebook, in turn, predicted greater educational usage. Again, adoption was based on multiple elements working together. It is also important to note that the college students in this sample also were not *required* to use Facebook as part of a course or any part of their formal learning. Instead, this study examined the spontaneous integration of Facebook from informal to formal educational contexts. In other words, students, once experienced with Facebook, began to expand its use to the formal educational environment. These results are encouraging because they suggest that students do indeed see the potential for Facebook to contribute to their formal educational experience so much so that they begin to employ it without formal instruction to do so.

24.1.5   How Do Students Employ Facebook for Formal Educational Purposes?

There are various built-in features of Facebook that may encourage use of the site for more formal educational purposes. For instance, Facebook has recently made changes which now allow users to create specific groups that can be based around shared interests, activities, and even academic study. Users have the ability to control the privacy settings for each individual group by setting their preferences accordingly, thus controlling access to their academic and personal information. In addition to specialized groups, Facebook gives users the option to add various education-related applications. For example, "I'm Reading" lets users display lists of books they are currently reading, browse through books their friends are reading, and look at book reviews friends have written. "Philosophers + Philosophy" is an educational application that displays biographical information and famous quotes from 400 philosophers. Users are also given the opportunity to engage in philosophical debates with other users. According to Facebook statistics as of November 2010, "I'm Reading" had 41,817 monthly active users and "Philosophers" had 13,784 monthly active users, indicating that these applications are popular.

A recent qualitative examination of the wall postings of 612 university students indicated that only 4% of 68,169 postings observed dealt with education-related issues (Selwyn 2009). The vast majority of communications dealt with personal and relationship concerns. The relatively negligible frequency of educationally relevant references in wall postings is not surprising when one considers that the study, similar to the studies mentioned above, again, examined informal use of Facebook. Students were not required to use Facebook as part of an experimental manipulation, but instead these students spontaneously adapted a primarily social connectivity tool to include educationally relevant content. Interestingly, the educational references included exchanges about the students university experience (what their most recent lecture was like), providing basic practical information (due dates for assignments), as well as more detailed academic information (interpretation of assignment expectations), support seeking (for poor performance), and also fun exchanges. The fact that spontaneous exchanges occurred and could be noted for only one of the many features available through Facebook suggests the potential and desire for SNSs to include formal educational experiences as part of the natural exchange of ideas, opinions, and thoughts that typically are exchanges in SNSs. There is some caution, however, in that some of the language and references to individuals depicted in the postings were unflattering, to say the least, and would lead to potential problems if accepted "as is" within a classroom context. This issue raises two concerns. First, there is the issue of rules of conduct for the use of SNSs. In general, there are no current overarching rules that dictate what should and should not be present information posted through Facebook (barring legal issues related to posting hateful, threatening, or pornographic information). The second issue is that constraining the nature and content of postings may change the nature of Facebook and what makes it appealing. This is a sensitive issue which is explored below in the consideration of digital citizenship.

24.1.6   What Is Digital Citizenship?

Digital citizenship evolved with the ever-increasing prevalence of technology in social contexts. Digital citizenship deals with the appropriate use of technologies in social contexts, including educational contexts. The need for this construct has become apparent more recently because as technologies become more pervasive, there are more opportunities for the use of technologies to clash with social expectations of how social communication should occur. For example, should you or should you not post pictures of your friends who were at party with you among your Facebook photos? Different people will answer this question differently and that is the challenge. People have different expectations because there are, as yet, no formally accepted conventions for most digital technologies and this is also true for SNSs. Whereas rules of turn-taking and "acceptable" language and levels of sharing are fairly well defined within cultures, the social pragmatics regarding digital technologies lags far behind that of traditional forms of social interaction. The introduction of SNSs in the classroom, therefore, might best be concomitant with a discussion of social expectations and appropriate codes of conduct. Although etiquette issues often arise (Ribble et al. 2004) as a nuisance or annoyance in day-to-day interactions when using SNSs, there are more serious issues that demand immediate attention.

Practical issues regarding expectations of privacy for oneself and others, for example, are important considerations for avoiding potentially embarrassing or harmful content from appearing and for avoiding potential liability issues. Perhaps the most serious considerations for educators are potential abuses that can result in cyberbullying, harassment, and/or deliberate embarrassment (Kiriakidis and Kavoura 2010), or threats to academic integrity such as cheating (sharing test questions and answers) and plagiarism. For example, a Canadian university student was recently accused of academic cheating because of his involvement in the creation of a Facebook study group that gave students the opportunity to post homework questions and answers online (www.cbc.ca, 2008). Unbeknownst to the student, this was grounds for expulsion from the institution. Explicit instructions regarding expectations is a necessary function that educators need to be prepared to provide before requiring Facebook as part of their course or program (Ribble et al. 2004). This however is not an easy task as many school boards do not have well-developed protocols regarding digital citizenship, leaving educators to develop these protocols on their own. Educators themselves may differ with respect to their expectations and this could lead to disparities and unnecessary conflicts or confusion across courses, teachers, and programs. Individual educators may also have limited expertise with SNSs which will inhibit their ability to anticipate potential challenges. Clearly, digital citizenship is a critical foundation when introducing SNSs as an educational tool. Effective development of digital citizenship expectations requires that educators work collaboratively with one another and with their students and, ideally, as a whole school or system approach, to devise consistent, clear codes of conduct to facilitate effective, culturally appropriate communication.

24.1.7 The Perfect Setting! Privacy and Safety Issues in Social Media

Although SNSs may represent potentially new learning tools, their introduction requires careful consideration in order to avoid pitfalls that could lead to vulnerabilities for the user. Access, information, building relationships, and sharing with others are the hallmarks of social network sites. By simply typing in a person's name, an abundance of information can be accessed, ranging from relatively benign pieces of personal details such as favorite quotes, to highly personal pieces of information including profile pictures, home addresses, and birth dates. Users may not consider the implications of their disclosures online and may not realize that they can put themselves and others at risk, either directly or indirectly, by sharing information in an open forum. The very openness, connectedness, and accessibility offered through SNSs have the potential to place users at risk, but the sites also have mechanisms to minimize risks.

24.1.8 What Are the Associated Risks with SNSs?

When users initially sign up for a Facebook account, they are required to provide at least a few personal details (date of joining, school status, e-mail address, and name). Once a member, many users go beyond just the bare minimum and provide a wide variety of personal information in their profiles (location, mobile phone number, sexual orientation, personal photos). The default setting for a new profile allows public access to any other user within the new user's specified network. As well, the new user's profile is accessible to the friends of all the other users within their network. Given that users are providing sensitive information online, they may place themselves at considerable risk. For example, Facebook users may subject themselves to potential embarrassment, identity theft, "lurking" or stalking by other users, and blackmailing (Gross et al. 2005).

Nosko et al. (2010) conducted an archival examination of 400 randomly selected, preexisting, open (publicly accessible) Facebook profiles to examine the issue of disclosure – and more importantly, over-disclosure. Disclosure is the act of revealing information about the self to another (Collins and Miller 1994) and may be conveyed either in verbal or written form (Derlega et al. 1993). Over-disclosure involves providing information which can potentially be used in a variety of harmful ways. For example, to injure a person legally through online identity theft, to injure a person physically by placing oneself in a position where they could be stalked, assaulted, or robbed, and, finally, to injure a person psychologically by opening oneself to public criticism or threat as a function of holding certain views or customs that differ from others. One concern with SNSs is that users may provide information about themselves that opens them to one or more of these kinds of threats. We explored this concern systematically by constructing a comprehensive coding scheme that allowed all the pieces of information present in each profile to be identified (Nosko et al. 2010). The pieces of information were then organized into categories that could be used to assess the potential of risk for identity theft, personal security threats, and stigmatization. Results confirmed that these risks were present in the sample. Almost everyone in the sample provided at least one piece of information for each of these threat categories (94%, 100%, and 99% for identity, personal security, and stigmatizing information threats, respectively). In addition, on average, about 50% of potential pieces of information were provided for each category by members of the sample. Clearly, the potential threats identified in earlier research were evident in this research.

Our study (Nosko et al. 2010) examined whether certain factors, including gender, relationship status, and age, were related to the likelihood of disclosing certain types of information online. Interestingly, some groups were at higher risk. Younger, rather than older, users were at greater risk. As age increased, the likelihood of disclosing all three types of information decreased. Users who indicated they were single disclosed more stigmatizing information. Indicating any relationship status was related to an increase in disclosure of identity theft information and information that could compromise personal security. Gender, however, did not predict disclosure in the three categories. Results suggest that certain groups may be more inclined to put themselves at risk, including younger individuals and those who declare themselves single.

24.1.9   Just How Serious Can Over-Disclosure Be?

In some cases, Facebook users have posted directions to personal residences and cottages along with wall updates notifying others that they are out of town for the weekend–providing an open invitation to thieves to come over to an empty, unsupervised house. During a 2-month-long investigation that tracked more than a dozen Canadians through their open social networking profiles, a reporter for a national newspaper, "The Globe and Mail," built profiles for individual users (Hartley 2008). Here are examples of some of the information extracted about individual users:

> A 24-year-old Calgary woman posts her cell phone number, e-mail address, and the name of the Kelowna motel where she and three of her friends will spend a June weekend partying. In addition to nicknaming the event the "Erotic Party," the women joke about finding "some hot men to buy us dinner and drinks."
> A Toronto teen posts comments about her favorite sexual positions; a 24-year-old Saskatchewan man posts details for a huge house party he plans to hold while his parents are out of town.

The reporter went on to explain that while some of these standalone details may not amount to much, through use of freely available Web tools including directory searches (Canada411) and Google (using the reverse phone search on Canada411), other users could easily look up related personal information, including home addresses and directions to personal residences. In one instance, the reporter even went so far as to meet up with a 17-year-old female, whose profile he found on Facebook. The teenager's cell phone number was posted on her open Facebook profile, and this is how he contacted her. After agreeing to meet, he showed her the profile he had constructed for her based on information she had posted, including, but not limited to, where she lived, where she worked, her home and cell phone numbers, and her birth date.

24.1.10   How Is Online Information Accessed?

Informational privacy theory: Informational privacy theory defines privacy as the control an individual possesses over the flow of their personal information, including both the transfer and exchange of their personal information (Tavani 2004). While transfer and exchanging information may seem like a simple and innocuous task, the reality is that there are a host of information theft-related risks online. Three main dangers include: data gathering, data exchanging, and data mining.

Data gathering occurs when personal information is collected and recorded, for example, on certain SNSs, user information is gathered by third parties through means of a "free flow of cookie-based information" (Rucker 2008). Basically, a cookie is a string of text that a Web server can store on a user's computer, whenever a person visits a Web site. Web sites use cookies so that information about the user can be stored on the user's computer, and then retrieved by the Web site on a later date. Usually, this consists of a simple name–value string, which is basically a user ID. Cookies essentially allow Web site owners to glean information about an individual's online browsing preferences (Tavani 2004).

Data exchanging occurs when personal information is transferred and exchanged across and between computer databases. Tavani (Tavani 2004) defines computer merging, a data exchanging technique, as a way of "extracting information from two or more unrelated databases, which contain data about some individual or group of individuals, and incorporating it into a composite file" (p. 127). For example, a user first signs into Facebook and provides his/her age, gender, and location, and then signs into another site that asks for their income and credit history. The user has voluntarily and knowingly provided different pieces of personal information to two legitimate and separate sites. These personal pieces of information provided to two apparently independent sites are then combined through computer merging, and can be freely disclosed, exchanged, or even sold without the user's awareness or consent.

Data mining occurs when personal information is searched in an effort to find patterns implicit in large databases. This is done so that third parties (ad agencies) can generate consumer profiles based on behavioral patterns discovered in certain groups. An example of data mining can be found on Facebook where the site targets ad delivery based on profile information provided by Facebook users. This essentially allows marketers to "predict what products and services users might be interested in even before they have specifically mentioned an area" (Vara 2007).

While data gathering, exchanging, and mining occur frequently online, there are ways to control and limit what happens with personal information online. For example, there are features built into social media outlets that are available to protect user information and to control the degree to which their information is accessible to other users. Ensuring that users are aware of potential risks and taking steps to reduce risks is clearly a critical concern, especially since these are not salient features of SNSs.

24.1.11 How Can You Protect Yourself and Others?

Facebook, for example, gives users the opportunity to change privacy settings for their personal profile information and photo and video information (www. Facebook.com). Users can also control the ability of others to contact them and can limit third-party access to their personal information. Moreover, users have the ability to control who can see their profile, and who cannot. For instance, a user can choose to strictly limit what a stranger (someone who is not yet on their friends list) can see when they come across their profile in Facebook. Alternatively, users may also keep an "open" profile, allowing anyone to freely browse through their information regardless of whether or not they are friends. Users can also set their privacy controls so that only certain people can search for them and find them on Facebook. There are varying degrees of accessibility, and users who choose "anyone" agree to allow everyone who is a member of Facebook to locate their profiles on Facebook. If a user is particularly open with their information, they can opt to have their profiles entered into search engines such as Google and Yahoo. When this option is selected, a simple Google search of a user name will pull up a profile and list it in the search results.

Privacy features not only protect the user, but also any information that the user may have posted about other people (pictures, posts, and personal details). The only problem is that while privacy safeguards exist, getting user's to employ them is a different story.

24.1.12 Privacy Settings: Are They Being Used?

Most people are concerned about their privacy, both offline and online (Cranor et al. 1999; Nosko et al. in preparation; Statistics Canada). While the general consensus is that privacy is important (Acquisti and Gross 2006), there appears to be a discrepancy between attitudes and behaviors (Acquisti and Gross 2006; Govani and Pashley unpublished manuscript). Gross and Acquisti (2005) found that the majority of Facebook users did not employ the available privacy settings, allowing for complete access to their profiles. If any settings were used, they were minimal, and allowed, for example, friends of friends or a user's entire network to view their profile. In keeping with Gross and Acquisti's findings, in an archival examination of existing Facebook profiles, Nosko et al. (2010) found that out of 800 randomly generated profiles, half of the profiles accessed were publicly accessible – meaning that complete strangers could access user's personal details.

24.1.13 How Does Awareness Affect Outcomes?

Unfortunately, it appears that even though users boast that they are aware of the privacy settings, and even given the provision of information regarding settings, some users still choose not to employ them. Govani and Pashley (unpublished manuscript) found that while most users were well aware of the privacy settings available to them, less than half actually employed any (40%). Nosko, Wood, and Kenney (Nosko et al. in preparation) are currently completing an investigation examining privacy setting use for newly created Facebook accounts. Preliminary findings indicate that the vast majority of users did not employ any settings at all (97%), even when they were given explicit instructions explaining how each setting functioned and where to find the setting in Facebook.

Failure to use available safeguards presents a challenge for educators and students who are using social media as a teaching and learning tool. In the context of online social media, there is a fine balance between disclosing personal information (even for educational purposes), while, at the same time, maintaining a degree of informational privacy. One could argue that what an individual does with his/her personal information and how s/he uses privacy settings is a personal choice. But is it? If educators require their students to use SNSs, are they responsible for ensuring that appropriate safeguards are being employed? If the responsibility falls on the students, what motivates them to protect themselves when using social media? Ethical and legal issues are important considerations when it comes to privacy and SNSs.

24.1.14 Privacy and Policy Considerations to Protect Users: "But I Just Don't Care About My Privacy" (Male/26)

The development of social network sites has also necessitated the development of laws to protect the privacy of users. In order to convey the kinds of legal considerations that have been developed, this section addresses current laws in the United States that are in place for SNSs (Arendt 2009); however, other countries have also developed laws some of which are more stringent and others less so. The purpose in presenting this information is to highlight policies that have emerged and to present some suggestions about how educators and policy makers can ensure safer use of social media.

There are various data protection laws in place that stipulate that individuals "must be allowed to control the collection, use and transfer of personal information about them" (JISC Legal, 2008a, as cited in Arendt 2009). SNSs such as Facebook are considered external sites, such that they are not moderated by educational institutions. This, therefore, poses a risk to students and educators whose information may be shared on these external sites. Arendt (2009) advises that "before adopting the use of an externally-provided Web 2.0 service, the organizer shall appraise the stability and security of that service, the loss, damage and/or disruption that would be caused by failure of the service, and the corresponding benefit that using the service brings" (p. 21). Cate (2009) suggests that educators who choose to use social media should make an effort to explicitly outline in their syllabi or course descriptions the privacy rights of students. Arendt also suggests that all users familiarize themselves with the SNS of choice and the existing site policies prior to using the media. For example, Facebook boasts two core principles of privacy (www.Facebook.com):

(a) You should have control over your personal information.
(b) You should have access to the information others want to share.

The Higher Education Academy and the Joint Information Systems Committee (2009) goes on to suggest that it is the responsibility of the policy makers to make information and advice available and accessible to users, and most importantly, to educators and administrators. The committee notes that there are a few key points to keep in mind when creating policies surrounding use of social networking in education, including:

(a) Assume that new users have no prior knowledge or experience with the technology
(b) Demonstrate how the technology will be used
(c) Use layperson language and communicate clearly (Cate 2009)

As self-disclosure increases as a function of social media use, so does the need for strategies to protect user information. Ribble and colleagues (2004) highlight how students need to be educated about protecting their electronic data (by using virus software, by backing up information, and by protecting their identities). In terms of responsibility, students need to know that it is their responsibility to protect not only themselves, but others in the community through the use of various protection strategies.

Another potential issue for educators to consider when employing Facebook for educational purposes is whether or not faculty and teachers should "friend" students. Given that both students and teachers may possess active Facebook accounts, the possibility remains that students may seek out their teachers and request to be added as their "friend." Debate over this issue was posted on the Facebook discussion board and the consensus was that this was not considered to be professional or an appropriate practice. In many cases, educators are accountable for teacher–student communication, and may be faced with a host of issues if communication is deemed inappropriate or misinterpreted by either party.

24.1.15   Can We Encourage Greater Consideration of Privacy Concerns: Interventions and Their Impact?

Typically, legal privacy policies have been the main mode of communicating to users about their privacy rights and options, but our current research has shown that these widespread and commonly used documents have little bearing on the amount of information that users actually disclose (Nosko et al. in preparation). Specifically, this study contrasted the adoption of the different privacy settings users employed while constructing a Facebook account as a function of exposure stories provided prior to constructing the profile.

The study contrasted three different exposure stories: a legal privacy statement taken directly from the privacy statement on the Facebook online Web site, a personal privacy story that was an adaptation of a story that appeared in the Globe and Mail (September 2008) which outlined potential consequences of putting personal information online, or a control story that described the history of the Internet and its popularity. Although it was expected that the anecdotal personal story might be particularly salient (Stanovich 2009) for drawing attention to the need to employ settings, there were no significant differences between the groups in terms of privacy settings use, overall disclosure, or for disclosure of information related to identity theft, personal security, and stigmatization (Nosko et al. in preparation). Clearly, encouraging users to adopt privacy settings requires more than simple interventions.

To address this concern, more intensive, explicit interventions may be required. For example, just-in-time instruction provided as the user begins to build each component of his/her profile may encourage thoughtful consideration of the impact of decisions regarding use of privacy settings. With just-in-time instruction, questions are addressed immediately (Anderson and Wood 2009). By providing support at the time when it is needed, memory demands are reduced and students are able to reduce the time it takes to figure out the solution to their problem, thus permitting faster and easier progression through learning tasks (Kester et al. 2001; VanLehn 1996). In the case of Facebook privacy settings, students would be taught about privacy and privacy settings with examples and hands-on activities to accompany the material. Most importantly, any questions that arise should be addressed immediately.

What is needed is additional research that explores why privacy settings are or are not used and what influences individual's decisions to employ them. These will yield testable training programs that can be supported through research and that can be implemented in the community. Training may be especially important for younger students, who may be more naïve and less able to understand the importance of privacy issues, but may be, at the same time, very active users of social media.

24.1.16   The Digital Divide

In all contexts where new technologies are being integrated into formal classroom environments, the issue of the digital divide must be considered. Three structures depict the issues inherent in digital divide considerations. The first structure reflects the width of the divide. This structure is the one most frequently associated with digital divide concerns as it represents access to the necessary technology. In the case of SNSs, a potential user would need to have access to a computer, the Internet, and to a system which would allow for ease of use with the SNS requirements (digital camera with interface to take and upload pictures). Although access to computers is generally becoming less and less of a concern, especially in industrialized world, there are still some groups, especially low socioeconomic groups, who may be at risk for lack of access especially to components needed for some applications within SNSs. The second structure involves the slope of the divide. The slope reflects beliefs or cultures which can support or hinder the use of technologies (some educators view technology as an integrated part of curriculum that allows students experiences that would otherwise be unavailable to them while others see little value in using technology). The research above indicates that this may be one of the most important challenges facing integration of social networking technologies within the classroom today as many instructors and students do not intend to use these technologies for educational purposes. The third structure of the divide is depth. Depth reflects how technology is being used (surface or peripheral level vs. deep and meaningful level) (Willoughby and Wood 2008). To date, little information is available regarding how to implement SNSs effectively in the classroom. Educators and researchers need to be encouraged to develop and execute innovative studies that will define how, when, and where SNSs might become tools for learning.

24.1.17 Using Facebook in the Classroom Reflections and Considerations for Those Integrating This Technology

1. Facebook evolved in an informal learning context. Harnessing this technology might be most beneficial if it is not overly constrained. If educators can find a way to work with the design of the software rather than constraining the design to fit the formal teaching format, then the software will most likely retain the highly interactive and motivating features that make it so popular.
2. An initial point for adoption of this technology should be for adult learners. The greatest numbers of users of Facebook fall between the ages of 18 and 25 (Gross et al. 2005; Selwyn 2009). Adults in this range are typically in college or University contexts. Initial adoption and experimentation within the college/university context would be beneficial for three reasons. First, features of distance and online education courses offered in higher education contexts typically already have tools that share some similar features with Facebook. Most notably, bulletin boards where information can be posted and communication exchanged with fellow students and/or instructors. Second, developing the protocols required for digital citizenship, privacy, and academic integrity may be more expedient with this age group because they are a mature and experienced

group of collaborators and, hence, can contribute more efficiently to the process, and their advanced cognitive skills may make them more effective at understanding, generating, and navigating the decision making required in each of these contexts, Finally, the youngest age for approval of membership for Facebook is 13, this means that members would at the very earliest be in high school or equivalent. Parents may need to be required to provide consent and active supervision in order to introduce Facebook as an instructional tool. This may lead to challenges in uniformity of access in initiating any program and liability issues should anything go wrong.

3. Given what we know about digital divide issues, access to technology compatible with Facebook requirements must be established and secured for each participant in the adoption and integration of this technology.
4. Support services need to be in place to ensure confidence in all users' ability to use the SNS independently.
5. Collaboration is useful, among instructors, programs, and schools in order to ensure uniformity of expectations within the Facebook environment.
6. Clearly identifying the pedagogical advantage for using Facebook vs. other technologies and sharing these pedagogical considerations with students will build awareness of the expectations and limitations of the technology.

Considering these issues will assist in putting in place the mechanisms to make sure the adoption of Facebook is more seamlessly integrated. According to Albion (2008), "Social media represents a more participative and potentially paradigm-changing environment for building and sharing knowledge. Some educators have begun to apply these tools in classrooms but, as their use in society expands, there will be expectations for their wider application in schools" (p. 181).The challenge is clear, innovative technologies are taking hold in our upcoming and current generations of learners. It now falls to researchers, educators, schools, and communities to determine how to translate these technologies into salient and motivating learning tools in both formal and informal learning environments. SNSs are one new technology waiting to be effectively and safely incorporated as part of a repertoire of tools to promote learning.

References

Acquisti, A., Gross, R.: Imagined communities: awareness, information sharing, and privacy on facebook. PET 2006. http://privacy.cs.cmu.edu/dataprivacy/projects/Facebook/Facebook2.pdf (2006)

Aduwa-Ogiegbaen, S.: Nigerian in-service teachers. Self-assessment in core technology competences and their professional development needs in ICT. J. Comput. Teach. Educ. **26** (1), 17–28 (2009)

Ajjan, H., Hartshorne, R.: Investigating Faculty Decisions to Adopt Web 2.0 Technologies: Theory and Empirical Tests. Internet High. Educ. **11**(2), 71–80 (2008)

Albion, P.: Social media in teacher education: two imperatives for action. Comput. Sch. **25**(3/4), 181–198 (2008)

Anderson, D.M., Haddad, C.J.: Gender, voice, and learning in online course environments. J. Asynchronous Learn. Netw. **9**(1), 3–14 (2005)

Anderson, A., Wood, E.: Implementing technology in the classroom: assessing teachers' needs through the use of a just-in-time support system. In: Society for Information Technology and Teacher Education (SITE), Charleston (2009)

Arendt, A.M.: Social media tools and the policies associated with them. In: Best Practices in Policy Management Conference, Utah Valley University (2009)

Bandura, A.: Social cognitive theory of mass communication. Media Psychol. **3**(3), 265–299 (2001)

Bartlett-Bragg, A. Reflections on Pedagogy: Reframing Practice to Foster Informal Learning with Social Software. http://www.dream.dk/uploads/files/Anne%20Bartlett-Bragg.pdf (2006)

Birch, A.: Preservice teachers' acceptance of ICT integration in the classroom: applying the UTAUT model. Educ. Media Int. **46**(4), 295–315 (2009)

Boneva, B., Kraut, R., Frohlich, D.: Using e-mail for personal relationships: the difference gender makes. Am. Behav. Sci. **45**(3), 530–549 (2001)

Bostock, S.J., Lizhi, W.: Gender in student online discourse. Innov. Educ. Teach. Int. **42**(1), 73–85 (2005)

Boyd, D.M., Ellison, N.B.: Social network sites: definition, history, and scholarship. J. Comput.-Mediated Commun. **13**(1), article 11 (2007) http://jcmc.indiana.edu/vol13/issue1/boyd.ellison.html

Bugeja, M.: Facing the facebook. Chronicle High. Educ. **52**(21), 1–4 (2006)

Bull, G., Thompson, A., Searson, M., Garofalo, J., Park, J., Young, C., Lee, J.: Connecting informal and formal learning experiences in the age of participatory media. Contemp. Issues Technol. Teach. Educ. **8**(2), 100–107 (2008)

Cate, B.: The law and policy of Web 2.0: much old, some new, lots borrowed, so don't be blue. Educuase Learn. Initiative (2009) http://hosted.mediasite.com/mediasite/Viewer/?peid=98e83dc76b9749f3a08996bfb0f5904b

Collins, N.L., Miller, L.C.: Self-disclosure and liking: a meta-analytic review. Psychol. Bull. **116**, 457–475 (1994)

Cranor, L.F., Reagle, J., Ackerman, M.S.: Beyond concern: understanding net users' attitudes about online privacy. AT&T Labs-Research Technical Report (1999) http://www.research.att.com/library/trs/TRs/99/99.4

Crombie, G., Pyke, S.W., Silverthorn, N., Jones, A., Piccinin, S.: Students' perception of their classroom participation and instructor as a function of gender and context. J. High. Educ. **74**(1), 51–76 (2003)

Cuban, L., Kirkpatrick, H., Peck, C.: High access and low use of technologies in high school classrooms: explaining an apparent paradox. Am. Educ. Res. J. **38**, 813–834 (2001)

Derlega, V.J., Metts, S., Petronio, S., Margulis, S.T.: Self disclosure. Sage, London (1993)

Drent, M., Meelissen, M.: Which factors obstruct or stimulate teacher educators to use ICT innovatively? Comput. Educ. **51**, 187–199 (2008)

Ellison, N.B., Steinfield, C., Lampe, C.: The benefits of facebook "friends:" social capital and college students' use of online social network sites. J. Comput-Mediat. Commun. **12**(4), 1143–1168 (2007)

Govani, T., Pashley, H.: (Unpublished Manuscript): Student Awareness of the Privacy Implications when Using Facebook, http://lorrie.cranor.org/courses/fa05/tubzhlp.pdf

Granger, C.A., Morbey, M.L., Lotherington, H., Owston, R.D., Wideman, H.H.: Factors contributing to teachers' successful implementation of IT. J. Comput. Assist. Learn. **18**, 480–488 (2002)

Gross, R., Acquisti, A.: Information revelation and privacy in online social networks (the Facebook case). In: 2005 ACM Workshop on Privacy in the Electronic Society, pp. 71–80, (2005)

Hartley, M.: Social networking comes with a price. http://www.theglobeandmail.com/news/technology/article709699.ece(2008)

Hartshorne, R., Ajjan, H.: Examining student decisions to adopt web 2.0 technologies: theory and empirical tests. J. Comput. High. Educ. **21**(3), 1042–1726 (2009)

Higher education academy and the joint information systems committee. Higher education in a Web 2.0 world. http://www.jisc.ac.uk/media/documents/publications/heweb20rptv1.pdf (2009)

History of MySpace. http://www.randomhistory.com/2008/08/14_myspace.html

Jackson, L., Ervin, K., Gardner, P.D., Schmitt, N.: Gender and the internet: women communicating and men searching. Sex Roles **44**(5/6), 363–379 (2001)

Kester, L., Kirschner, P.A., van Merrienboer, J.J.G., Baumer, A.: Just-in-time information presentation and the acquisition of complex cognitive skills. Comput. Hum. Behav. **17**, 373–391 (2001)

Kiriakidis, S.P., Kavoura, A.: Cyberbullying: a review of the literature on harassment through the internet and other electronic means. Family & Community Health: The Journal of Health Promotion & Maintenance **33**(2), 82–93 (2010)

Koehler, M.J., Mishra, P.: What is technological pedagogical content knowledge? Contemp. Issues Technol. Teach. Educ. **9**(1), 60–70 (2009)

Lenhart, A., Madden, M.: Social networking websites and teens: an overview. Pew internet and American life project report. http://www.pewinternet.org/PPF/r/198/report_display.asp (2007)

Lim, C.P., Khine, M.S.: Managing teachers' barriers to ICT integration in Singapore schools. J. Technol. Teach. Educ. **14**(1), 97–125 (2006)

Madge, C., Meek, J., Wellens, J., Hooley, T.: Facebook, social integration and informal learning at university: 'it is more for socializing and talking to friends about work than for actually doing work'. Learn. Media Technol. **34**(2), 141–155 (2009)

Maloney, E.: What web 2.0 can teach us about learning. Chronicle High. Educ. **53**(18), 26 (2007)

Mason, R.: Learning technologies for adult continuing education. Stud. Contin. Educ. **28**(2), 12–33 (2006)

Mazer, J.P., Murphy, R.E., Simonds, C.J.: The effects of teacher self-disclosure via facebook on teacher credibility. Learn. Media Technol. **34**(2), 175–183 (2009)

Mazman, S.G., Usluel, Y.K.: Modeling educational usage of facebook. Comput. Educ. **55**(2), 445–453 (2010)

Mejias, U.: Nomad's guide to learning and social software. http://knowledgetree.flexiblelearning.net.au/edition07/html/la_mejias.html (2005)

Mueller, J., Wood, E., Willoughby, T., Ross, C., Specht, J.: Identifying discriminating variables between teachers who fully integrate computers and teachers with limited integration. Comput. Educ. **51**, 1523–1537 (2008)

Nosko, A., Wood, E., Molema, S.: All about me: disclosure in online social networking profiles: the case of FACEBOOK. Comput. Hum. Behav. **26**, 406–418 (2010)

Nosko, A., Wood, E., Kenney, M., Archer, K., Depasquale, D., Molerma, S., Zivcakova, L.: To tell or not to tell: the impact of anecdotal privacy invasion story and gender on disclosure and privacy settings usage in Facebook profiles. Comput. in Hum. Behav. (under review)

Olson, D.R., Bruner, N.: Folk psychology and folk pedagogy. In: The Handbook of Education and Human Development: New Models of Learning, Teaching and Schooling, pp. 9–27. Blackwell Publishing, Malden (1996)

Paraskeva, F., Bouta, H., Papagianni, A.: Individual characteristics and computer self-efficacy in secondary education teachers to integrate technology in educational practice. Comput. Educ. **50**, 1084–1091 (2008)

Pempek, T.A., Yermolayeva, Y.A., Calvert, S.L.: College students' social networking experiences on facebook. J. Appl. Dev. Psychol. **30**, 227–238 (2009)

Ribble, M.S., Bailey, G.D., Ross, T.W.: Digital citizenship: addressing appropriate technology behaviour. Learn. Leading Technol. **32**(1), 6–12 (2004)

Rucker, J.D.: Facebook user-data gathering goes viral. Soshable. Social media blog. http://soshable.com/Facebook-user-data/ (2008)

Sadker, M.P., Sadker, D.M.: Failing at Fairness: How America's Schools Cheat Girls. Scribners Sons, New York (1994)

Sang, G., Valcke, M., Van Braak, J., Tondeur, J.: Student teachers' thinking processes and ICT integration: predictors of prospective teaching behaviors with educational technology. Comput. Educ. **54**(1), 103–112 (2010)

Savioki, V., Kelley, M., Lingenfelter, D.: Gender group composition and task type in small task groups using computer mediated communication. Computers in Human Behavior. **12**, 549 565 (1996)

Selwyn, N.: Screw blackboard. Do it on facebook! An investigation of students' educational use of facebook. http://www.scribd.com /doc/513958/Facebook seminar-paper-Selwyn (2007)

Selwyn, N.: Faceworking: exploring students' education-related use of facebook. Learn. Media Technol. **34**(2), 157–174 (2009)

Shapley, K., Sheehan, D., Maloney, C., Caranikas-Walker, F.: Effects of technology immersion on teachers' growth in technology competency, ideology, and practices. J. Educ. Comput. Res. **42**(1), 1–33 (2010)

Stanovich, K.: What Intelligence Tests Miss: The Psychology of Rational Thought. University Press, Yale (2009)

Statistics Canada.: Internet use by individuals, by internet privacy concern and age. http://www40.statcan.gc.ca/l01/cst01/comm31a-eng.htm (2008)

Stutzman, F.: Our lives, our Facebooks. In: 26th INSNA Conference, Vancouver (2006)

Sullivan, P.: Gender differences and the online classroom. Male and female college students evaluate their experiences. Community Coll. J. Res. Pract. **25**, 805–818 (2001)

Tavani, H.: Ethics and Technology: Ethical Issues in an Age of Information and Communication Technology. Wiley, Hoboken (2004)

Valkenburg, P.M., Schouten, A.P., Peter, J.: Adolescents' internet-based identity experiments: an exploratory survey. New Media Soc. **7**, 383–402 (2005)

VanLehn, K.: Cognitive skill acquisition. Annu. Rev. Psychol. **47**, 513–539 (1996)

Vara, V.: Facebook gets personal with Ad targeting plan. http://online.wsj.com/article/NA_WSJ_PUB:SB118783296519606151.html (2007)

Watson, G.: Technology professional development: long-term effects on teacher self-efficacy. J. Technol. Teach. Educ. **14**(1), 151–166 (2006)

Wiley, C., Sisson, M.: Ethics, accuracy and assumption: the use of facebook by students and employers. In: Southwestern Ohio Council for Higher Education Special Topics Forum, Dayton (2006)

Willoughby, T., Wood, E.: Children's Learning in a Digital World. Blackwell, Oxford (2008)

Yum, K.: Facebook says 'Thanks, Canada'. National Post, May 18, 2007

Ziegler, S.: The (mis)education of Generation M. Learn. Media Technol. **32**(1), 69–81 (2007)

Chapter 25
myLearningSpace: Engaging Education

Nathan Bailey, Katharina Franke, and Gordon Sanson

Abstract Traditional approaches to educating university students, where the instructor "transmits" content from the front of the class to students, are still popular at universities in Australia. It is clear that these approaches are increasingly failing to engage a digitally connected generation of social learners. Traditional lectures provide students with little opportunity to explore lecture content, collaborate with peers, or interact with the instructor. Monash University has been developing a collaborative learning environment that encourages students to participate in a personal learning journey independent of their physical location. This is enhanced by flexible learning spaces designed to facilitate a peer-based educational approach. Initial results indicate that these educational innovations are transforming the pedagogy, space, and technology of education to better meet the needs of twenty-first century learners.

25.1 Introduction

The traditional university lecture's generic, information-rich delivery increasingly fails to recognize individual learning styles, the very different expectations of a new generation and the demands of an information-rich global workplace (cf. Hughes 2009; Ito et al. 2008).

While educators are better at understanding student learning needs, their learning styles, preferences, motivations, and backgrounds (for an overview, see BECTA 2006), it is difficult to apply this knowledge to large classes where students essentially share the same experience. Large classes also limit student contributions and feedback to the instructor. These classes almost invite an impersonal and passive learning experience. However, a successful educational environment should provide some mechanism for mass personalization: a way to give students

N. Bailey (✉) • K. Franke • G. Sanson
eEducation Centre, Monash University, Melbourne, Australia
e-mail: Nathan.Bailey@monash.edu; Katharina.Franke@monash.edu; Gordon.Sanson@monash.edu

B. White et al. (eds.), *Social Media Tools and Platforms in Learning Environments*,
DOI 10.1007/978-3-642-20392-3_25, © Springer-Verlag Berlin Heidelberg 2011

the optimal learning experience for *them*, even in large classes. Education should challenge every student to *stretch* to their full potential, it should give every student an opportunity to *contribute* to the learning of their peers and it should support each student through a *learning journey that ensures mastery* of one level of knowledge before progressing to the next.

To mediate this personalized experience, today's students will need some kind of device. The device needs to be small enough for students to carry all the time but large enough for them to be able to interact with rich images and masses of text. In the future, this may be an iPad with Google-based tools. At present, Monash University is using Tablet PCs with custom collaborative software.

Tablet PCs allow students to manage normal documents but also to interact with visual information by annotating, highlighting, and drawing. The authors' research (Logan et al. 2010; Logan et al. 2009) shows that these features add significant value to the learning experience, and when combined with appropriate software, can enable participation in a far more active form of learning; a change that appears well overdue.

Students already enter the classroom with Web-enabled devices,[1] but little use is made of them and students are often asked to turn them off or put them away (Fang et al. 2009; Foster 2008). In contrast, many of today's students study with multiple sources of input; socializing and collaborating is part of their learning paradigm. When these are taken away, the boredom and the decreasing attention span and focus observed by Mann and Robinson (2009) and Young et al. (2009) can be exacerbated.

Although some argue that multitasking is detrimental to attention spans and cognitive task performance (Hembrooke and Gay 2003; Ophir et al. 2009), educational institutions nevertheless have an opportunity to take advantage of technology with which today's students are highly familiar, and integrate it into a sound pedagogical framework.

These changes need to be part of an holistic approach to address widespread student disengagement with the university experience, low retention and performance rates, decreased class attendance, a lack of peer-based instruction, and increased expectations of technology based on exposure within the K-12 environment and outside the classroom (see, e.g., ACER 2010; Crosling and Heagney 2009; Kennedy et al. 2009; Massingham and Herrington 2006; Moyle 2010).

Students and teachers, however, are not the only ones feeling dissatisfied. Employers are expressing concerns that graduates do not have the fundamental skills they require. The modern workplace is primarily built on teams with agile processes, but most grading schemes focus on individual performance and primarily measure the outcome (grade) rather than the process (learning journey). Successful employees collaborate beyond organizational boundaries to include informal networks of internal colleagues and external peers and friends.

---

[1] Network logs indicate that 53% of students at Monash University connect to the wireless network. In 2010, 79% of incoming Monash students reported owning a laptop or notebook, 41% have a Web-enabled phone (e.g., iPhone, BlackBerry), and 61% participated in social networking, e.g., Facebook, MySpace (Monash University 2010).

The skills, experience, and resources of incoming students are rapidly changing. The Australian Federal Government has initiated a rapid increase in technology adoption in the K-12 sector,[2] growing participation in higher education (from 29% to 40% by 2020 (Bradley 2008)), and a program for a National Broadband Network[3] that will create a range of new collaborative and educational possibilities. Incoming students will increasingly be used to highly social, digitally collaborative learning and, therefore, unprepared for a disconnected learning environment where digital devices are turned off and peer learning is limited.

Moreover, the predicted additional 11% of tertiary students are likely to come from families who have had limited exposure to higher education, (students with less experience, support, and familiarity with the demands of tertiary learning). Peer-based instruction, crowdsourcing, and other mechanisms that allow engagement and enquiry in a safe, exploratory environment will be key to the success of these students.

25.2 The Need for a New Approach: *myLearningSpace*

Monash University is a research-intensive institution, based in Melbourne, Australia, with eight campuses, including South Africa and Malaysia. Nearly 60,000 students are enrolled in its broad program of education, from medicine and law through to arts and business.

Instructors and students seek vigorous, engaging discussions that actively explore the topic at hand; this can, however, be difficult in early year courses, with large enrolments of more than 1,000 students. Instructors can feel overwhelmed as they repeat the same lecture two or three times to groups of 300–400 students. Students can feel disengaged and isolated, as only a few of the most confident have an opportunity for a brief exchange with the instructor.

The *myLearningSpace* approach is intended to address these issues – to provide a personalized learning environment that helps students to learn collaboratively during the class and then continue beyond the classroom. *myLearningSpace* focuses on three spheres of change: technology, space, and pedagogy. When these spheres are integrated, they provide a learning experience that today's students find invigorating, challenging, and effective. Instructors also feel energized and engaged – and challenged to review their teaching. They are encouraged to explore their educational objectives and approach, experiment with new ways of teaching, and seek greater interaction and feedback from students in class. As instructors drive the change, students begin to respond and engage (e.g., Logan et al. 2009).

---

[2]http://www.deewr.gov.au/Schooling/DigitalEducationRevolution/Pages/default.aspx
[3]http://www.dbcde.gov.au/broadband/national_broadband_network

25.2.1 Technology: Feedback, Inking, and Crowdsourcing

In designing appropriate technology for the *myLearningSpace* approach, in 2008 Monash considered a number of available technologies for improving classroom interaction. Audience response systems (e.g., "clickers", SMS voting) were increasing in popularity (e.g., MacGeorge et al. 2008; Medina et al. 2008), and new opportunities like the iPod and iPhone were becoming more widely available.

The value of in-class quizzing, especially in large classes, is increasingly well understood and utilized (e.g., Mollborn and Hoekstra 2010; Stowell and Nelson 2007), but many of the existing approaches have limitations. Table 25.1 shows a variety of ways to seek feedback from a class – from students raising their hands to in-house software, *Monash MeTL*.

Students are often wary of providing public feedback in class for fear of appearing ignorant or foolish – either to their peers or the instructor. They may also be shy or simply lack the confidence to respond to a question or an activity publicly. Some form of anonymous feedback is required, and ideally, through a device students already have and carry – such as a Web-enabled phone.

Web-enabled phones make it easy for instructors to seek responses from students to multiple-choice or short-answer quizzes. However, their screen size is very limited, which makes it difficult to engage with visually rich information or large amounts of text, and to provide visual information back to the instructor. These limitations led to an exploration of the potential offered by Tablet PCs and associated interactive software.

The Tablet PC's capacity to make casual annotations is attractive to instructors whose blackboards and whiteboards are being replaced with data projectors. Whiteboards are ineffective in large lecture theaters; document cameras can help fill this gap but hands can block the image, the image is not digitally available to students and the activity is separate from the presentation. In losing this capacity for spontaneous visual exposition, instructors lost a valuable pedagogical capability: the capacity to take a complex visual artifact (a cross section of a worm) and simplify it to its essential characteristics (endoderm, mesoderm, and ectoderm).

myLearningSpace encourages instructors to regularly use their virtual whiteboard space, to create an adaptive, spontaneous presentation that allows them to respond to

Table 25.1 Comparison of (selected) mechanisms for collecting in-class feedback

Technology	Question Complexity	Anonymity	Presentation Integration	Data capture
Hands	Y/N	×	×	×
Cards	Y/N; A/B/C	×	×	×
Clickers	Y/N; A/B/C; short text	√	√	√
Web quiz	Y/N; A/B/C; text	√	×	√
Interactive software[a]	Y/N; A/B/C; slide content	√	√	√
Monash MeTL	Multimodal	√	√	√

[a]E.g., Classroom presenter

student feedback and introduce complexity in an incremental way, encouraging students to participate in a co-created learning journey. The shared journey is accelerated as the whiteboard moves from an instructor-controlled space into a communal whiteboard, enabling crowdsourced-based peer instruction (cf. Sect. 25.2.3) among students and structured feedback between students and the instructor. This facilitates a shift in teaching styles from a static, one-way delivery mode (e.g., by using information-heavy, complex PowerPoint slides) to a more dynamic, interactive mode where instructors and students are both expected to contribute – a realization of the "guide on the side" mode of pedagogy frequently discussed in educational literature (King 1993).[4]

25.2.2 *Exploring Tablet PCs and Interactive Software*

Although Tablet PCs have been available for nearly a decade, they have had limited uptake, largely due to their higher cost and the lack of a compelling "killer app." However, Tablet PCs have two very interesting capabilities for educators – OneNote and inking in PowerPoint. OneNote provides a powerful electronic notebook for faculty and students to make handwritten notes individually or in small groups, to search the handwritten notes and to convert them to text (see Jeschke et al. 2009). The addition of inking functionality to PowerPoint has had a dramatic impact on the potential for PowerPoint to engage and educate students (Gibson et al. 2008; Johnson 2008).

Studies have shown that Tablet PCs can more easily provide a platform for collaborative, peer-based instruction, and incremental learning approaches (see, e.g., the contributions in Berque et al. 2009). These benefits are most powerfully felt when both instructor and students have Tablet PCs and are able to collaborate on the content together. Such approaches can improve student engagement, motivation and interaction, help students to understand the content and keep pace with the instructor, even in large classes (e.g., Anderson et al. 2006; Lafontant 2008).

Classroom Presenter (CP) was one of the earliest systems to implement a collaborative approach. Developed by the University of Washington, CP extends the static presentation style of PowerPoint with improved inking, quizzing, screen (slide) submissions, and shared annotation (Anderson 2003).[5] Anonymous submissions allow student voices to be heard in an environment where it is safe to be wrong. By including students into the presentation, these features can help the

---

[4]King's (1993) article "From sage on the stage to guide on the side" has been cited 171 times according to Google Scholar.

[5]CP provides other benefits to make ink-based instruction easier, including larger buttons, easier navigation, extra writing space, and whiteboard functionality.

lecture theater become a vibrant, conversational environment that provides rich feedback and insight for the instructor as the class progresses.

PowerPoint, on the other hand, provides a comfortable starting space for instructors to explore tablet-based teaching, but limitations in inking and sharing have led instructors to explore alternative approaches like *OneNote 2007* and CP. OneNote allows small groups of students to share a document with each other and the instructor, which can be an effective tool for tutorials, but does not provide a presentation mode for lectures.

Table 25.2 reviews the capabilities of PowerPoint and OneNote 2007 in contrast to more collaborative learning tools such as CP and current versions of *Monash MeTL*.

CP's third version (CP3) also provides special "instructor-only" content as private notes (prompts) to the instructor. This allows instructors to reduce the content on slides, improving clarity for students while still retaining key information to be covered. Some instructors draw pictures, graphs, or notes in this "private" mode and then trace over them in the lecture to provide a more dynamic experience for students. This capacity for private reminders to the lecturer is a powerful tool.

Table 25.2 Summary of current tablet-based collaborative software

	PowerPoint	OneNote 2007	CP3	*MeTL (v1.0)*	*MeTL (v2.0)*
Inking options	Difficult	Medium	Easy	Easy	Easy
Extra writing space	×	Unlimited	Limited	Unlimited	Unlimited
Whiteboard	Blank screen can be used	Insert new or extend current	Insert new (separate deck)	Insert new or extend current	Insert new or extend current
Instructor notes	Off-slide; text only	×	On-slide; text and object	On-slide; text and object	On-slide; text and object
Media support	Images; audio; video	Images; audio; video	Images	Images; Web	Images
Distributed to students	×[a]	√ (limited)	√	√	√
Quizzes	Only with add-ins	×	√	×	√
Screen submissions	×	×	√	√	√
Moveable ink	×	√	×	√	√
Student sharing	×	√	×	√	√
Scale (number of students in a live session)	Instructor-only	~10 students	~80 students	~40 students (peer-to-peer); ~100 students (instructor–students)	~800 students

[a]PowerPoint 2010 supports web-based live distribution

CP has been adopted by a number of institutions across the world (especially in league with the "HP in Education" program[6]). As open-source software, it has been customized and extended, including support for screencasts,[7] platform independence, and peer instruction. The results of these adaptations have informed the Monash approach.

Almeida and Azevedo's (2009) work with video playback and annotation (highlighting where students most needed to review) affirmed the authors' interest in data mining to improve the learning experience. *Ubiquitous Presenter* (developed at UC San Diego) allows students to participate from any Web-enabled platform (cf. Bales et al. 2009) and, with the addition of "note blogging", explores peer instruction-based approaches (Simon et al. 2008). This substantiated the authors' ideas for crowdsourcing[8] as an incredible opportunity to engage large classes in helping each other to learn – drawing on each other's strengths, knowledge, and expertise.

By connecting students with a peer-to-peer model, crowdsourcing can create learning environments where it is more powerful to have 500 students learning together than 50. Crowdsourcing, peer instruction, and affiliation-based collaborations can help to challenge and stretch the strongest students and reconnect the weaker ones. With Monash seeking to facilitate a rich collaborative learning experience in classes of 300–400, CP3's lack of student–student interaction[9] and 80 user limitation[10] prompted an in-house solution – *Monash MeTL*.

25.2.3 Incremental Development Approach

25.2.3.1 Monash MeTL (v1.0)

Monash MeTL (v1.0) was designed to support large-scale collaboration over a very flexible set of resources. A thin membrane over a fully functional Web browser

---

[6]See http://www.hp.com/hpinfo/grants/education.html for more information. Under the program, institutions receive a class set of HP Tablet PCs as a grant for exploring new ways of engaging and educating students. Of the 80 institutions that received HP Technology for Teaching Grants during 2004–2008, at least 12 explored the potential of CP.
(http://www.hp.com/hpinfo/grants/us/programs/tech_teaching/hied_global.html)

[7]Screencasts are very popular with tablet-based instruction, allowing the capture of complex sequences of annotations, e.g., science-based slides such as mathematical formulae, chemical structures, or ICT architectures.

[8]Crowdsourcing is 'group intelligence', allowing every student to contribute their individual insights and experiences in an incrementally developed learning experience.

[9]Student notes in *Ubiquitous Presenter* are an addendum to the slide rather than part of the slide deck.

[10]Although CP3 is generally robust for up to about 80 students, if three or four students enter after the start of the presentation, CP3 can become unstable for as little as 20 users. This instability can be avoided by requiring all students to connect to the session before the lecture begins; however, this is not a sustainable or practical approach.

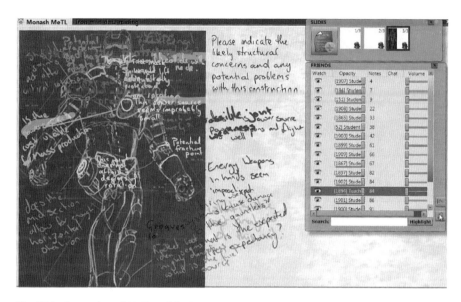

Fig. 25.1 Screenshot of *MeTL (v1.0)* showing slide annotations by multiple students

allowed instructors to annotate any Web-based resource, from slide decks to Web-based documents and even videos. The "crowdsourcing" mode was individually controllable, enabling students to turn any participant on or off. They could ignore the annotations of students they felt were irrelevant, or, where strokes appeared over the top of each other, dim one annotation to read another.[11] Students could also move annotations around on the membrane. *MeTL (v1.0)* included traditional presentation features (slides) and inking-style features (like CP3) (Fig. 25.1).

In mid-2009, *Monash MeTL (v1.0)* was first piloted with student cohorts in biology and psychology. Whilst feedback was generally positive and the early version proved effective, especially for tutorials and small practical classes, significant scaling limitations surfaced.

Despite thorough testing of *MeTL (v1.0)* before its first release, some last minute improvements to data integrity had the side effect of significantly impacting performance. As a result, *MeTL (v1.0)* in full "peer-to-peer" mode was unsuitable for large classes, although it could be used if students turned off the peer-instruction capabilities. *MeTL (v1.0)'s* crowdsourcing design allowed every student to see other students' annotations, notes, images, and other contributions live (or dim/hide them). Ultimately, the performance ceiling of *MeTL (v1.0)* related to limitations in Microsoft's TCP/IP implementation in WCF,[12] which led to a redesign for *MeTL (v2.0)*.

---

[11]A major limitation of CP3 is that a student's annotation can be obstructed by subsequent instructor annotations. Being able to move one's annotations out of the way was a far more amenable solution than having to erase them.

[12]The networking implementation in .NET's *Windows Communication Foundation*.

Nevertheless, *MeTL (v1.0)* was still a success. Its internal use (meetings and planning sessions), and the pilots with biology and psychology students helped to clarify requirements and identify what was most important in a collaborative presentation and annotation tool that supported a rich peer-to-peer model.

25.2.3.2 Monash MeTL (v2.0)

Monash MeTL (v2.0) (hereafter *MeTL*) incorporates a range of key features that were explored, prototyped, trialed, and then implemented for broader use. In addition to agile and user-centered design methodologies, the development of *MeTL* has been informed by research, drawing on literature from peers exploring similar approaches and from internal research and evaluation activities to meet the expectations of instructors and students, and project goals. Usability testing ensured the end product met the needs and expectations of instructors using a collaborative teaching approach.

Technologically, *MeTL* is designed for large amounts of parallel communications. It uses *ejabberd*, an XMPP daemon that supports distributed and highly concurrent communications.[13] This makes *MeTL's* collaborative annotations far more scalable and robust than *MeTL (v1.0)*. Design-wise, it draws on a broader range of academics who have participated in tablet-based teaching at Monash, as well as a deeper understanding of the literature relating to Tablet PCs in education across a variety of levels, disciplines, and institutions.

MeTL slide decks are called "conversations." A conversation can be based upon a PowerPoint slide deck[14] or a blank slate. The conversation can be access-controlled using LDAP[15] groups (departments, courses, or individuals). The creator of the conversation becomes the instructor, with certain extra capabilities, including:

(a) Capacity to add extra slides
(b) Ability to enable synchronized navigation (students follow instructor on slide changes)
(c) Ability to switch between "lecture" (only instructor can write publicly) and "tutorial" (anyone can write publicly).

Any user can write, draw, type, or add images in the shared space (Fig. 25.2). This input can be public (seen by all users) or private (only viewable by that user). This allows instructors to write private notes to themselves (like CP3) and students to share annotations with peers or write privately. *MeTL* can also support text-based chat and a private notepad (both in separate panes to the main slide). The canvas

---

[13]*ejabberd* is used by *Facebook* and others to support large numbers of instant messaging clients talking to each other; XMPP is the protocol most modern instant messaging clients use.

[14]These can be imported as images to look exactly like the PowerPoint slide or as individual objects on the slide to allow editing.

[15]LDAP groups are directory services filters based on roles and group memberships.

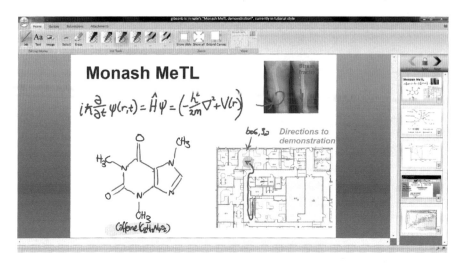

Fig. 25.2 Screenshot of *MeTL (v2.0)* showing an annotated lecture slide

Table 25.3 Overview of class size, teaching mode, and software used across cohorts in the Faculty of Medicine, Nursing and Health Sciences in 2010

Class size	Teaching mode and software	Courses
Lab or tutorial (<30)	Instructor-only (PowerPoint or *MeTL*)	n/a
Small lecture (<80)	Instructor–student (CP3)	6
Medium lecture (80–150)	Instructor–student (*MeTL*)	2
Large lecture (>150)	Instructor-only (PowerPoint or CP3)	2

size automatically extends as strokes continue beyond the right or bottom margin. Zooming allows the user to focus on particular parts of the canvas as it gets larger.

In 2010, *myLearningSpace* was implemented across a substantial proportion of the Faculty of Medicine, Nursing and Health Sciences at Monash University. Over 75 instructors and 1,000 students from ten courses and four campuses participated. Depending on class size and instructor preference, instructors used PowerPoint, CP3, or *MeTL* for teaching purposes. Table 25.3 shows the breakdown across the ten courses, although some instructors opted to use PowerPoint or CP3 in instructor-only mode (without students connected).

An initial analysis of the protocols of CP3 and *MeTL* indicated that the standard wireless service at Monash would be inadequate. An alternative, high-performance wireless solution was identified, tested, and implemented. Automated stress testing of CP3 and *MeTL* determined their probable limitations and a comprehensive, in-person test with 100 participants in a lecture theater confirmed these limitations. This information informed the subsequent deployment of the software. The in-person testing of *MeTL* was very successful, showing that it could easily cope with 100 concurrent users and appeared to cope effectively with 800 virtual users (each in-person user simulating eight separate users). This confirmed the capability of both the product and the underlying wireless infrastructure.

However, given previous experience, the decision was made to move safely, allocating classes according to their tested limits (Table 25.3). Another factor informing this decision was storage. *MeTL* stored high-fidelity ink; if every student wrote in every class very heavily, it was possible that new storage might be required on short notice. Restricting the scale of adoption limited this risk. The deployment approach could be reviewed as the semester progressed, with the possibility of inviting further classes across to experiment with *MeTL*.

In parallel to the technology preparations, a comprehensive change program was developed and implemented. An experienced change consultant provided leadership of the change program, developing a range of resources and activities to ensure that instructors and students were fully engaged, prepared, and equipped to successfully participate in collaborative learning and teaching.

25.2.4 On the Way to Collaborative Education: Adopting Change

Although innovators are keen to explore new opportunities, it can be much more difficult to implement comprehensive change across institutions. Rogers' (1962) "diffusion of innovations" model implies that 2.5–15% of faculty would be willing to explore new approaches, but the majority would want to see strong evidence of the positive impact combined with significant commitment from their department for support, coaching, and expert advice before committing their time and resources to change.

A key part of the *myLearningSpace* approach was ensuring that instructors and students were prepared and supported through the change, and felt confident in the technological and pedagogical support that was available. The project adopted "start small" as an important part of the change philosophy: Instructors were encouraged to adopt the new approach at a level with which they were comfortable, and to build upon success once they were ready. This "succeed and grow" model draws on project-based change management models (e.g., Kotter 1996) and endeavors to minimize the impact and maximize the opportunities of concurrently developing a new pedagogy with a new technology.

Through a successful trial in 2009, the Faculty of Medicine, Nursing and Health Sciences had developed a strong collaborative partnership with the project team. The Faculty's Academic Director for Information Technology played a key role in ensuring engagement, facilitating change, and monitoring for success. The change program began with initial consultations with Heads of School, representatives who had academic, financial, and administrative oversight of the proposed courses and the instructors who taught them.

With Heads of Schools' support, a change process was initiated that included information sessions, training, and practice to ensure instructors and students were fully prepared and equipped to participate in the program (Table 25.4).

Table 25.4 Overview of change activities to prepare and equip participants

	Instructors	Students	In-class support staff
Awareness	Faculty; Heads of School; sponsor sessions	Postal and e-mail notifications	Recruitment; group induction
Engagement	1-on-1 inductions; training sessions; dress rehearsals	'Getting prepared' and 'Let's go' sessions	Training; 100 person testing; dress rehearsals
Monitoring	KPI and incidents; sponsor check-ups	Metrics; support staff feedback	Check-ups with instructors; meetings
Review	Focus groups; sponsor check-ups	Focus groups; surveys	Debriefing sessions; in-class support

An initial "advocacy" session explored current challenges in education, why *myLearningSpace* was being introduced, and promoted the potential benefits. Each instructor was given a personal induction session when they received their Tablet PC[16] and were encouraged to explore the device prior to group-based training sessions in CP3 or *MeTL*. Subsequent "dress rehearsals" allowed instructors to practice with a group of support staff acting as students.

It became clear that this dress rehearsal was a crucial activity for instructors. Most instructors were quite experienced teachers and entered the session fairly confidently. After experiencing a live session, they tended to reevaluate the preparation and level of change that might be required. Conducted in advance of the commencement of the teaching semester, the sessions gave instructors time to rethink their approaches, to prepare further, and to incorporate the opportunities (and challenges!) of *myLearningSpace* more effectively.

Perhaps the most valued part of supporting the change was the provision of in-class technical support. As much as possible, the same support staff was scheduled to the same instructors to allow a level of relationship, understanding, and trust to be developed. Instructors reported feeling far safer and more confident with the support staff on hand. It allowed them to begin at a comfortable level of risk, and then to take further steps, secure in the knowledge that if things broke (as they sometimes did), someone was right there to quickly get things back on track. Instructors frequently commented on the value of this support in helping them more confidently adopt the *myLearningSpace* approach.

The in-class support staff (a casual workforce, primarily students) went on a parallel change journey that ensured that, as the "coal face" representatives of the project, they understood what the project was endeavoring to achieve, and were available to provide appropriate levels of support and refer more complex issues to the project team. Regular reporting against KPIs and of incidents ensured a good feedback channel from classes to the project.

As part of the incremental adoption path for instructors, an instructional designer participated in the training, dress rehearsals, and subsequent 1-on-1 coaching and exploration sessions with instructors. This allowed instructors to seek feedback and

---

[16]This included an overview of the hardware and how to ink in OneNote, PowerPoint, and Word.

advice about their content and approach, and proved to be a service in significant demand throughout the life of the project.

Finally, students participated in a two-phase process; a "Getting prepared" session provided them with information about *myLearningSpace* – what it was, why they were being given the opportunity, and the potential benefits. A "Let's go!" session gave them a live experience of CP3 or *MeTL* prior to the instructor commencing teaching with the software the following week.

The Faculty's Academic Director helped to maintain strong working relationships with academic staff. He regularly contacted instructors to review preparations, how lectures were going, and how instructors felt about the project. Feedback from these conversations provided the richest source of insight into problems and potential solutions, as well as some outstanding praise reports and successes. This was by far the most valuable feedback channel from instructors, despite the many other forms of engagement that were conducted.[17] Focus groups, surveys, and other research activities explored the impact of *myLearningSpace* and informed a continuous improvement cycle.

25.2.5 Conclusion: Where to from Here?

The pedagogical power of *Monash MeTL* lies within the collaborative learning experience that the software allows students and instructors to have. Since its early versions, *MeTL* has undergone significant design changes to provide a more user-friendly interface, to deliver robust performance on a large scale, and to offer a solution that instructors and students across disciplines and with varying competence levels can explore and utilize.

Throughout the pilot phase (2008–2009) and the wider rollout (2010 onward), instructors have found the *myLearningSpace* approach to be positive, with students being more engaged and, in some cases, learning far quicker or more deeply than before. Some instructors have reported receiving standing ovations, classes where students have learned more in 4 weeks than in the previous entire semester and students who are producing assignments with more depth and breadth than previously. Perhaps most potently, a number of instructors have made statements such as "I've thought more about my teaching in the last 7 weeks than I have in the last 7 years."

The feedback from participating students has generally been strongly positive in favor of the approach. In addition to the benefits of collaborative learning, students have also appreciated the capacity to have all the digital resources associated with their studies in one place, a place they could take with them, and a place that could

---

[17]Ongoing regular evaluation activities analyzed the health, success, and impact of the project, including in-class data collection, individual consultations, focus groups, surveys, and technology performance data.

be connected back to Monash for further information when required. Throughout the pilots, anecdotes emerged of students using their Tablet PCs on the bus and train, on their travels during semester break, in their favorite coffee shop, and in the park while walking the dog!

It is clear that there is opportunity to do better. In particular, the resilience of CP3 has had an impact on instructor trust and participation, and guest lecturers have tended not to participate, leading to some disenfranchisement from students (Logan et al. 2010). Instructional design and 1-on-1 support with academics is in great demand, and further resources are needed. Throughout Semester 1, 2010, students could have been better engaged and activated as supporters and facilitators of the change, both with their peers and instructors.

Despite these limitations, a great deal has been achieved. A resilient infrastructure and software environment has been prepared, tested, and proven to deliver. A range of efforts in preparing instructors for change has helped them to feel more confident and in control. Providing in-class technical support has helped instructors to start small and then take risks. Moreover, students report feeling more engaged, having better interaction, and, in some cases, are learning far quicker and more deeply than in previous semesters. But this success is also strongly influenced by the design of the learning spaces where these classes are conducted.

Beyond basic technological support (data projection, power, wireless,...), learning spaces need attractive and provocative designs that reinforce to students that a different mode of learning is occurring in this space. They also need flexible furniture that allows students to collaborate in groups and support different modes of collaboration. Unfortunately, the design of many current spaces acts as a major inhibitor to active engagement and collaboration. The presentation, fixed structures, and lack of facilities encourage a monochromatic, didactic approach. Concurrent to the educational and technological change advocated by the *myLearningSpace* approach, Monash University has been exploring the changes required in physical learning space design, presentation, and fitout to maximize effective collaborative learning.

25.3   Continuing Research

Typically, universities spend millions of dollars on building learning spaces; and a large part of their income relates to the activity that occurs in those spaces. The performance of those spaces is coming under increasing attention with case studies and well-developed models for evaluation and post-occupancy review (e.g., Jamieson 2003; Oblinger 2006; Pearshouse et al. 2009; Radcliffe et al. 2009).

However, to better understand the impact of factors such as comfort, lighting, or color on learning, and to improve the effectiveness of its own learning spaces, Monash has begun to conduct experimental research into the design and impact of higher education learning spaces. This appears to be an area that is quite under-researched,[18] but offers huge opportunities to better understand education from a holistic perspective.

By exploring the correlation between in-class activity (such as space utilization, class attendance, and device usage) and activity occurring outside of class (e.g., accessing the my.monash portal, course management systems, or lecture recordings), it is hoped to develop powerful insights into how effectively the integrated learning environment is operating. Early findings indicate that some factors have a very significant impact on attendance and a likely flow through to learning outcomes.

myLearningSpace adds a valuable dimension to this understanding by integrating online and in-class activity. Are student annotations correlating with the most important points in the lecture? Did participation wane at a point in time? Do students at the back participate and perform differently from others? And how is this class performing and responding against the norms for this course, degree, or the entire university?

The ultimate goal of this research activity is to move from an assessment model that focuses on the "outcome" (grade) to the "learning path" (How did student get the grade?) to better measure capability in action instead of artifacts at the end.

25.4 myLearningSpace: An Integrated Learning Environment

myLearningSpace is already having a significant positive impact on education at Monash University – both directly (through more engaging learning experiences) and indirectly (by encouraging instructors to reexamine their approach to education). This change synergizes with improvements in learning spaces that invite more collaborative approaches and accelerate the exploration, adoption, and value of new, technology-enabled collaborative learning experiences. Together, they encourage a more personalized, challenging, and engaging model of learning; they provide instructors with more detailed and real-time insights into students' learning; and they provide the institution with greater insight into the relative performance and impact of the various elements of their learning environment.

The integrated learning environment, *myLearningSpace*, provides a dynamic, collaborative environment that invites participation. While this environment allows more traditional approaches, it is sufficiently provocative to make it slightly uncomfortable to continue in these modes, inviting instructors to explore new approaches and exciting students with the collaborative potential.

Acknowledgments The authors wish to acknowledge the leadership of Prof. Adam Shoemaker in establishing the eEducation Centre at Monash University and supporting the *myLearningSpace*

---

[18]As far as the authors are aware, there is no research exploring learning space design and impact from an experimental design perspective.

program. The authors also acknowledge the contributions of Chris Hagan, Helen Palmer, and the rest of the eEducation Centre team, as well as Dr George Kotsanas and other colleagues from the Faculty of Medicine, Nursing and Health Sciences and ITS to the *myLearningSpace* program.

References

ACER: Doing More for Learning: Enhancing Engagement and Outcomes. Australian Council for Educational Research, Melbourne (2010)

Almeida, P., Azevedo, R.: Active learning and screencasting with tablet PCs: a detailed evaluation. In: Berque, D.A., Konkle, L.M., Reed, R.H. (eds.) The Impact of Tablet PCs and Pen-Based Technology on Education: New Horizons, pp. 3–11. Purdue University Press, West Lafayette (2009)

Anderson, R.: University of Washington Classroom Presenter. University of Washington, Seattle (2003)

Anderson, R., Anderson, R., Chung, O., Davis, K.M., Davis, P., Prince, C., Razmov, V., Simon, B.: Classroom presenter: a classroom interaction system for active and collaborative learning. In: Berque, D., Prey, J.C., Reed, R.H. (eds.) The Impact of Tablet PCs and Pen-Based Technology on Education: Vignettes, Evaluations, and Future Directions, pp. 21–30. Purdue University Press, West Lafayette (2006)

Bales, E., Griswold, W., Simon, B., Hieber, A., Kelly, M.J., Lintern, J., Ouyang, D.: Use of ubiquitous presenter: 2006–2009. In: Berque, D.A., Konkle, L.M., Reed, R.H. (eds.) The Impact of Tablet PCs and Pen-Based Technology on Education: New Horizons, pp. 13–19. Purdue University Press, West Lafayette (2009)

BECTA: Learning Styles: An Introduction to the Research Literature. British Educational Communication and Technology Agency (BECTA), Coventry (2006)

Berque, D.A., Konkle, L.M., Reed, R.H.: The Impact of Tablet PCs and Pen-Based Technology on Education: New Horizons. Purdue University Press, West Lafayette (2009)

Bradley, D.: Review of Australian Higher Education. Department of Education, Employment and Workplace Relations, Canberra (2008)

Crosling, G., Heagney, M.: Improving student retention in higher education: improving teaching and learning. Aust. Univ. Rev. **51**(2), 9–18 (2009)

Fang, B.: From distraction to engagement: wireless devices in the classroom. Educause Q., **32**(4) (2009) http://chronicle.com/article/Law-Professors-Rule-Laptops/29745

Foster, A.L.: Law professors rule laptops out of order in class. Chron. High. Educ. (2008) http://www.educause.edu/EDUCAUSE+Quarterly/EDUCAUSEQuarterlyMagazineVolum/FromDistractiontoEngagementWir/192959

Gibson, B., Friend, J., Yeo, L.: Digital ink for simple cognitively effective recorded lectures: making way for student centred engineering classrooms. In: World Conference on Educational Multimedia, Hypermedia and Telecommunications 2008: AACE (2008)

Hembrooke, H., Gay, G.: The laptop and the lecture: The effects of multitasking in learning environments. J. Comput. High. Educ. **15**(1), 46–64 (2003)

Hughes, A.: Higher Education in a Web 2.0 World. The Committee of Inquiry into the Changing Learner Experience. JISC, Bristol (2009)

Ito, M., Horst, H., Bittanti, M., Boyd, D., Herr-Stephenson, B., Lange, P.G., Pascoe, C.J., Robinson, L.: Living and learning with new media: summary of findings from the digital youth project. In: The John, D., Catherine, T. (eds.) MacArthur Foundation Reports on Digital Media and Learning. MacArthur Foundation, Chicago (2008)

Jamieson, P.: Designing more effective on-campus teaching and learning spaces: a role for academic developers. Int. J. Acad. Dev. **8**(1), 119–133 (2003)

Jeschke, S., Knipping, L., Natho, N., Schröder, C., Zorn, E.: Information management in education using tablet PCs and OneNote. In: 37th Annual Conference of SEFI. Rotterdam (2009)

Johnson, A.E.: Digital ink: in-class annotation of PowerPoint lectures. J. Chem. Educ. **85**(5), 655–657 (2008)

Kennedy, G., Dalgarno, B., Bennett, S., Gray, K., Waycott, J., Judd, T., Bishop, A., Maton, K., Krause, K.-L., Chang, R.: Educating the Net Generation. Australian Learning and Teaching Council (ALTC), Strawberry Hills (2009)

King, A.: From sage on the stage to guide on the side. Coll. Teach. **41**(1), 30–35 (1993)

Kotter, J.: Leading Change. Harvard Business Press, Cambridge (1996)

Lafontant, P.: Using tablet PCs and DyKnow vision to enhance student engagement in a human anatomy class. In: Reed, R.H., Berque, D.A., Prey, J.C. (eds.) The Impact of Tablet PCs and Pen-Based Technology on Education: Evidence and Outcomes, pp. 89–93. Purdue University Press, West Lafayette (2008)

Logan, M., Bailey, N., Franke, K., Sanson, G.: Patterns of tablet PC use across multiple learning domains: a comparison program. In: Berque, D.A., Konkle, L.M., Reed, R.H. (eds.) The Impact of Tablet PCs and Pen-Based Technology on Education: New Horizons, pp. 83–92. Purdue University Press, West Lafayette (2009)

Logan, M., Franke, K., Bailey, N.: Is tablet-based teaching for everyone? an exploration of teaching with tablet PCs across science and humanities classes. In: Berque, D., Reed, R.H. (eds.) The Impact of Tablet PCs and Pen-Based Technology on Education: Going Mainstream. Purdue University Press, West Lafayette (2010)

MacGeorge, E., Homan, S., Dunning, J., Elmore, D., Bodie, G., Evans, E., Khichadia, S., Lichti, S., Feng, B., Geddes, B.: Student evaluation of audience response technology in large lecture classes. Educ. Technol. Res. Dev. **56**(2), 125–145 (2008)

Mann, S., Robinson, A.: Boredom in the lecture theatre: an investigation into the contributors, moderators and outcomes of boredom amongst university students. Br. Educ. Res. J. **35**(2), 243–258 (2009)

Massingham, P., Herrington, T.: Does attendance matter? an examination of student attitudes, participation, performance and attendance. J. Univ. Teach. Learn. Pract. **3**(2), 82–103 (2006)

Medina, M.S., Medina, P.J., Wanzer, D.S., Wilson, J.E., Er, N., Britton, M.L.: Use of an Audience Response System (ARS) in a dual-campus classroom environment. Am. J. Pharm. Educ. **72**(2), 1–7 (2008)

Mollborn, S., Hoekstra, A.: "A meeting of minds": using clickers for critical thinking and discussion in large sociology classes. Teach. Sociol. **28**(1), 18–27 (2010)

Monash University: Commencing Student Information and Communication Technology (ICT) Usage Survey 2010. Client Services, ITS Division. Monash University, Clayton (2010)

Moyle, K.: Building innovation: learning with technologies. In: Australian Education Review. Australian Council for Educational Research (ACER), Melbourne (2010)

Oblinger, D.G.: Learning Spaces. Educause, Washington, DC (2006) http://www.amazon.com/Learning-Spaces-Diana-G-Oblinger/dp/0967285372/sr=1-10/qid=1162831109/ref=sr_1_10/102-9593341-0281740?ie=U

Ophir, E., Nass, C., Wagner, A.D.: Cognitive control in media multitaskers. Natl. Acad. Sci. USA **106**(35) (2009)

Pearshouse, I., Bligh, B., Brown, E., Lewthwaite, S., Graber, R., Hartnell-Young, E., Sharples, M.: A Study of Effective Evaluation Models and Practices for Technology Supported Physical Learning Spaces. Learning Sciences Research Institute. University of Nottingham, Nottingham (2009)

Radcliffe, D., Wilson, H., Powell, D., Tibbets, B.: Learning Spaces in Higher Education: Positive Outcomes by Design. The University of Queensland, St Lucia (2009)

Rogers, E.M.: Diffusion of Innovations. Free Press, Glencoe (1962)

Simon, B., Davis, K., Griswold, W.G., Kelly, M., Malani, R. Noteblogging: taking note taking public. In: SIGCSE '08, Portland. (2008)

Stowell, J.R., Nelson, J.M.: Benefits of electronic audience response systems on student participation, learning, and emotion. Teach. Psychol **34**(4), 253–258 (2007)

Young, M.S., Robinson, S., Alberts, P.: Students Pay attention!: combating the vigilance decrement to improve learning during lectures. Active Learn. High. Educ. **10**(1), 41–55 (2009)

Printed by Printforce, the Netherlands